COLLECTIBLES
HANDBOOK & PRICE GUIDE

COLLECTIBLES
HANDBOOK & PRICE GUIDE

Judith Miller
and Mark Hill

MILLER'S

Miller's Collectibles Handbook & Price Guide 2014-2015

First published in Great Britain in 2014 by Miller's, a division of Mitchell Beazley,
imprints of Octopus Publishing Group Ltd., 189 Shaftesbury Avenue,
London, WC2H 8JY UK.
An Hachette Livre UK Company.
www.hachette.co.uk

Distributed in the USA by Hachette Book Group USA,
237 Park Avenue, New York NY 10017, USA.
Distributed in Canada by Canadian Manda Group,
165 Dufferin Street, Toronto, Ontario, M6K 3H6, Canada.

Miller's is a registered trademark of Octopus Publishing Group Ltd.
www.millersonline.com

Copyright © Octopus Publishing Group Ltd. 2014

———————————————

While every care has been exercised in the compilation of this guide,
neither the authors nor publishers accept any liability for any financial or
other loss incurred by reliance placed on the information contained in
Miller's Collectibles Handbook & Price Guide.

ISBN 9781845337902

A CIP catalog record for this book is available from the Library of Congress.

Set in Frutiger

Color reproduction by United Graphics, Singapore
Printed and bound in China by 1010 Printing International Ltd.

Authors Judith Miller & Mark Hill

Editorial Director Tracey Smith
Editorial Co-ordinator Katy Armstrong
Copy-editor and Proofreader John Wainwright
Editorial Assistant Brianna Weber
Indexer Hilary Bird
Design and Prepress Ali Scrivens, TJ Graphics
Production Lucy Carter

Photographs of Judith Miller and Mark Hill by Simon Upton, Chris Terry
and Graham Rae

CONTENTS

LIST OF CONSULTANTS

BEER CANS
Nick West
Private Collector

BOOKS
Roddy Newlands
Dreweatts & Bloomsbury
www.bloomsburyauctions.com

CERAMICS
Beth Adams
Alfie's Antiques
www.alfiesantiques.com

Dr Graham Cooley
Private Collector

Will Farmer
Fieldings
fieldingsauctioneers.co.uk

Kevin Graham
potteryandglass.forumandco.com

Steven Moore
Anderson & Garland
www.andersonandgarland.com

Ron Pook
Pook & Pook
www.pookandpook.com

David Rago
Rago Arts
www.ragoarts.com

COMMEMORATIVES
Andrew Hilton
Historical & Collectable
www.historicalandcollectable.com

FASHION & ACCESSORIES
Leslie Hindman
Leslie Hindman Auctions
www.lesliehindman.com

FIFTIES & SIXTIES
Ian Broughton

GLASS
Robert Bevan-Jones
Private Collector

Dr Graham Cooley
Private Collector

Will Farmer
Fieldings
fieldingsauctioneers.co.uk

Mike Moir
manddmoir.co.uk

MARBLES
Mark Block
blockglass.com

MARINE
Charles Miller
Charles Miller Ltd.
www.charlesmillerltd.com

ORIENTAL
Richard Cervantes
Freeman's
www.freemansauction.com

POSTERS
Nicholas D Lowry
Swann Galleries
www.swanngalleries.com

SPORTING
Graham Budd
Graham Budd Auctions
www.grahambuddauctions.co.uk

We are also grateful to all our friends and experts who gave us so much help and support – Diane Baynes of Sworders, Sue Belshaw of Halls, Nigel Benson of 20thcentury-glass.com, Tori Billington of Dreweatts, Tamzin Corbett of Woolley & Wallis, James Gooch of the 'weird and wonderful' Doe & Hope, Jeanette Hayhurst, Kevin Harris of undercurrents.biz, Clive Hillier of Louis Taylor, Lindsay Hoadley of Summers Place Auctions, Michael Jeffrey of Woolley & Wallis, Jindrich Parik, Wesley Payne of Alfie's Antiques Market, Thomas Plant of Special Auction Services, Alan & Sue Poultney of Scarab Antiques, Geoffrey Robinson of Alfie's Antiques Market, Adam Schoon of Tennants, Simon Smith of Vectis, Alison Snowdon of Fieldings, Max Sobolevskij of Tennants, Ron & Ann Wheeler of artiusglass.co.uk, Nigel Wiggin of The Old Hall Club and Lee Young of Lyon & Turnbull.

HOW TO USE THIS BOOK

Subcategory heading Indicates the sub-category of the main heading.

Page tab This appears on every page and identifies the main category heading as identified in the Contents List on pages 5-6.

Caption The description of the item illustrated, including when relevant, the period, the maker or factory, medium, the year it was made, dimensions and condition. Many captions have **footnotes** which explain terminology or give identification or valuation information.

The price guide These price ranges give a ballpark figure for what you should pay for a similar item. The great joy of collectibles is that there is not a recommended retail price. The price ranges in this book are based on actual prices, either what a dealer will take or the full auction price.

Judith/Marks Picks Items chosen specifically by Judith and Mark, either becuase they are important or interesting, or because our experts believe that these pieces are good investments.

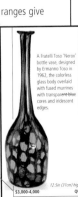

Quick Reference Gives key facts about the factory, maker or style, along with stylistic identification points, value tips and advice on fakes.

Closer Look Does exactly that. These are where we show identifying aspects of a factory or maker, point out rare colors or shapes, and explain why a particular piece is so desirable.

The object The collectibles are shown in full color. This is a vital aid to identification and valuation. With many objects, a slight color variation can signify a large price differential.

Source code Every item has been specially photographed at an auction house, a dealer, an antiques market or a private collection. These are credited by code at the end of the caption, and can be checked against the Key to Illustrations on pages 408-10.

INTRODUCTION

Welcome to the new edition of the 'Miller's Collectibles Handbook & Price Guide'. The first edition of this guide was launched just over 25 years ago and both the guide and the market it represents have changed enormously since then. What hasn't changed is the fact that this guide contains an all-new selection of collectibles from across the world, each accompanied by a full caption and price guide.

You'll find a wealth of extra information in our 'Closer Look' and 'Quick Reference' features and our in-depth footnotes. We've also continued our popular 'Judith Picks' and 'Mark Picks' features, which we hope will give you an insight into our personal thoughts on certain items in today's marketplace.

We're delighted to be able to include many new sections in this edition, including beer cans, buckles, fishing memorabilia, wall masks and even collectibles from outer space in the form of meteorites! The years covered by the guide (2014 and 2015) also see two important anniversaries: a hundred years since the start of World War I in 1914 and two hundred since the Battle of Waterloo in 1815. So you'll also find sections dedicated to items and memorabilia relating to and from these important events.

A 1930s Myott 'Beaky' jug. $150-250 FLD

industry is still as vibrant and varied as ever shows that it's far from dead – change can be a sign of growth and nothing should remain static.

One notable thing that certainly hasn't remained static is the price of silver, which has leapt up over the past few years. Unfortunately many pieces have been scrapped in an attempt to cash in on high prices, but values for many small, high quality items, such as pepperettes, have risen far and above their scrap value. Quality always sells.

This surge in the price of small silver objects is largely driven by a group of dedicated collectors, who represent one side of a market that is clearly stratifying into two camps. On one side are the ever-keen, ever-dedicated collectors who vie against each other to build and complete their collections and push the boundaries of knowledge; on the other are primarily new and young buyers, who collect antiques largely for their visual and decorative appeal. Not bothering to 'keep up with the Joneses', they're creating their own individual 'vintage' style. Although this look focuses on decorative pieces from the 1930s and the 1950s and '60s, other antiques and collectibles are also an important part of this. The look of an object has always been important and objects that speak of the style of the day they were made in are always sought after.

A George V silver salt, in the form of a pig, by C Saunders & F Shepherd, Birmingham. 1912 $500-700 LC

There are definitely still many opportunities for buying wisely with an eye for the future. For example, although Clarice Cliff remains ever popular, similar Art Deco ceramics by Myott seem extremely good value now.

In this business, knowledge is money and the best way of learning is by reading books and handling as many objects as possible. We hope you enjoy both.

'I WANT YOU FOR U.S. ARMY', designed by James Montgomery Flagg. $8,000-12,000 HER

Although many have seen the general downturn in prices across the industry as the beginning of the end of collecting, we at Miller's believe that nothing could be further from the truth. People have collected for centuries and collecting itself has been in and out of fashion many times during that period. The fact that the

A late 1950s French magazine rack. $120-180 MA

QUICK REFERENCE - ADVERTISING

- The majority of advertising memorabilia available to collectors today dates from the early 20thC at the very earliest, with most pieces dating from the 1960s onwards. The market is driven by nostalgia, meaning that items from well-known brands, such as Cadbury's, tend to be the most valuable.
- Collectors tend to focus on one brand or on one type of advertising object, such as enamelled signs. Food- and drink-related advertising and packaging is consistently popular and tobacco advertising has increased in desirability recently. Pieces that have cross-market interest, for example signs that feature trains, are also likely to be desirable.
- A popular style, such as Art Nouveau, Art Deco or 1950s kitsch, will usually add value to a piece of advertising.

The style can also help with dating, as can the format of names, logos, postcodes and telephone numbers.
- Signs are one of the most popular collecting areas and can be extremely valuable, particularly if they have eye-catching visuals. Condition is very important, so examine surfaces carefully for damage, such as scratches, losses to the surface or dents. Signs in mint condition will usually fetch many times the value of worn equivalents.
- Counter-top display pieces can be rare, as fewer were made than other forms of advertising and they were often damaged or discarded when a newer version arrived in the shop.
- In general, look for visually appealing items in good condition that represent the brand, subject area or period as these are likely to be the most valuable.

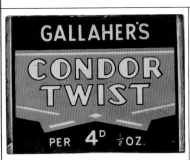

'FRANKLYN'S FINE SHAGG ALWAYS GOOD TO THE END', a double-sided enameled-metal advertising sign, with white lettering on red ground.

'GALLAHER'S CONDOR TWIST PER 4D 1/2 OZ', an enameled-metal advertising sign, the reverse enameled 'Park Drive 10 For 4d, 5 For 2d - Plain or Cork Tipped'.

16in (40.5cm) wide

$100-150   GWRA

14in (35.5cm) wide

$350-450   GWRA

'PLAYER'S "DIGGER" TOBACCOS', a double-sided enameled-metal advertising sign, with wall-mounting flange, in excellent condition.

16in (40.5cm) wide

$200-300   GWRA

'Player's Please', an enameled-tinplate advertising sign, depicting a sailor wearing an HMS 'Invincible' cap, in good condition.

22.5in (57cm) wide

$120-180   GWRA

'Smith's PINEWOOD Cigarettes', a double-sided enameled-metal advertising sign.

20in (50cm) wide

$400-600   GWRA

ADVERTISING

'BLUE CROSS TEAS', an enameled-metal advertising sign, with some restoration.

Restoration can often best be observed with the fingers, as it will usually feel different from the totally smooth original shiny enamel. You'll feel a slight bump or 'line' followed by the restored area, which can feel more matt to the touch.

44in (111cm) wide

$300-500   GWRA

'LIPTON'S TEA', a double-sided enameled-metal advertising sign, with lion and unicorn coat-of-arms, with areas of enamel loss and rust damage.

12in (30.5cm) wide

$150-250   GWRA

'LIPTON'S TEA', a double-sided enameled-metal advertising sign, with wall-mounting flange, in excellent condition.

18in (46cm) wide

$250-350   GWRA

'LYONS' TEA' 'Always the Best' 'Over One Million Packets Sold Daily', an enameled-metal advertising sign, in very good condition.

39in (99cm) high

$200-300   GWRA

'LYONS' TEA SOLD HERE', a double-sided enameled-metal advertising sign, with wall-mounting flange, in very good condition.

18in (46cm) wide

$150-250   GWRA

'MAZAWATTE TEA RECALLS THE DELICIOUS TEAS OF THIRTY YEARS AGO', an enameled-metal advertising sign, in good condition, with enamel damage and rust to the edges.

Much Mazawattee memorabilia is sought after, particularly if it includes the old lady who is so closely associated with the brand.

12in (30.5cm) wide

$300-500   GWRA

'Geo Payne's G.P. TEA', a large enameled-metal advertising sign, in the form of a tea packet, with some damage to edges.

Shaped signs, especially those that suggest perspective and depth, are often sought after and valuable.

33in (84cm) high

$650-850   GWRA

'SUNNY ISLAND CEYLON TEA TRY IT', a large enameled-metal advertising sign, by Chromo Wolverhampton, with some restoration.

54in (137cm) wide

$650-850   GWRA

'Bass IN BOTTLE', a glass and slate advertising sign, with mounting fixings, in very good condition.

20in (50cm) high

$500-700   GWRA

'THOUSANDS OF PEOPLE EAT Bermaline Bread', an enameled-metal advertising sign, in excellent condition, with chipping around bolt holes.

24in (61cm) high

$150-250   GWRA

'BURMA SAUCE THE ONLY SAUCE I DARE GIVE FATHER', an enameled-metal advertising sign, with some restoration.

30in (76cm) high

$1,500-2,000   GWRA

A CLOSER LOOK AT AN ADVERTISING SIGN

This very large sign dates from 1890 and is one of the earliest Cadbury advertising signs known to exist.

Founder John Cadbury (1802-89) had a flair for advertising and promotion that was inherited by his sons Richard and George, who took over the business in 1861.

This sign was part of Cadbury's campaign promoting the medicinal, health-giving benefits of cocoa.

The purity of Cadbury's cocoa was stressed at a time when the British government was concerned about cheap ingredients being added to food to increase profit margins.

'Cadbury's COCOA Absolutely PURE Therefore BEST', an enameled-metal advertising sign, with losses around the bolt holes and left-hand edge.

95in (241cm) long

$1,000-1,500   GWRA

'ICE COLD Coca-Cola SIGN OF GOOD TASTE', a late 20thC printed-tinplate advertising sign.

The current popularity of 1950s advertising has led to the manufacture of fakes and reproductions. The screen-printed surface, light weight and unusually perfect condition of this sign reveal its origins as a modern piece.

27in (68.5cm) wide

$30-50   PC

'EAT COLMAN'S MUSTARD WITH OUR PRIME BEEF, MUTTON ETC. AND ENJOY THEM MORE.', an enameled-metal advertising sign, with some restoration to edges.

22in (56cm) wide

$300-500   GWRA

'EVERARD'S BURTON ALES IN BOTTLE', an enameled-metal advertising sign, in excellent condition.

16in (41cm) wide

$250-350   GWRA

ADVERTISING

Mark Picks

Founded c1759, Fry's was the first company to introduce the chocolate bar as we know it today. It caught on and they introduced the 'Chocolate Cream' bar in 1866. This image was so successful that the bar it adorned, produced from 1902-76, became known as 'Five Boys' chocolate. Many still remember this childhood treat nostalgically and related memorabilia is hotly collected.

'FRY'S CHOCOLATE', a rare 'Five Boys' enameled-metal advertising sign, with some restoration to edge and fifth boy.

18in (46cm) wide

$2,000-3,000   **GWRA**

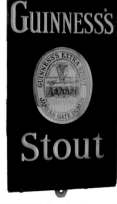

'GUINNESS'S Stout', a glass and slate advertising sign, with fittings for wall mounting, in very good condition.

20in (51cm) high

$300-500

'LYONS CAKES', a double-sided enameled-metal advertising sign, further inscribed 'BY APPOINTMENT CATERERS TO THE LATE KING GEORGE VI J.LYONS & CO. LTD. LONDON W.14', in very good condition.

The wording regarding the death of George VI is helpful as it allows the sign to be dated to a specific period. George VI died in 1952 and was succeeded by Queen Elizabeth II.

c1953   *25in (63.5cm) high*

$200-300   **GWRA**

'LYONS' CAKES', a double-sided enameled-metal advertising sign, with wall-mounting flange, in very good condition.

17in (43cm) wide

$120-180   **GWRA**

'LYONS SWISS ROLLS The roll of fame with a famous name - 1/8 each', a 1960s printed-tinplate advertising sign, in very good condition, with some scratches.

Lyons Swiss Roll advertising may seem a niche area, but pieces are sought after by a number of collectors. This is a rare sign.

12in (30.5cm) wide

$300-500   **GWRA**

'MEW'S ISLE OF WIGHT W.B.MEW,LANGTON & Co.. LTD..', a large enameled-metal advertising sign, in mint condition.

39in (99cm) high

$500-700   **GWRA**

'ROWNTREE'S CHOCOLATES', an enameled-metal advertising sign, with lion and unicorn coat-of-arms, in good condition, with some edge chipping.

25in (63.5cm) wide

$550-750   **GWRA**

'Milkmaid BRAND Milk LARGEST SALE IN THE WORLD As a Guarantee of Quality see the Milkmaid on every Tin', an enameled-metal advertising sign, with some professional restoration.

24in (61cm) high

$1,500-2,500   **GWRA**

'BRASSO', an enameled-metal advertising sign, in the form of a tin of Brasso, with some edge restoration.

Brasso liquid polish was introduced by Reckitt & Sons in 1905 after a senior member of staff saw a similar product being used in Australia. It replaced paste-based polishes. The instantly recognisable can was similar to early 'cone top' beer cans, often causing unpleasant confusion. For more information about cone-topped beer cans, see pp.31-32.

10in (25.5cm) high

$250-350   **GWRA**

'BOND'S SOAP' 'CLEANS & POLISHES', an enameled-metal advertising sign, with some edge restoration.

$1,200-1,800   **GWRA**

'HUDSON'S' '1/4lb. Packets' 'SOAP', an enameled-metal advertising sign, in the form of a clover leaf, in good condition, with some restoration.

12in (30.5cm) wide

$350-450   **GWRA**

'JEYES' FLUID THE BEST DISINFECTANT', an enameled-metal advertising sign, with some edge chipping.

8in (20.5cm) wide

$150-250   **GWRA**

QUICK REFERENCE - SUNLIGHT SOAP

● 'Sunlight' was the world's first branded and packaged laundry soap bar. It was developed by Bolton chemist William Hough Watson and launched by Lever Brothers (now Unilever) in 1884.

● 'Sunlight' was hugely successful across the world and the brand is still in use in some countries.

● The '£1000' featured on the sign below related to the Victorian concerns with purity of products - that vast sum (around $150,000 today!) would be awarded to anyone who could prove 'Sunlight' was adulterated or contained 'injurious' chemicals.

● The bold red, yellow and blue packaging not only attracted housewives' eyes, but also became an iconic design that evokes both reliability and nostalgia in many today. Beware of the many reproductions that this demand has caused.

'LIFEBUOY ROYAL DISINFECTANT SOAP', an enameled-metal advertising sign, with lion and unicorn coat-of-arms, further inscribed 'LEVER BROS LTD SOAPMAKERS TO H.M. THE QUEEN', in good condition, with some restoration.

15in (38cm) wide

$250-350   **GWRA**

'SUNLIGHT SOAP' 'Does Double Work In Half the Time', an enameled-metal advertising sign, in good condition, with some edge chipping.

18in (46cm) wide

$550-750   **GWRA**

'SUNLIGHT SOAP' '£1000' 'GUARANTEE OF PURITY', an enameled-metal advertising sign, with a few small chips.

33in (84cm) wide

$650-850   **GWRA**

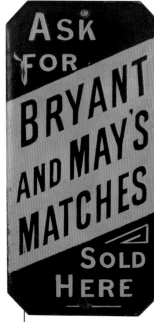

'ASK FOR BRYANT AND MAY'S MATCHES SOLD HERE', an enameled-metal fingerplate advertising sign, in good condition, with some professional restoration.

Fingerplate signs were placed on the area of a door most people would push to open it. The idea was that you would glance down at where you were putting your hands and thus the sign.

7in (18cm) high

$120-180   GWRA

'EVANS' Antiseptic Throat Pastilles For all affections of the throat', an enameled-metal advertising sign, in good condition, with chips to edges.

24in (61cm) wide

$250-350   GWRA

'HALL'S DISTEMPER The Oil-Bound Water Paint', a large 1920s enameled-metal advertising sign, inscribed 'SISSONS BROTHERS & CO. LTD. HULL', in excellent condition, with minor chipping.

The excellent condition and charming 1920s image complete with 'Metroland' house is what makes this sign as valuable as it is.

66in (168cm) wide

$650-850   GWRA

'Exide THE LONG LIFE BATTERY SOLD HERE', an enameled-metal advertising sign, with some fading.

30in (76cm) high

$400-600   GWRA

'Agent for P. & R. HAY. Dyers & French Cleaners Edinburgh.', an enameled-metal advertising sign, in good condition.

22in (56cm) high

$250-350   GWRA

'SOLD HERE THE PATENT STRAINING SAUCEPANS & COVERS', an enameled-metal advertising sign, further inscribed 'NO EXTRA PRICE SOLE MANUFACTURERS JOSEPH & JESSE SIDDONS, WEST BROMWICH', in very good condition, with some edge loss.

Very few of these signs would have been made as Siddons (founded 1846) is a small company compared to Cadbury and Lever Brothers. As an iron and steel foundry, cooking wares were only a part of their business. These factors make this sign very rare.

20in (51cm) wide

$550-750   GWRA

'REPAIRS REDFERN RUBBERS', an enameled-metal advertising sign, in excellent condition.

12in (30.5in) wide

$250-350   GWRA

'Rexall Chemists' and 'Rexall Orderlies', a double-sided enameled advertising sign, in excellent condition, mounted in its original wooden frame, with strengthened corners and twin hanging hooks.

17in (43cm) wide

$200-300   GWRA

A CLOSER LOOK AT A HOTEL SIGN

From the geometric form and design to the angular, brightly colored stylisation of the figure, this sign is typical of the Art Deco era.

It is in excellent condition given its age and particularly given its material. Painted wood is usually more badly affected by the weather than enameled metal.

The fact it has been handmade and painted implies that this sign is either unique or part of a very small number of similar signs.

It is for the world-famous Savoy Hotel. The gilt implies the luxury of the hotel as well as the general high class and perfect level of service. All these factors make the sign desirable.

'SAVOY HOTEL', a 1930s Art Deco wooden sign, with gilt and painted geometric and chequered design surrounding a stylized military general figure.

46in (117cm) high

$4,000-6,000   L&T

'SELO FILMS' 'THE POWER BEHIND THE LENS', a double-sided enameled-metal hanging sign, with minor chips.

23in (58.5cm) high

$250-350   GWRA

'Stephens' Ink', a 1920s-30s enameled-metal advertising sign, with some enamel losses and rust to the corners and sides.

In 1832 Henry 'Inky' Stephens (1796-1864) developed an 'indelible' blue-black ink, which became the core product of the company that bore his name for over 130 years. This sign probably dates from the 1920s. Stephens' signs are more commonly found in white enamel with inset thermometers.

$300-500   GWRA

'VENOS Lightning COUGH CURE for COUGHS, COLDS, FLU, BRONCHITIS, ASTHMA & Children's Coughs', an enameled-metal advertising sign, in excellent condition with very minor edge chipping.

30in (76cm) high

$300-500   GWRA

'VIROL THE FOOD FOR HEALTH', an enameled-metal advertising sign, in excellent condition, with minor marks around the bolt holes.

This is a classic and typical sign for Virol.

48in (122cm) wide

$200-300   GWRA

'Waterman's Ideal Fountain Pen', an enameled-metal advertising sign, in very good condition, with some small chips.

This sign would appeal to both fountain pen collectors and advertising collectors. The pen shown is a No.12 Slip Cap and predates the adoption of the lever-filling system by Waterman in 1915. This helps to date the sign to the late 1900s-1910s.

20in (51cm) wide

$400-600   GWRA

ADVERTISING

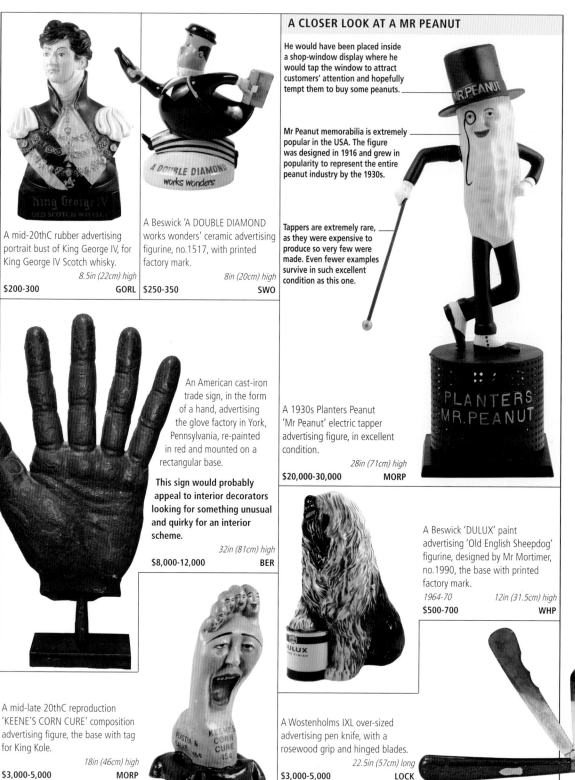

A mid-20thC rubber advertising portrait bust of King George IV, for King George IV Scotch whisky.

8.5in (22cm) high

$200-300 GORL

A Beswick 'A DOUBLE DIAMOND works wonders' ceramic advertising figurine, no.1517, with printed factory mark.

8in (20cm) high

$250-350 SWO

A CLOSER LOOK AT A MR PEANUT

He would have been placed inside a shop-window display where he would tap the window to attract customers' attention and hopefully tempt them to buy some peanuts.

Mr Peanut memorabilia is extremely popular in the USA. The figure was designed in 1916 and grew in popularity to represent the entire peanut industry by the 1930s.

Tappers are extremely rare, as they were expensive to produce so very few were made. Even fewer examples survive in such excellent condition as this one.

A 1930s Planters Peanut 'Mr Peanut' electric tapper advertising figure, in excellent condition.

28in (71cm) high

$20,000-30,000 MORP

An American cast-iron trade sign, in the form of a hand, advertising the glove factory in York, Pennsylvania, re-painted in red and mounted on a rectangular base.

This sign would probably appeal to interior decorators looking for something unusual and quirky for an interior scheme.

32in (81cm) high

$8,000-12,000 BER

A Beswick 'DULUX' paint advertising 'Old English Sheepdog' figurine, designed by Mr Mortimer, no.1990, the base with printed factory mark.

1964-70 *12in (31.5cm) high*

$500-700 WHP

A mid-late 20thC reproduction 'KEENE'S CORN CURE' composition advertising figure, the base with tag for King Kole.

18in (46cm) high

$3,000-5,000 MORP

A Wostenholms IXL over-sized advertising pen knife, with a rosewood grip and hinged blades.

22.5in (57cm) long

$3,000-5,000 LOCK

A 'Y & N DIAGONAL SEAM CORSETS' advertising mirror, with a printed vignette-style image of a corseted woman, in excellent condition.

21in (53.5cm) high

$100-150   GWRA

A 'FRY'S CHOCOLATE' advertising mirror, with lion and unicorn coat-of-arms, in original wooden frame, in excellent condition.

28in (71cm) high

$650-850   GWRA

A 'DAY & NIGHT WEAR "Viyella" DOES NOT SHRINK' beveled advertising mirror, with gilt and gilt-lined black lettering, in original wooden frame, in very good condition, with minor mottling.

20in (51cm) wide

$120-180   GWRA

A 'ROWNTREE'S CHOCOLATES' mahogany and glass shop display cabinet, with glazed front and sides and two glass shelves.

23.75in (68cm) high

$800-1,200   LC

A 'CARR'S BISCUITS' mahogany and glass shop display unit, with three sections, brass handles and marble top.

c1910   53.75in (134cm) high

$2,000-3,000   LC

A CLOSER LOOK AT A COCA COLA DISPLAY

This very rare piece was designed to show that Coca-Cola could be enjoyed all year round and in a variety of places – from the beach to the bar to a frozen lake.

All the characters look healthy and attractive, thereby promoting the drink's supposed health benefits.

For a cardboard item made for display in a shop window, it is in surprisingly good condition and the colors are not faded.

This 'Four Seasons' image was also used in the late 1980s for an advertising mirror, a printed tin tray and a limited-production printed-glass shop display. The latter can fetch over $1,000, with the other two typically fetching less than $80 each.

The complex images were printed in many colors using the lithographic-printing technique.

The form was die-cut.

The Art Nouveau style of the piece is highly appealing and typical of the period

A 'JACOB'S BISCUITS' wooden biscuit dispenser, with image of packet of cream crackers above six slots, in very good condition.

23in (58.5cm) wide

$400-600   GWRA

'ENGLAND'S CROCODILE SHOES', a color lithograph-printed advertisement, further inscribed 'For Contentment and Peace of Mind wear England's Crocodile Shoes'.

22in (55cm) high

$120-180   FLD

A very rare Coca-Cola die-cut and printed cardboard 'Four Seasons' window display, with original black tape links, in very good condition, with some blemishes and scuffs.

1922   60in (152cm) wide

$20,000-30,000   JDJ

QUICK REFERENCE

- These free-standing or wall-mounted vending machines were once commonly found in British towns, villages and railway stations. Produced at a time when pre-packaged goods, consumerism and the middle classes began to boom, they provided quick treats for the weary traveller or sweet-toothed child.
- Examples are rare today, as the majority were melted down during World War I and II. The metal was more valuable for the war effort, but additionally the contents (sweets, chocolates, etc) changed in size and format, meaning machines that had been built to dispense the older shapes and sizes were no longer suitable.
- This is a large and particularly elaborate machine, with a total of eight different dispensers. It is likely it would have been placed in a busy location.
- This example can be dated to the 1890s. The Southwark Street, London-based company that made it closed in 1904.
- Despite only having a limited appeal with advertising collectors living in adequately large homes, these machines fetch consistently high prices as demand exceeds supply, particularly for those that have their original paint or are more complex.

A 'NESTLÉ'S' cast-iron wall-mounted vending machine, for chocolate bars costing '1D', finished in red with white lettering, in excellent condition.

29in (74cm) high

$2,000-3,000 GWRA

A rare 'NESTLÉ'S' cast-iron twin-column vending machine, for milk chocolate at '1D' and Smokers' chocolate at '2D', re-painted and with professional restoration.

71.5in (182cm) high

$5,000-7,000 CA

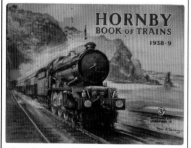

A folding wooden advertising chair, with a 'SMOKE Piedmont "THE CIGARETTE OF QUALITY"' enameled-metal advertising sign inserted into the back panel, in excellent condition.

It is likely that this very rare chair was only made in small quantities, perhaps for one location only.

$300-500 GWRA

A rare late 19thC 'SWEETMEATS' Automatic Delivery Co. 'column and drawer' cast-iron vending machine, re-painted and with professional restoration.

73.5in (187cm) high

$15,000-20,000 CA

A 'Hornby Book of Trains' catalog, with rusted staples, light tears and rust mark to cover.

The image of the speeding steam train helps to raise the value and desirability of this catalog.

1938-39

$120-180 TOV

Six different Meccano catalogues, including those for 1931-32, 1933-34, 1934-35, 1935-36 and 1937, with creased edges and tears.

$250-350 TOV

'The Peerless Series of Private Greeting Cards', a hardback album with 32 patriotic color cards, mounted with costs for different quantities of cards.

1914 *12in (31cm) wide*

$40-60 FLD

A late 1950s Stewart's pressed-glass advertising beer glass, with printed red branding.

Stewart's, known for their whisky, launched beer in the 1950s and produced promotional materials, such as this glass, to help advertise their new product. Unfortunately, it wasn't successful and was consequently withdrawn quickly. As a result, promotional pieces can be scarce.

6in (15.5cm) high

$10-15   MA

A 1950s Godwin 'Champagne Perry' 'Ooh la la!' champagne coupe glass.

4.5in (11.5cm) high

$10-15   MA

A 1920s Gray's Pottery advertising jug, handpainted with the 'Cubist' pattern, inscribed 'ROSS'S BELFAST GINGER ALE', the base with printed factory marks.

4.5in (11.5cm) high

$250-350   SWO

A large 1950s-60s Beswick 'Babycham' ashtray, with transfer-printed motif.

9.25in (23.5cm) wide

$30-50   WHP

A Bourjouis & Cie. 'Pudre de Riz' printed card powder box, sealed, the base printed with five languages.

These were made in the same design 1832-1932.

c1919

$70-100   PC

Judith Picks

Huntley & Palmers are celebrated for their biscuit tins and, looking at this tin, it's clear why! This is a particularly good example. Novelty forms are always sought after, but not only is this a novelty form, it's also clockwork and it's a bus! Transport themes are very popular with collectors. Condition is also important to value. Many biscuit tins were used as toys or storage for keys, spare change and other bits and bobs and were consequently damaged over time. That means examples in good condition are rare and sought after. Although this example is slightly worn, the majority of the printed design is still there - and what a wonderful printed design it is, right down to the different faces of the commuters.

A Huntley & Palmers tinplate clockwork six-wheel 'General' doubledecker omnibus biscuit tin, manufactured by Huntley, Boorne & Stevens, lithographed in red with cream hinged roof, with 'BREAKFAST BISCUITS' advertising on sides, in good condition, with wear to edges.

1930   *9.5in (24.5cm) long*

$5,500-6,500   SAS

A 'MAXIM'S' of Paris menu, handwritten on headed paper, framed and glazed, slightly faded.

16in (40.5cm) high

$25-35   CAPE

QUICK REFERENCE - ART DECO FIGURES

- During the 1920s & '30s, elegant figurines of dancers, acrobats and ladies at leisure became popular. The idealized characters shown were typically very slim, with elongated limbs, short, bobbed hair and fashionable clothes of the day. Pierrots, children and figurines in national costume were also popular. Most are modeled as though in the middle of dancing or executing an acrobatic move.
- Apart from their light, porcelain-like skin tones, ceramic figurines were typically brightly painted and intricately detailed. Clothing became an important design feature and flowing skirts or sleeves are often held up and out to give large flat areas that could be decorated.
- Many companies produced ceramic Art Deco figurines, with the best known being Goldscheider, founded in Vienna in 1885. Goldscheider produced many hundreds of high quality designs, some of which, such as 'Captured Bird', are rare and sought after. Values generally range from low hundreds to high thousands of dollars. Look out for the work of key designers such as Stefan Dakon and Josef Lorenzl.
- Other British and Continental European factories produced similar designs, which are often more affordable. Look out for designs by Katzhütte in Germany, Lenci in Italy, Robj in France and Royal Dux in Bohemia (now Czech Republic).

- The scarcest, most desirable and valuable Art Deco figures are made from cast bronze and ivory, a combination known as chryselephantine. Important sculptors include Ferdinand Preiss (1882-1943), Demetre Chiparus (1886-1947) and Bruno Zach (1891-1935). Of these, Chiparus's designs are perhaps the most sought after and in 2007 a 'Les Girls' group sold at Sotheby's for $950,000. The secondary tier of sculptors includes Josef Lorenzl (1892-1950) and Pierre Le Faguays, known as Fayral (1892-1935). Their work can fetch hundreds or thousands of dollars. All these sculptors were widely imitated in their day. These copies, which were often produced in alloys such as spelter, were and still are much more affordable than original, signed pieces. Contemporary imitations can usually be found for well under $1,200.
- As well as the maker, the quality, size, elegance and eye appeal of the figure count toward value. Examine every part for damage or restoration, as limbs are prone to damage.
- Art Deco figures have been widely reproduced in the last 30 years, as the style has returned to fashion. Learn to spot authentic examples by handling as many as possible. Metals used in reproductions are different, ivory is often replaced by plastic and reproductions will not have the patina or signs of age that original pieces have.

A Katzhütte figurine of a lady, holding her skirt, on an oval base with printed mark and impressed 'No. 67', with cracked and re-glued arm and other damage.

By comparing the value of this figurine to that of the others on this page, it's easy to see how seriously damage reduces desirability and consequently value.

13in (33cm) high

$25-35   CAPE

A large Katzhütte figurine of a woman, wearing a long flowing dress, glazed in graduated pinks, purples and greens, with printed marks, with original paper label.

17in (43cm) high

$700-1,000   WW

A small Katzhütte figurine of a lady, wearing a pink dress and hat, the base with printed mark, with small chip to rim.

8in (21cm) high

$120-180   WW

A large Katzhütte figurine of a dancing couple, the base with printed factory mark, with professional restoration to base.

Katzhütte gained its name from its mark, which shows a stylized cat (katze) inside a stylized house (haus). The company was founded as Porzellanfabrik Hertwig & Co. (Hertwig & Co. Porcelain Makers) by Christoph Hertwig and Benjamin Beyermann in 1864. It became known as Katzhütte in 1958 when it was nationalized, but earlier figures are known by this name as well. From the late 1950s, production was limited to purely decorative items.

20in (5cm) high

$1,200-1,800   WW

A Katzhütte figurine of a lady, wearing a shawl suit with tied scarf belt and broad-rimmed hat, the base with printed mark, with restoration to hat.

11in (27cm) high

$300-500   WW

A Goldscheider pottery figurine of an exotic dancer, designed by Albert Dominique Rosé c1915, model no.5171, the base with impressed and printed marks.

Apart from the fact that he was born in Amiens, France in 1861, little is known about Rosé. He is one of Goldscheider's lesser-known modellers, specializing in clocks and figurines of girls and dancers. Although at first sight this figurine is visually impressive, the quality of the painted pattern is not very high.

10in (25cm) high

$900-1,100   WW

A Goldscheider pottery figurine of a lady, holding a pink scarf, designed by Josef Lorenzl in c1925, model no.5600, the base with impressed and printed marks, with chips to fingers.

18in (45cm) high

$1,000-1,500   WW

A Goldscheider pottery figurine of a Spanish dancer, wearing a shawl and holding a fan, designed by Josef Lorenzl in c1925, model no.5616, the base with impressed and printed marks and facsimile signature.

This figurine is sometimes known as 'Dolores del Río', who was a famous Mexican film star and great beauty. Del Río (1905-83) was the first Latin American star to achieve international success and was considered a counterpart to Rudolph Valentino.

19in (48cm) high

$3,000-5,000   WW

A CLOSER LOOK AT A GOLDSCHEIDER FIGURINE

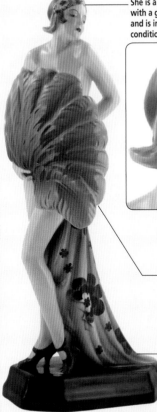

She is a large and rare model with a great burlesque pose and is in excellent, undamaged condition.

She is very well painted with a characterful face and plenty of detail on the scarf and textile.

She protects her naked body with an exotic, pink ostrich-feather fan and a floral textile. Erotic subjects are popular with collectors.

She was designed and originally modeled by Stefan Dakon (1904-92), who was one of Goldscheider's most talented designers. His work is highly sought after today.

A Goldscheider pottery figurine of a performer, holding a large ostrich feather fan, designed by Stefan Dakon in c1926, model no.5876, the base with impressed and printed marks and facsimile signature.

19in (48cm) high

$12,000-18,000   WW

A Goldscheider pottery figurine of a lady with a guitar, model no.6901, designed by Stefan Dakon in c1934, the base with impressed and printed marks, with hairline crack to the rim.

17in (42cm) high

$1,500-2,000   WW

A Goldscheider pottery figurine of a lady, designed by Stefan Dakon in c1934, model no.6912, with impressed and printed marks, with minor chips to the rim, can be fitted for electricity.

12in (31cm) high

$2,500-3,500   DOR

A Goldscheider pottery figurine of a dancing lady, designed by Josef Lorenzl in c1935, model no.7053, the base with printed and impressed marks.

The pose, as if caught mid-dance, allows for dramatic curves, elegantly outstretched arms and plenty of space to display the colorful pattern. For more information about Lorenzl, see p.26.

16in (41cm) high

$3,000-5,000   WW

QUICK REFERENCE - CLAIRE WEISS

● The Hungarian-born Claire Weiss (1906-97) was also known as Claire Weiss-Herczeg or Klára Herczeg. She studied at the Budapest Academy before moving to Paris and Berlin in the late 1920s. Her speciality at Goldscheider was elegant women, but she also modeled lamps and figurines of children. She also designed large sculptures for public display and worked for Rosenthal and Bing & Grøndahl.

A Goldscheider pottery figurine of a lady, strolling with a parasol, designed by Claire Weiss, model no.8138, with impressed and printed marks.

13in (32cm) high

$800-1,200   WW

A Goldscheider pottery figurine of a tambourine dancer, designed by Stefan Dakon, model no.7699, the base with impressed and printed marks and original paper label, with restoration to one hand.

17in (42cm) high

$2,000-3,000   WW

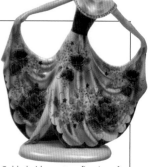

A Goldscheider pottery figurine of a lady, 'Suzette', designed by Stefan Dakon, model no.8083/9, with minor chip to hem of skirt.

This lady is modeled on British/German actress and singer Lilian Harvey (1906-68).

c1938   13.25in (33.5cm) high

$1,500-2,500   DOR

A Goldscheider pottery figurine of a lady, designed by Josef Lorenzl, model no.8167, on a domed black base with impressed factory marks and facsimile signature.

9in (22cm) high

$1,000-1,500   WW

A Goldscheider pottery figurine of a lady, wearing a lace dress and holding her skirts, model no.8301, the circular black base with printed marks.

12.5in (32cm) high

$800-1,200   GORL

A Goldscheider pottery figurine of a young girl, wearing a tartan dress and holding a Pekingese dog, model no.7524, the base with impressed marks.

Goldscheider is best known for figurines of elegant women, but they did produce other models, such as this figurine of a young girl. Values are relatively similar.

10in (26cm) high

$650-850   WW

A Fieldings Crown Devon figurine of a dancer, model no.2271, with bobbed hair and gypsy earrings and wearing a draped gilt-embellished green shawl, the black oval base with printed marks.

13in (33cm) high

$1,000-1,500   AH

A large Fieldings Crown Devon figurine of a lady, wearing a blue shawl, the base with printed marks.

18in (46cm) high

$1,000-1,500   WW

A Fieldings Crown Devon figurine of a dancer, wearing a green bikini top and tiered long skirt, the base with printed marks.

8in (20cm) high

$300-500   AH

A 1990s Kevin Francis for Peggy Davies Ceramics Art Deco-style figural group, 'Tea with Clarice Cliff', no.258 from a limited edition of 2,000, with original box and certificate.

This piece was produced during the most recent peak in the market for Clarice Cliff, the late 1990s and early 2000s. It was part of a series of Art Deco-style figurines featuring Clarice Cliff at various stages of her life. This was the standard colorway for general release.

9in (23cm) high

$150-250   WHP

A Lenci figurine of a kneeling nude lady, holding a celestial globe, modeled by Celia Bertelli, incised 'Le Bertelli' and with painted factory marks.

8.5in (22cm) high

$900-1,200   SWO

QUICK REFERENCE - CELLULOSE DECORATION

● Cellulose was an inexpensive way of decorating plaster and ceramic figurines. It was cheaper than other methods of decoration as it did not require a second firing and could be simply left to dry after being painted.

● The shiny, painted finish is very prone to peeling and damage. At Wade it was only used c1927-37. Many surviving examples of cellulose-decorated figurines have chipped or scuffed paintwork, which reduces value.

● Before producing their famous 'SylvaC' range of animals, Shaw & Copestake also made similar cellulose-decorated figurines, many of which were used as prizes at fairs.

A 1930s Wade cellulose-decorated figurine of 'Gloria', designed by Jessie van Halen, the base with printed marks.

5in (13.5cm) high

$120-180   LSK

A 1930s Wade cellulose-decorated figurine of a 'Conchita', designed by Jessie van Halen, the base with printed marks.

8in (21.5cm) high

$120-180   LSK

ART DECO FIGURES

A Continental porcelain figurine of a dancing girl, wearing a flowing red robe, the base with impressed marks.

10in (26cm) high

$400-600   WW

A German Art Deco porcelain figurine of a dancer, wearing a pink floral dress with blue flowers, unmarked.

11in (28cm) high

$120-180   FLD

A Czechoslovakian Art Deco figurine of a topless dancing girl, wearing a yellow skirt with a blue belt, unmarked.

12in (30cm) high

$400-600   GORL

A Continental ceramic figurine of a lady, wearing a pink flowing dress, the base with impressed and printed marks.

12in (31cm) high

$400-600   WW

A Czechoslovakian Art Deco figural group of dancers, wearing matching bright orange costumes and striking a dramatic pose, the gilt-highlighted base impressed 'Cechoslov, 14600/33'.

The impressed mark is not a limited edition number, but rather a mold or shape number. Many factories in Central Europe impressed shape numbers into the bodies of ceramics.

16in (40.5cm) high

$300-500   AH

QUICK REFERENCE - ATELIER PRIMAVERA

- Atelier Primavera was a French design studio and separate department within the Parisian department store Les Printemps. Founded in 1912 to provide the burgeoning middle classes with stylish decorative wares for their homes, its first director was the influential critic Réné Guillère. An admirer of Renaissance arts, he coined the name of the department, which means 'Spring' in Italian. The store, 'Les Printemps', is 'Spring' in French.
- Designers included Charlotte Cauchet, who eventually married Guillère.
- The department produced and sold ceramics, glass, textiles and furniture.
- Following the influential 1925 Paris Exhibition, they adopted the Art Deco style for which they are best known today.
- The angularity, shape of the base and use of glazes on this figurine are typical of some of Primavera's designs. The minimal and modern style of this piece is popular with collectors and interior decorators today.

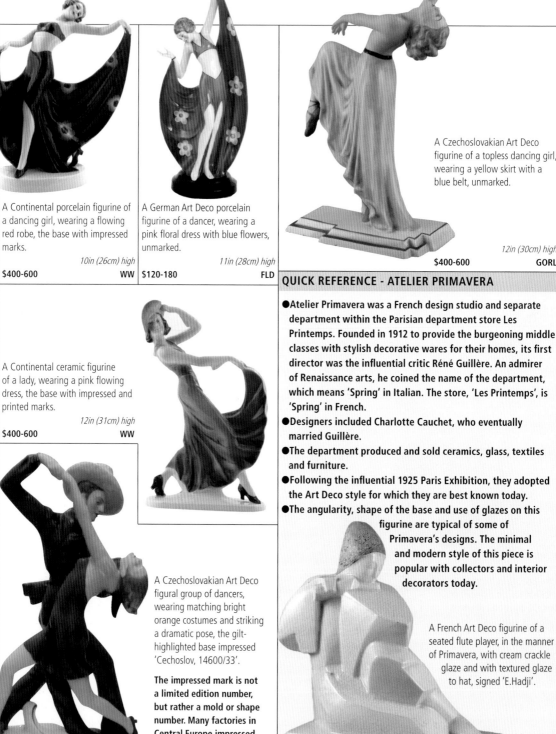

A French Art Deco figurine of a seated flute player, in the manner of Primavera, with cream crackle glaze and with textured glaze to hat, signed 'E.Hadji'.

11.5in (29cm) high

$300-500   GORL

A German Art Deco ormolu figure of a 'A Dancer', designed by E Beck, the black marble plinth inscribed 'A Dancer'.

c1930   16in (39.5cm) high
$1,200-1,800   **DOR**

An Art Deco bronze figure of an 'Andalusian Dancer', designed by Claire Jeanne Roberte Colinet, converted to a table lamp with a conical glass shade and mounted on a marble plinth, the plinth etched 'C.J.R. Colinet'.

c1925   20.5in (52cm) high
$1,200-1,800   **L&T**

A late 20thC Art Deco-style bronze figure of a lady, 'Beloved', wearing a hooded Art Deco-style silvery costume and pendant strands of beads, designed by Erté, on a stepped base, signed 'AP16/37 Fine Art Acquisitions ©1987'.

Erté was the name used by the prolific Russian-born, French artist, designer and costume designer Romain de Tirtoff (1892-1990). The name 'Erté' is derived from the French pronunciation of his initials 'R T'. He is best known for his supremely elegant Art Deco costume designs, but he also designed over 200 covers for 'Harper's Bazaar' and designed sets and costumes for many films, including 'Ben-Hur' (1959). His work enjoyed a revival from the 1960s and particularly from the 1980s onward when the Art Deco style started becoming popular again.

17.5in (44cm) high
$2,500-3,500   **IMC**

A large Art Deco metal and ivorine figural group of a lady feeding pheasants, designed by G Gori, the elongated octagonal marble plinth with inset black marble panels and inscribed 'G.GORI'.

Ivorine is a form of plastic that resembles ivory. The internal streaks in ivorine are more regular than those on natural ivory.

c1927
$2,500-3,500   **L&T**

A mid-late 20thC Art Deco-style bronze figure of a female warrior, after a design by Pierre Le Faguays (1892-1962), on a green marble plinth, with etched signature.

The dramatic, angular pose and athletic, physically-fit body are typical of Faguays' style. The Ancient Greek 'Tanagra' figures provided much inspiration for his work. He also used the (male or female) warrior as subject matter frequently. Many of his designs bear the words 'Fayral' or 'Guerbe' molded into the metal base.

20in (52cm) high
$400-600   **ROS**

An Austrian Hagenauer silvered-bronze figure of a dancer, designed by Karl Hagenauer, on a circular base with stamped factory marks.

Hagenauer was founded by Carl Hagenauer (1872-1928) in 1898. Many of the Art Deco figures produced by the company were designed by his son Karl (1898-1956), who joined the family firm in 1919. Such figures are typically highly stylized, with unembellished surfaces.

6.25in (16cm) high
$700-1,000   **WW**

QUICK REFERENCE - JOSEF LORENZL

- The Austrian sculptor and ceramicist Josef Lorenzl (1892-1950) is best known for his range of bronze sculptures of slim, elegant and often elongated dancers. They typically feature only one figure, delicately balanced on a base.
- Little is known about Lorenzl's early life, but he seemed to have learnt about bronze casting while working at the Vienna Arsenal.
- Pieces are often signed with his name, the name of the model/design or sometimes 'Enzl' or 'Lor'.
- Works marked 'Crejo', a painter who worked with Lorenzl and decorated many of his models, are highly sought-after.
- Lorenzl also designed ceramic figurines for Austrian companies Goldscheider (see pp.21-22), Hertwig and Keramos.

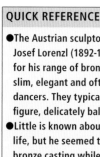

An Art Deco patinated bronze figure of a dancer, designed by Josef Lorenzl, the base with signature, on a green onyx plinth.

13.25in (34cm) high

$2,500-3,500   GORL

An Art Deco patinated-bronze figure of 'Rebecca', cast from a model by Josef Lorenzl, the green striated marble plinth signed 'Lorenzl'.

9in (22.5cm) high

$1,200-1,800   WW

An Art Deco patinated-bronze and ivory figure of a dancing girl, designed by Josef Lorenzl, the green onyx plinth signed 'Lorenzl', missing one hand.

9.25in (23cm) high

$1,500-2,500   DUK

An Art Deco patinated and painted bronze figure of a girl, designed by Josef Lorenzl, the base with impressed mark, on an onyx plinth.

8.5in (22cm) high

$2,000-3,000   DUK

An Art Deco patinated-bronze figure of a nude, cast from a model by Josef Lorenzl, the base signed 'Lorenzl made in Austria', on an onyx plinth.

9.75in (25cm) high

$2,000-3,000   WW

An Art Deco silvered-bronze figure of 'Vivian', cast from a model by Josef Lorenzl, signed 'Vivian real bronze', on a Brazilian onyx plinth.

9in (23cm) high

$2,000-3,000   WW

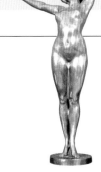

An Austrian Art Deco silver-patinated bronze figure of 'Le Reveil', designed by Paul Philippe for the Goldscheider foundry, the base with Goldscheider foundry seal and numbered 'VB 63/1413'.

This rare figure is large, which is desirable, and in excellent condition, retaining its original patinated surface. It is also extremely well modeled and life-like, lacking much of the strong stylisation found on other, similar sculptures.

c1930   *30in (75cm) high*

$5,500-6,500   SWO

An Art Deco silvered- and bronzed-spelter figure of 'La Danseuse', on a mottled white marble plinth, unsigned.

Spelter is an alloy usually made of zinc and lead, but sometimes also including copper. It was commonly used for lower quality cast figures and other such items. It is surprisingly fragile and brittle.

15.25in (39cm) high

$500-700   DA&H

An Art Deco bronze figure of 'The Faun', by Alexander Proudfoot, signed 'A. PROUDFOOT'.

Alexander Proudfoot (1878-1957) is best known for his public works in and around Glasgow. He taught at the Glasgow School of Art, became an Associate of the Royal Society of Arts in 1921 and a Fellow of the Royal Society of British Sculptors in 1938.

8.5in (21.5cm) high

$550-750   L&T

An Art Deco bronzed-alloy figural table lamp, modeled as a seated semi-nude figure holding a crackle-glass globe shade, on a stepped onyx plinth.

$650-750   RW

An Art Deco gilded plaster figurine, 'La Fille Du Soleil Set De Le Mer', modeled after a design by F Wanczak, missing the fingers of one hand and with other damage.

If you weren't wealthy enough to afford a bronze and ivory or bronze figure by sculptors such as Demetre Chiparus, Ferdinand Preiss or even Josef Lorenzl, you could get the look by buying a plaster copy like the one shown. Molded from plaster in their thousands, such figurines were painted to look like they were made from metal and sold in department stores across the world. Few have survived in good condition as plaster is more delicate than metal, even brittle spelter.

8.5in (22cm) high

$35-45   TRI

An Art Deco cold-painted spelter figural lamp, modeled as a semi-nude exotic dancer poised on one leg holding aloft a glass globe light shade, on an alabaster plinth.

22in (56cm) high

$900-1,200   ROS

An Art Deco-style 'verdigris'-patinated spelter figure of a warrior, holding a javelin, on a stepped natural stone plinth, unmarked.

This is in the style of Pierre Le Faguays (see p.25). It is likely that this figure is a recent copy of an earlier figure, as the patina looks too bright and the stone base looks wrong in comparison with early 20thC examples.

15in (38.5cm) high overall

$650-850   PC

AUSTRIAN BRONZES

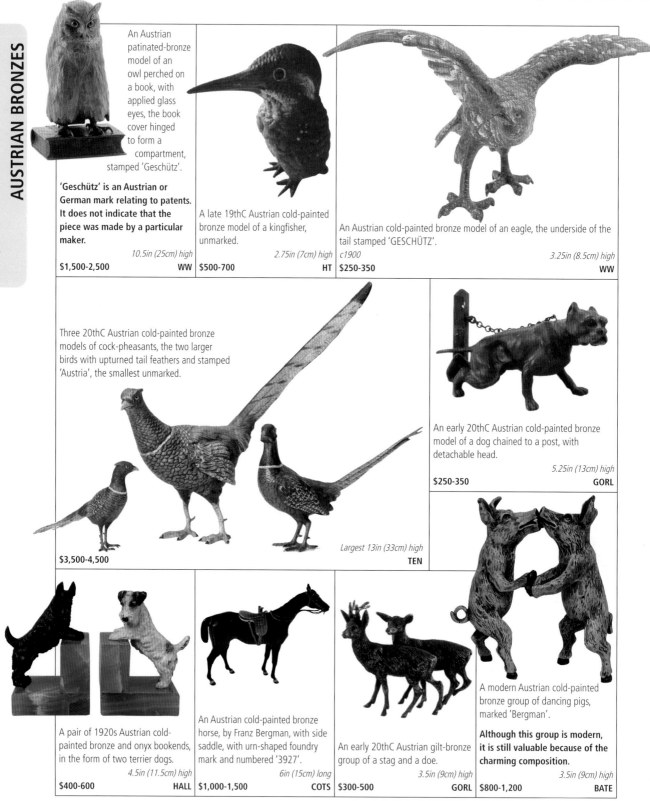

An Austrian patinated-bronze model of an owl perched on a book, with applied glass eyes, the book cover hinged to form a compartment, stamped 'Geschütz'.

'Geschütz' is an Austrian or German mark relating to patents. It does not indicate that the piece was made by a particular maker.

10.5in (25cm) high

$1,500-2,500   WW

A late 19thC Austrian cold-painted bronze model of a kingfisher, unmarked.

2.75in (7cm) high

$500-700   HT

An Austrian cold-painted bronze model of an eagle, the underside of the tail stamped 'GESCHÜTZ'.

c1900   *3.25in (8.5cm) high*

$250-350   WW

Three 20thC Austrian cold-painted bronze models of cock-pheasants, the two larger birds with upturned tail feathers and stamped 'Austria', the smallest unmarked.

Largest 13in (33cm) high

$3,500-4,500   TEN

An early 20thC Austrian cold-painted bronze model of a dog chained to a post, with detachable head.

5.25in (13cm) high

$250-350   GORL

A pair of 1920s Austrian cold-painted bronze and onyx bookends, in the form of two terrier dogs.

4.5in (11.5cm) high

$400-600   HALL

An Austrian cold-painted bronze horse, by Franz Bergman, with side saddle, with urn-shaped foundry mark and numbered '3927'.

6in (15cm) long

$1,000-1,500   COTS

An early 20thC Austrian gilt-bronze group of a stag and a doe.

3.5in (9cm) high

$300-500   GORL

A modern Austrian cold-painted bronze group of dancing pigs, marked 'Bergman'.

Although this group is modern, it is still valuable because of the charming composition.

3.5in (9cm) high

$800-1,200   BATE

QUICK REFERENCE - SIGNED LETTERS

● The value of a signed letter depends on more than simply who the person who wrote it is or was. The context and contents will also affect value. For example, a letter that reveals something personal about the writer, or one that is related to an important part of their career or life, will be more highly valued than one that deals with everyday matters. Similarly, if a letter is written to an important person, or one closely connected to the writer, its value will normally increase.

● This is a pleasant letter to an important person, but monarchs send out many letters of thanks for gifts throughout their reign. It is not particularly rare and relatively impersonal, leading to a comparatively low value. Compare it to the Sassoon letter on this page, in which the great writer discusses working on his famous novel series!

A rare signed 'Apollo 11' beta cloth, signed 'Neil Armstrong', 'Buzz Aldrin' and 'Michael Collins', featuring the 'eagle landing' mission insignia.

Beta cloth is a fabric that is fireproof up to 650 degrees Celsius. It was used in the Apollo spacesuits after the fatal 1967 'Apollo 1' fire.

6in (15cm) high

$2,500-3,500   NDS

A typewritten letter, from and signed in ink by Winston S Churchill and James of Hereford, typed on Board of Trade, Whitehall Gardens notepaper.

$650-850   TRI

A handwritten letter, from and signed by King George V, dated June 4th 1918, thanking Lord Iveagh for a 'lovely old box', which he gave to the king for his birthday, on personal notepaper, with a crowned embossed envelope.

1918

$400-600   TRI

A fragment of crossed cheque, signed by Charles Dickens.

$400-600   TRI

A signed photograph, signed by Stan Laurel and Oliver Hardy, with inscription 'HELLO MAJORE!', in good condition, with minor soiling, creasing and paste residue.

9.75in (24.5cm) wide

$1,500-2,500   NDS

One of a set of two handwritten letters, between Siegfried Sassoon and Alexander Scott, Scott's dated June 1929, Sassoon's dated July 2nd 1929, with envelope.

Sassoon's letter includes a discussion of his work on the Sherston trilogy: 'my object is demonstrate, in a delicate way, the value of peace rather than the horror of war... But I find great difficulty in recovering the authentic detail of my war experience & psychologically it is a most unpleasant task.'

$1,500-2,500 set   L&T

A signed ink sketch of Snoopy, signed by Charles Schulz, on light card stock.

Snoopy is Charles Schulz's (1922-2000) best-known and most-loved creation. The autographs of cartoonists are worth considerably more if accompanied by drawings, particularly if the character depicted is posed typically.

7.75in (20cm) high

$1,200-1,800   NDS

An autograph album, containing the signatures of Julie Andrews, Cliff Richard, Stan Laurel and Oliver Hardy.

$300-500   FLD

A chrome-plated bronze 'Vesta' car mascot, on a hinged radiator cap.

11in (28cm) high

$250-350   **SAS**

A 1920s chrome-plated bronze 'Speed Nymph' car mascot, possibly manufactured by A E Lejeune, on a later plinth base.

8.75in (22cm) high

$250-350   **SAS**

A Rolls-Royce radiator grille, with 'Spirit of Ecstasy' mascot, on a hardwood display base with two Rolls-Royce 'RR' plaques.

28in (72cm) high

$1,000-1,500   **SWO**

A Bentley chrome-plated 'Flying B' car mascot, numbered 'EG807924'.

Most of these mascots were made by Joseph Fray Ltd., although some were made by A E Lejeune.

$150-250   **LSK**

'RAC APPROVED', a double-sided enameled-metal sign, marked with the maker's name 'Bruton Palmers Green N13', in good condition, with a few small chips.

22in (56cm) wide

$80-120   **GWRA**

'Mobiloil', a shield-shaped enameled-metal advertising sign, with red Pegasus, in very good condition, with minor edge defects.

12in (30.5cm) wide

$300-500   **GWRA**

'CROISIERE BLEUE', a Belgian Art Deco transcontinental car race promotional poster, printed by Ciné-Studio, Brussels, in very good condition, with some restoration.

The 38,000 kilometre journey advertised is billed as the world's longest car race.

c1925   *32.25in (82cm) high*

$1,500-2,500   **SWA**

'SUPER SHELL', a petrol pump globe, in excellent condition, on a wooden stand, wired with a bulb, but with cable removed to comply with safety regulations.

$550-750   **GWRA**

QUICK REFERENCE - BEER CANS

- Other foods had been tinned since c1812, but it wasn't until 1933 in the USA and 1936 in the UK that beer was tinned - or canned. Beer cans had to be able to withstand the pressure of the beer and were lined either with plastic or a waxy substance so that the taste of the beer wasn't affected by the metal.
- Aided by close connections to the tinplate industry that was centered in South Wales, the Felinfoel Brewery in South Wales was the first British brewery to can beer. The company's first cans were 'cone tops', sealed with 'crown caps'. These were only replaced with 'flat tops' in 1964.
- Some early cans were flat tops. These were opened by puncturing two holes in the top flat surface.
- Opening was made easier and safer with the invention of the ring-pull tab in 1967. This was used until 1990 when the current 'stay tab' was developed.
- The highest prices are fetched by early cans, designs that cross collecting markets and rare designs. Most beer cans cost under $50 each, often under $15 each.
- Condition is paramount, with dents, rust or damage to the image reducing value dramatically.

A 'H & G. SIMONDS LTD' 'CORONATION BREW' cone-top beer can, issued by H G Simonds.

Once dubbed the world's rarest beer can, this can is actually relatively common. It is the royal connection that increases its value.

1937   280ml
$500-700   NWST

A 'SIMONDS PALE ALE' cone-top beer can, issued by H G Simonds.

The beer was specially brewed for the Royal cruise to Australia and New Zealand in 1949.

1949   280ml
$800-1,200   NWST

A 'THE FELINFOEL BREWERY CO. LITD. PALE ALE' cone-top beer can, issued by the Felinfoel Brewery Co., in very good condition.

This is the first ever British beer can and is both very rare and highly desirable, especially in such good condition.

1936   280ml
$1,200-1,800   NWST

A 1950s 'LONDON PRIDE Export Special Premium Beer' flat-top beer can, issued by Fuller, Smith & Turner, in excellent condition.

340ml
$150-250   NWST

A 1950s 'BLACK BEAUTY Sweet STOUT' flat-top beer can, issued by Hull Brewery.

This iconic design is highly collectible in the 275ml size

275ml
$40-60   NWST

A 1950s 'McEWANS INDIA PALE ALE' flat-top beer can, issued by Scottish Brewers, in mint condition.

340ml
$80-120   NWST

A 'JACKPOT COURAGE BITTER ALE' party can, issued by Courage Barclay & Perkins.

This was one of the UK's first ever 4-pint party cans. Its iconic design makes it very popular with collectors.

1961-62   272ml
$30-50   NWST

A 'TENNENT'S' lager flat-top beer can, 'Scottish Series' 'Forth Bridge', issued by J & R Tennent, missing base.

This design is one of a series of twelve export cans.

1962   340ml
$150-250   NWST

A 1960s 'Anchor Export Beer' ring-pull beer can, issued by Hull Brewery.

With an iconic design, this can is highly collectable in the 275ml size.

275ml
$70-100   NWST

A 'TENNENT'S PALE ALE' ring-pull beer can, 'Ann' 'At the deep end', issued by Tennent Caledonian Breweries.

This can is one of a series of twelve cans. It is the less common 'Pale Ale' version

1965   *440ml*
$30-50   NWST

A rare 'TENNENT'S HOUSEWIVES' CHOICE' lager flat-top beer can, 'Jane Recommends this Recipe: HAM AND CHEESE TOPPERS', issued by J & R Tennent.

One of a series of 20 different recipes from 20 different 'Housewives'.
1964   *440ml*
$1,000-1,500   NWST

A 'TENNENT'S' lager flat-top beer can, 'Ann's Day', issued by Tennent Caledonian Breweries.

This design is part of a series of twelve export cans depicting what happens across 'Ann's day' and is highly desirable.

1965   *333ml*
$500-700   NWST

A 1970s 'JOHN BROWN Badger EXPORT BROWN ALE' ring-pull beer can, issued by Hall & Woodhouse.

Its attractive design makes this can more valuable than other cans of a similar age.

331ml
$15-25   NWST

A rare 'TENNENT'S DRAUGHT LAGER' test ring-pull beer can, issued by Tennent Caledonian Breweries.

This was a test can and only on the market for a short period.
1993   *480ml*
$15-25   NWST

A limited edition 'CARLING' ring-pull beer can, issued by Carling Brewing Co.

This can was available in a silver (very common) version and this gold version. The gold version was only produced in strictly limited quantities and was hidden in multipacks. Finders were entitled to claim a prize. As a result, most gold cans were destroyed because people sent them back to the company.
1999   *520ml*
$15-25   NWST

A rare 'STELLA ARTOIS Strong Continental Lager' ring-pull beer can, issued by Whitbread & Co.

This special black can was released to celebrate the solar eclipse on 11 August 1999. It was available on Plymouth Hoe (one of the best places in the UK to view the eclipse) for one day only, making it unusual and rare.
1999   *440ml*
$8-12   NWST

QUICK REFERENCE - BOOKS

- First editions by popular writers from the last 150 years, such as Agatha Christie, Ian Fleming, Graham Greene and George Orwell, are likely to be collectible. Although famous, iconic titles by these authors are likely to be sought after, an author's earlier books might be more valuable than their later books, as fewer first edition copies of the earlier title will have been printed.
- First editions can have multiple print-runs (or impressions) in which errors are corrected, but these are typically less desirable than what is known as 'true first' editions. The number of true firsts (those copies from the first print run of a book) can be very limited and the smaller the print run, the more valuable a book is likely to be.
- To identify a first edition, check that the publishing date and copyright date match and that these match the original publishing date and publisher for the title. Some publishers state that a book is a first edition or use a series of letters or a number '1' in the series of numbers.
- The presence of the author's signature generally adds value, particularly if the book is a limited or special edition. Dedications are typically less desirable than plain signatures, unless the recipient is famous or connected to the author in some way.
- Condition is of paramount importance. Check that the book is complete and not defaced or damaged, with a dust jacket in good condition. If the jacket is missing, value can fall by up to 50 percent or more. Damaged dust jackets can often be restored. You should also check to see if the price on the inside front has been cut away or 'clipped', as this can reduce the desirability and value to some collectors. Mint condition first editions will always command a premium.

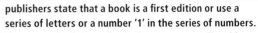

'Lucky Jim', by Kingsley Amis, first British edition, published by Gollancz, with signed presentation inscriptions from the author, one on an endpaper, one on a sticker on the endpaper, with dust jacket, in fine condition.

This was Amis's first book. Signed examples of this great literary debut are extremely rare – only one other signed example is known and that was dedicated to the poet Philip Larkin.
1953
$14,000-16,000   BLO

'I, Robot', by Isaac Asimov, first British edition, published by Grayson & Grayson, with dust jacket, in very good condition.

This was Asmiov's first published collection. It introduces his concept of the Three Laws of Robotics.
1952
$600-800   BLO

'Empire of the Sun', by J G Ballard, first British edition, published by Gollancz, signed by the author on the title page, with dust jacket, in near mint condition.
1984
$400-600   BLO

'Psycho', by Robert Bloch, first edition, published by Simon & Schuster, New York, with dust jacket, in excellent condition, with a little rubbing.
1959
$800-1,200   BLO

'The Postman Always Rings Twice', by James M Cain, first edition, published by Alfred A Knopf, New York, with dust jacket, in excellent condition.

This is a superb copy of the author's first book, which was a landmark in the development of noir fiction.
1934
$5,000-7,000   BLO

'Peril at End House', by Agatha Christie, first British edition, published by Collins Crime Club, in very good condition, the dust jacket with darkened spine, repairs and restorations to head and foot.

This is the correct dust jacket for a first edition.
1932
$8,000-12,000   BLO

'Death on the Nile', by Agatha Christie, first edition, published by Collins Crime Club, with four pages of advertisements and dust jacket, in excellent condition with light foxing and some wear.
1937
$5,500-6,500   BLO

'Appointment with Death', by Agatha Christie, first edition, published by Collins Crime Club, with dust jacket, in very good condition with some browning and small stains and losses.
1938
$5,500-6,500   BLO

A CLOSER LOOK AT A FIRST EDITION

The dust jacket is rare.

Although the creases on the dust jacket can be satisfactorily repaired, the large loss around the title cannot.

The British edition includes the author's 'Preface', which isn't in the first American edition.

The true first edition has a comma after 'Essex' in the publisher's address.

The last page of advertisements in the true first edition is dated '8/5/15' at the end.

'Victory', by Joseph Conrad, first British edition, first issue, with slight browning but internally fine, the bright dust jacket with some losses, rubbed, chipped and creased.
1915
$1,500-2,500   BLO

'Hercule Poirot's Christmas', by Agatha Christie, first edition, published by Collins Crime Club, in excellent condition, the dust jacket with some rubbing, repairs and restoration.

This book was published in 1938 but its copyright page is dated 1939.
1938
$3,000-5,000   BLO

'Sharpe's Sword', by Bernard Cornwell, first edition, published by Collins, with dust jacket, in excellent condition, with small repairs to spine.
1983
$650-850   DW

'The Sound and the Fury', by William Faulkner, first English edition, published by Chatto & Windus, with brown cloth boards, with small inked owner's inscription, price clipped and some surface soiling.
1931
$400-600   BLO

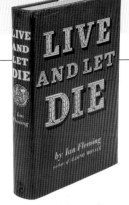

'Live and Let Die', by Ian Fleming, first edition, published by Jonathan Cape, in fine condition, with ink ownership inscription to title verso, the first issue dust jacket in excellent condition, with minor restorations.

The first issue of the dust jacket can be identified as it does not feature a credit for jacket designer Kenneth Lewis. All subsequent printings do credit Lewis, although the location of this credit is not the same from printing to printing.

1954
$10,000-15,000   BLO

A CLOSER LOOK AT A FIRST EDITION

Some copies of the first issue (print run) of the first edition of this book have 'shoot' spelt 'shoo' at the end of the line of page 10. Examples in which 'shoot' is spelt correctly are preferred by collectors, but there isn't much difference in value and the presence or absence of the 't' does not indicate a different issue or print run. It's believed that the 't' became dislodged during printing!

The dust jacket artwork is by Kenneth Lewis, an artist at the Sunday Times who Fleming knew. Lewis produced the cover designs for the first three of Fleming's books.

The first print-run was 9,900 copies, which were printed on two types of paper (19mm and 15mm). The thinner paper is more prone to browning.

'Moonraker' is the third of Fleming's Bond novels. In 1979 it became the eleventh Bond film.

'Moonraker', by Ian Fleming, first edition, published by Jonathan Cape, in excellent condition, with bumped corners, the dust jacket in excellent condition, with darkened spine, some soiling and chipping.

1955
$4,000-6,000   BLO

'Diamonds Are Forever', by Ian Fleming, first edition, first issue, published by Jonathan Cape, in fine condition, the dust jacket in excellent condition, with some browning and chipping.

The true first issue (shown here) has mis-numbered contents. The first print run numbered 14,700 copies.

1956
$3,000-5,000   BLO

'From Russia, With Love', by Ian Fleming, first edition, published by Jonathan Cape, in fine condition, the dust jacket in very good condition.

This edition of 'From Russia, With Love' (marked 'Cape') is considered by collectors to be a true first edition, even though there was an earlier batch. Unfortunately, the first batch of printed pages were of such poor quality that they were rejected by the publisher and sold to a book club instead. Therefore, the book club edition is actually the real first edition, but collectors favor the better printing!

1957
$3,000-5,000   BLO

'Dr. No', by Ian Fleming, first edition, published by Jonathan Cape, second issue, in fine condition, the dust jacket with very light rubbing to head and foot, with custom-made box.

The silhouette of heroine Honeychile Ryder on the front black cloth cover indicates that this example is from the second issue of 'Dr. No'. The first issue, which does not have a silhouette, is rarer.

1958
$3,000-5,000   BLO

'On Her Majesty's Secret Service', by Ian Fleming, uncorrected proof copy published by Jonathan Cape, with 'Proof Only' printing on inside front flap, in good condition, the dust jacket with creases, soiling and tears.

Proof copies of this title are rare and bear a hostile review from the Soviet newspaper 'Izvestia' on the lower panel: 'Obviously American propagandists must be in a bad way if they need to have recourse to the help of an English free-booter - a retired spy who has turned mediocre writer. ('Ouch !' I.F.)'. When the book was actually printed, British reviews of Fleming's four previous Bond titles were used instead.

1963
$1,500-2,500   BLO

'Chitty Chitty Bang Bang The Magical Car', by Ian Fleming, first edition in three volumes, with illustrations by John Burningham, all in very good condition, one with inked owner's inscription.

1964-65
$650-850   BLO

'England Made Me', by Graham Greene, first edition, published by Heinemann, the title page with signed presentation inscription from the author, in very good condition, the dust jacket with chipping and light soiling.

This novel was drawn in part from Greene's own uncomfortable memories of English boarding school. He later wrote of 'England Made Me' – 'I have always had a soft spot in my heart for my fifth published novel…Kate, Anthony's sister, seems to me the woman I have drawn better than any other.'
1935
$15,000-20,000   BLO

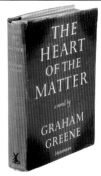

'The Heart of the Matter', by Graham Greene, first edition, published by Heinemann, the title page with signed presentation inscription from the author, in excellent condition, the dust jacket with some chipping, losses and soiling.
1948
$2,500-3,500   BLO

'A Sense of Reality', by Graham Greene, first edition, published by The Bodley Head, the endpaper with signed presentation from the author possibly to John Sutro, in excellent condition, the dust jacket with small chip and light soiling.

John Sutro (1903-1985) was British film producer and a long-standing friend of Greene.
1963
$1,000-1,500   BLO

'The Power and the Glory', by Graham Greene, first edition, published by Heinemann, the title page with signed presentation inscription from the author, in very good condition, the dust jacket with rubbing and restoration.

Perhaps Greene's greatest novel, 'The Power and the Glory' was so popular in France that it was denounced by two Catholic bishops on two separate occasions. In 1953 Greene was summoned to Westminster Cathedral by Cardinal Griffin. There he was read a letter from the Holy Office demanding changes to the text.
1940
$12,000-18,000   BLO

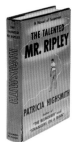

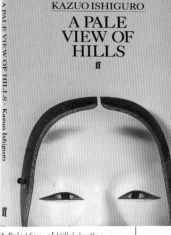

'The Talented Mr. Ripley', by Patricia Highsmith, first edition, published by Coward McCann, New York, in excellent condition, the dust jacket in very good condition, with custom-made box.
1955
$2,000-3,000   BLO

'All the Conspirators', by Christopher Isherwood, first edition, published by Jonathan Cape, in very good condition, the dust jacket in very good condition with price clipped.

This is Isherwood's first novel. The dust jacket is very rare today, particularly in such good condition.
1928
$5,000-7,000   BLO

'Goodbye to Berlin', by Christopher Isherwood, first edition, published by Hogarth Press, in excellent condition, with lightly foxed endpapers, the dust jacket with rubbing, minor chipping and darkened spine.

A semi-autobiographical account of Isherwood's time in Berlin in the late 1930s, 'Goodbye to Berlin' was adapted into the popular and award-winning musical 'Cabaret'.
1939
$5,000-7,000   BLO

'A Pale View of Hills', by Kazuo Ishiguro, first edition, published by Faber & Faber, London, in very good condition, with dust jacket, with usual sunning.

This was the author's first book.
1982
$1,000-1,500   BLO

'On the Road', by Jack Kerouac, first edition, published by Viking, New York, in excellent condition, the first issue dust jacket in very good condition with fading, restoration and abrasions.
1957
$4,000-6,000 **BLO**

'Carrie', by Stephen King, first British edition, published by New English Library, the endpapers with signed presentation inscription from the author, in excellent condition, with some bumping and browning, the dust jacket in very good condition, with faults.
1974
$1,500-2,500 **BLO**

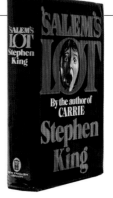

'Salem's Lot', by Stephen King, first British edition, published by new English Library, the title page with signed presentation inscription from the author, the dust jacket in fine condition, with rubbing and fading.
1975
$500-700 **BLO**

QUICK REFERENCE - BRITISH & AMERICAN FIRSTS

● **Note the difference in price between the American first edition, which was the actual first printed edition, and the first British edition, which came out later in the year. It is true that the market for first editions is larger in the USA than it is in the UK, and many collectors do prefer to collect the first edition for their own country. However, the main reason for the disparity in value between the UK and USA editions of 'To Kill a Mockingbird' is that most collectors prize the true first edition of a book, which in this instance is the American edition.**

● **This copy is particularly valuable as it is also signed by Harper Lee. Signed copies are extremely rare.**

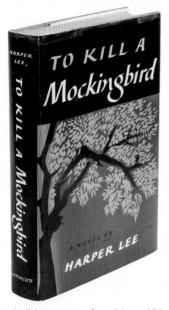

'To Kill a Mockingbird', by Harper Lee, first edition, published by Lippincott, New York, the endpapers with signed presentation inscription from the author, with a card signed by the author, in fine condition, with some bumping and fading, the dust jacket in fine condition.
1960
$20,000-30,000 **BLO**

'To Kill a Mockingbird', by Harper Lee, first British edition, published by Heinemann, in excellent condition, the dust jacket in excellent condition.
1960
$700-1,000 **DW**

'The Naked and the Dead', by Norman Mailer, first edition, published by Rinehart, New York, first issue with publisher's device on copyright page, the half-title page with signed presentation inscription from the author, in excellent condition, the dust jacket with restoration and rubbing.
1948
$1,200-1,800 **BLO**

'Death of a Salesman', by Arthur Miller, first edition, published by Viking Press, New York, with pictorial endpapers with photo of Arthur Miller to rear flap, the dust jacket frayed and with slightly chipped extremities.
1949
$550-750 **DW**

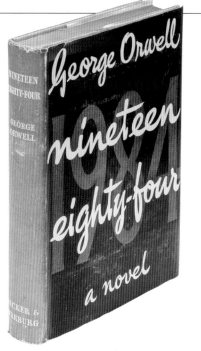

'Under the Net', by Iris Murdoch, first edition, published by Chatto & Windus, the title page with signed presentation inscription from the author, in near-fine condition, the dust jacket in excellent condition, with faded spine, small chips to corners and spine ends.
1954
$1,500-2,500 BLO

'The Flight from the Enchanter', by Iris Murdoch, first edition, published by Chatto & Windus, the tile page with signed presentation inscription from the author, in fine condition, with dust jacket, in fine condition, with rubbing, soiling and fading.
1956
$1,500-2,500 BLO

'Nineteen Eighty-Four', by George Orwell, first edition, published by Secker & Warburg, in fine condition, the first-issue red dust jacket in excellent condition, with faded spine, chipped ends and corners, rubbed.

The main difference in value between the two copies of 'Nineteen Eight-Four' shown on this page is down to the dust jackets.
1949
$3,000-5,000 BLO

'Nineteen Eighty-Four', by George Orwell, first edition, published by Secker & Warburg, in very good condition, with fading at spine and head, the second-issue green dust jacket in excellent condition, with repairs and restorations to spine ends, joints and corners, rubbed, creased and soiled.
1949
$1,200-1,800 BLO

'The Flood', by Ian Rankin, first paperback edition, published by Polygon, Edinburgh, the title page with full-page inscription from the author, the original wrappers in very good condition.

'The Flood' is Rankin's first book and was issued simultaneously in hardback and paperback. The inscription refers to 'the oddity of Fife and its people.'
1986
$300-500 BLO

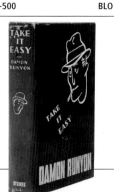

'Take it Easy', by Damon Runyon, first edition, published by Stokes, New York, in very good condition, with slightly darkened and bumped spine, the dust jacket in very good condition, with slightly faded spine and some rubbing and chipping.
1938
$300-500 BLO

'Nine Stories', by J D Salinger, first edition, published by Little, Brown, Boston, first issue with color variation to fore-edge, in fine condition, with spine ends a little bumped, the dust jacket in fine condition.
1953
$2,000-3,000 BLO

'Tortilla Flat', by John Steinbeck, first edition, published by Covici-Friede, New York, in excellent condition, spine ends a little bumped, slightly mottled and darkened, the dust jacket in excellent condition, with chipping, darkening and short split.
1935
$4,000-6,000 BLO

'The Prime of Miss Jean Brodie', by Muriel Spark, first edition, published by Macmillan, the endpapers with signed presentation inscription from the author, in near-fine condition, with spine ends and corners a little bumped, the dust jacket in near-fine condition, with spine ends and corners a little rubbed and chipped.
1961
$800-1,200   **BLO**

'East of Eden', by John Steinbeck, first edition, published by The Viking Press, New York, first issue, in fine condition, with spine ends a little bumped, the first-issue dust jacket in near-mint condition, with small chip to upper panel.

This prized first issue of this first edition has 'bight' spelt as 'bite' on line 38 of page 281. The correct matching dust jacket has the author's photo on the lower panel and no reviews.
1952
$2,000-3,000   **BLO**

'In a Yellow Wood', by Gore Vidal, first edition, published by Dutton, New York, the endpapers signed by the author, in excellent condition, with spine ends a little bumped, the dust jacket with excellent condition, with spine ends and corners a little chipped.

Vidal later said that this book was so bad he couldn't bear to re-read it!
1947
$300-500   **BLO**

'Decline and Fall', by Evelyn Waugh, first edition, first issue, with original patterned cloth, in excellent condition, with slight fraying to spine ends, the dust jacket in excellent condition, with browning, chipping to spine and two short tears.

This first issue has the names 'Martin Gaythorne-Brodie' and 'Kevin Saunderson' on pp.168-69.
1928
$10,000-15,000   **BLO**

A CLOSER LOOK AT A FIRST EDITION

This is the only known copy of this legendary book to be signed by Waugh to be found so far.

The inscription is interesting, relates to the title and will increase the desirability and value. It reads: 'For this body which you call vile, my Lord Jesus Christ was not ashamed to die.'

First editions of this title with their dust jackets are very hard to find.

It is also from the preferred issue, with a price of 7/6 and advertisements on the lower panel ending with 'Second Choice', rather than 'Miss Veil Intervenes'.

'Vile Bodies', by Evelyn Waugh, first edition, first issue, published by Chapman & Hall, the endpapers with signed presentation inscription from the author, the title page printed in red and black with design by the author, with two pages of reviews of 'Decline & Fall' at end, with bookplate of Janet Marston, in near-fine condition, with bumping to spine, the dust jacket in very good condition, with darkening, restorations and rubbing.
c1930
$15,000-20,000   **BLO**

'Officers and Gentlemen', by Evelyn Waugh, first edition, published by Chapman, London, with original blue cloth boards and un-clipped dust jacket, in very good condition.
1955
$400-600   **GORL**

'A Prefect's Uncle', by P G Wodehouse, first edition, second issue, published by A & C Black, with eight illustrations by R Noel Pocock, with eight pages of publisher's advertisements at end, with owner's inscription to rear pastedown, light stains to endpapers, spine a little faded.
1903
$1,200-1,800   **DW**

'William Tell Told Again', by P G Wodehouse, first edition, first issue, published by A & C Black, with color illustrations by Philip Dadd, with two pages of advertisements at end, with a few light spots, the endpapers with owner's inscription.
1905
$500-700   DW

'Love Among the Chickens', by P G Wodehouse, second edition, with original pictorial cloth, with plates, with occasional light finger-soiling to margins, spine darkened, spine ends frayed and a little rubbed.
1906
$500-700   BLO

'The Swoop! or How Clarence Saved England', by P G Wodehouse, first edition, published by Alston Rivers Ltd., with illustrations by C Harrison, with four pages of advertisements, with later cloth, the original upper cover of pictorial wrappers bound-in, with sticker for '1/6' price.

'The Swoop' was designed to be sold for a shilling in railroad bookstalls and similar places. It is consequently among the rarest Wodehouse first editions, as most copies were discarded after reading or treated poorly until they fell apart.
1909
$2,500-3,500   BLO

'If I Were You', by P G Wodehouse, first edition, published by Jenkins, with original cloth, with eight pages of publisher's advertisements, with some spotting, the dust jacket designed by W Heath Robinson, with a few chips and tears.
1931
$1,200-1,800   DW

'Enter Psmith', by P G Wodehouse, first edition, published by A & C Black, with original cloth, with browning to endpapers and spine faded, the dust jacket with tears, chipping, creasing and light surface soiling.

This story was originally published as one half of the novel 'Mike' in 1909. This section was published as a separate novel, 'Enter Psmith', in 1935 and as 'Mike and Psmith' in 1953.
1935
$550-750   BLO

'Three Guineas', by Virginia Woolf, first edition, published by The Hogarth Press, with five plates, in excellent condition, the dust jacket designed by Vanessa Bell, with foxing, spine faded and chipped.
1938
$200-300   BLO

'The Caine Mutiny', by Herman Wouk, first edition, published by Doubleday, New York, in excellent condition, with spine ends a little bumped, the dust jacket in excellent condition, with slightly faded spine, a little rubbed and creased.
1951
$500-700   BLO

'Native Son', by Richard Wright, first edition, published by Harpers, New York, first issue, with first-issue endpapers browned, with first-issue blue cloth stamped in red and white, in fine condition, the first-issue dust jacket with minor restorations to spine ends.

The rare first issue of the first edition has 'first edition' and the publisher's code 'A-P' on the copyright page and '1940' printed in red on the title page. The first-issue dust jacket has no blurb on the spine.
1940
$5,500-6,500

BLO

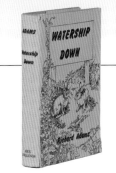

'Watership Down', by Richard Adams, first edition, published by Rex Collings, with folding map, with small mark to rear endpaper and on rear cover, the dust jacket with slight split to spine ends.
1972
$400-600   DW

'Orlando (The Marmalade Cat) Keeps a Dog', by Kathleen Hale, first edition, published by Country Life, with color illustrations throughout, patterned endpapers and original cloth-backed pictorial boards, in very good condition, the dust jacket with clipped price and some faint spotting.
1949
$300-500   DW

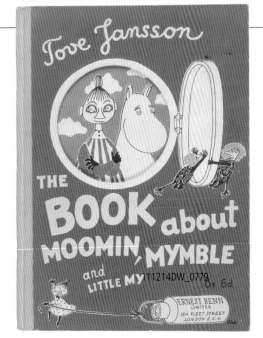

'The Book about Moomin, Mymble and Little My', by Tove Jansson, first British edition, published by Ernest Benn, with color illustrations throughout, with slight rubbing and marks to spine.
1953
$700-1,000   DW

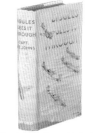

'Biggles - Air Commodore', by W E Johns, first edition, published by Oxford University Press, with color frontispiece, seven illustrations, a few light spots, original gray cloth, dust jacket priced at 3/6, small snagged tear to spine, light water stain and a few nicks and closed tears.
1937
$1,000-1,500   DW

'Biggles Sees It Through', by W. E Johns, first edition, published by Oxford University Press, with color frontispiece, six illustrations, with original orange pictorial cloth, one or two light stains, the dust jacket priced at '4/-', with some stains and abrasions.
1941
$400-600   DW

'Biggles and the Deep Blue Sea', by W E Johns, first edition, published by Brockhampton Press, with original cloth, in very good condition, the dust jacket with a few minor tears and nicks.
1968
$650-850   DW

'The Jungle Book', by Rudyard Kipling, first edition published by Macmillan, with illustrations throughout, foxing spots, owner's inscription, spine ends a little rubbed, upper cover with faint discoloration to one edge.
1894
$1,200-1,800   DW

'Just So Stories for Little Children', by Rudyard Kipling, first edition published by Macmillan, with illustrations by the author, pictorial red cloth cover, overall a bright copy.
1902
$300-500   DW

'War Horse', by Michael Morpurgo, first edition, published by Kaye & Ward, Kingswood, with original pictorial boards and light yellowing to spine, with minor spots to edges and neat owner's inscription.

This is a good copy of a rare title, which has been very successfully adapted for stage and film, thereby increasing the value of the first edition of the book.

1982
$1,000-1,500   DW

'The Railway Children', by Edith Nesbit, first edition, published by Wells Gardner, with pictorial title page and 19 plates by C E Brock, with original cloth but endpapers renewed, slightly rubbed in places.
1906
$400-600   DW

'The Tale of the Flopsy Bunnies', by Beatrix Potter, first edition, published by Warne, with color illustrations, with green cloth, in good condition, with faded spine.
1909
$800-1,200   DW

'The Tale of Timmy Tiptoes', by Beatrix Potter, first edition, published by Warne, with color illustrations and pictorial endpapers, with brown boards.
1911
$350-450   DW

'Scouts in Bondage. A Story of Boy Scouts in Strange Adventure', by Geoffrey Prout, first edition, with color frontispiece, the original red pictorial cloth with fading to spine, the dust jacket with some losses, tears and light staining.

A must for the bizarre books collector. The author's other books include 'Trawler Boy Dick'!
1935
$100-150   DW

'Mary Poppins', by P L Travers, first American edition, published by Reyna & Hitchcock, with illustrations, spine a little faded and ends rubbed, with price-clipped dust jacket, and darkened and chipped spine ends, in generally good condition.
1934
$200-300   BLO

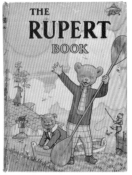

'The Rupert Book', first edition, published by the Daily Express, with rubbing, spine ends split.
1941
$300-500   DW

'Rupert in More Adventures', first edition, published by the Daily Express, with previous owner's inscription, not price-clipped, with slight rubbing.
1944
$650-850   DW

'The Rupert Book', first edition published by the Daily Express, not price-clipped, neat inscription to 'belongs to' box and inside front cover, original wrappers, base of spine slightly rubbed, couple of minor marks.
1948
$150-250   DW

A late-Victorian brass-bound coromandel wood writing box, with inkwells, letter slots, pen holders, fold-out leather-covered writing surface and calendar with moving hand.

A complex interior (in terms of slots, drawers, etc), high quality wood and the presence of unusual features (such as the calendar shown here) will add to the value of writing boxes.

17in (42cm) wide

$700-1,000   LSK

QUICK REFERENCE - BRAMAH LOCKS

- **Prolific inventor Joseph Bramah (1748-1814) patented his first lock in 1784 and displayed an 'unpickable' lock in the window of his London shop from 1790. This highly complex lock used a cylindrical key.**
- **Bramah's 'unpickable' lock remained unbeaten for over 67 years until 1851 when American locksmith Alfred Hobbs opened it after 51 hours of work over 16 days at the Great Exhibition in London. He was awarded a prize of 200 guineas for his achievement.**
- **Bramah's company is still renowned for its high quality, secure locks today.**
- **A Bramah lock fitted on a typical, but large size, box such as this can only add value, so always look at the lock!**

An Edwardian oak domed top writing cabinet, with sloping compartments, three drawers, glass ink bottle, pen tray, gilt-tooled leather-covered writing surface and Bramah lock.

11.5in (29cm) high

$300-500   CAPE

A Victorian coromandel wood stationery box, the satin-birch interior with plate dated '13th December 1879', with five ivory writing tools.

1879   *9in (23cm) wide*

$500-700   GORL

An Edwardian morocco-leather-covered mahogany stationery and writing box, the lid with recessed brass handles, with fall-front blotter/writing surface, two fold-out fitted letter racks and fitted interior with letter racks, inkwell and pen tray.

12in (30cm) wide

$120-180   CAPE

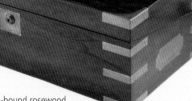

A mid-19thC brass-bound rosewood writing slope, with a gilt-tooled leather writing surface, two lidded compartments, brass topped inkwells and a pen tray, above three secret drawers and a lift-out tray, the lock stamped 'SECURE BRAMAH', the lid with brass plaque inscribed 'G. Cooper'.

21in (53cm) wide

$800-1,200   WW

A Victorian coromandel wood writing slope, with brass mounts, fitted interior and gilt-tooled leather folding slope, with Bramah lock and key.

16in (40cm) wide

$250-350   RW

A Victorian brass-bound rosewood writing slope, with a plush and gilt-tooled leather writing surface with printed label for 'J.J.Meche, No.4 Leadenhall St., London', the side with a base drawer, the lid with brass plaque initialled 'A.G.'.

16in (40.5cm) wide

$250-350   WW

A William IV rosewood sarcophagus-form tea chest, the hinged lid with nulled moldings, the interior with twin lidded pull-out canisters and an associated glass bowl, with ring handles.

12.75in (32.5cm) wide

$300-500   **WW**

A William IV bird's-eye maple sarcophagus-form tea caddy, the hinged lid with a plated navette-shape handle, the interior with two lidded compartments flanking a sugar bowl recess, on gilt-brass ball feet.

12in (30.5cm) wide

$400-600   **WW**

A Victorian rosewood sarcophagus tea chest, the interior with a pair of hinged-lid containers flanking a later glass bowl, with ring handles, on flattened bun feet.

14.5in (37cm) wide

$300-500   **WW**

A William IV rosewood sarcophagus shape tea chest, the hinged lid with a cast brass handle, the interior with twin pull-out lidded canisters, missing glass bowl, with damage to interior.

12in (30.5cm) wide

$200-300   **WW**

A Victorian burr-walnut tea caddy, with engraved brass and ivory mounts, the interior with a bowl recess and a lidded compartment.

9.5in (24cm) wide

$200-300   **WW**

A Victorian burr walnut tea caddy, with engraved brass mounts, the divided interior with a pair of facet-edged covers.

9in (23cm) wide

$150-250   **WW**

A Regency green tortoiseshell tea caddy, with pewter stringing, the cover with replaced plaque, missing feet.

Green is the rarest color of tortoiseshell, followed by the brown/ beige light blond color. This green color is obtained by placing the translucent, almost colorless, tortoiseshell material against a green background. As well as the condition, date, size and form of a tea caddy, the brightness and quality of the mottling and patterning will affect the value. This example would have fetched considerably more if it had been a brighter green and if it had its original feet.

6in (15cm) wide

$2,000-3,000   **WW**

An early 19thC Chinese Canton carved ivory gaming box, carved with roses and forget-me-nots, with a set of carved mother-of-pearl gaming counters each initialed 'GI'.

A William IV kingwood and ivory sarcophagus-form jewelry box, with nulled scrolled moldings, the interior with a padded pouch to the lid and a previously divided lift-out tray.

10.5in (26.5cm) wide

$150-250   **WW**

An early 19thC Tunbridgeware bombe-form work box, with specimen wood cube-parquetry, with a later paper-lined interior, on embossed brass leaf paw feet, with damage to back of top, with bent feet and cracked veneers on lid.

8.5in (21.5cm) wide

$300-500   **WW**

Along with similarly carved card cases, 19thC Cantonese boxes have risen steeply in value over the past five years. This swift and large rise has been driven by the Chinese, who are buying back their heritage through antiques. Although porcelain and jade fetch the highest prices, other areas are also seeing values rising as the number of wealthy Chinese buyers grows. With Cantonese boxes, the complexity and quality of the carving will affect the value, as well as the size and use of the box itself. Games boxes are particularly sought-after.

$3,000-5,000   **GORL**

An Indian carved and pierced sandalwood box, decorated with leaves, animals and trailing foliage, the cover centered with a figure lying on his front, the front edge carved 'PRESENTED BY D. S. RAO IN MEMORY OF JOG FALLS'., missing feet.

Jog Falls is the highest plunge waterfall in India. It is in the Shimoga District, South West India.

7in (18cm) wide

$120-180   **WW**

A Victorian brass-bound coromandel wood dressing box, with a side drawer and fitted jewelry drawer, with eleven silver-topped bottles, the silver by William Nash, London, engraved with leafy scrollwork surrounding circular cartouches engraved with monograms within foliate borders.

Despite their lavish appearance and vast original cost, dressing boxes often do not fetch as much as they perhaps ought to and can be tricky to sell. This is simply due to the fact that there are few serious collectors and dressing boxes are of no real practical use today. Excellent condition, fine quality and completeness all count toward value. The presence of a well-known maker or previous owner's name will also help.

1863   *13in (33.5cm) wide*

$2,500-3,500   **SWO**

Mark Picks

The value of straw-work pieces depend on their complexity and condition, what the pattern depicts and what the object is. Some of the most valuable straw-work pieces were made by Napoleonic prisoners-of-war. A great many pieces were also made by ordinary people at home - this box was probably made by and for a Victorian lady. To fetch the highest prices, the straw should be intact and preferably retain its original color.

Although this particular box needs replacement hinges and has some wear and damage, particularly on the outside, it's a pleasing and typical example of a piece that combines a good variety of different patterns - from stripes to chequers to chevrons and even an inset scenic print - with a currently fashionable 'folk-art' appeal. The fact that this piece is a box also adds to its appeal, as boxes are usually popular with collectors.

An early-mid 19thC straw-work box, decorated with geometric panels, the fitted interior with a small drawer beneath, the lid interior decorated with printed scenes of buildings in landscapes.

14in (36cm) wide

GHOU

$120-180

QUICK REFERENCE - BUCKLES

- The word buckle is derived from the Latin 'buccula', which indicated the cheek or chin strap of a soldier's helmet. Some of the earliest buckles were used to strap parts of body armor together. A buckle is made up of four parts: the frame, the prong, the bar and the chape, the latter being the part attached to the strap or belt.
- In Britain, the buckle-making industry was focused on Birmingham, where factories produced thousands of different types of buckles, many of which were exported to Europe and the USA. Although silver was commonly used, buckles were also made from copper alloy or pinchbeck (a gold-tone metal alloy).
- Shoe buckles have been known since medieval times and were often used as a way of displaying the wearer's wealth and status. They returned to fashion in the late 17thC century and reached a high point in the late 18thC. Sizes became larger as the 18thC progressed. Inset stones became fashionable in the 1740s, although most were made from foil-backed 'paste', a type of lead glass, rather than being genuine precious stones.
- The shoe buckle began to fall out of favor from the 1790s onward. Laces, which had previously been seen as effeminate, began to replace shoe buckles during this period, although shoe buckles were still widely made into the late 19thC.
- The materials used are important to value - the more precious they are, the more valuable a buckle will be. Look out for hallmarked examples and learn about the different marks used for silver and gold in different countries by consulting a reference book, such as 'Miller's Antiques Marks'. The age and style of a buckle will also contribute to its value. Art Nouveau and particularly Art Deco buckles are highly sought after. Always look for quality in terms of design and manufacture.

A late Victorian silver nurse's belt buckle, maker's mark 'SJ', London, of typical scroll pierced form, with heart and cherub motifs, on original elasticated belt.

1897   5in (12cm) wide

$250-350   LSK

A Victorian silver nurse's belt buckle, maker's mark 'D & E', Birmingham, with cast decoration of scrolls and foliage.

1898-99

4in (10.5cm) wide

$80-120   MAR

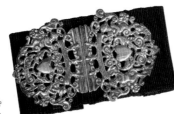

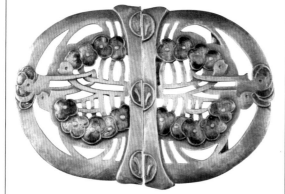

A silver and enamel belt buckle, designed by Jessie M King for William Haseler.

Jessie Marion King (1875-1949) was a Scottish illustrator who also designed jewelry, fabric and pottery. She was appointed as the tutor of book design at the Glasgow School of Art in 1899 and ran the Sheiling Atelier School in Paris, with her husband Ernest Archibald Taylor, from 1910 to 1915. She was heavily influenced by Art Nouveau design and her work is considered to have influenced the Art Deco movement. Her curving and enameled jewelry was often sold by Liberty and is highly sought after today.

3in (7.5cm) wide

$650-850   GORL

A silver belt buckle, by John Maitland Talbot, of pierced Celtic knot form, with a hammered finish, the reverse with stamped marks.

5in (13cm) diam

$800-1,200   WW

A Scottish provincial belt buckle, the design attributed to Alexander Ritchie in Iona, manufactured by Cornelius Saunders & Francis Shepherd, Chester, decorated with stylized vine leaves and branches, with registration no.' 391329' for 1902.

Saunders & Shepherd produced much of Ritchie's silver before 1910, at which point he began producing his own silver and registered his own mark. Based on the remote Scottish island of Iona, Ritchie (1856-1941) and his wife Euphemia were inspired by Celtic art.

1905-06   5.5in (14cm) wide 3.7oz

$400-600   L&T

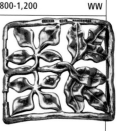

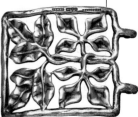

A Liberty & Co. silver belt buckle, designed by Jessie Marion King, one piece hallmarked Birmingham, decorated with stylized birds and flowers

1909-10. 2.5in (6cm) wide

$1,200-1,800 **L&T**

A Liberty & Co. silver 'Cymric' belt buckle, designed by Archibald Knox, Birmingham, cast with stylized foliate panels.

This buckle was also produced with mottled blue and green enamel on the flat panels. The color combination was most commonly used during the Arts & Crafts and Art Nouveau periods.

1903 3in (8cm) wide

$600-800 **WW**

A Liberty & Co. silver 'Cymric' belt buckle, designed by Archibald Knox, in the form of a stylized bunch of tulips.

'Cymric' was the name of the range of silver tableware, decorative objects and jewelry designed for and sold by Liberty & Co., London. 'Cymric' (pronounced coomrick) means 'of, or having to do with, Wales, Welsh or Welsh culture' and many of the designs were inspired by Celtic art. The similar pewter range was known as 'Tudric'. Archibald Knox (1864-1933) began designing for Liberty in 1899.

1902 3in (8cm) wide

$800-1,200 **TEN**

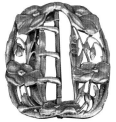

An Art Nouveau silver belt buckle, by William Comyns, London, with pierced design of stylized poppies.

1899 2.5in (6.5cm) high

$300-500 **SWO**

An Art Nouveau silver and enamel belt buckle, by Reynolds & Westwood, Birmingham, decorated with blue-green enamel.

1910 3in (8cm) long

$350-450 **FLD**

A silver and enamel belt buckle, possibly designed by Oliver Baker for Liberty & Co., Birmingham, decorated with blue, green and yellow enamel, set with foil-backed cabochons.

Oliver Baker (1856-1939) was a painter and designer, who exhibited frequently at the Royal Academy from 1883 onward. He produced designs for Liberty's 'Cymric' and 'Tudric' ranges, but is less well known than Archibald Knox. The choice of red, yellow and other bright colors lends an exotic near-Eastern feel to this design.

1901 2.5in (7cm) long

$1,000-1,500 **FLD**

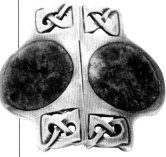

A silver belt buckle, by William H Haseler, Birmingham, with blue-green panels and Celtic knot stylized decoration to borders, with marker's marks for William H Haseler and hallmarks for Birmingham.

William Haseler founded his silver and goldsmiths company in Birmingham in c1848. A London office was opened in 1876 and the company became known as W H Haseler from 1901. Liberty & Co. was one of the company's most famous clients, with much of Liberty's famous 'Cymric' wares being produced by Haseler. In 1946 the company became Haseler & Restall.

1907 2.5in (4cm) long

$350-450 **FLD**

A Piel Frères bronze and cloisonné belt buckle, in the form of a peacock's feather, set with a blue glass cabochon, stamped with maker's marks and 'depose'.

c1900 4in (11cm) wide

$1,500-2,500 **L&T**

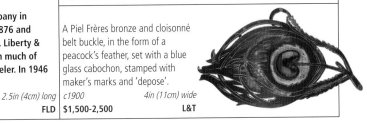

BUCKLES

A CLOSER LOOK AT A BUCKLE

Theodor Fahrner was founded in Pforzheim, Germany in 1855 by Theodor Fahrner Senior and his business partner Georg Seeger.

In 1883, Theodor died and his son, also called Theodor, took over and revitalised the company by hiring leading designers who worked in the modern styles of the day.

The company won a silver medal at the Exposition Universelle in Paris in 1900 and became widely known for its high quality jewelry in the Art Nouveau and particularly the Art Deco styles.

The company declined after World War II and closed in 1979. Today, Fahrner jewelry is highly sought-after, particularly if a piece can be attributed to a known designer.

An early 20thC, possibly French, cloisonné belt buckle, decorated with stylized thistles, unmarked.

2.5in (6.5cm) wide

$150-250   FLD

A Theodor Fahrner silver and enamel belt buckle, molded with Art Nouveau stylized flowers, marked 'T F Depose 900'.

$1,500-2,500

2in (5cm) wide

DA&H

An Art Deco brass and enamel belt buckle, decorated with a multicolored geometric chevron design.

2.75in (7cm) wide

$80-120   TRI

An Art Deco enamel belt buckle.

c1925   *2.5in (6.5cm) wide*

$120-180   PC

A 1930s Art Deco black and amber-red plastic belt buckle.

3.5in (9cm) wide

$70-100   PC

A 1930s Art Deco black and red plastic belt buckle, with carved decoration.

3.25in (8cm) high

$30-50   PC

An early 20thC Japanese belt buckle, decorated in relief with Samurai warriors, unmarked.

3.75in (9.5cm) wide

$300-500   TRI

A Chinese silver belt buckle, by Wang Hing, the two panels decorated in low relief with flowering prunus branches.

c1890   *2.5in (6cm) wide*

$150-250   SWO

A Japanese silver-wire cloisonné belt buckle, the rui-shaped halves decorated with a lily and a bird, with minor stress damage at rear.

c1900   *3.25in (8.5cm) wide*

$300-500   SWO

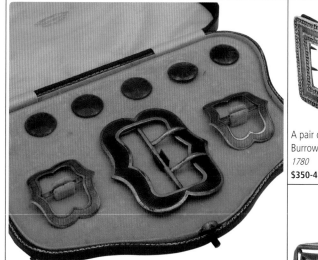

A pair of George III mounted steel and silver shoe buckles, one by George Burrows, London, the other with maker's mark 'IC' and lion passant only.
1780   *2.5in (6.5cm) wide*
$350-450   **WW**

A set of Edwardian silver-gilt and enamel buckles and buttons, by L Emmanuel, Birmingham, comprising a belt buckle, shoe buckle and five buttons, with original fitted case.
1908   *Shoe buckles 2.5in (6.5cm) wide*
$250-350   **WW**

A pair of George III mounted steel and silver shoe buckles, probably by John Northam, London, with pierced and fine bead borders.
1796   *3in (7.5cm) wide*
$300-500   **WW**

A George III steel and nickel gentleman's shoe buckle, set with colorless faceted paste stones.

A pair of Victorian silver shoe buckles, Birmingham, bright cut with stylized flowers and banding.
1897

2.5in (5.5cm) wide   *1in (2.5cm) wide 0.22oz*
$80-120   **WHP**   **$50-70**   **DA&H**

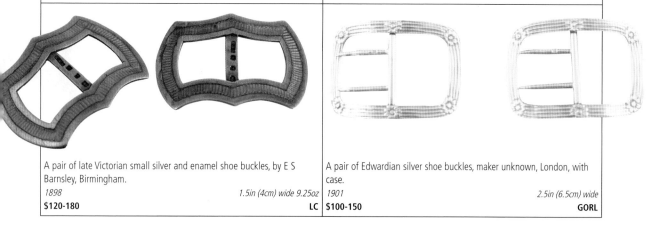

A pair of late Victorian small silver and enamel shoe buckles, by E S Barnsley, Birmingham.
1898   *1.5in (4cm) wide 9.25oz*
$120-180   **LC**

A pair of Edwardian silver shoe buckles, maker unknown, London, with case.
1901   *2.5in (6.5cm) wide*
$100-150   **GORL**

A Thornton-Pickard 'Triple Victo' Honduran-mahogany and brass plate-camera, with plates and leather case.

The Victo was introduced in 1898 and a triple extension bellows was added to the model in 1904. The 1911 model had a Houghton self-capping shutter.

$300-500   DN

Two Kodak 'Rainbow Hawk-eye' No. 2 folding model-B cameras, one in green, the other in blue, in good condition, with some wear.

Most Kodak cameras of this type are worth around $10-20, particularly those with black covering and standard lenses. Brightly colored models, such as these, or those with enameled Art Deco patterns are worth more.

1930-33

$200-300   FLD

An E Krauss of Paris mahogany, brass and leather 'Protar-Zeiss' stereoscopic camera, with dual Zeiss Protar lenses, with leatherette exterior, with original canvas case.

Stereoscopic cameras have two lenses side by side, which capture two similar images of the same target. This creates the effect of a three-dimensional image. The stereoscope viewer was developed by Charles Wheatstone in 1838. Stereoscopy peaked during the 1840s-90s and has returned recently to our cinema screens.

10.5in (27cm) wide

$500-700   GORL

A 1920s Franke & Heidecke 'Heidoscope' stereo triple-lens camera, with Zeiss Tessar 1:45 lenses and strap, with a separate cartridge in leather case.

$400-600   FLD

A Leica Ic camera, serial no. 50211, with some paint loss, with a Leitz Elmar 1:3.5 f=50mm lens, with a leather travel case.

The model number, lens type and condition of a Leica are essential to its value. If you don't know the model number, you can find it by looking up the serial number. This will also give you the year of manufacture.

1930

$1,500-2,500   DN

A Leica IIIa camera, serial no.205351, with a Leitz 'Summar' f=5cm 1:2 lens, no.248335, with leather travel case, 'Pocket Leica Book' from 1954 and a Sixtino exposure meter.

1936

$450-650   DN

A Leica IIIa camera, serial no.196949, with a Summar f=5cm 1:2 lens, no.287430, with accessories.

1936

$800-1,200   DN

A 1930s Russian copy of a Leica camera, serial no.168939, with a Cyrillic-named retracting lens, with leather case.

$200-300 GORL

A Rolleiflex twin-lens reflex camera, with original leather case.

$120-180 REEM

A Rolleiflex 3.5f camera, with leather case and instructions.

$700-1,000 CHT

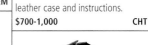

A late 1960s Zenza 'Bronica' S2 6x6 camera, with scratches, with a Nippon 'Kogaku Nikkor'-P 1:2.8 f=75mm lens, 2X Vivitar automatic tele converter and a Tamron 1:2.5 24mm lens.

Zenza is a Japanese company.

$200-300 DN

A subminiature late 1940s Petal 'spy' camera, with fixed-focus 12mm lens, two speeds B and I, the reverse marked 'CPO' within a diamond stamp.

This camera was made in Japan.

$200-300 FLD

A CLOSER LOOK AT A GROUP OF 'MIDGET' CAMERAS

Introduced and sold around the mid-1930s, the Coronet 'Midget' originally cost five shillings. It took a six-exposure film.

Although there are variations in terms of features, for example some cameras have handles while others have domed knobs for winding on film, these variations do not have much of an effect on value. Color is far more important.

As with all Bakelite, most 'Midget' cameras are found in black and brown. Jazzy Art Deco colors, particularly blue, are rarer and more valuable.

A Bolex 'Paillard H16 Reflex' camera, with a Switar 1:1,9 f=75mm lens, no.923315, Switar 1:1,4 f=25mm lens, no.903082, and Switar 1:1,6 f=10mm lens, no.911558, with a leather travel case.

1956

$650-850 DN

Condition is of paramount importance. They must be undamaged to achieve the prices shown here.

c1935

A group of miniature Coronet 'Midget' cameras, with differently colored mottled Bakelite bodies, each with leather flip case (not shown).

2.5in (6.5cm) high

Red: $150-250 Brown: $120-180 Green: $150-250 Blue: $500-700 Black: $100-150 FLD

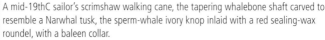

A mid-19thC sailor's scrimshaw walking cane, the tapering whalebone shaft carved to resemble a Narwhal tusk, the sperm-whale ivory knop inlaid with a red sealing-wax roundel, with a baleen collar.

A spiraling barleytwist design was added to this stick to make it resemble the rare tusk of the Narwhal, a type of Arctic-dwelling whale. Narwhal tusks were once thought to be unicorn horns and were consequently highly prized by kings and emperors! For more information, see p.405.

34.5in (88cm) long

$1,200-1,800   WW

A late 17th/early 18thC malacca walking cane, with a turned ivory handle, the pierced silver mount initialed 'T*D'.

35.75in (91cm) long

$1,000-1,500   WW

A sailor's walking cane, the ivory knop incised with diamond-forms, with gold-mounted 'Zebra'-wood (stained malacca) shaft, with brass ferrule.

35in (89cm) long

$300-500   WW

A walking cane, the large ivory ball-knop carved to resemble a knot, the silver by an unknown maker, with Birmingham hallmarks.

1890
34in (86cm) long

$550-750   WW

A mid-19thC sailor's scrimshaw whalebone walking cane, the carved sperm-whale ivory handle in the form of a clenched fist holding a snake, with a metal ferrule.

The clenched fist is a commonly found form for sailor's canes. Value depends on the material as well as the depth and detail of the carving.

32in (81.5cm) long

$1,000-1,500   WW

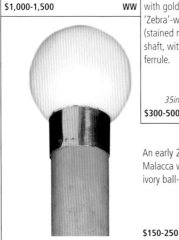

An early 20thC gentleman's Malacca walking stick, with carved ivory ball-finial and 9ct gold collar.

34.5in (88cm) long

$150-250   FLD

A Victorian wooden walking cane, the handle in the form of a parrot's head with inset glass eyes and polychrome decoration, the iron cap revealing an iron protruding spike.

A walking cane, the ivory handle in the form of a hare's head with glass eyes, with silver collar.

36.5in (93cm) long

$650-850   GHOU

43.5in (110.5cm) long

$300-500   WW

A walking cane, the handle in the form of a dog's head.

37.75in (96cm) long

$350-450   DA&H

QUICK REFERENCE - BESWICK

- Founded in Loughton, Staffordshire in 1894, the Beswick Pottery initially focused on vases and tableware, but it has now become best known for its animal figurines. These were introduced in c1900 and were a major part of production by 1930. Values for all but the rarest and most desirable models have fallen recently, which could mean this is a good time to start a collection.
- Collectors tend to focus on one type of animal, such as dogs or cats, which are widely popular. Cattle, particularly large and impressive bulls, tend to be the most valuable pieces, as they are sought after often by butchers and farmers. Calves are generally less valuable than adult cattle, but collectors often buy calves to match their bulls and cows.
- Notable modellers include Arthur Gredington (who designed most of Beswick's animals produced 1939-57), Colin Melbourne, Graham Tongue, Albert Hallam and Alan Maslankowski.
- Value varies greatly based on variation in the type of glaze (typically gloss or matt), form (such as a differently positioned tail) and color. Matt-glazed pieces are usually more valuable than gloss-glazed pieces and 'rocking horse' gray pieces are generally more valuable than brown, but this is not always the case. If you have or are considering beginning a collection, it is worth investing in a specialist guide.
- Beswick was sold to Royal Doulton in 1969, but pieces marked 'Beswick' were still produced until 1989 when production of animal figurines was consolidated under the Royal Doulton name. The 'Beswick' name was used again from 1999 until the factory closed in 2002.
- Collectors always aim to buy pieces in mint condition.

A Beswick yellow, black and blue gloss-glazed model of 'Balitmore Orioles', designed by Arthur Gredington, model no.926.

1941-65   5in (12.5cm) high

$70-100   WHP

A Beswick pink, blue and yellow gloss-glazed model of a small 'Cockatoo', model no.1180, designed by Arthur Gredington.

1949-75   8.5in (21.5cm) high

$120-180   WHP

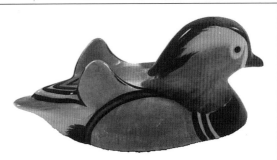

A Beswick gloss-glazed model of a medium 'Mandarin Duck', model no.1519, designed by Arthur Gredington, from the 'Peter Scott Wildfowl' series.

1958-71   3.75in (9.5cm) long

$150-250   WHP

A Beswick dark brown gloss-glazed model of a 'Golden Eagle', designed by Graham Tongue, model no.2062, from the 'Connoisseur' series.

1966-74   9.5in (24cm) high

$100-150   WHP

A Beswick brown matt- and gloss-glazed model of an 'Owl', designed by Harry Sales, model no.2238, from the 'Moda' range.

The highly stylized 'Moda' range was introduced in 1968. Unfortunately designs were too modern for Beswick's main customer base, who generally preferred traditional animal figurines. As a result, few 'Moda' pieces were sold and the range was quickly withdrawn. Examples are rare and can be surprisingly valuable today.

1968-71   6.75in (17cm) high

$250-350   LT

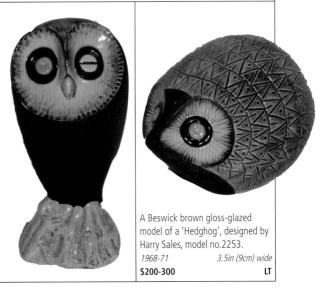

A Beswick brown gloss-glazed model of a 'Hedghog', designed by Harry Sales, model no.2253.

1968-71   3.5in (9cm) wide

$200-300   LT

A Beswick brown gloss-glazed model of a 'Cantering Shire', designed by Arthur Gredington, model no.975.

1943-89   8.75in (22cm) high

$70-100   **WHP**

A Beswick brown matt-glazed model of a 'Shire Horse' (large action shire), designed by Alan Maslankowski, model no.2578.

1978-89

8.25in (21cm) high

$220-280   **WHP**

A Beswick model of a 'Canadian Mounted Cowboy', designed by Mr Orwell, model no.1377.

The fact that this model is rare adds value, as does the fact that it depicts a horse, one of the most popular types of Beswick figure. This particular model is enormously desirable in Canada.

1955-73   *8.75in (22cm) high*

$1,500-2,500   **LT**

A Beswick dun gloss-glazed model of a 'Norwegian Fjord Horse', designed by Albert Hallam, no.2282.

6.5in (16.5cm) high

$400-600   **LT**

A Beswick gray gloss-glazed model of a large 'Elephant', designed by Arthur Gredington, model no.998.

1943-75   10.25in (26cm) high

$150-250   **WHP**

A Beswick dark brown gloss-glazed model of a 'Bison', designed by Arthur Gredington, model no.1019. 1945-73

5.75in (14.5cm) high

$120-180   **WHP**

A Beswick gloss-glazed model of a 'Tiger', designed by Graham Tongue, model no.2096.

Examples are known in a black satin glaze, but these are exceptionally rare.

1967-90   7.5in (19cm) high

$120-180   **WHP**

A Beswick brown and white gloss-glazed model of a 'Dairy Shorthorn bull', 'Gwersylt Lord Oxford 74th', designed by Arthur Gredington, model no.1504.

1957-73   *5in (13cm) high*
$550-750   **WHP**

A Beswick brown and white gloss-glazed model of a 'Hereford Bull', designed by Arthur Gredington, model no.949.

1941-57   *5.75in (14.5cm) high*
$300-500   **WHP**

A Beswick red-brown gloss-glazed model of an 'Irish Setter', 'Sugar of Wendover', designed by Arthur Gredington, model no.966.

This is a very rare model - only around 90 were made.

1941-89   *5.75in (14.5cm) high*
$2,000-3,000   **LT**

A Beswick tan gloss-glazed model of a 'Goat', designed by Arthur Gredington, model no.1035.

1945-71   *5.5in (14cm) high*
$200-300   **WHP**

A Beswick black and tan gloss-glazed model of a 'Dachshund', designed by Albert Hallam, model no.2286, from the 'Fireside Models' series.

1969-81   *10.5in (26.5cm) high*
$200-300   **WHP**

QUICK REFERENCE - TRENTHAM ART WARE

● In 1934, Beswick signed an agreement to design and produce a range of ceramics for a Nottingham-based distributor called Hardy. Marketed under the 'Trentham Art Ware' name, the range of 200 shapes included vases, jugs and 30 animal models.

● After the deal ended in 1941, Beswick was free to continue to produce the range under its own name, which it did until around the late 1960s. Considering the glazes, this donkey probably dates from that later period.

A Beswick gloss-glazed model of a 'Golden Trout', designed by Arthur Gredington, model no.1246.

1952-70   *6in (15cm) high*
$250-350   **WHP**

A 1960s Beswick (Trentham Art Ware) model of a donkey, glazed in green with red spots, the base impressed '181'.

      7in (17.5cm) high
$15-25   **M20C**

An early 19thC Rogers meat plate, printed in blue with the 'Elephant' pattern within a floral border, the reverse with impressed marks.

c1810-20   *19in (48cm) wide*

$300-500   **GORB**

A large pearlware 'Nelson in Memoriam' serving dish, printed in blue with Neptune in a conch carriage, the border containing four sillhouettes of Nelson.

c1820

18.25in (46.5cm) wide

$250-350   **H&C**

QUICK REFERENCE - CONDITION, SHAPE & PATTERN

- The incredibly low price here shows quite how far values for some blue-and-white transfer-printed wares have fallen! Of course, this particular price is especially low as a result of the disfiguring browning caused by frost - without it, this platter may have been worth around $80-120. In a depressed market, even mint condition pieces are likely to be relatively inexpensive, so buyers will generally ignore damaged pieces.

- As well as condition, the pattern and shape are also very important factors to consider when valuing transfer-printed pottery. Rare and desirable patterns, such as 'Durham Ox' or those from the 'Indian Sporting Series', will be worth more than common patterns, such as the 'Long Bridge'. Baby feeders are generally rarer and more sought after than plates and platters.

A Leeds Pottery meat platter, printed in blue with the 'Long Bridge' pattern, with frost staining.

c1810-20   *21in (53cm) wide*

$40-60   **DA&H**

A Joshua Heath pearlware meat dish, printed in blue with the 'Reindeer' pattern, the reverse impressed 'IH'.

c1800   *18.25in (46cm) long*

$300-500   **DN**

A Spode pearlware 'Well and Tree' serving dish, printed in blue with the 'A Triumphal Arch of Tripoli in Barbary' pattern, from the 'Caramanian' series, the reverse with impressed mark.

c1815   *20.75in (52.5cm) wide*

$1,000-1,500   **DN**

A Spode pearlware serving dish, printed in blue with the 'Principle Entrance to the Harbour of Cacamo' pattern, from the 'Caramanian' series, the reverse with printed and impressed marks.

c1815   *14.5in (37cm) wide*

$300-500   **DN**

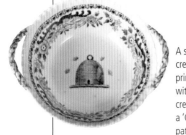

A small Spode crested basket, printed in blue with a beehive crest within a 'Geranium' pattern border, the gadrooned rim with two rope twist handles, the reverse with printed mark.

c1825   *5in (12.5cm) diam*

$350-450   **DN**

An early 19thC Spode foot bath, printed in blue with a river landscape scene featuring buildings, bridges and cows, the base with impressed and printed marks.

With handles 20.5in (52cm) wide

$650-850   **DA&H**

QUICK REFERENCE - BOCH FRÈRES

- Boch Frères was founded in Belgium in 1841 and is still in existence today.
- It produced affordable, mid-market stoneware, typically decorated in a style similar to that of Longwy.
- In 1906, Boch Frères hired the French designer Charles Catteau (1880-1966), who had studied at the National Ceramics School and the National Porcelain Factory in Sèvres. He had also previously worked at Nymphenburg in Germany.
- Appointed design director in 1907, Catteau introduced the fashionable Art Deco style to the factory in the 1920s. Today it is pieces in this style, particularly those by Catteau himself, that are the most valuable. Many of the best pieces bear a facsimile of his signature on the base.
- Catteau's importance was formalized when one of his designs won a gold medal at the landmark 1925 Paris Exhibition that launched the 'Art Deco' style.
- Catteau remained at the company until 1948.
- Simple, clean-lined forms with highly stylized, often geometric patterns, in strong colors are the most sought after, especially if they feature animals.
- The market reached a peak around 2008 and has declined slightly for all but the best and rarest pieces.

A Boch Frères vase, designed by Charles Catteau, pattern no.D1433, painted with geometric stylized flowers in black and green on a cream ground, the base with printed marks and facsimile signature.

12in (31cm) high

$550-750   WW

A Boch Frères vase, designed by Charles Catteau, pattern no.D1174, painted with geometric flowers on a white crackle ground, the base with printed marks.

10in (28cm) high

$500-700   WW

A Boch Frères vase, designed by Charles Catteau, decorated with panels of abstract birds and foliage in purple, black, green and white over an oxide-glazed ground, the base with impressed marks.

13in (33cm) high

$1,500-2,500   FLD

A Boch Frères vase, decorated with stylized floral patterns, the base with mark.

5in (13cm) diam

$200-300   DRA

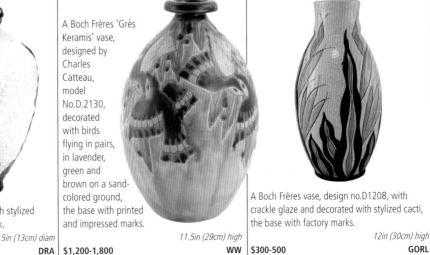

A Boch Frères 'Grès Keramis' vase, designed by Charles Catteau, model No.D.2130, decorated with birds flying in pairs, in lavender, green and brown on a sand-colored ground, the base with printed and impressed marks.

11.5in (29cm) high

$1,200-1,800   WW

A Boch Frères vase, design no.D1208, with crackle glaze and decorated with stylized cacti, the base with factory marks.

12in (30cm) high

$300-500   GORL

CERAMICS

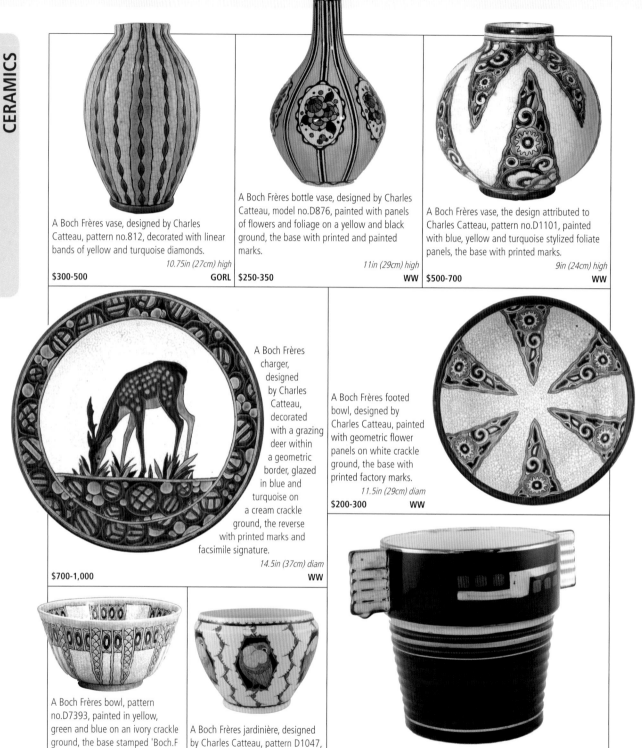

A Boch Frères vase, designed by Charles Catteau, pattern no.812, decorated with linear bands of yellow and turquoise diamonds.

10.75in (27cm) high

$300-500   **GORL**

A Boch Frères bottle vase, designed by Charles Catteau, model no.D876, painted with panels of flowers and foliage on a yellow and black ground, the base with printed and painted marks.

11in (29cm) high

$250-350   **WW**

A Boch Frères vase, the design attributed to Charles Catteau, pattern no.D1101, painted with blue, yellow and turquoise stylized foliate panels, the base with printed marks.

9in (24cm) high

$500-700   **WW**

A Boch Frères charger, designed by Charles Catteau, decorated with a grazing deer within a geometric border, glazed in blue and turquoise on a cream crackle ground, the reverse with printed marks and facsimile signature.

14.5in (37cm) diam

$700-1,000   **WW**

A Boch Frères footed bowl, designed by Charles Catteau, painted with geometric flower panels on white crackle ground, the base with printed factory marks.

11.5in (29cm) diam

$200-300   **WW**

A Boch Frères bowl, pattern no.D7393, painted in yellow, green and blue on an ivory crackle ground, the base stamped 'Boch.F Made in Belgium' and marked 'D.739.3 Ct.'

9in (23cm) diam

$300-500   **DRA**

A Boch Frères jardinière, designed by Charles Catteau, pattern D1047, painted with birds within abstract decoration.

7.75in (20cm) high

$400-600   **GORL**

A Boch Frères two-handled jardinière, decorated with a geometric pattern in silver and orange, the base impressed '1275'.

6.75in (17cm) high

$300-500   **GORL**

QUICK REFERENCE - 1920S-30S CARLTON WARE

- The Carlton Works were founded in Stoke-on-Trent in 1890 as Wiltshaw & Robinson.
- The Carlton Ware name was first used in 1894. It only became the company's official name in 1958, although most of the company's earlier production is also known as 'Carlton Ware'.
- The company entered a 'golden age' in terms of design and sales with the appointment of Horace Wain as design director in 1912. He introduced richly decorated chinoiserie patterns and forms, of which 'Mikado' is one of the most popular.
- In c1921, Wain moved to Wilton and was replaced by Enoch Boulton who had been at the factory since 1908. Chinoiserie styles were continued and augmented by vibrant Art Deco patterns inspired by the 1925 Paris Exhibition. These were successful and continued to be sold into the 1930s and '50s after Boulton moved to Fielding's Crown Devon in 1929.
- Boulton was succeeded by Violet Elmer, who was known for her dramatic and bold Art Deco patterns.
  - Elmer left in the late 1930s and was replaced by Rene Pemberton, who worked for Carlton Ware until the outbreak of war in 1939.

A 1920s Carlton Ware 'Rouge Royale' pattern 'Kangxi' vase, designed by Horace Wain, decorated with Chinese pavilions in a landscape.

11in (28cm) high

$500-700   **GORL**

A late 1920s-30s Carlton Ware 'Chinese Figures' pattern vase, designed by Enoch Boulton in c1927, pattern no.3199, gilded and enameled with figures before pagodas with a frieze of Oriental writing.

8in (20.5cm) high

$80-120   **TRI**

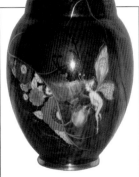

A Carlton Ware 'Fairy' pattern vase.

This vase is well painted, has a rare background color and was featured on the cover of a well-known book.

6in (15cm) high

$5,000-7,000   **LT**

A late 1930s Carlton Ware 'Jacobean Figures' pattern vase, probably designed by Violet Elmer in c1935, pattern no.3956, decorated with gilt and enamel, the base printed 'Carlton Ware', inscribed '3958' and molded '1676'.

6in (15.5cm) high

$1,000-1,500   **CHT**

A 1930s Carlton Ware 'Floral Comets' pattern jug, designed by Violet Elmer in c1929, pattern no.3387, gilt and enameled with flowers and streaks of color, the base with factory marks and 'The Kosniowski Collection' label, with minor restoration to handle.

c1930   *6.75in (17cm) high*

$500-700   **TOV**

A rare Carlton Ware 'Anemone' pattern wall charger, designed by Violet Elmer in c1939, pattern no.3694, printed and painted in colors and gilt on an orange ground, the reverse with printed and painted marks.

13in (32cm) diam

$1,200-1,800   **WW**

A late 1930s Carlton Ware 'Heron and Magical Tree' pattern coffee set, probably designed Violet Elmer in c1937, pattern no.4159, comprising coffee pot and cover, sugar basin and cover, milk jug and six cups and saucers, shape no.1582, all pieces with factory mark.

7.5in (19cm) high

$1,000-1,500   **MLL**

CERAMICS

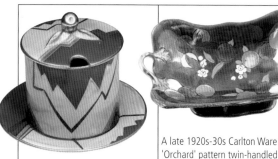

A late 1920s-30s Carlton Ware 'Zig Zag' pattern jam pot, cover and stand, pattern no.3356, from the 'Handcraft' range, the bases with printed factory mark.

Stand 4.75in (12cm) diam

$250-350   MLL

A late 1920s-30s Carlton Ware 'Orchard' pattern twin-handled footed bowl, designed by Enoch Boulton in c1924, pattern no, 2885, printed and enameled with fruiting boughs with gilt highlights, the base with painted marks.

12in (30.5cm) wide

$150-250   WW

A rare 1950s Carlton Ware 'Poppy & Daisy' pattern molded bowl, the base molded '2042' and with printed factory marks, designed in c1949.

Molded 'Embossed' floral and fruiting patterns, often on leaf-shaped bases, were produced in the 1920s and '30s as well as the 1950s. This pattern is very rare today as the colors were deemed too bold for period tastes or interiors. Large pieces, such as this, are also quite fragile, so many of the pieces that were bought were damaged or broken.

c1949-c1959   *9.5in (24cm) diam*

$250-350   BETH

A rare 1930s Carlton Ware 'Poppy & Daisy' pattern molded dish, designed in c1949.

c1949-c1959   *14in (35cm) long*

$120-180   BETH

A 1930s Carlton Ware yellow 'Waterlily' pattern teapot, the base molded '1786/3' and with printed factory mark, designed in c1937.

5.25in (13cm) high

$250-350   BETH

A 1930s Carlton Ware pink 'Calla Lily' spill vase, the base with printed factory mark and impressed '1710'.

5.5in (14.5cm) high

$120-180   BEV

A 1950s-60s Carlton Ware Guinness toucan advertising jug and stand, the base with printed marks.

7in (18cm) high

$120-180   WHP

An early 1920s Carlton Ware advertising figure of a boy, printed with 'I'M FOREVER BLOWING BUBBLES', the base with registered design no.681378 for 1921.

4.5in (11.5cm) high

$50-70   H&C

QUICK REFERENCE – CLARICE CLIFF

● Clarice Cliff (1899-1972) is one of the most collectible names in 20thC British ceramics, with prices rising to many thousands of dollars for rare and desirable pieces.

● After beginning her career as an apprentice decorator at Linguard Webster & Co., Cliff joined A J Wilkinson in 1916. By 1925 factory owner Colley Shorter had spotted her as an emerging talent and had given her her own studio. There she painted defective wares with brightly colored, geometric patterns, which covered the flaws in the ceramic. A team of women (know as the 'Bizarre Girls') were later trained by Cliff to paint her designs.

● Her first range, 'Bizarre', was launched in 1928. The 'Bizarre' heading was used until 1935 and featured numerous pattern names under the general title. The name 'Fantasque' was added to the 'Bizarre' title during 1928-34.

● Value is dependent on the shape and size of a piece, the pattern and the colors used. Orange is a relatively common colorway for many patterns, while purple and blue are generally rarer. Geometric patterns in the Art Deco style are hotly sought after by collectors, particularly if they are painted onto a similarly Art Deco shape. In general, pieces that display the pattern well, such as chargers, vases, jugs and plates are likely to be sought after.

● Damage or wear will reduce the value of any piece, so watch out for cracks and chips.

● Fakes do exist, so it is a good idea to handle as many authenticated pieces as you can, so you can learn the difference. Always look at the mark and check that it is underneath the glaze. If in doubt, be sure to buy from a reputable auction house or dealer.

A Clarice Cliff Bizarre 'Orange Picasso Flower' pattern vase, shape no.264, the base with printed factory marks.

8in (20cm) high

$1,500-2,500   WW

A Clarice Cliff 'Branches and Squares' pattern 'Isis' vase, the base with printed marks, with scratched orange areas and base rim.

c1930   *10in (25.5cm) high*

$1,000-1,500   SWO

A Clarice Cliff Bizarre 'Original Bizarre' pattern vase, shape no.269, the base with printed factory mark, with hairline crack to top rim.

This form was reputedly designed by Clarice Cliff herself. It was produced in two sizes 1928-c1933.

6in (15.5cm) high

$400-600   WW

A Clarice Cliff Bizarre 'Lightning' pattern vase, shape no.265, the base with printed and painted marks, with minor loss to black border.

This vase was featured in the book 'The Best of Clarice Cliff', by renowned experts and collectors Sevi Guatelli and Leonard Griffin. This shape was produced 1928-c1936.

c1929   *6in (15.5cm) high*

$3,000-5,000   SWO

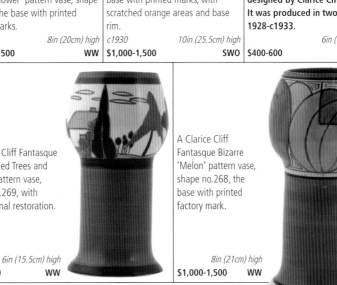

A Clarice Cliff Fantasque Bizarre 'Red Trees and House' pattern vase, shape no.269, with professional restoration.

6in (15.5cm) high

$400-600   WW

A Clarice Cliff Fantasque Bizarre 'Melon' pattern vase, shape no.268, the base with printed factory mark.

8in (21cm) high

$1,000-1,500   WW

CERAMICS

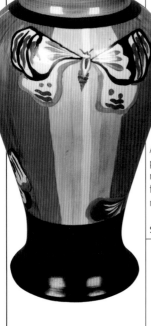

A Clarice Cliff Bizarre 'Umbrellas' pattern stepped vase, shape no.366, the base with printed factory mark, with professional restoration to top rim.

6in (15.5cm) high

$3,000-4,000   WW

A Clarice Cliff Bizarre 'Moonlight' pattern stepped vase, shape no.366, the base with printed factory mark.

6in (15cm) high

$2,500-3,500   WW

A Clarice Cliff Bizarre 'Double V' pattern square-section stepped vase, shape no.369, the base with printed mark and 'Sevi Guatelli Collection' paper label.

This rare form was designed by Clarice Cliff and was produced 1929-34 in one size. Always examine the corners carefully, as they are often chipped. Sevi Guatelli is a major Clarice Cliff collector, expert and author. He sold the majority of his collection in 2009.

7.75in (19.5cm) high

$2,500-3,500   WW

A large Clarice Cliff Fantasque Bizarre 'Butterfly' pattern vase, decorated with orange and yellow vertical stripes and overpainted butterflies, the base with 'Fantasque' mark.

16.5in (42cm) high

$2,500-3,500   DUK

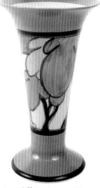

A Clarice Cliff Fantasque Bizarre 'Autumn' pattern trumpet-shaped vase, shape no.280, the base with printed mark, with tiny chips to glaze on rim.

c1931   *6in (15.5cm) high*

$800-1,200   SWO

QUICK REFERENCE - CLARICE CLIFF FAKES

- As prices have risen for Clarice Cliff's work, so have the number of fakes. Although her geometric patterns and 'Lotus' jugs are the usual targets, don't get caught out by fakes of less valuable pieces, such this 'Indian Tree' pattern vase (the vase shown is authentic).
- Fake 'Indian Tree' pattern vases have cruder molded details and the colors are typically less balanced and delicate. The background of fakes tends to have a yellow tone, while the greens and trunk colors are usually considerably stronger in tone.

A miniature Clarice Cliff salesman's sample vase, painted with a geometric pattern, the base with remains of marks, with restoration to neck.

2.75in (7cm) high

$400-600   WW

A miniature Clarice Cliff 'Original Bizarre' pattern vase, painted with a banded geometric pattern, the base with printed factory marks.

2.25in (6cm) high

$300-500   WW

A 1940s-50s Clarice Cliff 'Indian Tree' pattern vase, shape no.989, molded with a flowering tree on cream ground.

8in (20cm) high

$120-180   DA&H

QUICK REFERENCE - 'CONICAL' SUGAR SIFTERS

● The 'Conical' sugar sifter, shape no.489, is one of Clarice Cliff's most iconic and recognisable designs. It was designed by Cliff herself and issued in 1931 in one height.

● It was produced in large quantities and was decorated with a huge number of handpainted and transfer-printed patterns until around 1938. As a result, some collectors choose to focus on collecting this shape exclusively.

   ● Always examine the edges and particularly the top for damage or restoration, as any damage will affect the value.

   ● The pattern on this sugar sifter hasn't been seen before and may be unique. Unfortunately, it's not terribly well painted and is only in a single color that isn't very vibrant. This means that it is relatively unattractive and unlikely to appeal to many buyers As such, it's a good example of how rare (and even unique) pieces are not always the most valuable!

A 1930s Clarice Cliff 'Conical' sugar sifter, shape no.489, decorated in red with a pattern of a cottage, bands and blocks, the base with printed marks.

5.5in (14cm) high

$400-600   **L&T**

A Clarice Cliff 'Cabbage Flower' pattern 'Conical' sugar sifter, shape no.489, the base with printed marks.

c1934   *5.5in (14cm) high*

$550-750   **L&T**

A Clarice Cliff 'Chalet' pattern 'Conical' sugar sifter, shape no.489, the base with printed marks.

c1936   *5.5in (14cm) high*

$800-1,200   **L&T**

A Clarice Cliff 'Chintz' pattern 'Conical' sugar sifter, shape no.489, the base with printed marks.

c1934   *5.5in (14cm) high*

$550-750   **L&T**

A Clarice Cliff 'Coral Firs' pattern 'Conical' sugar sifter, the base with printed 'Bizarre' marks.

c1933   *5.5in (14cm) high*

$800-1,200   **FLD**

A Clarice Cliff 'Blue Firs' pattern 'Conical' sugar sifter, shape no.489, the base with printed 'Bizarre' marks.

c1933   *5.5in (14cm) high*

$800-1,200   **FLD**

A Clarice Cliff 'Honolulu' pattern 'Conical' sugar sifter, shape no.489, the base with printed marks.

c1933   *5.5in (14cm) high*

$1,200-1,800   **L&T**

A Clarice Cliff 'Killarney' pattern 'Conical' sugar sifter, shape no.489, the base with printed marks, with professional restoration to rim.

c1930   *5.5in (14cm) high*

$550-750   **WW**

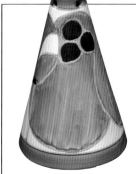

A Clarice Cliff 'Pastel Melons' pattern 'Conical' sugar sifter, shape no.489, the base with printed marks.

c1934   *5.5in (14cm) high*

$900-1,200   **L&T**

Judith Picks

This sifter is decorated in the highly collectable 'Poplar' pattern, but it lacks the cottage usually found by the trees on the horizon. Little differences like this show that the Bizarre Girls (Clarice Cliff's decorators) had free reign to change patterns if they wished, thereby adding a charming human element to collecting these pieces. This pattern is also quite rare, having been sold only briefly in c1932.

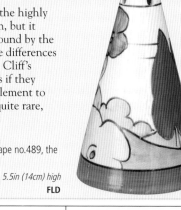

A Clarice Cliff 'Poplar' pattern 'Conical' sugar sifter, shape no.489, the base with printed 'Bizarre' marks.

c1932   *5.5in (14cm) high*

$1,200-1,800   **FLD**

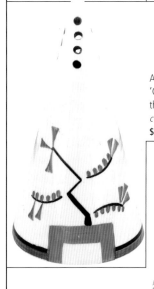

A Clarice Cliff 'Ravel' pattern 'Conical' sugar sifter, shape no.489, the base with printed marks.

c1932   *5.5in (14cm) high*

$650-850   **L&T**

A Clarice Cliff 'Sungold' pattern 'Conical' sugar sifter, shape no.489, the base with printed marks.

c1934   *5.5in (14cm) high*

$550-750   **L&T**

A Clarice Cliff 'Tartan' pattern 'Conical' sugar sifter, shape no.489, the base with printed marks.

c1934   *5.5in (14cm) high*

$300-500   **L&T**

A Clarice Cliff 'Tulips' pattern 'Conical' sugar sifter, shape no.489, the base with printed marks.

c1930   *5.5in (14cm) high*

$1,200-1,800   **L&T**

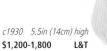

A Clarice Cliff 'Farmhouse' pattern 'Bonjour' sugar sifter, the base with printed factory marks.

5in (12.5cm) high

$500-700   **L&T**

A Clarice Cliff 'Rhodanthe' pattern 'Lynton' sugar sifter, the base with printed factory marks, with some crazing, paint loss and small chips.

c1934   *4.75in (12cm) high*

$300-500   **SWO**

QUICK REFERENCE - HONEY & PRESERVE POTS

- This form was produced 1926-38 in two heights: 3in (7.5cm) and 3.25in (8.5cm). It's clear that it is intended to hold honey, due to its quirky beehive form, which includes a bee acting as the handle.
- The small hole on all of these pots would have once held a spoon, which was typically made of silver or chrome-plated metal.
- Along with the cylindrical pot shown on this page, this form is one of the most commonly found preserve pots.
- The 'Beehive' honey pot was produced in a variety of different patterns.
- Always check the lid and around the inside of the rim for chips and cracks.

A Clarice Cliff Fantasque Bizarre 'Berries' pattern 'Beehive' honey pot and cover, the base with printed factory marks.

c1931   *3in (7.5cm) high*

$550-750   **WW**

A Clarice Cliff Bizarre 'Autumn Crocus' pattern preserve pot and cover, the base with printed marks, with broken and re-glued knop handle.

c1932   *3.75in (9.5cm) high*

$150-250   **SWO**

A Clarice Cliff Bizarre 'Orange Battle' pattern preserve pot and cover, shape no.230, with printed factory marks, with hairline crack to rim.

This is one of Cliff's more unusual patterns. It looks like amorphous, one-eyed oranges fighting for space (hence the name) among green lines. The pattern was only produced in small quantities in 1930, so is comparatively rare today. This form is more common and was produced 1926-36.

c1930   *3.25in (8.5cm) high*

$300-500   **WW**

A Clarice Cliff 'Original Bizarre' pattern preserve pot and cover, the base with printed marks.

5in (12cm) high

$300-500   **WW**

A Clarice Cliff 'Autumn Crocus' pattern 'Bonjour' preserve pot and cover, the base with printed marks.

The 'Bonjour' preserve pot was produced 1933-38. There are two types of finial: disc (shown here) and spherical.

4in (10cm) high

$250-350   **SWO**

A Clarice Cliff 'Autumn Crocus' pattern 'Beehive' honey pot, the base with printed factory marks.

4in (10cm) high

$250-350   **GORB**

A large Clarice Cliff Bizarre 'Liberty Band' pattern 'Beehive' honey pot and cover, the base with printed factory marks, with restoration.

4in (10cm) high

$120-180   **WW**

A Clarice Cliff Fantasque Bizarre 'Summerhouse' pattern preserve pot and cover, shape no.230, the base with printed mark.

c1931   *4in (8cm) high*

$300-500   **SWO**

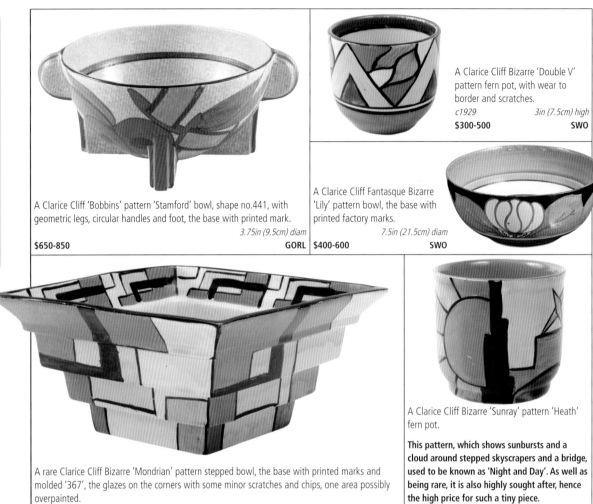

A Clarice Cliff 'Bobbins' pattern 'Stamford' bowl, shape no.441, with geometric legs, circular handles and foot, the base with printed mark.

3.75in (9.5cm) diam

$650-850 GORL

A Clarice Cliff Bizarre 'Double V' pattern fern pot, with wear to border and scratches.

c1929 *3in (7.5cm) high*

$300-500 SWO

A Clarice Cliff Fantasque Bizarre 'Lily' pattern bowl, the base with printed factory marks.

7.5in (21.5cm) diam

$400-600 SWO

A rare Clarice Cliff Bizarre 'Mondrian' pattern stepped bowl, the base with printed marks and molded '367', the glazes on the corners with some minor scratches and chips, one area possibly overpainted.

c1930 *9in (23cm) wide*

$2,500-3,500 SWO

A Clarice Cliff Bizarre 'Sunray' pattern 'Heath' fern pot.

This pattern, which shows sunbursts and a cloud around stepped skyscrapers and a bridge, used to be known as 'Night and Day'. As well as being rare, it is also highly sought after, hence the high price for such a tiny piece.

1929-30 *2.75in (7cm) high*

$1,200-1,800 SWO

A Clarice Cliff Fantasque 'Sunrise Blue' pattern sugar bowl, the base with printed mark.

c1929 *3in (8cm) high*

$300-500 SWO

A Clarice Cliff Fantasque 'Red Trees and House' pattern 'Ivor' bowl, the base with printed mark, with minor loss to black on one tall tree and minor spotting on the red interior.

This shape was produced 1924-36 in three different sizes ranging from 5.5in (14cm) to 7.75in (19.5cm).

c1929 *5.5in (14cm) diam*

$500-700 SWO

A late 1930s-50s Clarice Cliff 'Water Lily' bowl, shape no.973, the base with printed mark.

Designed by Clarice Cliff in 1938, this bowl was produced and sold in very large quantities, making it one of the more common pieces of Clarice Cliff found today.

9in (22.9cm) diam

$120-180 CAPE

A Clarice Cliff Fantasque Bizarre 'Original Bizarre' pattern plate, the base with factory mark, with wear to paint.

Plates display patterns very well, so they tend to be popular with collectors. As they were usually sold in sets they're more common than other forms and can be a comparatively less expensive way to buy into a pattern.

9in (23cm) diam

$200-300   WW

A Clarice Cliff Bizarre 'Circus' pattern plate, designed by Dame Laura Knight, from the 'Artists in Industry' Range, the reverse with printed factory mark, the reverse with grind marks and crazing.

1934   6.5in (16.5cm) diam

$650-850   SWO

QUICK REFERENCE - 'BLUE FIRS'

● 'Blue Firs' is a rarer variation of the best-selling yellow and orange 'Coral Firs'. Both colorways were introduced in 1933. A green variation is known, but currently only one example has been found.

● The 'number 5 blue' color used for 'Blue Firs' caused problems because its firing temperature was so much higher than that of the other colors used in the pattern - the ideal solution would have been to fire the blue at the high temperature, then add the other colors and fire again at the lower temperature. However, with the exception of large pieces and samples, this was not done. Instead, 'Blue Firs' pieces were fired only at the lower temperature, which meant the blue fused inadequately to the honeyglaze surface. Workers were instructed to pack 'Blue Firs' pieces with lots of paper in an attempt to stop colors from running.

● The 'Blue Firs' colorway was dropped in around 1938.

● The pattern sometimes includes part of a cliff and the roof of a house, which aren't present on this example.

A Clarice Cliff Fantasque Bizarre 'Honolulu' pattern plate, the front with minor wear and scratches, the base rim with wear.

c1933   10in (25.5cm) diam

$650-850   SWO

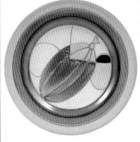

A Clarice Cliff Fantasque Bizarre 'Pastel Melon' pattern plate, the glaze with a few tiny surface chips.

c1932   9in (23cm) diam

$250-350   SWO

A Clarice Cliff Bizarre 'Blue Firs' pattern side plate, the reverse with printed factory mark and impressed date mark.

1934   7in (17.5cm) diam.

$550-750   WW

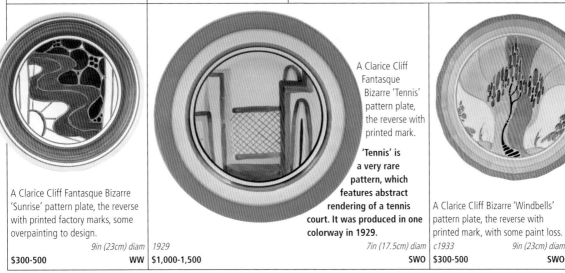

A Clarice Cliff Fantasque Bizarre 'Sunrise' pattern plate, the reverse with printed factory marks, some overpainting to design.

9in (23cm) diam

$300-500   WW

A Clarice Cliff Fantasque Bizarre 'Tennis' pattern plate, the reverse with printed mark.

'Tennis' is a very rare pattern, which features abstract rendering of a tennis court. It was produced in one colorway in 1929.

1929   7in (17.5cm) diam

$1,000-1,500   SWO

A Clarice Cliff Bizarre 'Windbells' pattern plate, the reverse with printed mark, with some paint loss.

c1933   9in (23cm) diam

$300-500   SWO

A Clarice Cliff Bizarre 'Autumn Crocus' pattern matched coffee set, comprising a 'Conical' coffee pot and lid, sugar bowl and cream jug and four 'Tankard' coffee cans and saucers, with printed and painted marks.

This coffee set has been built up by a collector from various parts - an original set would have had 'Conical' cups (like the example shown on this page), which have triangular handles, to match the coffee pot and jug. 'Crocus' was Clarice's best-selling and most prolifically produced pattern, making it easier to build up sets in this way.

c1930   *Coffee pot 7.75in (19.5cm)*
$1,500-2,500   **SWO**

A large Clarice Cliff 'Bobbins' pattern 'Globe' cup and saucer, with printed 'Fantasque' and 'Bizarre' marks.

c1931   Saucer 6in (15cm) diam
$400-600   **FLD**

A Clarice Cliff 'Castellated Circle' pattern 'Empire' tea cup and saucer, with printed 'Bizarre' mark.

c1928
$500-700   **FLD**

A Clarice Cliff Bizarre 'Blue Ravel' pattern 'Conical' cup and saucer, the base with printed marks.

Issued from 1929 onward, the 'Conical' cup was designed by Clarice's sister, Dolly Cliff. Examples made 1929-36 had solid flat-sided handles, while handles made 1932-36 had shallow depressions. The handles produced 1936-40 were hollow or 'open'. Shelley were also known for their Art Deco solid handles on tea cups.

1929-c1935   *2.75in (7cm) high*
$300-500   **WW**

A Clarice Cliff Bizarre 'Newport' pattern 'Stamford' tea-for-two set, comprising a teapot, milk jug, sugar basin, two cups and saucers and a side plate, all with printed factory marks, the teapot dated.

1932   *Teapot 5in (12.5cm) high*
$2,500-3,500   **WW**

A Clarice Cliff 'Original Bizarre' pattern 'Tankard' coffee can and saucer, with gold-printed mark, with crazing and some paint loss.

c1928
Saucer 4.25in (10.5cm) diam
$250-350   **SWO**

A Clarice Cliff Bizarre 'Summerhouse' pattern 'Tankard' coffee can and saucer, the cup with printed mark, with tiny glaze chips.

c1931-33   Saucer 4.25in (10.5cm) diam
$300-500   **SWO**

A Clarice Cliff Bizarre 'Blue W' pattern 'Tankard' coffee can and saucer, with printed marks.

c1930   2.5in (6cm) high
$500-700   **WW**

A CLOSER LOOK AT A PAIR OF CANDLESTICKS

Early catalogs refer to this 'Octagonal' shape as the 'Elton' shape. It was produced 1925-36 in two heights: 8in (20cm) high and 12in (30cm) high.

The 'Elton' shape was probably inspired by a piece by Frank Lloyd Wright.

The shape was very popular up until 1930 and then became rapidly less popular, possibly due to electric lighting taking over in homes. Clarice continued to promote candlesticks as decorative accessories.

The 'Café au Lait' wording in the pattern name refers to the stippled or mottled background over which the 'Bobbins' pattern is painted. Here it is in a desirable green, but it can also be found in other colors, such as brown.

A pair of Clarice Cliff Bizarre 'Café au Lait Bobbins' pattern 'Octagonal' candlesticks, with printed factory marks, one with restored foot.

12in (30cm) high

$1,500-2,500   **WW**

A Clarice Cliff Fantasque 'Broth' pattern candlestick, shape no.310, the base with printed mark.

This shape was produced c1926-39. The 'Broth' pattern is rare and desirable.

c1928   *4.5in (11.5cm) high*

$300-500   **SWO**

A Clarice Cliff Bizarre 'Coral Firs' pattern figural candlestick, in the form of a Turkish boy.

6in (15cm) high

$1,500-2,500   **GORL**

A Clarice Cliff Bizarre 'Delecia Citrus' pattern candlestick, shape no.331, with printed factory mark.

c1930   *3.5in (9cm) high*

$150-250   **SWO**

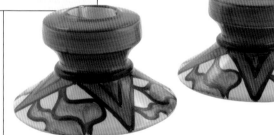

A pair of Clarice Cliff Bizarre 'Double V' pattern candlesticks, shape no.331, painted in colors and with printed factory marks.

3.5in (9cm) diam

$550-750   **WW**

A pair of Clarice Cliff Bizarre 'Gayday' pattern candlesticks, shape no.310, one with printed and painted marks.

c1930   *4.5in (11.5cm) high*

$500-700   **SWO**

A Clarice Cliff 'Original Bizarre' pattern 'Octagonal' candlestick, the base with gold printed mark.

'Original Bizarre' is one of the most common patterns found on the 'Octagonal' candlestick, along with 'Autumn Crocus', 'Appliqué' patterns and early landscape patterns, such as 'Trees & House' and 'Autumn'.

c1927-28   *12in (30.5cm) high*

$550-750   **SWO**

A Clarice Cliff Fantasque Bizarre 'Red Trees and House' pattern candlestick, shape no.310, with printed factory mark.

4.5in (11.5cm) diam

$400-600   **WW**

CERAMICS

A late 1930s Clarice Cliff 'Marlene' wall mask, with gilt details, with printed script mark, the reverse with crack from hanging aperture to top.

First sold in 1931, this mask was based on famous actress and singer Marlene Dietrich, who shot to global fame in 1930 with her film 'The Blue Angel'. Pale versions tend to date from after 1934. Compare this version with the brighter variation of the same model on the right and note how widely the effects differ depending on the colors used and where they are used.

7in (18cm) high

$300-500   FLD

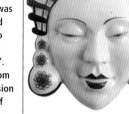

A 1930s Clarice Cliff Bizarre 'Marlene' wall mask, with yellow and orange headpiece, with some restoration.

7in (18cm) high

$400-600   PC

A Clarice Cliff 'Chahar' wall mask, with printed marks.

The 'Chahar' mask was inspired by a column depicted in Owen Jones' influential book 'Grammar of Ornament'. 'Chahar' was Cliff's first decorative mask and was produced until c1930, primarily in these colors although details can differ.

c1930   11in (28cm) high

$2,500-3,500   PC

An early 1930s Clarice Cliff 'Jack' wall mask, decorated with an 'Inspiration' glaze, yellow, pink and blue.

7in (18cm) high

$300-500   PC

A CLOSER LOOK AT A MASK

This mask was released in 1929.

It seems to have been inspired by ancient Italian gargoyles, here given a modern twist with Art Deco colors and geometry.

Ron Birks was the son of ceramics designer and factory owner Lawrence Birks. He worked briefly for Clarice Cliff and his initials are often found on earlier examples.

This piece is in excellent condition, with no damage or restoration.

This mask is also available in a patterned variation, which could be worth $8,000-15,000 depending on pattern and condition.

A rare Clarice Cliff 'Grotesque' mask, designed by Ron Birks, painted in shades of green, red and black, the reverse with printed factory mark.

11in (28cm) high

$5,500-6,500   WW

A 21stC Wedgwood for the Clarice Cliff Collectors' Club 'Grotesque' mask, originally designed by Ron Birks, painted in shades of orange, yellow and black, the reverse with printed mark and dated.

The marks on these officially licensed reproductions are different from those on originals. The two versions are also decorated very differently - the colors are glossier and more even.

2001   11.25in (28.5cm) high

$80-120   WW

A Clarice Cliff 'Pan' wall mask, the reverse with printed factory marks.

c1925   9in (23cm) high

$450-650   PC

A miniature Clarice Cliff wall-mask pendant, in the form of a lady with a green scarf, the reverse with printed factory marks, with crack.

3in (7.5cm) high

$400-600   PC

A Clarice Cliff Bizarre wall mask, in the form of a lady wearing a beret.

c1925   8.75in (22cm) high

$550-750   PC

QUICK REFERENCE - SAMSON & CIE.

- As well as producing their own designs, French ceramics company Samson, Edmé & Cie (1845-1969) were well-known for copying the work of other illustrious ceramics companies. Such companies included Meissen, Sèvres, Worcester, Chelsea and Derby.
- Samson did not intend its replicas to be passed off as originals. Reportedly each piece was made with a letter 'S' contained within the copied factory's mark. However, this 'S' can easily be removed!
- Some copies are so close to the originals that they can only be identified scientifically. Often, however, the difference can be seen in the body, the way a piece is made and the quality of the painting.

A late 19thC German cabinet cup and saucer, painted with cherubs and gilded, the handle molded with a face, the base with an 'S' within crossed swords mark.

It wasn't just the French firm of Samson that produced copies and imitations - the mark on this German piece is an imitation of the famous Sèvres mark. The 'S' in this mark does not refer to Samson, but is a copy of a Sèvres date letter.

c1910-20   *Saucer 5.25in (13cm) diam*

$120-180   **BETH**

A late 19thC Continental fluted coffee cup and saucer, possibly Samson, enameled with a landscape and floral bouquets within gilt on cobalt borders, the base with Worcester-style fret mark.

$100-150   **FLD**

Two Wedgwood Orient Line 'Heartsease' pattern tea trios, designed by Edward Bawden, the reverses of the saucers and plates with printed factory marks.

c1952   *Side plates 6in (15.5cm) diam*

$550-750   **WW**

An early 20thC Staffordshire teacup and saucer, printed in blue with the 'Willow' pattern, the reverse of the saucer impressed 'ENGLAND'.

Saucer 5.75in (14.5cm) diam

$15-25   **PC**

Two of a set of six Paragon Art Deco coffee cans and saucers, printed and painted with large stylized daffodil blooms over a black ground, with green banded saucers, one saucer damaged.

$100-150 set   **FLD**

A Wedgwood 'Carnaby Daisy' coffee set, designed by Susie Cooper, comprising six cups and saucers, the bases with printed backstamps, with original box.

As the pattern name suggests, Cooper was inspired by the Swinging Sixties and Pop Art.

c1968   *Saucers 5.5in (14cm) diam*

$250-350   **MLL**

A 20thC Richard Ginori coffee can and saucer, the can printed with a gentleman riding a horse, the saucer printed with riding crop and boots, the design attributed to Gio Ponti, the bases with printed factory marks.

Saucer 4.75in (12cm) diam

$100-150   **WW**

CERAMICS

QUICK REFERENCE – DOULTON

- Doulton was founded in 1815 in the south London borough of Lambeth. In 1877 founder Henry Doulton acquired a share in the Staffordshire Nile Street pottery, which he renamed Doulton & Co. in 1882. Doulton soon became one of the world's most prolific producers of fashionable art pottery. The company became known as Royal Doulton in 1901.
- The 'fussy' High Victorian style and muddy coloring of much of the late 19thC and early 20thC stoneware, which is no longer seen as desirable, has led to a serious downturn in values over the past fifteen years. The most sought after pieces today are typically the work of noted decorators, such as Hannah and Florence Barlow (see p.79), George and Arthur Tinworth and Mark Marshall. Higher prices are also commanded by pieces in interesting shapes or stylish patterns inspired by Moorish or Art Nouveau styles, as well as large sized (or miniature!) pieces.
- Figurines were first made at Doulton in the 1880s under George Tinworth, but it was under Charles Noke that a range was developed - first in 1889 but more seriously from 1912 when a small collection was released. All figurines are assigned an 'HN' number, the HN' standing for Harry Nixon who ran the painting department.
- Values for figurines have declined over the past decade, with those produced in large quantities for long periods of time (such as 'Top O' The Hill', introduced in 1937) being most affected. In general, the most desirable figurines are those that were produced before World War II.
- Many collectors choose to collect by designer, such as Leslie Harradine, or theme. Some ranges or themes, such as 'Middle Earth', have proven particularly popular due to their connection to TV and film. In all instances, look for rare colorways and variations and always consider condition and how long a figurine was produced for.

A Royal Doulton figurine of 'Henry Lytton as Jack Point', designed by Charles Noke, HN610, the base with printed marks.

Henry Lytton (1865-1936) was a celebrated English singer and actor known for his comic baritone roles in Gilbert & Sullivan operettas. 'Jack Point', a strolling jester character in 'The Yeoman of the Guard', was his favorite role. When this figurine was modeled, Lytton would have been as famous as a successful soap star or singer is today, making this the equivalent of a model of Neil Patrick Harris!

1924-49
6.5in (16.5cm) high
$650-850   CENC

A Royal Doulton figurine of 'The Mask', designed by Leslie Harradine, HN656, with some restoration.
1924-38   6.75in (17cm) high
$1,200-1,800   LT

A Royal Doulton figurine of a 'Butterfly' lady, designed by Leslie Harradine, HN720, the base with printed marks.

This figurine is desirable and valuable in all the different colors it was produced in, but the extremely rare and visually striking black and gold colorway is the most sought after. Goldscheider (see pp.21-22) produced similar figurines of elegant dancing girls holding their extravagant and exotic cloaks aloft to reveal their bodies and legs. This type is popular with collectors.
1925-40   6.5in (18.5cm) high
$1,500-2,500   CENC

A Royal Doulton figurine of 'Pierrette', designed by Leslie Harradine, HN731, the base with factory marks.

Look out for the later, second style of this figurine, numbered HN795 and HN796, which is extremely rare.
1925-38   7.25in (18.5cm) high
$1,500-2,500   CENC

A Royal Doulton figurine of a 'Chelsea Pensioner', designed by Leslie Harradine, HN689, the base inscribed and with printed mark.
1924-38   5.75in (15cm) high
$700-1,000   SWO

A CLOSER LOOK AT A DOULTON FIGURINE

This double-sided figurine, made at Doulton's Burslem factory during the 1890s, is larger in size than the 7.75in (20cm) high standard 'Mephistopheles and Marguerite' figurines made 1925-49.

This figurine is chipped and damaged, which has reduced the value by around 50%.

The smaller, later figurines were more commonly produced in orange and purple glazes (HN755) or orange and cream glazes (HN775). The delicate ivory glaze used here is rare but less representative of the characters.

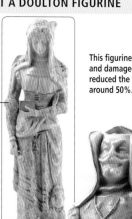

The depictions of Mephistopheles and Marguerite may have been inspired by Ellen Terry and Henry Irving who appeared together in 'Faust' at London's Lyceum Theatre in 1886.

A Royal Doulton, Burslem double-sided figurine of 'Mephistopheles and Marguerite', designed by Charles Noke, HN755, glazed in ivory and highlighted in gilt, the base with printed marks, with minor chips to sword and petals.

12in (31cm) high
$800-1,200
WW

A Royal Doulton figurine of 'London Cry-Carrots & Turnips', designed by Leslie Harradine, HN771.

The purple, red, black and green version is worth around the same as this version. A similar model, HN772, shows a lady and young girl selling strawberries and is, again, worth around the same. They may have been inspired by the popular series of late 18thC prints of street sellers entitled 'Cries of London'.

1925-38   *6.75in (17cm) high*
$1,200-1,800   **CENC**

A Royal Doulton figurine of 'The Flower Seller's Children', designed by Leslie Harradine, HN1206.

Look out for the ultra-rare green and blue glazed variation or equally rare blue, orange and yellow glazed variation. They are so rare that it's likely that, if found, one could fetch well over twice the value of this example!

1926-49   *8.25in (21cm) high*
$1,000-1,500   **CENC**

A rare Royal Doulton figurine of 'Harlequinade', designed by Leslie Harradine, HN780, the base with factory marks.

1926-40   *6.5in (15.5cm) high*
$1,500-2,500   **CENC**

A Royal Doulton figurine of a 'Boy with Turban', designed by Leslie Harradine, HN1210, the base with factory marks.

This figurine was produced in many different color variations, all of which are worth roughly the same. That said, different people have different personal preferences and this can cause peaks in value for different colors at different times. The dramatic color combination of orange (or red) with black shown here can also be found on many British and European Art Deco ceramics, including those by Myott and Clarice Cliff.

1926-36   *3.75in (9.5cm) high*
$650-850   **CENC**

A Royal Doulton figurine of a 'Lady Jester', style one, designed by Leslie Harradine, HN1222, the base with factory marks.

The colorful red, blue and black version (HN1332) can fetch marginally more than this version. This is 'style one' of this figurine. For 'style two', see p.75.

For 'style two', see p.75.

1927-38   *7in (18cm) high*
$1,500-2,500   **CENC**

CERAMICS

A Royal Doulton figurine of 'The Wandering Minstrel', designed by Leslie Harradine, HN1224, the base with factory marks.

1927-36   *7in (18cm) high*

$1,500-2,500   **CENC**

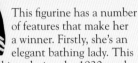

Judith Picks

This figurine has a number of features that make her a winner. Firstly, she's an elegant bathing lady. This was a popular subject during the 1920s and '30s, an area that is hotly collected today. Also note the strongly Art Deco stylized flowers on her cushion. Similar designs can be found on ceramics and textiles of the period.

She recalls more expensive figurines by Lenci, but she's clothed, which makes her a little more widely appealing. The curve of her posture is good and shows life and movement.

A Royal Doulton figurine of 'Negligée', designed by Leslie Harradine, HN1228, the base with factory marks.

1927-36   *5in (12.5cm) high*

$1,500-2,500   **CENC**

A rare Royal Doulton figurine of 'Susanna', designed by Leslie Harradine, HN1233.

1927-36   *6in (15cm) high*

$2,000-3,000   **CENC**

A Royal Doulton figurine of 'The Bather', designed by Leslie Harradine, HN1238, the base with printed and painted marks, with restoration.

1927-38   *8in (20cm) high*

$1,500-2,500   **DN**

A Royal Doulton figurine of 'Ko-Ko', designed by Leslie Harradine, HN1266, the base with factory marks.

1928-36   *5in (12.5cm) high*

$1,200-1,800   **CENC**

A Royal Doulton figurine of 'The Alchemist', designed by Leslie Harradine, HN1282, the base with factory marks.

1928-38   *11.25in (28.5cm) high*

$1,200-1,800   **CENC**

A rare Royal Doulton figurine of 'Lady Jester', style two, designed by Leslie Harradine, HN1284, the base with factory marks.

This is 'style two' of this figurine, for 'style one', see p.73. This figurine can be more difficult to find than 'style one', probably due to its size. As it is smaller, 'style two' probably didn't seem as good value as the standard sized figurine and consequently fewer were sold, leading to a smaller number being on the market today.

1928-38	4.25in (11cm) high
$1,500-2,500	CENC

A Royal Doulton figurine of 'Folly', designed by Leslie Harradine, HN1335, the base with factory marks.

1929-38	9in (23cm) high
$1,200-1,800	CENC

A rare Royal Doulton figurine of 'Dulcinea', designed by Leslie Harradine, HN1419, the base with factory marks.

1930-38	5.5in (14cm) high
$1,500-2,500	CENC

QUICK REFERENCE - DAMAGE

● Damage always destroys the value of a common Doulton figurine. As the majority of figurines were mass-produced, there is generally a large number of examples to choose from. This means collectors are often able to buy examples that are in mint condition for relatively low sums.

● Always check all protruding areas, such as heads, fingers, flowers and the edges of hats and dresses, for any damage.

● This figure still fetched a good sum of money because 'Barbara' (HN1432) is a relatively rare pre-war figurine. The fact that it was damaged allowed a collector with a smaller pocket to add an otherwise expensive and sought-after figurine to their collection without having to pay the usual price. Had it been in perfect condition, this figurine might have fetched over four times this value.

A Royal Doulton figurine of 'Anthea', designed by Leslie Harradine, HN1527, the base with factory marks.

1932-40	6.5in (16.5cm) high
$550-750	CENC

A Royal Doulton figurine of 'Barbara', designed by Leslie Harradine, HN1432, the head broken and repaired.

1930-37	7.75in (19.5cm) high
$250-350	CAPE

A rare Royal Doulton figurine of a 'Fairy', designed by Leslie Harradine, HN1532.

This figurine is small and depicts a relatively unusual subject matter for Doulton. Both factors undoubtedly contributed to its unpopularity at the time, meaning that it was only produced for six years. It is now rare and valuable today!

1932-38	4in (10cm) high
$1,200-1,800	CENC

CERAMICS

A Royal Doulton figurine of 'Miss Demure', designed by Leslie Harradine, HN1560, the base with printed and painted factory marks.

1933-49   *7in (18cm) high*

$350-450   **WW**

A Royal Doulton figurine of 'Marion', designed by Leslie Harradine, HN1582, the base with inscribed and printed marks.

1933-40   *6.5in (16.5cm) high*

$800-1,200   **SWO**

A Royal Doulton figurine of 'Virginia', designed by Leslie Harradine, HN1693, the base with factory marks.

1935-49   *7.5in (19cm) high*

$650-850   **CENC**

A Royal Doulton figurine of the 'Coming of Spring', designed by Leslie Harradine, HN1722, the base with inscribed and printed marks.

This large and impressive figurine was also made in pale green. That variation is worth roughly the same as this one.

1935-49   *12.5in (31.5cm) high*

$1,200-1,800   **CENC**

A Royal Doulton figurine of 'The Lambeth Walk', designed by Leslie Harradine, HN1881, with some damage.

This figurine is very rare, due to the fact that war began a year after it was introduced! Materials for making colored glazes were also strictly controlled for the first few years after World War II ended.

1938-49   *10in (25.5cm) high*

$1,200-1,800   **LT**

A Royal Doulton figurine of 'The Jersey Milkmaid', designed by Leslie Harradine, HN2057, the base with factory marks.

This blue, red and white version is worth around a third more than the green, brown and white version, which was made later (1975-81).

1950-59   *6.5in (16.5cm) high*

$120-180   **CAPE**

A Royal Doulton figurine of the 'Royal Governor's Cook', designed by Peggy Davies, HN2233, from the 'Figures of Williamsburg' series, the base with printed mark.

1960-83   *6in (15cm) high*

$120-180   **CAPE**

A Royal Doulton figurine of 'Katrina', designed by Peggy Davies, HN2327, the base with printed factory marks.

1965-69   *7.5in (19cm) high*

$100-150   **WW**

A Royal Doulton limited edition figurine of 'Florence Nightingale', designed by Pauline Parsons, HN3144, no.744 from a limited edition of 5,000 for Lawleys By Post, the base with printed marks, with certificate.

8.5in (21.5cm) high

$150-250   **CAPE**

A Royal Doulton figurine of 'King Charles I', designed by Charles Noke and Harry Tittensor, HN3459, from a limited edition of 350.

1992   *16.75in (42.5cm) high*

$1,500-2,500   **LT**

A Royal Doulton figurine, perhaps intended as a prototype for 'Alice' from 'Alice in Wonderland'.

This figure has some similarities to 'Alice' (HN2158) designed by Peggy Davies in 1960, but looks as though it must be an earlier prototype.
$3,000-4,000   **LT**

QUICK REFERENCE - PROTOTYPES

- **Prototype figurines are usually among the most valuable Royal Doulton figurines.**
- **Typically, three figurines were cast from the first master 'production' mold, which was made using the original clay model created by a Doulton artist, such as Leslie Harradine. Each of the three figurines was decorated with different colors before being shown to the company's management.**
- **Figurines and colorways that were approved were given an HN number. Those that were not were usually put into the company's archive. Many were not marked, but can be authenticated by comparison to the Doulton pattern books. Marks that were used include 'Not For Re-Sale' and 'Design Sample'.**
- **In the late 1990s, Royal Doulton began selling its archive of prototypes. Many fetched high prices.**

A Royal Doulton prototype figurine of a 'Dancer', by an unknown designer, un-numbered, with some damage.

This figurine is damaged, which has lowered its value - if it were undamaged, the value might be several thousand dollars higher! It may have been intended to be in the same series as 'Dancing Figure' (HN311), which was designed in 1918.

$2,500-3,500   **LT**

A Royal Doulton prototype figurine of a 'Jester', by an unknown designer, un-numbered, the base marked 'Property of Royal Doulton Factory'.

This figurine was never put into production.

9.5in (24cm) high
$10,000-15,000   **LT**

CERAMICS

A large Royal Doulton model of a 'Bulldog Draped in Union Jack with Trinity Cap', designed by Charles Noke, D6181, the back with printed mark.

1941   *7in (18cm) high*

$1,200-1,800   **LSK**

A Royal Doulton model of 'Bonzo Character Dog', style four, designed by Charles Noke, D393, with red buttons and jacket edge.

1923-c1946   *2in (5cm) high*

$650-850   **LT**

A Royal Doulton model of 'Mother Bunnykins', designed by Charles Noke, inscribed 'D6004' and incised '8305', the base with printed marks.

The colors and marks show that this was the earliest 'Mother Bunnykins' figurine produced.

1939-c1940   *7in (17.5cm) high*

$650-850   **SWO**

A CLOSER LOOK AT A BRITISH BULLDOG

This patriotic bulldog was introduced during World War II in 1941.

Look out for versions wearing hats (such as the other example on this page), as they are much rarer and more valuable.

The three rarest variations are the 2.25in (5.7cm) high version of this model (which was made in 1941 only), the bulldog wearing a sailor's uniform and hat and the khaki-colored bulldog with a Union Jack.

This version was re-released by Royal Doulton in 2012, as an example is featured on M's desk in the James Bond film 'Skyfall'. The re-released version bears a special 'DD007' number and backstamp.

A medium Royal Doulton model of a 'Bulldog Draped In Union Jack', designed by Charles Noke, D5913, the base with factory marks.

4in (10cm) high

$120-180   **GORL**

A Royal Doulton flambé-glazed model of a 'Leaping Salmon', designed by Charles Noke, model no.666, the base with printed mark.

c1940-50   *12in (30.5cm) high*

$300-500   **CAPE**

A Royal Doulton limited edition model of 'Desert Orchid', style one, designed by Graham Tongue, DA134, with printed and painted marks, with wooden base.

13.5in (34cm) wide

$150-250   **WW**

An early 20thC Royal Doulton Lambeth stoneware vase, decorated by Hannah Barlow with a wide border of incised horses, within borders in olive green, burnt sienna, pale blue and dark blue/green glazes, the base with impressed mark and incised monogram, with repaired chip to rim.

18.25in (46cm) high

$650-850   CAPE

A large late 19thC Doulton Lambeth stoneware vase, designed and decorated by Florence Barlow with panels of native birds among foliage, with stylized pink, green and brown glazed flowers, the base with impressed marks, with small chip to rim.

20.75in (53cm) high

$800-1,200   SWO

An early 20thC Royal Doulton Lambeth stoneware jardinière and stand, molded in low relief with a floral cartouche in shades of mottled green, blue, white and brown impressed marks, with minor damage.

35.5in (90cm) high

$500-700   WW

A late 19thC Doulton Lambeth stoneware jug, designed and decorated by Hannah Barlow, with a family of donkeys, the neck with an incised foliage border, decorated in green and blue on a buff ground, the base with impressed and incised marks and dated, with hairline crack to handle, and other minor damage.

1874   *11in (27cm) high*

$400-600   WW

Judith Picks

The work of Hannah Barlow and her sister Florence has been written about many times and is the focus of many collections. Florence is known for her painting of flowers and birds, while Hannah is known for her horses and other animals. Lions, however, are something quite different. Both sisters usually portrayed native animals. Exotic, foreign animals, such as lions, are extremely rare. This jardinière may have been a special commission. Even though the stand is missing and the rest of the decoration is standard, the lions make this bowl the king of the saleroom.

A late 19thC Doulton Lambeth stoneware jardinière bowl, designed and decorated by Hannah Barlow, with a sgraffito border of lions and lionesses among green scrolling foliage and impressed patterns, the base with impressed mark, inscribed initials and dated.

1887   *7.5in (19cm) high*

$5,000-7,000   DUK

A pair of early 20thC Royal Doulton 'Slater's Patent' 'Chiné' vases, with bulbous and flared necks, the base with impressed marks.

For more information about Slater's Patent, see 'Miller's Collectibles Handbook 2012-2013', p.83. The vases pictured here are more desirable than many other examples of 'Slater's Patent' vases as the form is complex and they are an undamaged pair. However, the gilding is missing in some areas, such as at the shoulder, which will decrease value.

8in (21cm) high

$200-300   LOC

An early 20thC Royal Doulton Lambeth stoneware vase, designed and decorated by Frank Butler, with tubelined Art Nouveau floral decoration, the base with impressed and incised marks.

14in (36cm) high

$500-700   ECGW

A pair of late 19thC Doulton Lambeth 'Faience' vases, decorated by Mary M Arding, with fruiting blackberry stems on a shaded turquoise ground, the bases with impressed and incised factory marks and painted monogram, with some restoration.

11in (28.5cm) high

$500-700   TOV

A late 19thC Doulton Lambeth stoneware ginger jar and cover, probably by John Huskinson, decorated with a matt-glazed design of chrysanthemums on an ivory and gilt sponged ground, with brown and gilt foliate scroll borders, the base with factory marks.

10in (25cm) high

$70-100   CAPE

Mark Picks

For me this 'Foliage' pattern is the perfect union between nature, art and industry that typifies Doulton. As they walked to work through the autumnal streets of south London, decorators (typically girls or ladies) would pick up leaves they saw and thought were beautiful. These would then be impressed into the body of a pot and glazed over. When the piece was fired, the leaves would burn away leaving the form and delicate veining. Due to this process, every piece is unique.

Despite all of this, prices for 'Foliage' pieces remain largely affordable, particularly for smaller examples. But for how long?

A large early 20thC Royal Doulton Lambeth 'Foliage' pattern jardinière bowl, the impressed leaves glazed in tonal salt-glazed brown, on a mottled gray ground, the base with impressed marks.

14in (35cm) wide

$300-500   FLD

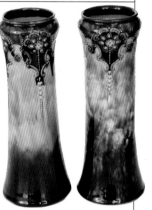

A large pair of early 20thC Royal Doulton Lambeth vases, decorated with tubelined floral garlands on a blue and green glazed ground, the base with impressed marks.

13in (33cm) high

$300-500   FLD

An early 20thC Royal Doulton Lambeth stoneware vase, decorated with tubelined flowers in pinks, beige, cream, green and brown glazes, the base with impressed marks.

8.25in (21cm) high

$250-350   WW

A tall early 20thC Royal Doulton Lambeth stoneware vase, designed and decorated by Elisa Simmance with a rambling rose border in shades of cream and green on a blue ground, the base with impressed marks and incised monogram.

13.75in (35cm) high

$400-600   WW

A late 19thC Doulton baluster-shaped vase, painted with a continuous coastal scene featuring a young lady seated on a breakwater, with gilt and dark blue lace-style borders, the base with printed marks.

21in (53cm) high

$300-500   DA&H

A Royal Doulton 'Rhuddlan Castle' vase, painted in colors by J Hughs, the base with printed and painted marks.

6in (15cm) high

$120-180   WW

A Doulton Burslem ewer, decorated by Fred Hancock with flowerheads, shape no.RA2280, decorated in monochrome ruby and highlighted in gilt, signed, the base with printed and painted marks, with small frit to top rim.

6in (15cm) high

$120-180   WW

A rare miniature Royal Doulton 'Chang'-glazed vase, by Charles Noke, covered in a running thick white glaze, with 'sang de boeuf' and green patches, with impressed marks.

3in (8cm) high

$700-1,000   WW

QUICK REFERENCE - CHANG GLAZE

- The 'Chang' glaze was inspired by ancient Chinese glazes and was produced 1925-39.
- Several layers of thick glazes were applied to heavy bodies and were allowed to run and drip freely, making the painterly effects on each piece unique.
- The 'Chang' glaze was the brainchild of Charles Noke, but much of the decorating work was done by Harry Nixon, whose monogram often appears on the base.
- The 'Chang' glaze was 'avant garde' and expensive in its day and continues to be so today. Even miniature vases are desirable.

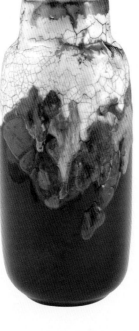

A Royal Doulton 'Chang'-glazed stoneware vase, by Charles Noke and Harry Nixon, decorated in shades of green, yellow and flambé on a flambé ground and under a crackled white glaze, the base with printed factory mark, painted signature and monogram.

11.5in (29.5cm) high

$5,000-7,000   WW

A Royal Doulton 'Chang'-glazed stoneware vase, by Charles Noke and Harry Nixon, decorated in shades of yellow, gray and veined white on a rich flambé and electric blue streaked ground, the base with printed factory mark, painted Chang mark, painted signature and monogram, with professional restoration to rim.

10in (25.5cm) high

$1,200-1,800   WW

A very rare Doulton Lambeth stoneware pin tray, in the form of a kookaburra, with impressed factory mark.

4.25in (11cm) high

$800-1,200   WW

An early Émile Gallé pottery vase, painted with a scene of rooster, hen and chicks in farmyard, the side signed 'M. Latoche', the base signed 'E.G.' and impressed '244'.

7in (18cm) high

$2,000-3,000   JDJ

An Émile Gallé faience wall pocket, in the form of a fan, decorated with a chinoiserie pattern in the Imari palette, the reverse marked 'Gallé, Nancy E&G Depose', with damage.

12in (30.5cm) high

$300-500   GHOU

An Émile Gallé faience basket, in the form of an Oriental man in a foliate shawl swinging from a fruiting vine handle, the base marked 'E Gallé Nancy'.

7.5in (19cm) high

$300-500   GHOU

An Émile Gallé pottery ewer, decorated with a dancing couple in a country landscape on a dimpled ground, signed 'É Gallé Nancy, E & G Dopose', with small chip to rim.

12.5in (31.5cm) high

$550-750   GHOU

An unusual Émile Gallé faience model of a begging dog, with glass eyes, the base with impressed dog mark and signed 'Gallé', with broken tail, with traces of retail label.

Gallé took over his father's glass and faience factory in 1874.

13in (33cm) high

$500-700   GHOU

A rare Émile Gallé faience rabbit spill vase, with glass eyes, the base signed 'É Gallé Nancy' and with impressed factory mark.

14in (35.5cm) high

$2,500-3,500   GHOU

Miller's Compares

The faces of Gallé's cats are more expressive and characterful than the face of the cat opposite. Genuine examples often have a superior air.

The quality of modeling and painting is much finer on the genuine example.

The pattern is more typical of the period.

Delft-style landscapes are not found on authentic Gallé cats. Patterns are usually more abstract or floral.

This example has been damaged and restored, which further lowers its value. If it was in perfect condition, it might be worth around $250-350.

An Émile Gallé faience model of a cat, with glass eyes, signed 'É Gallé Nancy'.

13in (33cm) high

$3,000-5,000   DRA

An early 20thC Émile Gallé-style pottery model of a cat, printed and painted with a blue and white Dutch landscape scene, with glass eyes, with professional restoration to paw.

13.5in (34cm) high

$50-70   WW

QUICK REFERENCE - ITALIAN CERAMICS

- Ceramics have been produced on the Italian peninsula for centuries, with the area becoming well known for its tin-glazed maiolica by the 13thC. The first few decades of the 20thC, known as the 'Novecento', saw the birth of modern ceramic design under designers such as Galileo Chini, Luigi de Vecchi, Riccardo Gatti and others. Pieces by these designers are widely collected today.
- Ceramics from the post-war period can be divided into two areas – unique 'studio' pieces and mass-produced factory ceramics. Both types were decorated by hand. Most were also made by hand, but some of the factory ceramics were slip-molded on a production line.
- A comparatively large amount is known about the unique studio and high-end factory ceramics. Influential names include Guido Gambone (1909-69), Marcello Fantoni (1915-2011) and Gio Ponti (1891-1979).
- The work of those designers inspired many other designers and factories, which produced and exported fashionable designs in larger quantities. Thanks to new research, this contribution to 20thC ceramic design is now beginning to be understood. Important names to consider and look for include Fratelli Fanciullacci (1862-1988), which was one of the largest producers and exporters of affordable ceramics in a variety of modern styles during the 1910s-60s, and Bitossi (founded 1921). During this period, Bitossi's designer was the innovative and productive Aldo Londi (1911-2003).
- Styles tended to be modern, with curving and clean-lined forms and abstract or highly stylized patterns executed in bright colors. Forms, patterns and marks on the base can help to identify a maker.
- For more information see 'Alla Moda' by Mark Hill (2012).

A 1950s-60s ARS Artigiana vase, decorated with circles and applied dots on a white ground, the inside glazed in blue, the base marked 'ARS ARTIGIANA DERUTA'.

This is a high price for this vase, even though it is large, undamaged and an unusually modern shape for this range. This general design was also produced by other companies in Deruta.

11.75in (30cm) high

$500-700   QU

A Fantoni majolica vase, designed by Marcello Fantoni in 1953, decorated with a figure in ocher, red, petrol-blue and blue on alkali-black glaze, the base marked 'Fantoni 1953'.

1953   19in (48cm) high

$1,200-1,800   QU

A Fantoni majolica ewer, designed by Marcello Fantoni in c1955, decorated with stylized figures in blue, dark-red, white and brown glazes, the base marked 'Fantoni'.

c1955

20.5in (52cm) high

$1,200-1,800   QU

A Fantoni majolica 'Horseman by Night' vase, designed by Marcello Fantoni in c1955, decorated in anthracite-gray, blue, red, yellow, green and petrol blue on dark blue enamels and glazes, the base signed 'Fantoni, Italy'.

c1955   13in (33.5cm) high

$1,200-1,800   QU

A Fantoni majolica ewer, designed by Marcello Fantoni in 1956, decorated with knights and horses on an alkali white ground, the base marked '(...)90, 1956 Fantoni ITALY'.

1956   15.5in (39cm) high

$1,000-1,500   QU

A 1950s Fantoni earthenware vase, designed by Marcello Fantoni, decorated in black, turquoise, red, yellow, pink and white enamels and glazes, the base marked 'Fantoni Italy'.

11in (28cm) high

$550-750   QU

CERAMICS

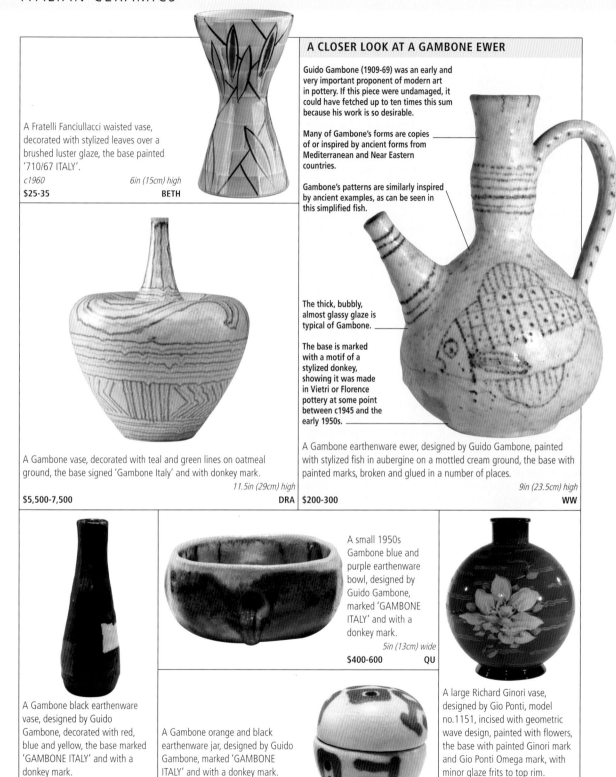

A Fratelli Fanciullacci waisted vase, decorated with stylized leaves over a brushed luster glaze, the base painted '710/67 ITALY'.

c1960   *6in (15cm) high*
$25-35   **BETH**

A CLOSER LOOK AT A GAMBONE EWER

Guido Gambone (1909-69) was an early and very important proponent of modern art in pottery. If this piece were undamaged, it could have fetched up to ten times this sum because his work is so desirable.

Many of Gambone's forms are copies of or inspired by ancient forms from Mediterranean and Near Eastern countries.

Gambone's patterns are similarly inspired by ancient examples, as can be seen in this simplified fish.

The thick, bubbly, almost glassy glaze is typical of Gambone.

The base is marked with a motif of a stylized donkey, showing it was made in Vietri or Florence pottery at some point between c1945 and the early 1950s.

A Gambone vase, decorated with teal and green lines on oatmeal ground, the base signed 'Gambone Italy' and with donkey mark.

11.5in (29cm) high
$5,500-7,500   **DRA**

A Gambone earthenware ewer, designed by Guido Gambone, painted with stylized fish in aubergine on a mottled cream ground, the base with painted marks, broken and glued in a number of places.

9in (23.5cm) high
$200-300   **WW**

A Gambone black earthenware vase, designed by Guido Gambone, decorated with red, blue and yellow, the base marked 'GAMBONE ITALY' and with a donkey mark.

10.5in (27cm) high
$2,500-3,500   **QU**

A Gambone orange and black earthenware jar, designed by Guido Gambone, marked 'GAMBONE ITALY' and with a donkey mark.

1948   *3in (7.5cm) high*
$500-700   **QU**

A small 1950s Gambone blue and purple earthenware bowl, designed by Guido Gambone, marked 'GAMBONE ITALY' and with a donkey mark.

5in (13cm) wide
$400-600   **QU**

A large Richard Ginori vase, designed by Gio Ponti, model no.1151, incised with geometric wave design, painted with flowers, the base with painted Ginori mark and Gio Ponti Omega mark, with minor glaze frits to top rim.

14in (35cm) high
$2,500-3,500   **WW**

A 1920s-30s Richard Ginori two-handled vase, probably designed by Gio Ponti, with molded panel decoration, the base with printed marks.

8in (20cm) high

$1,000-1,500 **GORL**

A Richard Ginori porcelain bowl, designed by Gio Ponti, overglazed with geometric chains in blue and gold, the base marked 'RICHARD GINORI E, 986 E'.

Gio Ponti was the artistic director of Richard Ginori from 1923 to 1930. He was succeeded by Giovanni Gariboldi, who was artistic director from 1930 to 1970.

c1925 *8.25in (21cm) diam*

$4,000-6,000 **QU**

A late 1920s-30s Richard Ginori porcelain vase, overglazed in rust-red with stylized chess pieces, the base marked 'RICHARD GINORI'.

7.75in (20cm) high

$2,500-3,500 **QU**

A very rare 1950s-60s Italo Casini jug-vase, decorated with gray-green, ocher-gold, white and green lava glazes in a triangle and dot pattern, the base with paper label reading '679/30'.

Little is known about Italo Casini, apart from the fact that they were based in Sesto Fiorentino. A ceramic in Mark Hill's collection is printed on the base with the company's name, location and 'Produzione Brevettata', implying that the glaze formulae and/or designs were patented.

12in (30cm) high

$1,200-1,800 **MODO**

A late 1950s Carlo Marelli 'San Giminiano' vase, designed by Carlo Marelli, signed three times by the artist, with printed marks.

18in (46cm) high

$1,000-1,500 **QU**

A Società Ceramica Italiana Laveno jug, designed by Antonia Campi, from the 'C205' teaset.

This jug was also available in other colors including white, blue, pink and burgundy.

1953 *5.75in (14.5cm) high*

$350-450 **MODO**

A 1950s-70s Italian majolica model of a 'Bull', by an unknown maker, with wrought-iron horns, the base marked 'Italy'.

16.5in (42cm) long

$650-850 **QU**

CERAMICS

A Lladró group of a boy and a donkey, 'Platero and Marcelino', designed by Juan Huerta, model no.1181.

The title of this figurine alludes to Juan Ramón Jiménez's poem 'Platero y Yo' (Platero and I), which is about a boy and his donkey.
1974-81   *7.75in (20cm) high*
$100-150   **TRI**

A Lladró figurine of a boy with puppies, 'Sweet Dreams', designed by Antonio Ramos, model no.1535.
1988-2005   *4in (10cm) high*
$80-120   **DMC**

A Lladró figurine of a girl washing a puppy, 'Bashful Bather', designed by Juan Huerta, model no.5455.
1987-92   *5in (12.5cm) wide*
$100-150   **DMC**

A Lladró figurine of the 'Virgin Mary', designed by Juan Huerta, model no.5477, from the 'Nativity Set'.
Issued 1988   *6.75in (17cm) high*
$100-150   **DMC**

A Lladró figurine of a girl on vanity stool with hand mirror, 'I Feel Pretty', designed by Antonio Ramos, model no.5678.
1990-92   *6.25in (16cm) high*
$100-150   **DMC**

QUICK REFERENCE - LLADRÓ

- Founded in 1953 in Almacera, near Valencia in Spain, Lladró has produced over 4,000 designs.
- Pieces from the 1950s are rare. They can be identified by their incised marks. Impressed marks were standardized around 1960, with the blue stamp being introduced in 1971. The accent over the 'o' was added in 1974.
- Pieces in matt glazes are rarer than those decorated in other glazes and can fetch more, as can pre-production pieces with a creamy finish. Look out for pieces produced in small limited editions or for short periods of time.
- Facial expressions are usually full of character. Lladró never used black for eyes, lids or brows - a factor that can often be used to identify fakes.
- Always examine the protruding extremities, such as flowers, hat brims etc, as any damage reduces value considerably.
- Complex moldings and large sizes are usually highly sought after.

A Lladró figurine of the Virgin Mary, 'Our Lady With Flowers', designed by Vicente Martinez, model no.5171.
1982   *12.25in (31cm) high*
$80-120   **TRI**

A Lladró figurine of a girl with dog, 'Who's The Fairest', designed by Juan Huerta model, no.5468.
Issued 1982-98   *5.5in (14cm) high*
$100-150   **DMC**

A Lladró group of two children, 'Big Sister', designed Francisco Polope, model no.5735, with damage.
1990-2007   *6.5in (16.5cm) high*
$60-80   **TRI**

A Lladró figurine of a mother and baby, 'Dressing the Boy', designed by Joan Coderch, model no.5845.

Retired 2005   8in (20.5cm) high
$100-150   **DMC**

A Lladró limited edition Christmas tree-topper figurine, 'Angelic Cymbalist', designed by Joan Coderch, model no5876G, from the 'Angel Symphony' range of tree toppers.

1992
$50-70   **DMC**

A Lladró figurine of a young girl, 'Petals of Love', designed by Antonio Ramos, model no.6346.

1997-2007   8in (20.5cm) high
$200-300   **DMC**

A Lladró figurine of a mother and child, 'My Little Treasure', designed by Francisco Polio, model no.6503.

This figurine displays the elegant, curving elongation of form for which Lladró is celebrated. The delicate blue, white and pink glaze combination is also another hallmarks of the company's work and was used by nearly all designers.

1998-2004   9in (23cm) high
$150-250   **DMC**

A Lladró figurine of a sleeping boy, 'Bedtime Buddies', designed by José Javier Malavia, model no.6541.

1998-2004   6in (15cm) long
$80-120   **DMC**

A Lladró figurine of a young girl, 'Rosey Posey', designed by Francisco Polope, model no.6690.

Retired 2005   5in (12.5cm) high
$150-250   **DMC**

A Lladró model of a dog in a boot, 'A Well Heeled Puppy', designed by Francisco Polope, model no.6744, the base with Lladró trade mark.

Retired 2005   8.5in (21.5cm) high
$100-150   **DMC**

A Lladró figurine of a child on a blanket, 'Counting Sheep', designed by José Alvarez, model no.6790.

2001-08   4in (10cm) high
$80-120   **DMC**

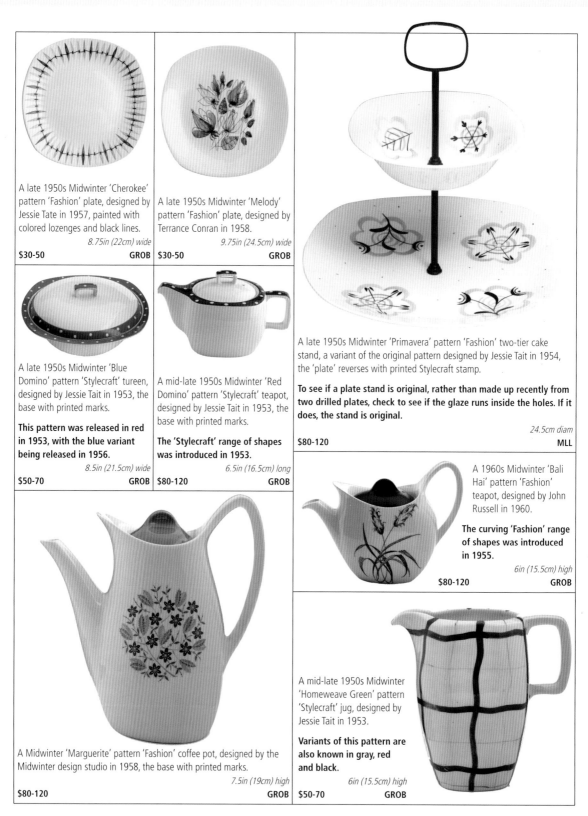

A late 1950s Midwinter 'Cherokee' pattern 'Fashion' plate, designed by Jessie Tate in 1957, painted with colored lozenges and black lines.

8.75in (22cm) wide

$30-50   GROB

A late 1950s Midwinter 'Melody' pattern 'Fashion' plate, designed by Terrance Conran in 1958.

9.75in (24.5cm) wide

$30-50   GROB

A late 1950s Midwinter 'Blue Domino' pattern 'Stylecraft' tureen, designed by Jessie Tait in 1953, the base with printed marks.

This pattern was released in red in 1953, with the blue variant being released in 1956.

8.5in (21.5cm) wide

$50-70   GROB

A mid-late 1950s Midwinter 'Red Domino' pattern 'Stylecraft' teapot, designed by Jessie Tait in 1953, the base with printed marks.

The 'Stylecraft' range of shapes was introduced in 1953.

6.5in (16.5cm) long

$80-120   GROB

A late 1950s Midwinter 'Primavera' pattern 'Fashion' two-tier cake stand, a variant of the original pattern designed by Jessie Tait in 1954, the 'plate' reverses with printed Stylecraft stamp.

To see if a plate stand is original, rather than made up recently from two drilled plates, check to see if the glaze runs inside the holes. If it does, the stand is original.

24.5cm diam

$80-120   MLL

A 1960s Midwinter 'Bali Hai' pattern 'Fashion' teapot, designed by John Russell in 1960.

The curving 'Fashion' range of shapes was introduced in 1955.

6in (15.5cm) high

$80-120   GROB

A Midwinter 'Marguerite' pattern 'Fashion' coffee pot, designed by the Midwinter design studio in 1958, the base with printed marks.

7.5in (19cm) high

$80-120   GROB

A mid-late 1950s Midwinter 'Homeweave Green' pattern 'Stylecraft' jug, designed by Jessie Tait in 1953.

Variants of this pattern are also known in gray, red and black.

6in (15.5cm) high

$50-70   GROB

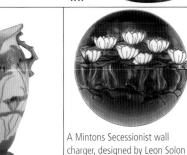

A Mintons Secessionist twin-handled vase, designed by Leon Solon and John Wadsworth, decorated with tubeline flowers and foliage in shades of green, blue and mustard on a yellow ground, the base with printed marks.

6.75in (17.5cm) high

$300-500　　　　WW

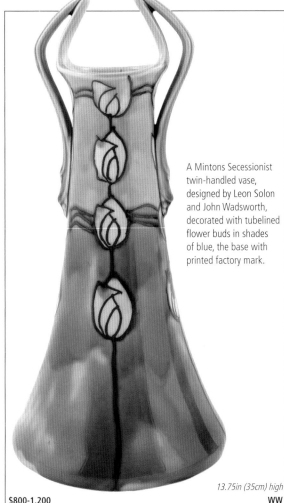

A Mintons Secessionist twin-handled vase, designed by Leon Solon and John Wadsworth, decorated with tubelined flower buds in shades of blue, the base with printed factory mark.

A Mintons Art Nouveau vase, painted and gilded with stylized tulips, the base with printed mark.

6.5in (17cm) high

$300-500　　　　GORL

A Mintons Secessionist wall charger, designed by Leon Solon and John Wadsworth, decorated tubelined waterlilies in shades of green and blue on a purple ground, the reverse with printed marks.

15in (38cm) diam

$1,200-1,800　　　　WW

13.75in (35cm) high

$800-1,200　　　　WW

A CLOSER LOOK AT A MINTONS VASE

Minton was established in 1793 and was called Mintons from 1873. The factory was keen to embrace the Secessionist and Art Nouveau styles, it seemed less keen to produce pieces in the Art Deco style. Such pieces are therefore much harder to find today.

This vase was designed by John Wadsworth (1879-1955), who joined Mintons in 1901. Wadsworth is best known for his highly traditional 'Haddon Hall' printed pattern, which was introduced in 1949. This vase is poles apart from his usual work!

The pared down, Modernist ball-form with turned and carved decoration is clearly based on Keith Murray's commercially successful designs for Wedgwood (see p.142).

Although the form is derivative of Murray's work, Wadsworth has used a more complex and highly appealing glaze than Murray.

A Mintons Secessionist jardinière, decorated with tube-lined and enameled peacocks on a swirling cream and brown ground.

14.25in (36cm) high

$400-600　　　　DA&H

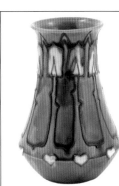

A Mintons Secessionist vase, designed by Leon Solon and John Wadsworth, no.21, decorated with tubelined flower stems, the base with printed marks.

5.25in (13.5cm) high

$500-700　　　　WW

A very rare early 1930s Mintons ball vase, designed by John Wadsworth, glazed in mottled gray-blue, the base with printed Mintons and facsimile John Wadsworth signature marks.

$300-500　　　　MHC

CERAMICS

QUICK REFERENCE – MOORCROFT

- William Moorcroft (1872-1945) was the son of a potteries-based ceramics designer and painter. After graduating from the Burslem School of Art, William joined James MacIntyre & Co. in 1897. His considerable talents led to him being appointed manager of Ornamental Ware the following year.

- His first ranges, 'Aurelian' and 'Florian', were highly successful. Both ranges feature stylized curving foliate and floral motifs that are typical of the Art Nouveau style of the day. Some patterns were also inspired by exotic Moorish designs.

- Moorcroft's vases, bowls and jars for James MacIntyre & Co. were all thrown and decorated by hand, making each piece unique even though the designs were produced in quantity. Moorcroft employed the tube-lining process where liquid clay was piped on to the surface, creating a raised outline to the desired pattern. The resulting 'cells' were then filled with liquid glaze.

- Moorcroft left James MacIntyre & Co. in 1912 and founded his own company with backing from his leading customer, the prestigious London retailer Liberty & Co.

- By 1929, Moorcroft had been awarded the Royal Warrant.

- After William's death, his son Walter continued to devise designs, as well as develop his father's ideas.

- Moorcroft designs are typically inspired by the natural world and include flowers, leaves, plants and, more recently, animals. Many of William's original patterns were so popular that they were produced throughout the 20thC. Colors tend to be strong and rich, including greens, blues and pinks. The marks on the base of a piece can help to date it to a period, as can the pattern and colorway.

- Patterns produced for many decades tend to be the most affordable, particularly on pieces in small sizes. The most valuable pieces tend to be the early Art Nouveau pieces made from the early 1900s-20s, including 'Florian', 'Claremont' and the early landscape patterns.

- More recently, independent designers have been employed, the first being Sally Tuffin (b.1938) who joined the company in 1986. Other late 20thC designers include Rachel Bishop (b.1969) and Nicola Slaney (b.1975), who both joined the 1990s. Some of these recent designs can also fetch strong prices when resold. This is particularly the case for pieces from small limited editions and very large pieces.

A James Macintyre & Co. 'Florian Ware' jar and cover, designed by William Moorcroft, decorated with a frieze of poppies and panels of spring flowers, the base with printed mark and green signature, the cover re-stuck.

c1900   *2in (5.5cm) high*

$650-850   **L&T**

A small James Macintyre & Co. 'Florian Ware' vase, designed by William Moorcroft, decorated with the 'Peacock Feathers' pattern, the base with printed 'Florian Ware' mark and painted signature 'W.Moorcroft des.', with printed registration number.

c1900   *5in (12.5cm) high*

$2,500-3,500   **L&T**

A small James Macintyre & Co. 'Florian Ware' vase, designed by William Moorcroft, decorated with the 'Lilac' pattern, the base with green painted signature and no.'M2838/4', with printed 'TOWNSEND & CO. NEWCASTLE' retailer's mark, with some damage.

c1902   *3.75in (9.5cm) high*

$150-250   **L&T**

A James Macintyre & Co. 'Florian Ware' vase, designed by William Moorcroft, decorated with harebells against a cream ground, the base with printed mark and green painted signature.

12in (30cm) high

$5,500-7,500   **DUK**

A James Macintyre & Co. 'Florian Ware' vase, designed by William Moorcroft, decorated with the 'Landscape' pattern, the base with printed mark and green painted signature, with chip to foot.

c1908   *12in (30.5cm) high*

$2,000-3,000   **DN**

A small Moorcroft 'Anemone' bottle vase, designed by William Moorcroft, with flambé glazes, the base with impressed factory marks and green signature.

Both William and Walter Moorcroft experimented with flambé glazes on many different patterns and a special kiln was built in 1921. William guarded the secrets he had learnt, only revealing them to his son who continued to develop them. Pieces with flambé glazes are very popular with collectors today and typically fetch more than pieces with normal glazes.

c1920   *6in (15cm) high*
$650-850   **DN**

Miller's Compares

This vase and shape dates from the early period of Moorcroft's designs.

This pattern is from a later range devised by William in 1937 and developed by his son Walter. The later version is much more common and less valuable than the earlier version.

The colors are much more commonly found and less deep and dramatic.

This vase is larger, meaning it would have been more expensive in its day.

This shape is later and not as appealing as the earlier one.

A rare large Moorcroft 'Orchid' vase, designed by William Moorcroft, painted in shades of purple, green and yellow on a blue green ground, the base with impressed marks and painted green signature.

The orchid flower was first used by William Moorcroft around 1918, probably after he was inspired by botanical drawings by his father Thomas.

c1918   *10.5in (27cm) high*
$6,500-8,500   **WW**

A Moorcroft 'Orchids' ovoid vase, designed by William and developed by Walter Moorcroft, on a green ground, the base with impressed factory stamps and blue painted signature.

c1945   *5in (13cm) high*
$1,000-1,500   **PC**

A Moorcroft 'Orchid and Spring Flowers' vase, designed by William Moorcroft, the base with impressed and painted factory marks and impressed 'Potter to H.M. The Queen', the glaze crazed.

8in (21cm) high
$1,000-1,500   **TEN**

A Moorcroft 'Pansies' bottle vase, designed by William Moorcroft, the base with impressed factory marks and green signature.

$550-750   **L&T**

A Moorcroft 'Pansies' footed bowl, designed by William Moorcroft, the base with impressed factory marks and green signature.

c1920   *10in (25cm) diam*
$300-500   **L&T**

CERAMICS

A Moorcroft 'Pomegranate' footed bowl, designed by William Moorcroft, the base with impressed factory marks, green signature and dated.

1918   *9in (23cm) diam*

$300-500   **L&T**

A tall Moorcroft 'Pomegranate' vase with flared rim, designed by William Moorcroft, with a blue ground, the base with impressed factory marks and green signature.

7.5in (19cm) high

$550-750   **SWO**

A Moorcroft 'Pomegranate' biscuit barrel and cover, designed by William Moorcroft, with a green and blue ground, the base with impressed factory marks, paper label and green signature.

This is a rare and desirable shape. The handles and lid are easily damaged, but this example is in very good condition, further adding to its desirability. 'Pomegranate', introduced in 1910, was one of Moorcroft's best-sez patterns and is not hard to find today.

4.25in (11cm) high

$1,200-1,800   **TOV**

A Moorcroft 'Pomegranate' jar and cover, designed by William Moorcroft, with a blue ground, the base with impressed factory marks and green signature.

4.25in (11cm) high

$500-700   **SWO**

A 1920s Moorcroft 'Big Poppy' biscuit barrel, designed by William Moorcroft, no.2245, with a green and blue mottled ground, the base with impressed factory marks and blue painted initials, with an electro-plated swing handle, cover and rim.

Metal parts are very rarely found on Moorcroft ceramics.

4.25in (11cm) high

$2,000-3,000   **DN**

A 1920s Moorcroft 'Spanish' attenuated vase, designed by William Moorcroft, the base with impressed factory marks and green signature, with chips to rim and foot rim.

15.75in (40cm) high

$2,000-3,000   **DN**

A Moorcroft 'Springflowers' baluster vase, designed by William Moorcroft, the base with impressed factory marks and blue painted signature.

8.5in (22cm) high

$650-850   **WW**

A small Moorcroft 'Bramble' dish, designed by Sally Tuffin, on a cream ground, the base with impressed marks.

1991-99   *4.75in (12cm) diam*

$30-50   CAPE

A Moorcroft limited edition 'Crown Imperial' vase, designed by Rachel Bishop, on a cream ground, numbered 203 from an edition of 600, the base with impressed marks.

c1998   *12in (30.5cm) high*

$300-500   SWO

A Moorcroft 'Daisy' vase, designed by Sally Tuffin for the Moorcroft Collectors' Club, the base with painted and impressed marks and stamped 'Moorcroft Collectors' Club' in an oval.

1988   *8in (20.5cm) high*

$250-350   SWO

A CLOSER LOOK AT A MOORCROFT VASE

This is a very large vase, with great visual impact. It was very expensive when introduced.

It was given a full page in Paul Atterbury's landmark book on Moorcroft and captures the Moorcroft look perfectly in terms of the form, colors and pattern.

It was designed by Sally Tuffin, whose work attracts a legion of dedicated fans and collectors.

Only 100 examples of this vase were made - a very small quantity given the size of the Moorcroft market.

A large Moorcroft limited edition 'Carp' baluster vase, designed by Sally Tuffin in 1991, on a celadon ground, numbered 77 from an edition of 100, the base with painted signature, 'ST' initials and edition number.

23.25in (67cm) high

$6,500-8,500   WW

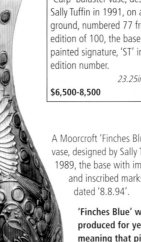

A Moorcroft 'Finches Blue' bottle vase, designed by Sally Tuffin in 1989, the base with impressed and inscribed marks and dated '8.8.94'.

'Finches Blue' was produced for years meaning that pieces decorated in it are unlikely to be rare and valuable. However, this vase is very large, leading to a higher value than most 'Finches Blue' pieces.

1994   *16.5in (42cm) high*

$1,000-1,500   SWO

A Moorcroft 'Finches Green' vase, designed by Sally Tuffin, the base with impressed and painted marks.

The green colorway of this pattern was only produced for two years.

1991-92   *7.25in (18.5cm) high*

$300-500   SWO

A Moorcroft 'Honeycomb' ginger jar and cover, designed by Philip Richardson, the base with 'WM' monogram and impressed marks, with original box.

1987-89   *6in (15.5cm) high*

$550-750   **SWO**

QUICK REFERENCE - INSPIRATION

- Moorcroft's designers take their inspiration from many places. Flowers and nature are most common. Here the specific inspiration was one of the world's best known and most successful Arts & Crafts designers, William Morris. This pattern was based on, and named after, Morris's famous 'Strawberry Thief' textile design.
- Morris was inspired to create his design after watching thrushes stealing fruit in his garden at Kelmscott Manor. Introduced in the early 1880s and initially printed using the complex indigo-discharge method, 'Strawberry Thief' became one of his most popular patterns, despite being expensive.

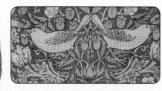

A Moorcroft 'Strawberry Thief' vase, designed by Rachel Bishop, the base with inscribed and impressed marks.

1995   *5.25in (13cm) high*

$300-500   **SWO**

A Moorcroft 'Nasturtium' ginger jar and cover, designed by Sally Tuffin for the Moorcroft Collectors' Club, the base with printed and impressed marks and numbered '337'.

Moorcroft Collectors' Club pieces were produced annually and offered to members of the club for that year only. The piece may be in a special shape, colorway or size that marks it out from standard production.

1992   *6in (15.5cm) high*

$400-600   **SWO**

A Moorcroft 'Peacock Feather' vase, designed by Sally Tuffin, signed with initials by the decorator Wendy Mason.

This pattern was originally introduced for London department store Liberty's, which enjoyed a close business relationship with William Moorcroft in the early days of his factory. The pattern was designed in 1988 and was withdrawn in 1990.

10in (25.5cm) high

$500-700   **SWO**

A Moorcroft 'Pole to Pole' 'Arctic Foxes' vase, designed by Kerry Goodwin, the base with impressed and painted marks, dated, with original box.

2007   *5.5in (14cm) high*

$300-500   **WW**

A Moorcroft 'Pole to Pole' 'Rabbits' vase, designed by Kerry Goodwin, the base with impressed and painted marks, dated, with original box.

2007   *4in (10cm) high*

$300-500   **WW**

A Moorcroft trial 'Ryden Lane' ginger jar and cover, designed and decorated by Wendy Mason, the base with impressed and painted marks, dated '8.I.98'.

Many collectors vie to own trial pieces, which often show variation in terms of the pattern or colors. These can reveal parts of the story of the development of a pattern. Many trials are very finely painted and detailed. Wendy Mason began working as a paintress at Moorcroft in 1979.

1998 *6in (15.5cm) high*

$500-700 **SWO**

A rare early 1990s Moorcroft model of 'Peter The Pig', designed by Roger Mitchell in 1990, painted in the 'Temptation' pattern with apples and blossoms, the base with impressed marks.

12in (30cm) long

$1,500-2,500 **AH**

A Moorcroft limited edition 'Tree Bark Thief Caravan' baluster vase, designed by Rachel Bishop, shape no.65/16, the base with impressed and painted marks, numbered 87 from an edition of 100, signed 'Rachel J Bishop'.

Although it still counts as part of the edition, this vase was marked as a second.

17in (43cm) high

$1,000-1,500 **TEN**

A Moorcroft limited edition 'Underwood' vase, designed by Debbie Hancock, numbered 304 from an edition of 350, the base with impressed and painted marks.

1998 *6.5in (17cm) high*

$550-750 **SWO**

A Moorcroft 'Windrush' vase, designed by Debbie Hancock, the base with impressed and painted marks.

2000 *12in (30.5cm) high*

$500-700 **SWO**

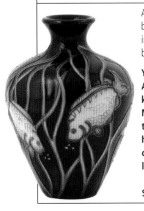

A Moorcroft 'Ysselmeer Carp' vase, designed by Marie Penkethman, the base with impressed and painted marks, with original box.

Ysselmeer is a lake, situated north of Amsterdam in the Netherlands, which is known for its carp fishing. Marie's husband Mark is a fisherman and Marie was inspired to produce this design after accompanying him to the lake where she noted that the carp there were golden in color and had large scales.

5in (10cm) high

$200-300 **WW**

A Moorcroft vase in the form of a bottle oven/kiln, designed by Rachel Bishop, the base with painted marks.

These vases were produced in different sizes, this being the largest.

2008 *10.25in (26cm) high*

$550-750 **WW**

CERAMICS

QUICK REFERENCE - POOLE POTTERY

- In 1921, the Carter & Co. Pottery in Poole, England, acquired a subsidiary pottery that was soon renamed Carter, Stabler & Adams. Recognized for its decorative wares, the pottery was known from early on as 'Poole Pottery'. All pieces were thrown and decorated by hand.
- During the 1920s and '30s, the key designer was Truda Carter. Her modern designs were stylized floral and foliate that fitted in well with the Art Deco style of the day. Animals, such as gazelle and deer, were sometimes included in designs, which are among the more valuable Poole patterns.
- Although Truda Carter's designs continued to be produced after World War II, the most important range of the post-war period was the 'Contemporary' range designed by Alfred Burgess Read, decorator Ruth Pavely and potter Guy Sydenham. Although nature was still a

key inspiration, patterns were even more stylized and were often repeated. New forms were added, but they remained simple and clean-lined. Period Scandinavian pottery was also strongly influential.
- In 1958, Robert Jefferson became the resident designer and, together with Sydenham and designer Tony Morris, devised the 'Delphis' range. This landmark range bridged the divide between commercial factory-produced wares and increasingly fashionable studio pottery.
- This aspect was built on further in 1966 when the Craft Section was founded. It produced unique works, as well as designs for other ranges including the 'Ionian', 'Aegean' and 'Atlantis 'ranges. Although interest in pieces from the 1920s-30s is returning, unique or short-run pieces from the 1960s-70s tend to fetch the highest prices.

A 1920s-30s Poole Pottery urn vase, pattern 'CE', designed by Truda Carter, decorated by Anne Hatchard, the base with impressed and painted marks.

9.5in (24cm) high

$700-1,000   **WW**

A 1920s-30s Poole Pottery 'Bluebird' pattern urn vase, pattern 'HE', designed by Truda Carter, decorated by Ruth Pavely, the base with impressed and painted marks.

9in (24cm) high

$550-750   **WW**

A large late 1920s-30s Poole Pottery vase, pattern 'BX', designed by Truda Carter, decorated by Anne Hatchard, the base with impressed factory mark and decorator's monogram.

12in (30.5cm) high

$1,000-1,500   **L&T**

A late 1920s-1930s Poole Pottery vase, pattern 'LJ', designed by Truda Carter, decorated by Anne Hatchard, the base with impressed marks and decorator's mark.

This shape is rare and was designed by Truda Carter in 1921. Another example of this pattern and shape combination, also decorated by Anne Hatchard, can be seen on p.64 of 'Poole Pottery', by Paul Atterbury, published by Richard Dennis Publications, 2002.

11in (28cm) high

$650-850   **WW**

A 1920s-30s Poole Pottery vase, pattern 'GVY', designed by Truda Carter, decorated by Margaret Atkins, the base with impressed and painted marks.

8in (20.5cm) high

$700-1,000   **WW**

A 1930s Poole Pottery vase, pattern 'VY', designed by Truda Carter, the base with impressed and painted marks.

9in (23cm) high

$1,000-1,500   **WW**

A Poole Pottery vase, shape no.803, pattern 'PC', decorated by Sheila Jenkins.

After World War II, the 'Traditional' range devised in the 1920s and '30s was simplified – more space was added between the motifs or alternatively, as here, motifs were used almost as 'decals'. This is a rare shape to find with banded decoration.

1949-61   *5.75in (14.5cm) high*

$80-120   **PC**

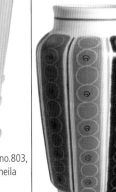

A late 1950s Poole Pottery 'Contemporary' vase, shape no.595, probably designed by John Adams in 1930-35, pattern 'E/PLC', designed by Alfred Read in 1954, the base with printed and painted marks.

9in (22.5cm) high

$250-350   **WW**

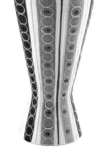

A late 1950s Poole Pottery 'Contemporary' vase, shape no.717 designed by Alfred Read and Guy Sydenham, pattern 'X/PLC', designed by Alfred Read in 1954, painted with columns in mushroom, the base with gray printed and painted marks.

7.75in (20cm) high

$300-500   **WW**

A late 1950s-60s Poole Pottery 'Contemporary' 'Ravioli' pattern plant pot, shape no.721, designed by Alfred Read and Guy Sydenham in c1956, pattern 'HOL', designed by Ruth Pavely in c1956, the base with printed and painted factory marks.

9in (23cm) high

$400-600   **WHP**

A Poole Pottery 'Freeform' 'Butterflies' pattern vase, shape no.352 designed by Alfred Read and Guy Sydenham in c1956, pattern 'PTH', designed by Ruth Pavely, the base with printed and painted factory marks.

1956-57   *6.25in (16cm) wide*

$300-500   **DS**

A Poole Pottery 'Festival of Britain' hors d'oeuvres dish, shape no.362, designed by John Adams in c1937, pattern designed by Claude Smale in 1951, the base with impressed and printed marks.

Most of the memorabilia produced for the Festival of Britain is of surprisingly poor quality. Notable exceptions are the Wedgwood mug designed by Norman Makinson and this very rare dish. Poole's next commemorative pieces were created for the 1953 Coronation. These are considerably more common than 'Festival of Britain' pieces.

1951   *8.75in (22cm) diam*

$400-600   **WW**

A large mid-1960s-70s Poole Pottery 'Delphis' vase, painted in colors on a yellow ground, the base with printed and painted marks.

13.5in (34cm) high

$120-180   **WW**

A mid-1960s-70s Poole Pottery 'Delphis' carved vase, shape no.85, decorated with wax-resist geometric motifs, the base with printed factory marks.

15.5in (39cm) high

$550-750   **WW**

A late 1960s-70s Poole Pottery 'Atlantis' vase, decorated by Alan White, incised and glazed in mottled ocher and white, the base with impressed mark and incised monogram.

8.25in (21cm) high

$250-350   WW

A late 1960s-70s Poole Pottery 'Atlantis' vase, designed and made by Guy Sydenham, glazed in pale blue and white over a terracotta body, the base with impressed marks.

6.5in (16.5cm) high

$150-250   WW

A late 1960s-1970s Poole Pottery 'Atlantis' vase, decorated by Carol Kellett, with incised corn and line motifs, glazed in speckled blue, the base with impressed and incised marks, with minor restoration to top rim.

7.25in (18.5cm) high

$120-180   WW

A Poole Pottery 'Studio' vase, probably designed by Robert Jefferson, glazed and incised with decoration in rust glazes, the shoulder and foot glazed in white, the base with printed and impressed 'Studio' mark.

A Poole Pottery 'Studio' vase, probably designed by Robert Jefferson, resist decorated with geometric motifs in shades of green on a white ground, the base with printed 'Poole Studio' mark.

3.5in (8.5cm) high

$200-300   WW

A 1970s Poole Pottery 'Delphis' carved vase, shape no.85, incised and glazed in turquoise and blue over orange, the base with printed factory marks.

15.5in (39cm) high

$500-700   WW

12.5in (31.5cm) high

$650-850   WW

A 1970s Poole Pottery 'Atlantis' carved vase, shape no.A51, decorated by Suzanne Dipple, the base with impressed marks.

3.5in (9cm) high

$150-250   TRI

A 1970s Poole Pottery flower vase, shape no.A5/2, decorated by Carol Cutler, with raised abstract ridge glazed in a metallic brown, the base with marks.

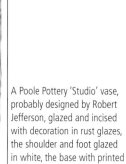

4.5in (11.5 cm) high

$120-180   WHP

A late 1960s Poole Pottery 'Delphis' charger, shape no.54, painted with a geometric design, the reverse with printed and painted marks.

16.25in (41cm) diam

$650-850   **WW**

A 1960s Poole Pottery 'Studio' plate, painted with a geometric design, the reverse with printed 'Poole Studio' mark.

10.75in (27.5cm) diam

$800-1,200   **WW**

A 1960s Poole Pottery 'Studio' plate, painted with an abstract design, with concealed mark.

10.75in (27.5cm) diam

$300-500   **WW**

A 1960s Poole Pottery 'Studio' plate, painted with geometric panels, the reverse with printed 'Poole Studio' mark.

8.25in (21cm) diam

$250-350   **WW**

A Poole Pottery 'Studio' charger, by Janice Tchalenko, painted with a pointillist design, the reverse with printed and painted marks and dated.

1999   *16.25in (41cm) diam*

$120-180   **WW**

Mark Picks

Janice Tchalenko (b.1942) is one of Britain's most influential late 20thC studio potters (see p.131 for two examples). Breaking from the Oriental- and Leach-inspired traditions in studio pottery, she championed a new avenue of design typified by bright colors and stylized floral patterns on simple forms. Her inspirations include Persian and Russian ceramics, the work of potter Bernard Palissy and that of painters such as Matisse.

As well as producing designs for Poole from 1996, she has also designed for the Dart Pottery since 1984, produced designs for Next (see p.283) in 1985 and is a fellow of the Royal College of Art. Tchalenko's work is still slightly too 'new' for many collectors, so in my opinion now is the time to buy. Her work is affordable and I believe that she is certainly a key name to watch for the future.

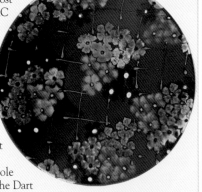

A Poole Pottery 'Studio' charger, by Janice Tchalenko, painted with flowers, the reverse with printed and painted marks and dated.

1999   *16.25in (41cm) diam*

$120-180   **WW**

A Poole Pottery 'Studio' charger, designed and painted by Nicky Massarella, the reverse with printed factory mark, painted signature and 'TF7 1/1', with original presentation box.

A similar design built up with spots was produced in two variations (one with the face on the left, one on the right). Each variation was made in a limited edition of 50 pieces.

16.25in (41cm) diam

$200-300   **WW**

CERAMICS

QUICK REFERENCE - RICARDIA WARE

- Ricardia art pottery was produced from the late 1920s until 1939 by Richards Tiles, which was, at the time, one of Britain's largest tile companies.
- Richards was inspired by other tile companies, such as Mintons and Candy & Co., and by the art pottery produced by companies such as Ruskin, Pilkington and Doulton. Like those companies, Richards was also inspired by ancient Chinese forms and glazes.
- Ricardia's fine quality glazes are complex and used selenium and uranium.
- Forms are balanced and proportional.
- Pieces are rare as they were seemingly never produced for sale and were instead used promotionally, being displayed in stockists or given to key or prestigious clients.
- For more information, visit www.ricardia.com

A Richards Tiles 'Ricardia Ware' ginger jar, shape no.10, glaze no.EE11, the base with printed mark.

Ginger jars without necks (such as the example shown here) are rarer than those with necks.

7.25in (18.5cm) high

$400-600   MHC

A Richards Tiles 'Ricardia Ware' 'Leaf vase', shape no. unknown, glaze no. unknown, the base with printed mark.

This rare form recalls American art pottery by Rookwood, Teco and Grueby

7.5in (19cm) high

$300-500   MHC

A Richards Tiles 'Ricardia Ware' ginger jar, shape no.1, glaze no.EE18, the base with printed mark and painted '1 - EE18'.

7.25in (18.5cm) high

$400-600   MHC

A large Richards Tiles 'Ricardia Ware' 'Angular Vase', shape no.13, glaze no.EE45, the base with printed and painted marks.

7.75in (19.5cm) high

$300-500   MHC

A Richards Tiles 'Ricardia Ware' 'Footed Baluster Vase', shape no.5, glaze no.EE2, the base with printed and painted marks.

5.5in (14cm) high

$200-300   MHC

A Richards Tiles 'Ricardia Ware' bowl, shape no.5, glaze no.EE42, the base with printed and painted marks.

6in (19cm) diam

$120-180   MHC

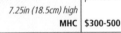

A Richards Tiles 'Ricardia Ware' lidded cigarette box, shape no. unknown, glaze no.EE47 with black details, the lid acting as a cigarette rest, the base with printed and painted marks.

6in (15cm) long

$150-250   MHC

A Richards Tiles 'Ricardia Ware' matchbox-holder ashtray, shape no. unknown, glaze no.EE4, the base with printed mark.

Ashtrays are the most common form found. They sometimes bear presentation marks on the base.

4.25in (10.5cm) diam

$50-70   MHC

QUICK REFERENCE - ROOKWOOD

- The Rookwood Pottery was founded as a 'hobby business' in Cincinnati, Ohio, USA by heiress Maria Longworth Nichols. In 1883, she was joined by William Watts Taylor, who became Production Manager and who made the pottery into a commercial success.
- Rookwood's first major glaze range was the shiny brown- and beige-toned 'Standard' glaze, introduced in 1884. Flowers and leaves are commonly found motifs, portraits are much rarer.
- Over the next two decades, the company released a series of different high-quality glazes, including 'Sea Green', 'Iris' and 'Vellum'.
  - Marks on the base will help to date a piece and identify who decorated it.
  - After 1905, Rookwood began to produce its 'Production' ware range, which was not artist signed.
  - Although the company thrived into the 1930s by adapting to the changing styles of the day, it suffered after the war and closed in 1967.

A Rookwood 'Standard' glaze ewer, decorated by Emma Foertmeyer, the base with flame mark and initials 'EDF'.

1890   *8in (20.5cm) high*
$650-850   **DRA**

A Rookwood 'Iris' glaze pottery vase, decorated by Olga Geneva Reed, the base with flame mark, '732/C' and 'O.G.R.'.

The clear, glossy 'Iris' glaze was introduced in 1894.

1896   *7in (18cm) high*
$550-750   **DMC**

A Rookwood 'Matt' glaze bowl, decorated by Jens Jensen, the base with flame mark and artist's monogram.

1901   *7in (17.5cm) diam*
$400-600   **DRA**

A Rookwood 'Standard' glaze vase, painted with opium poppies, the base with impressed marks.

10in (24cm) high
$650-850   **WW**

A Rookwood 'Matt' glaze vase, decorated by Jens Jensen, the base with flame mark and decorator's monogram 'JJ'.

1927   *5.5in (14cm) high*
$1,000-1,500   **DRA**

A Rookwood 'Matt' glazed vase, decorated by Vera Tischler, the base with flame mark and decorator's monogram 'VT'.

Although Rookwood experimented with matt glazes as early as 1886, matt-glazed pieces were not introduced to the market until 1901. Sea creatures and human figures are very rare motifs. Designs with low-relief carved details are usually highly sought after.

1922   *9in (23cm) high*
$700-1,000   **DRA**

A Rookwood 'Vellum' vase, decorated by E T Hurley, the base with flame mark and decorator's monogram 'ETH'.

1921   *8in (20.5cm) high*
$500-700   **DRA**

QUICK REFERENCE - THE VELLUM GLAZE

- The Vellum glaze was introduced in 1900. It 'diffused' the painted pattern it covered, giving it a misty appearance.
- Flowers are more common motifs than landscapes. Most were painted in delicate shades of green, cream and blue.
- Landscapes, which typically contain trees, recall those by glassmakers Gallé and Daum, who worked during the same period.
- The 'V' in the mark was used to signify the Vellum glaze.

A Rookwood 'Scenic Vellum' glaze vase, decorated by Ed Diers, the base with flame mark, '904C', 'V' and decorator's monogram 'ED'.

1909   *12.5in (32cm) high*

$2,500-3,500   **DRA**

A Rookwood 'Scenic Vellum' glaze vase, decorated by Sara Sax, the base with flame mark, '952E', 'V' and decorator's monogram 'SS'.

1915   *7.75in (19.5cm) high*

$2,500-3,500   **DRA**

A Rookwood 'Banded Scenic' vase, decorated by Lenore Asbury, the base with flame mark, '938D' and decorator's monogram 'LA'.

1918   *7in (18cm) high*

$1,500-2,500   **DRA**

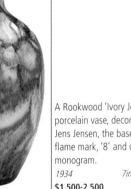

A Rookwood 'Ivory Jewel' porcelain vase, decorated by Jens Jensen, the base with flame mark, '8' and decorator's monogram.

1934   *7in (18cm) high*

$1,500-2,500   **DRA**

A Rookwood 'Jewel' porcelain vase, decorated by Jens Jensen, the base with flame mark, 'S' and decorator's monogram.

1933   *4.25in (10.5cm) high*

$1,000-1,500   **DRA**

A Rookwood 'Jewel' porcelain vase, decorated by Jens Jensen, the base with flame mark, 'S' and decorator's monogram.

1933   *5.5in (14cm) high*

$1,000-1,500   **DRA**

A Rookwood 'Iris' glaze vase, decorated by E T Hurley (1869-1950), the base with flame mark, '927D' and decorator's monogram 'ETH'.

1902   *8.25in (21cm) high*

$1,200-1,800   **DRA**

A Rookwood 'Jewel' porcelain vase, decorated by Sara Sax, the base with flame mark, '6197C' and decorator's monogram 'SS'.

1931   *9in (23cm) high*

$4,000-6,000   **DRA**

QUICK REFERENCE - ROSEVILLE

- The Roseville Pottery was founded in 1890 in Zanesville in the 'pottery state' of Ohio, USA.
- Its first art pottery range, 'Rozane' was introduced in 1900 and its success led to many more ranges being released.
- After 1908, when the art pottery boom began to tail off, the company began to produce molded wares, typically focusing on stylized natural motifs such as flowers and leaves.
- The company employed notable designers such as Frederick Hurten Rhead (1904-08) and Frank Ferrell (1917-54) and glaze-maker George Krause (1915-54)
- Look for rare ranges and crisply molded designs that are well decorated as these are likely to be the most valuable. Shapes and colors also affect value. Damage, such as cracks, always devalues a piece seriously.
- The company closed in 1954.

A rare Roseville 'Aztec' jardinière and pedestal, the pedestal with decorator's monogram.

c1915   *35.5in (90cm) high*
$2,500-3,500   **DRA**

A Roseville green 'Bleeding Heart' pattern jardinière and pedestal, the base with factory marks.

32in (81cm) high
$1,200-1,800   **DRA**

A 20thC Roseville blue 'Clematis' pattern jardinière and pedestal, the base stamped '667-8'.

24.5in (61cm) high
$250-350   **DRA**

A 1930s Roseville 'Earlam' pattern sand jar, with foil label.

'Earlam' was introduced in 1930 with popular color combinations including mottled matt green-tan (shown here) or tan-purple.

14.5in (37cm) high
$2,500-3,500   **DRA**

A Roseville red 'Imperial II' pattern vase, with foil label.

7in (18cm) high
$400-600   **DRA**

A Roseville 'Imperial I' jardinière and pedestal.

28.5in (72.5cm) high
$150-250   **DRA**

A Roseville 'Imperial II' pattern vase, decorated in golden ocher over a frothy blue glaze, with shadow of former label.

11.25in (28.5cm) high
$700-1,000   **DRA**

CERAMICS

A Roseville red 'Nude Silhouette' pattern rose bowl, the base with raised mark.

8in (20.5cm) diam

$500-700   DRA

A Roseville brown 'Pinecone' pattern pitcher, shape no.5, unmarked.

9.5in (24cm) high

$500-700   DRA

A Roseville 'Sunflower' pattern wall pocket.

For two more examples of this pattern on different shapes, see 'Millers Collectibles Handbook 2012-2013' p.108.

7.5in (19cm) high

$700-1,000   DRA

A Roseville 'Woodland' pattern twisted vase, with some glaze pops to bisque and minor chip to base, unmarked.

10.5in (27cm) high

$350-450   DRA

A Roseville brown 'Zephyr Lily' pattern pedestal, the base with mark.

16.75in (42.5cm) high

$150-250   DMC

A CLOSER LOOK AT A ROSEVILLE VASE

'Della Robbia' was designed in 1906 by notable British ceramics designer Frederick Hurten Rhead. He was Art Director at Roseville 1904-08.

'Della Robbia' pieces were made by combining sgrafitto patterns with cast forms in two differently colored slips. It was time-consuming to make and required great skill from the decorators.

This example is an attractive shape.

It is large, which is appealing to buyers.

It has a pierced (or cut-out) rim, which is a rare feature.

Described as 'unlike anything else' in its day, 'Della Robbia' is one of the most sought-after Roseville ranges. Pieces decorated with a number of colors, such as this example, are the most desirable.

A rare Roseville 'Della Robbia' vase, decorated with wild roses, with a cut-out rim, the base with raised 'Rozane Ware' seal, with incised decorator's monogram.

c1910   *15.5in high*

$55,000-75,000   DRA

A 1950s Roseville 'Raymor' swinging coffee pot and stand, designed by Ben Seibel in 1952, shape no.176, decorated in 'Autumn Brown'.

This piece was designed as part of the Raymor 'Modern Stoneware' oven-to-table range. Ben Seibel (1918-85) was a notable American Industrial designer. He produced this design in 1952 as part of Roseville's attempts to stay in business - unfortunately the company closed two years later.

13in (33cm) high

$300-500   FRE

QUICK REFERENCE - ROYAL COPENHAGEN

- Royal Copenhagen was founded in 1775 under the patronage of Queen Julianne Marie of Denmark. Its founder, Heinrich Frank Müller, had unlocked the secret of producing porcelain, which was only known to a few factories in Europe.
- Its first range, 'Blue Fluted', is also its most popular and longest-lived tableware range. Most collectors focus on decorative designs from the early- to mid- 20thC. Colors are pale and usually include a blue and creamy white.

- Important designers include Nils Thorsson (1898-1975), Knud Kyhn (1880-1969) Arnold Krog (1856-1931), Axel Salto (1889-1961)and Johanne Gerber.
- Designs were usually inspired by the natural although characters from Danish stories and everyday life were also used. Look out for the modern designs produced from the 1950s to the 1970s, as these are currently very popular.
- Marks on the base can help to date a piece, but you will need a specialist reference guide.

A 1920s Royal Copenhagen figural group, 'The Rock & The Wave', designed by Professor Theodor Lundberg in 1897, model no.1132, the base with printed marks.

A 20thC Royal Copenhagen porcelain figurine of 'The Little Mermaid', designed by Edvard Eriksen, model no. 4431.

This figurine is modeled after Eriksen's (1876-1959) sculpture, unveiled in 1913 on Copenhagen's coast.

A Royal Copenhagen figurine of a young girl with a goose, model no.527, the base painted with artist's initials 'TM'.

9.25in (23.5cm) high

$120-180   CAPE

8.75in (22cm) high

$500-700   PC

A mid-late 20thC Royal Copenhagen model of a seated polar bear, designed by Carl Frederik Liisberg, model no.502.

Carl Frederik Liisberg (1860-1909) was a sculptor and decorator at Royal Copenhagen 1885-1909. This model was part of a series of polar bears he designed.

Lundberg (1852-1926) was a Swedish sculptor. His work is typified by expressive poses and a strong feeling for realism and character.

18in (46cm) high

$800-1,200   L&T

13in (33cm) high

$120-180   WHP

A 1920s Royal Copenhagen charger, decorated by Jenny Meyer, with painted signature in the design, the reverse with printed and painted marks.

Jenny Sofie Meyer (1866-1927) was a notable decorator at Royal Copenhagen 1892-1927. She trained under Arnold Krog and specialized in floral motifs. Her work received a Gold Medal at the 1893 World's Fair in Chicago.

A Royal Copenhagen 'Lobster' dish, designed by Jorgen Bolslov, model no.3277, the base with maker's mark.

1969-74   6.25in (16cm) wide

$300-500   KAU

11.75in (30cm) diam

$650-850   WW

A 1920s Royal Copenhagen vase, model no.1217, pattern no.2635, the base with decorator's mark.

9.25in (26cm) high

$400-600   KAU

CERAMICS

A 1970s Royal Copenhagen 'Baca' vase, designed by Johanne Gerber, the base with printed marks.

This Japanese-inspired design is one of the most commonly found Royal Copenhagen patterns of this period.

9in (23cm) high

$100-150   PC

An early 1970s Royal Copenhagen 'Baca' vase, designed by Nils Thorsson, the base with painted and printed factory marks and painted '726/3259'.

This design was also produced in blue, as can be seen on the dish below.

8.75in (22.5cm) high

$100-150   SAS

A late 1960s/mid-1970s Royal Copenhagen 'Tenera' chimney vase, designed by Berte Jessen, the base with printed factory marks, painted '436/3121' and impressed '3259'.

7.5in (19cm) high

$120-180   GAZE

A 1970s Royal Copenhagen 'Baca' vase, designed by Johanne Gerber or Marianne Johnson, the base with printed marks and printed and inscribed '799/3101'.

14.25in (36cm) high

$250-350   AH

A large Royal Copenhagen 'Tenera' square dish, designed by Inge-Lise Kofoed, the base with printed factory marks and painted '156/2885' and '4'.

10.5in (26.5cm) wide

$70-100   GAZE

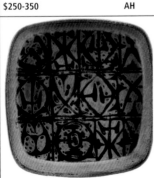

A Royal Copenhagen 'Baca' square dish, designed by Nils Thorsson, with painted and printed factory marks to base and painted '704/2883'.

6.5in (16.5cm) wide

$80-120   SAS

A Royal Copenhagen 'Tenera' mug, designed by Inge-Lise Koefoed, shape no.3113, pattern no.454, the base with printed factory marks, designer's monogram and decorator's mark.

c1986-89   *5.5in (14cm) high*

$70-100   PC

A 1960s-70s Royal Copenhagen 'Anette' pattern 'Tenera' teapot, designed by Berte Jessen, the base painted '601/3151', with 'B' chop mark and decorator's monogram.

4.25in (10.5cm) high

$100-150   GC

A 1970s Royal Copenhagen 'Tenera' wall plaque, designed by Beth Breyen, shape no.2866, pattern no.162, the reverse with printed 'Aluminia' backstamp, with designer's monogram 'BB' and decorator's monogram 'BA'.

c1961   *11.75in (30cm) high*

$120-180   **PC**

An early 1960s Royal Copenhagen stoneware dish, designed by Jorgen Mogensen, model no.21941, modeled in low relief with a bird, the reverse with printed and painted marks and incised monogram.

11.5in (29.5cm) wide

$150-250   **WW**

A CLOSER LOOK AT A VASE

Axel Salto (1889-1961) is considered one of the most important Danish ceramic designers of the 20thC. He favored sculptural over purely functional forms.

Salto used the rich and deep 'Sung' glazes developed by the company in the late 1910s. These were heavily influenced by Japanese ceramics and glazes.

As this cone or seed pod design shows, Salto was heavily inspired by nature. This theme would become one of the central ideas of Scandinavian Modernism.

This vase is part of a series of rare vases and bowls, designed from c1949 onward. All are more expressive in their form and surface design than earlier or contemporaneous work at the company.

A Royal Copenhagen stoneware 'Budding' vase, designed by Axel Salto, decorated with the 'Sung' glaze, the base with green 'Royal Copenhagen Denmark' three line factory mark, and inscribed 'SALTO 20701'.

7.5in (19cm) high

$5,500-7,500   **DRA**

A 1950s-60s Royal Copenhagen 'Marselis' gourd-shaped vase, designed by Nils Thorsson, the base with 'Aluminia' mark.

5in (13cm) high

$120-180   **PC**

A mid-late 20thC Royal Copenhagen pottery bust of a woman, designed by Johannes Hedegaard, model no.159/2897, the base with printed and painted marks.

12.5in (33cm) high

$400-600   **WW**

A Royal Copenhagen stoneware vase, designed by Axel Salto, with sculpted rim glazed in blue and mustard mottle, the base marked '21439/DENMARK/ SALTO' and with paper label.

5.25in (13cm) high

$3,000-5,000   **DRA**

A Royal Copenhagen stoneware model of a bear, designed by Knud Kyhn, model no.21453, decorated with a 'Sung' glaze, the base impressed 'KK' and with printed marks.

4in (10cm) high

$50-70   **PC**

CERAMICS

A Pilkington's 'Royal Lancastrian' luster-glazed vase, decorated by Richard Joyce, mold no. 3152, the base with impressed factory mark, mold number and painted artist's monogram.

4.75in (12cm) high

$800-1,200   CAPE

A Pilkington's 'Royal Lancastrian' luster-glazed vase, decorated by William S Mycock, mold no.3152, the base with impressed factory mark, mold number, painted artist's monogram and date code.

1926   4.75in (12cm) high

$550-750   CAPE

A Pilkington's 'Royal Lancatrian' luster-glazed vase, decorated by Gladys Rogers, mold no.2507, the base with indistinct impressed factory mark, mold number and painted artist's mark.

4.25in (11cm) high

$250-350   CAPE

QUICK REFERENCE - ROYAL LANCASTRIAN

- Pilkington's was founded in Manchester in 1892 and became known for its tiles.
- Decorative wares with high-fired and luster glazes were introduced in 1906. They were sold under the brand name 'Lancastrian', which came from the location of the factory in Lancashire.
- In 1913, the company received a Royal Warrant, thereby becoming Royal Lancastrian.
- Production of 'Royal Lancastrian' lustered wares reached its peak in the 1910s and ceased in 1938, as fashion had changed and sales had fallen.
- Egyptian themes, inspired by the discovery of Tutankhamun's tomb in 1922, are comparatively rare and highly sought after. This particular piece is also large, possibly by one of the most skilled and popular artists and in excellent condition: all factors that make it desirable.

A Pilkington's 'Royal Lancastrian' luster-glazed vase, possibly decorated by Richard Joyce, mold no.2634, the base with impressed factory mark, mold number and painted artist's monogram.

7.75in (18.4cm) high

$1,000-1,500   CAPE

A Pilkington's 'Royal Lancastrian' luster-glazed vase, decorated by William S Mycock, mold no.503, the base with impressed factory mark, mold number and painted artist's monogram.

5in (12.5cm) high

$500-700   CAPE

A Pilkington's 'Royal Lancastrian' luster-glazed vase, mold no.3019, the base with impressed factory mark, mold number and date code, with restoration.

1913   9in (23cm) high

$250-350   CAPE

A Pilkington's 'Royal Lancastrian' low-fired mottled orange-glazed vase.

$120-180   WHP

A Pilkington's 'Royal Lancastrian' dish, decorated by William S Mycock, mold no.3225, the base with impressed factory mark, mold number and painted artist's monogram and date code, the interior heavily rubbed.

1930   9in (22.9cm) diam

$80-120   CAPE

QUICK REFERENCE – ROYAL WORCESTER

- The Worcester factory was founded in England in 1751. The factory gained its first Royal Warrant from George III in 1788. It became known as Royal Worcester in 1862.
- Forms and decoration were often inspired by Oriental porcelain, the work of competing British and European porcelain factories.
- Notable names include the modeller James Hadley, sculptor Charles Toft and the Stinton family of decorators.
- The early 20thC saw the company suffer as sales fell. This led to Royal Worcester declaring bankruptcy in 1930. The company was saved by C W Dyson Perrins

and, led by Joseph Grimson, entered another 'golden age'. New freelance modellers were introduced and the product range was refreshed and expanded. Today Royal Worcester continues to sell many of the figurines designed during this period by names such as Doris Lindner.

- As production is typically traditional in style, many Royal Worcester ceramics have gone out of fashion. As a result, values for much of Worcester's 19thC and 20thC production has fallen, making it more affordable to collectors than ever. The very rarest and most desirable objects still command a premium.

A Royal Worcester figurine of 'January', modeled by Freda Doughty, no.3452, from the 'Months of the Year' series, the base with black printed mark.

c1950-85   *6in (15cm) high*
$80-120   **AH**

A Royal Worcester figurine of 'February', modeled by Freda Doughty, no.3453, from the 'Months of the Year' series, the base with black printed mark.

c1950-85   *7in (18cm) high*
$80-120   **PC**

A Royal Worcester figurine of 'March', modeled by Freda Doughty, no.3454, from the 'Months of the Year' series, the base with black printed marks.

c1950-85   *5.5in (14cm) high*
$120-180   **AH**

A Royal Worcester figurine of 'October', modeled by Freda Doughty, no.3417, from the 'Months of the Year' series, the base with black printed mark.

1951-85   *7in (18cm) high*
$80-120   **FLD**

A Royal Worcester figurine of 'November', modeled by Freda Doughty, no.3418, from the 'Months of the Year' series, the base with black printed mark and dated.

This model was produced in this colorway and under this name c1950-1985. Examples without the registered 'R' in a circle mark date from before 1962 and are more desirable. A miniature version known as 'Peace' (model no.4167) was produced 1982-c1985. The version with pink coat and hat and only two doves is known as 'Fantails' (model no.3760). It was produced 1963-c1982 and is worth roughly the same as 'November'.

1957   *7in (18cm) high*
$150-250   **AH**

A Royal Worcester figurine of 'Monday's Child is Fair of Face', modeled by Freda Doughty, no.3257, from the 'Days of the Week' series, the base with black printed mark.

'Monday's Child' can also be found with a blue dress trimmed in yellow on a white plinth with a blue and yellow design. That version is worth roughly the same as this one, but look out for a very rare version with a purple dress trimmed with yellow. Known as 'Susie', she was only produced 1982-83 and could fetch more than twice as much as this piece.

1938-84, 1996-2002

6in (16.5cm) high

$70-100   **CHT**

A Royal Worcester figurine of 'Tuesday's Child is Full of Grace', modeled by Freda Doughty, no.3258A, from the 'Days of the Week' series, the base with black printed mark.

A variation of this figure with a white tutu and red shoes, known as 'Red Shoes', was produced 1982-83 and is extremely rare. It would be worth around five times as much as this example.

1938-84, 1996-2002

9in (22.5cm) high

$70-100   **CHT**

A Royal Worcester figurine of 'Wednesday's Child is Full of Woe', modeled by Freda Doughty, no.3521, from the 'Days of the Week' series, the base with black printed mark.

The 3in (7.5cm) high miniature version of this model was produced 1982-c1985 and is known as 'Poor Teddy' (no.4195).

1938-84, 1996-2002

7in (18cm) high

$80-120   **CHT**

A Royal Worcester figurine of 'Wednesday's Child', no.4487, modeled by Carol Gladman.

1990   *6in (15cm) high*

$70-100   **CHT**

A Royal Worcester figurine of 'Thursday's Child Has Far to Go', modeled by Freda Doughty, no.3260, from the 'Days of the Week' series, the base with black printed mark.

Look out for the version with a brown hat, walking stick and sandals. Known as 'Smiling Through', it was only produced 1982-83. It is consequently relatively rare and could fetch more than twice the value of this more common version.

6in (16cm) high

$100-150   **CHT**

A Royal Worcester figurine of 'But the Child that is Born on the Sabbath Day is Fair and Wise and Good and Gay', modeled by Freda Doughty, no.3256, from the 'Days of the Week' series, the base with black printed mark.

Look out for examples with a puce printed mark. These were produced 1938-40 and can fetch more than twice the value of figurines with black printed marks. This model is one of the most desirable from the 'Days of the Week' series.

1938-85   *5in (12.5cm) high*

$250-350   **WHP**

A Royal Worcester figurine of 'Ireland', modeled by Freda Doughty, no.3178, from the 'Children of the Nations' series, the base with black printed mark, dated, produced 1936-58.

Examples with puce marks, rather than black marks, are more desirable and valuable.

1951   *5.75in (15cm) high*
$250-350   **AH**

A Royal Worcester figurine of 'Peter Pan', modeled by Frederick Gertner, no.3011, the base with puce printed mark, dated, produced 1933-c1958.

The relatively high value of this figurine is due to three factors: Peter Pan is a popular character, this model was produced for a comparatively short period of time and pre-war examples with puce marks are rare.

1936   *8in (20cm) high*
$250-350   **AH**

A Royal Worcester figurine of 'Scotland', modeled by Freda Doughty, no.3104, from the 'Children of the Nations' series, the base with black printed mark, dated, produced 1935-59.

1953   *5.5in (14cm) high*
$250-350   **AH**

A Royal Worcester figurine of 'The Duchess's Dress', modeled by Freda Doughty, no.3106, the base with black printed mark.

This is the second version of this figurine. The first version, produced during the same time period, has the hand underneath, rather than to the side of, the rose. It can fetch more than twice the value of this version.

1935-59
$70-100

QUICK REFERENCE - FREDA DOUGHTY

- Freda G Doughty (1895-1972) was one of Royal Worcester's most prolific and popular modellers and her designs arguably revived Royal Worcester's fortunes. On July 4th 1930, the company went bankrupt due to falling sales and financial problems. At this point, it was acquired (and subsidized) by Charles Dyson Perrin. One of the directors was staying with Freda's cousin, saw her work and invited her to submit some designs to Royal Worcester. Her charming children in lively poses caught the public's imagination and quickly became some of the company's bestselling products.
- 'Boy with Parakeet' remained very popular into the 1950s and is said to have helped keep the company afloat during that decade!
- One of Doughty's most successful series for Royal Worcester was 'Days of the Week', initially comprising 14 children (each day of the week was thus represented by a boy and a girl). Introduced in 1938, the range was so popular that an additional seven designs were added in 1954. When the range was re-introduced in 1991, colors were paler. Early examples have the name of the figurine painted by hand on the base.

A Royal Worcester figurine of 'Boy with Parakeet', modeled by Freda Doughty, no.3087, the boy wearing a yellow suit with white frills, the base with black printed mark.

1935-83   *6.5in (17cm) high*
$30-50   **ECGW**

A Royal Worcester limited edition figurine of 'The Spirit of Summer', modeled by Peter Holland, no.66 from an edition of 9,500, the base with printed and painted marks.

7.5in (16.5cm) high | *2002*   *10.5in (26.5cm) high*
FLD | **$80-120**   **CAPE**

CERAMICS

QUICK REFERENCE - DORIS LINDNER'S HORSES

- Doris Lindner (1896-1979) first produced designs for Royal Worcester in 1931, making her a part of the team of new modellers who helped turn the company around.
- In 1935 she began producing her celebrated horse figurines, with the first limited edition being 'Princess Elizabeth on Tommy' in 1948. Only 100 examples were produced and it is one of her most valuable and sought-after designs today, regularly fetching in excess of $5,000.
- Her limited edition range of horses reached a peak in popularity during the 1960s and 1970s, but remains popular today.
- Look for small edition sizes, well known (often Royal) riders and elegant horses, such as this. Also try to ensure that the model is complete with the relevant paperwork, wooden stand and packaging, as this will ensure the highest values.

A Royal Worcester limited edition model of 'Hackney Stallion', no.3935, modeled by Doris Lindner, no.103 from an edition of 500, with wooden base, certificate and original box.
1973

$2,500-3,500

11in (28cm) high

GORL

A Royal Worcester limited edition model of 'Appaloosa Imboden's Driftwood Bob', modeled by Doris Lindner, no.3869, no.308 from an edition of 750, with wooden base and framed certificate.
1968   *9.75in (25cm) high*

$1,000-1,500   **SWO**

A Royal Worcester limited edition model of 'Galloping Dartmoor Ponies' modeled by Doris Lindner, no.3922, no.117 from an edition of 500, with wooden base, certificate and original box.

This model was also produced in white. That version is worth around half of the value of this version.

1972   *8.75in (22cm) high*

$2,000-3,000   **GORL**

A Royal Worcester limited edition model of 'Foxhunter and Lt. Col. H M Llewellyn CBE', modeled by Doris Lindner, no.3678, from an edition of 500, with printed marks, with wooden base.
1959   *12in (30.5cm) high*

$800-1,200   **SWO**

A Royal Worcester limited edition model of 'H.R.H. Prince Charles on Pans Folly', modeled by Lorne McKean, no.4031, no.53 from an edition of 250, with printed mark, with wooden base and fitted 'Tri-Mite' carrying case.
1979   *14.5in (37cm) high*

$600-800   **CAPE**

A Royal Worcester limited edition model of 'George Washington' on a horse, modeled by Bernard Winskill, no.3897, from the 'Famous Commanders' series, no.111 from an edition of 750, with wooden base and certificate.
1972   *18in (46cm) high*

$1,200-1,800   **L&T**

QUICK REFERENCE - THE STINTON FAMILY

- The Stinton family name has been associated with finely painted Worcester porcelain for over 160 years. Henry Stinton began the tradition after being taken on at the Grainger factory (later part of Worcester) in 1805.
- Henry's son John Snr. discovered that oil of cloves prevented his paints from drying out too quickly, enabling him to work on his paintings for longer.
- The best known Stintons are Henry's grandsons, John Jnr. and James, and John Snr.'s brother Harry.
- John Jnr. is particularly renowned for his delicate and evocative scenes of Highland cattle in misty landscapes. Other typical subjects related to the family include castles, game birds and other cattle.
- The 'Stinton' name adds great value to a piece of Worcester and many collectors choose to collect only works painted by one of them.

A Royal Worcester baluster vase, painted by John Stinton Jnr. with Highland cattle, signed, the base with green mark and date code.

1913   *5.5in (14cm) high*

$1,200-1,800   **DN**

A Royal Worcester trumpet-form spill vase, painted by John Stinton Jnr. with Highland cattle, signed, the base with puce printed mark and date code.

1935   *7.5in (19cm) high*

$1,200-1,800   **DN**

A Royal Worcester pin, painted by Harry Stinton with Highland cattle, signed, in a silver-colored metal mount, the reverse with puce printed mark and date code.

This is a rare form, hence the high price for such a small piece.

1928   *3in (7.5cm) wide*

$550-750   **DN**

A small Royal Worcester pin dish, painted by William Roberts with peaches and berries over a mossy ground, the reverse with black printed mark.

4in (10cm) diam

$120-180   **FLD**

A Royal Worcester cabinet plate, painted by Raymond Rushton with a view of Durham Cathedral, the reverse signed, inscribed and with printed mark and date code.

1938   *11in (28cm) wide*

$400-600   **A&G**

A Royal Worcester cream jug, painted by William Powell with a bullfinch, with branch-like angled handle, signed, the base with printed mark and date code.

1921   *2.75in (7cm) high*

$120-180   **ECGW**

A pair of Royal Worcester blush ivory wall pockets, in the form of hunting horns, shape no.933, painted with loose bouquets of summer flowers, with gilt strapwork molded borders, the reverses with green printed marks and dated.

1898   *11.75in (30cm) high*

$700-1,000   **HT**

CERAMICS

A CLOSER LOOK AT A WORCESTER TEA SET

Scottie Wilson (c1890-1972) was a Scottish artist who was an early proponent of 'outsider' art, rejecting commercialism and living a life of poverty.

A resident in both Canada and Britain, he began drawing in 1932, aged 44. Within a few years his work was being collected by Pablo Picasso and Jean Dubuffet. His work can now be found in major public galleries.

Wilson was commissioned to produce this pattern for Royal Worcester in the early 1960s. It was based on Native North American totem poles.

The 'Scottie Wilson' range was produced at the Palissy Pottery in Stoke-on-Trent. The factory was owned by Royal Worcester from 1958 until 1989 when it closed.

The 'Scottie Wilson' pattern was available on a white ceramic body or on the terracotta-colored 'Samian' body, shown here.

Although it was popular with design aficionados, the 'Scottie Wilson' range was expensive and did not sell well. It was discontinued in 1965.

A Royal Worcester 'Scottie Wilson' pattern tea service, designed by Scottie Wilson, comprising a teapot and cover, milk jug, covered sugar basin and six cups, saucers and side plates, printed in black on a terracotta ground, the bases or reverses with printed marks and facsimile signatures.

Teapot 5in (13cm) high

$250-350   **WW**

A Royal Worcester candle snuffer, 'Abbess', the base with puce printed mark.

This model was produced for many years from the late 19thC.

c1900   *3.75in (9.5cm) high*

$80-120   **DA&H**

A Royal Worcester candle snuffer, in the form of a Geisha in a yellow kimono, the base with puce printed mark and date mark.

1902   *6in (6.5cm) high*

$100-150   **ROS**

A Royal Worcester candle snuffer, in the form of a bust of an old lady, the base with printed factory mark.

Candle snuffers are placed over a candle to extinguish the flame. Most are only used decoratively and they have become very popular with a small number of Royal Worcester collectors.

c1912   *2.75in (7cm) high*

$150-250   **DA&H**

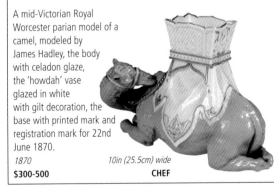

A mid-Victorian Royal Worcester parian model of a camel, modeled by James Hadley, the body with celadon glaze, the 'howdah' vase glazed in white with gilt decoration, the base with printed mark and registration mark for 22nd June 1870.

1870   *10in (25.5cm) wide*

$300-500   **CHEF**

A Royal Worcester model of an 'English Bulldog', modeled by Doris Lindner, no.2945, from the 'Small Dogs' series, the base with black mark, designed in 1932.

2.5in (6cm) high

$200-300   **WHP**

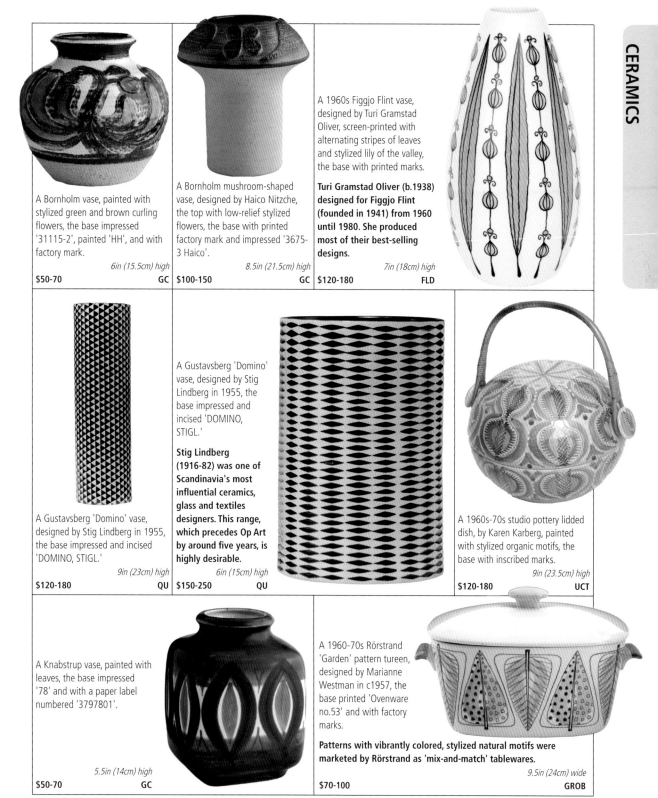

A Bornholm vase, painted with stylized green and brown curling flowers, the base impressed '31115-2', painted 'HH', and with factory mark.

6in (15.5cm) high

$50-70   GC

A Bornholm mushroom-shaped vase, designed by Haico Nitzche, the top with low-relief stylized flowers, the base with printed factory mark and impressed '3675-3 Haico'.

8.5in (21.5cm) high

$100-150   GC

A 1960s Figgjo Flint vase, designed by Turi Gramstad Oliver, screen-printed with alternating stripes of leaves and stylized lily of the valley, the base with printed marks.

Turi Gramstad Oliver (b.1938) designed for Figgjo Flint (founded in 1941) from 1960 until 1980. She produced most of their best-selling designs.

7in (18cm) high

$120-180   FLD

A Gustavsberg 'Domino' vase, designed by Stig Lindberg in 1955, the base impressed and incised 'DOMINO, STIGL.'

9in (23cm) high

$120-180   QU

A Gustavsberg 'Domino' vase, designed by Stig Lindberg in 1955, the base impressed and incised 'DOMINO, STIGL.'

Stig Lindberg (1916-82) was one of Scandinavia's most influential ceramics, glass and textiles designers. This range, which precedes Op Art by around five years, is highly desirable.

6in (15cm) high

$150-250   QU

A 1960s-70s studio pottery lidded dish, by Karen Karberg, painted with stylized organic motifs, the base with inscribed marks.

9in (23.5cm) high

$120-180   UCT

A Knabstrup vase, painted with leaves, the base impressed '78' and with a paper label numbered '3797801'.

5.5in (14cm) high

$50-70   GC

A 1960-70s Rörstrand 'Garden' pattern tureen, designed by Marianne Westman in c1957, the base printed 'Ovenware no.53' and with factory marks.

Patterns with vibrantly colored, stylized natural motifs were marketed by Rörstrand as 'mix-and-match' tablewares.

9.5in (24cm) wide

$70-100   GROB

CERAMICS

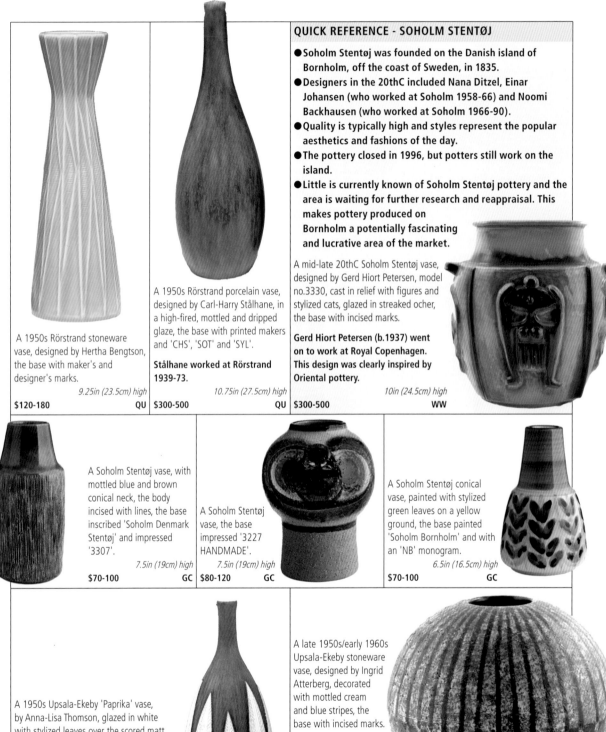

A 1950s Rörstrand stoneware vase, designed by Hertha Bengtson, the base with maker's and designer's marks.

9.25in (23.5cm) high

$120-180 QU

A 1950s Rörstrand porcelain vase, designed by Carl-Harry Stålhane, in a high-fired, mottled and dripped glaze, the base with printed makers and 'CHS', 'SOT' and 'SYL'.

Stålhane worked at Rörstrand 1939-73.

10.75in (27.5cm) high

$300-500 QU

QUICK REFERENCE - SOHOLM STENTØJ

- Soholm Stentøj was founded on the Danish island of Bornholm, off the coast of Sweden, in 1835.
- Designers in the 20thC included Nana Ditzel, Einar Johansen (who worked at Soholm 1958-66) and Noomi Backhausen (who worked at Soholm 1966-90).
- Quality is typically high and styles represent the popular aesthetics and fashions of the day.
- The pottery closed in 1996, but potters still work on the island.
- Little is currently known of Soholm Stentøj pottery and the area is waiting for further research and reappraisal. This makes pottery produced on Bornholm a potentially fascinating and lucrative area of the market.

A mid-late 20thC Soholm Stentøj vase, designed by Gerd Hiort Petersen, model no.3330, cast in relief with figures and stylized cats, glazed in streaked ocher, the base with incised marks.

Gerd Hiort Petersen (b.1937) went on to work at Royal Copenhagen. This design was clearly inspired by Oriental pottery.

10in (24.5cm) high

$300-500 WW

A Soholm Stentøj vase, with mottled blue and brown conical neck, the body incised with lines, the base inscribed 'Soholm Denmark Stentøj' and impressed '3307'.

7.5in (19cm) high

$70-100 GC

A Soholm Stentøj vase, the base impressed '3227 HANDMADE'.

7.5in (19cm) high

$80-120 GC

A Soholm Stentøj conical vase, painted with stylized green leaves on a yellow ground, the base painted 'Soholm Bornholm' and with an 'NB' monogram.

6.5in (16.5cm) high

$70-100 GC

A 1950s Upsala-Ekeby 'Paprika' vase, by Anna-Lisa Thomson, glazed in white with stylized leaves over the scored matt brown ground, the base with impressed marks.

16in (40.5cm) high

$450-650 SWO

A late 1950s/early 1960s Upsala-Ekeby stoneware vase, designed by Ingrid Atterberg, decorated with mottled cream and blue stripes, the base with incised marks.

Atterberg designed for Upsala-Ekeby 1944-63.

11.75in (30cm) high

$300-500 WW

A late 1930s Shelley twenty-piece part tea set, pattern no.Y.0169. comprising five 'Ascot' shape cups, six saucers and side plates, milk jug, a 'Court' sugar bowl and sandwich plate.

Cups 2.5in (6cm) high

$80-120   CAPE

A 1930s Shelley part tea service, comprising three 'Eve' cups and four saucers, four side plates, a sandwich plate and a sugar bowl.

Cups 2.5in (6cm) high

$50-70   WHP

A 1930s Shelley Art Deco part dinner service, decorated with gray and yellow geometric patterns, the bases with printed marks.

$150-250   WHP

QUICK REFERENCE - SHELLEY

- The pottery was founded in 1822 in an area known as 'The Foley' near Longton in Staffordshire. Due to changes in ownership, the company was renamed Wileman & Co. in 1872 and used a Foley China mark until 1910, when the mark was changed to Shelley.
- The company was renamed Shelleys in 1925, when the Shelley mark began to be used officially.
- Notable Art Directors included Frederick Rhead (1896-1905) Walter Slater (1905-37) and Eric Slater (from 1937-1960s).
- The company is best known for its bone china teasets

produced from the 1920s until the 1940s, which can fetch many hundreds of dollars depending on the size of the set, the shape, color and pattern. The more modern and angular the shape, and the more angular and colorful the pattern is, the better.
- Teapots are typically the most valuable and desirable individual shapes, followed by teacups and saucers, and milk jugs and sugar bowls.
- Condition is paramount to value.
- In 1966, Shelley was taken over by Allied English potteries and in 1971 it was absorbed into Royal Doulton.

A Shelley Art Deco tea set, pattern no.W12131, comprising an 'Eve' teapot and stand, milk jug and sugar basin, five 'Regent' cups and six saucers, side plates and one sandwich plate, the bases and reverses with printed and painted marks.

Sandwich plate 9.75in (24.5cm) wide

$550-750   WW

A Shelley 'Orange Block' pattern 'Mode' tea set, pattern no.11792, comprising a teapot, two cups and saucers, one plate and one sugar bowl, with crack to one cup and smudging to teapot handle.

Cups 2.5in (6.5cm) high

$300-500   SWO

Two Shelley 'Sunray' pattern 'Mode' cups and saucers, pattern no.11742, with crack and chip.

Cups 2.5in (6.5cm) high

$300-500   SWO

A mid-late 1930s Shelley 'Phlox' pattern 'Regent' teapot, pattern no.W12325, the base with marks and registered no. '781613' for 1933.

5in (12.5cm) high

$100-150   BETH

CERAMICS

A large 1930s Shelley ribbed 'Harmony' jug, designed by Eric Slater, the base with printed factory mark.

9.75in (25cm) high

$150-250   GORL

A 1930s Shelley 'Harmony' 'Dripware' jug, designed by Eric Slater, decorated with graduated brown, beige, green, black and pink drips, the base with green printed factory mark.

c1932   5in (10.5cm) high

$150-250   BETH

A 1930s Shelley 'Harmony' washing jug and bowl, designed by Eric Slater, decorated in graduated green glazes, the base with a printed mark.

$30-50   WHP

A Shelley 'Harmony' 'Dripware' conical vase, decorated with green, cream, orange, and blue drips, the base with green printed factory mark.

Geometric-shaped 'Harmony' ware items decorated in bold colors (particularly purple) are highly sought after.

5in (10.5cm) high

$100-150   BETH

A Shelley figurine of 'The Curate', designed by Mabel Lucie Attwell, model no.LA4, painted in colors, the base with printed and painted marks.

6.75in (17cm) high

$1,200-1,800   WW

A 1930s Shelley 'Harmony' 'Dripware' jam pot, decorated with graduated brown, beige, pink, and green drips, the base with printed green factory mark.

4in (10cm) high

$70-100   BETH

A rare Shelley porcelain figurine of 'Patricia', designed by Mabel Lucie Attwell, painted in colors, the base with printed factory marks.

7in (18cm) high

$1,200-1,800   WW

A Shelley Pottery 'Boo Boo' milk jug, designed by Mabel Lucie Attwell, the base with printed marks including a facsimile signature, with some paint loss.

Due to their popularity, some Mabel Lucie Attwell pieces are being copied today, while some brand new designs in her style are also being produced. Some are made by re-decorating authentic Shelley pieces that were originally blank or very minimally decorated. As the 'Attwell' designs are applied over the glaze rather than under it on these fakes, it is often possible to scratch some of the design away with a fingernail. Others reproductions use different colors or printing methods to the originals.

6in (15.5cm) high

$120-180   WW

A late 18thC Staffordshire creamware figure of a hare or leveret, decorated in a Whieldon-type glaze, on a hollow dome base.

While other Staffordshire figures have dropped in value, these figurines have remained popular because they are much earlier, much rarer and have a wonderful 'folk art' charm to them. The form of a hare is also rare.

4.25in (11cm) high

$1,500-2,500   HW

A CLOSER LOOK AT STAFFORDSHIRE FIGURES

Pearlware is a form of English earthenware that has a slightly blue-tinted tin glaze. It was made in Staffordshire, Yorkshire and Wales from c1770 into the first half of the 19thC.

The word 'bocage' is derived from the 14thC French word 'bosc', meaning bushes or a wood. With Staffordshire figures, the word is used to describe the stylized trees or branches placed behind or around figures.

As these figures are unmarked, they are impossible to attribute with absolute certainty.

The broad-leaf design and placement of the trees is typical of John Walton's sought-after and popular work, which was produced 1806-35.

A pair of early 19thC Staffordshire Walton-type bocage pearlware figures of musical shepherdesses, on molded dome bases, damaged.

Taller 4.5in (11cm) high

$200-300   HW

A late 18thC Staffordshire pearlware figure of a fox and its prey, decorated in a Whieldon-type mottled glaze, on a molded base.

4.25in (11cm) wide

$1,000-1,500   HW

A late 18thC Staffordshire pearlware figure of a piper and a musician, decorated in green-manganese and iron-black glazes, on molded hollow bases.

Piper 8in (20cm) high

$1,500-2,500   HW

Left: An early 19thC Staffordshire pearlware bocage figure of a gardener, probably by Samuel Hall of Burslem, titled 'GARDNERS' (sic), the base impressed 'Hall'.

6.5in (16cm) high

$80-120   HW

Right: An early 19thC Walton-type pearlware bocage figure of a shepherdess, titled 'SHEPERDISS' (sic).

6in (15cm) high

$80-120   HW

An early 19thC Staffordshire Pratt-type pearlware bocage group of a pair of roosting birds and nest, on a square molded base.

9.5in (24cm) high

$1,200-1,800   HW

An early 19thC Staffordshire pearlware bocage figure of 'Saint Peter', the base with sprigged detail and inscribed 'SAINT PETER'.

9in (23cm) high

$150-250   HW

A Victorian Staffordshire group of a Highland lad and lassie, seated over a clock face.

14in (35.5cm) high

$70-100   DA&H

CERAMICS

Miller's Compares

In the late 18thC and early 19thC, figures were more detailed and had more time and care devoted to them - this can be seen in the molding of the legs and the separate arm.

The decoration is bright, detailed and well painted.

By the 1870s, the quality of Staffordshire figures had fallen dramatically. Figures were mass-produced by pouring liquid slip into molds and had scant decoration.

Over the past few years, recent Chinese copies of Staffordshire figures have swamped the market. Combined with a dramatic drop in demand from collectors, this has caused values for all but the rarest Staffordshire figures to plummet.

An early 19thC Staffordshire pearlware figure of a general, probably meant to represent the Duke of Wellington.

11.5in (29cm) high

$650-850   **HW**

A late Victorian Staffordshire 'Robin Hood' spill vase.

15in (38cm) high

$70-100   **DA&H**

An early 19thC Staffordshire Neale-type pearlware group of Faith, Hope and Charity, on a square base.

8in (20cm) high

$200-300   **HW**

An early 19thC Staffordshire pearlware group of 'Vicar and Mosses'.

8.5in (22cm) high

$300-500   **HW**

An early 19thC Staffordshire Prattware 'Pan and Bacchus' figural water jug.

12in (30cm) high

$1,200-1,800   **HW**

An early 19thC Staffordshire creamware figure of a captive bear, on a hollow dome base.

3in (7.5cm) wide

$800-1,200   **HW**

An early 19thC pearlware whistle, in the form of a parakeet, with yellow-ocher detail.

3.25in (8cm) high

$800-1,200   **HW**

QUICK REFERENCE - STONEWARE SPIRIT FLASKS

- Stoneware spirit flasks reached the height of their popularity during the 1820s-50s. They were used to drink spirits, most notably gin, as people went about their daily, working lives.
- They were produced in large quantities by large potteries and sold inexpensively.
- Many were molded in the form of politicians or royalty who were notable at the time. If they existed today, we'd find them in the shapes of Prince William and Kate, or Barack Obama. Lord Brougham (pronounced 'broom') (1778-1868) was a British statesman and Lord Chancellor 1830-34. He passed the Reform Act of 1832 and supported the Slavery Abolition Act of 1833. He also established the Central Criminal Court. At the time some people said that London Gin tasted better when drunk from the head of the Lord Chancellor!

A T Oldfield & Co. stoneware flask, in the form of Lord Brougham, the base with impressed mark.
c1832 6in (15.5cm) high
$350-450 H&C

A Doulton & Watts stoneware spirit flask, in the form of Lord Brougham, the reverse impressed 'Harris, York buildings, New Road', the base with impressed mark.
c1832 7in (17.5cm) high
$200-300 H&C

A T Oldfield & Co. stoneware spirit flask, in the form of Lord Gray.
c1832 9.75in (24.5cm) high
$500-700 H&C

A Bourne Potteries stoneware spirit flask, in the form of Alexandrina Victoria, the reverse with impressed name and maker's mark.

Made in anticipation of her ascension, it was not until Victoria's first Privy Council meeting that she signed herself 'Victoria' rather than with her actual first name 'Alexandrina'.
1837 7.75in (20cm) high
$500-700 H&C

A Bourne Potteries stoneware spirit flask, in the form of Queen Victoria, the base with impressed mark.
c1838 8in (20.5cm) high
$250-350 H&C

A Bourne Potteries stoneware spirit flask, in the form of William IV, the base with impressed mark.
c1835 7.5in (19cm) high
$300-500 H&C

A Doulton Lambeth stoneware flask, in the form of Herbert Asquith.
c1910 7.25in (18.5cm) high
$150-250 H&C

A stoneware spirit flask, in the form of a man wearing a tailcoat pinned with the Garter Star, with small chip to base.

This flask may represent the Duke of York, George IV or even William IV.

c1830   *9.5in (24cm) high*

$400-600   H&C

A Doulton & Watts stoneware flask, decorated to one side with Mr and Mrs Caudle, the reverse with Miss Prettyman.

Mr Job Caudle was the hen-pecked husband in Douglas Jerrold's amusing 1845 column for 'Punch' magazine. A bedroom scene would show Mrs Caudle telling her husband off for whatever misdemeanour had occurred that day.

c1845   *7.25in (18.5cm) high*

$250-350   H&C

A Queen Victoria commemorative stoneware spirit flask, decorated with Queen Victoria, the reverse with the Hanovarian coat-of-arms, the base indistinctly inscribed in italics 'Published by...July 20 1837'.

7.75in (19.5cm) high

$200-300   H&C

A '1854-55 Crimean War' commemorative stoneware spirit flask, impressed 'War Declared March 23 1854' and 'Peace Proclaimed April 29 1855', the base impressed 'WM. Wenham,Gun, Church St, Croydon'.

7in (17cm) high

$1,500-2,500   H&C

A brown stoneware flask, in the form of a fish.

c1850   *10.5in (26.5cm) long*

$550-750   H&C

A Queen Victoria commemorative stoneware spirit flask, impressed 'T. Walker, Northampton'.

c1840   *7in (18cm) high*

$650-850   H&C

A large stoneware spirit flask, in the form of Souter Johnny, with chip to base.

c1845   *12.25in (31cm) high*

$150-250   H&C

A Doulton & Watts 'Triumph of the Pen' stoneware flask, impressed mark, with small chip to base.

c1845   *7in (18cm) high*

$250-350   H&C

QUICK REFERENCE - STUDIO POTTERY

- Studio Pottery is the term used to describe ceramics made by a potter in their own studio, or by a small team of potters working together, sometimes under the guidance of a lead potter. Beginning in the late 19thC, the movement strengthened in the early 20thC and boomed in size and popularity from the 1960s onward.

- Every piece of studio pottery is made and decorated by hand, making each piece unique. Although decorative, most pieces of studio pottery are also functional, and include vases, bowls and tableware. However, over the past three decades, many potters have adapted studio pottery so it conveys a message. Grayson Perry (b.1960) is a good example.

- The most important and often most valuable work was made by a first generation of potters including Bernard

Leach (1887-1979) and his family, Shoji Hamada (1894-1978), Lucie Rie (1902-95), Otto (1908-2007) and Gertrud (1908-71) Natzler, and Hans Coper (1920-81). The same is true of today's top contemporary artist potters, such as Grayson Perry (b.1960) and Magdalene Odundo (b.1950).

- Look at and around the base for impressed, printed or inscribed marks as these can help identify the potter or pottery, and can sometimes indicate a period of manufacture. Investing in a reference guide showing these marks is essential. Always look for skill and quality in terms of glaze, potting, form, and overall design.

An Aldermaston Pottery vase, by Alan Caiger-Smith, decorated in shades of yellow and green, the base with painted mark.

10in (25cm) high

$700-1,000   WW

An Aldermaston Pottery tin-glazed vase, by Alan Caiger-Smith, decorated in black and red, the base with painted mark, with hairline crack.

10in (25cm) high

$120-180   WW

An Aldermaston Pottery footed bowl, by Alan Caiger-Smith, decorated with a frieze of running deer in a luster glaze on a blue ground, the base with painted marks.

Both the pattern and the colors used are unusual for Aldermaston (which operated 1955-2006) and Caiger-Smith. For more information about this pottery, see 'Miller's Collectibles Handbook 2012-2013', p.121.

7.5in (19cm) high

$1,200-1,800   WW

An Aldermaston Pottery candlestick, by Alan Caiger-Smith, decorated in shades of rust, the base with painted marks.

7.75in (20cm) high

$250-350   WW

An Aldermaston Pottery twin-handled vase, by Alan Caiger-Smith, painted in ruby luster, the base with painted marks, dated.

1986   *6in (15cm) high*

$400-600   WW

An Aldermaston Pottery charger, by Alan Caiger-Smith, painted in ruby and copper luster on a tin glaze, the reverse with painted marks, dated.

1990   *14in (35cm) diam*

$300-500   WW

A rare Aldermaston Pottery model of a peacock, by Alan Caiger-Smith, the base with painted marks, dated, with some repairs.

1964   *11in (28cm) wide*

$1,200-1,800   WW

CERAMICS

QUICK REFERENCE - CELTIC POTTERY

- Celtic Pottery was founded in the mid-1960s in Mousehole, Cornwall by Canadian Maggie Fisher and her husband Bill.
- Bill designed the 'Folk' range, which is typically decorated with spiky motifs and 'sprayed' spots.
- During the early 1970s, Maggie joined another potter, Everidge Stevens, who had been running the Gwavas Pottery. Stevens devised Celtic's 'Medallion', which became the company's second most successful range after 'Folk'.
- In the late 1970s, both ranges were discontinued and the pottery changed its name to Sunset Ceramics.
- Examples of Celtic pottery are not hard to find, particularly in small sizes, and rarely exceed $300.
- Marks comprise a label and the company name boldly painted on the base.

A large Celtic Pottery lampbase, decorated with a phoenix, the base with gilt label.

18in (46cm) high

$250-350   GC

A large Celtic Pottery 'Folk' dish, decorated with a stylized phoenix on a yellow-mottled white ground, unmarked.

10.5in (27cm) diam

$40-60   GROB

A Celtic Pottery 'Folk' wall charger, decorated with a bird on a yellow ground.

9in (23cm) diam

$50-70   PC

A Celtic Pottery 'Folk' egg-shaped dish, decorated with a fish, unmarked.

6.5in (16.5cm) long

$25-35   GROB

A small Celtic Pottery 'Folk' cylinder vase, decorated with a stylized cockerel or phoenix, unmarked.

6in (15cm) high

$25-35   GROB

A Celtic Pottery 'Folk' mug, decorated with a stylized plant, unmarked.

4.5in (11.5cm) high

$25-35   GROB

A Celtic Pottery 'Folk' square dish, decorated with a bull on a yellow, blue and white ground.

The bull is a rare choice of subject matter for Celtic.

8.25in (21cm) wide

$50-70   GROB

Two Celtic Pottery models of cats.

$100-150   CHEF

A 1970s Celtic Pottery 'Medallion' coffee service, comprising a coffee pot, milk jug, sugar bowl and six cups and saucers, some pieces with marks.

The 'Medallion' pattern can also be found in green and bronze, as well as a matt finish.

$70-100   WHP

A small Dennis Chinaworks 'Tiger' pattern 'Mr T' vase, designed by Sally Tuffin, the base with impressed and painted marks, numbered '31', dated.

2004   *3.5in (9cm) high*
$150-250   **WW**

A Dennis Chinaworks 'Midnight Hare' jar and cover, designed by Sally Tuffin, the cover with a lying hare finial, the base with impressed and painted marks, marked 'no.3', dated.

2005   *5in (12cm) high*
$300-500   **WW**

A Dennis Chinaworks 'Blackberry' vase and cover, designed by Sally Tuffin, modeled in low relief with fruiting branches, the base with impressed and painted marks, marked 'no.2', dated.

2006   *8in (20cm) high*
$300-500   **WW**

A Dennis Chinaworks trial 'Poppy' vase, designed by Sally Tuffin, inscribed 'HERE IS THE FLOWER OF DREAMS FOR THEE - THEN WLL YOU SOMETIMES DREAM OF ME', the base with impressed and painted marks, dated.

1997   *7.25in (18.5cm) high*
$120-180   **WW**

A pair of Dennis Chinaworks 'Wisteria' candlesticks, designed by Sally Tuffin, the bases with impressed and painted marks, marked 'No.1', dated.

2006   *6.25in (16cm) high*
$250-350   **WW**

A large Dennis China Works vase, by Sally Tuffin, decorated with two red and blue macaws, the base with impressed and painted marks, numbered '21', dated.

2000   *12.5in (32cm) high*
$550-750   **FLD**

A Dennis Chinaworks limited edition 'Angel' vase, designed by Sally Tuffin after a design by William Morris, no.8 from an edition of 25, on a blue ground, the base with painted marks.

Sally Tuffin (b.1938) worked as a textile and fashion designer in the 1960s and '70s before turning her creative eye to pottery. In 1986, she became the first designer at Moorcroft who was not a member of the Moorcroft family. She founded Dennis Chinaworks with her husband Richard Dennis in 1985 and has designed there full time from 1993 until the present day.

2002   *11in (32cm) high*
$800-1,200   **WW**

A Dennis Chinaworks 'Indian Elephant' footed jar and cover, designed by Sally Tuffin, the cover with an elephant finial, on four elephant-feet feet, the base with impressed and painted marks, dated.

Carefully modeled animal forms used as finials, handles, feet and three-dimensional decoration are a recurring feature in Tuffin's work.

2005   *6in (15.5cm) high*
$300-500   **WW**

CERAMICS

QUICK REFERENCE - QUENTIN BELL'S POTTERY

- Author, potter and artist Quentin Bell (1910-96) was the son of key Bloomsbury Group members Vanessa and Clive Bell.
- Bell learnt how to pot in the Staffordshire potteries in 1935 and continued to pot throughout his life. Much of his output was decorative, rather than functional.
- His bright, freely painted designs owe much to the work of his mother and her Bloomsbury Group colleagues, such as Duncan Grant.
- The historically important Fulham Pottery was founded by John Dwight in c1667. Bell worked there in the 1970s-80s.

A Fulham Pottery plate, by Quentin Bell, decorated with a dancing maiden.

10.75in (27cm)

$300-500   GORL

A Fulham Pottery plate, by Quentin Bell, incised and painted with the head and shoulders of a woman wearing a broad-rimmed hat, the reverse with incised marks.

10in (24.5cm) diam

$1,200-1,800   WW

A Fulham Pottery stoneware charger, by Quentin Bell, incised with a head portrait and glazed swirls, the reverse with black dash, blue lines and incised mark.

13.25in (34cm) diam

$800-1,200   AH

A Fulham Pottery plate, by Quentin Bell, decorated with a mythical creature, the reverse with marks.

10in (25.5cm) diam

$650-850   WW

A Fulham Pottery rectangular dish, by Bruce McLean, decorated with an abstract pattern and two incised stylized heads, one smoking a pipe, the reverse marked 'JPL' and with impressed marks.

Bruce McLean is a Scottish performance artist and painter. He studied at the Glasgow School of Art 1961-63 and the St Martin's School of Art in London 1963-66. He was Head of Graduate Painting at the influential Slade School in London and his work has featured in one-man shows, including at the Tate Gallery. He worked sporadically with the Fulham Pottery in the late 1980s and early 1990s.

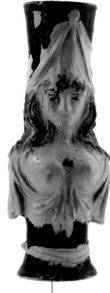

A Fulham Pottery 'Janus' vase, by Quentin Bell, modeled to both sides with portrait busts, glazed in dark purple and white, the base painted 'QB'.

Although this is a rare vase and similar examples can be found in publications by the Charleston Trust, it is not highly desirable. Most collectors prefer Bell's colorful portrait plates.

15in (38cm) high

$400-600   WW

A Fulham Pottery blue and copper-luster plate, by Quentin Bell, decorated with a stylized design.

It has been suggested that this design represents an owl's head.

11.75in (30cm) diam

$400-600   GORL

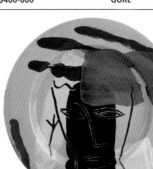

A Fulham Pottery plate, by Bruce McLean, decorated with an abstract pattern and a stylized incised head, the reverse with painted signature.

c1990

12in (30.5cm) diam

$500-700   L&T

c1990   *26in (65cm) diam*

$1,200-1,800   SWO

An Allander Pottery vase, by Hugh Allan, decorated in a running flambé glaze, the base with etched marks and monogram, dated.

1906   8.5in (22cm) high

$200-300   WW

A small 1960s-70s Ambleside flower-pot cover or vase, sgrafitto decorated with stylized flowers and bands, the base with factory mark.

4in (10cm) high

$25-35   PC

An Ashtead Pottery 'Harvest Putti with Pigeons' figural bookend, designed by Percy Metcalfe, model no.M73, the base with printed and painted marks and molded artist's mark.

6.75in (17cm) high

$500-700   WW

Judith Picks

Yes, it does seem like this vessel is worth a great deal of money, but Gordon Baldwin (b.1932) is high regarded as an artist and potter. Outside studio pottery and gallery circles, Baldwin's work is frequently overlooked, but I think this is likely to change in the near future.

Inspired by music and the natural landscape, Baldwin was important in moving ceramics toward sculptural forms and away from traditional functional pots. Nevertheless, many of his pieces do retain a hint of a domestic vessel in their forms - here, a jug. In some ways he can be seen in the same light as America's highly influential potter Peter Voulkos (see p.132), albeit in a more formal and geometric style.

Baldwin taught at Eton College and was awarded an OBE in 1992. In my opinion, pieces like this are sure to appreciate in value as his work and importance becomes more widely known.

A 'Developed Bottle' sculptural vessel, by Gordon Baldwin, decorated in green and blue and with incised decoration, the base with painted signature.

1982   13.75in (35cm) high

$3,000-4,000   WW

A large vase, by Peter Beard, decorated with blue, green and turquoise glazes in a scale-like pattern, the base marked 'P 12 PFBV' and with illegible inscription.

c1980   12in (31.5cm) high

$800-1,200   QU

A stoneware vase, by Nora Billington, decorated in a streaked brown glaze, the base with incised marks, dated.

1921

10.5in (27cm) high

$200-300   WW

A geometric vase, by Eric and Chuy Boos, painted in black, pink and blue, dated.

The style of this vase is typical of the geometric Postmodern movement of the 1980s and early 1990s.

1988   10.5in (26cm) high

$150-250   SWO

A bowl, by Iain Denniss, decorated with stylized fish in beige, brown and silvery blue glazes, the base with impressed mark.

9.5in (24cm) diam

$25-35   CAPE

CERAMICS

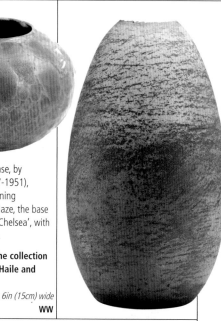

A Coldrum Pottery vase, by Reginald Wells (1877-1951), decorated with a running strawberry-colored glaze, the base impressed 'Coldrum Chelsea', with small chip to top rim.

Provenance: From the collection of key potters Sam Haile and Marianne de Trey.

6in (15cm) wide

$250-350   **WW**

A stoneware vase, by Joanna Constantinidis (1927-2000), with textured bark-like body, the base impressed with a 'C' in a circle seal mark.

16.75in (42cm) high

$1,000-1,500   **SWO**

A small stoneware bowl, by Emmanuel Cooper, decorated with a vivid blue volcanic glaze, with impressed seal mark.

4.25in (11cm) high

$300-500   **DN**

Mark Picks

Bernard Forrester (1908-90) trained at the Minton factory, where he served an eight-year apprenticeship from the age of 14. During the early 1930s the art critic Herbert Read persuaded Forrester to work at the Leach Pottery - this bowl is typical of the style he developed there.

Having trained under Bernard Leach, Forrester then took over the Dartington Pottery from Leach's son David and taught pottery at the Dartington Hall School until 1971. He also ran his own pottery, Bramblemoor, from 1952 until his death.

It is said that no two pots made by Forrester are alike. Due to the quality and visual appeal of his designs, I feel his work should rise in value. I think that his work is currently affordable for a 'second generation' studio potter who studied directly under Leach, so now could be a good time to buy if you like this style.

A bowl, by Bernard Forrester, incised with panels of flower stem and mon, highlighted in gilt, the reverse painted 'F'.

12in (30cm) diam

$350-450   **WW**

A vase, by Jonathan Cox, tubelined and painted with mushrooms, the base with indistinct inscription, the glaze crazed throughout.

Cox studied ceramics at Staffordshire University 1980-83 and now runs his own gallery and pottery studio in Carmarthen, Wales. His work recalls the work of Moorcroft designers.

8.75in (22cm) high

$200-300   **SWO**

A beaker vase, by Bernard Forrester, incised and painted with flower sprays, highlighted in gilt, the base with painted gilt 'F'.

6in (15cm) high

$300-500   **WW**

A large Ewenny vase, with incised floral and foliate motifs and with geometric banding, with Welsh inscriptions.

One of the inscriptions translates as 'Three observations to consider, are they beautiful, are they talented and can they be completed.'

c1900   *21.25in (54cm) high*

$500-700   **L&T**

A ceramic sculpture, 'The Cosmic Egg,' by David Gilhooly, signed 'Gilhooly The Cosmic egg', the top and base with different dates.

1975-78   *20in (51cm) high*

$250-350   **DRA**

An Iden Pottery vase, by Dennis Townsend, decorated with a wax-resist pattern, the base with printed mark.

3.75in (9.5cm) high

$50-70   GC

An earthenware jug on stand, by Walter Keeler, decorated in a 'Whieldon' glaze, with a 'thorned' handle, the base with impressed mark.

Keeler (b.1942) is one of Britain's leading ceramicists and already has a large following of collectors. His visually functional forms question the definitions of art and utility.

2002   *9in (23.5cm) high*

$1,000-1,500   WW

A Leach Pottery vase, by Bernard Leach, resist decorated with a tenmoku glaze, the base with impressed marks.

7.5in (19cm) high

$1,500-2,500   DN

A miniature Leach Pottery stoneware vase, by Bernard Leach, glazed with mottled ash glaze and decorated with a repeated painted chevron pattern, the base with impressed seal marks.

3.5in (9cm) high

$800-1,200   WW

A Leach Pottery stoneware vase, by Bernard Leach, decorated with running hares in an iron-red glaze over a celadon ground, the base with impressed marks.

The work of studio pottery pioneer Bernard Leach is always sought after and desirable, but it is the size and quality of this vase that makes it as valuable as it is. The left hand mark above is for the St Ives pottery and the right hand mark ('BL') is Leach's personal mark, which was only used on pottery made by him.

10.5in (25.5cm) high

$6,500-8,500   DN

A CLOSER LOOK AT AN IDEN POTTERY VASE

Dennis Townsend founded the Iden Pottery in Sussex in 1959 after he left the important Rye Pottery. Iden was successful and moved to Rye in 1966. Many pieces were exported and the pottery remained in business until Townsend retired in 2002.

This wax-resist technique is typical of Townsend's designs. Wax was applied to areas where an additional glaze was not required. It burnt off in the kiln, leaving clear lines and the under pattern showing.

Iden pieces produced after 1974 can often be dated to a specific year - count the notches/gaps in the blue ring around the mark and add them to 1974 to find the likely date. The two notches on this mark suggest a date of 1976.

An Iden Pottery vase, by Dennis Townsend, decorated with a wax-resist pattern, the base with printed mark, dated.

1976   *4in (10.5cm) high*

$50-70   GC

A stoneware vase, by David Leach, decorated with a wax-resist willow tree motif in a tenmoku glaze on a celadon ground, the base with impressed seal mark.

David Leach (1911-2005) was Bernard Leach's son. This type of form and decoration is typical of his work.

11.25in (28.5cm) high

$800-1,200   WW

A large gouged and incised ceramic sculpture, by Jim Leedy, signed 'Leedy 89 U of Or'.

This sculpture recalls the work of Peter Voulkos.

1989   *40in (102cm) high*

$1,200-1,800   DRA

CERAMICS

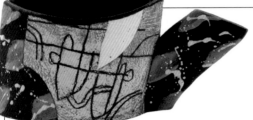

A stoneware mug form, by John Maltby, slip decorated with abstract ships in a harbour design, the base painted 'Maltby'.

8.75in (22.5cm) wide

$1,200-1,800 WW

A 1980s stepped pedestal platter, by Carol McNicoll, the base with painted signature, with minor restoration.

$40-60

12in (30cm) wide

WW

A Mortlake Pottery earthenware vase, by George J Fox, decorated with a lavender-blue and streaked sang de boeuf glaze, the base incised 'Mortlake', 'CJC' and 'A', dated.

Mortlake pottery was produced from 1910 until 1914 in Upper Richmond Road, Mortlake, London. Its founder, George J Cox, immigrated to the USA after 1914.

1913   *9in (23cm) high*

$650-850 L&T

A Mortlake Pottery shouldered vase, by George J Cox, decorated in a purple glaze with lavender to the shoulder, the base with incised mark, dated, with hairline cracks to top rim.

1913   *7in (17.5cm) high*

$200-300 WW

An Oxshott Pottery model of a seated cat, by Denise Wren (1891-1979), with impressed bird cypher and incised Oxshott.

6.25in (16cm) high

$250-350 WW

A Bushey Heath Pottery stoneware flaring vase, by Fred Passenger, decorated with a radiating sunray design above a band of stylized flowerheads, in pink and yellow on a golden luster ground, the base with printed factory mark and painted artist monogram.

9in (22.5cm) diam

$1,200-1,800 WW

A large stoneware vase, by Katharine Pleydell-Bouverie, with vertical ribs, decorated in a blue ash glaze, the base with impressed mark, with restoration to rim.

8.75in (22cm) high

$500-700 WW

A small stoneware beaker vase, by Katharine Pleydell-Bouverie, decorated in a tenmoku glaze, the base with impressed seal mark.

4.25in (11cm) high

$30-50 WW

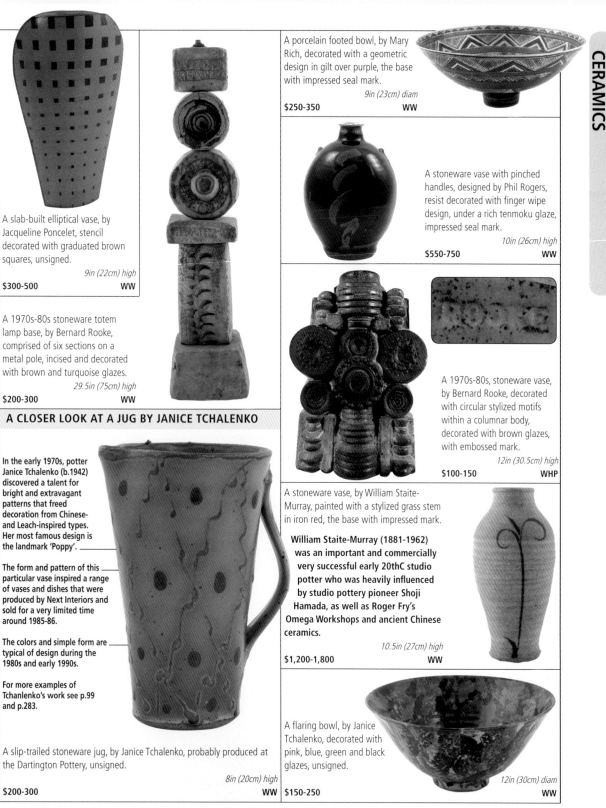

A slab-built elliptical vase, by Jacqueline Poncelet, stencil decorated with graduated brown squares, unsigned.

9in (22cm) high

$300-500   WW

A 1970s-80s stoneware totem lamp base, by Bernard Rooke, comprised of six sections on a metal pole, incised and decorated with brown and turquoise glazes.

29.5in (75cm) high

$200-300   WW

A porcelain footed bowl, by Mary Rich, decorated with a geometric design in gilt over purple, the base with impressed seal mark.

9in (23cm) diam

$250-350   WW

A stoneware vase with pinched handles, designed by Phil Rogers, resist decorated with finger wipe design, under a rich tenmoku glaze, impressed seal mark.

10in (26cm) high

$550-750   WW

A 1970s-80s, stoneware vase, by Bernard Rooke, decorated with circular stylized motifs within a columnar body, decorated with brown glazes, with embossed mark.

12in (30.5cm) high

$100-150   WHP

A CLOSER LOOK AT A JUG BY JANICE TCHALENKO

In the early 1970s, potter Janice Tchalenko (b.1942) discovered a talent for bright and extravagant patterns that freed decoration from Chinese- and Leach-inspired types. Her most famous design is the landmark 'Poppy'.

The form and pattern of this particular vase inspired a range of vases and dishes that were produced by Next Interiors and sold for a very limited time around 1985-86.

The colors and simple form are typical of design during the 1980s and early 1990s.

For more examples of Tchalenko's work see p.99 and p.283.

A slip-trailed stoneware jug, by Janice Tchalenko, probably produced at the Dartington Pottery, unsigned.

8in (20cm) high

$200-300   WW

A stoneware vase, by William Staite-Murray, painted with a stylized grass stem in iron red, the base with impressed mark.

William Staite-Murray (1881-1962) was an important and commercially very successful early 20thC studio potter who was heavily influenced by studio pottery pioneer Shoji Hamada, as well as Roger Fry's Omega Workshops and ancient Chinese ceramics.

10.5in (27cm) high

$1,200-1,800   WW

A flaring bowl, by Janice Tchalenko, decorated with pink, blue, green and black glazes, unsigned.

12in (30cm) diam

$150-250   WW

CERAMICS

A Scheier glazed and incised earthenware vessel with figures, dark brown ground, signed.

6.5in (16.5cm) diam

$5,000-6,000   **DRA**

A large Upchurch Pottery vase, decorated in a green-streaked glaze, with applied handles, the base incised 'Upchurch'.

14.5in (37cm) high

$300-500   **WW**

QUICK REFERENCE - PETER VOULKOS

- Despite its somewhat underwhelming appearance, this piece is representative of a landmark in studio pottery. Peter Voulkos (1924-2002) was one of the USA's most influential studio potters. A leader of the 'Revolution in Clay', he rejected and tore apart the functional vessel - sometimes quite literally with random tears, holes and gouges. Rather than pursue perfection, he explores the sculptural potential and the raw qualities of clay.
- His work, and that of his followers and students Paul Soldner (1921-2011) and Ken Ferguson (1928-2004), is highly sought after and often very valuable.

A stoneware vase, by Charles Vyse, decorated with a band of chrysanthemums in a tenmoku glaze over a beige ash glaze, the base incised 'CV', dated.

1933   8.75in (22cm) high

$1,000-1,500   **WW**

A large gas-fired stoneware charger, by Peter Voulkos, with glazed details, the reverse with signature, dated.

1978   25in (61cm) diam

$8,000-12,000   **DRA**

A baluster vase, by Charles Vyse, decorated with stylized Oriental motifs in a tan glaze on a brown ground, the base initialed, dated.

Charles Vyse (1882-1971) was a key figure in the development of British studio pottery in the early 20thC. During his career he worked at Doulton and the Royal College of Art, taught at the Farnham School of Art and ran a studio pottery with his wife in Chelsea, London.

1931   10.5in (27cm) high

$1,000-1,500   **GORL**

A stoneware 'Poppy Seadhead' vase, by Alan Wallwork, decorated in gray and ocher glazes, the base incised 'AW'.

7.5in (19cm) high

$300-500   **WW**

A bone china vase, by Sasha Wardell, spray-glazed with geometric panels, the base painted 'S K W'.

3.75in (9.5cm) high

$120-180   **WW**

A stoneware vase, by Robin Welch, with painted blue panels on a bronze ground, the base with impressed seal mark.

5.25in (13.5cm) high

$400-600   **WW**

QUICK REFERENCE - SUNFLOWER POTTERY

- The Sunflower Pottery was founded by a member of the landed gentry, Sir Edmund Harry Elton (1846-1920).
- Elton inherited his uncle's title and estate at Clevedon in 1883 and founded a pottery at around the same time. Although he designed and initially potted many of the designs himself, he also employed an assistant, George Masters, to help him.
- Due to his wealth and connections in society and business, Elton was able to solve many problems inherent in founding a small studio pottery by visiting other successful ceramics factories and potteries and learning from their example. For example, in c1879 he visited Pountney's Victoria Pottery in Bristol to examine their kilns.
- Sunflower Pottery is best known for simple red earthenware forms, decorated with a lustrous gold- or silver-colored crackle glaze. These pieces were produced primarily between c1902 and 1912. Platinum-colored glazes tend to be rarer than gold. Earlier pieces had been more traditional forms, decorated with carved and applied floral and foliate designs on a smooth, glossy blue or dark green ground.
- Artist potter William Fishley Holland joined the pottery after Elton's death in 1920 and began his own pottery in Clevedon after the Sunflower Pottery closed in 1922.
- Many pieces are signed 'Elton' on the base, although some of these marks were lost during the glazing process, meaning genuine pieces may appear to be unmarked.
- All Sunflower Pottery wares are fragile. Before buying, make sure you examine any piece carefully for signs of damage or restoration, as both reduce value considerably.
- Elton's work and place in British ceramic history has recently been reappraised and values are rising.

An early Sunflower Pottery vase, by Sir Edmund Elton, with low relief and slip-decorated flowers and butterfly and incised foliage in shades of green and blue on a blue ground, slip decorated with pink and blue dots to the inside of the neck, the base signed 'Elton' and dated.

1881   *5in (12.5cm) high*

$550-750   **WW**

A Sunflower Pottery vase, by Sir Edmund Elton, slip decorated with flowers and foliage in green, with flaring serrated rim, the base signed 'Elton'.

9.25in (23.5cm) high

$400-600   **WW**

A large Sunflower Pottery vase, by Sir Edmund Elton, slip decorated with flowers and foliage in shades of red on a running red, green and blue ground, with flaring, pinched rim, unsigned, with minor glaze nicks to top rim.

This vase was sold with a letter of authentication by Patricia Elton.

12.5in (30cm) high

$300-500   **WW**

A Sunflower Pottery vase, by Sir Edmund Elton, slip decorated with flowers and foliage in coral and ocher on a streaked blue ground, with knopped neck, the base signed 'Elton'.

6.5in (17cm) high

$400-600   **WW**

CERAMICS

A Sunflower Pottery handled jug vase, by Sir Edmund Elton, slip decorated with flowers in shades of red and blue on a green ground, the base signed 'Elton', with hairline crack to top rim.

The damage and less appealing form and pattern mean that this vase is worth less than others in this section. But beauty is said to be in the eye of the beholder!

14.25in (36.5cm) high

$250-350   WW

A Sunflower Pottery jug, by Sir Edmund Elton, slip decorated with narcissus in blue on a streaked blue ground, the base signed 'Elton'.

6in (15cm) high

$300-500   WW

A CLOSER LOOK AT A SUNFLOWER POTTERY VASE

This vase is an important crossover point from Elton's early slip-decorated wares to designs with lustrous metallic glazes.

Elton began experimenting with luster glazes around 1902 and initially used them simply as background glazes, as shown on this vase.

This combination of shape and decoration is rare. A similar example is shown in 'Elton Ware: The Pottery of Sir Edward Elton', by Malcolm Haslam.

It is a large size, which is appealing to collectors.

The appealing design shows inspirations from both Japanese art and the Art Nouveau style of the day.

A rare Sunflower Pottery vase, by Sir Edmund Elton, slip decorated with flowers in ocher and green on a blue ground with two-tone gold luster, with knopped neck, the base signed 'Elton'.

8.5in (22.5cm) high

$3,000-5,000   WW

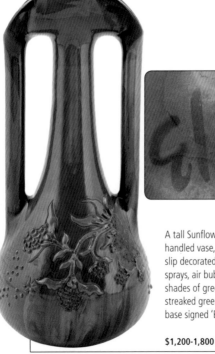

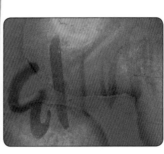

A tall Sunflower Pottery twin-handled vase, by Sir Edmund Elton, slip decorated with flowering coral sprays, air bubbles and a butterfly in shades of green, blue and ocher on a streaked green and blue ground, the base signed 'Elton'.

15.25in (39cm) high

$1,200-1,800   WW

A Sunflower Pottery vase, by Sir Edmund Elton, slip decorated with berried foliage in shades of red on a streaked blue and red ground, with loop handles, the base signed 'Elton', with minor frits to glaze.

This form is strongly Arts & Crafts in style.

8in (20cm) high

$300-500   WW

A tall Sunflower Pottery vase, by Sir Edmund Elton, slip decorated with a butterfly above sunflowers in blue and green on a streaked green and blue ground, the base signed 'Elton'.

17.5in (46cm) high

$700-1,000   WW

A Sunflower Pottery jug, by Sir Edmund Elton, decorated with a gold crackle glaze over a green ground, with pinched rim, the base signed 'Elton'.

5in (12.5cm) high

$300-500 WW

A Sunflower Pottery ewer, by Sir Edmund Elton, decorated with a gold crackle glaze over a green ground, with knopped neck, the base signed 'Elton', with professional restoration to the neck.

10in (25.5cm) high

$300-500 WW

A Sunflower Pottery jug, by Sir Edmund Elton, modeled in low relief with a mask face, decorated with a gold crackle glaze, with loop handle, the base signed 'Elton'.

The clean-lined form and angle of the spout is startlingly modern.

7.5in (21cm) high

$550-750 WW

A Sunflower Pottery vase and cover, by Sir Edmund Elton, decorated with a gold crackle glaze over a white ground, with everted rim, the lid with low-relief mask finial, the base signed 'Elton', with restoration to lid.

5in (12cm) high

$800-1,200 WW

A Sunflower Pottery vase by Sir Edmund Elton, with modeled roundels, decorated with a gold crackle glaze over a green ground, the base signed 'Elton'.

9in (23cm) high

$1,200-1,800 WW

A Sunflower Pottery vase, by Sir Edmund Elton, decorated with a platinum crackle glaze over a green ground, with everted neck and serrated rim, the base with indistinct painted 'Elton' signature.

5.25in (13.5cm) high

$800-1,200 WW

A Sunflower Pottery vase, by Sir Edmund Elton, decorated with a platinum crackle glaze, the base signed 'Elton'.

8in (20cm) high

$1,000-1,500 WW

A Sunflower Pottery gourd-form vase, by Sir Edmund Elton, decorated with a platinum crackle glaze over a green ground, the base signed 'Elton'.

This vase was illustrated in 'British Ceramic Art 1870-1940', by John Bartlett, published by Schiffer.

8.5in (21cm) high

$1,500-2,500 WW

CERAMICS

A CLOSER LOOK AT A TROIKA VASE

This is a common shape for Troika.

Troika patterns with figural forms are extremely rare.

The oxide glazes used are rare and early in date. Some have a slightly gloss finish to them, which was only used very rarely after c1974.

Early Troika glazes tend be dark and austere in color and tone, imitating Scandinavian pottery of the period.

Early pieces do not always have the textured surfaces that became typical of the company's designs from c1974 onward.

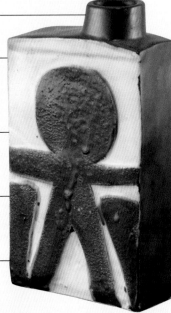

A very rare early Troika Pottery 'Chimney' vase, decorated with a 'Gingerbread Man' pattern, the reverse decorated with a stylized mask in blue and browns.

7.75in (19.5cm) high

$3,000-5,000 GORL

An early 1970s Troika Pottery vase, decorated by Linda Taylor, cast and incised with geometric decoration, the base with painted pottery marks and 'LT' monogram.

The 'LT' monogram is for Linda Taylor, not Linda Thomas, who worked at Troika from the late 1960s to the early 1970s.

6.75in (17.5cm) high

$400-600 WW

A Troika slab-form vase, decorated by Ann Jones, incised and molded with geometric designs, the base with painted pottery marks and 'AJ' monogram.

1976-77   6.75in (17cm) high

$150-250 HW

A Troika Pottery 'Chimney' vase, decorated by Avril Bennet, cast in low relief with geometric designs, the base with painted marks.

1973-79   7.75in (20cm) high

$300-500 WW

A Troika Pottery 'Slab' vase, decorated by Louise Jinks, cast in low relief with a female torso to one side and a river to the other, the base with painted pottery marks.

1976-81   6.75in (17.5cm) high

$300-500 WW

QUICK REFERENCE - TROIKA POTTERY

- Troika Pottery was founded in 1963 in St Ives, Cornwall by potter Benny Sirota, painter Lesley Illsley and architect Jan Thompson.
- In 1970, success allowed Troika to move to larger premises in Newlyn, Cornwall.
- Shapes were slip molded, but all decorating was done by hand.
- By 1974, the matt-textured style had become the main decorative treatment.
- Although it was successful, the pottery closed in 1983.
- Size, color and shape are the main indicators to value.
- Practical, small rectangular vases and pots are the most common forms.
- Marks on the base can identify the period a piece was made in and the decorator.
- Date ranges given here indicate (if known) the period that the decorator was working at Troika, not the date of the shape or design. Knowing where a design was introduced or discontinued can sometimes help dating further. In such cases the date range has been modified

A Troika Pottery 'Chimney' vase, decorated by Honor Curtis, cast in low relief with an archway motif, the base with painted pottery marks and monogram.

1970-74   7.75in (20cm) high

$800-1,200 WW

A Troika Pottery vase, decorated by Honor Curtis, modeled in low relief with geometric panels, the base with painted pottery marks and 'HC' monogram.

1970-73 8.75in (22.5cm) high

$400-600 WW

A Troika Pottery 'Rectangle' vase, decorated by Simone Kilburn, modeled in low relief with figures and masks, glazed in brown on a blue ground, the base with painted marks and 'SK' monogram.

1975-77 8.75in (22cm) high

$300-500 WW

A Troika Pottery vase, decorated by Marilyn Murphy, incised with geometric shapes, the base with painted pottery mark and 'MM' monogram.

Marilyn Murphy married and became Marilyn Pascoe. She studied at the Redruth College of Art and the Chelsea Pottery and worked at Troika from the late 1960s until 1974.

1970-74 12.5in (31.5cm) high

$400-600 SWO

A Troika Pottery vase, decorated by Ann Lewis, incised with geometric shapes, the base with painted pottery mark and monogram.

1970-72 12.25in (31cm) high

$400-600 SWO

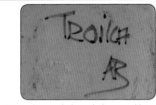

A Troika Pottery 'Marmalade Pot', decorated by Alison Brigden, the base with painted pottery mark and 'AB' monogram.

Pieces marked simply with the company name and 'Cornwall' were made in or after 1970, when Troika moved to Newlyn. Pieces from before the move bear marks reading 'St Ives' or, if very early in date, a stylized trident motif. The town name 'Newlyn' does not appear in Troika marks.

1977-83 3.5in (9cm) high

$120-180 WHP

A 1970s Troika Pottery 'Marmalade Pot', decorated with geometric designs, glazed in blue and mottled gray, the base with painted pottery marks.

3.75in (9.5cm) high

$100-150 MLL

A Troika Pottery 'Cube' vase, probably decorated by Avril Bennet, incised with circular motifs, the base with painted marks.

1973-79 3.5in (8.5cm) high

$120-180 WHP

CERAMICS

A Troika Pottery footed 'Cube' vase, decorated by Alison Brigden, modeled in low relief with geometric panels, the base with painted marks.

To see how different colors and glaze-effects vary the look of a piece, see p.129 of 'Miller's Collectibles Handbook 2012-2013'. That book features an identical form with an identical pattern, but a very different look and feel!

c1977-83   *6.75in (17.5cm) high*
$300-500   **WW**

A Troika Pottery vase, decorated by Marilyn Murphy, the base with painted pottery mark and monogram, with small chip to base.
1970-74   *14.5in (36.5cm) high*
$400-600   **SWO**

A 1970s Troika Pottery vase, decorated with a band of geometric shapes, with stained interior, the rim painted with 'Troika Cornwall'.
                  7.25in (18.5cm) high
$120-180   **WHP**

QUICK REFERENCE - REPRODUCTION & FAKE TROIKA

- This vase is an authentic Troika production from the 1970s, but the form is being reproduced and faked.
- Around 2009, Fosters Pottery in Cornwall re-introduced Troika forms, colors and designs, but produced them in mainly larger sizes. These look-alikes also bear different marks to the Troika original. Although never intended to be original Troika, they are collected.
- When Troika Pottery closed in 1983, the stock of undecorated white biscuitware was sold and these have slowly trickled into the market over the years. Some people have decorated these blanks to look like Troika, sometimes marking them and selling them as authentic Troika. Although the body will be identical, the tones and balance of colors are often different. Marks are often clumsily executed and may have been applied with a marker pen, not a brush.
- Similarly, new pieces have been produced using original molds and decorated in the same manner described above.
- Molds have been made using original Troika pieces as 'masters'. These can then be used to produce 'reproductions'. The clay material is often different and these copies may weigh more or less than authentic pieces.
- The best way to avoid being caught out by a fake or reproduction is to buy from reputable sources and handle as much authentic Troika as possible to learn about weights, clays and glaze colors.

A 1970s Troika Pottery 'Double Base' lamp base, molded in low relief with geometric forms, the base with painted marks.
                  14in (36cm) high
$700-1,000   **HW**

A Troika Pottery 'Double Base' lamp base, decorated by Alison Brigden, modeled in low relief with geometric panels, the base with painted marks.
1977-83   *14.25in (36cm) high*
$500-700   **WW**

A Troika Pottery 'Anvil' vase, decorated by Teo Bernatowitz, modeled in low relief, the base with painted pottery marks.
c1974   *8.5in (21.5cm) high*
$650-850   **WW**

A late 1970s Troika Pottery 'Wheel' lamp base, decorated by Annette Walters, modeled in low relief with geometric panels, the base with painted marks.
                  10.75in (27.5cm) high
$250-350   **WW**

A Troika Pottery 'Wheel' lamp base, incised with geometric decoration, the base with painted pottery marks and monogram probably for Jane Fitzgerald.

1976-83   *10.75in (27.5cm) high*

$300-500   **LT**

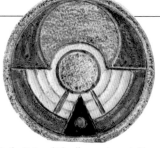

A Troika Pottery 'Wheel' vase, decorated by Avril Bennet, cast in low relief with geometric motif, the base with painted pottery marks and monogram.

1973-79   *6.25in (16cm) high*

$400-600   **WW**

A Troika Pottery 'Wheel' vase, decorated by Avril Bennet, modeled in low relief with geometric panels, the base with painted pottery marks and monogram.

1973-79   *6.25in (16cm) high*

$500-700   **WW**

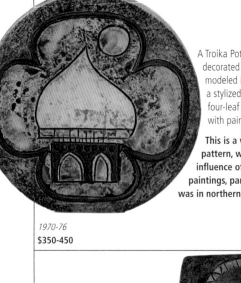

A Troika Pottery 'Wheel' vase, decorated by Penny Black, modeled in low relief with a stylized building inside a four-leaf clover, the base with painted pottery marks.

This is a very unusual pattern, which shows the influence of Paul Klee's paintings, particularly when he was in northern Africa.

1970-76   *7.75in (20cm) high*

$350-450   **WW**

A 1970s Troika Pottery 'Aztec' mask sculpture, the base with painted pottery mark, with restoration to top corner.

'Aztec' mask sculptures are rare and have been known to fetch well over $1,500 in the past. The low price for this example is due to the damage and restoration and also to the presence of fakes and reproductions (see previous page), which has resulted in falling prices for all but the most exceptional pieces.

9.75in (25cm) high

$700-1,000   **L&T**

A 1970s Troika Pottery 'Aztec' mask sculpture, modeled in low relief, the base with painted pottery mark and blurred monogram.

13.75in (35cm) high

$800-1,200   **WW**

A rare Troika Pottery 'Celtic Cross' vase, decorated by Simone Kilburn, modeled in low relief, the base with painted pottery marks and monogram.

1975-77   *10.25in (26cm) high*

$500-700   **WW**

A rare 1970s Troika Pottery model of a tin mine, the base with blue painted pottery marks and 'CF' monogram.

8.75in (22cm) high

$1,000-1,500   **WW**

CERAMICS

QUICK REFERENCE - VALLAURIS

- Vallauris is a town between Cannes and Antibes in the south of France. Pottery has been made there since medieval times, but production grew markedly during the 19thC with the success of companies, such as Massier and Foucard-Jourdan.
- When Pablo Picasso visited the town in 1948 and began producing his own designs at Madoura, a second golden age of Vallauris pottery began as many others were inspired to follow his example. The 1950s saw many potteries being founded or revived. An influx of designers led to a vast array of modern designs being produced.
- Some of the best pieces were produced by notable designers, such as Roger Capron and Jean Derval. Such works inspired a huge range of mass-produced, slip-molded ceramics decorated in glazes that range from bright and glossy to bubbling 'lava'-like glazes.
- It is currently difficult, if not impossible, to identify the company behind many of these pieces, but more research may yield the answers. If this happens, interest in and values paid for these pieces are sure to rise.

A large 1970s Vallauris leaf-shaped dish, with mottled and striated white, yellow, brown and green glazes on an orange ground, unmarked.

17.75in (45cm) long

$80-120　GC

A large 1970s Vallauris leaf-shaped dish, decorated with striated glossy brown and yellow glazes, unmarked.

18in (46cm) long

$80-120　GC

A 1970s Vallauris oval dish, with scalloped rim, decorated with mottled pink, white and brown glossy glazes, with gold foil factory label.

16.75in (42.5cm) long

$80-120　GC

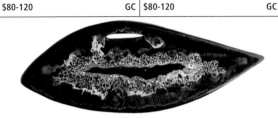

A large 1970s Vallauris elliptical dish, with integral handle, decorated with mottled and striated pink, brown, cream and white glazes on a rich browny-burgundy ground, the base impressed 'VALLAURIS'.

24.5in (62.5cm) long

$80-120　GC

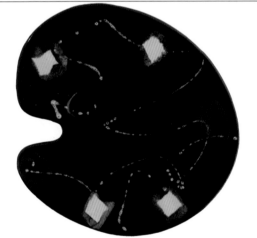

A 1950s-60s Vallauris pallet-shaped dish, with trailed turquoise foamy glaze and squares in turquoise, red and yellow, unmarked.

12in (30.5cm) widest

$80-120　MA

A 1950s-60s Vallauris bowl, decorated with a volcanic glaze, with original paper label, the base painted 'Vallauris'.

19in (49cm) wide

$120-180　WW

A small 1970s Vallauris shell-shaped dish, decorated with striated green, yellow and brown glossy glazes, unmarked.

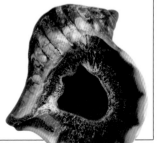

8in (20.5cm) wide

$70-100　GC

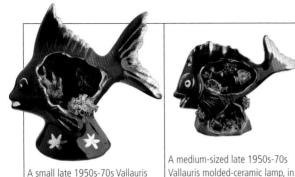

A small late 1950s-70s Vallauris molded-ceramic lamp, in the form of a fish, the interior with an applied fish and coral, with gilt highlights, in mint condition.

9in (23cm) high

$70-100   **MA**

A medium-sized late 1950s-70s Vallauris molded-ceramic lamp, in the form of a fish, the interior with an applied fish, the base with rocks and coral, with gilt highlights, in mint condition.

13in (33cm) long

$80-120   **MA**

A late 1950s-70s Vallauris molded-ceramic lamp, in the form of a fish, the interior with an applied fish and flowers, with gilt highlights, in mint condition, with 'Véritable Céramique Vallauris' foil label.

You either love them or hate them, but these quirky lamps can be quite valuable. Always look out for damage as the ceramic used is very easy to chip and damaged examples are worth a fraction of the value of one in mint condition. Some can be found without the lamp fittings.

17.5in (44.5cm) long

$120-180   **MA**

A CLOSER LOOK AT A VALLAURIS BOWL

Jean Derval (1925-2010) was a key mid-20thC French potter and ceramics designer.

He founded the important 'Les Trois Coqs' (The Three Roosters) movement in Vallauris.

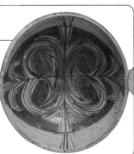

He worked alongside other important Modern ceramicists of the time including Roger Capron, for whom he made ceramics 1968-73, and Robert Picault.

Antique Greek and Mediterranean forms were an inspiration to many European ceramics artists and designers during the mid-20thC. Their influence can be clearly seen in this form.

This piece shows the influence of Pablo Picasso's ceramics - indeed Derval worked at the Madoura pottery 1948-51, throwing pottery to Picasso's designs.

A Vallauris sculptural bowl, by Jean Derval, in the form of a two-headed beast of burden supporting a bowl, with stylized floral decoration, the base painted 'JEAN DERVAL'

16in (40.5cm) wide

$1,200-1,800   **MLL**

A 1950s Vallauris asymmetric jug vase, by an unknown designer, decorated with a textured green-black glaze, red spot, inverted rim, unmarked.

14in (35.5cm) high

$120-180   **MHC**

A 1950s Vallauris earthenware 'WHISKY' jar, three mugs and a matching vase, by Roger Capron, each decorated with multicolored bands and stripes.

Jar 13in (33cm) high

$650-850   **QU**

A mid-late 1930s Wedgwood 'Matt Blue'-glazed ribbed vase, designed by Keith Murray, the base with printed factory mark and 'KM' monogram.

7.5in (19cm) high

$650-850　　　　**WW**

A 1930s Wedgwood 'Matt Straw'-glazed vase, designed by Keith Murray, the base with printed factory mark and 'Keith Murry' facsimile signature.

6in (15cm) high

$350-450　　　　**WW**

An early 1930s Wedgwood 'Matt Green'-glazed ribbed vase, designed by Keith Murray, the base with printed factory mark and 'Keith Murray' facsimile signature.

7.5in (19cm) high

$500-700　　　　**WW**

An early 1930s Wedgwood 'Bronze Basalt' vase, designed by Keith Murray, shape no. 3991, the base with impressed and printed factory marks and 'Keith Murray' facsimile signature.

'Bronze Basalt' is one of the rarest colors, being rarer even than 'Black Basalt'.

8.75in (22cm) high

$1,200-1,800　　　　**WW**

A Wedgwood 'Black Basalt' vase, designed by Keith Murray, with turned decoration, the base with impressed factory mark and 'Keith Murray' facsimile signature.

8in (20cm) high

$1,000-1,500　　　　**WW**

A CLOSER LOOK AT A MUG

These mugs were also produced in two sizes (this is the smaller) and were available with pink, blue or yellow stripes. A jug and a bowl were also made.

The letters A-X are illustrated by an object or person on the exterior, with Y and Z appearing on the interior.

Ravilious's choice of images is charmingly retrospective, (particularly the choice of a biplane) and hark back to a gentler past age. Many of the images are directly inspired by 19thC nursery ware.

As the work of Eric Ravilious (1903-42) has become increasingly sought after, this mug design has been recently re-released, with a slightly different shape and with different marks. Modern versions are currently worth around $15.

A Wedgwood nursery ware 'Alphabet' mug, designed by Eric Ravilious in 1937, the base with printed factory marks.

3.25in (8.5cm) high

$650-850　　　　**MLL**

An early 1930s Wedgwood 'Black Basalt' coffee set, designed by Keith Murray, the bases with impressed and printed marks and 'Keith Murray' facsimile signature.

Although they can be rarer than decorative forms, tablewares are generally less desirable and valuable.

Coffee pot 7.75in (19.5cm) high

$250-350　　　　**DN**

A Wedgwood earthenware vase, designed by Norman Wilson, glazed with an experimental brown glaze with gold-foil inclusions, the base with impressed and printed Wedgwood marks and 'NW' monogram.

Norman Wilson (1902-85) was inspired by Chinese ceramics and glazes. For more information about Wilson, see p.131 of the 'Miller's Collectibles Handbook 2010-2011'.

11in (27cm) high

$1,500-2,500　　　　**WW**

A large Wemyss twin-handled vase, glazed in a rich red glaze, the base with impressed Wemyss mark.

15in (37cm) high

$400-600   **WW**

A Wemyss 'Cabbage Roses' beaker vase, decorated by Karel Nekola, the base painted and impressed 'Wemyss'.

Czech-born decorator Karel Nekola (d.1915) was one of Wemyss' most talented painters and came up with the pottery's hallmark floral and fruiting patterns.

c1900   *11in (28.5cm) high*

$900-1,200   **L&T**

A Wemyss 'Cabbage Roses' pin tray, the base with impressed 'R.H.& S.' mark and puce retailer's mark.

The 'R.H.& S.' mark is for the Robert Heron & Son pottery of Fife, which began branding its wares 'Wemyss Ware' in the 1880s. The pottery was founded by Robert Methven Heron in c1790.

12in (30cm) long

$400-600   **L&T**

An early 20thC Wemyss water jug, decorated with nasturtiums, the base impressed 'WEMYSS'.

7.5in (19cm) high

$1,500-2,500   **L&T**

An early 20thC Wemyss 'Cabbage Rose' stationery rack, decorated by James Sharp, the base incised 'Wemyss'.

8.75in (22.5cm) wide

$1,200-1,800   **L&T**

A large Wemyss preserve jar and cover, decorated with damsons, the base impressed 'Wemyss Ware' and 'R.H.& S.' and printed 'T. Goode & Co.', with minor damage.

c1900   *6.25in (16cm) high*

$500-700   **L&T**

A large Wemyss cat figurine, decorated by Joe Nekola with black sponge ware on a white ground, the base painted 'Wemyss', with minor restoration.

In 1930 the Wemyss molds and designs were sold to the Bovey Tracey pottery in Devon. Karel Nekola's son, Joe Nekola, moved with them.

12.5in (32cm) high

$1,200-1,800   **L&T**

A small Wemyss lavender-blue model of a pig.

Pigs are among the most desirable and valuable Wemyss forms, particularly if they are small or lying down and sleeping!

c1900   *6in (15cm) long*

$4,000-6,000   **L&T**

A Wemyss model of a pig, decorated with shamrocks including a four-leaf clover, impressed 'Wemyss Ware' and 'R. H. & S.' and printed 'T. Goode & Co.'

c1900   *6in (16.5cm) long*

$1,000-1,500   **L&T**

CERAMICS

QUICK REFERENCE - WEST GERMAN POTTERY

- Known to many as 'Fat Lava', the ceramics produced in West German factories during the 1950s-70s have become enormously popular and increasingly valuable over the past eight years. Bright, colorful and largely affordable, they were exported across the world before they went out of fashion in the 1980s.
- Notable factories include Scheurich, Bay, Carstens, Ceramano, Roth and Ruscha. Many closed in the 1990s due to competition from Far Eastern factories.

- In general, the most valuable pieces are those with thick, bubbling 'lava' glazes and futuristic forms or those by notable designers, such as Bodo Mans, Gerda Heuckeroth and Heinz Siery. Avoid traditional forms with flat glazes in browns and beiges, as these tend to be the least valuable and desirable. Large 'floor' sizes are often highly sought after by interior decorators as well as collectors.
- The shape, glaze and marks on the base will help identify a factory, particularly when considered in combination.

A 1960s West German Bay Keramik 'Paris' pattern conical jug, designed by Bodo Mans in 1960, with angled handle, the base molded 'WEST-GERMANY 7770-20', with silver-foil factory label.

8in (20.5cm) high

$100-150   **GC**

A West German Carstens vase, designed by Scholtis, from the 'Ankara' range, decorated in gun-metal gray and mottled blue glazes with a resist pattern of circles, squares and triangles, the base molded 'W.GERMANY 663-25', with original factory label.

10.25in (26cm) high

$120-180   **GC**

A 1960s West German Ceramano 'Ceralux' bowl, designed by Gerda Heuckeroth or or Hans Welling in 1960, with applied short columns to the rim, decorated in deep turquoise glazes with cobalt-blue highlights, the base with inscribed marks.

6.25in (16cm) diam

$80-120   **GC**

Mark Picks

I'm often asked which of the West German ceramics companies I rate the most. Personally, it has to be Ceramano. The bases are typically inscribed by hand with the shape number, range name, artist's initials and company name, so they should be easy to identify (see below).

Active from 1959 to 1984, Ceramano specialized in producing high-end, studio-like ceramics. The range of designs is vast, moving from the 'fat lava' 'Rubin' or 'Incrusta' ranges to the prehistoric cave-painting-inspired 'Apulia' and 'Pergamon'. The shapes and glazes are very high quality and, because everything was individually artist-decorated, every piece is a truly unique ceramic artwork.

It's this high quality, the comparative scarcity of pieces and the great design that makes Ceramano a winner for me.

A large 1960s West German Ceramano 'Apulia' pattern jug, designed by Hans Welling in 1959, decorated with beige glaze and resist pattern of bands of squiggles and lines and stylized deer, the base with inscribed marks.

13in (33cm) high

$150-250   **GC**

A West German Ceramano 'Toscana' tapering vase, designed by Hans Welling, the base hand-inscribed '170 Toscana Cermano Handarbeit'.

10.25in (26cm) high

$100-150   **RET**

A mid-late 1970s West German Dümler & Breiden 'Polar' vase, designed by Rudolf Kügler in 1973, from the 'Relief' range, the base molded '22/25' and with other marks.

10in (25.5cm) high

$120-180   **GAZE**

A 1970s West German Emons & Söhne (ES) Keramik jug-vase, decorated with white-veined cobalt-blue glaze, unmarked.

7.5in (19cm) high

$100-150   **GC**

A 1970s West German Kreutz Keramik jug-vase, decorated with glossy orange glaze and band of black lava glaze, the base molded '208'.

7.25in (18.5cm) high

$70-100   **GC**

A 1970s West German 'Jasba' jug, decorated with creamy white glaze over dark-brown matt glaze with a resist pattern of stylized circles and lines, the base with indistinct marks, with gold-foil factory label.

14in (35.5cm) high

$120-180   **GC**

A 1970s West German 'Jopeko' jug, decorated with glossy orange glaze under a mottled beige, white and black salt glaze, the base impressed '7201 15', with gold-foil factory label.

6in (15cm) high

$50-70   **GC**

QUICK REFERENCE - ROTH & MAREI

- Changes in attributions in the world of collecting are not rare events. They happen most often in new markets, such as West German ceramics, where new information is constantly being uncovered. In late 2012, a number of catalogs for a lesser-known company called Marei were discovered by a German collector. These catalogs contained photographs of many shapes that, until then, were thought to have been made by Roth Keramik, including this 'chimney vase'.
- Marei was founded in 1929 by Jean Fuss and was, until 1948, part of Emons & Söhne.
- Many shapes were designed by Hans Kraemer and many glazes were devised by Willi Hack. During the 1950s, Bodo Mans also produced designs for the company.
- It is possible that Roth acted as a distributor for or re-labeled some of Marei's production.

A 1970s West German Kreutz Keramik vase, decorated with orange bubbled-lava glaze, the base with indistinct three-digit mark beginning in a '4', with gold-foil factory label.

10in (25.5cm) high

$120-180   **GC**

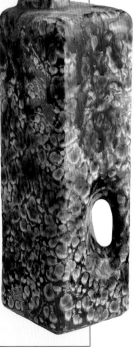

A 1970s West German Marei Keramik vase, decorated with a mottled brown, beige, blue and green 'snakeskin' effect glaze, unmarked.

12in (30.5cm) high

$120-180   **GC**

A large 1970s West German Roth double-ring-handled jug-vase, possibly designed by Dorothea Roth, decorated with glossy yellow panels and matt black bubbled-lava glaze, the base impressed 'MADE IN W.Germany 314'.

16in (40.5cm) high

$700-1,000　　　　GC

A large 1960s West German Ruscha jug, no.311/5, decorated with a 'Vulkano' glaze designed by Otto Gerharz, the base with molded numbers.

This form is unusually Classical and traditional for West German ceramics.

13.75in (35cm) high

$70-100　　　　GC

A 1970s West German Scheurich tapered vase, decorated with thick cobalt-blue and almost iridescent gold bubbled-lava glaze, the base molded 'W.GERMANY 520-28'.

11in (28cm) high

$100-150　　　　GC

A 1970s West German Walter Gerhards Töpferei vase, molded with a stylized flower, decorated with mottled glossy black and orangey-red glaze, the base impressed '520/21 Foreign'.

8.25in (21cm) high

$40-60　　　　GC

A 1970s West German Scheurich handled jug-vase, decorated with the 'Regebogen' (rainbow) decor devised by Oswald Kleudgen, the base molded 'W.GERMANY 401-28'.

11in (28cm) high

$100-150　　　　GC

A 1970s West German Walter Gerhards Töpferei jug-vase, decorated with dark gray tube-lined lava-glaze zig-zags over a striated orangey-red glossy ground, the base impressed 215/25.

Walter Gerhard's pottery may have used the name Kera Modern and Kera Keramik as brand names.

10in (25cm) high

$100-150　　　　GC

A large 1970s West German Steuler jug vase, designed by Cari Zalloni, the base molded with the Steuler logo and '226/30'.

This type of mark was used from 1960 into the 1980s. From 1918 until 1960, the mark was a similarly molded 'ST' monogram inside a tall vase shape. Cari Zalloni (1937-2012) produced innovative and quintessentially Modern designs for Steuler 1960-76. After he left Steuler, he designed and made eyewear and produced designs for Rosenthal and WMF. His work is typically clean-lined and decorated in vibrant colors.

11.5in (29cm) high

$300-500　　　　GC

A large Ault Pottery jardinière, with dripped yellow, green and red glazes and pulled handles, the base with red impressed mark, with some restoration.

13.5in (34cm) high

$300-500   **WW**

A 1960s Denby 'Glynbourne' vase, designed by Glyn Colledge in 1960, hand-painted with stylized leaves in muted tones of green and brown, the base with printed marks.

11in (28cm) high

$50-70   **CAPE**

Judith Picks

Although this piece looks naively potted, Austrian Walter Bosse (1904-79) was primarily a Modernist designer. He studied at the Vienna School of Applied Arts under Michael Powolny, had his work included in the famous Paris 'International Exposition of Modern Industrial and Decorative Arts' of 1925 and worked for Goldscheider (see pp.21-22 and p.391). He was also mentored by Josef Hoffman. This rare figurine was made when he was at his shop and pottery in Kufstein, which he opened in 1923 and closed in 1937. Although he continued working in ceramics in Vienna from 1938, he was working mainly in brass by the 1950s.

Collectors clamour to own original pieces by Bosse, especially those that exhibit this level of detail and humor.

A Walter Bosse figurine of a man with a unicorn, the base with impressed mark.

6.25in (16cm) high

$5,500-6,500   **DOR**

A large C H Brannam vase, painted and incised with geometric flowers and foliage on a blue ground, with twin lug handles, the base with impressed marks.

For more examples of Brannam ceramics, see the Miller's 'Antiques Handbook & Price Guide 2014-2015' p.497.

16.5in (42cm) high

$500-700   **WW**

A Burmantofts Pottery faience jardinière and stand, molded with sunflowers, with a ripple-effect treacle ground, the jardinière base marked 'Burmantofts Faience England 1947A', the stand impressed and numbered '1948B'.

36in (91.5cm) high

$400-600   **TRI**

A Bursley Ware hexagonal vase, designed by Charlotte Rhead, pattern no.1554, decorated with tubelined flowers and foliage in orange, purple and green, the base with printed and painted marks.

5.75in (14.5cm) high

$120-180   **WW**

A pair of Burmantofts Pottery faience vases, shape no.2049, painted and molded with turquoise and blue flowers on an ivory ground, with geometric borders, the base with impressed mark and signed.

13.75in (35cm) high

$700-1,000   **TRI**

A Bursley Ware vase, designed by Charlotte Rhead, pattern no.1554, decorated with tubelined flowers and foliage in orange, purple and green, highlighted in gilt, the base with printed and painted marks.

The shape of this vase is harder to make, rarer and much more desirable than the other vase shown in the same pattern.

6.25in (16cm) high

$350-450   **WW**

A Susie Cooper Pottery 'Art Ware' jug, no.E325, incised with a leaping antelope and glazed in orange-yellow, the base incised 'Susie Cooper'.

c1933   *8.5in (21.5cm) high*
$200-300   **SWO**

A 1920s Clews & Co. Ltd. 'Chameleon ware' vase, designed by David Capper in c1914, painted with stylized leaves on a blue ground.

6.5in (17cm) high
$100-150   **DA&H**

A 1920s Clews & Co. 'Chameleon Ware' vase, pattern no.53/125, designed by David Capper in c1914, the base with printed factory mark.

10in (25.5cm) high
$200-300   **GHOU**

A Thomas Forester & Sons vase, designed by A Dean, painted with a frieze of ducks, with knopped neck and pinched flaring rim, the base with painted mark.

7.75in (20cm) high
$250-350   **WW**

A tall Thomas Forester & Sons vase, designed by A Dean, painted with scrolling foliage, the base with printed factory mark and facsimile signature, with restoration to neck and rim.

14.5in (37cm) high
$250-350   **WW**

A Thomas Forester & Sons vase, designed by A Dean, painted with a band of pelicans and stylized cypress trees, the base with printed factory mark and facsimile signature.

Thomas Forester took his sons into partnership in 1883. The company closed in 1959.

8.75in (22cm) high
$300-500   **WW**

A Thomas Forester & Sons Art Deco 'Syrian ware' vase and cover, molded with stylized flowers and foliage.

12in (30cm) high
$300-500   **SWO**

A Fulper Pottery pedestal bowl, glazed in rich pink, the rim highlighted in green, the base painted 'Fulper'.

7.5in (19cm) diam
$80-120   **WW**

A Fulper Pottery vase, modeled in low relief with mushrooms, glazed in flambé and ocher luster glazes, the base printed 'Fulper', with hairline crack.

9.5in (24cm) high
$150-250   **WW**

A Fulper Pottery vase, glazed in a streaked blue glaze, the base with impressed mark.

11.75in (30cm) high

$300-500 **WW**

A 1920s-30s Théodore Haviland porcelain model of a parrot, designed by Édouard-Marcel Sandoz, the base with white printed factory marks.

Édouard-Marcel Sandoz (1881-1971) was a Swiss sculptor who is best known for his highly stylized Art Deco tea and coffee services produced by Haviland in Limoges, France from 1916 onward. He also worked for Sèvres and Richard Ginori.

7.5in (19cm) high

$400-600 **WW**

A Linthorpe Pottery vase, designed by Dr Christopher Dresser, model no.106, glazed in streaked green and ocher, the base with impressed marks and facsimile signature, with repair to neck.

12.5in (32cm) high

$250-350 **WW**

QUICK REFERENCE - 'MORRISWARE'

- Sampson Hancock & Sons was founded in 1857 in Tunstall, Staffordshire and closed in 1937 after having moved to other locations in the Potteries.
- The company produced affordable tablewares, toilet wares and crested china, but is mainly celebrated today for its 'Morrisware' range of decorative wares.
- Designs were tubelined and resemble (and thus were undoubtedly inspired by and competed with) William Moorcroft's ceramics for James Macintyre & Co.
- Tile designer and ceramicist George Cartlidge (1868-1961) was the first and most important designer. He trained at the Hanley School of Art, worked for Sherwin & Cotton and ran his own company before working for Hancocks from c1918-26.
- Art Director F X Abraham produced designs during the 1920s. He was followed by Edith Gater (née Smith) during the 1930s.
- The richly colored, often complex 'Morrisware' designs have risen dramatically in value over the past few years and are now highly sought after.
- Look for unusual shapes and detailed patterns that sum up the Art Nouveau style.

An early 20thC Sampson Hancock & Sons 'Morrisware' vase, designed by George Cartlidge, decorated with tubelined cornflowers, the base with printed marks and numbered 'C10-12'.

c1905 *8.5in (21cm) high*

$550-750 **SWO**

A 1930s Myott 'Beaky' jug, hand-painted with geometric bands in orange, green, blue and black, the base with printed marks and numbered 'BG62'.

Myott wares have fallen dramatically in value recently. At the peak of the market, this rare 'Beaky' jug may have fetched over $1,500. Such pieces now represent amazing value for money, especially compared to Clarice Cliff and prices may yet rise again. If you like this style, get in now while you can!

9in (22.5cm) high

$150-250 **FLD**

A 1920s Noritake vase, decorated with an elephant and rider in a tropical landscape within gilded black and orange borders, the base with printed mark.

10in (25cm) high

$550-750 **GORL**

An early 20thC Pewabic vase, glazed externally and internally with a green iridescent glazed, the mouth with incised ribbed motif, the base impressed with illegible mark and with paper label inscribed 'Pewabic Pottery'.

5.25in (13.5cm) high

$500-700 **DMC**

CERAMICS

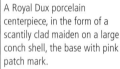

A 1950s-60s Red Wing cornucopia vase, glazed in chartruese, the base with indistinctly molded numbers.

7.75in (19.5cm) high

$50-70   PC

A Ridgway 'Homemaker' 62-piece tea and breakfast set, designed by Enid Seeney in 1957, comprising nine large plates, nine medium-sized plates, eight small plates, nine large bowls, eight small bowls, nine saucers, eight cups, a milk jug and a sugar bowl.

The wonderfully ovoid coffee pot is the rarest and most sought-after form from the 'Homemaker' set and can easily fetch over $250 on its own.

1957-70

$550-750 set   SWO

A Royal Dux porcelain centerpiece, in the form of a scantily clad maiden on a large conch shell, the base with pink patch mark.

16in (40.5cm) high

$800-1,200   HT

A Royal Stanley 'Jacobean' vase, decorated with tubelined fruit and foliage, the base with printed factory marks.

7in (18cm) high

$300-500   WW

A CLOSER LOOK AT A TECO VASE

Teco Art Pottery was produced by the American Terracotta & Ceramic Co. (Gates Pottery) from 1902 until the mid 1920s. It is highly sought after today.

Many forms are bud-like or molded with or into leaf or flower forms. This almost geometric form with its buttress handles is also typical.

Teco designs are typically clean-lined with undecorated surfaces, focusing on the heavy and monumental architectural form.

The high quality matt green glaze is a hallmark feature of the company. It was inspired by French ceramics seen at the World's Columbian Exposition in 1893.

A Teco gourd-shaped vase, glazed in a matt dark green, with four buttressed handles, the base stamped 'Teco', with short hairline crack to one handle.

6.5in (16.5cm) high

$3,000-5,000   DRA

A Teco vase, glazed in smooth matt green, with three twisted handles, the base stamped 'Teco 284'.

11.25in (28.5cm) high

$2,500-3,500   DRA

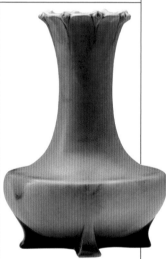

A Teco bottle-shaped vase, glazed in smooth matt green, with floriform rim and four feet, the base stamped 'Teco', with hairline cracks and restoration to feet and rim.

This elegant vase combines natural motifs, seen on the flower shaped rim, with geometric feet and a simple, elegant form. It is also large in size, which is desirable.

13.5in (34cm) high

$2,000-3,000   DRA

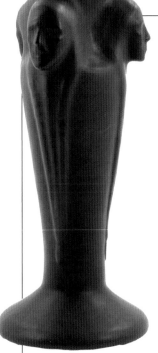

A Van Briggle vase, modeled in relief with three native American heads, glazed in deep red and blue, the base with etched marks.

12.25in (31cm) high

$650-850   WW

A Wade pottery figurine of a seated girl, 'June', the base with printed marks.

7.5in (19cm) high

$300-500   WW

An H J Wood 'Bursley Ware' vase, designed by Charlotte Rhead, pattern no.1432, decorated with tubelined flowers and foliage, the base with marks.

For more ceramics see: Art Deco figures pp.20-27; Chinese 'Red' Collectibles pp.154-57; Commemoratives pp.167-71; Disneyana p.177; Fishing pp.190-92; Oriental pp.263-71; Postmodern Design pp.282-83; Pot Lids pp.301-05; Tiles pp.351-55; Wall Masks pp.390-95

8.25in (21cm) high

$250-350   WW

Mark Picks

Almost certainly produced in Belgium during the late 1910s-30s, these vases are typified by their dripping green, brown, beige and yellow glazes and Arts & Crafts style forms. The quality can vary widely. Many are rather naively and 'rustically' modeled with bubbles and skips in the glazes, but the best are well-potted, well-glazed and have complex, extravagent forms, sometimes with animals curling around the body.

It is likely that more than one factory produced them, but the factory most commonly associated with them is Faiencerie Thulin. Most are unmarked, but some bear model numbers and 'BELGIUM' marks. I think they're a great way of obtaining the Arts & Crafts look affordably, as most examples can be found for $15-25 and there are plenty of quirky forms to collect.

A Belgian Ault-style vase, in the manner of Dr Christopher Dresser, with three curving handles, unmarked.

13in (34cm) high

$25-35   WHP

A Continental porcelain night-light, in the form of a man in a turban, in the manner of Robj, unsigned.

Robj was active in Paris in the 1920s-30s. His ceramic designs were made under commission by various suppliers.

7.5in (19cm) high

$150-250   WW

A Continental pottery model of a grotesque creature, glazed in bright blue, with applied glass eyes, with restoration to beak.

12.25in (31cm) high

$100-150   WW

A 20thC porcelain cabinet plate, painted by Terence Nutt with apples, blackberries, cherry and blossom on moss, the reverse signed 'T Nutt' within gilt line border.

Nutt used to decorate ceramics for the world-famous Royal Worcester factory, which explains the similarity of this design to theirs. Along with many other ex-decorators, such as Harry Ayrton, he continued decorating blanks after his departure.

9in (23cm) diam

$150-250   FLD

QUICK REFERENCE - CHESS

- Chess probably originated in India in the 6thC, but developed into the game we know today in 15thC Italy.
- It boomed in popularity during the 19thC and 20thC, which is when most of the sets on the market today date from.
- The Eastern export markets of China and India were among the most prolific producers, but chess sets were also made in German, Britain and France.
- Look out for high quality materials and design. The more finely carved and detailed the pieces, the better.
- Aim to buy complete sets, as finding replacement pieces to match in terms of color, size and detail is very difficult.
- Be aware of national limitations on the trade and export of materials such as ivory, particularly for modern sets.

A 19thC Cantonese carved and stained-ivory 'puzzle-ball' chess set, in the form of Eastern figures, with mahogany box.

Largest king 6in (15cm) high

$700-1,000   **GORL**

A 19thC Cantonese carved and stained-ivory figural chess set, in the form of the emperor and empress and their retinue, each piece supported on a puzzle-ball knop and lotus-form base.

c1850   *Kings 5.25in (13.5cm) high*

$800-1,200   **TEN**

A late 19thC Chinese carved and stained-ivory harlequin chess set, on puzzle-ball knops, missing one white knight, with two replaced bishops.

Tallest king 6in (15cm) high

$400-600   **WW**

A 19thC Indian ivory chess set, with damage to three pieces, with box.

Kings 4in (10cm) high

$250-350   **DA&H**

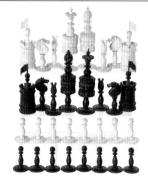

A 19thC Indian stained-bone chess set, the kings and queens decorated with leaves within beaded borders.

Kings 5in (12.5cm) high

$400-600   **TEN**

A Vizagapatam carved ivory and horn chess set.

This is an elegant set in an uncommon shape. Vizagapatam is a town on the South East coast of India. It produced and exported furniture, boxes and other accessories that were typically Western in forms. Decoration was typically a fusion of Indian and Western styles.

c1820   *King 4.5in (11.5cm) high*

$2,000-3,000   **SWO**

A late 19thC ebony and boxwood Staunton chess set, by Jacques, London, with associated mahogany box.

King 3.75in (9.5cm) high

$550-750   **GORB**

CHESS

A boxwood and ebonized Staunton chess set, with weighted bottoms, two rooks marked with a red crown mark.

$500-700   CHT

An early 20thC carved and turned stained-ivory Staunton chess set.

King 2.75in (7cm) high

$800-1,200   SWO

A CLOSER LOOK AT A CHESS SET

This set retains its original box, which adds to the desirability. Carton-pierre is a type of papier-mâché strengthened with glue and calcium carbonate. It can be successfully molded into all manner of detailed shapes.

In 1849, British games company Jaques revolutionized the chess world by designing a new standard set for competitions. The set was named after chess champion Howard Staunton (1810-74).

The Staunton design was copied widely, but this is an original Jaques set and bears their name and crown mark stamped into the bases of certain pieces.

Ivory Staunton sets are more rare than those made from fruitwoods.

This is large and well detailed set.

A 19thC Staunton stained-ivory chess set, by Jaques, London, four pieces stamped with crown mark, the white king with maker's mark, the original carton-pierre box from a design by Joseph L Williams, the lid with central roundel with bishop's mitre and crozier, knight's visor, king and queen's crowns, on a castle-form base.

8in (21cm) high

$5,500-6,500   TEN

A boxwood and ebony Staunton chess set, by Jaques, London, the white king stamped at base, two rooks and two knights stamped with a red crown, with associated Morocco-leather case, with a rosewood and satin-birch chessboard.

King 4.25in (11cm) high

$3,000-5,000   GORL

A mid-19thC English turned and stained bone 'Barleycorn' chess set.

Kings 4in (10.5cm) high

$400-600   DN

A set of early- to mid-20thC molded-plastic chessmen, in the form of medieval figures, with a faux-snakeskin box.

$30-50   WHP

A late Victorian sycamore-cased games compendium, the hinged cover with a folding board for chess, backgammon and horse race, the lift-out tray with Cribbage board, turned bone counters, Bezique and Whist markers, a gavel, dominoes, lead horses, with boxwood and ebony chess pieces, four pieces marked with a red crown, three pieces replaced.

13in (33cm) high

$700-1,000   WW

CHINESE 'RED' COLLECTIBLES

QUICK REFERENCE - CHINESE 'RED' COLLECTIBLES

- Communist design is a new and emerging collecting field, but it has been admired since Communism began to fall in Eastern Europe in the late 1980s. Few people from the countries where Communism ruled wish to collect Communist memorabilia, making it more of a Western European preoccupation, although this may yet change.
- Posters are the most popular item of Chinese Communist memorabilia. They give a fascinating insight into the social, political and economic changes that occurred in China after World War II. Earlier posters are more traditional in design and imagery, focusing on Chinese traditions and landscapes. From the 1950s onward, this was swept away by a bold, modern and clean-lined style with dynamic perspectives, which reflected the revolution.
- Chairman Mao Zedong naturally features large in many posters, both as the leader of China and as an intrinsic part of Communism. The Chinese military also features regularly, either in relation to specific wars or as part of a constant battle against the West. The Chinese are shown as strong, hard working and full of passion.
- Although the market for Chinese Communist design is new, reproductions are significantly more common than authentic examples, even in China and the former Soviet states. Without cast-iron provenance, it can be hard to tell the difference between originals and reproductions, as they are often made using the same production methods. The weight of a ceramic, the printing method and paper used for some posters and the exact size or any piece may provide clues as to whether it is an original or reproduction. Always buy from a reputable dealer or auction house and remember - if something looks too good to be true, it probably is!

['Railway Workers Support the Ouster of Americans'], a Chinese propaganda poster, printed by the Cultural and Education Department of Northern China District Committee of the China Railway Workers' Union, featuring a caricature of President Harry S Truman holding his invasion plan and running away from a Chinese soldier poking him with bayonet, with stains, with restoration.

The Chinese text at the bottom of the poster calls for 'All staff members [to] take immediate action to enhance production, [and] support the Chinese People's Volunteer Army to Smash the invasion plan of the American Imperialists.'

1950   30.5in (77.5cm) high
$3,500-4,500   BLO

['The Glory of Marxist-Leninist-Mao Zedong Thought Shines Over New China'], a Chinese propaganda poster, designed by Zhou Cheng Lun, printed by the People's Art Publishing House, Beijing, depicting Chairman Mao in brown uniform with a topographic rendition of New China behind him and a waving flag with portraits of the other great figures of Communism, with some tears and creases.

1953   42.5in (108cm) wide
$2,500-3,500   BLO

中苏两国人民和军队的友谊万岁

['Long Live the Friendship Between the People and Army of China and the Soviet Union'], an early 1950s Chinese propaganda poster, printed by the People's Liberation Army Pictorial Publishing House, Beijing, depicting a Russian and Chinese sailor, both in white uniform on deck, with creases.

30.5in (78cm) wide
$650-850   BLO

我们一定要解放台湾

['We Must Liberate Taiwan'], a Chinese propaganda poster, depicting stylized portraits of a worker, soldier and a peasant holding the red flag and Mao's 'Selected Works' over the Taiwan strait filled with ships from a naval armada, with jets overhead, with creases and restored edge tears.

c1962   41.5in (105.5cm) wide
$650-850   BLO

['Congratulate the Vietnamese People's Victory in Defeating the Military Invasion of the USA'], a Chinese propaganda poster, designed by Yin Su Sheng, printed by the People's Art Publishing House, Beijing, depicting a victorious Vietcong soldier and his comrades-in-arms with firearms raised, and a group planes falling from the sky, with edge tears and restoration.

This example is from the first printing of 15,000 copies and has wider than usual left and right margins as it comes from the printer's own company archive. It was published in August 1964, just after the Gulf of Tonkin incident that began the American involvement in the Vietnam war.

1964   30.5in (77.5cm) wide
$2,000-3,000   BLO

['20th Anniversary of the Great Victory in the Anti-Japanese War'], a Chinese film exhibition poster, printed by the Cultural Department of People's Republic of China, depicting a victorious soldier straddling two bunkers with raised rifle and holding a red flag, with horizontal creases and repaired edge tears.

c1965   41.5in (105.5cm) high
$650-850   BLO

A CLOSER LOOK AT A CHINESE PROPAGANDA POSTER

'Sailing the Seas depends on the Helmsman' is the English title of a popular Chinese revolutionary song. It reached the height of its popularity during the Cultural Revolution (1966-76), which is when this poster was made.

Mao Tse-Tung (1893-1976) was Chairman of the Communist party 1945-76 and was depicted as more and more god-like in posters as his stewardship of China progressed.

The buildings depicted include TianAnMen tower, a symbol of 'modern' China; Yan'An, celebrated as the birthplace of the revolution; the rural buildings of Mao's childhood home; and JiaXing where the first national Chinese Communist congress was held.

Made from three panels, this huge poster has great visual appeal, is an excellent example of Chinese propaganda posters and is very hard to find in such great condition with such bold, original colors.

['Sailing the Seas Depends on the Helmsman, Carrying on Revolution Depends on Mao Tse-Tung's Thoughts'], a Chinese three-panel propaganda poster, printed by the Central Art and Handicraft Institute, Beijing, with handling creases, folds and edge tears.

1968   87in (221cm) wide
$3,000-5,000   BLO

['Propaganda Against Liu Shao Qi and Deng Xiao Ping'], a Chinese silk-screened propaganda poster, depicting Red Guards waving Mao's 'Selected Works' and forging ahead under the flag of Chairman Mao with the support of soldiers, peasants and workers, while at the bottom right corner are caricatures of Liu and Deng cowering, with patched tear.

The text on the bottom reads 'The Shanxi Province Completely Smashing the Anti-Revolution Revisionist Route of Liu Shao Qi and Deng Xiao Ping Exhibition'.

c1967   31in (78.5cm) wide
$2,500-3,500   BLO

['We Will Destroy Whoever Dares to Attack Us'], a Chinese propaganda poster, printed by the Ying Tan County Mao Tse-Tung Thoughts Propaganda Center, Jiangxi Province Xinhua Bookstore, depicting a peasant, militia member and soldier with relics of war including US soldiers' helmets, a tattered Japanese flag and a wrecked tank, beneath the Chinese flag and with a copy of Mao's 'Selected Works', with some creases, folds and repaired edge tears.

1970   30in (76cm) high
$650-850   BLO

['Warmly Hail the Revolutionary Integration Within Hubei Province Literature and Art Circle'], a Chinese propaganda poster, printed by the Hubei Province Literature and Art Association Xinhua Printing Factory, depicting Red Guards celebrating and brandishing red flags, Mao's 'Quotations' book and a board reading 'Headquarters for Literature and Art', with some creases.

c1970   29in (73.5cm) wide
$250-350   BLO

['People and Soldiers are the Basis for Victory'], a Chinese propaganda poster, printed by the Beijing 76th High School, depicting a miner, PLA and peasant militia man in front of a crowd of militant Chinese people, with some stains.

1970   41.75 (106cm) high
$300-500   BLO

CHINESE 'RED' COLLECTIBLES

Mark Picks

I like a challenge and, in this case, that would be finding the two flanking posters that complete this extremely rare three-panel poster. Even though this is only one of three parts, it's the most important part, being highly desirable due to a number of features. The poster depicts a pyramid of supporters rising up beneath a benevolent, god-like Mao who salutes the proletariat with his right hand. Mao's work and achievements are 'backed' by the presence of Lenin and Marx. These two figures appear frequently with Mao and are sometimes joined by Engels and Stalin, showing the unity (and strength in unity) of the Communist nations. As such this poster represents much of what this collecting area represents, and is rare and visually appealing. Because it's incomplete, it's also more affordable than many other similar examples.

['United We Stand - Long Live the Great Marxism-Leninism-Mao Tse-Tung Thought!'], the central panel of a three-panel Chinese propaganda poster, printed by Tianjin People's Art Publishing House, depicting a mass of people of different nationalities rising up with flags and the Little Red Book, beneath a half portrait of Mao, with similar portraits of Lenin and Marx behind him.

1969

41.25in (104.5cm) high

$500-700   **BLO**

['Long Live the Great Marxism, Leninism and Mao Tse-Tung's Thoughts'], a Chinese propaganda poster, produced by Shaanxi Province Class Education Exhibition, printed by the Shaanxi People's Publishing House, depicting a half-portrait of Chairman Mao with bust portraits of the four other 'Greats' of Communism on a waving flag behind him, in the area below the masses are uniting and rising up, with some discoloration to top margin and edge tears.

1971   *42.25in (107.5cm) wide*

$650-850   **BLO**

['Completely Devoted to Supporting the Volunteer Army to Help Korea and Fight Against the USA'], a Chinese original gouache watercolor drawing produced for a propaganda poster, depicting Chinese Volunteer Army soldiers fighting against the devastated American troop, depicted behind them is support from China, including letters from home, medical supplies, food and money, with some edge stains.

1951   *30.5in (77.5cm) wide*

$4,000-6,000   **BLO**

'Selected Works', by Mao Zedong [Mao Tse-Tung], first collected edition of Mao's writings and speeches, published by the North East Railway Printing Factory for the North East China Bookstore, with mounted blue-tinted photo portrait of Mao with tissue-guard, with original gilt-titled embossed blue cloth covers, bumped.

This copy was part of an initial print run of 20,000 copies, issued 17 months before the founding of the People's Republic of China. Reputedly, only four libraries hold copies of this version: Harvard, the University of Chicago and Sweet Briar College in Virginia in the USA and the Bibliotheque Nationale de France in Europe.

1948

$800-1,200   **BLO**

A large 1960s Chinese molded plaster half-bust of Chairman Mao Tse Tung, the base incised 'Wishing Chairman Mao Long Life', with chip to base.

This huge size of Mao bust was produced for the halls or entrances of schools or government buildings. Sometimes such busts were also used in small gatherings or ceremonies. The quality of molding on this example is much higher than the molding on many later copies.

c1966   *43in (109cm) high*

$7,000-10,000   **BLO**

A 1970s Chinese molded pale opaque green glass bust of Chairman Mao Tse Tung, the rounded square base with molded wording reading 'Long Live Chairman Mao', on original red-painted wood shrine pedestal.

Bust 11.25in (28.5cm) high

$2,000-3,000   **BLO**

A 1970s Chinese porcelain figural group, 'Defending the Motherland Against Foreign Aggression', depicting figures representing the Chinese navy, army and militia standing on a beach, with minor chips and restoration, with replaced flag and placard.

The militaristic subject matter of this rare and very large figural group makes it valuable, as does the fact that it is well painted in colors.

17.5in (44.5cm) high

$5,000-7,000   BLO

A Chinese 'blanc de Chine' figural group, 'Exposing a Landlord, Re-educating a Landlord', depicting a female Red Guard with a megaphone and a young pioneer boy with spear in his hands disciplining a landlord, with a placard around his neck reading 'Down with the Gang who follows the Capitalist route'.

This is a very rare and detailed figurine with a politically and economically interesting subject matter. As well as these factors, its provenance also contributes to the high price guide shown - this figure was part of a batch created for export sale in Singapore, but never sold. The batch was recently discovered in a storage warehouse.

c1970   *7.5in (19cm) high*

$4,000-6,000   BLO

Two 1970s porcelain sculptural lamp bases, each with a figure in tattered orange robes and a balletic pose representing the main character of the Revolutionary Opera, one with original metal switch.

The Revolutionary Operas (or eight model plays) were planned and engineered by Jiang Qing, deputy director of the Central Cultural Revolution Group and the wife of Chairman Mao Zedong. Rather than featuring the traditional figures of Beijing opera (emperors, kings, beauties, etc), they featured stories from China's recent revolutionary struggles against foreign and class enemies.

8.5in (21.5cm) high

$550-750   BLO

Two Jingdezhen commemorative porcelain jars and lids, produced to celebrate the publication of volume four of the 'Selected Works of Mao Tse-Tung', the lids with Chinese text reading 'Four Volumes of Heroic Works', the bodies painted with the fourth volume, banners, flowers and panels of script reading 'Selected Works of Mao Tse-Tung Volume Four', 'Four Volumes of Heroic Works' and 'Spread Their Thoughts Around the World', one knop chipped.

1960   *11.25in (28.5cm) high*

$650-850   BLO

A 1970s Chinese porcelain teapot, large plate and cup, decorated with a Revolutionary Opera design on a white ground, illustrating a ballet between the white haired girl (Xi'er) and the PLA soldier (Dachun) who rescues her, the teapot inscribed 'Long Live Chairman Mao'.

Teapot 7.5in (19cm) high

$250-350   BLO

Three early-mid 1960s molded glass bottles, each molded with a tractor and slogans, the green bottle by the San Huang factory with 'Grasp Revolution, Promote Production', the blue bottle with 'Rely on Ourselves, Work Hard Despite Hardship', the yellow bottle with 'Grasp Revolution, Promote Production'.

The arrival of the tractor in rural China was a 'revolutionary' development, completely changing the face of Chinese farming.

Tallest 11.5in (29cm) high

$1,200-1,800   BLO

COMICS

QUICK REFERENCE - COMICS

- Comics have been collected by childen for decades, but only began to be taken seriously as a collecting area in the 1960s, when the first conventions were organized.
- The area became established by the 1970s and has developed since and collectors now include millionaires! The most expensive comic ever sold fetched a staggering $2.16million. Said to be the first 'modern' comic book, it was 'Action Comics' No.1. Another copy of this comic was found recently inside a wall! For more information about this lucky find see p.164.
- The first issue of a title is often the most desirable and valuable, with values dropping considerably for subsequent issues. Most comics had large print runs.

- Other sought-after issues include those that feature the first appearance or death of a character or a major event in their story arc. Historical topicality, such as the first nuclear explosion or wartime propaganda, can also increase desirability.
- Values can also rise if a successful film or TV series is released and this revives interest in a character. A good example is Spider-Man, the subject of four recent films.
- Condition is vitally important, so look for bright colors, no tears, scuffs, browning or written annotations. Be aware that although some superhero comics, such as those by Marvel, are collected internationally, others may have appeal in one country only.

'The Beano Comic', No.2, 6th August 1938, the bright cover with 0.1in (0.25cm) trim to right-hand edge to front, with cream/light tan pages.
$5,500-6,500   CBA

'The Beano Comic', No.3, 13th August 1938, in fine condition, the bright cover with 0.25in (0.5cm) chip from top right-hand edge, with cream/light tan pages.
$4,000-6,000   CBA

'The Beano Comic', No.1, 30th July 1938, in very good condition, with several tape repairs to spine, upper cover and one leaf.

This is a bright example of this extremely rare comic and comes from the collection of Dennis Gifford, a notable collector and author of many books on comics.
$8,000-12,000   DW

'The Beano Comic', No.6, 3rd September 1938, in fine condition, the bright covers with a few small tears to edge overhang, with cream/light tan pages.
$1,200-1,800   CBA

'The Beano Comic', No.27, 28th January 1939, in fine condition, with bright cover and cream/light tan pages.
$450-550   CBA

'The Beano Comic', No.100, 22nd June 1940, in very fine condition, with bright, fresh colors and cream pages.

This wartime propaganda issue contains a story called 'Down with Lord Haw-Haw'. The name 'Lord Haw-Haw' generally applies to William Joyce, who (among others) broadcast pro-German propaganda on the radio in Great Britain in an attempt to demoralize the country.
$500-700   CBA

'The Beano Comic', No.74, 23rd December 1939, Christmas issue, in very good condition, with bright cover, with cream/light tan pages and some light margin foxing.
$550-750   CBA

QUICK REFERENCE - WARTIME ISSUES

● Issues of 'The Beano Comic' from before 1948 are much harder to find than later editions. During the war, paper supplies not used for the war effort were strictly rationed. Children were encouraged to share their comics with family and friends and to hand them in for other uses after they were finished, rather than collect them. As a result, the few examples that survive are usually in poor condition as they have been read many times!

● Many wartime issues also contained anti-Nazi propaganda, which was sometimes subtle, but often not. Here, Big Eggo has a swastika shaved into his body.

'The Beano Comic', No.77, 13th January, 1940, in very fine condition, with bright, fresh covers and cream pages.
$300-500   CBA

'The Beano Comic', No.195, 19th December 1942, Christmas issue, 'Jerry Won't Be Merry This Xmas If You Do Your Bit!', in fine condition.
$500-700   CBA

'The Beano Comic', No.218, 6th November 1943, in very good condition.
$30-50   PCOM

A 'THE BEANO BIG-BANG FUN-GUN' free gift, from 'The Beano Comic' No.36, in very good condition, with paper tape on the top and front of the 'bang'.

From the time of its launch in July 1938 until war rationing took its toll, 'The Beano Comic' was accompanied by a number of free gifts, including toys and sweets. Most toy gifts were damaged, lost or thrown away, making surviving examples, such as the one pictured, rare today. The free sweets were even less likely to survive, as most were eaten!
1939
$70-100   PCOM

'The Beano Comic', No.452, 17th March 1951, in fine condition, with bright covers, the cream/light tan pages with slightly darker edges.

This issue is worth as much as it is because it contains the first appearance of the infamous character Dennis The Menace, created by David 'Davey' Law (1908-71).
$650-850   CBA

A bound set of the complete issues of 'The Beano Comic' for 1962, comprising Nos.1016-67, some with penciled addresses to the covers, generally in very good to very fine condition.

Early 1960s issues of 'The Beano Comic' are rare, due to lower distribution by the publisher.
1962
$1,000-1,500   CBA

COMICS

'The Dandy Comic', No.10, 5th February 1938, in fine condition, the bright cover with neatly repaired 1in (2.5cm) cover tear, with cream/light tan pages.
$400-600   CBA

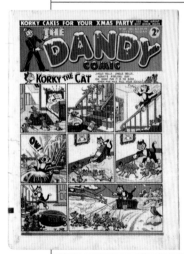

'The Dandy Comic', No.107, 16th December 1939, Christmas issue, in very good condition, with two neatly repaired 0.5in (1.5cm) tears inside the cover.

This wartime propaganda issue saw the first appearance of 'Addy And Hermy, The Nasty Nazis', created by comic-book artist Sam Fair.
$250-350   CBA

'The Dandy Comic', No.282, 23rd December 1944, Christmas issue, with crayon delivery name to lower cover margin, otherwise in fine condition.
$250-350   CBA

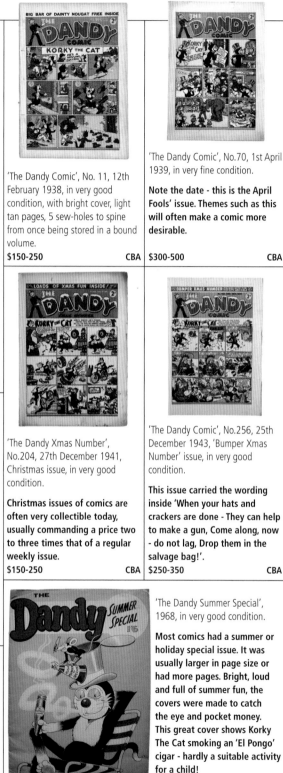

'The Dandy Comic', No. 11, 12th February 1938, in very good condition, with bright cover, light tan pages, 5 sew-holes to spine from once being stored in a bound volume.
$150-250   CBA

'The Dandy Comic', No.70, 1st April 1939, in very fine condition.

Note the date - this is the April Fools' issue. Themes such as this will often make a comic more desirable.
$300-500   CBA

'The Dandy Xmas Number', No.204, 27th December 1941, Christmas issue, in very good condition.

Christmas issues of comics are often very collectible today, usually commanding a price two to three times that of a regular weekly issue.
$150-250   CBA

'The Dandy Comic', No.256, 25th December 1943, 'Bumper Xmas Number' issue, in very good condition.

This issue carried the wording inside 'When your hats and crackers are done - They can help to make a gun, Come along, now - do not lag, Drop them in the salvage bag!'.
$250-350   CBA

'The Dandy Summer Special', 1968, in very good condition.

Most comics had a summer or holiday special issue. It was usually larger in page size or had more pages. Bright, loud and full of summer fun, the covers were made to catch the eye and pocket money. This great cover shows Korky The Cat smoking an 'El Pongo' cigar - hardly a suitable activity for a child!
$15-25   PCOM

COMICS

QUICK REFERENCE - THE DANDY MONSTER COMIC

- 'The Dandy Monster Comic' was an annual comic book released in August each year in time for Christmas.
- The first was released in 1938.
- It was renamed 'The Dandy Book' in 1952 and 'The Dandy Annual in 2002'. After 1965, the year was added to the title, but it was the year following the publication and release, not the year of release.
- In line with the comics themselves, Korky The Cat adorned the cover until 1985 when Desperate Dan took over.
- Many examples were given as Christmas gifts, so were inscribed with a dedication. Other owners wrote their names inside, so they could be returned if lent to a friend. Uninscribed copies are consequently prized by collectors.
- Compare this example to the other example of this issue on this page to see how condition affects desirability and value.

'The Dandy Monster Comic', 1946, in very good to fine condition, with bright boards, spine with medium wear, neat ink dedication inside and cream/off-white pages.
$800-1,200　　　　　CBA

'The Dandy Monster Comic', 1946, with 3in (7.5cm) scrape damage to lower front cover and two upper cover corner creases, with cream/off-white pages.

$250-350　　　　　CBA

'The Dandy Book', 1958, in near mint condition, with bright boards and spine, no dedication and cream/off-white pages.

This edition is very rare in this condition.
$400-600　　CBA

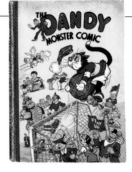

'The Dandy Monster Comic', 1942, in good to very good condition, with bright boards, intact slightly loose spine, overall general wear and rubbed-out inscription, the cream/light tan pages with a hint of foxing and some finger marks.
$650-850　　　　　CBA

'The Dandy Monster Comic', 1945, in very good condition, with bright boards, complete spine, neat dedication and light-medium overall wear, with cream/off-white pages.
$800-1,200　　　　　CBA

'The Dandy Monster Comic', 1944, in very good condition, with bright boards, complete spine, neat dedication and overall general wear, with off-white pages.
$800-1,200　　　　　CBA

'The Dandy Monster Comic', 1947, in fine condition, with some wear to boards and no dedication.
$400-600　　　　　DW

'The Amazing Spider-Man', No.1, 1963, British copy with price in pence, the bright detached cover with worn spine, the back cover with biro name.
$1,000-1,500　　CBA

'The Amazing Spider-Man', no.2, 1963, British copy with price in pence.

This was the first appearance of 'The Vulture'.
$350-450　　　　　DW

'The Amazing Spider-Man', No.22, 1965, American copy with price in dollars, CGC graded 8.5, with off-white pages.
$250-350　　　　　HER

COMICS

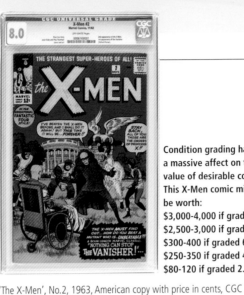

Condition grading has a massive affect on the value of desirable comics. This X-Men comic might be worth:
$3,000-4,000 if graded 9.2
$2,500-3,000 if graded 9.0
$300-400 if graded 6.0
$250-350 if graded 4.0
$80-120 if graded 2.0

'The X-Men', No.1, 1963, British copy with price in pence, in very fine condition.
$1,500-2,500   DW

'The X-Men', No.2, 1963, American copy with price in cents, CGC graded 8.0.
$1,200-1,800   HER

'The X-Men', No.3, 1964, American copy with price in cents, in fine condition.

This issue saw the first appearance of the Blob.
$300-500   DW

QUICK REFERENCE - CGC RATINGS

- Launched in 2000, Comics Guaranty LLC, better known as CGC, is an independent assessor that grades comic books on their condition.
- The books are examined using strict criteria and are given a condition grade number from 0.5 to 10. The comic is then sealed in a plastic holder bearing its grade and extra details pertaining to its condition.
- This independent appraisal of condition makes it easier to trade comic books, partly because it preserves the comic in that precise condition and partly because it removes the personal opinions of the sellers and buyers.

'The X-Men', No. 5, 1964, British copy with price in pence, in fine condition.
$150-250   DW

'The X-Men', No.12, 1965, American copy with price in cents, CGC graded 8.0.
$500-700   HER

'The X-Men', No.35, August 1967, 'Along Came A Spider' issue with Spider-Man and first appearance of the Changeling, American copy with price in cents, CGC graded 9.2, with off-white to white pages.
$500-700

'The X-Men', No. 29, 1967, American copy with price in cents, in near mint condition with full cover gloss, with cream pages.
$150-250   CBA

'Giant Size X-Men', No.1, 1975, American copy with price in cents, in near mint condition, with full cover gloss and cream/off-white pages.

This issue saw the first appearance of The New X-Men.
$1,000-1,500   CBA

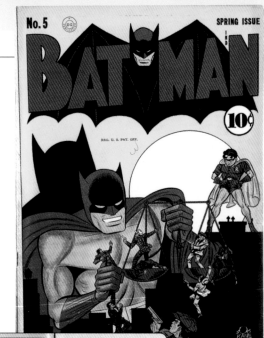

'Batman', No.11, June-July 1942, American copy with price in cents, in good condition, the front cover missing bottom right corner, the back cover missing part of top right corner, with tan interior covers and light tan pages with several pin gouges and worn lower right-hand page edges.
$400-600 CBA

'Batman', No.5, Spring 1941, American copy with price in cents, in very good condition, with bright cover with lower center edge wear, with stains to lower page margins.

The 'Scales of Justice' cover is deemed a classic. The fact that there is a Joker story inside also makes 'Batman' No.5 desirable and valuable.
$800-1,200 CBA

'Batman', No.12, August-September 1942, American copy with price in cents, in very good condition with restored spine and cover edges, color touched in, with cream/light tan pages, with generally neat amateur restoration.
$150-250 CBA

'Batman', No.45, February-March 1948, 'A Batman And Robin Christmas Adventure', American copy with price in cents, in fine condition, the bright cover with light date stamp and some small pinholes, with cream pages.
$250-350 CBA

'Batman', No.77, June-July 1953, American copy with price in cents, in fine condition, with good cover gloss, the back cover with 3in (7.5cm) crease to lower margin, with cream pages.
$250-350 CBA

'Batman', No.85, August 1954, American copy with price in cents, in very good to fine condition.
$120-180 CBA

'Batman', No.94, September 1955, American copy with price in cents, CGC graded 7.5, with off-white/white pages.
$250-350 CBA

'Batman', No.183, August 1966, American copy with price in cents, featuring the second appearance of Poison Ivy, CGC graded 9.0, with cream/off-white pages.
$120-180 CBA

COMICS

'Atom', No.1, July 1962, American copy with price in cents, CGC graded 5.5, with off-white pages.

$120-180   CBA

'Bunty', No.1000, 12th March 1977, in very good condition with some damage to bottom right of front cover.

Girls' comics are becoming increasingly collectible as the girls who read them grow into women with disposable incomes. Titles such as 'Bunty', 'Mandy', 'Judy' and 'School Friend' are popular.

$3-5   PCOM

'Buster', 23rd December 1967, Christmas issue, in good to very good condition.

'Buster', named after its main character, ran 1960-2000. He wears a flat cap as he was initially billed as being the son of Andy Capp, the 'Daily Mirror's' famous and long-standing comic strip character, who was introduced in 1957.

$5-10   PCOM

'Commando' 'War Stories in Pictures', No.80, 1962, in good to very good condition.

This 64-page small-format comic was first released in 1961 and is still being published today. The artwork is typically detailed and dramatic and encourages patriotism. Issues 50-100 are generally worth around $10-30 each.

$12-18   PCOM

'Daredevil', No.1, 1st April 1964, American copy with price in cents, in very good condition, with light tan pages.

$400-600   CBA

'Daredevil', No.2, 1964, American copy with price in cents, CGC graded 8.5.

'Daredevil' No.1 is generally more valuable than No.2. The difference in value between this and the No.1 shown left is due entirely to condition. A copy of No.1 in similar condition might be worth $3,000-4,000.

$700-1,000   HER

'Dick Tracy', No.1, 1937, published by Dell, in very good to excellent condition, with bright covers and tan pages.

Titled 'Dick Tracy Meets The Blank', with the same illustration on the back cover, this 76-page comic is also known as 'Large Feature Comic' No.1.

$500-700   CBA

Judith Picks

You never know what treasures might be tucked away in your house - in cupboards, attics and even the walls! David Gonzalez, a builder and decorator in Hoffman, Minnesota, USA bought a small house for $10,500 and set to work on fixing it up for re-sale. When he took down one of the walls, he found this copy of 'Action Comics' No.1 being used as insulation. As you can see from the cover, this was the comic that introduced the most famous superhero of all time: Superman! That made it a very valuable find indeed.

The comic was in very bad condition and was further damaged during an argument between Gonzalez and his mother-in-law, but such is its rarity and importance that it still fetched this astonishing sum when auctioned in 2013. Perhaps even more astonishingly, if it had been in near-mint condition (CGC graded 9 or higher) it could have fetched over $1.5 million!

'Action Comics', No.1, June 1938, CGC graded 1.5.

$200,000-300,000   COC

'It's Gametime', No.1, September-October 1955, in very good condition, with bright cover, the back page with brittle corner piece taped back in place and two puzzles filled in.

This is a rare comic.

$100-150   CBA

'June and School Friend', 23rd December 1967, Christmas issue, in very good condition.

The two titles merged in 1965 to gain popularity. Bessie Bunter, one of its characters, was the sister of Billy Bunter from 'Magnet' comic.

$5-10   PCOM

A CLOSER LOOK AT A SET OF COMICS

'The Hotspur' comics from the 1930s and '40s are usually worth up to $5-10 each.

This collection is the highest grade of 'The Hotspur' comics ever offered at auction.

This set comes complete with the rare gifts for No.78, 'The Big Spoof Book', and No.107, a 'Wallet Album for Foreign Stamps'.

'The Hotspur' is one of the original 'Big Five' comics from DC Thompson. The others are 'Adventure', 'The Rover', 'The Wizard' and 'The Skipper'.

These comics were hugely successful with generations of boys until World War II. Around this period TV, space and the humor comics of the 1960s made these prose stories seem old-fashioned.

A bound set of issues of 'The Hotspur' for 1935, comprising Nos.71-122, in very fine to near mint condition except for No.105 in fine condition.

1935

$500-700   CBA

'The Magic Comic', No.3, 5th August 1939, in very good condition, with bright covers, some minor foxing spots and small margin tears, with cream/light tan pages.

$300-500   CBA

'Silver Surfer', No.1, August 1968, American copy with price in cents, in very fine condition, with bright cover, light margin mark to splash page and cream/light tan pages.

$300-500   CBA

'Tales Of Suspense', No.24, December 1961, American copy with price in cents, in very fine condition, with high cover gloss, with cream pages.

$200-300   CBA

'Tales of Suspense', No.5, September 1959, American copy with price in cents, in very fine condition, with full cover gloss, theback cover with two small tears, the cream/light tan pages with slightly darker edges and narrow dust shadow.

$200-300   CBA

'Tiger', No.5, 9th October 1954, in good to very good condition.

Roy of the Rovers appeared on the cover of Tiger from 1954 to 1976, after which he had his own comic that lasted until 1993. Issues from the 1950s are generally worth around $5-10 each, depending on issue and condition.
$5-10   PCOM

'The Topper', No.3, 21st February 1953, in good to very good condition.
$8-12   PCOM

'TV Comic', No.683, 16th January 1965, in good to very good condition.
$8-12   PCOM

'TV Century 21', No.28, 1965, in good to very good condition.

This science fiction comic ran from 1965 to 1969 when it merged with 'Joe90'. It featured 'Fireball XL5', 'Thunderbirds' and 'Captain Scarlet', as well as other TV series created by Jerry and Sylvia Anderson. Issues featuring 'Doctor Who' often fetch the largest sums of money.
$25-35   PCOM

A bound set of the complete issues of 'Union Jack' for 1915 and 1917, comprising issues 586-637 and 717-42, in fine to very fine condition, contained in three bound volumes.

These were from the publisher's archives.
$1,000-1,500   CBA

A complete set of issues of 'Union Jack' for 1909, comprising Nos.273-324, contained in two volumes with a four-page pull-out 'Blackmail' story and flyers for 'Family Journal' No.1, 'Answers Competition' and 'Art Offer', in fine to very fine condition.

These were from the publisher's archives.
$1,000-1,500   CBA

'The Victor', 25th February 1961, in good condition with some tears to edges.
$5-10   PCOM

'Whizzer and Chips', 25th December 1971, Christmas issue, in good condition with some folds.

1970s issues of this comic, which ran 1969-90, usually fetch around this price.
$3-5   PCOM

An '1851 Great Exhibition' nursery plate, printed in purple with a view of the Crystal Palace, with foliate-molded border.

7.75in (19.5cm) diam

$120-180   H&C

A Contintental porcelain 'Shah of Persia' plate, decorated with a foliate design in blue, red and gilt, the center with color-printed portrait of Naser al-Din Shah Qajar.

Naser al-Din Shah was born in 1831 and reigned from 1834 until 1896 when he was assassinated. He was the first Persian Shah to visit Britain, doing so in 1873 (when he was made a Companion of the Order of the Garter) and again in 1878 and 1889.

c1880   *8in (20.5cm) diam*

$120-180   H&C

A Copeland '1899-1900 Transvaal War' three-handled loving cup, printed and painted with various patriotic vignettes and inscriptions, the base with printed 'Copeland' mark, retailer's mark for Thomas Goode & Co.' and 'Subscriber Copy'.

6in (15cm) high

$500-700   LT

A group of three early 20thC women's suffrage items, comprising an enamel badge inscribed 'VOTES FOR W.S.P.U', a tin badge inscribed 'NATIONAL UNION OF WOMEN'S SUFFRAGE SOCIETIES' and a cloth rosette with pinned 'VOTES FOR WOMEN' badge, the enamel badge stamped 'W.O. Lewis, Birmingham'.

$1,000-1,500   DW

A Paragon '1938 Munich Peace Conference' loving cup with a named sepia-printed portrait of Neville Chamberlain, with floral shaped handles.

3in (7.5cm) high

$250-350   H&C

A mid-20thC 'Henry Herbert Asquith' toby jug, wearing a black coat and top hat and holding an umbrella, the base numbered '435', with glaze chips to rim.

6.5in (16.5cm) high

$120-180   H&C

A mid-20thC Staffordshire 'David Lloyd George' toby jug, holding a leek, the base numbered '459'.

6.75in (17cm) high

$250-350   H&C

A mid-20thC Staffordshire 'Stanley Baldwin' toby jug, wearing top hat and with characteristic pipe, the base numbered '451'.

6.75in (17cm) high

$300-500   H&C

COMMEMORATIVES

A composition 'Winston Churchill' character mug.

The amateur look and use of composition are both due to wartime restrictions on materials and on the production of non-essential colored ceramics.

c1945   *6.25in (16cm) high*

$150-250   **H&C**

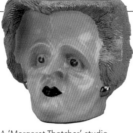

A 'Margaret Thatcher' studio pottery caricature jug, the base inscribed 'C. Haslock 14 November '79'.

1979   *6.25in (15.5cm) high*

$120-180   **H&C**

A pair of 1980s 'Margaret Thatcher' and 'Neil Kinnock' salt and pepper shakers.

4in (10cm) high

$80-120   **H&C**

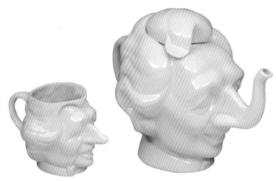

A Luck & Flaw 'Spitting Image' 'Margaret Thatcher' teapot and milk jug, the bases with impressed marks.

c1983   *Teapot 8.5in (22cm) high*

$150-250   **MLL**

A pair of Kevin Francis 'Spitting Image' character jugs of John Major and Neil Kinnock.

c1992   *4.25in (11cm) high*

$60-80   **H&C**

QUICK REFERENCE - OBAMA 'HOPE' POSTER

● **Designed in a single day, Shepherd Fairey's iconic image of Barack Obama quickly became one of the most widely recognized symbols of Obama's 2008 election. 'Hope' was the most common version, although other posters were also produced using the words 'Progress' or 'Change'.**

● **The poster was initially produced and distributed independently by Fairey but with the approval of the Obama campaign. Of the first 700 posters (all of which were screen-printed), Fairey sold 350 and put the rest up on public display. He then printed another 4,000, which were distributed at rallies before Super Tuesday, and posted a printable digital version of the image online for everyone to use.**

● **In total, it is estimated that by October 2008 over 300,000 versions of this poster had been produced using different printing methods.**

'HOPE', an American election poster, designed by Shepard Fairey.

2008   *36in (91.5cm) high*

$300-500   **FRE**

'PROGRESS', an American election poster, designed by Shepard Fairey, first printing of 700, with 'OBEY' symbol in campaign badge, signed by Shepard Fairey.

2008   *12in (30.5cm) high*

$800-1,200   **FRE**

QUICK REFERENCE - ROYAL COMMEMORATIVES

- Although royal memorabilia has been produced since the mid-17thC, production boomed during the reign of Queen Victoria (1837-1901). The variety of memorabilia available is large, so collectors tend to focus on one monarch or one event such as a coronation or jubilee.
- Ceramics were the first and most common item to be produced. With the advent of transfer-printing, railways and canals, they could be produced and distributed economically and widely.
- Always consider the maker and quality of the piece. The work of well-known makers, such as Royal Worcester and, Mintons, is likely to be desirable, but providing a piece is well decorated and well made, it is likely to be of interest.
- The event commemorated is also important to value, as some pieces can be rare as they were produced in small quantities. For example, many more pieces were produced for Victoria's Golden Jubilee than for her marriage.
- Consider condition too, as damage always reduces value.

A late Victorian briar pipe, in the form of a veiled bust of Queen Victoria, with a Vulcanite mouthpiece.

c1897   *6in (15cm) long*
$120-180   DN

A large '1887 Queen Victoria, Golden Jubilee' official silver medal, designed and modeled by Sir Joseph Edgar Boehm and Frederick, Lord Leighton, the obverse with a veiled crowned bust left, the reverse with the Queen enthroned attended by allegorical figures, with original red leather case.

1887   *3in (7.5cm) diam*
$700-1,000   DN

A wooden capstan inkwell, with plaque reading 'THIS IS MADE OF TIMBER WHICH WAS USED IN THE CONSTRUCTION OF HER LATE MAJESTY QUEEN VICTORIA'S YACHT "OSBOURNE."', with hinged lid.

HMY 'Osborne' was a paddle-steamer Royal Yacht of the Royal Navy of the United Kingdom. Designed by Edward James Reed, she was launched on 19 December 1870 at Pembroke Royal Dockyard and replaced a yacht of the same name, which had formerly been known as the HMY 'Victoria and Albert'.
$200-300   DN

A '1981 Queen Victoria in Memorium' gold pendant, with a bust of the Queen surrounded by a black enamel ring and split pearls, the reverse molded 'In memory of H.M. Queen Victoria, Obt. 1901 - Det.81', the case marked 'Joseph Hemming & Co., 28 Conduit St.'

1981   *0.75in (2cm) diam 0.2oz*
$300-500   DN

A pair of Royal Doulton Lambeth '1911 George V and Queen Mary Coronation' stoneware vases, decorated with portrait medallions and gloss glazes, the bases with impressed factory marks.

1911   *11.5in (29cm) high*
$500-700   H&C

An Adie & Lovekin '1911 George V and Queen Mary Coronation' silver pin cushion, in the form of the royal crown on a mounted square cushion, with Chester hallmarks, loaded.

1910   *1.5in (4cm) high*
$400-600   LC

A Royal Doulton Lambeth '1911 George V and Queen Mary Coronation' stoneware tankard, the base with impressed factory mark to base and numbered '7455'.

1911   *4.75in (12cm) high*
$100-150   TRI

COMMEMORATIVES

A Shelley '1924 Prince of Wales Visit to uMgungundlovu' mug, decorated with colored-printed portrait, the reverse with inscription, the base with factory marks.

This mug was produced for retailer Henwoods of Pietermaritzburg to commemorate the Prince's visit to the former seat of King Dingane of the Zulus in South Africa. Memorabilia for smaller, foreign events associated with lesser royals is usually much rarer than memorabilia produced for more important monarchs, because smaller amounts would have been produced. However, memorabilia for minor royals and minor events only appeals to a a relatively small number of collectors, so values are not often as high as one may hope.

1924
$120-180   PC

QUICK REFERENCE - EDWARD VIII MEMORABILIA

- **Unfortunately most Edward VIII memorabilia is not nearly as rare or valuable as many people think. The potteries began mass-production of a range of designs many months before the Coronation itself. As a result, many thousands of pieces were produced and sold before the Abdication was announced. This mug is an unusually valuable example of Edward VIII memorabilia. It's value comes from its rarity and cross-market interest.**
- **Pieces commemorating the Coronation and Abdication on the same object are rare, partly as the whole affair was deemed rather distasteful and embarrassing at the time.**
- **Musical jugs and mugs are a niche collecting market in their own right, further adding to the desirability of this mug.**

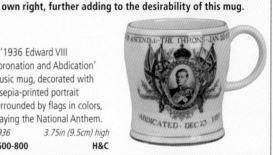

A '1936 Edward VIII Coronation and Abdication' music mug, decorated with a sepia-printed portrait surrounded by flags in colors, playing the National Anthem.

1936   *3.75in (9.5cm) high*
$600-800   H&C

A Paragon '1926 Princess Elizabeth Birth' baby's plate, printed in sepia with a portrait after Marcus Adams, lined in red and gilt.

1926
$200-300   H&C

A Royal Doulton '1935 George V and Queen Mary Silver Jubilee' limited edition loving cup, from an edition of 1,000.

1935   *10.25in (26cm) high*
$400-600   DA&H

A Bovey Pottery '1936 Three Kings' tyg, decorated with sepia-printed portraits surrounded by flags and heraldic devices in colors, the inside rim with inscription, the base with factory marks.

The 'year of the three kings' refers to the year 1936 when Edward VIII succeeded his father, George V, as King of the UK and British Dominions, but abdicated in favor of his brother, George VI.

1936
$150-250   H&C

A Shelley '1937 Edward VIII Coronation' loving cup, decorated with a sepia-printed portrait, with gilt handles and highlights, the base with printed factory marks.

1937   *4.5in (11.5cm) high*
$150-250   H&C

A Paragon '1937 George VI & Queen Elizabeth Coronation' serving dish, decorated in colors with central heraldic shield.

17in (43cm) wide
$400-600   H&C

A Paragon '1939 George VI and Queen Elizabeth Visit to Canada' plate, decorated with sepia-printed portraits among colored borders and heraldic motifs, the reverse with printed factory marks.

1939
$300-500   H&C

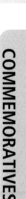

A Burleigh Ware '1953 Queen Elizabeth II Coronation' character jug, in the form of the Queen enthroned, decorated with national emblems and 'ER' cypher, the base with impressed and painted marks.

8.75in (22cm) high

$120-180   **GORB**

A Beswick figurine of 'HM Queen Elizabeth II on Imperial', designed by Mr Folkard, model no.1546.

1958-81   *10.5in (26.5cm) high*

$250-350   **CAPE**

A Royal Doulton limited edition figurine of 'HM Queen Elizabeth The Queen Mother', designed by E J Griffiths, no.HN2882, from an edition of 1,500, with wooden stand, certificate and box.

1980   *8in (20.5cm) high*

$200-300   **CHT**

A CLOSER LOOK AT A COMMEMORATIVE JUG

Slipware pottery, decorated with trails of colored liquid clay called slip, has been made for centuries. It was much used as a way of commemorating an event in ceramic before the development of porcelain.

Parts of the design are incised into the surface. This technique is known as sgrafitto and has been a hallmark of pottery in Devon since the 17thC

Harry Juniper (b.1933) is a studio potter who works in Torrington and then Bideford. He is known for his 'Harvest Jugs', which commemorate national or local events or personalities.

He made his first jug in 1958. Each piece can take up to six weeks to make and decorate, meaning they are all either one-offs or from a small series.

A '1981 Prince Charles and Lady Diana Spencer Betrothal' pottery 'Harvest Jug', with incised and slip-trailed decoration and wording, the base incised 'Made by Harry Juniper of Bideford'.

1981   *9in (21cm) high*

$400-600   **H&C**

A Paragon China '1980 Queen Elizabeth, The Queen Mother, 80th Birthday' limited edition loving cup, from an edition of 750, with original fitted case.

1980

$120-180   **DN**

A KK Outlet '2011 Prince William and Kate Middleton Wedding' plate, 'THANKS FOR THE FREE DAY OFF', designed by Angela Lidderdale in 2011, the reverse printed 'Edwardian Bone China Made in Stoke On Trent England'.

Initially only available through the KK Outlet store in East London, these humorous plates were soon also stocked by major chains, such as John Lewis. Each piece cost around $30. As they captured the youth of the couple and the design zeitgeist of the time, it will be interesting to see how they perform in the future.

2011   *10.5in (26.5cm) diam*

$25-35   **KKO**

A KK Outlet '2011 Prince William and Kate Middleton Wedding' plate, 'Facebook', designed by Üte Geisler in 2011, the reverse printed 'Edwardian Bone China Made in Stoke On Trent England'.

2011   *10.25in (26.5cm) diam*

$25-35   **KKO**

COSTUME JEWELRY

QUICK REFERENCE - COSTUME JEWELRY

- When costume jewelry was brought into the BBC 'Antiques Roadshow' ten, or even five, years ago we tended to admire its design and quality but regularly announced that there was little commercial value in the piece. That has certainly changed.

- Pieces by the major players, such as Trifari, Miriam Haskell, Stanley Hagler, Christian Dior and Chanel, are now making hundreds and, in some cases, thousands of dollars. Many of the main costume jewelry companies mass-produced their ranges and these pieces do still turn up in charity shops and job lots at auction, but certainly not as often as they did.

- Quality is of paramount importance to value. Companies such as Trifari made jewelry for every budget, so just because a piece is marked 'Trifari' doesn't mean it will be valuable. Attention should always be paid to the design and manner of construction.

- For Trifari's top-end range, chief designer Alfred Philippe set the tone by using fine, facet-cut, skilfully hand-set Austrian rhinestones in extremely convincing imitations of precious jewelry. Such pieces are generally the most valuable Trifari jewels today, however many other pieces are beginning to fetch high-end prices. Jelly belly pins, animal pins and Trifari's famous crown pins have also risen significantly in value.

- Don't disregard unsigned pieces, which can sometimes be bought at bargain prices. Look for high quality 'stones', which have been well selected for color tones and variation of style. Pieces that achieve a highly desirable three-dimensional effect are often valuable.

- Be careful to examine any piece of costume jewelry carefully, as damage dramatically reduces values. Although replacement stones can be found, they may not match the original stones exactly in either size or color.

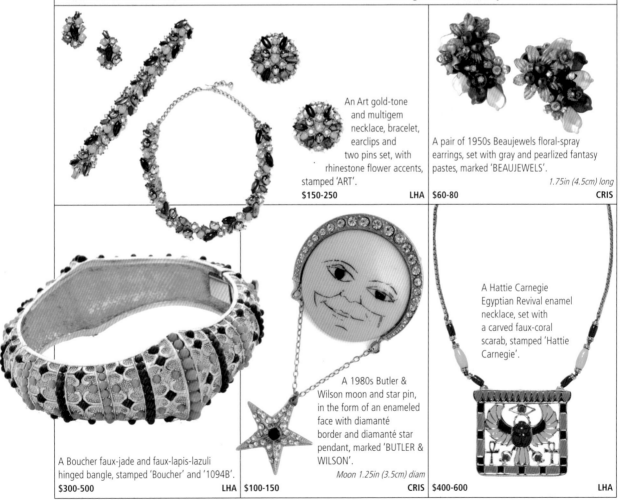

An Art gold-tone and multigem necklace, bracelet, earclips and two pins set, with rhinestone flower accents, stamped 'ART'.

$150-250   LHA

A pair of 1950s Beaujewels floral-spray earrings, set with gray and pearlized fantasy pastes, marked 'BEAUJEWELS'.

1.75in (4.5cm) long

$60-80   CRIS

A Boucher faux-jade and faux-lapis-lazuli hinged bangle, stamped 'Boucher' and '1094B'.

$300-500   LHA

A 1980s Butler & Wilson moon and star pin, in the form of an enameled face with diamanté border and diamanté star pendant, marked 'BUTLER & WILSON'.

Moon 1.25in (3.5cm) diam

$100-150   CRIS

A Hattie Carnegie Egyptian Revival enamel necklace, set with a carved faux-coral scarab, stamped 'Hattie Carnegie'.

$400-600   LHA

Judith Picks

I love Hattie Carngie's jewels, but I love her story, too. In 1904, aged 18, Henrietta Kanengesier immigrated to the USA from Vienna and on the ship she asked who was America's richest man. Her subsequent adoption of Andrew Carnegie's surname proved appropriate. From a single shop opened in 1909 she went on to found a chain of exclusive boutiques. In 1918 she launched her first collection of high quality costume jewelry. Her pieces range from the very classical, such as this necklace, to the quirky, such as goat's head and anteater pins. I feel all her pieces are still undervalued today and are likely to prove good investments.

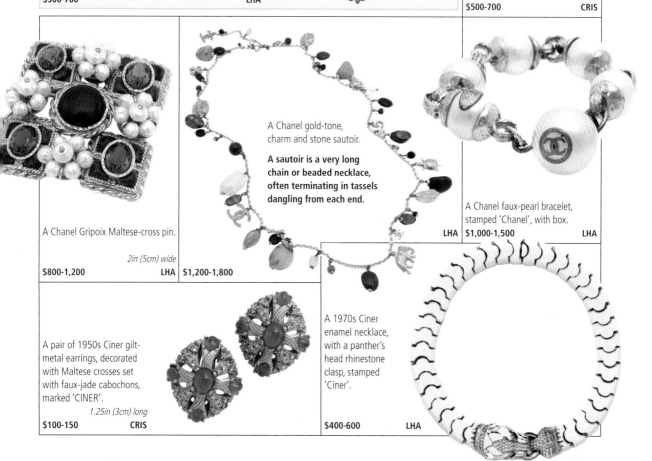

A Hattie Carnegie gold-tone and carved faux-lapis-lazuli necklace, with rhinestone surround, with a colorless resin and gold-tone link chain, stamped 'Hattie Carnegie'.
$500-700   LHA

A 1950s Joan Castle 'Russian gold' crown pin, set with a clear diamanté, marked 'JOAN CASTLE'.

Joan Castle was the widow of Eugene Joseff, founder of Joseff of Hollywood (see p.174). This pin is reputed to have been made as a gift for contestants on the television show 'Queen for a Day'.

2in (5cm) high
$500-700   CRIS

A Chanel Gripoix Maltese-cross pin.

2in (5cm) wide
$800-1,200   LHA

A Chanel gold-tone, charm and stone sautoir.

A sautoir is a very long chain or beaded necklace, often terminating in tassels dangling from each end.

$1,200-1,800

A Chanel faux-pearl bracelet, stamped 'Chanel', with box.
                          LHA **$1,000-1,500**   LHA

A pair of 1950s Ciner gilt-metal earrings, decorated with Maltese crosses set with faux-jade cabochons, marked 'CINER'.
1.25in (3cm) long
$100-150   CRIS

A 1970s Ciner enamel necklace, with a panther's head rhinestone clasp, stamped 'Ciner'.
$400-600   LHA

COSTUME JEWELRY

A William deLillo cabochon cross pendant-necklace, stamped 'William deLillo'.

$700-1,000 LHA

A Miriam Haskell amber 'Art Glass' pin, stamped 'Miriam Haskell'.

$150-250 LHA

A 1950s Har gilt-metal genie pin, set with colorless and blue rhinestones and a faux-amethyst cabochon, marked 'HAR' with copyright symbol.

2.25in (5.5cm) high

$550-750 CRIS

A Miriam Haskell double-strand necklace, stamped 'Miriam Haskell'.

$300-500 LHA

An Hermès orange alligator-skin 'Collier de Chien' bracelet, with palladium hardware, blindstamp square 'K', stamped 'Hermes', with pouch and box.

2007

8.75in (22.5cm) long

$3,000-4,000 LHA

An Hermès enamel bangle, stamped 'Hermes', with pouch.

Size 70

$500-700 LHA

A pair of Jomaz white-beaded floral earclips, stamped 'Jomaz'.

$50-70 LHA

Judith Picks

Eugene Joseff (the founder of Joseff of Hollywood) is one of my favorite costume jewelry designers and his 'Sun God' and 'Moon God with Ruff' pins are some of the most frequently worn items from my collection.

Joseff's career took off in 1931 when he began producing historically accurate jewelry for Hollywood films. In 1937, he created a series of commercial lines based on his designs for the Silver Screen. The design for this fabulous snake pin was used for a belt worn by Elizabeth Taylor in one of her most legendary roles: Cleopatra (1963). Joseff of Hollywood produced the snake pin with a variety of different colors of glass 'stone, but the green shown here is the same as the film. Prices for Joseff jewels continue to rise, so if you like his work - buy now!

A 1960s Joseff of Hollywood 'Russian gold' snake pin, the head set with a green glass, the reverse with applied 'Joseff' plaque.

$300-500 MHC

QUICK REFERENCE - KENNETH JAY LANE

- Born in Detroit, Michigan, Kenneth Jay Lane (1930-) started work in the fashion world in the mid-1950s. Having worked in the art department at 'Vogue', he went on to design shoes for Christian Dior and shoes and jewelry for Arnold Scaasi. He established his own business in 1963.
- During the 1980s he designed for Avon and in the 1990s he re-issued his 'Jewels of India' line via shopping channel QVC.
  - Lane's pieces are typically very large and made from good quality materials.
    - Many of his designs are inspired by the Renaissance and Eygpt, as well as Roman, Oriental and Medieval styles.
    - Figural themes are also common, with popular motifs including gods, snakes, dancers and religious figures. Pieces such as his 'Big Cats' pins or those with rams' heads, walrus, mermaids or chameleons are particularly sought after today.
  - Lane's designs from before the 1970s are marked 'K.J.L.' His pieces from the late 1970s onward are signed 'Kenneth Jay Lane' or 'Kenneth Lane'.

A Kenneth Jay Lane bead necklace, with an Indian-style faux-coral and faux-turquoise pendant, stamped 'KJL'.

$250-350   LHA

A pair of 1950s Kramer faux-jade and gilt-metal earrings, with twisted-rope setting, marked 'KRAMER'.

0.75in (2cm) diam

$40-60   CRIS

A 1950s Kramer New York bracelet, comprising four strands of twisted gilt-mesh and beads, marked 'KRAMER OF NEW YORK'.

6.75in (17.5cm) long

$65-85   CRIS

A pair of Karl Lagerfeld gold-tone ear-pendants, engraved and stamped 'KL'.

$150-250   LHA

A Lanvin gold-tone and enamel 'L' necklace, stamped 'Lanvin Paris'.

$250-350   LHA

A pair of 1950s Napier gitl-metal and faux-cornelian earrings, marked 'NAPIER PAT PENDING'.

1.25in (3.5cm) long

$60-80   CRIS

A pair of 1950s Leru gilt-metal and diamanté earrings, marked 'LERU' with copyright symbol.

1.5in (4cm) long

$70-100   CRIS

A 1950s Matisse enameled copper palette pin, marked 'MATISSE'.

4.5in (11cm) long

$100-150   CRIS

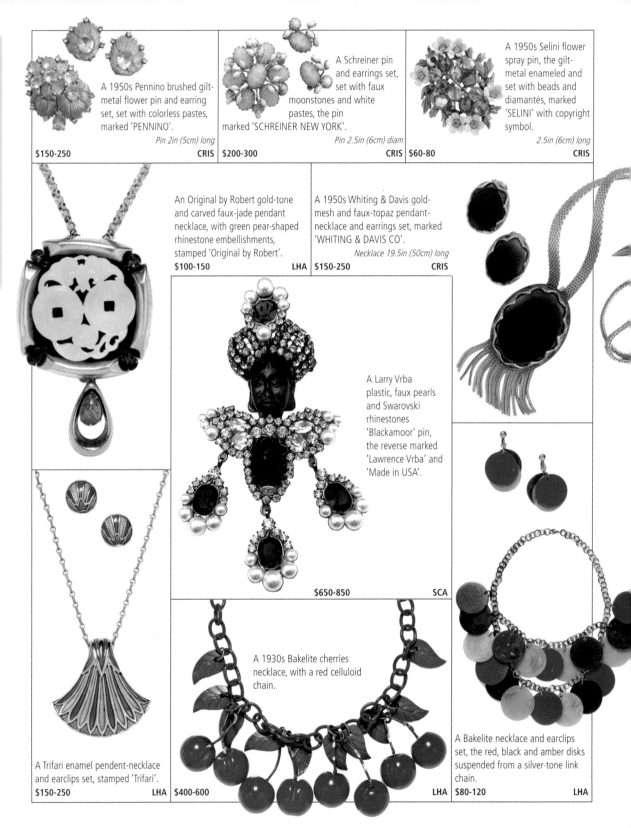

A 1950s Pennino brushed gilt-metal flower pin and earring set, set with colorless pastes, marked 'PENNINO'.

Pin 2in (5cm) long

$150-250   CRIS

A Schreiner pin and earrings set, set with faux moonstones and white pastes, the pin marked 'SCHREINER NEW YORK'.

Pin 2.5in (6cm) diam

$200-300   CRIS

A 1950s Selini flower spray pin, the gilt-metal enameled and set with beads and diamantés, marked 'SELINI' with copyright symbol.

2.5in (6cm) long

$60-80   CRIS

An Original by Robert gold-tone and carved faux-jade pendant necklace, with green pear-shaped rhinestone embellishments, stamped 'Original by Robert'.

$100-150   LHA

A 1950s Whiting & Davis gold-mesh and faux-topaz pendant-necklace and earrings set, marked 'WHITING & DAVIS CO'.

Necklace 19.5in (50cm) long

$150-250   CRIS

A Larry Vrba plastic, faux pearls and Swarovski rhinestones 'Blackamoor' pin, the reverse marked 'Lawrence Vrba' and 'Made in USA'.

$650-850   SCA

A Trifari enamel pendent-necklace and earclips set, stamped 'Trifari'.

$150-250   LHA

A 1930s Bakelite cherries necklace, with a red celluloid chain.

$400-600   LHA

A Bakelite necklace and earclips set, the red, black and amber disks suspended from a silver-tone link chain.

$80-120   LHA

A Beswick Walt Disney black, white and red gloss-glazed model of 'Mickey Mouse', designed by Jan Granoska, model no.1278, the base with gilt mark.
1952-65   *4in (10cm) high*
$200-300   **CAPE**

A Beswick Walt Disney white and blue gloss-glazed model of 'Donald Duck', designed by Jan Granoska, model no.1283.
1953-65   *4in (10cm) high*
$200-300   **CAPE**

A large 1930s Dean's Rag Book Walt Disney 'Minnie Mouse', with velvet stuffed body, the left foot with Dean's label.

Minnie can be rarer than Mickey, as most children, even girls, wanted Mickey himself, not his girlfriend!
10.5in (27cm) high
$250-350   **DW**

A 1930s-40s American cardboard Mickey Mouse hoop-la game, with string and ring.

Images of Mickey can often be dated to a rough period by how he looks. He was initially very rodent-like and then became more rounded and 'friendly', losing his teeth, during the 1930s-60s.
5in (12.5cm) high
$120-180   **CBA**

A Johnson Walt Disney film-strip projector, with instructions, a box of six Disney filmstrips and an additional single film strip, in good condition, within scratch-built wooden box.
$30-50   **VEC**

'Mickey Mouse in King Arthur's Court', by Walt Disney, first edition, published by Blue Ribbon Books, New York, with four color pop-ups and other illustrations, the dust jacket with two short closed tears along folds.
1933
$800-1,200   **DW**

'Flip the Frog Annual', by Walt Disney, published by Dean & Son, with four color plates and numerous black and white illustrations by Wilfred Haughton, the spine neatly glued to head of lower joint.

This was the first and only edition of 'Flip the Frog Annual'.
1931
$400-600   **DW**

A Wade Walt Disney pottery 'Fantasia' vase, printed with stylized designs, with gilt-lined rim, the base with printed mark.
8in (20.5cm) high
$80-120   **CAPE**

DOLLS & DOLL'S HOUSES

QUICK REFERENCE - DOLL MATERIALS

- It is possible to date a doll to a period by considering the material it is made from. Considering other features such as clothing, wear, style and any marks will help narrow the period down further. Bear in mind that most materials described here were also used after the dates given.
- Painted wooden dolls date from the first half of the 18thC or earlier, but those that survive today are usually from the late 18thC or early to mid-19thC.
- The golden age of bisque-head dolls was from the late 19thC to the early 20thC. Such dolls usually had wooden or composition bodies.
- Fabric dolls have been made for centuries, but most that have survived date from the late 19thC into the 1930s.
- Composition and celluloid dolls generally date from the 1920s to the 1940s, with dolls made from other hard plastics taking over in the 1950s.
- Soft plastics and vinyls were mainly used from the 1960s onward.

An Armand Marseille bisque-head girl doll, mold no.1894, with fixed blue glass eyes, open mouth and brown mohair wig, the head marked '1894 AM 9/0 DEP', with composition bent limbed body, with crochet bonnet and lace and cotton dress.

8in (20cm) high

$120-180   AH

An Armand Marseille bisque-head child doll, mold no.390, with brown sleeping eyes and brown mohair wig, with jointed composition body, in original sailor's clothes.

14in (36cm) high

$120-180   SAS

A Tête Jumeau bisque-head doll, with blue fixed eyes, closed mouth and original auburn mohair wig and cork pate, the head printed in red 'DEPOSE TETE JUMEAU BtehS.G.D.G.6', signed with artist checkmarks 'L H III' and impressed '6', with re-painted composition and wood ball jointed body, with size 3 lace-up shoes and other clothes, with crack to head.

This doll's head is cracked on the front of her head from the top of the wig-rim down to her eyebrow, which has reduced her value considerably. Jumeau's high quality dolls are among the most sought after in the world. Had she not been damaged, her value could have tripled or more.

c1886

$1,000-1,500   VEC

A J D Kestner bisque-head child doll, mold no.171, with blue sleeping eyes and blonde mohair wig, with jointed composition body, with white cotton frock, the body stamped 'Germany', with repainted hands.

25in (64cm) high

$400-600   SAS

A Kammer & Reinhardt bisque socket-head doll, mold no.403, the head manufactured by Simon & Halbig, with sleeping brown glass eyes and brown wig, the head impressed 'K & R / Simon & Halbig / 403 / Germany / 62', with a ball-jointed composition body with movable wrists.

25.5in (65cm) high

$550-750   DN

A Simon & Halbig bisque-head child doll, mold no.1079, with blue sleeping eyes and blonde mohair wig, with jointed composition body with fixed wrists, with white muslin dress, underclothes and lace bonnet, with restoration to arms.

19.5in (49cm) high

$250-350   SAS

A bisque-head doll, mold no.4, with fixed blue eyes and modern blonde wig, with French papier-mâché and wooden body, with later dress, bonnet, underclothes and bible.

21.75in (55cm) high

$400-600   SAS

A CLOSER LOOK AT A FABRIC DOLL

Martha Chase (1851-1925) began making stockinette dolls for her children and their friends in 1889. In 1891 they were spotted by a retailer, who began to stock them and, by 1900, they were being sold nationally in the USA.

Chase dolls have raised, realistic features, heads and body forms, unlike many other fabric dolls. They are also more durable than bisque dolls.

In 1913, Martha Chase designed her first life-sized hospital adult doll for nurses to practice on. These were realistically proportioned and weighted. The success of the life-sized versions led to the production of 'Baby Chase' baby hospital dolls. Chase hospital dolls can be distinguished from toy dolls as they have open nose and ear holes.

All Chase's dolls from the 1930s have 'jointed' shoulders, like this. They do not have similar joints at the elbow. After 1939, the shoulder joints were made from metal.

A rare 1930s Martha Chase painted cloth 'Baby Chase' Hospital Doll, with floppy joints at shoulders, elbows and hips, with weighted stuffing, with transfer label under right arm reading 'CHASE HOSPITAL DOLL TRADE MARK PAWTUCKET, R.I. MADE IN U.S.A.', with wear and flaking to joints.

26.5in (67.5cm) high

$150-250   **SAS**

A 1930s Lenci pressed-felt boy doll, from the '300' series, with inserted auburn mohair hair, with swivel head and jointed body, with original felt and hand-knitted clothes and leather shoes, the left foot stamped 'Lenci', with slight fading.

17in (43.5cm) high

$1,500-2,500   **SAS**

A rare Art Fabric Mills printed-cloth doll, with a blue and white striped cotton romper.

Printed fabric dolls such as this were often sold on flat sheets to be cut out, stuffed and sewn together at home.

c1900-02   *4in (61cm) high*

$250-350   **SAS**

A Dean's Rag Book composition and cloth 'Dutch Boy' doll, with original felt costume, the left foot with label.

17in (43cm) high

$100-150   **VEC**

A rare 1920s Louise R Kampes Studios 'Kamkins' cloth doll, with blonde mohair wig, with possibly original dress, coat and hat, the feet with ink stamps.

19in (48cm) high

$400-600   **SAS**

A late 20thC Maggie Made Dolls limited edition pressed-felt artist doll, 'Hannah', by Maggie Iacono, from an edition of 70, with auburn hair, fully jointed, with cotton and felt clothing, in mint condition, with near-mint condition box.

15in (38cm) high

$500-700   **VEC**

A late 20thC Maggie Made Dolls limited edition pressed-felt artist doll, 'Mia', by Maggie Iacono, from an edition of 100, with blonde hair, fully jointed, with cotton and felt clothing, in mint condition, with near-mint condition box.

11in (28cm) high

$300-500   **VEC**

A rare 18thC wooden doll, with gesso and painted head blonde hair wig, with replaced kid arms, redressed in the 19thC, but retaining original stockings and under slip, with Jumeau size 6 shoes with bee mark, with some repainting and wear.

An accompanying letter of provenance explains that this doll was owned by six generations of the same family. She was named Lady Louisa Elizabeth Huntingdon.

c1766   21.5in (54cm) high

$12,000-18,000   SAS

A mid-19thC wax over papier-mâché doll, with blue fixed eyes, white curled mohair wig, with stuffed body and kid lower arms, with remains of blue silk dress, plush hat and undergarments, with some cracks.

22in (56cm) high

$150-250   SAS

A 1920s-30s French celluloid doll, possibly by Convert, with painted eyes and features, the Rayon and cotton muslin body with celluloid hands, with original cotton dress and bonnet, with original card label to left wrist reading 'Fabrication Parisienne, Les Poupess Gina', in excellent condition.

14in (36cm) high

$80-120   VEC

A rare 1920s German composition gnome doll, possibly by Cuno & Otto Dressel, with blue glass eyes and white wool beard, with jointed composition and wood body, with original clothing and molded lace-up shoes with blue cloth socks, with crack to head, missing some finger tips.

Cloth socks held in place with composition shoes was a feature of many early Dressel dolls.

15.5in (39.5cm) high

$500-700   SAS

A Pedigree black hard-plastic 'Mandy Lou' walking doll, with flirting eyes, black astrakhan wig, with inoperative 'mama' voice box and grille to front torso, with Pedigree cotton dress, nylon undergarments, cotton socks and Cinderella shoes, in very good condition.

The hands are the earlier type with a seam across the palm.

c1953   20in (51cm) high

$200-300   VEC

A Pedigree 'Fashion Girl' 'Sindy' doll and a 'Paul' doll, both fully dressed, Sindy lacking necklace, Paul with chinos rather than jeans and missing plimsoles, Sindy with stand, both with boxes, in good condition.

The little girl who owned these dolls was obviously very careful with them. However, she enjoyed brushing Sindy's hair, as can be seen from its current 'style'. Sindys produced from 1968 had longer hair that curled in a flip at the ends. It's important that hair on plastic dolls is in the original style and condition for them to reach the highest values. The outfit that Sindy is currently wearing was redesigned in pink in 1969.

1965-68

$800-1,200   HT

A late 20thC-early 21st C Abigail Sandy's Babies 'One-of-a-Kind' Cernit newborn doll, signed 'Sandy Faber', with knitted coat and bonnet and cream trousers, in mint condition.

Cernit is a moldable and carvable plastic and clay compound that can be fired in home ovens.

22in (56cm)

$100-150   VEC

A late 19thC 'Box Back' wooden doll's house, in the manner of Silber & Fleming, the front opening to reveal four rooms with hall, stairs and landing, fireplaces and chimney breasts.

24in (61cm) high

$120-180   SAS

A Victorian painted wooden doll's house, in the form of a terrace house, the front opening to reveal four rooms with wallpaper and floor coverings, with some faults and wear.

27.5in (72cm) high

$550-750   TOV

A 19thC wooden doll's house, in the form of a palace-front townhouse, the hinged front with brickwork parquetry inlay, opening to reveal six rooms, with hall and landings, on mahogany plinth base.

51.5in (131cm) high

$400-600   DN

A 1930s-50s Tri-ang painted wooden doll's house, the front opening to reveal two rooms.

16.25in (41cm) high

$100-150   DN

A 1920s Schoenhut clapper-board wooden doll's house, with pressed card tiled roof and tinplate windows, the back opening to reveal four rooms, with electric lighting and 24 pieces of carved wood Schoenhut doll's house furniture.

24.5in (62cm) wide

$250-350   SAS

A 1930s-50s Tri-ang wooden doll's house, the front opening to reveal two rooms.

16.25in (41cm) high

$100-150   DN

Judith Picks

Most doll's houses were made to resemble houses of the period. They either reflected a house the little girl was used to, or acted as an 'ideal' home to aspire to.

By the 1920s, the combination of urban sprawl, inner city slums and a nostalgia for rural values meant that most little girls aspired to the 'Tudorbethan' style of houses that were being built in many London outer suburbs. Such houses combined traditional architecture with spacious rooms, a garden and the convenience of town-living. The other Tri-ang houses on this page are good examples of this style.

Meanwhile, this Modernist- or Art Deco-style house would have been too avant-garde for most parents and their children. It would have sold in considerably lower numbers than the more traditional houses, meaning that it is rare today and is consequently worth almost four times as much!

A rare 1930s Tri-ang Art Deco painted wooden doll's house, the front opening to reveal four rooms, the roof with a sun lounge.

29.25in (74cm) wide

$550-750   DN

FASHION

A Balenciaga brown
bouclé skirt suit,
fully lined, labeled
'Balenciaga/10, Avenue
George V. Paris/53482'.
$400-600　　　**LHA**

A Bill Blass for Maurice Rentner daywear ensemble, comprising a dress and coat, with black and white anchor motif, labeled 'Bill Blass for Maurice Rentner/Bonwit Teller', with yellowing around the shoulders.

Maurice Rentner (1889-1958) founded his company in 1923 and became known for high quality suits and dresses during the 1930s. After he died in 1958, the company merged with his sister's company, Anna Miller. Bill Blass was the designer there and became the head designer at Maurice Rentner. In 1967 Blass bought the company (Maurice Rentner) and in 1970 he renamed it Bill Blass Ltd.
c1960　　　　　　　　　　　　　　　　Size 12
$2,000-3,000　　　　　　　　　　　　**LHA**

QUICK REFERENCE - FASHION

- The most valuable pieces are usually those by notable designers, particularly those that pioneered a look or a style, such as Coco Chanel. Learn to identify the different styles of labels as most designers had or have a less valuable or desirable diffusion range as well as a sought-after haute couture collection.
- Clothes from the 1950s-70s tend to be the most desirable, partly as earlier clothes are generally rarer and less immediately wearable, due to size or (often perceived) fragility. Pieces from the 1980s are currently rising in value, particularly those pieces by designers who founded and led trends, such as Gianni Versace (1946-97) and Vivienne Westwood (b.1941).
- The most desirable pieces will sum up the style of the period and have 'eye appeal'. Other factors to consider include the shape, cut, color and pattern. You should also always consider the quality of the stitching and fabric used, regardless of whether it is a 'designer piece' or not. If you are buying with an eye for the future, learn which collections made a designer's name as these pieces are mostly likely to rise in value if the designer becomes popular.
- Condition is also important. Take time to examine a piece all over and avoid stained or torn pieces (unless that was intentional!) and pieces that have been dramatically altered at a later date, for example in size.

A Chanel navy-blue tweed skirt suit, the jacket with gold lion's head buttons and cropped sleeves, labeled 'Chanel/13171'.
$1,200-1,800　　　**LHA**

A Chanel tan and cream tweed skirt suit, the jacket with green braided trim and lion's head buttons, labeled 'Chanel/14726'.
$1,200-1,800　　　**LHA**

A Chanel cream silk dress, the back with logo buttons, labeled 'Chanel Boutique'.
$1,000-1,500　　　**LHA**

A Chanel pink and orange jacket, from the 'Cruise 2001' collection, with red metallic buttons, labeled 'Chanel'.
Size 40
$500-700　　　**LHA**

A 1960s Courrèges lime-green wool mod dress and matching jacket, the dress with cream buttons and a cream leather belt, labeled 'Courrèges/38445/Made in Paris'.
Size B
$1,500-2,500　　　**LHA**

A 1980s Romeo Gigli 'Jester' ensemble, comprising a red velvet jacket and matching sash and a gold glitter vest, labeled 'Romeo Gigli'.

A 1960s Courrèges orange vinyl jacket, with white snaps and logo, with full detachable lining, labeled 'Courrèges/Paris'.
$500-700   LHA

A Christian Dior coral and cream wool coat, with coral lining, labeled 'Christian Dior New York Inc.'
$500-700   LHA

Romeo Gigli (b.1949) had his major international breakthrough in 1986 when he launched his Spring/Summer collection inspired by the Italian Renaissance. This ensemble may have been part of, or inspired by, that collection.

Size 42
$700-1,000   LHA

A 1980s Givenchy ash-gray and yellow dress, with a fitted boned bodice, labeled 'Givenchy/Paris'.
$550-750   LHA

A Madame Grès green printed chiffon dress, fully lined, labeled 'Grès'.
$1,200-1,800   LHA

An Hermès beige coat, labeled 'Hermès'.
Size 40
$650-850   LHA

An Hermès ocean-print lycra dress, with clear paillettes throughout, labeled 'Hermès'.
Size 40
$650-850   LHA

A Marc Jacobs orange 'Button' sweater dress, with large navy button motifs at neckline and sleeves, labeled 'Marc Jacobs'.
1987
$400-600   LHA

FASHION

An Issey Miyake pleated tunic, labeled 'Issey Miyake'.

$300-500   LHA

A Moschino green 'Coin Purse' coat, with two detachable velvet coin purse pockets, labeled 'Moschino Cheap and Chic'.

Size 10

$200-300   LHA

A Moschino black 'Dinner Suit' jacket and matching skirt, the jacket decorated with gold-colored knives, spoons and forks, labeled 'Moschino Couture!'.

Size 12

$800-1,200   LHA

Mark Picks

Emilio Pucci's instantly recognisable designs never fall far out of fashion and always make an eye-catching investment that's practical to wear.

Dashing aristocrat and wartime flying-ace Emilio Pucci (1914-1992) launched his career as a fashion designer in 1947 when a ski suit he designed was featured in 'Harper's Bazaar'. In 1950, he opened a boutique in Capri, Italy, where he sold elegant, flattering silk dresses, sportswear and lingerie, all printed with psychedelic swirling or geometric patterns in a vibrant palette. Beloved by the fashionable 'jetset' of the 1960s, Pucci's hallmark look quickly went global. In 1965, he even designed avant-garde uniforms for the stewardesses of Braniff Airlines, which included clear plastic 'space helmets'. After falling from favor during the 1980s and '90s, the brand and designs were re-launched and re-developed by the luxury group LVMH, owned by French billionaire Bernard Arnault.

Over the decades, Pucci's signature style has been widely copied, so always look out for labels and the word 'Emilio' printed in the design, as shown in the image opposite. Look out for Pucci menswear, as it tends to be much harder to find than womenswear. I often wear my vintage Pucci tie to the BBC 'Antiques Roadshow' and it always attracts envious looks and admiring comments!

A 1960s Emilio Pucci geometric printed silk jumpsuit, with a V-neck and wide leg pants, labeled 'Emilio Pucci'.

$500-700   LHA

An Emilio Pucci pink and brown print dress, labeled 'Emilio Pucci for Formfit Rogers'.

Size P

$150-250   LHA

An Emilio Pucci two-piece silk evening ensemble, with a sequined top and long pink skirt, labeled 'Emilio Pucci Firenze'.

Size 12

$400-600   LHA

A 1960s Emilio Pucci pink and gray silk organza dress, with a ruffled hemline, labeled 'Emilio Pucci'.

Size 10

$300-500   LHA

An Oscar de la Renta floral sheath dress, fitted with pink cord straps, missing label.
$300-500   LHA

An Oscar de la Renta pink 'watercolor' print bustle-dress, labeled 'Oscar de la Renta'.
Size 6
$550-750   LHA

An Oscar de la Renta Studio color-block sequin dress, the blocks separated by black velvet strips, labeled 'Oscar de la Renta Studio'.
Size 4
$70-100   LHA

A Zandra Rhodes blue silk beaded dress, decorated with a face motif, labeled 'Zandra Rhodes London/ Marshall Field'.
$300-500   LHA

A 1980s Yves Saint Laurent black and gold lurex jacket and trouser set, labeled 'Saint Laurent'.
Jacket size 38
$300-500   LHA

A 1980s Yves Saint Laurent black and red taffeta blouse, with all-over multicolored embroidery, labeled 'Saint Laurent'.
Size 38
$300-500   LHA

A 1970s Malcolm Starr 'Circus' skirt, decorated with felt appliqués of an elephant, labeled 'Malcolm Starr'.
$250-350   LHA

A 'shocking pink' wool shift daywear ensemble, comprising a dress and jacket, labeled '28 Shop Marshall Field & Company'.

Marshall Field & Company was a chain of American department stores based in Chicago. In 2005 it was acquired by and merged into Macy's.
$500-700   LHA

FASHION

A 1920s German silver purse-clasp, embossed and molded with cherubs among foliage, stamped '800', with original chain, with a mid-20thC 'shocking pink' damask fabric bag.

$70-100   DN

A two-color gold-mesh purse, the foliate engraved and pierced mounts set with sapphires and diamonds, with chamois lining

5in (15.5cm) high 12oz

$7,000-10,000   WW

QUICK REFERENCE - WHITING & DAVIS

- Whiting & Davis was established in Massachusetts, USA, in 1876 and is best known for metal-mesh purses. Initial designs were hand-soldered, but by 1920 this laborious process had been mechanized and designs became more complex.
- Renowned fashion designers Elsa Schiaparelli (1890-1973) and Paul Poirot (1879-1944) were among those who produced designs for the company.
- Bright colors and angular designs, such as the one shown here, typify bags from the 1920s and '30s.
- Whiting & Davis bags fell out of fashion after World War II, so the company began to focus more on jewelry. The bags returned to fashion again during the disco craze of the 1970s and are now highly sought after by collectors, particularly if they have vibrantly colored patterns.

A Whiting & Davis mesh purse, stamped 'Whiting and Davis Co.'

7in (18cm) high

$200-300   LHA

A gray lucite purse, with a carved floral handle and top, stamped 'Florida Purses'.

8in (20cm) high

$100-150   LHA

A large 1970s crocodile-skin purse, with divided interior.

$150-250   DN

A Chanel black quilted caviar-leather purse, no. 3548117, stamped 'CHANEL, MADE IN FRANCE', the shoulder chain converting to double handles, with authenticity card and care booklet.

9in (23cm) wide

$1,500-2,500   DN

A Chanel cinnamon-colored woven-straw and calf-leather mini purse, no. 1323958, stitched 'CC' under top flap, stamped 'CHANEL, MADE IN ITALY', with plastic identity card.

8in (20cm) wide

$700-1,000   DN

A Chanel blue woven-straw and leather purse, no. 362332, stamped 'CHANEL, MADE IN ITALY'.

9.25in (23cm) wide

$500-700   DN

A Chanel wine-red quilted lizard-skin clutch-style purse, no. 295409, stamped 'CHANEL, MADE IN ITALY'.

9.5in (24cm) wide

$1,200-1,800   DN

A 1960s Gucci black patent-leather box purse, stamped 'MADE IN ITALY by Gucci'.

9.5in (24cm (9.5in) wide

$300-500   DN

A Gucci brown 'logo' tapestry and leather purse, no. 001.3814 003754, with chrome-plated fittings, stamped 'MADE IN ITALY' and with leather Gucci label to interior.

$300-500   DN

An Hèrmes coral taurillon-clemence-leather 'Evelyne' purse, with palladium hardware, unlined, blindstamp square 'M', stamped 'Hèrmes'.

Taurillon clemence is a type of calf's leather.

2009   *12in (31cm) wide*

$2,500-3,500   LHA

QUICK REFERENCE - HERMÈS BAGS

● Hermès (founded 1837) is best known for the iconic 'Kelly' and 'Birkin' purses. The 'Kelly' was designed in the 1930s but shot to fame in 1956 when it was carried by Grace Kelly. The 'Birkin' was designed for actress Jane Birkin in 1984 and was based on a design from 1894. Both bags are symbols of wealth, success and luxury - as well as high style.

● Hermès bags are produced in a huge variety of different leathers and skins. The particular skin used, the color and any precious metals used for the fittings indicate the value. Some are purely 'in fashion' at the time so fetch a high price, while others are extremely rare or may even be unique. Prices can vary from high hundreds of dollars for a worn bag in a common leather, right up to over $150,000 for a rare skin and color! As well as the material, also pay attention to the condition, as considerable wear reduces value. Some wear is accepted.

● Fakes are known and can be extremely good, so it is no longer sufficient to look for metal parts stamped with the company name. Consider the type of metal, the quality of the plating, stitching and the style of the lettering, numbering and lining. If in doubt, take the bag to Hermès for identification.

An Hermès green ostrich-leather 'Market' tote bag, with drawstring closure, stamped 'Hermès'.

This bag was designed to resemble a sailor sac that Hermès produced for the beach.

11in (27cm) high

$2,500-3,500   LHA

An Hermès marron foncé ostrich-leather 'Birkin' purse, with palladium fittings and hardware, blindstamped, stamped 'Hermès Paris', with CITES papers.

The fact that this bag has the necessary papers allowing it to be exported overseas makes it a more commercial item. If it did not have these papers, then the market would be limited.

2006   *12in (30cm) wide*

$12,000-18,000   LHA

An Hermès chartreuse togo-leather 'Birkin' purse, with palladium hardware, blindstamped, stamped 'Hermès'.

2008 14.5in (35cm) wide

$15,000-20,000   LHA

A Moschino blue leather 'Sand Pail' bag, decorated with beach-motif appliques, with suede lining, stamped 'Moschino'.

7in (18cm) high

$400-600   LHA

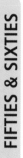

A 1950s painted-plaster table lamp, in the form of an exotic lady, with original shade, both in mint condition.

This lamp is worth as much as it is due to its unusual style, which brings to mind Vladimir Tretchikoff's highly popular prints. The lamp is complete with its rare original shade and both parts are in mint condition, which is also vital to value.

23.5in (60cm) high

$300-400   MA

A 1950s painted-plaster 'Chinese Girl' table lamp, in mint condition, the original ovoid shade in mint condition.

24in (61cm) high

$250-350   MA

A 1950s Japanese painted-plaster 'Calypso' table lamp, stamped 'FOREIGN', with original shade.

15in (38.5cm) high

$150-250   MA

A 1960s-70s rocket-style lamp, with teak three-legged base and orange spun-fiberglass shade.

Any damage to the brittle shade will reduce the value. Some shade colors, such as peach, are rare but the classic orange is always popular.

44.5in (113cm) high

$150-250   WHP

A late 1950s Formica-topped coffee table, the Formica printed with musical instruments in gray and black on a hatched background.

48in (122cm) long

$300-500   MA

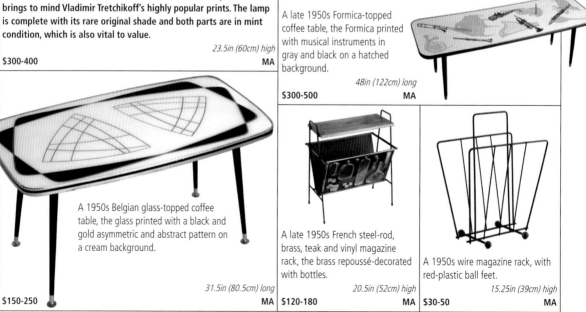

A 1950s Belgian glass-topped coffee table, the glass printed with a black and gold asymmetric and abstract pattern on a cream background.

31.5in (80.5cm) long

$150-250   MA

A late 1950s French steel-rod, brass, teak and vinyl magazine rack, the brass repoussé-decorated with bottles.

20.5in (52cm) high

$120-180   MA

A 1950s wire magazine rack, with red-plastic ball feet.

15.25in (39cm) high

$30-50   MA

Mark Picks

These wall decorations were highly fashionable during the mid-1950s and were mass-produced and sold inexpensively. As they were cheap to buy, most were thrown away as fashion changed. This means they are relatively rare today, particularly in such good condition, since the thin metal is easily bent and, if it does bend, the paint usually flakes off.

Although these decorations are fashionable once again, these particular examples aren't that valuable as the Chinese man motifs aren't particularly sought after. Skiers and musicians are more desirable and can fetch up to $70 each.

A pair of mid-1950s painted-wire and pressed-metal octagonal wall decorations, one showing a Chinese man pulling a cart, the other showing a Chinese man with an umbrella.

11.25in (28.5cm) high

$30-50   MA

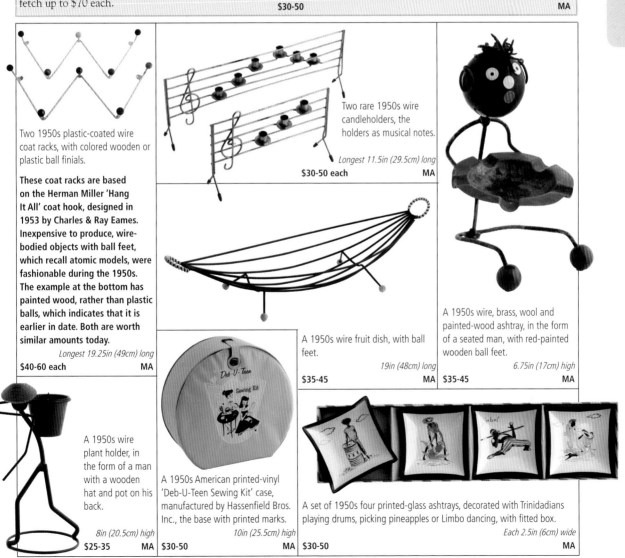

Two 1950s plastic-coated wire coat racks, with colored wooden or plastic ball finials.

These coat racks are based on the Herman Miller 'Hang It All' coat hook, designed in 1953 by Charles & Ray Eames. Inexpensive to produce, wire-bodied objects with ball feet, which recall atomic models, were fashionable during the 1950s. The example at the bottom has painted wood, rather than plastic balls, which indicates that it is earlier in date. Both are worth similar amounts today.

Longest 19.25in (49cm) long

$40-60 each   MA

Two rare 1950s wire candleholders, the holders as musical notes.

Longest 11.5in (29.5cm) long

$30-50 each   MA

A 1950s wire fruit dish, with ball feet.

19in (48cm) long

$35-45   MA

A 1950s wire, brass, wool and painted-wood ashtray, in the form of a seated man, with red-painted wooden ball feet.

6.75in (17cm) high

$35-45   MA

A 1950s wire plant holder, in the form of a man with a wooden hat and pot on his back.

8in (20.5cm) high

$25-35   MA

A 1950s American printed-vinyl 'Deb-U-Teen Sewing Kit' case, manufactured by Hassenfield Bros. Inc., the base with printed marks.

10in (25.5cm) high

$30-50   MA

A set of 1950s four printed-glass ashtrays, decorated with Trinidadians playing drums, picking pineapples or Limbo dancing, with fitted box.

Each 2.5in (6cm) wide

$30-50   MA

FISHING

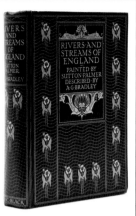

'Angling & Art in Scotland', by Ernest E Briggs, first edition, published by Longmans, Green & Co., the half title page inscribed by the author to 'H.D.B. Anderson', with 32 color plates, captioned tissue guards and illustrations, with catalog of watercolors by Briggs loosely inserted, with original pictorial cloth.

Anderson was Ernest Briggs's favorite ghillie - a ghillie is a man or boy who acts as an attendant on a fishing, fly fishing, hunting, or deer stalking expedition.

1908

$700-1,000 BLO

'Blacker's Art of Fly Making', by William Blacker, second edition, published by George Nichols, with engraved frontispiece, engraved title and 20 plates, with original blind-stamped green cloth, with very slight rubbing.

The first edition (1842) was only 48 pages. The 1855 edition was considerably expanded by Blacker with hand-painted, colored illustrations and 252 pages.

1855

$650-850 BLO

'The Rivers and Streams of England', by A G Bradley, first edition, published by A & C Black, with color plates by Sutton Palmer, with original decorated cloth.

1909

$120-180 BLO

QUICK REFERENCE - FISHING

- The most recognisable and common item of fishing memorabilia is, of course, the stuffed fish (for examples, see p.343). However, a wide variety of other items are also available to fans of the relaxing art of fishing.
- The high point of production was during the first half of the 20thC, although fishing memorabilia was produced before this.
- Pieces that feature fish or fisherman as prominent motifs are likely to be the most desirable.
- Always look for quality in terms of design and craftsmanship.
- Appealing novelty forms and precious materials will usually add desirability and value.
- Books are always popular, particularly if the cover is decorative and appealing.

'The Practical Fisherman', by John Harrington Keene, first edition in book form, published by L Upcott Gill, with wood-engraved frontispiece and plates, the front free endpaper with previous owner's signature, with original pictorial cloth, gilt, with slight rubbing.

1881

$300-500 BLO

'Trouting in Norway', by General E F Burton, first edition, published by Carlisle & London, with photographic plates, with original cloth.

1897

$150-250 BLO

'The Fly', by Andrew Herd, first edition, published by Medlar Press, one of 99 specially-bound copies from a limited edition of 599, with original tan leather.

2001

$400-600 BLO

'Fishing Tackle, its Materials and Manufacture', by John Harrington Keene, first edition, published by Ward Lock & Co., with wood-engraved frontispiece, 4 folding plates and illustrations, with original decorated cloth, with some rubbing and soiling.

1886

$400-600 BLO

'Tips by the Author of The Salmon Fly', by George M Kelson, first edition, published by the author, with illustrations, with original cloth, with slight rubbing and a few stains.

1901

$400-600 BLO

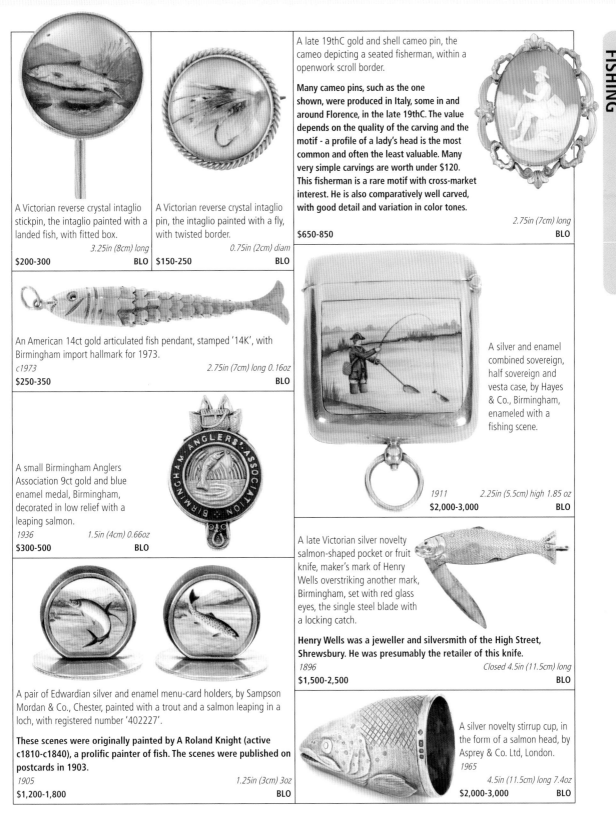

A Victorian reverse crystal intaglio stickpin, the intaglio painted with a landed fish, with fitted box.

3.25in (8cm) long

$200-300   **BLO**

A Victorian reverse crystal intaglio pin, the intaglio painted with a fly, with twisted border.

0.75in (2cm) diam

$150-250   **BLO**

A late 19thC gold and shell cameo pin, the cameo depicting a seated fisherman, within a openwork scroll border.

Many cameo pins, such as the one shown, were produced in Italy, some in and around Florence, in the late 19thC. The value depends on the quality of the carving and the motif - a profile of a lady's head is the most common and often the least valuable. Many very simple carvings are worth under $120. This fisherman is a rare motif with cross-market interest. He is also comparatively well carved, with good detail and variation in color tones.

2.75in (7cm) long

$650-850   **BLO**

An American 14ct gold articulated fish pendant, stamped '14K', with Birmingham import hallmark for 1973.

c1973   *2.75in (7cm) long 0.16oz*

$250-350   **BLO**

A small Birmingham Anglers Association 9ct gold and blue enamel medal, Birmingham, decorated in low relief with a leaping salmon.

1936   *1.5in (4cm) 0.66oz*

$300-500   **BLO**

A silver and enamel combined sovereign, half sovereign and vesta case, by Hayes & Co., Birmingham, enameled with a fishing scene.

1911   *2.25in (5.5cm) high 1.85 oz*

$2,000-3,000   **BLO**

A late Victorian silver novelty salmon-shaped pocket or fruit knife, maker's mark of Henry Wells overstriking another mark, Birmingham, set with red glass eyes, the single steel blade with a locking catch.

Henry Wells was a jeweller and silversmith of the High Street, Shrewsbury. He was presumably the retailer of this knife.

1896   *Closed 4.5in (11.5cm) long*

$1,500-2,500   **BLO**

A pair of Edwardian silver and enamel menu-card holders, by Sampson Mordan & Co., Chester, painted with a trout and a salmon leaping in a loch, with registered number '402227'.

These scenes were originally painted by A Roland Knight (active c1810-c1840), a prolific painter of fish. The scenes were published on postcards in 1903.

1905   *1.25in (3cm) 3oz*

$1,200-1,800   **BLO**

A silver novelty stirrup cup, in the form of a salmon head, by Asprey & Co. Ltd, London.

1965

4.5in (11.5cm) long 7.4oz

$2,000-3,000   **BLO**

FISHING

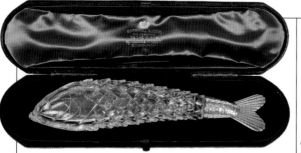

Fish

A very rare late 18thC child's stained-ivory alphabet roundel, for the letter F.

1.5in (4cm) diam

$100-150   **BLO**

A late Victorian inlaid tortoiseshell cigar case, one side decorated with a seated man fishing, the other with a vacant shield, the blue silk interior with pockets and a sanded striker paper.

6in (15cm) long

$800-1,200   **BLO**

A Victorian silver-mounted cut-glass novelty perfume bottle, in the form of a fish, the silver screw-on cover by Sampson Mordan & Co., London the leather case from Marshall & Sons, Goldsmiths to the Queen, Edinburgh with an applied plaque reading 'Gwendoline from Johnnie 15:II:87'.

This form is rare, high quality and would appeal to collectors of perfume bottles as well as to collectors of fishing memorabilia.

1884   *6.75in (17cm) long*

$1,500-2,500   **BLO**

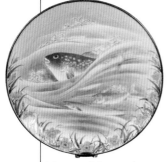

A Japanese Fukagawa charger, decorated with a fish swimming in waves, the reverse with prunus blossoms.

c1900   *13.5in (34.5cm) diam*

$120-180   **BLO**

A late 19thC French majolica dish, in the Palissy style, modeled in relief with a fish, insects, lizard and ferns.

7.5in (19cm) long

$500-700   **BLO**

Left: A Royal Worcester majolica pike's head jug, the base with impressed mark.

c1870   *12.25in (31cm) high*

$300-500   **BLO**

Right: A Royal Worcester parian pike's head jug, the base with impressed mark.

11.75in (30cm) high

$250-350   **BLO**

A 20thC cold-painted bronze model of a salmon, by Fritz Bermann, the underside impressed 'BERMANN WIEN'.

A late 19thC Bohemian pale-green glass vase, probably Harrach, enameled with carp among pondweed.

9.5in (24cm) diam

$250-350   **PC**

A late 19thC French patinated-bronze figure of a fisher boy, after 'Geo. Omer' (probably Georges Ormerth), signed in the maquette.

12.75in (32.5cm) high

$300-500   **BLO**

Mathias Bermann established a bronze foundry in Hernals, near Vienna, Austria in 1850. His descendent Fritz Bermann expanded the company from 1927 until his death in 1967, widening the range of animal models. Since 1991 the company has been owned and run by Alfred Kirchner. Similar to the work of the more famous Bergmann company, this model is well cast and naturalistically painted. It is also large, which is desirable.

9.5in (24cm) long

$1,000-1,500   **BLO**

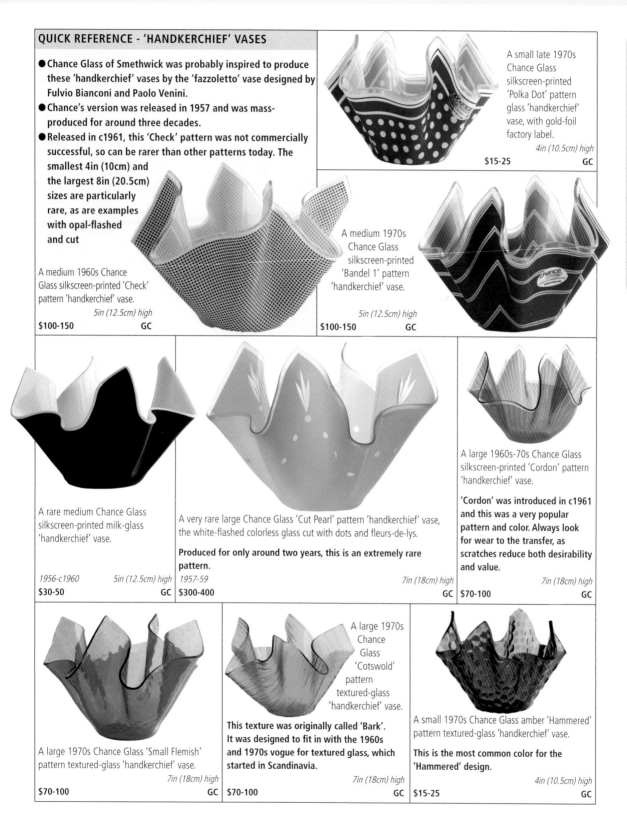

QUICK REFERENCE - 'HANDKERCHIEF' VASES

- Chance Glass of Smethwick was probably inspired to produce these 'handkerchief' vases by the 'fazzoletto' vase designed by Fulvio Bianconi and Paolo Venini.
- Chance's version was released in 1957 and was mass-produced for around three decades.
- Released in c1961, this 'Check' pattern was not commercially successful, so can be rarer than other patterns today. The smallest 4in (10cm) and the largest 8in (20.5cm) sizes are particularly rare, as are examples with opal-flashed and cut

A small late 1970s Chance Glass silkscreen-printed 'Polka Dot' pattern glass 'handkerchief' vase, with gold-foil factory label.

4in (10.5cm) high

$15-25   GC

A medium 1960s Chance Glass silkscreen-printed 'Check' pattern 'handkerchief' vase.

5in (12.5cm) high

$100-150   GC

A medium 1970s Chance Glass silkscreen-printed 'Bandel 1' pattern 'handkerchief' vase.

5in (12.5cm) high

$100-150   GC

A rare medium Chance Glass silkscreen-printed milk-glass 'handkerchief' vase.

1956-c1960   5in (12.5cm) high

$30-50   GC

A very rare large Chance Glass 'Cut Pearl' pattern 'handkerchief' vase, the white-flashed colorless glass cut with dots and fleurs-de-lys.

Produced for only around two years, this is an extremely rare pattern.

1957-59   7in (18cm) high

$300-400   GC

A large 1960s-70s Chance Glass silkscreen-printed 'Cordon' pattern 'handkerchief' vase.

'Cordon' was introduced in c1961 and this was a very popular pattern and color. Always look for wear to the transfer, as scratches reduce both desirability and value.

7in (18cm) high

$70-100   GC

A large 1970s Chance Glass 'Small Flemish' pattern textured-glass 'handkerchief' vase.

7in (18cm) high

$70-100   GC

A large 1970s Chance Glass 'Cotswold' pattern textured-glass 'handkerchief' vase.

This texture was originally called 'Bark'. It was designed to fit in with the 1960s and 1970s vogue for textured glass, which started in Scandinavia.

7in (18cm) high

$70-100   GC

A small 1970s Chance Glass amber 'Hammered' pattern textured-glass 'handkerchief' vase.

This is the most common color for the 'Hammered' design.

4in (10.5cm) high

$15-25   GC

GLASS

QUICK REFERENCE - HARRACH

- The first mention of a glassworks on the location where Harrach stands was in 1684. The noble Harrach family acquired the area in 1701 and the first official mention of a 'new glassworks' in Neuwelt, Bohemia (now Czech Republic) is in 1712.
- The 19thC saw the glassworks enter a 'golden age' of design quality and production. Harrach took part in many prestigious international exhibitions from 1828 onward.
- Designs from the 18thC to the early 20thC were produced or overseen by the following administrators: Anton Erben (d.1795), Martin Kaiser (d.1808), Johann Pohl (1769-1850, director of the factory 1808-50), Wilhelm Erben, Josef Petricek and Julius Jelinek.
- Key later designers in the 20thC include Rudolf Schwedler and Milan Metelak.
- Much of the company's production was exported to other European countries.
- The extent, influence and importance of Harrach's tens of thousands of designs are only just being uncovered and reappraised. It is therefore likely that Harrach may soon be recognized as one of the major producers of glass in Europe.

A Harrach cameo-glass vase, the orange glass overlaid with green, deeply cut with a stylized flower, with gilded highlights.
c1898   *8in (20.5cm) high*
$1,500-2,500   **MDM**

A Harrach glass vase, the top half cut with a flower and the bottom with stems, with raised trefoil and stylized floral designed rim and foot decoration, the base with shape code.

This shape was produced in four sizes and was one of the most commonly used for the 1900 World's Fair in Paris. The form and the patterns used to decorate it were probably designed by Julius Jelinek.
c1900   *7in (17.5cm) high*
$1,000-1,500   **MDM**

A large Harrach cameo-glass vase, the colorless glass overlaid with pink blackberries, stems and leaves, with gilded highlights.
c1898
$2,500-3,500   **MDM**

A Harrach Art Nouveau mold-blown glass 'Maigrün' (dark green) vase, decorated with raised and gilded lotus flowers, stems and leaves.
1901   *11in (28cm) high*
$1,000-1,500   **MDM**

A small Harrach glass japonaiserie vase, designed by Josef Petricek, the white opal-glass body partially overlaid with green glass, decorated with raised and gilded leaves, vines, flowers and bugs, the base with Harrach plume mark.
c1885
$500-700   **MDM**

A pair of large Harrach mold-blown glass 'Bamboo' vases, the agate-glass with colored and foil inclusions, decorated with raised, gilded and painted bamboo leaves and bands.
c1890
13in (33cm) high
$2,000-3,000 MDM

A Harrach glass 'Formosa' vase, designed by Julius Jelinek in 1900, the red opal-glass with green and gold-foil inclusions, painted and gilded with mistletoe leaves and berries.
c1900-05   *6in (15cm) high*
$1,000-1,500   **MDM**

A tall Harrach glass vase, from the 'Moravia' range, the colorless glass body with applied and melted-in blue and green combed swirls, the gilt rim with stylized floral motifs.

c1901

$1,000-1,500   MDM

A small Harrach glass vase, the amber glass body applied with enameled and gilded blue-glass trails in the form of fish, with blue and red opal-glass fishing line and worm.

A similar example can be found in the Harrach factory museum. This technique and look was used at Harrach from 1880, when it was used to produce glass enameled with Japanese motifs similar to that produced by Auguste Jean (c1830-active until 1904).

1898

$1,200-1,800   MDM

A small Harrach glass vase, the gray body applied with blue rim and dripped trails on the neck, decorated with red, gray and blue stylized leaves, flowers and stems.

The form, decoration and colors are typical of this type of Harrach vase.

c1880   *4in (10cm) high*

$250-350   MDM

A Harrach glass dish, in the form of a lily pad, the brown glass body applied with blue rim and dripped trails and hand-cut with radiating lines.

c1880   *8in (20.5cm) diam*

$400-600   MDM

A Harrach glass japonaiserie vase, the gray glass body with applied blue pendant trails and bosses, enameled with cartouches containing stylized bugs, flowering branches, and geometric patterns.

c1895

$800-1,200   MDM

A Harrach copper-mounted glass vase, the iridized white on red glass body with combed trail decoration, with a Secessionist-style copper mount.

c1900   *8in (20.5cm) high*

$1,200-1,800   MDM

A Harrach bronze-mounted mold-blown glass vase, molded and gilded with a flower and leaves, the mount with marks for Carl Deffner, with wear to gilding.

Carl Deffner (1856-1948) was a metalware manufacturer based in Esslingen am Neckar, near Stuttgart in Germany. His work and that of his company was strongly influenced by the Art Nouveau style and the work of the Weiner Werkstätte.

c1900

$1,200-1,800   MDM

GLASS

A 1960s Harrach glass 'Evening Blue' vase, designed by Milan Metelàk in 1961, the bubble inclusions containing mica chips.

9.25in (23.5cm) high

$150-250   **DA&H**

A late 1950s-60s Harrach 'Evening Blue' glass bud vase, designed by Milan Metelàk in 1957, overlaid in colorless glass.

8in (20.5cm) high

$120-180   **MHC**

A 1960s Harrach 'Topaz' glass bud vase, no.4/4357, designed by Milan Metelàk in 1961, overlaid in colorless glass.

7in (18cm) high

$200-300   **MHC**

QUICK REFERENCE - 'HARRTIL' RANGE

- The 'Harrtil' range was designed by Harrach's Technical Director Milos Pulpitel in 1955.
- It was inspired by Venetian lace glass. Rather than the net being composed of applied trails, as in the Venetian version, the 'Harrtil' design is composed of a net of woven glass fibers sandwiched between two layers of glass. This creates the more regular mesh effect. Vases with additional applied streaks (such as the colorless and blue vase on this page) are unique as the streaks were applied by hand.
- 'Harrtil' vases are considerably rarer than bowls and ashtrays, which are relatively common. Facet-cut 'Harrtil' is particularly rare.
- Designers of shapes included Milan Metelàk, Rudolf Schwedler, Milena Velísková and Maria Stáhlíková.

A late 1950s-60s Harrach glass vase, designed by Milan Metelàk and Milos Pulpitel in 1957, from the 'Harrtil' range.

8in (20.5cm) high

$350-450   **MHC**

A Borské Sklo blue glass 'Large Olives' barrel vase.

14in (35.5cm) high

$70-100   **GAZE**

A late 1950s-60s Harrach green glass vase, designed by Rudolf Schwedler and Milos Pulpitel in 1957, from the 'Harrtil' range, with colorless applied pad-foot.

8in (20.5cm) high

$350-450   **MHC**

A mid-late 1970s Chlum u Třeboně glass 'Clown' vase, designed by Jan Gabrhel in 1974, the mottled yellow waisted body overlaid with colorless glass, with a sprayed matt red enamel band.

8in (20.5cm) high

$200-300   **MHC**

A unique glass bottle-vase, designed by Pavel Hlava and probably made at the Chlum u Třeboně glassworks, with metal-oxide foil inclusions and internal air bubbles, the base signed by Pavel Hlava and dated.

1966   17.5in (44.5cm) high
$1,200-1,800   **QU**

A late 1970s Chlum u Třeboně glass 'Clown' vase, designed by Jan Gabrhel in 1974, the mottled yellow double-waisted body overlaid with colorless glass and with sprayed matte red enamel bands and spots.

A column of dots is a recurring motif in Gabrhel's work. Where they are applied to forms that resemble stylized torsos, they can appear like buttons on clothing. Gabrhel was one of Czechoslovakia's most mercurial designers, producing a vast range of very different designs.

8in (20.5cm) high
$200-300   **MHC**

A mid-late 1980s Chřibská glass bowl, designed by Josef Hospodka in 1986, the pink body with thin vertical lines of tiny particles and folded rim.

5.25in (13cm) high
$80-120   **MHC**

A 1960s-70s Chřibská glass organic vase, designed by Josef Hospodka in the 1950s, with 'CJ' foil label.

The 'CJ' label is for Jones & Co, a British distributor of Czech glass and other items. Many of Hospodka's organic designs were highly successful and were consequently produced into the 1990s.

4.75in (12cm) high
$50-70   **WHP**

A 1960s-70s Exbor glass model of a fish, designed by Josef Rozinek and Stanislav Honzík in 1958, unknown model number, the base with acid-etched mark and foil sticker.

8.75in (22cm) high
$550-750   **PC**

A late 1960s-80s Exbor glass vase, designed by Pavel Hlava in 1964, the blue glass overlaid with metal-oxide foil spiral and with air-bubble inclusions, with a broad-cut facet, overlaid with yellow and colorless glass, the base with circular acid-etched mark.

8.75in (22.5cm) high
$400-600   **QU**

An Exbor glass 'Monolith' vase, designed by Pavel Hlava in 1958, with flat polished front and back, the base with circular 'Exbor' acid-etched mark and 'PH' monogram.

The presence of Hlava's monogram indicates that he made this piece himself or oversaw its production directly - this is extremely rare. Other, similar forms from the same range were produced into the 1990s and probably beyond. Unmarked examples in very bright colors or those with internal bubbles or 'creases' are likely to be of more recent manufacture.

1958-65   7.25in (18.5cm) high
$1,200-1,800   **MHC**

GLASS

A (Sklo Union) Hermanova Glassworks light-blue pressed glass vase, no.20047, designed by František Vizner in 1962.

7.75in (19.5cm) high

$200-300   MHC

A 1950s-70s Karlovarske Sklo glass freeform organic vase, overlaid in amber, light green, dark green and colorless glass.

The designer of these large and extravagant vases is not yet known. The hallmark curving 'wings' were created by shooting compressed air at the molten glass. The asymmetric rim was cut and swung as well as being manipulated with compressed air.

12.5in (32cm) high

$250-350   MHC

A Mstisov or Moser glass 'Romana' vase, designed by Hana Machovska in c1961, with applied blue and pink stripes on an amber and colorless glass body.

8.5in (22cm) high

$200-300   MHC

A CLOSER LOOK AT A CZECH GLASS VASE

The simple forms of this futuristic range appear almost machine-like, while the applied prunts look like something from outer space.

The prunts are in blue glass, but appear green due to light passing though the amber glass. They can also be found with rounded and leaf-shaped patterns.

The desirable range was also produced with the main body in vivid light green, pink and light and dark blue. The colorway shown is the most common.

This is an unusually large, rare size for this range.

It has many prunts, which is a desirable feature.

A 1970s Prachen glass 'Applied Vase', designed by Josef Hospodka in 1969, no.40114, the amber glass with applied blue prunts impressed with a grid design, with polished base.

12.5in (32cm) high

$500-700   MHC

A mid-late 1970s Prachen glass 'Knobbly Pineapple' vase, designed by František Koudelka in 1972.

The glass used here contains colloidal gold, which turns through oranges into deep red depending on how long it is reheated.

5in (12.5cm) high

$80-120   MHC

A Rosice pressed-glass vase, designed by an unknown designer in c1957, no.959, the yellow glass overlaid with green, decorated bands of lenses.

This shape is usually found in colorless glass, with that variation usually being worth around $30-50. This colorway is very unusual. Available in three sizes, this shape was also found with alternating frosted and clear lenses.

8in (20cm) high

$50-70   MHC

A very rare Crystalex mold-blown, overlaid and trailed glass vase, designed by Ivo Rozsypal in 1978.

10.25in (26cm) high

$300-400   MHC

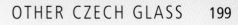

A multi-colored glass 'Cake' sculpture, by Miluse Roubíckovà, with applied colored trails and spots and crimped border.

Miluse Roubíckovà (b.1922) is married to one of the Czech Republic's leading glass designers, Réné Roubicek (b.1923). Together, Réné and Miluse built up an international reputation from the 1950s onward and were highly influential and inspirational to glass designers from Czechoslovakia and other countries. These 'Cake' forms were first shown at the International Exposition in 1967 in Montréal, but this example may have been made later.

10.5in (26.5cm) wide

$1,500-2,500   QU

A Skrdlovice glass vase, designed by Milena Velíšková in 1959, no.5925, with internal pink stripes, with original 'ARCADIA Czechoslovakia' distributor's label.

10.25in (26cm) high

$120-180   FIS

A Skrdlovice amber glass vase, designed by Jan Kotik in 1954, no.54132, with asymmetric opening and well, with original foil label.

4.5in (11.5cm) high

$80-120   GROB

A very rare Skrdlovice glass vase, designed by František Vizner in 1967, no.6763, the toffee-brown colored glass overlaid with a heavy olive-green foot, with 'HAND MADE BOHEMIAN CRYSTAL CZECHOSLOVAKIA' silver-foil importer's label.

7.75in (17.5cm) high

$500-700   GC

A 1990s Skrdlovice glass vase, designed by Ladislav Palecek in 1977, no.7719, the colorless glass thickly overlaid in green and blue, with paper factory label, with polished base.

6.75in (17.5cm) high

$150-250   GC

A 1960s-80s Železný Brod Sklo (ZBS) glass bud-like vase, probably designed by Miloslav Klinger or Josef Cvrček, with pulled rim and blown bubble in base, with blue and silver foil factory label.

Many ZBS designs have been in continuous production since they were introduced in the 1950s and onward. As a result, some pieces are very common. This vase - or the label at least - predates 1989 as the label reads 'Czechoslovakia' rather than 'Czech Republic'. At the time of writing, many ZBS designs are still available in souvenir shops across the Czech Republic, although color tones tend to be bolder and brasher.

9.5in (24cm) high

$80-120   GC

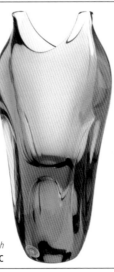

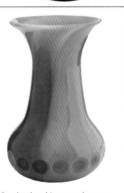

A Czechoslovakian translucent 'Lithyalin'-type glass vase, the bottom cut with lenses, with broken pontil mark.

Lithyalin glass was developed by Frederick Egermann in 1828 and mimics stone.

c1900   5in (12.5cm) high

$80-120   PC

A Czechoslovakian dichroic-glass wine goblet, with a colorless stem.

The color of this glass changes from pink and blue to yellow-green under different lights.

5.25in (13cm) high

$25-35   GROB

GLASS

QUICK REFERENCE - D'ARGENTAL & PAUL NICOLAS

- D'Argental was a brand name created in c1918 by the St Louis glassworks, predominantly for its Gallé- and Daum-style cameo-glass range. D'Argental glass was relatively unsuccessful until Paul Nicolas (a former protégée of Émile Gallé and also his chief designer) and other ex-Gallé employees were persuaded to work for St Louis in 1919.
- Cameo pieces signed 'D'Argental' with a small 'SL' (for St Louis) are often unconnected to Nicolas and his colleagues. Early Nicolas-designed pieces were signed 'St Louis Nancy', but this soon changed to 'D'Argental' with Nicolas adding a Cross of Lorraine to any piece he made personally. He also made pieces for his own sales, which were signed 'Paul Nicolas' (often with 'Nancy'). These are rarer.
- Nicolas continued to work with St Louis throughout most of the 1920s. After that he mostly made one-off commission pieces until his death in 1952.
- D'Argental cameo glass is usually made of lead crystal, which allowed for high levels of wheel-cut detail. Dark, reddish brown, caramelly colors are typical.
- Although not as well known as their competitors, Paul Nicolas and D'Argental produced very high quality pieces. Interest in and prices being paid for pieces are rising. They could be a good investment for the future.

A D'Argental cameo-glass vase, designed and made by Paul Nicolas, signed 'D'Argental' with a Cross of Lorraine within the design.
c1925   *9in (23cm) high*
$3,000-5,000   **MDM**

A D'Argental cameo-glass vase, designed by Paul Nicolas, the colorless glass overlaid in blue and violet, acid etched with clematis, with frosted ground, signed 'D'Argental' within the design.
c1925   *7.5in (17.5cm) high*
$1,200-1,800   **DOR**

A D'Argental cameo-glass vase, designed and made by Paul Nicolas, the yellow-orange glass overlaid with red, decorated with leaves, signed 'D'Argental' with a Cross of Lorraine within the design.
c1925   *9in (23cm) high*
$3,000-5,000   **MDM**

A Paul Nicolas cameo-glass vase, partly made at the St Louis glassworks, designed and made by Paul Nicolas for his own private sales, signed 'Paul Nicolas Nancy' within the design.
                    6in(15cm) high
$2,500-3,500   **MDM**

A D'Argental cameo-glass vase, designed and made by Paul Nicolas, orange glass overlaid in dark red, decorated with thistles, signed 'D'Argental' with a Cross of Lorraine within the design.
c1925   *6in (15.5cm) high*
$1,800-2,200   **MDM**

A D'Argental cameo-glass vase, designed by Paul Nicolas, the yellow glass overlaid with deep red, carved with stylized flowers, signed 'D'Argental' within the design.
                    8in (20cm) high
$2,000-3,000   **PC**

A D'Argental cameo-glass vase, designed and made by Paul Nicolas, the orange glass overlaid in dark red, decorated with orchids, signed 'D'Argental' with a Cross of Lorraine within the design.
                    6in (15cm) high
$1,500-2,500   **MDM**

A D'Argental cameo-glass vase, designed by Paul Nicolas, the orange glass overlaid with red and brown, decorated with a landscape, signed 'D'Argental' within the design.

c1925   6in (15.25cm) high
$2,000-3,000   **MDM**

A D'Argental cameo-glass vase, designed and made by Paul Nicolas, decorated with datura, signed 'D'Argental' with a Cross of Lorraine within the design.

c1925   9in (22.5cm) high
$2,500-3,500   **MDM**

A D'Argental cameo-glass vase, designed by Paul Nicolas, the orange glass overlaid with brown, decorated with a landscape, signed 'D'Argental' within the design, with original retailer's label.

c1925   12in (30.5cm) high
$3,000-5,000   **MDM**

A D'Argental cameo-glass vase, designed by Paul Nicolas, the orange glass overlaid with red, decorated with a landscape, signed 'D'Argental' within the design.

c1925   4in (10cm) high
$2,000-3,000   **MDM**

A rare early D'Argental fire-polished cameo-glass box and cover, designed and made by Paul Nicolas, signed 'St Louis Nancy' within the design.

c1919   5in (12.5cm) diam
$2,500-3,500   **MDM**

A rare D'Argental cameo-glass lamp, designed and made by Paul Nicolas, signed 'D'Argental' with a Cross of Lorraine within the design.

A D'Argental cameo-glass vase, designed and made by Paul Nicolas, decorated with a landscape, signed 'D'Argental' signed D'Argental' with a Cross of Lorraine within the design.

c1925   6in (15.5cm) high
$2,000-3,000   **MDM**

c1925   14in (35.5cm) high
$4,000-6,000   **MDM**

A small D'Argental cameo glass bowl, designed and made at St Louis, inscribed 'trois châteaux d'eguisheim' (probably as a tourist piece), signed 'D'Argental SL' within the design.

c1923   4in (10cm) high
$1,500-2,500   **MDM**

GLASS

QUICK REFERENCE - LOETZ

- The glass factory that became known as Loetz was founded in Klostermühle, Austria in 1836 by Johann Eisner.
- It became known as Loetz Witwe (Loetz Widow, more commonly just 'Loetz') when Susanna Loetz, widow of glass entrepreneur Johann Loetz, acquired the factory in 1852.
- In 1879 it passed to her descendent Max Ritter von Spaun and began to flourish as a result of the designs of von Spaun himself, as well as E Prochaska and Franz Hofstätter. Other notable Loetz designers include Michael Powolny, Koloman Moser and Josef Hoffmann.
- During the late 19thC and early 20thC, Loetz was one of the largest glassmakers in Central Europe and exported its products widely.
- Loetz's best-known ranges were heavily iridized and trailed in the Art Nouveau style. This 'Phänomen' vase is typical. As fashions changed, the company began to produce more brightly colored pieces, such as those pictured on p.203.
- The factory was enormously influential and many competitors copied or were inspired by Loetz designs. Today, this can cause problems as regards correct attributions.
- The company closed in 1947.
- For further information, visit www.loetz.com

A Loetz iridescent glass 'Medici' vase, the colorless glass overlaid in red-brown, the lower half covered with silver-yellow splashes pulled upward into four prongs.

c1902　　　　10in (26cm) high

$1,500-2,500　　　　**DOR**

A Loetz iridescent glass bottle-vase, with conical neck and lobed body, the base signed 'Loetz Austria'.

9.25in (23cm) high

$300-500　　　　**LHA**

A small Loetz iridescent glass 'Candia Papillon' vase, the colorless glass overlaid with silver-yellow powdered enamels.

4in (10cm) high

$150-250　　　　**FIS**

A small Loetz iridescent glass 'Titania' vase, the colorless glass overlaid with yellow and craquelure iridescent blue, overlaid with colorless glass.

c1905　　　　5.25in (13cm) high

$250-350　　　　**FIS**

A Loetz iridescent glass 'Phänomen' trumpet vase, the red glass trailed with combed silver-yellow bands, one pulled into a rosette, the base inscribed 'Loetz Austria'.

c1901　　　　7.5in (16.5cm) high

$5,000-7,000　　　　**DOR**

A Loetz iridescent glass 'Candia Silberiris Diaspora' vase, with pinched rim and cratered finish, the base etched 'Loetz Austria'.

c1900　　　　7.5in (19cm) high

$550-750　　　　**LHA**

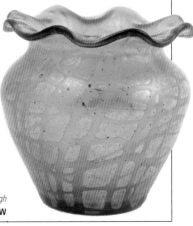

A Loetz iridescent glass vase, with veined-blue lustrous finish, unsigned.

4.5in (11.5cm) high

$500-700　　　　**WW**

GLASS

A small late 19thC Loetz iridescent glass model of an elephant, the colorless glass overlaid with silver-yellow powdered enamel, with applied ears, legs and tusks.

6.25in (16cm) high

$500-700   FIS

A late 19thC Loetz glass 'Karneol Marmoriertes' vase, the neck enameled with stylized leaves.

'Marmoriertes' (marbled) glass was intended to look like a semi-precious stone. It was introduced in the late 1880s and was issued in new colors, such as yellow and white, in 1906.

6in (15cm) high

$120-180   TRI

A small Loetz glass 'Streifen und Flecken (Stripes and Spots)' pattern vase, with applied orange stripes and patches.

c1900   *5in (10cm) high*

$650-850   DOR

A Loetz glass vase, with applied black trails and spots, overlaid in colorless glass.

c1925   *6in (15cm) high*

$350-450   FIS

A Loetz glass vase, with a black foot and applied black bosses and spiral trail.

c1925   *6.25in (16cm) high*

$250-350   FIS

A Loetz glass vase, from the 'Tango' range, with amethyst-colored threaded columns and rims, overlaid in colorless glass, unsigned.

Loetz's brightly colored 'Tango' designs (produced from c1905) are often all attributed to the Austrian ceramicist Michael Powolny (1871-1954). Although he certainly designed a number of shapes for the company, potentially including some three-handled and striped pieces, most 'Tango' designs were not by him.

11in (28cm) high

$650-850   WW

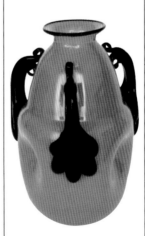

A Loetz glass vase, from the 'Tango' range, with 'knocked' sides and applied black scroll-work handles.

c1920   *8in (21cm) high*

$300-500   FLD

A Loetz glass vase, the blue glass overlaid in colorless, with applied black handles and rim.

c1915   *5.5in (14cm) high*

$200-300   FIS

QUICK REFERENCE - MDINA & ISLE OF WIGHT STUDIO GLASS

- Mdina Glass was founded by glassmaker Michael Harris (1933-94) in 1968 on the Mediterranean island of Malta. Harris used the newly developed studio glass techniques to produce unique, handmade glass that was different to the factory-produced glass of the period.
- The range he designed included vases, bowls, sculptures and paperweights. These pieces were made by newly trained Maltese glassmakers and two Italian glassmakers, who had trained at the British glass company Whitefriars.
- Colors are reminiscent of the Mediterranean, from the deep blue-green of the sea to the ochers and yellow of sandy beaches. Forms are typically chunkily blown, meaning that most pieces are heavy in weight. Production was aimed at the tourist market, but Harris's designs were also highly successful in export markets, such as the USA and Europe.
- Harris left Mdina in 1972 and founded a new glass studio on the Isle of Wight in the same year. The first ranges he designed at his new studio, for example 'Aurene' and 'Tortoiseshell', featured the same swirls and colors of his work on Mdina, but were more finely blown.
- The company's turning point came in 1978 with the introduction of the 'Azurene' range. It used 22ct gold and silver foil on the surface, initially on a very deep purple 'black' glass, but other colors were also used on later pieces. It was hugely successful and was exported across the world. The use of these fragmented foils became a hallmark of the company's designs. Values depends on the range (some are very rare), the shape and size.
- After Harris' death, the studio was run by his son and widow until it closed in January 2013. It reopened in different, smaller premises later that year.

A Mdina Glass 'Sculpture', designed and made by Michael Harris, in blue, green and yellow swirling glass, the base signed.

This a good example with a range of strong colors, but collectors obviously preferred the example to the right. It's also worth comparing the values of these two sculptures, which were both made and signed by Michael Harris, with the values of the taller, later examples on this page. As you can see, the signature makes a 'significant' difference!

c1970
$650-850

10in (25.5cm) wide
GAZE

A Mdina Glass 'Sculpture', designed and made by Michael Harris, in green and blue swirling glass, the base signed.

11in (28cm) high
$1,000-1,500
WW

A late 1970s Mdina Glass 'Sculpture', in blues, turquoise and colorless glass, the base inscribed 'Mdina'.

10in (25cm) high
$100-150
FLD

A large 1970s Mdina Glass freeform sculptural knot, in turquoise, blue and colorless glass, the base inscribed 'Mdina'.

8in (21cm) high
$100-150
FLD

A mid-late 1970s Mdina Glass 'Pulled Lobe' vase, designed by Michael Harris, in mottled and streaked ocher, green and blue glass, overlaid in colorless glass.

6in (15cm) high
$30-50
WHP

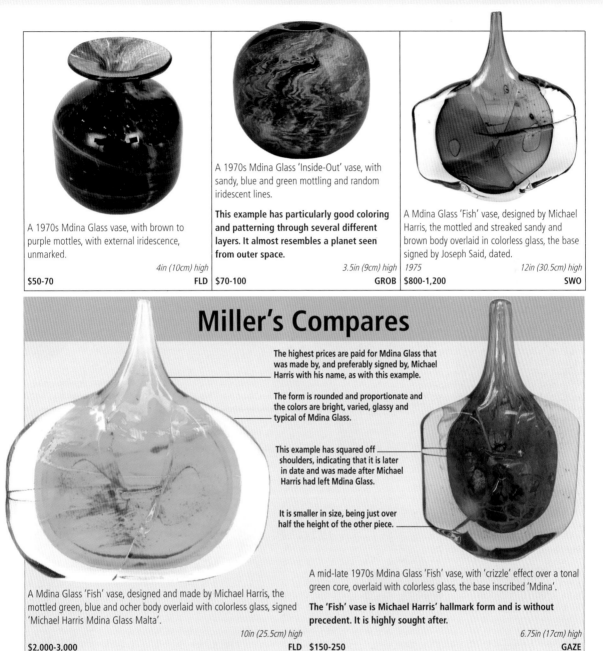

A 1970s Mdina Glass vase, with brown to purple mottles, with external iridescence, unmarked.

4in (10cm) high

$50-70   **FLD**

A 1970s Mdina Glass 'Inside-Out' vase, with sandy, blue and green mottling and random iridescent lines.

This example has particularly good coloring and patterning through several different layers. It almost resembles a planet seen from outer space.

3.5in (9cm) high

$70-100   **GROB**

A Mdina Glass 'Fish' vase, designed by Michael Harris, the mottled and streaked sandy and brown body overlaid in colorless glass, the base signed by Joseph Said, dated.

1975   *12in (30.5cm) high*

$800-1,200   **SWO**

Miller's Compares

The highest prices are paid for Mdina Glass that was made by, and preferably signed by, Michael Harris with his name, as with this example.

The form is rounded and proportionate and the colors are bright, varied, glassy and typical of Mdina Glass.

This example has squared off shoulders, indicating that it is later in date and was made after Michael Harris had left Mdina Glass.

It is smaller in size, being just over half the height of the other piece.

A Mdina Glass 'Fish' vase, designed and made by Michael Harris, the mottled green, blue and ocher body overlaid with colorless glass, signed 'Michael Harris Mdina Glass Malta'.

10in (25.5cm) high

$2,000-3,000   **FLD**

A mid-late 1970s Mdina Glass 'Fish' vase, with 'crizzle' effect over a tonal green core, overlaid with colorless glass, the base inscribed 'Mdina'.

The 'Fish' vase is Michael Harris' hallmark form and is without precedent. It is highly sought after.

6.75in (17cm) high

$150-250   **GAZE**

A Mdina Glass 'Fish' vase, shape designed by Michael Harris, from the 'Earthtones' color range designed by Eric Dobson or Joseph Said, unsigned.

10in (25.5cm) high

$200-300   **WW**

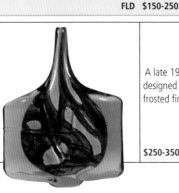

A late 1990s Mdina Glass 'Fish' vase, designed by Michael Harris, with frosted finish, unmarked.

12in (29.5cm) high

$250-350   **WW**

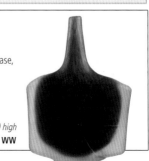

GLASS

A Mdina Glass bowl, designed and made by Michael Harris, with applied zigzag band in blue, the base signed 'Michael Harris Mdina Glass Malta 1967' and with applied paper label.

Dated signatures by Harris are extremely rare. This is a very early piece.

c1969   *5in (12.5cm) high*

$650-850   **WW**

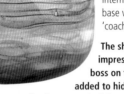

Two 1970s-80s Mdina Glass bowls, in colorless, blue and yellow mottled glass, one with a pulled and curled rim.

Taller 4.25in (11cm) high

$12-18 each   **WHP**

A mid-1970s-80s Mdina Glass stoppered bottle, with applied trails, the base inscribed 'Mdina', with paper label.

12in (30.5cm) high

$70-100   **FLD**

A 1980s Mdina Glass stoppered bottle, the orange body with applied blue-green trails, the base inscribed 'Mdina'.

8in (20.5cm) high

$50-70   **FLD**

An Isle of Wight Studio Glass squat vase, with pinky-beige striations and internal bubbles, the base with plain concave 'coachbolt' pontil mark.

The shallow, plain, impressed and applied boss on the base was added to hide the scar left by the removal of the pontil rod. It is known as the coachbolt mark because it was made by pushing a coachbolt into the hot, molten glass. This style of boss was only used in 1973 after which the 'flame' pontil mark was introduced. This piece is a rare, experimental colorway.

1973   *3in (7.5cm) high*

$150-250   **GC**

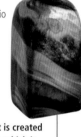

An Isle of Wight Studio Glass 'Blue Aurene' stoppered bottle, designed by Michael Harris, the base with impressed 'flame' pontil mark, missing stopper.

The iridescent effect is created when silver chloride, which is used to create the coloring, escapes from the area where the gob of glass joins the pontil. The silver chloride is then spread across the body as the piece is formed.

1974-c1982   *5.25in (14cm) high*

$120-180   **GC**

An Isle of Wight Studio Glass globe vase, designed by Michael Harris, from the 'Pink & Blue Swirls' range, the base with impressed 'flame' pontil mark.

1974-c1976   *5.5in (14cm) high*

$80-120   **GC**

Mark Picks

Any Isle of Wight Studio Glass piece engraved with a limited edition number from an edition of 500 was produced for export to American retailers, such as JC Penney. All the pieces from these editions were signed by Harris, immediately adding a premium.

Although the intention was to make 500 pieces, fewer were made and those that were crossed a number of ranges. This means that only a small number of each shape and size were made in each range. The green-toned 'Landscape' is the rarest of the three 'scapes' designed by Harris - 'Nightscape' and 'Seascape' continued to be produced for many years.

In general, the limited edition pieces were excellent examples of each design. I think they are sure to continue to be popular and sought after by collectors in the future.

An Isle of Wight Studio Glass limited edition 'Landscape' vase, designed by Michael Harris, the mottled green body with gold leaf inclusions and applied trails, the base signed 'Michael Harris, England, 30/500'.

c1987   *6in (15cm) high*

$500-700   **SWO**

A late 1920s-30s John Moncrieff Ltd. 'Monart' glass ovoid vase, shape CD, the colorless glass with swirling lemon and white inclusions and with further green and pink inclusions.

8.25in (21cm) high

$500-700 L&T

A late 1920s-30s John Moncrieff Ltd. 'Monart' glass vase, shape MF, the colorless glass with swirling lemon and white inclusions and with further green and pink inclusions.

7in (18cm) high

$400-600 L&T

A late 1920s-30s John Moncrieff Ltd. 'Monart' glass ovoid vase, shape JA, the mottled red core overlaid in colorless glass, with aventurine inclusions, with bruise to base.

6.75in (17cm) high

$300-500 WW

QUICK REFERENCE - MONART GLASS

- Monart glass was produced by John Moncrieff Ltd. in Perth, Scotland 1924-61. Design and manufacture was led by Salvador Ysart and his sons.
- Over 300 designs were produced, with many shapes inspired by Chinese ceramics.
- Monart glass is typified by mottled, colored patterns with internal sparkling aventurine specks - such mottled or cloudy glass was fashionable during the 1920s and '30s. Prices reached a peak in the early 2000s, but have declined somewhat. A revival of interest, and hopefully values, is widely anticipated.

A late 1920s-30s John Moncrieff Ltd. 'Monart' glass flared trumpet vase, shape TC, with applied foot, the colorless glass with swirling lemon and white inclusions and with further green and pink inclusions.

10.25in (26cm) high

$500-700 L&T

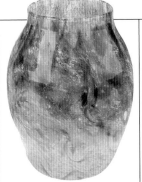

A late 1920s-30s John Moncrieff Ltd. 'Monart' glass ovoid vase, shape A, the pink glass with colored splashes, the base with paper label reading 'VI.A.455A'.

The detail on the label include the shape (A), the intended size (VI = 8in (20.5cm) high) and the colors (455: pinks, mauves, white and gold aventurine). Most labels have been lost over time or were removed after purchase.

7.75in (20cm) high

$300-500 DN

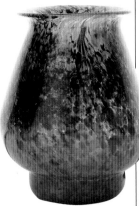

A late 1920s-30s John Moncrieff Ltd. 'Monart' glass vase, shape RA, with orange, yellow, green, amethyst and aventurine inclusions.

8.5in (21.5cm) high

$350-450 L&T

A late 1920s-30s John Moncrieff Ltd. 'Monart' glass baluster vase, shape FA, the mottled blue and green glass overlaid with colorless glass, the base with polished pontil mark.

7.25in (18.5cm) high

$400-600 WW

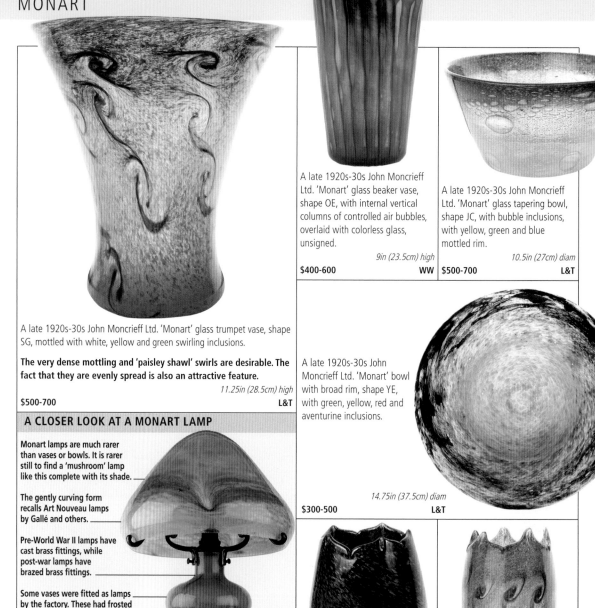

A late 1920s-30s John Moncrieff Ltd. 'Monart' glass beaker vase, shape OE, with internal vertical columns of controlled air bubbles, overlaid with colorless glass, unsigned.

9in (23.5cm) high

$400-600   WW

A late 1920s-30s John Moncrieff Ltd. 'Monart' glass tapering bowl, shape JC, with bubble inclusions, with yellow, green and blue mottled rim.

10.5in (27cm) diam

$500-700   L&T

A late 1920s-30s John Moncrieff Ltd. 'Monart' glass trumpet vase, shape SG, mottled with white, yellow and green swirling inclusions.

The very dense mottling and 'paisley shawl' swirls are desirable. The fact that they are evenly spread is also an attractive feature.

11.25in (28.5cm) high

$500-700   L&T

A late 1920s-30s John Moncrieff Ltd. 'Monart' bowl with broad rim, shape YE, with green, yellow, red and aventurine inclusions.

14.75in (37.5cm) diam

$300-500   L&T

A CLOSER LOOK AT A MONART LAMP

Monart lamps are much rarer than vases or bowls. It is rarer still to find a 'mushroom' lamp like this complete with its shade.

The gently curving form recalls Art Nouveau lamps by Gallé and others.

Pre-World War II lamps have cast brass fittings, while post-war lamps have brazed brass fittings.

Some vases were fitted as lamps by the factory. These had frosted interiors.

The 'P' in the code on the label stands for 'pedestal'.

A late 1920s-30s John Moncrieff Ltd. 'Monart' 'mushroom' pedestal lamp, the pale orange mottled glass with pulled 'silver' banding, the base with paper maker's label reading 'V.P/3.200'.

18.75in (48cm) high

$3,000-5,000   L&T

A John Moncrieff Ltd. 'Monart' glass table lamp, with aventurine flecks.

10.25in (26cm) high

$400-600   SWO

An Ysart Brothers 'Vasart' glass tulip lamp, with pink and blue swirled decoration.

c1950   *11in (28cm) high*

$300-500   L&T

QUICK REFERENCE - MURANO

- Glass has been made in Venice since the 11thC. During the 13thC, manufacture moved to Murano to avoid the risk of fire damaging the mercantile capital.
- Many different styles were developed on the island and many of these traditional techniques and styles are still made today.
- Following World War II, there was an explosion of innovation and experimentation on the island. Artists and architects provided much of the impetus and produced designs that combined clean-lined, simple forms and bright, vibrant colors. Traditional techniques were modified and updated, and new techniques developed.
- The work of influential designers and Murano's best-known factories tends to fetch the highest prices. Notable factories include Venini (founded 1921), Seguso Vetri D'Arte (1933-92) and Barovier & Toso (founded 1942). Notable designers include Fulvio Bianconi (1915-96), Flavio Poli (1900-84) and Dino Martens (1894-1970).
- Many of the best designs were and still are copied by other factories, particularly if successful. Most Murano glass is unmarked, so handle as many correctly attributed pieces as possible in order to build up a good knowledge of forms, color tones and sizes.

A Venini & C. glass 'Incalmo' bottle with stopper, designed by Fulvio Bianconi in 1956, the blue glass centered with a band of colorless glass densely packed with spiraling orange 'mezza filigrana' threads, the base acid-etched with round 'venini murano' stamp and with factory label.

Although it appears to be the same as the 'A Fasce' banded bottles, the bottle is made using a different and much more complex and time-consuming technique. The bands on 'A Fasce' bottles are applied on top of the body and then melted in, but this 'Incalmo' bottle is made of three different parts of blown glass, which are joined together when still hot and ductile. This is why the blue body does not show through the orange and colorless glass band. The vase on the right was made using the same technique.

15in (38cm) high

$1,000-1,500   QU

A Venini & C. glass 'handkerchief' vase, designed by Fulvio Bianconi and Paolo Venini in 1950, the colorless glass body overlaid with opaque white and yellow, the base with three line acid-etched 'venini murano ITALIA' mark.

10in (25.5cm) high

$1,200-1,800   FIS

A late 1960s-70s Venini & C. glass 'A Fasce' bottle with stopper, designed by Fulvio Bianconi, with applied bands, the base acid-etched with three-line 'venini murano ITALIA' mark.

Although it may have been designed some 10-15 years before, this shape can be found in the 1969 Venini trade catalog.

16.5in (42cm) high

$1,500-2,500   WW

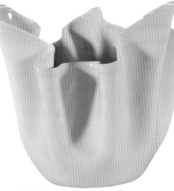

A Venini & C. glass 'Doppio Incalmo' vase, designed by Fulvio Bianconi in c1952, in blue, colorless and green glass with round base and square section rim, the base with factory marks.

6in (15cm) high

$1,200-1,800   QU

A Venini & C. glass 'A Fasce Verticali' bottle vase, designed by Fulvio Bianconi, the colorless body with overlaid broad multicolored stripes.

c1960   *6.5in (17cm) high*

$650-850   FRE

GLASS

QUICK REFERENCE - 'FORATO' RANGE

● 'Forato' means hole in Italian. Some pieces have more than one hole, in which case they are known as 'Forati' (holes).

● Shapes tend to be free-formed and fluid. This is typical of 1950s asymmetry and also Bianconi's free approach to glass making and design.

● Although there would have been guidelines to the shapes and placement and sizes of the holes, each piece from this range is unique, as they were made by hand.

● The range was popular and was reintroduced in the late 1980s, but few later pieces were cased.

● The two-line inscribed mark on this example was only used 1966-70.

A late 1960s Venini & C. glass 'Forato' vase, designed by Fulvio Bianconi in c1951, the red-brown core overlaid with yellow and colorless glass, the base engraved 'venini italia'.

1966-70   *11.5in (29cm) high*
$1,200-1,800   **QU**

A Venini & C. turquoise and red glass 'Forati' vase, designed by Fulvio Bianconi in 1989, with red-lined hole to the middle, applied red rim, and kicked-up base, the base signed 'venini Fulvio Bianconi 89'.

1989   *16in (41cm) high*
$3,000-4,000   **FIS**

A Venini & C. glass 'Inciso' vase, designed by Paolo Venini in 1956, the turquoise core overlaid in light-green and colorless glass, the exterior matted with densely packed shallow cuts, the base engraved 'venini 1998/14' and with original factory label.

1998   *12.5in (31.5cm) high*
$2,000-3,000   **FIS**

A 1950s-60s Venini & C. glass 'Inciso' bottle with stopper, designed by Paolo Venini in 1956, the turquoise glass overlaid with colorless glass, the exterior matted with densely packed shallow cuts, the base with three-line 'venini murano ITALIA' mark.

1998   *10in (25.5cm) high*
$1,000-1,500   **QU**

A Venini & C. glass 'Arado' vase, designed by Alessandro Mendini in c1988, the colorless body overlaid with vertical canes in different colors, the base engraved 'venini archivio storico'.

Not only is this a hallmark design by one of the founding fathers of the Postmodern design movement, it is also from Venini's own company archives. These factors make this piece valuable.

c1988   *12.5in (32cm) high*
$10,000-15,000   **QU**

A Venini glass 'Monofiori' bottle with stopper, designed by Laura Diaz de Santillana in c1996, with cobalt-blue body, the colorless stopper with applied amber beads, the base engraved 'Venini '96'.

1996   *5.5in (14cm) high*
$250-350   **FRE**

A Venini & C. glass 'Sette Colori' 'A Canne' tapering vase, designed by Gio Ponti in c1950, the colorless body overlaid with vertical canes in seven different colors.

6in (15cm) high
$1,200-1,800   **FIS**

A Venini & C. glass 'Opalino' vase, the white core overlaid with blue, the base engraved 'venini 99' and with original factory label.

1999   *19.5in (50cm) high*
$300-500   **FIS**

A 1970s Gino Cenedese & C. 'sommerso'-glass vase, designed by Antonio da Ros in 1959, the olive-green core overlaid with light-blue, unmarked.

Founded in 1946 by Gino Cenedese (1907-73), Cenedese is best known for its 'sommerso' (cased) vases, which often have three or four layers. This D-shape is typical of da Ros's designs.

13.5in (34.5cm) high

$1,200-1,800   FIS

A 1970s Gino Cenedese & C. 'sommerso'-glass vase, designed by Antonio da Ros in c1959, the red-brown core overlaid with a thick pink layer.

This form of 'vase' seems to question whether the piece is a functional form or a sculptural display object.

9.75in (25cm) wide

$2,000-3,000   FIS

A 1960s Gino Cenedese & C. 'sommerso'-glass bottle, designed by Antonio da Ros c1960, the purple glass core overlaid with yellowy-green, unmarked.

19.25in (49cm) high

$1,000-1,500   QU

A 1970s Gino Cenedese & C. glass bowl, designed by Fulvio Bianconi in c1955, the opalescent body with applied turquoise and violet canes and applied rim, the base inscribed 'Cenedese'.

15.25in (39cm) diam

$400-600   FIS

A 1970s Gino Cenedese & C. Alexandrit-glass bowl, designed by Antonio da Ros in c1969, with asymmetric opening and band of blue, purple and yellow circular murrines, unmarked.

6.75in (17cm) diam

$550-750   QU

A Gino Cenedese & C. glass sculpture of a stylized figure, designed by Antonio da Ros in c1960, with red, green and Alexandrit glass.

The use of Alexandrit glass (also known as neodymium glass) is unusual on Murano. It is more commonly associated with Czech glass. It changes from violet in incandescent light to an icy blue under fluorescent light.

13.5in (34cm) high

$1,000-1,500   QU

A CLOSER LOOK AT AN 'AQUARIUM' BLOCK

The 'Aquarium' range was designed by Riccardo Licata (b.1929) for Cenedese in 1952, but some of the later designs were by Alfredo Barbini.

The value depends on the size, scale and the complexity of the piece - the more fish and seaweed and the more detailed they are, the higher the price is likely to be, especially if it is a large piece.

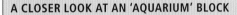
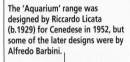

Designs were copied widely and it is extremely hard to tell the difference between authentic Cenedese examples and copies, particularly as Cenedese examples are very rarely marked or labeled.

Always consider the complexity of the elements and the brightness of the colorless glass (period examples will not usually be crystal clear and bright). Most authentic period examples have great detail, such as finely edged brown blades of seaweed.

A 1960s Gino Cenedese & C. glass 'Aquarium' block, probably designed by Riccardo Licata c1960, with internal detailing of three fish among seaweed.

12.5in (32cm) wide

$700-1,000   QU

A 1960s Seguso Vetri d'Arte 'sommerso'-glass vase, with blue, violet and ruby red layers, designed by Flavio Poli in c1955.

Seguso Vetri D'Arte was founded in 1933 by a number of glassmakers and designers, including Archimede Seguso. In 1942, Seguso left and founded his own company, Vetreria Archimede Seguso, where he pursued numerous techniques, including filigrana.

8in (20cm) high

$1,000-1,500   FIS

A late 1960s Seguso Vetri d'Arte 'sommerso'-glass bottle vase, designed by Mario Pinzoni in c1966, the purple core overlaid with light blue and colorless glass.

Mario Pinzoni (1933-93) joined Seguso Vetri d'Arte in 1954 and began working with Flavio Poli. In 1963 he succeeded Poli as Art Director, a position he held until 1971.

12.75in (32.5cm) high

$1,200-1,800   QU

A Vetreria Archimede Seguso 'sommerso'-glass vase, designed by Archimede Seguso, the tapering teardrop form with pulled rim and colorless, green and light yellow layers, unmarked.

15.5in (39cm) high

$650-850   QU

A late 1960s Seguso Vetri d'Arte 'sommerso'-glass bottle vase, designed by Mario Pinzoni in c1966, the purple core overlaid with light green, yellow and colorless glass.

8.25in (21cm) high

$650-850   QU

A 1950s-60s Vetreria Archimede Seguso 'Sommerso a bollicine' glass vase, designed by Archimede Seguso in c1950, the turquoise core overlaid with colorless glass with trapped bubbles of air and gold-foil inclusion in between, unmarked.

8in (20cm) high

$800-1,200   QU

A 1950s Vetreria Archimede Seguso glass 'Polveri' vase, designed by Archimede Seguso in c1953-54, the colorless glass with gold-foil and purple and red powder inclusions, unmarked.

'Polveri' is Italian for dust and indicates the thick application of powdered colored enamel and gold-foil specks between layers of colorless glass that give this range its unique look. With this form, Seguso took the 1950s obsession with asymmetric organic form right to the 'heart' of living things!

7.5in (19cm) high

$1,000-1,500   QU

A 1960s Seguso Vetri d'Arte glass bottle with stopper, designed by Archimede Seguso in c1960, in orange, yellow and colorless glass, unmarked.

17in (43cm) high

$650-850   QU

A 1950s Vetreria Archimede Seguso glass 'Polveri' bowl, designed by Archimede Seguso in c1952-53, with asymmetric lobed rim, the colorless glass with orange and purple powder and gold-foil inclusions, unmarked.

12in (30cm) wide

$1,000-1,500   QU

A CLOSER LOOK AT AN AURELIANO TOSO EWER

The 'Oriente' range is highly sought after as it exemplifies the explosion in color and creativity on Murano after World War II.

The asymmetric form is typical of the range, but the extended spout and spout used to form the handle adds extravagance and flair, making this early piece even more desirable.

Dino Martens (1894-1970) was a painter and brought his experience of modern art to this range, which was launched at the 1952 Biennale.

A number of techniques are used, including gold-foil inclusions, filigrana, a large black and white star murrine, as well as freeform patches of color. The pattern on every piece is unique.

An Aureliano Toso glass 'Oriente' ewer, designed by Dino Martens, in 1952, with pulled spout and handle, with irregular internal decoration, including gold-foil and latticino patches, unmarked.

9.25in (23cm) high

$12,000-18,000   SWO

An Aureliano Toso glass vase, designed by Dino Martens in the 1950s, the blue body overlaid with spiraling bands of extended yellow, red, blue, white and green melted-in chips, and with applied crimped 'wings', unmarked.

9in (21.5cm) high

$300-500   QU

A Barovier & Toso glass 'Spacchi' bowl, designed by Toni Zuccheri in c1984, the colorless glass body overlaid with thick bands of white and deep purple (black) glass, the base engraved 'barovier & toso murano tz 85'.

Spacchi means 'slits' in Italian and relates to both the Postmodern cut side and the narrow 'slits' created by the different colors of glass.

1985   7in (18cm) high

$1,500-2,500   QU

An Effetre International red and colorless glass 'Saturno' vase, designed by Lino Tagliapietra in 1987, unmarked.

11.25in (28.5cm) diam

$1,000-1,500   QU

A Memphis 'Alioth' vase, designed by Ettore Sottsass in 1983, manufactured by Toso Vetri d'Arte, the green, blue and yellow glass with deep purple (black) threads, the base engraved 'E. SOTTSASS PER MEMPHIS by TOSO VETRI d'ARTE'.

1983   18in (46cm) high

$1,500-2,500   QU

A late 1970s VeArt glass 'Otri' vase, designed by Toni Zuccheri in 1972, the orange body with slanted neck and internal protrusion in the base, the base with original maker's label.

Otri is the Italian word for 'wineskin' - a portable leather sack-like flask used for storing water or wine. VeArt was founded in 1965.

32.5in (82cm) high

$1,000-1,500   QU

A Vetreria Vistosi limited edition glass 'Vase', designed by Ettore Sottsass in 1977, the yellow body with dark purple (black) neck and collar and band to base, the base engraved 'E. SOTTSASS 202/250 VISTOSI'.

1977   8in (20.5cm) high

$2,500-3,500   QU

GLASS

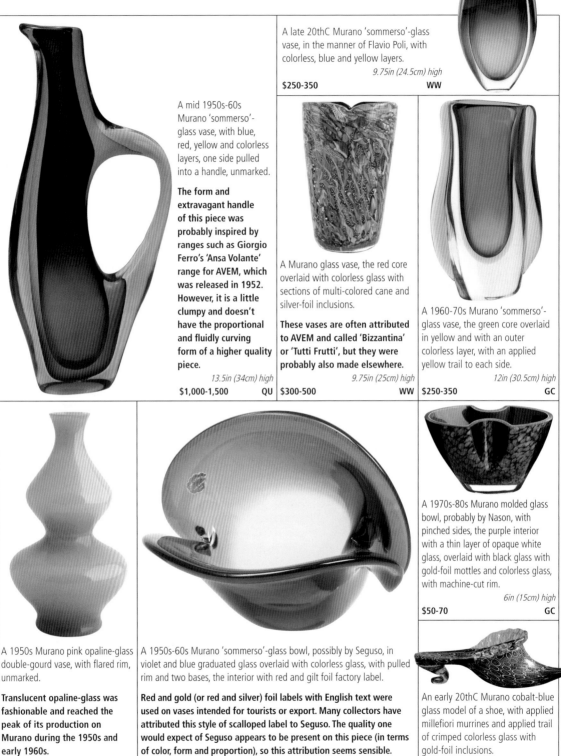

A mid 1950s-60s Murano 'sommerso'-glass vase, with blue, red, yellow and colorless layers, one side pulled into a handle, unmarked.

The form and extravagant handle of this piece was probably inspired by ranges such as Giorgio Ferro's 'Ansa Volante' range for AVEM, which was released in 1952. However, it is a little clumpy and doesn't have the proportional and fluidly curving form of a higher quality piece.

13.5in (34cm) high
$1,000-1,500 QU

A late 20thC Murano 'sommerso'-glass vase, in the manner of Flavio Poli, with colorless, blue and yellow layers.
9.75in (24.5cm) high
$250-350 WW

A Murano glass vase, the red core overlaid with colorless glass with sections of multi-colored cane and silver-foil inclusions.

These vases are often attributed to AVEM and called 'Bizzantina' or 'Tutti Frutti', but they were probably also made elsewhere.

9.75in (25cm) high
$300-500 WW

A 1960-70s Murano 'sommerso'-glass vase, the green core overlaid in yellow and with an outer colorless layer, with an applied yellow trail to each side.

12in (30.5cm) high
$250-350 GC

A 1950s Murano pink opaline-glass double-gourd vase, with flared rim, unmarked.

Translucent opaline-glass was fashionable and reached the peak of its production on Murano during the 1950s and early 1960s.

10.75in (27cm) high
$80-120 GC

A 1950s-60s Murano 'sommerso'-glass bowl, possibly by Seguso, in violet and blue graduated glass overlaid with colorless glass, with pulled rim and two bases, the interior with red and gilt foil factory label.

Red and gold (or red and silver) foil labels with English text were used on vases intended for tourists or export. Many collectors have attributed this style of scalloped label to Seguso. The quality one would expect of Seguso appears to be present on this piece (in terms of color, form and proportion), so this attribution seems sensible.

7.5in (18cm) high
$650-850 DOR

A 1970s-80s Murano molded glass bowl, probably by Nason, with pinched sides, the purple interior with a thin layer of opaque white glass, overlaid with black glass with gold-foil mottles and colorless glass, with machine-cut rim.

6in (15cm) high
$50-70 GC

An early 20thC Murano cobalt-blue glass model of a shoe, with applied millefiori murrines and applied trail of crimped colorless glass with gold-foil inclusions.

6in (15cm) long
$400-600 TRI

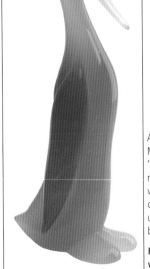

A 1950s-60s Murano 'sommerso'-glass model of a swan, with blue, pink and colorless layers, unmarked, the beak shortened.

Had the beak been intact, it would have crossed down over the neck and would have increased the value to well over $150.

11.75in (29.5cm) high

$100-150   **GROB**

A 1950s-60s Murano green opaline-glass duck, with applied opaline beak and feet.

12in (30.5cm) high

$100-150   **GC**

A 1960s-70s Murano glass model of a bird, with applied and hot-worked features, with gold-foil inclusions, on a spiraling base.

17.25in (46cm) high

$65-85   **WW**

A Vetreria Archimede Seguso glass model of a horse's head, designed by Archimede Seguso, the colorless glass with gold-foil inclusions, the base etched 'Archimede Seguso, Murano, 1981', with small chips to mane.

1981   *7.75in (19.5cm) high*

$150-250   **WW**

A Vetreria Archimede Seguso 'Polveri'-type glass model of a duck, probably designed by Archimede Seguso, the body with gold-foil inclusions, the head with pink streaks, unmarked.

6in (15cm) long

$100-150   **GROB**

A 1960s-70s Murano Alexandrit-glass model of a chamois head, possibly by Seguso.

7.5in (19.5cm) high

$70-100   **GROB**

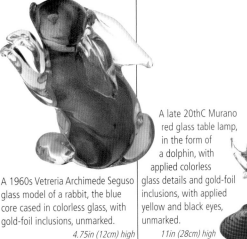

A 1960s Vetreria Archimede Seguso glass model of a rabbit, the blue core cased in colorless glass, with gold-foil inclusions, unmarked.

4.75in (12cm) high

$80-120   **GROB**

A late 20thC Murano red glass table lamp, in the form of a dolphin, with applied colorless glass details and gold-foil inclusions, with applied yellow and black eyes, unmarked.

11in (28cm) high

$80-120   **WW**

GLASS

QUICK REFERENCE - SCANDINAVIAN GLASS

- Over the past two decades, Scandinavian glass produced during the 1950s–70s has boomed in popularity as the area has been reappraised by collectors and design historians. This reappraisal has caused many pieces to rise dramatically in value.
- There are two main styles that, generally speaking, conform to particular decades. The 1950s saw an asymmetric style with curving forms and cool colors inspired by nature and forms such as buds and leaves. The late 1960s-70s saw clean–lined geometric forms and textured surfaces, both executed in bright colors.
- Always consider the factory and the designer as work by the best names is typically the most valuable. Important factories include Orrefors (founded 1726), Kosta (founded in 1942) Kosta Boda (formed 1976), Holmegaard (founded 1825) and Riihimäen Lasi Oy (1910-90).

- Key designers include Vicke Lindstrand (1904-83), Tapio Wirkkala (1915-85), Sven Palmqvist (1906-84), Per Lütken (1916-98) and Simon Gate (1883-1945). Many of their designs continued to be produced and be influential for long periods. Some designers moved between factories.
- Most collectible glass is unmarked, but unusually many pieces by the major Scandinavian factories are marked on the base with inscribed marks. These usually include the company name and a code that indicates different aspects from the form number to the designer.
- When examining any piece of Scandinavian glass, consider how it was made, as this will often have a bearing on value. Those made using complex, time-consuming techniques will be nearly always be worth more than a mold-blown design. Also pay attention to the style, color and size of the piece.

A Kosta Boda glass 'Unicum' (Unique) vase, designed by Ulrica Hydman-Vallien, decorated with colored powdered and painted enamels over a pink ground, with applied curving blue snake, the base painted 'Ulrica HV', and engraved 'KOSTA BODA UNIQUE 13734.90054 Ulrica HV'.

c1990   *13.75in (35cm) high*

$1,200-1,800   **QU**

A late 1930s Kosta glass beaker vase, designed by Elis Bergh, with internal horizontal ribbing.

Elis Bergh (1881-1954) was design director at Kosta 1929-50. His name was promoted as a 'brand' on factory stickers: a relatively common practice today, but rare at this early date.

10in (25cm) high

$60-80   **DUK**

A mid-1960s Boda Afors glass bottle-vase, designed by Bertil Vallien, the base with 'BODA Afors Bruk SWEDEN' paper label.

9in (23cm) high

$200-300   **GROB**

A late 1950s-60s Kosta vase, designed by Vicke Lindstrand in c1954, the ruby-red core overlaid with white trails and with colorless glass, the base with factory marks.

6.75in (17cm) high

$400-600   **QU**

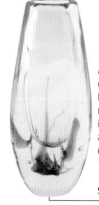

A Kosta glass vase, designed by Vicke Lindstrand, with randomly applied internal green trails and bubbles, the base etched 'Kosta LH 1803'.

7.5in (19cm) high

$250-350   **WW**

An Orrefors glass 'Ariel' vase, designed by Ingeborg Lundin in 1978, decorated with a band of stylized faces on a graduated olive-green and purple ground, the base inscribed 'Orrefors Ariel Nr 197-E8 Ingeborg Lundin'.

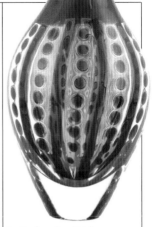

A small Orrefors glass 'Ariel' vase, designed by Edvin Öhrström, the base with inscribed marks.

2.5in (6cm) high

$300-500   TRI

$3,000-4,000

7.5in (19cm) high

QU

An Orrefors glass 'Ariel' vase, designed by Edvin Öhrström, the base with etched signature and factory marks.

8in (21cm) high

$1,200-1,800   WW

QUICK REFERENCE - ORREFORS 'KRAKA' RANGE

- Developed by Sven Palmqvist (1906-84) in 1941, 'Kraka' was produced in a similar manner to 'Graal'.
- 'Kraka' vases were made up of two differently colored layers of glass - here blue over purple. Early examples tend to be in one color (typically brown) and colorless glass. Two-color examples like this tend to be later.
- Once the two layers of glass had cooled and hardened, mesh was applied to the surface and the areas not covered were sandblasted away, revealing the underlying glass (purple) and creating a 'net' pattern (blue).
- The body was then reheated, covered in a layer of colorless glass to 'seal' the pattern, reblown and finished.
- This form and colorway can be found in Orrefors's 1975 catalog.

An Orrefors glass 'Kraka' vase, designed by Sven Palmqvist, decorated with a graduated blue and purple hatched design, the base inscribed 'ORREFORS, Kraka No. 537, Sven Palmqvist'.

1972   *6in (15.5cm) high*

$650-850   QU

A late 1950s-60s Orrefors glass vase, designed by Nils Landberg in 1956, from the 'Dusk' range, the base engraved 'Orrefors No.393XXX',

The 'Dusk' range was one of the inspirations behind Geoffrey Baxter's Scandinavian-style designs for Whitefriars in the late 1950s.

5in (13cm) high

$120-180   GROB

A late 1950s-60s Orrefors glass vase, designed by Nils Landberg in c1954-56, from the 'Dusk' range, the base with engraved signature.

12.5in (29cm) high

$150-250   FLD

An Orrefors amethyst-colored smoked-glass urn and cover, designed by Simon Gate in c1918.

c1918   *20in (50cm) high*

$800-1,200   WW

GLASS

An early 1960s Aseda glass vase, designed by Bo Borgstrom, with tightly turned-over rim and internal gray-powder inclusions and tiny bubbles.

6.25in (15.5cm) high

$40-60   TRI

An 1960s Ekenas glass bowl, designed by John Orwar Lake, with graduated mottled blue to green powdered enamel and bubble inclusions, the base with inscribed marks.

6.5in (16.5cm) diam

$100-150   PC

Mark Picks

This form shows the influence of nature and asymmetry, which were both important themes in 1950s Scandinavian glass design. Hugo Gehlin (1889-1953), who joined Gullaskruf in 1930, was one of the first Swedish designers to work with organic forms.

Neither the designer nor the company are currently particularly sought after by collectors, so pieces like the one shown are often passed by. However, they are good quality, almost certainly under-rated and provide an unusual and affordable entry point into the design ethos of the decade.

A Gullaskruf 'Double Walled Coiled Bowl', designed by Hugo Gehlin, the polished base engraved 'Gehlin, Gullaskruf'.

7.25in (18.5cm) wide

$50-70   PC

A Holmegaard glass vase, no.15469, designed by Per Lütken in 1955, the base with inscribed marks and dated.

1957   *10in (25.5cm) high*

$250-350   TRI

A Holmegaard blue glass 'Rondo' vase, designed by Per Lütken in c1955, the base inscribed 'HOLMEGAARD PL58'.

1958   *4.5in (11.5cm) high*

$200-300   TRI

A 1970s Holmegaard yellow glass vase, designed by Per Lütken in 1968, from the 'Carnaby' range, overlaid in colorless glass.

9in (23cm) high

$200-300   GC

A large Holmegaard glass 'Gulvase' bottle-vase, designed by Otto Brauer in 1962, unsigned.

17.5in (44cm) high

$250-350   WW

A collection of Holmegaard 'Smoke' drinking ware, designed by Per Lütken in c1955, including three 'Aristocrat' decanters, nos.16588, a Roskilde jug, designed in 1960, no.161430, a set of matching waisted 'Canada' glasses and twenty similar glasses.

c1955-c1990

$650-850 set   SWO

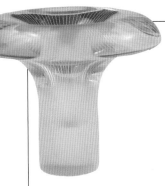

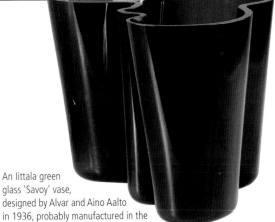

An Iittala glass 'Tatti' vase, designed by Tapio Wirkkala in 1953, no.3552, the exterior cut with vertical flutes, the base with incised signature, '55' and other marks.

4.25in (10.5cm) high

$300-500   WW

An Iittala green glass 'Savoy' vase, designed by Alvar and Aino Aalto in 1936, probably manufactured in the 1940s-50s, the base inscribed 'ALVAR AALTO - 3030'.

Designed for the luxurious Savoy restaurant in Helsinki, Finland, this landmark vase is still produced today in a range of colors and sizes. The highest prices are fetched by large vintage examples, such as the one shown above, that display wear commensurate for their age as well as the correct color-tone and inscribed marks.

6in (15cm) high

$3,000-4,000   QU

A Kastrup blue glass vase, designed by Jacob Bang in 1959, with original paper label.

A larger version of this shape, measuring 10in (25.5cm) high, was produced as a decanter with a wooden stopper. It is shown in the company's 1960 catalog.

7in (18cm) high

$50-70   BETH

A Kastrup glass vase, by Jacob Bang in 1964, pattern no.32708, from the 'Antik Grøn' series, with applied prunt with impressed head.

1964-70   6in (15cm) high

$80-120   PC

An Arabia green glass bowl, designed by Björn Weckström in 1980, manufactured by Nuutajärvi Notsjö, the base engraved 'Björn Weckström Nuutajärvi Notsjö' and with Arabia distributor's label.

Arabia (founded in 1873) is Finland's leading ceramics and tableware company.

7.5in (17cm) high

$300-500   QU

A 1960s Neiman Marcus mold-blown green glass 'People' bottle, designed by Erik Höglund.

Renowned Swedish artist and glass designer Erik Höglund (1932-98) designed these whimsical bottles for American company Neiman Marcus, which sold bath salts or shampoo inside them during the late 1960s. Rather than being made in Sweden as you might expect, these bottles were made in Italy, probably in a factory in or around Empoli.

A large Riihimäen Lasi Oy glass 'Aurinko' (Sun) bottle vase, designed by Helena Tynell in 1964.

Lighter weight and slightly rougher examples are potentially copies by the Italian Bormioli glass works and are generally less valuable than originals. However, 'Aurinko' vases with narrow lips were made by Riihimäen Lasi Oy, so don't judge authenticity based on this feature!

9.25in (23.5cm) high

$150-250   WHP

A Riihimäen Lasi Oy blue glass vase, possibly designed by Tamara Aladin.

1965-71   10.75in (27.5cm) high

$50-70   DA&H

6.75in (17.5cm) high

$25-35   GROB

A mid-late 1980s Glasform glass vase, by John Ditchfield, with flared rim and three button feet, with combed and pulled trailed decoration and iridescent finish.

6.25in (16cm) high

$300-500   **FLD**

A glass paperweight, by Sam Herman, the mottled iridescent exterior with silver-chloride inclusions and melted-in applied trails, with a ground base.

For more paperweights, see p.272-73.

3in (7.5cm) diam

$120-180   **PC**

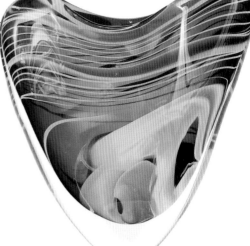

A glass 'Ariel V' freeform sculptural vase, by Peter Layton, with pulled and swung rim, with tonal ocher whiplash lines over a blue ground, the base with engraved signature.

12.5in (32cm) high

$1,000-1,500   **FLD**

A glass vase, by Isgard Moje-Wohlgemuth, with iridescent stripes, oxide bands and matt finish, the base inscribed 'MOJE M 74'.

1974   *6in (15cm) high*

$550-750   **QU**

A glass abstract vase, in the form of a stylized hand, by Joel Philip Myers, with an iridescent combed pattern over a deep amber ground, the base with engraved signature and dated.

Joel Philip Myers (b.1934) is perhaps best known as the Design Director of Blenko glass 1963-70. His studio work is part of many important private and public collections and, at a price like this, could be a good bet for the future.

1973   *10.25in (26cm) high*

$550-750   **FLD**

An Okra glass vase, by Dave Barras, with applied and melted-in iridescent leaves, purple stylized flowerheads and trailed on a yellow mottled ground, the base etched 'DB' and with other marks.

6.5in (17cm) wide

$200-300   **AH**

A glass paperweight, by Paul Stankard, depicting a bee over a botanical composition of flowers, insects and a root system containing 'root spirit', the base inscribed 'Paul J. Stankard F3 1999'.

Paul Stankard's (b.1943) highly detailed and fine quality work is very sought after by collectors. For more information, see 'Miller's Collectibles Handbook 2012-2013' p.273. Stankard obelisks are rarer than paperweights, but this does not mean they are necessarily worth more. Generally values for Stankard pieces are dependent on the desirability and complexity of the contents. The 'root spirit', which represents the spirit of nature for Stankard, featured in this piece is a highly desirable feature.

1999   *5.5in (14cm) high*

$4,000-6,000   **LHA**

QUICK REFERENCE - WHITEFRIARS

● Whitefriars was founded in London in 1680. In 1834, it was acquired by James Powell and became known as 'Powell & Sons'. In 1923, the factory moved to Wealdstone, just outside London, and became known as Whitefriars again in 1962. For ease, most collectors refer to all glass produced by the company as 'Whitefriars'.

● Many 19thC and early 20thC designs are highly sought after, particularly if they are in the Venetian, Arts & Crafts or Art Nouveau styles. Designs from the 1920s–30s tend to be less desirable and, as a result, are currently less expensive. This may change if interest is revived.

● The most popular 20thC designs were produced by Royal College of Art graduate Geoffrey Baxter (1922-95), who joined the company in 1954. His first designs were curving and influenced by the colors, clarity and clean lines of period Scandinavian glass.

● His 'Textured' range was released in 1967 and has since become the most sought after group of Whitefriars designs. Always pay attention to the color, size, level of texture and shape, as values vary depending on each factor. Despite the success of this range, and the 'Late Textured' range that followed, Whitefriars closed in 1980.

A late 19thC James Powell & Sons, Whitefriars glass 'Medieval' goblet vase, probably designed by Harry Powell, with applied 'Ruby'-red decoration.

4.5in (11.5cm) high

$150-250   WW

A James Powell & Sons, Whitefriars 'Sky Blue' drinking glass, the stem with gold-foil inclusions.

Many late 19thC and early 20thC James Powell & Sons designs were inspired by traditional and historic Venetian glass.

8.75in (22cm) high

$1,000-1,500   WW

A very rare James Powell & Sons, Whitefriars glass vase, probably designed by Harry Powell, the pink glass body with white and ocher striations, overlaid with colorless glass, unsigned.

9.75in (24.5cm) high

$1,500-2,500   WW

A late 1920s-30s Powell & Sons, Whitefriars 'Cloudy'-glass beaker vase, designed by Marriott Powell in c1930, no.L7, with mottled blue powder enamels graduating to green.

8.75in (22.5cm) high

$250-350   WW

A Powell & Sons, Whitefriars blue and green glass vase, no.3056A, designed by H J Dunne-Cooke, the base signed 'D. Cooke', numbered '6' and dated '32', with some chips and light scratches.

Captain Dunne-Cooke was a Director of Elfverson & Co., a British importer of Scandinavian glass. He also produced designs for Strömbergshyttan in Sweden.

1932   *7in (18cm) high*

$550-750   DN

GLASS

A late 1930s-50s Powell & Sons, Whitefriars 'Sapphire'-blue glass bowl, designed by James Hogan, pattern no.9169, with folded rim.

The line and clarity of color show the influence of Scandinavian glass.

c1937   *11in (28cm) diam*

$80-120   **TRI**

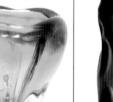

A late 1930s-50s Powell & Sons, Whitefriars 'Emerald'-green glass bowl, designed by Tom Hill in 1937, pattern no.9125m.

Tom Hill was a glassblower at the factory and produced a few designs during the late 1930s.

A 1930s Powell & Sons, Whitefriars turquoise glass vase, probably designed by Barnaby Powell in 1932, pattern no.8857, with applied purple dimple decoration.

10.25in (26cm) high

$400-600   **BATE**

10in (25.5cm) diam

$80-120   **TRI**

A 1950s-60s Powell & Sons, Whitefriars 'Golden Amber' glass vase, designed by William Wilson in the early 1950s, pattern no.9384, with applied wings.

7.75in (19.5cm) high

$100-150   **TRI**

Mark Picks

The landmark 'Blown Soda' range came about largely due to a mistake. Whitefriars's new range for 1962 was to be a range of freeblown blue or red vases with applied white trails. However, the white trails wouldn't adhere to the bodies in production and the range failed at the last minute. Lead designer Geoffrey Baxter had to come up with something new - fast.

The resulting range combined strong Scandinavian-inspired colors with clean-lined Modernist and modern shapes that could be economically blown into molds - some of which had previously been molds for lampshades. The pieces shown here were made from just such 'recycled' molds.

'Blown Soda' caught the fashions of the day perfectly and proved an instant hit. Even though these pieces were designed over half a century ago, they look as fresh today as they did then.

A Powell & Sons, Whitefriars glass lobed vase, designed by William Wilson, pattern no.9411, the blue core overlaid with colorless glass.

c1955   *6.25in (16cm) high*

$40-60   **WHP**

A mid-late 1960s Whitefriars 'Lilac' glass 'Knobbly' vase, designed by William Wilson and Harry Dyer in 1963, pattern no.9609, the purple core overlaid with colorless glass.

These 'Knobby' vases were produced in solid colors, as here, and with random streaky decoration.

7.25in (18.5cm) high

$100-150   **TRI**

Two mid-late 1960s Whitefriars 'Lilac'-glass vases, designed by Geoffrey Baxter in 1962, pattern nos.9596 and 9591, from the 'Blown Soda' range.

Taller 9.5in (24cm) high

$100-150   **TRI**

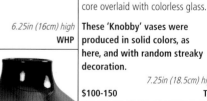

A mid-late 1960s Whitefriars 'Lilac' glass vase, designed by Geoffrey Baxter in 1962, pattern no.9600.

7in (17.5cm) high

$60-80   **TRI**

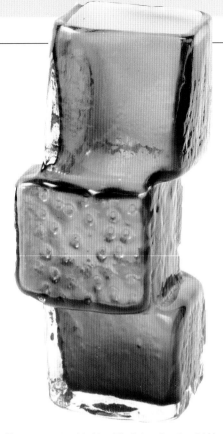

A small late 1960s-70s Whitefriars 'Tangerine' glass 'Drunken Bricklayer' vase, designed by Geoffrey Baxter in 1966, pattern no.9673, from the 'Textured' range, the orange core overlaid with colorless glass.

8.5in (21.5cm) high

$250-350   TRI

A small late 1960s-70s Whitefriars 'Meadow Green' glass 'Drunken Bricklayer' vase, designed by Geoffrey Baxter in 1966, pattern no.9673, from the 'Textured' range, the green core overlaid with colorless glass.

8.25in (21cm) high

$500-700   WW

A small late 1960s-70s Whitefriars 'Lilac' glass 'Drunken Bricklayer' vase, designed by Geoffrey Baxter in 1966, pattern no.9673, from the 'Textured' range, the purple core overlaid with colorless glass.

Look at how color affects the value for Whitefriars. Certain colors were only produced for a short length of time or were less desirable at the time, meaning they are rarer today. 'Tangerine' is one of the most frequently found, 'Lilac' less so, leading to the higher price.

8in (20.5cm) high

$800-1,200   SWO

A late 1960s-70s Whitefriars 'Ruby'-red glass 'Bark' vase, designed by Geoffrey Baxter in 1966, pattern no.9690, from the 'Textured' range, the red core overlaid with colorless glass.

9.5in (24cm) high

$100-150   TRI

A late 1960s-70s Whitefriars 'Cinnamon'-brown glass 'Basketweave Slab' vase, designed by Geoffrey Baxter, pattern no.9667, from the 'Textured' range, the brown core overlaid with colorless glass.

11in (28cm) high

$300-500   WW

A late 1960s-70s Whitefriars 'Willow'-gray glass 'Cello' vase, designed by Geoffrey Baxter, pattern no.9675, from the 'Textured' range, the gray core overlaid with colorless glass.

7in (18cm) high

$250-350   DS

A Whitefriars 'Cinnamon'-brown glass 'Pyramid' or 'Triangle' vase, designed by Geoffrey Baxter in 1966, pattern no.9674, from the 'Textured' range, the brown core overlaid with colorless glass.

6.75in (17cm) high

$150-250   DS

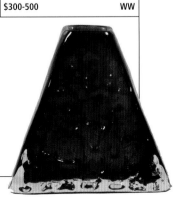

GLASS

Mark Picks

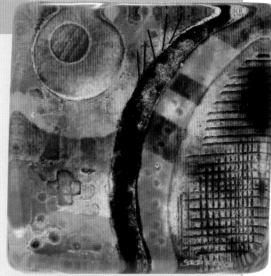

Sarah Peterson (b.1972) is the lead designer at Caithness Glass (est.1961) and has been producing sandcast blocks since 2002. A low-relief abstract pattern is impressed or scored into sand in a rectangular or square mold and then colored enamels are sprinkled over it. A thick layer of hot colorless glass is then poured into the mold and bonds with the enamels to give the finished block.

Peterson's designs are either produced serially, as limited editions or as unique examples. Although all her designs are likely to be collectible in the future, her unique designs are likely to be the most sought after and valuable.

A unique Caithness Glass sandcast-glass 'Ruby Twilight' display piece, designed by Sarah Peterson in c2010, decorated with an abstract landscape in colored powdered enamel, the base with engraved signature and numbered 1 of 1, with box and certificate.

7in (18cm) high

$300-500   **FLD**

A Caithness Glass sandcast-glass 'High Voltage' display piece, designed by Sarah Peterson in c2003, decorated with an abstract design with colored powdered enamel.

5.25in (13cm) high

$70-100   **GC**

A Caithness Glass sandcast-glass 'Clockwork' display piece, designed by Sarah Peterson in 2003, no.UO3123, decorated with an abstract design with colored powdered enamel.

7.75in (20.5cm) high

$80-120   **GC**

A Caithness Glass limited edition glass 'Poppies' bowl, designed by Helen MacDonald, from the 'Studio Collection', from an edition of ten.

13in (32cm) diam

$700-1,000   **CHT**

A 1930s Daum blue glass vase, decorated with concentric textured bands, the base inscribed 'Daum Nancy France'.

8.75in (22.5cm) high

$250-350   **DA&H**

A large 1930s Daum glass vase, the tonal amethyst and blue ground with gold-foil inclusions, overlaid in colorless glass, the footrim with engraved signature and Cross of Lorraine.

12.5in (33.5cm) high

$700-1,000   **FLD**

A late 20th/early 21stC Daum limited edition pâte-de-verre glass dolphin sculpture, designed by Claude Lhoste, numbered 62 from an edition of 300.

8.75in (22cm) high

$500-700   **WW**

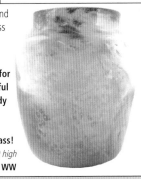

An Émile Gallé cameo-glass vase, the yellow glass overlaid with purple, decorated with violet flowers, signed 'Gallé'.

3.5in (9cm) high

$1,000-1,500   WW

An Émile Gallé cameo-glass vase, the white glass overlaid with red, acid etched with tiger lilies, signed 'Gallé'.

c1910   13in (33cm) high

$1,000-1,500   L&T

A Gray-Stan mottled green, yellow and brown glass vase, overlaid in colorless glass.

Gray-Stan was founded by Mrs Graydon-Stannus in 1926 and ran for ten years. As well as making colorful and fashionable mottled and cloudy art glass, such as this vase, the company was reputed to have produced fake antique Irish cut glass!

10in (24cm) high

$300-500   WW

A Gilbey's Gin commemorative glass decanter, designed by Ronald Stennett-Willson, with original packaging.

In 1957 Ronald Stennett-Willson was commissioned to design a decanter and glasses to commemorate the 100th anniversary of Gilbey's Gin. The order was too large for any British glass manufacturer to fulfil, so the order was fulfilled by Sandvik, a subsidiary of Orrefors, hence the 'MADE IN SWEDEN' wording on the Gilbey's label and box. It is very rare to find an example of this decanter complete with its avant garde packaging.

10in (25.5cm) high

$300-500   FLD

QUICK REFERENCE - HARTLEY WOOD

- ● Hartley Wood (1892-1989) was based in Sunderland. It was known for stained glass, hence the bright colors found in its vases.
- ● Decorative vases and bowls were probably only produced in the 1930s and the 1980s, although some pieces may have been made in the 1950s.
  - ● In 1992 a range of mold-blown vases was released under the 'Hartley Wood' name by Pilkington's. The pieces had new labels and a special pontil mark.
    - ● Hartley Wood pieces produced during the 1930s tend to be heavier in weight, more thickly blown and more irregularly shaped than their 1980s counterparts. They are also the most sought after and valuable.

A late 20thC Hartley Wood & Co. tonal-purple glass vase.

7.5in (19cm) high

$50-70   FLD

A 1930s Hartley Wood & Co. 'Antique Glass' vase, decorated with a random pink, yellow, orange and red swirling pattern, the base with broken-pontil mark.

13.25in (34cm) high

$250-350   GC

A 1930s Hartley Wood & Co. 'Antique Glass' vase, decorated with a random pink, blue, green and yellow swirling pattern, the base with broken-pontil mark.

12.5in (32cm) high

$200-300   GC

A Hocking Glass Co. 'Topaz' Depression-glass 'Princess' pattern tumbler.

This pattern was also made in blue, green, pink and apricot-yellow.

1931-35   5.25in (13.5cm) high

$12-18   PC

GLASS

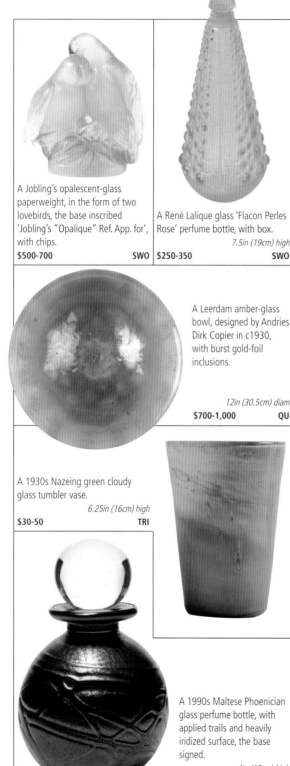

A Jobling's opalescent-glass paperweight, in the form of two lovebirds, the base inscribed 'Jobling's "Opalique" Ref. App. for', with chips.

$500-700   SWO

A René Lalique glass 'Flacon Perles Rose' perfume bottle, with box.

7.5in (19cm) high

$250-350   SWO

A Leerdam amber-glass bowl, designed by Andries Dirk Copier in c1930, with burst gold-foil inclusions.

12in (30.5cm) diam

$700-1,000   QU

A 1930s Nazeing green cloudy glass tumbler vase.

6.25in (16cm) high

$30-50   TRI

A 1990s Maltese Phoenician glass perfume bottle, with applied trails and heavily iridized surface, the base signed.

4in (10cm) high

$50-70   PC

QUICK REFERENCE - LALIQUE & CONSOLIDATED

- The Consolidated Glass Company of Pennsylvania, USA produced a range of glass called Martele from 1925 to the 1960s. Many of the designs were inspired by, and very similar to, designs by Lalique. Some Consolidated pieces were made with two differently colored layers of glass, but many were not.
- This piece is an almost direct copy of Lalique's 'Perruches' vase, which was designed in 1919. The main difference is that the Consolidated version has a slightly flared rim.
- This rim can be polished away and fake Lalique marks added, so handle as much authentic Lalique as possible to learn the weight and feel of authentic examples.

A 1930s-60s Consolidated Glass Co. lilac glass 'Love Birds' vase, after the 'Perruches' design originally designed by René Lalique.

10.25in (26cm) high

$1,000-1,500   WW

A 1920s-30s Le Verre Français/Verrerie Schneider glass ewer, with brown mottled neck, with acid etched body, the base with engraved mark.

12in (31.5cm) high

$250-350   DN

A 1920s Le Verre Français/Verrerie Schneider cameo-glass vase, the mottled light-blue glass overlaid in blue, acid etched with fruiting foliage, signed 'Charder' in the cameo, the base etched 'Le Verre Français'.

9.75in (25cm) high

$650-850   **L&T**

A Le Verre Français/Verrerie Schneider cameo-glass 'Garances' vase, the colorless glass with red and light-blue inclusions, overlaid with mottled purple, acid etched with stylized floral motifs, with a frosted ground, the base with needle-etched 'Le Verre Français'.

1924-27   14.5in (37cm) high

$2,500-3,500   **DOR**

A Le Verre Français/Verrerie Schneider cameo-glass 'Frenes' vase, the colorless glass with yellow and white inclusions, overlaid in mottled orange and dark purple, acid etched with stylized floral motifs, with frosted ground, the base acid etched 'Le Verre Français'.

1924–27   13.5in (34.5cm) high

$3,000-5,000   **DOR**

A pair of 1920s Stevens & Williams iridecent 'Abbey Glass' decanters with stoppers, with 'knocked in' sides, with compressed hollow blown stopper, the collars marked for Hukin & Heath.

1929   9in (23cm) high

$700-1,000   **FLD**

A Stourbridge blue cameo-glass plate, decorated with a butterfly above wild rose flowers.

8in (21cm) diam

$1,500-2,500   **WW**

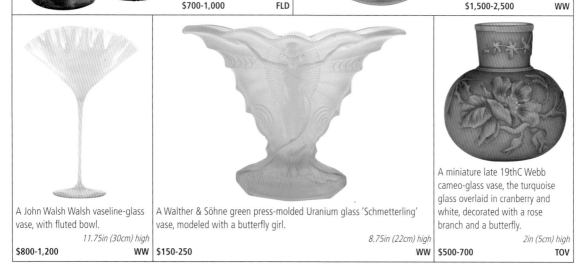

A John Walsh Walsh vaseline-glass vase, with fluted bowl.

11.75in (30cm) high

$800-1,200   **WW**

A Walther & Söhne green press-molded Uranium glass 'Schmetterling' vase, modeled with a butterfly girl.

8.75in (22cm) high

$150-250   **WW**

A miniature late 19thC Webb cameo-glass vase, the turquoise glass overlaid in cranberry and white, decorated with a rose branch and a butterfly.

2in (5cm) high

$500-700   **TOV**

GLASS

A King's Lynn Glass blue glass 'Lynn' wine goblet, designed by Ronald Stennett-Willson in 1967.

This goblet can be very hard to find today, hence the high price.
1967-69   *5in (12.5cm) high*
$150-250   **FLD**

A King's Lynn Glass blue glass pedestal fruit bowl, designed by Ronald Stennett-Willson in 1967, shape no.RSW52.
9in (23.5cm) high
$150-250   **FLD**

A King's Lynn Glass 'Topaz' glass candlestick, designed by Ronald Stennett-Willson, with a double inverted-baluster hollow-blown stem.

This is a complex and extremely unusual form. This example was from the personal collection of Ronald Stennett-Willson, which makes it particularly desirable.
7in (18cm) high
$150-250   **FLD**

A 1930s-50s WMF glass 'Ikora' bowl, the colorless glass internally-decorated with a red crackled design.
10.5in (27cm) diam
$150-250   **WW**

A CLOSER LOOK AT A CANDLE HOLDER

The nine-disc example was the largest 'Sheringham' candleholder made. The smallest had one disc. A handful of examples with no discs have been found, but most collectors do not count these as 'Sheringham'.

Each component is made from a separate gather of glass and each ring is made up of three components - meaning a staggering 21 gathers were used to make this candleholder!

Each piece is perfectly proportioned and sized and the piece is straight, showing the immense skill of the glassmakers.

The nine-ring candleholder was expensive in its day, so fewer were made and sold than of the smaller pieces. This piece is consequently comparatively rare today. Prices rise and fall and have gone over $1,500 a number of times in the past.

It won a Queen's award for design in 1967.

It was produced in other colors. 'Topaz' is the most common color.

A large King's Lynn Glass or Wedgwood Glass Topaz glass 'Sheringham' nine-ring candleholder, designed by Ronald Stennett-Willson in 1967, shape no.RSW13.
14in (35cm) high
$1,200-1,800   **FLD**

A 1930s WMF glass 'Ikora' vase, designed by Karl Wiedmann.

This is an unusual form and pattern for German company Württembergische Metallwarenfabrik (WMF). Baluster-shape vases and dishes are much more common.
c1930-35
$1,000-1,500   **FIS**

A late 1920s-30s WMF glass 'Ikora' vase, designed by Karl Wiedmann.
c1927   *9in (23cm) high*
$800-1,200   **FIS**

A 1930s WMF glass 'Ikora' vase, designed by Karl Wiedmann.
c1930-35   *17in (43cm) high*
$650-850   **FIS**

A 1930s-50s WMF glass 'Ikora' baluster-shaped vase.

9.75in (25cm) high

$120-180   FIS

A pair of oversized 1970s Italian display goblets, one in orange, one in blue, the bowls of both blown into molds.

Numerous wine glasses of this form were made in and around the town of Empoli, north of Florence, Italy. During the 1950s-70s, they were seen as inexpensive ways of adding Italian color to homes. Alas, during the 1980s they were deemed 'old-fashioned' and consigned to charity shops, lofts and rubbish bins. However, they are now seeing a revival among a younger generation, who see the same things in them as the original buyers did!

14.5in (37cm) high

$50-70   WHP

A 1930s French Art Deco green pressed-glass vase, with frosted, textured ribs and handles.

8.25in (21cm) high

$100-150   PC

An Art Deco enameled-glass vase, enameled with an Egyptian lotus-flower pattern.

7.25in (18.5cm) high

$250-350   WW

A 1930s French cameo-glass vase, in the manner of Le Verre Français, the amber and orange glass overlaid with brown, acid etched with stylized flowerheads and foliage.

9in (22cm) high

$400-600   FLD

QUICK REFERENCE - ZWEISEL GLASS TECHNICAL SCHOOL

- The 'Glasfachschule Zwiesel' (Zwiesel Glass Technical School) was founded in Germany in 1904 to provide a center for training in glass design and production. The school has been, and still is, a hotbed of experimental design.
- The area was already well known for its glass industry, with the major factory being Schott.
- Most of the pieces that are found on the market today were produced by students of the school. A small number of those students then went on to be important designers or artists.
- The most desirable pieces are of high quality in terms of design and eye-appeal and capture the aesthetics of the period they were made in.
- This high quality piece displays the influence of modern art in its stylized eye motifs and colorful geometric design.

A Zweisel Glass Technical School green glass bottle vase, the bubbly glass overlaid with a translucent white trail, the base etched '77' and with maker's signature.

1977   *13.75in (35cm) high*

$250-350   FIS

A 1950s Zweisel Glass Technical School enameled mold-blown glass vase, designed and hand-decorated by an unknown designer.

4in (10cm) high

$300-500   PC

INSTRUMENTS

QUICK REFERENCE - INSTRUMENTS

- Scientific instruments developed alongside a growing understanding of science and medicine during the Italian Renaissance. The discovery of America in 1492 and trade with the Far East also created a demand for accurate navigational instruments. The announcement that the sun was the center of the solar system by Nicolaus Copernicus in the 16thC, combined with advances in warfare and medicine, required better quality optical instruments.
- Instruments made before the 17thC are extremely rare and are usually very valuable. The majority of instruments bought, sold and collected today date from the 1700s, 1800s and early 1900s. Most collectors tend to focus on one category, such as microscopes.
- Factors to consider when determining value and desirability include the date, period and type of

instrument. Another important factor is the maker, with the work of high quality makers, such as Burge, Ramsden, Adams and Dollond, commanding a premium. Addresses stamped into the metal can help to date an instrument, as can the form and construction of the instrument. In general, look for complex, well-made instruments that retain their original boxes and accessories.
- Some instruments, such as compasses, microscopes and telescopes, are being replicated and reproduced today. Beware of any instrument that is in a bright, yellow brass and shows no signs of wear through use. Many fakes also have clunky movements, such as focusing. Antique technology has largely fallen in value over the past ten years. If interest refocuses on instruments, now could be a good time to buy.

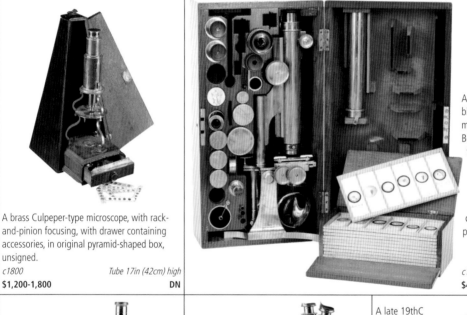

A brass Culpeper-type microscope, with rack-and-pinion focusing, with drawer containing accessories, in original pyramid-shaped box, unsigned.
c1800   *Tube 17in (42cm) high*
$1,200-1,800   **DN**

A 19thC lacquered-brass binocular compound microscope, by R & J Beck, with eyepieces, four objectives, 700 assorted slides and other accessories, with fitted mahogany case and later slide case, with dated presentation plaque.
c1869
$4,000-6,000   **FLD**

A mid-19thC lacquered-brass monocular microscope, signed 'POWELL & LELAND, 170 Euston Road, London', with rack and pinion focus above stage with X and Y adjustment, plano-concave mirror and triform frame support, incomplete.
15in (38cm) high
$1,200-1,800   **DN**

A late 19thC lacquered-brass binocular microscope, by Charles Collins, with rack and pinion focus adjustment and prism/filter above stage with X and Y adjustment, plano-concave mirror, engraved 'CHA'S. COLLINS, 77 Gt. Titchfield St. & Polytechnic Ins'in, LONDON', with original mahogany box and some accessories.
Box 18.5in (47cm) high
$1,200-1,800   **DN**

A late 19thC lacquered-brass binocular microscope, by Elliott Brothers, London, with sliding slide mount and aperture adjustable oculus, with pivoted plano-concave mirror, signed 'ELLIOTT BRO'S LONDON', with original case and accessories.
16in (40cm) high
$1,200-1,800   **DN**

A late 19thC patinated and lacquered brass monocular microscope, by 'HENRY CROUCH, LONDON', with rack and pinion focus and plano-concave mirror, in original mahogany box with some accessories.

Box 11.75in (30cm) high

$500-700   DN

A lacquered-brass traveling microscope, with stained wood case, one side used as the base of the microscope.

$800-1,200   A&G

Miller's Compares

Although often technically and optically of high quality, most microscopes made from the early 20thC onwards are of little interest to collectors, regardless of maker.

Microscopes of this type were produced in comparatively large quantities and many were used in educational institutions, such as schools and universities.

Its form and period of manufacture make this example appealing to collectors. If it was signed by a well-regarded 19thC maker, it would have fetched even more.

It retains its original mahogany box and its accessories. In general, the more accessories a microscope retains, the more it will fetch.

A late 19thC lacquered-brass and black-painted cast-iron monocular microscope, with two eyepieces and spare lenses, with original fitted wooden case.

11in (27cm) high

$150-250   FLD

An early 20thC lacquered-brass and black-finished cast-iron optical microscope, by Bausch & Lomb, with rack and pinion focus and revolving nosepiece for three objectives.

c1915-20   *14in (36cm) high*

$50-70   ECGW

An early 19thC lacquered-brass portable Withering-type botanical microscope, with three objectives, an up/down adjustable stage with central oculus and slots to take various accessories, with pivoted plano-concave mirror, with original wood case.

This form of portable botanical microscope was developed by Dr William Withering (1741-99) in around c1776. Portable botanical microscopes are a niche collecting area within microscopes.

4.25in (10.5cm) high

$2,000-3,000   DN

A late 19thC brass traveling drum compound monocular microscope, with rack and pinion focus, three objectives and other accessories, with fitted mahogany case.

9in (23cm) high

$300-500   ECGW

A late 19thC lacquered-brass drum compound monocular microscope, with original instruction sheet, plano-concave mirror, three bone sliders, two objectives and other accessories, with fitted mahogany case.

8in (20cm) high

$300-500   DN

INSTRUMENTS

QUICK REFERENCE - THE BACKSTAFF, OCTANT & SEXTANT

- The backstaff was invented by John Davis in c1594 and, as such, is often known as the Davis quadrant. It was held above and across a shoulder to measure the angle of the sun. It largely superseded the earlier and less accurate cross staff. Around 1730, the backstaff was transformed by John Hadley into the octant, which went into common usage during the 1750s. Although octants were still used until c1900, they were largely replaced from c1770 by sextants. The sextant, named because it represents one sixth of a circle, was more accurate than the octant and is still used today. Production boomed after 1800, with notable makers including John Bird (d.1776), Jesse Ramsden (d.1800) and Edward Troughton (d.1836).

A mahogany octant, by John Hardy Ratcliff, London, with inset ivory Vernier scale, with brass pinhole sights, interchangeable mirror pair and two brass feet, with maker's plate inscribed 'Made by Ino Hardy Ratcliff London', with erased owner's name and faded date '1777'.

1777   *16.25in (41cm) long*

$1,200-1,800   **CM**

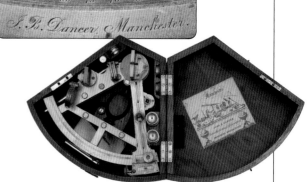

A mid-19thC polished brass sextant, by J B Dancer, Manchester, with 6.5in (16.5cm) radius, signed double frame, silvered scale, magnifier, mirrors and shades, with original fitted keystone case with accessories and printed paper trade label.

John Benjamin Dancer worked from 43 Cross Street in Manchester between 1847 and 1878, which means that this sextant can be dated to that period. Known for his high quality scientific and navigational instruments, Dancer (1812-87) also invented microphotography in 1839 and the stereographic camera in 1852.

12in (30.5cm) long

$2,500-3,500   **CM**

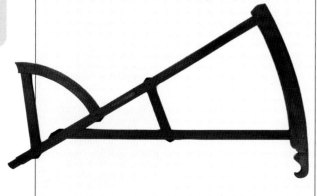

An 18thC rosewood and boxwood backstaff, divided over one side, the great arc to 35 degrees, the small arc to 60 degrees, unsigned.

25in (63.5cm) long

$5,000-7,000   **CM**

A mid-19thC oxidized and polished brass sextant, by Spencer Browning & Co., with 6in (15cm) radius, inset silvered Vernier scale, mirrors and shades, the original fitted case with dated trade label for William Heath, Portsmouth.

This sextant bears an inscription stating that it was owned by Captain Hay RN, Commander of the Royal Yacht 'Victoria & Albert'. Such a provenance will have added some value to the piece.

1884   *10in (25.5cm) long*

$700-1,000   **CM**

A late 19thC oxidized-brass 'Hezzanith' sextant, by Heath & Co. Ltd., signed on the arc, with silvered Vernier scale, magnifier, sighting objective shades, mirrors and fruitwood handle, with original fitted case, with test certificate for 1897.

This sextant was owned by George Louis Browne RN, who was awarded the China Medal of 1900 with a Relief of Pekin clasp, made lieutenant in 1903 and awarded the Croix de Guerre by the French President in 1918.

10.25in (26cm) long

$550-750   **CM**

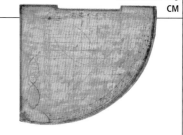

A late 19thC Turkish wood and paper quadrant, with an engraved trigonometric grid, punctuated with geometrically arranged dots and inscriptions to the edges, unsigned and undated, varnish discolored and with old wear and losses.

In general, middle and near Eastern versions of instruments are less desirable and valuable than European examples.

6.25in (16cm) long

$120-180   **CM**

An ivory Nuremberg compass
sundial, with string gnomon, the lid inscribed with a dog, the base with scratched doodles and possible 'H*G' maker's mark, the edge of the interior marked with common hours.

The string casts a shadow, which falls on the inscribed hour, thus telling the time. The 'H*G' mark may indicate that this dial was made by mid-16thC dial maker Johann Gebhart. Another dial by Gebhart, currently held in the Whipple Museum, is marked in a similar way.

3in (7.5cm) long

$2,500-3,500   CM

An 18thC mahogany-cased compass, with equinoctial silver-plated and brass ring.

3in (7.5cm) wide

$300-500   ECGW

A lacquered and silvered brass plane table compass, signed 'E. Kraft & Sohn in Wien No. 1360', the original mahogany case with sliding lid.

c1860   5in (12.5cm) wide

$300-500   DOR

A plane table compass, by Pierre Gourdin, Paris, the printed dial signed 'Gourdin à Paris', with half-blued-steel pointer, silvered outer ring and swivel mounted sight, the original wooden case signed and dated 'Gourdin à Paris 1780'.

1780   6.5in (16.5cm) diam

$400-600   CM

A 19thC brass surveyor's sighting compass dial, by Potter, London, the silvered dial with foliate-engraved eight-point compass rose signed 'Potter Poultry London', mounted in a brass case with opposing hinged sighting arms, with tripod stand.

8.25in (21cm) long

$1,000-1,500   DN

A 19thC surveying compass, by Cary, London, the silvered dial within a brass drum case on a square bedplate, with fixed pinhole sights, with brass cover.

3.75in (9.5cm) wide

$400-600   CM

A late 19thC gilt-brass pocket aneroid barometer and altimeter, by J Lizars, Glasgow, with signed silvered dial, blued-steel pointer, adjustable bezel and watch-form case with suspension ring, with original leather-covered fitted case.

2in (5cm) diam

$250-350   DN

INSTRUMENTS

A Regency 3in (7.5cm) pocket globe, probably by Nathaniel Lane, London, the original fishskin case lined with celestial maps, dated.

1818

$5,000-7,000   **GORL**

A CLOSER LOOK AT A BETTS'S GLOBE

This unusual globe expands like an umbrella, which allowed the globe to be easily portable, but also large enough to show detail.

Betts first made folding globes in the 1850s before selling out to George Philip & Sons after the 1880s. Philip's later, updated edition is more commonly found today.

This is an early edition with very different geography, political boundaries and cities (for example Chicago is not identified) than found on the Philip edition.

Condition is critical. This example is in superb condition and can still be expanded. The fact that the box is also present adds further value.

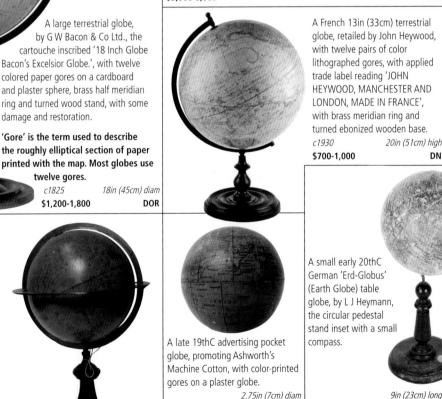

A Betts's Patent portable globe, with color lithograph-printed silk on an expandable metal frame, the original wooden box with printed advertisements inside and 'BETTS'S PATENT PORTABLE GLOBE' printed on three exterior sides.

Globe 15in (38cm) diam

$3,000-5,000   **LHA**

A large terrestrial globe, by G W Bacon & Co Ltd., the cartouche inscribed '18 Inch Globe Bacon's Excelsior Globe.', with twelve colored paper gores on a cardboard and plaster sphere, brass half meridian ring and turned wood stand, with some damage and restoration.

'Gore' is the term used to describe the roughly elliptical section of paper printed with the map. Most globes use twelve gores.

c1825   18in (45cm) diam

$1,200-1,800   **DOR**

A French 13in (33cm) terrestrial globe, retailed by John Heywood, with twelve pairs of color lithographed gores, with applied trade label reading 'JOHN HEYWOOD, MANCHESTER AND LONDON, MADE IN FRANCE', with brass meridian ring and turned ebonized wooden base.

c1930   20in (51cm) high

$700-1,000   **DN**

A late 19thC French celestial desk globe, by A Delamarche, Paris, with brass meridian ring and molded ebonized circular stand.

18.25in (46cm) high

$1,200-1,800   **AH**

A late 19thC advertising pocket globe, promoting Ashworth's Machine Cotton, with color-printed gores on a plaster globe.

2.75in (7cm) diam

$400-600   **TEN**

A small early 20thC German 'Erd-Globus' (Earth Globe) table globe, by L J Heymann, the circular pedestal stand inset with a small compass.

9in (23cm) long

$250-350   **CAPE**

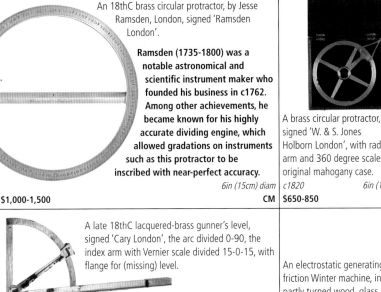

An 18thC brass circular protractor, by Jesse Ramsden, London, signed 'Ramsden London'.

Ramsden (1735-1800) was a notable astronomical and scientific instrument maker who founded his business in c1762. Among other achievements, he became known for his highly accurate dividing engine, which allowed gradations on instruments such as this protractor to be inscribed with near-perfect accuracy.

6in (15cm) diam

$1,000-1,500   CM

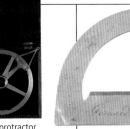

A brass circular protractor, signed 'W. & S. Jones Holborn London', with radius arm and 360 degree scales, with original mahogany case.

c1820   6in (15cm) diam

$650-850   DOR

A mid-18thC brass protractor, signed 'Renard à Paris', with scales from 180–0 and 0–180.

4in (10cm) wide

$150-250   DOR

A late 18thC lacquered-brass gunner's level, signed 'Cary London', the arc divided 0-90, the index arm with Vernier scale divided 15-0-15, with flange for (missing) level.

This was probably made at William Cary's workshop on the Strand between 1789 and 1821.

Arc 17.75in (45cm) long

$300-500   CM

QUICK REFERENCE - 'CURTA' CALCULATOR

- The 'Curta' calculator was designed by Curt Herzstak (1902-88) in the late 1930s and produced in Lichtenstein from the late 1940s until 1972.
- The Type I cost $125 and around 80,000 examples were produced until production ceased in 1972.
- The Type I and Type II 'Curtas' were considered the world's best portable calculators until they were replaced in c1970 by handheld electronic calculators.
- After the mid-1960s, the crank and metal carrying cases were made in plastic rather than metal. Early metal models can be dated from their serial numbers and are more desirable and valuable.

An electrostatic generating friction Winter machine, in partly turned wood, glass and brass, some parts missing.

Like the Van de Graaff generators found in schoolrooms across the world, this machine generated electricity, here using friction.

c1780   25in (64cm) high

$1,000-1,500   DOR

A Rema Patent mechanical calculator, serial no.6018, with wooden base and cover.

c1918   Cover 11in (29cm) long

$400-600   DOR

A Contina Type I 'Curta' mechanical calculator, serial no.38512, with minor damage, with matching metal case.

1959   3.5in (8.5cm) high

$900-1,200   DOR

A late 19thC mahogany-cased barograph with thermometer, by Ross, London, with clockwork drum movement, platform with balance guards, eight cell aneroid, cut glass ink bottle, case with beveled glass panels, base with frieze drawer.

15in (37.2cm) wide

$650-850   BELL

A 19thC 4in (10cm) brass reflecting telescope, by Henry Pyefinch, London, with rod adjustment, dust cover and sighting tube, engraved 'Pyefinch, Cornhill, London', with two spare objectives, on a folding tripod base, in need of restoration.

Henry Pyefinch (d.1790) studied under celebrated instrument maker Francis Watkins in 1753 and was in business on his own from 1763. In 1768 he was successfully sued by Dollond for infringing the patent on an achromatic lens. Although relatively large numbers of his telescopes are known, 4in (10cm) reflectors are rare.

26in (66cm) long

$1,000-1,500   L&T

QUICK REFERENCE - TELESCOPES TYPES

- There are two types of telescope - the reflecting and the refracting.
- The refracting telescope uses a series of lenses to capture and 'reflect' what is being viewed into an eyepiece. It was invented in 1608 by Zacharias Janssen, a spectacle maker in the Netherlands. Galileo devised his own version a year later, which he named the 'perspicillum'. Although the word telescope was first used in 1612, the Galilean telescope continued to be commonly known as a 'perspective glass' for several years. The reflecting telescope was invented in 1663 by John Gregory and was developed by Sir Isaac Newton. It uses mirrors of polished metal to do the same job. Barrels are usually short and wide.

A late 18th/early 19thC brass 'Gregorian' reflecting telescope, with internal rack focus adjustment for the secondary mirror, inscribed with repairer's name' J. Fuller, 1845', on a folding tripod base, with fitted box.

Body tube 15in (38cm) long

$1,200-1,800   DN

A presentation 1.5in (4cm) single-draw refracting telescope, by Troughton & Simms, London, inscribed 'Captain John Pollard for saving the crew of the schooner Lebanon of Dundee in 1863', with original fitted mahogany box.

28in (71cm) long

$1,500-2,500   CM

An early 19thC 1.25in (4cm) three-draw refracting telescope, by Ramsden, London, with nickel-plated tubes and wooden main tube, signed 'Ramsden, London', in original wood and leather case.

This form and type of telescope is extremely common. This example is only worth as much as it is because it is by Ramsden (see p.235). Most unmarked examples of this type are worth well under $150 or, if they are in worn condition, under $100.

7.75in (19.5cm) high

$200-300   CM

A mid-19thC lacquered-brass refracting telescope, by Merz & Son, Munich, with three-lens eyepiece, signed 'G. Merz und Sohn in München', with lens cap.

1858   *Extended 6in (15.5cm) long*

$400-600   DOR

A late 19thC lacquered-brass and wood refracting telescope, by Dollond, London, missing eyepiece mount.

Extended 13.75in (35cm) long

$70-100   GORB

A three-draw brass telescope, by Dollond, London, engraved 'Dollond, London, Day & Night', with mahogany hand grip.

Extended 86in (34cm) long

$300-500   A&G

A pair of late Victorian binoculars, by J Trotter, Optician, 24, Gordon Street, Glasgow, engraved 'Nathaniel Dunlop, April 7th 1891', with leather case.

$150-250 ROS

A late 18thC ivory-cased monocular, by Jesse Ramsden, London, with 1.5in (4cm) objective, the nickel-plated draw signed 'RAMSDEN LONDON', with original Morocco leather-covered wooden case.

3.75in (8.5cm) long

$800-1,200 CM

A late 18th/early 19thC pocket spy glass, with folding eyepiece and larger magnifying lens and finger ring, inscribed 'Bleuler-London'.

John Bleuler was an optician working at 27 Ludgate Street, London. He died in 1829.

1.75in (4.5cm) long

$400-600 LC

Mark Picks

Not all antique scientific, optical and precision instruments have been superseded by modern electronic versions! The camera lucida is still of enormous help to an artist. Although described 200 years earlier by Johannes Kepler, it was patented by William Wollaston in 1806. It uses a prism to enable the subject being viewed and the artist's paper or canvas to be seen together. The artist would place the subject a suitable distance away in front of the prism and the paper directly below it. By looking down through the prism, he or she could then create an accurate sketch of the subject on the paper without having to look up and check their work at every instance. Antique examples like this are often of very fine quality and add a certain romanticism to sketching. While using one, today's artist can wonder whose eyes looked through the prism before and at what?

A 19thC lacquered-brass camera lucida, by Dollond, London, with a stained wood box.

$250-350 A&G

A pair of late 19thC Lemaire mother-of-pearl cased opera glasses, stamped 'LEMAIRE FAB. PARIS', the original case with 'Taub Bros. & Co. Jewelers Detroit, MI.' retailer's stamp.

These opera glasses would have been a luxury item. The value of similar items would be reduced if any of the mother-of-pearl panels have been replaced or, worse, are missing.

$120-180 DMC

A Victorian figured walnut table-top stereoscope viewer, with easel support, fretwork fold-down card holder, twin lens viewer and a large single lens, on brass post supports.

16in (41cm) long

$200-300 CAPE

An early 20thC tinplate and lacquered-brass epidioscope, missing burner, with outer case.

Although this device resembles a magic lantern, it lacks the slide holder behind the front lens. This gives a clue to its function. An epidioscope is used for projecting and viewing opaque objects, such as leaves, rocks or book pages. As such, it is a predecessor to the overhead projector.

$50-70 CAPE

A late 19thC Rowsell rosewood graphoscope, with a 4.75 inch (12cm) adjustable lens, with an inset Ivorine disc stamped 'Rowsell's Graphoscope Patent'.

The finer the wood and decoration, the more graphoscopes tend to fetch.

15.5in (39.5cm) long

$150-250 WW

INSTRUMENTS

A late 19thC American medical amputation set, by L V Helmold, Philadelphia, the instruments with chequered ebony grip and stamped with the maker's name, with mahogany case, missing one small instrument.

Box 13.75in (35cm) wide

$1,200-1,800 **DN**

A 19thC mahogany medicine box, lined in red velvet and with two central lift-out trays, with seventeen bottles, missing one bottle and some stoppers.

10in (25.5cm) wide

$650-850 **DA&H**

An early 19thC steel and gilt surgical trepan/trephine, with steel crown bit and center pin with an adjustable screw, with a turned and diced ebony handle.

This instrument was designed to remove a small disc of bone from a skull in a process known as trepanning. Practiced since Prehistoric times, trepanning was used to treat a number of illnesses related to the head and brain.

4.25in (11cm) high

$300-500 **WW**

An early 19thC steel surgeon's bone saw, marked 'Laundy' and with a crown, with ivory handle.

The firm of Laundy was known at 12 St Thomas's Street, Borough, London 1783-1819.

c1810-15 *14.5in (37cm) long*

$400-600 **WW**

Twelve 19thC amber-glass apothecary bottles and stoppers, enameled with crested shields titled with the contents.

10in (25cm) high

$2,000-3,000 **WW**

An amusing temperature-demonstration model.

c1900 *3.75in (9.5cm) high*

$300-400 **DOR**

A painted plaster anatomical human head model, by Franz Jos. Steger, with minor damage.

c1870 *15in (37cm) high*

$1,200-1,800 **DOR**

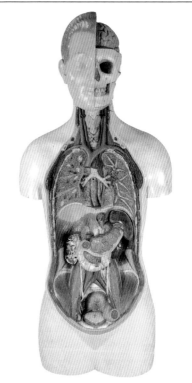

A painted composition anatomical male head and torso model, together with numbered internal organs.

35in (88.5cm) high

$500-700 **ROS**

Mark Picks

Over the past few years Pyrex kitchenware has become increasingly sought after by a younger generation of 'retro' collectors who buy to both decorate their kitchens and use them when they cook, especially for guests. Condition is paramount, so scratches or chips will make a piece almost unsaleable. The brighter the colors and more 'retro' or 'vintage' the pattern, the more it is likely to be worth. Don't book the cruise yet, though, as the trendsetters don't pay vast sums, and few pieces of Pyrex are worth over $50. This piece is only worth as much as it is because it a rare item in unused condition and retains its box.

A Pyrex 'Gaiety' pattern casserole dish on warmer stand, in unused condition, with original box and packaging.

Box 13.75in (35cm) wide

$70-100   **MA**

A mid-late 1950s Phoenix glass casserole dish, with applied color.

The mark can be read correctly when you look down into the bowl, but is reversed if you turn the base over and read it. Opaque Pyrex was introduced in the 1950s.

7.75in (20cm) wide

$15-25   **GROB**

A Pyrex glass 'Snowflake' pattern handled pouring bowl.

Pyrex was released by Corning Glass in 1924 and made in the UK by Jobling. Other companies, such as Phoenix Glass, also produced their own versions.

6in (15.5cm) wide

$15-25   **GROB**

A Pyrex glass butterdish, decorated with square motifs.

6in (15cm) long

$15-25   **GROB**

A Pyrex glass triangular dish, decorated with fruits.

6.25in (16cm) wide

$15-25   **GROB**

A Pyrex glass handled pouring bowl, no.320, with applied color.

6in (15.5cm) long

$15-25   **GROB**

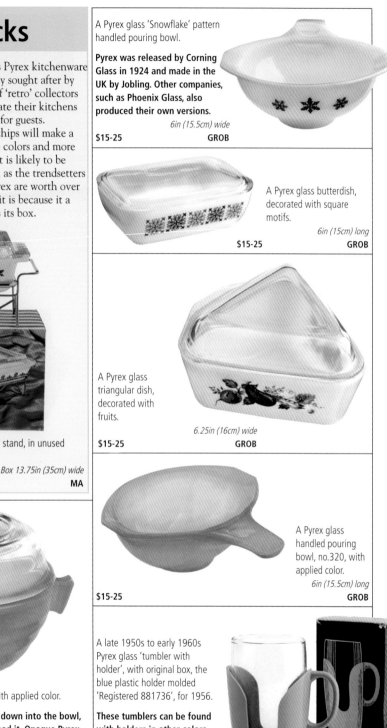

A late 1950s to early 1960s Pyrex glass 'tumbler with holder', with original box, the blue plastic holder molded 'Registered 881736', for 1956.

These tumblers can be found with holders in other colors, such as yellow or red.

5in (12.5cm) high

$15-25   **GROB**

KITCHENALIA

A CLOSER LOOK AT A COFFEE MAKER

This stove-top coffee machine was designed by Giordano Robbiati of Milan in 1946. Patents for manufacture in other countries and the USA were granted from 1946 to 1952.

Arguably ahead of its time, the curving design is very space-age, but also reflects streamlined design of the period.

The cup and the machine are made from aluminum, which was used for many household items in the late 1940s due to a desire to use 'new' materials and also to use up wartime stocks used for airplanes and other weapons.

Made until c1986, vintage models are highly sought-after by collectors of modern design. The coffee it produces is also legendary among aficionados!

An Italian Atomic for Sears Roebuck & Co. aluminum and Bakelite 'Atomic' espresso maker, designed by Giordano Robbiati in 1946, with cup and maker's plaque.

8in (20.5cm) high

$250-350   QU

A Dansk Designs teak 'Congo' ice bucket, model 810, designed by Jens Quistgaard, the base marked 'DANSK DESIGNS IHQ'.

Dansk was founded in 1954 and its main designer until the 1980s was Jens Quistgaard (1919-2008). His designs, identified by an 'IHQ' monogram on the base, have risen in popularity and value in recent years and look set to stay high. Made in two sizes (this is the larger), this design was inspired by the prow of a Viking longboat.

15.5in (39.5cm) high

$250-350   GC

A small Dansk Design teak bucket, designed by Jens Quistgaard, the base marked 'DANSK DESIGN IHQ'.

11in (28cm) high

$120-180   GC

A 1950s-60s chrome plated salt and pepper shaker and stand, in the form of a jet fighter.

4.75in (12cm) high

$250-350   SWO

A Scandinavian teak ice bucket and cover, with wickerwork finish handles, unmarked.

$120-180   WHP

A pair of Danish wenge candlesticks, the bases stamped 'ESP WENGE DENMARK'.

Wenge is a dark wood with a characteristic grain from the tropical Millettia Laurentii tree.

12in (30.5cm) high

$80-120   GC

A Victorian Kent's oak and cast iron knife sharpener, with brass and enamel maker's plaques reading 'Kent/Patentee of Manufacturer, 199 High Holborn, London'.

22in (55cm) high

$120-180   CHT

QUICK REFERENCE - LOUIS VUITTON

- Louis Vuitton founded his eponymous luggage and fashion company in 1854.
- Louis Vuitton was the first company to popularize the flat-topped trunk, which could be stacked easily on voyages. Before this dome-topped trunks had been standard.
- Vuitton used a Trianon canvas to ensure that its trunks remained waterproof. Beige and brown striped canvas was introduced in 1876, with the square 'Damier' canvas following in 1888. The 'LV' monogram canvas arrived in 1896 and became a hallmark of the company's designs.
- Vintage Louis Vuitton pieces have become hugely sought after by interior decorators, who use them as furniture or display them stacked in a room.
- Specially commissioned pieces or those with niche uses, such as musical instrument cases, can also fetch large sums.

An early 20thC Louis Vuitton canvas and wood lady's high trunk, the linen-lined interior with trays and compartments, the exterior painted with previous owner's initials, the label numbered 769096, the lock plate with addresses, '052567' and impressed name, scuffed, marked and worn.

35.75in (91cm) wide

$10,000-15,000   **DN**

A late 19thC Louis Vuitton canvas and wood trunk, with two internal trays, the label numbered '12589'.

32in (81cm) long

$7,000-10,000   **GORL**

A Louis Vuitton canvas and wood steamer trunk, with fitted interior, the label numbered '822142', with original keys.

Letters on labels indicate where a piece was made. The serial number can often be used to date a piece and identify its original use and sometimes even (for very special pieces) the identity of the original owner.

1941   *36in (91.5cm) long*

$7,000-10,000   **LHA**

A Louis Vuitton canvas and wood vanity case, the interior with lift-out tray, the label numbered '1027452', stamped, with original keys.

15.75in (40cm) long

$2,000-3,000   **DN**

A rare mid-late 20thC Louis Vuitton canvas and wood wine or aperitif hamper, the fall-front opening to a suede-lined interior with compartments for chrome and glass fittings, with stamped marks throughout, in good condition.

14.5in (37cm) high

$10,000-15,000   **DN**

A late 20thC Louis Vuitton canvas and wood hat box, stamped 'Louis Vuitton/Made in the USA under special license', with original keys.

18.5in (47cm) diam

$1,200-1,800   **LHA**

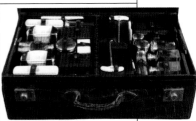

A Drew & Sons crocodile-skin suitcase, with lift-out tray and compartments containing silver-topped glass, ivory and leather-covered dressing accessories, the silver by George Neal, London, inscribed with monograms.

1919   *30in (76cm) wide*

$1,500-2,500   **DN**

A Mappin & Webb crocodile-skin suitcase, with internal pockets holding silver-gilt-topped glass accessories, the silver by Mappin & Webb, London, missing some pieces.

1927 *21.75in (55cm) wide*

$1,200-1,800 DN

An early Victorian leather-bound lady's traveling case, the fitted interior with silver-gilt-mounted jars and bottles and other accessories, the silver with hallmarks for London and monogrammed 'HBL', the case cover initialed 'HL'.

1838 *12in (30.5cm) wide*

$500-700 DN

A Victorian burr-walnut vanity case, the fitted interior with silver-mounted chequer-cut glass jars and bottles, the silver by John Howes, London, monogrammed 'KFA', the case with lock engraved 'Patent' beneath a crown and 'S. Mordan & Co. London', the drawer with blue leather cover over jewelry compartments.

The value of these vanity cases depends on the complexity and quantity of the fittings and contents, the quality of the materials and workmanship, and the maker. The work of prestigious names, such as Sampson Mordan, Asprey or Mappin & Webb, will fetch a premium.

1861 *12.75in (32cm) wide*

$1,200-1,800 DN

A 1950s Brexton faux-leather picnic hamper, containing crockery, cutlery, flasks, food containers and other items.

$70-100 WHP

A Hermès crocodile-skin traveling vanity case, with nickel fittings, the fall-front opening to black leather interior with compartments, with three brush surrounds, three boxes and a wallet, the lock plate with stamped marks, with label.

18.5in (47cm) wide

$1,500-2,500 DN

A late 20thC Asprey leather-covered writing case, with gilt-metal fittings, the interior with folders and detachable writing board, stamped 'Asprey London' in gilt.

12.5in (34.5cm) long

$350-450 WW

A crocodile-skin suitcase, with a pocketed fabric interior, and leather lining, with trade label for 'CUTHBERTSON & HARPER, CALCUTTA', with English lever locks and key.

20in (51cm) wide

$400-600 WW

An early 20thC leather 'leg of mutton'-shaped rifle case, with shoulder carrying strap and handle.

$70-100 ECGW

QUICK REFERENCE - ART GLASS MARBLES

- Early glass marbles were handmade, predominantly in Germany, from the 1860s to the 1920s. Marbles were machine-made from the early 20thC.
- The late 20thC saw a boom in the production of 'art glass' marbles and spheres that were not intended as playthings. Such marbles or spheres were made by independent studio glass artists.
- Many explore the reflective, refractive or magnifying properties of optical glass.
- Value is dependent on technique, size and maker. Notable artists include Paul Stankard, Jessie Taj and Daniel Benway.

A two-color plunge floral starburst borosilicate glass marble, by Jerry Kelly, with controlled air bubbles.
c2000-12   *1.5in (4cm) diam*
$50-70   **BGL**

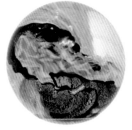

A dichoric glass 'Banded Swirl' marble, by Nina Paladino and Michael Hansen, with thick ribbon swirl.
2000-10   *3.25in (8.5cm) diam*
$50-70   **BGL**

A glass 'Lots of Mayhem' rake-pull marble, by Daniel Benway, with reverse design and applied opaque-white and transparent-purple blobs.
2000-10   *3.5in (9cm) diam*
$200-300   **BGL**

An 'end of day' glass frit marble, by Kris Parke, with a six-panel lobe core swirl.

'End of day' glass was made by the glassworkers in their own time at the end of the day. It usually uses up the remaining molten glass in the pots and therefore tends to be a mixture of colors.
c2000-12   *1.5in (4cm) diam*
$50-70   **BGL**

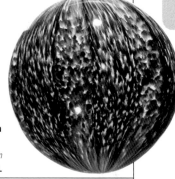

A glass 'Banded' marble, by Kris Parke, with green crosshatched design and orange separating bands over a black core.
2in (5cm) diam
$120-180   **BGL**

A glass 'Reticello' marble, by Joshua Sable, with multicolored filigrana surrounding a reticello design.
2000-10   *1.5in (4cm) diam*
$80-120   **BGL**

A floral glass marble, by Beth Tomasello, with two hemispheres of lampworked floral groups.
1.75in (4.5cm) diam
$150-250   **BGL**

A borosilicate glass 'Vortex' marble, by Chad Trent, the swirling vortex centered by a Gilson opal.

Pierre Gilson created the first synthetic opal in 1974.
2000-10   *1.5in (4cm) diam*
$70-100   **BGL**

A glass 'Abstract' marble, by Virginia Wilson Toccalino, containing multicolored ribbons.
2000-10   *3in (7.5cm) diam*
$150-250   **BGL**

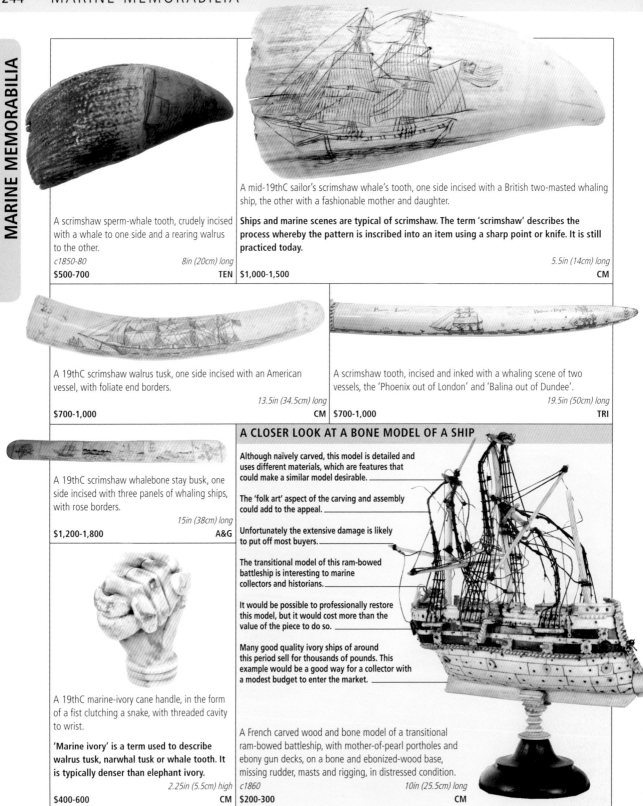

A scrimshaw sperm-whale tooth, crudely incised with a whale to one side and a rearing walrus to the other.

c1850-80   *8in (20cm) long*

$500-700   TEN

A mid-19thC sailor's scrimshaw whale's tooth, one side incised with a British two-masted whaling ship, the other with a fashionable mother and daughter.

Ships and marine scenes are typical of scrimshaw. The term 'scrimshaw' describes the process whereby the pattern is inscribed into an item using a sharp point or knife. It is still practiced today.

                                                  5.5in (14cm) long

$1,000-1,500   CM

A 19thC scrimshaw walrus tusk, one side incised with an American vessel, with foliate end borders.

                                        13.5in (34.5cm) long

$700-1,000   CM

A scrimshaw tooth, incised and inked with a whaling scene of two vessels, the 'Phoenix out of London' and 'Balina out of Dundee'.

                                        19.5in (50cm) long

$700-1,000   TRI

A 19thC scrimshaw whalebone stay busk, one side incised with three panels of whaling ships, with rose borders.

                                        15in (38cm) long

$1,200-1,800   A&G

A CLOSER LOOK AT A BONE MODEL OF A SHIP

Although naïvely carved, this model is detailed and uses different materials, which are features that could make a similar model desirable.

The 'folk art' aspect of the carving and assembly could add to the appeal.

Unfortunately the extensive damage is likely to put off most buyers.

The transitional model of this ram-bowed battleship is interesting to marine collectors and historians.

It would be possible to professionally restore this model, but it would cost more than the value of the piece to do so.

Many good quality ivory ships of around this period sell for thousands of pounds. This example would be a good way for a collector with a modest budget to enter the market.

A 19thC marine-ivory cane handle, in the form of a fist clutching a snake, with threaded cavity to wrist.

'Marine ivory' is a term used to describe walrus tusk, narwhal tusk or whale tooth. It is typically denser than elephant ivory.

                                        2.25in (5.5cm) high

$400-600   CM

A French carved wood and bone model of a transitional ram-bowed battleship, with mother-of-pearl portholes and ebony gun decks, on a bone and ebonized-wood base, missing rudder, masts and rigging, in distressed condition.

c1860   *10in (25.5cm) long*

$200-300   CM

A 20thC brass bridge binnacle and compass, by Sestrel, with liquid-filled compass bowl, gimbal mount, glazed cover, oil lamp and Kelvin magnetic correction spheres.

44in (111.5cm) high

$500-700   CM

A 19thC merchant carved and painted wooden figurehead, in the form of a woman, her dress terminating in a scrolled base.

40in (101.5cm) high

$3,000-4,000   CM

A brass ship's bell, from the River-class destroyer HMS 'Boyne', with molded rim and shoulder, with black-filled lettering.

Launched in 1905, HMS 'Boyne' survived World War I. She was sold for scrap in in 1919, but was instead sunk as a target. This bell was recovered from her wreck in 1988. It might have been worth considerably more if 'Boyne' had had a highly notable career.

1905   *12.5in (32cm) high*

$1,200-1,800   CM

A Russian three-bolt oxygen-helium deep-sea-diving helmet, in copper and brass, the front threaded for removal, with rebreathing inlets, adjustable exhaust valve, weight studs, hooks, threads and handle to top.

20in (52cm) high

$2,500-3,500   CM

A candle sconce or épergne, made from a converted speaking-tube whistle, inscribed 'H.M.S. T.B.D. ORIOLE', with drip tray, on silver-plated ball feet.

12in (30.5cm) high

$550-750   CM

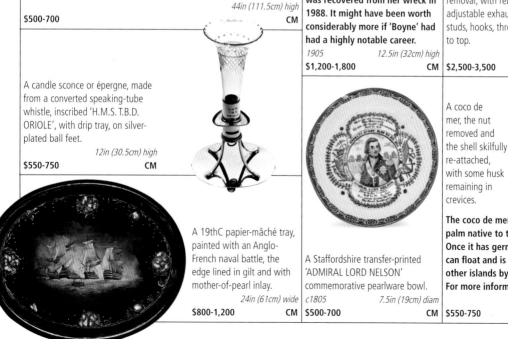

A 19thC papier-mâché tray, painted with an Anglo-French naval battle, the edge lined in gilt and with mother-of-pearl inlay.

24in (61cm) wide

$800-1,200   CM

A Staffordshire transfer-printed 'ADMIRAL LORD NELSON' commemorative pearlware bowl.

c1805   *7.5in (19cm) diam*

$500-700   CM

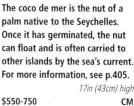

A coco de mer, the nut removed and the shell skilfully re-attached, with some husk remaining in crevices.

The coco de mer is the nut of a palm native to the Seychelles. Once it has germinated, the nut can float and is often carried to other islands by the sea's current. For more information, see p.405.

17in (43cm) high

$550-750   CM

METALWARE

QUICK REFERENCE - METALWARE

- Pewter (an alloy of tin, lead and antimony) has been used for tableware since medieval times, but few examples from before the late 17thC survive. Most early pewter wares were melted down, discarded or recast into other forms.
- As the 18thC progressed, ceramics, silver and Britannia metal increasingly replaced pewter. Production of spun- and electroplated pewter continued into the 20thC.
- Early forms from the 17thC and early 18thC, particularly those decorated with wrigglework, tend to be the most sought after and American pewter is often very desirable and valuable. In general, however, interest in pewter has dropped in the past few years. As a result, values for many objects have fallen and collections can be built up from affordable pieces. Most late 19thC and 20thC

pewter is currently not in demand, unless it is in the Arts & Crafts or Art Nouveau style and by a notable designer.
- Standard functional brass and copper pieces have also fallen in value over the past ten years. As with pewter, early forms and pieces in strong styles by notable designers can often fetch good prices, but these only make up around 10% of the market.
- By comparison, values for many designs in stainless steel (developed in 1913) and aluminum have risen dramatically. These pieces are designed in a modern style that fits with today's tastes and can also be put in a dishwasher, which is attractive to modern buyers. Key designers include Robert Welch, Stuart Devlin and Arne Jacobsen. Look out for designs that have a strong Mid-century Modern look, as these may rise in value.

An early 19thC pewter unlidded baluster gill measure, Newcastle, with shield-shape verification mark to rim, the inside stamped 'Imperial'.

3.5in (9cm) high

$250-350   WW

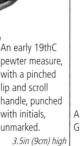

An early 19thC pewter measure, with a pinched lip and scroll handle, punched with initials, unmarked.

3.5in (9cm) high

$150-250   WW

A Scottish pewter Imperial half pint measure, Glasgow, with a shell thumbpiece.

5.5in (14cm) high

$80-120   WW

A pewter 'Spire' flagon, with a domed lid, 'chair back' thumbpiece and a double scroll handle, with a tapering drum and flared base, unmarked.

The knop of the lid, spout and handle are very decorative. Note the thumbpiece, used for opening the lid with one hand, which is shaped like the back of a chair. Flagons are one of the more sought-after pewter shapes.

13.25in (33.5cm) high

$500-700   WW

A late 19thC pewter coffee pot, by James Dixon & Sons, with a scroll handle.

10.75in (27cm) high

$80-120   DA&H

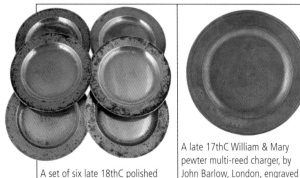

A set of six late 18thC polished pewter plates, by Burgum & Catcott, the bases with touch and hallmarks (Cott 708) and owner's monogram of a 'B' over 'SS'.

9.5in (24cm) diam

$400-600　　WW

A late 17thC William & Mary pewter multi-reed charger, by John Barlow, London, engraved with a later armorial, the rim with trailing wriggle work leaves and faux 'hallmarks', the reverse with touchmark (Cott 256).

16.5in (42cm) diam

$550-750　　WW

A CLOSER LOOK AT A PEWTER CHARGER

Tulip and wrigglework patterns are desirable. They are often found on painted furniture and other folk art.

The period of manufacture and date add value.

Timothy Fly was an important London maker whose works are sought after. He was working by 1710 and became a master in 1739.

The Cott number relates to Howard Cotterrell's landmark book of 1963, 'Old Pewter and its Makers and Marks', which lists many makers behind marks.

Chargers display patterns well and also have great eye appeal when displayed on a wall or oak dresser.

A George I wrigglework pewter charger, by Timothy Fly, London, the center decorated with a stylized tulip, the rim with owner's initials 'W' over 'TM' flanked by 'MW 1716' within a cartouche issuing trailing tulips and terminating with '1699', the reverse with touch mark (Cott 1704).

c1716　　*18in (46cm) diam*

$2,500-3,500　　WW

A French pewter bowl, with a shaped reeded edge, the base with indistinct crown mark and owners initials 'I G'.

12.25in (31cm) diam

$120-180　　WW

A pair of 17thC-style pewter trumpet candlesticks, with circular nozzle, drip trays and flared circular bases, the underside of each drip tray with 'B.B' touch mark.

7.5in (18cm) high

$1,000-1,500　　TOV

An early to mid-20thC pewter mug, by Travis Wilson & Co., Sheffield, the handle cast as a nude female, numbered '2699'.

6.85in (17cm) high

$150-250　　LHA

A 1930s five-piece pewter tea set, the hammered surface with rows of hemispherical discs, with Bakelite handles.

Although in a pleasing Arts & Crafts style, these sets are not hard to find and are largely undesirable as people believe that they can't be used.

$80-120　　WHP

METALWARE

QUICK REFERENCE - THE NEWLYN SCHOOL

● Due to a downturn in the income provided by fishing in Cornwall, unemployed fishermen were trained to produce works in copper (a commonly found Cornish asset), which they could then sell. In 1890, John McKenzie founded the Newlyn Industrial Class and invited artists and designers to collaborate with him. Functional domestic items such as dishes, frames and trays were produced with repoussé designs, often of marine subjects, in the Arts & Crafts or Art Nouveau styles. John Pearson (fl.1885-1910) was a master craftsman at Newlyn. This dish is typical of his work. Pearson worked with and was influenced by William de Morgan (see pp.351-52). He co-founded the Guild of Handicraft at Whitechapel, London with C R Ashbee in 1888. Newlyn copper is highly sought after today.

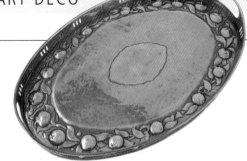

A Newlyn copper tray, hammered in relief with a frieze of apples, with raised, pierced gallery, stamped 'Newlyn'.

17.5in (47cm) wide

$400-600   WW

A Newlyn copper bowl, by John Pearson, repoussé hammered with a sailing boat, the reverse signed, numbered '2287' and dated.

1896   15in (38cm) diam

$2,500-3,500   GHOU

A Newlyn copper tapering square section jug, hammered in relief with a cormorant flanking a central sun motif, the base with stamped mark, with wicker handle.

7.5in (17cm) high

$550-750   WW

A Newlyn copper tea caddy, 'Longships', by Herbert Dyer, hammered in relief with the Longships lighthouse, a fish and a fishing boat, the base with stamped marks.

5in (15cm) high

$700-1,000   WW

A Newlyn copper vase, decorated with repoussé fish.

5in (13cm) high

$120-180   CHT

A Glasgow School brass wall sconce, attributed to Agnes Bankier Harvey, with repoussé design of an Art Nouveau maiden and stylized poppy heads above a drip tray and nozzle.

12in (30.5cm) high

$550-750   L&T

A brass wall candle sconce, by Alexander Ritchie, repoussé decorated with an Art Nouveau design of a longboat and entwined foliate motifs above a drip tray, missing nozzle.

For more information about Ritchie, see p.46.

c1920   10in (25.5cm) high
$500-700   L&T

A brass cigar box, by Alexander Ritchie, the lid repoussé decorated with a central oval panel of a longboat at sea, with a Celtic knot border.

c1920   8.25in (21cm) wide
$500-700   L&T

A WMF silver-plated condiment dish, in the form of a maiden arranging her hair, her robes flowing down to form the dishes, with stamped maker's marks to base, with glass bowls.

c1900   5.5in (14cm) high
$800-1,200   QU

An Art Deco copper bread bin, with Ivorine handles and feet.

10in (25.5cm) wide
$70-100   WHP

An Art Deco copper teapot, with ceramic interior and a black Bakelite finial, handle and base.
$30-50   WHP

A CLOSER LOOK AT A DRESSER HOT WATER JUG

Comprised of simple cones and cylinders, this geometric form is not too challenging for a metalworker to produce and is starkly modern for its early date.

Perry was known to have employed Dresser, although exact dates and details are unknown.

An identical jug signed by Dresser was included in a museum exhibition of his work in 2004.

Dr Christopher Dresser (1834-1904) is acknowledged as Europe's first industrial designer. His typically geometric and modern designs are sought after today.

A very similar form was produced in terracotta by the Watcombe Pottery, registered as a design on 3rd June 1872.

A Christopher Dresser copper and silver-plate hot water jug, probably manufactured by Richard Perry, Son & Co., the base stamped 'G1 3', with hardwood handle.

c1876-80   9.25in (23.5cm) high
$1,500-2,500   L&T

An American Wilcox Silver Plate Co. four-piece silver-plated tea set, designed by Gene Theobald, the bases with manufacturer's marks, with black Bakelite handles.

The use of silver-colored metal and black Bakelite on a clean-lined form is typical of the Art Deco style. This teaset, which exemplifies American Art Deco, is extremely rare.

c1928   8.5in (22cm) wide
$5,500-7,500   DRA

METALWARE

An early 1930s Wright Accessories spun aluminum table etagère, designed and made by Russel and Mary Wright, with two mugs or handled pots, stamped 'RUSSEL WRIGHT', with cork and cane fittings.

14in (33cm) high

$800-1,200   QU

An early 1930s Wright Accessories spun aluminum bun warmer, designed and made by Russel and Mary Wright, stamped 'RUSSEL WRIGHT', with wood and cane fittings.

These bun warmers were made by Wright and his wife Mary in a small studio in Midtown, New York City.

14in (33cm) high

$800-1,200   QU

A Stelton stainless steel ice bucket, designed by Arne Jacobsen, the base stamped 'Stelton Stainless Denmark A', designed c1965.

5.75in (14.5cm) high

$250-350   QU

A 1960s Old Hall stainless steel 'Alveston' tea set, designed by Robert Welch, the bases with stamped marks, designed 1962.

This is a landmark British design in stainless steel tableware. Harking back to the lines of the Modernist and Art Deco movements, the teapot in particular also recalls the shape of a UFO. Outer space was a key theme of the 1960s - a decade that culminated in man landing on the moon.

Teapot 4.25in (11cm) high

$200-300   WW

A Robert Welch cast-iron 'Hobart' nutcracker, molded 'R WELCH ENGLAND' under the top clamp.

6.25in (16cm) high

$50-70   GROB

A set of six Old Hall silver-plated stainless steel 'Alveston' spoons, designed by Robert Welch, in mint condition, with original box.

These spoons were usually made in stainless steel. Silver-plated versions were made to special commission so are considerably rarer today.

Box 6.25in (16cm) wide

$100-150   GROB

A Viner's set of six stainless steel 'Chelsea Steel' knives and forks, designed by Gerald Benney, in their original box, in mint condition.

Box 10.5in (27.5cm) wide

$100-150   GROB

A set of six Viner's stainless steel 'Studio' coffee spoons, designed by Gerald Benney, in mint condition, with original box.

Box 4.75in (12cm) long

$40-60   GROB

A set of six Viner's stainless steel 'Studio' knives and forks, designed by Gerald Benney, in mint condition, with original box.

Box 12in (30.5cm) long

$100-150   GROB

Mark Picks

Conrah was designed by Ronald Hughes in 1967 and produced in Wales during the 1970s. Anodized aluminum cut by machine with a pattern was expensive and challenging to produce, meaning that these pieces were not inexpensive. Their futuristic look, bright colors and sparkling faceted patterns make them typical of the late 1960s and '70s. Interest has only begun to rise over the past three years. As demand has increased prices have risen. I believe that they will continue to do so. This is a very unusual, rare and complex cut pattern. Green is also a rare color for Conrah. Buy while you can and group them together for maximum visual impact.

A large 1970s Conrah green anodized-aluminum vase, cut with bands of faceted X and ellipses, the base with incised factory mark.

10in (25.5cm) high

$150-250   GC

A 1970s Conrah aluminum vase, decorated with horizontal lines and a band of vertical faceted cut ellipses, the base with inset black plastic decal with printed factory marks.

9in (23cm) high

$120-180   GC

A 1970s Conrah rare butterscotch anodized-aluminum vase, cut with faceted stars, the base with inset black plastic decal with printed factory marks.

6in (15.5cm) high

$80-120   GC

A 1970s Conrah red anodized-aluminum bud vase, cut with faceted stars, with plain aluminum foot, unmarked.

6.75in (17.5cm) high

$30-50   GC

A small Conrah red anodized-aluminum vase, cut with faceted lozenge motifs, the base with inset black plastic Conrah mark.

8in (20.5cm) high

$50-70   GC

A 1970s Conrah red anodized-aluminum footed bowl, decorated with bands of faceted ellipses, the base with inset black plastic decal printed with factory marks.

6.75in (17.5cm) diam

$50-70   GC

METEORITES

QUICK REFERENCE - METEORITES

- A meteorite is a solid piece of debris from an asteroid or comet that survived its entry and impact into the Earth's atmosphere and surface. Before they land, these pieces of debris are known as meteoroids.
- Meteorites range from being 65 million years (meteorites from Mars) to 4.5 billion years old (meteorites from asteroids).
- They are always named after the place they were found, usually a nearby town or geographic feature.
- The best places to find meteorites are hot places, such as deserts, and Antarctica, which is the place that yields the most meteorites in the world. The oldest meteorite collected in Britain was found in 1795 and the most recent fell in 1991.
- The size and type of the meteorite and the fame of the fall contribute toward value.
- Always buy from a reputable dealer or auctioneer and make sure a meteorite comes with provenance. It should be recognized by the Meteoritical Society or come from a good reputable collection, such as a museum.

A fusion-crusted 'Campos Sales' meteorite, with deposits of oil to one end.

This meteorite is from a shower on 31st January 1991 over Ceara, Brazil. It was collected by a local resident and used as a stand to hold a can of heated peanut oil.

7in (18cm) long 71oz

$2,500-3,500   L&T

A polished part-slice from the 'Lance' meteorite.

'Lance' is one of only six stones recovered from the shower over Vendome, Loir-et-Cher, France on 23rd July 1872. 'Lance' is one of only two CO3.4's listed in the latest edition' Catalog of Meteorites'. It is rarely available to collectors.

2in (5cm) high 0.5oz

$1,000-1,500   L&T

A fragment of an L5 stone 'Mount Tazerzait' meteorite.

This meteorite fell on Mount Tazerzait, Tahoua, Niger on 21st August 1991.

4.25in (11cm) long 14oz

$800-1,200   L&T

A polished full-slice of one of the three 'Belle Plaine' meteorites.

The three 'Belle Plaine' meteorites were found across a two-mile strip near Belle Plaine, Sumner County, Kansas in 1950, 1960, and 1963.

Provenance: Monnig Meteorite Collection, Texas Christian University

8in (20.5cm) wide 21oz

$1,200-1,800   L&T

A fusion-crusted polished part-slice of one of the L6 brecciated 'L'Aigle' meteorites.

This slice is from one of the most important historic meteorite showers. It fell in L'Aigle, France and, along with the Ensisheim and Wold Cottage showers, played a major role in the general acceptance of 'stones which fall from the sky' due to the large number of eye witness accounts.

Provenance: Natural History Museum, London.

1.25in (3.5cm) long 0.17oz

$500-700   L&T

The largest piece of the 'Bechar 001' meteorite, an L5 chrondite meteorite, comprised of three reassembled fragments, the surface with dark fusion crust and deep regmaglypts.

This meteorite was found in Algeria in August 1998. Regmaglypts are thumbprint-like impressions that are formed as material erodes from the surface of a meteor passing through the Earth's atmosphere.

13.5in (34.5cm) high 511oz

$1,500-2,500   L&T

A fusion-crusted polished end piece of the H3-6 breccia 'Zag' meteorite.

This meteorite fell to Earth in Morocco during early March 1998.

2.5in (6.5cm) long 7.7oz

$1,000-1,500   L&T

QUICK REFERENCE - WORLD WAR I POSTERS

- World War I was arguably the first time that posters were used for mass propaganda purposes.
- The majority of World War I posters focused on recruitment, which was necessary on a vast scale due to the massive casualties in battles, such as those at the Somme. Other posters focused on themes such as lending to the government via bonds or stamps, or working hard on the Home Front.
- The soldier is the most commonly found motif, with the early enthusiastic soldier giving way to the more restrained image of a soldier bravely holding the trenches as the war progressed and the death toll grew.
- This poster is one of the best-known wartime posters. Alfred Leete's famous British version featuring Lord Kitchener was designed three years before this image.

'I WANT YOU FOR U.S. ARMY', an American recruitment poster, designed by James Montgomery Flagg in 1916, printed for the United States Army, in excellent condition, linen-backed.

1917   40.5in (103cm) high
$8,000-12,000   HER

'LORD KITCHENER SAYS:- ... ENLIST TO-DAY', a British recruitment poster, published by PRC No. 117, printed by David Allen, with folds.

1915   50in (127cm) wide
$200-300   ON

'Daddy, what did YOU do in the Great War?', a British Parliamentary Recruiting Committee poster, designed by Lumley Savile, printed by Johnson Riddle & Co.

This poster and its catchy subtitle have become famous. The poster aimed to attack the masculinity and responsibility of British men like the comfortably seated father.

1914-15   30in (75cm) high
$100-150   FLD

'Boys Come over here you're wanted', a British recruitment poster, designed by an anonymous designer, published by PRC No. 82, printed by David Allen, with folds.

1915   50in (127cm) wide
$150-250   ON

'AN APPEAL TO YOU,' a British recruitment poster, designed by an anonymous designer, published by PRC No. 88, printed by Roberts and Leete, with folds.

c1914   40.25in (102cm) high
$250-350   ON

'FALL IN ANSWER NOW IN YOUR COUNTRY'S HOUR OF NEED', a British recruitment poster, designed by E J Kealey, published by PRC No. 12, printed by Hill Siffken.

1914   30in (76cm) high
$200-300   ON

'NATIONAL RELIEF FUND TWO WAYS OF FIGHTING DISTRESS', a British wartime poster, designed by John Hassall, printed by David Allen.

John Hassall (1868-1948) was a prolific English illustrator, poster designer and artist. He worked for David Allen & Sons as an advertising illustrator 1895-1945. His best known design is perhaps the 'Jolly Fisherman' and the 'Skegness Is So Bracing' posters of 1908 for the London & North Eastern Railway. He was influenced by Alphonse Mucha's artwork and his style typically has flat planes of color with black outlines. Colors are often muted.

30in (76cm) high
$80-120   ON

A group of three World War I medals, comprising a 1914 Star, a War medal and a Victory medal, awarded to Sergeant George William Huston, Royal Sussex Regiment, with his memorial plaque, a 1912 Olympic Games competitor's medal, a 1899 Ferencvárosi Sports Club bronze medal in original case and archival material relating to his career as an athlete, including original photographs, press cuttings and an embroidered jersey badge worn by him at the 1912 Olympic Games, with original photographs relating to his short period of active service.

$4,000-6,000   WHP

A World War I General Service medal, awarded to 18-805 Private C H Clark of the Northumberland Fusilier's, with ribbon.

$40-60   A&G

A World War I War-end medal, awarded to 302727 Sergeant Hugh W Hodges, 5th London Regiment.

$550-750   WW

A World War I bronze death plaque, to commemorate Thomas Irwin, with card case.

$100-150   A&G

A World War I Royal Flying Corps pilot's furage.
c1915   11.5in (29cm) long
$150-250   PC

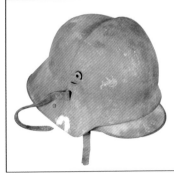

A rare German World War I Stahhelm M1916-17 helmet, with heavy steel bullet guard, with original leather interior cushions and strap.

$800-1,200   SWO

A rare World War I RAF lieutenant's tunic, with pilot's wings, with gilt crown/eagle badges, with a pair of overalls, marked 'S F J Fells'.

$1,200-1,800   W&W

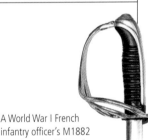

A World War I French infantry officer's M1882 sword, marked 'Manufacture Nationale d'Armes de Chatellerault, Janvier 1917, offre d'Infrie Mle 1882', with steel scabbard.

Blade 33.5in (85cm) long
$250-350   W&W

A World War I trench periscope, by Ross Ltd., London, with broad arrow mark, dated.

The 'arrow' or 'crow's foot' mark is made up of three lines, which together look like the tip of an arrow. The mark denotes a piece that was issued for military use and was not sold to the public.

1914

$100-150   MAR

A World War I military pocket compass, engraved 'Dennison, Birmingham VI 79124' and dated.

1918

$120-180   WHP

A pair of World War I 'Hezzanith' field binoculars, by Heath & Co., S-3, no.44976, with leather pouch, with later racing enclosure tags.

$100-150   RW

An early 20thC gold-mohair teddy bear, dressed in a gray uniform, with aluminum tag discs for Lieutenant A C M Walsh RFA, with medal ribbon.

This bear's owner, Lieutenant A C M Walsh of the Royal Fleet Auxiliary, was killed in action at Nieuwe Chappelle in France in 1915. Walsh was a cousin of Guy and David Campbell, who, as children, were given over 200 miniature bears, which became beloved toys and companions. They took their favorite bears to war with them and, unlike their cousin, they and their bears survived. In 1999, the by-then famous 'Campbell bears' were sold at auction at Sotheby's together with this bear.

12in (30cm) high

$1,000-1,500   SAS

A World War I silver officer's wristwatch, Birmingham, the case by Dennison with grill protector, the 15-jewel Rolex movement no.232031, with subsidiary seconds dial, on a tan strap.

1914   Case 1.3in (3.3cm) diam

$400-600   DN

QUICK REFERENCE - TRENCH ART

- The term 'Trench Art' usually refers to items made during World War I, but is often more widely applied to decorative items made during a recent period of armed conflict.
- Only a small percentage of trench art was made by soldiers actually in trenches or by prisoners of war. Most trench art, particularly larger and more complex pieces, was made either by civilians in occupied territories or on a commercial basis after the war had ended. Such pieces could then be sold to other soldiers during the war, or (after the war) to tourists and pilgrims to the battlefields.

A World War I colored photograph of a Royal Welsh Fusilier's Officer, indistinctly signed, in copper easel frame with Royal Welsh Fusilier's ribbon banding.

8in (20cm) high

$50-70   DA&H

A Trench Art shell and gilt-metal photograph frame, composed of four brass and cast-iron rounds enclosing a frame containing a portrait of an officer.

13in (32cm) high

$350-450   DN

MILITARIA

A Continental porcelain plate, printed in black with named portraits of the German commanders of World War I.

1914

$250-350 H&C

A Continental porcelain plate, printed with portraits of Wilhelm II and Franz Josef flanked by flags in colors, the border inscribed in gilt and dated '1914-16'.

$120-180 H&C

A German World War I cup, decorated with the iron cross below a crown, dated.

1914 *3in (7.5cm) high*

$80-120 GORL

An early 20thC carved sycamore nutcracker, in the form of Lord Kitchener's head.

8in (20.5cm) long

$100-150 PC

A silver novelty presentation table cigar lighter, in the form of a Mills No.5 grenade, by Mappin & Webb, Birmingham, with detachable ring, with a worn inscription.

In early 1915, William Mills (1856-1932) was asked by the War Department to improve his 'Mills Bomb' hand grenade. His new design included the distinctive pineapple appearance, which increased the grip for the thrower. By 1916, the Mills No.5 hand grenade was in wide scale production and over 75 million grenades were manufactured during World War I.

1918 *3.5in (9cm) high*

$2,500-3,500 WW

An early 20thC silkwork picture commemorating the end of World War I, depicting a lion and flags beneath '1914 WAR 1919'.

20in (51cm) wide

$300-500 GORL

A CLOSER LOOK AT A BOOK BY ROBERT GRAVES

Much of this autobiography describes Graves's wartime experience, including the futility, banality and intensity of his role as a British army officer.

This is the true first edition, as it has Siegfried Sassoon's poem on pp.341-43 printed in full. Sassoon objected to the form it was published in and it was not included in later editions.

Notable military historian Cyril Falls said of this book: the 'war scenes have been justly acclaimed to be excellent; they are, in fact, among the few in books of this nature which are of real historical value.'

The avant-garde cover design with a photograph of Graves taken by Alfred Cracknell was by Len Lye (1901-80), a notable New Zealand artist and sculptor.

'Good-Bye to all That', by Robert Graves, first edition, first issue, with original dust jacket, in near-fine condition, with bookplate on endpaper, with custom-made slipcase.

1929

$3,000-4,000 BLO

A Victorian officer's gilt and silver-plated helmet plate, for the Middlesex Regiment.
$250-350   W&W

A helmet plate, for the 2nd Volunteer Battalion, the Cameronians.
$300-500   W&W

A silver-plated pouch belt badge, for the Royal East Kent Mounted Rifles.
$400-600   W&W

A pre-1881 officer's waist belt clasp, for the 40th (2nd Somersetshire) Regiment.
$120-180   W&W

A Victoria Royal Niger Companies medal, with clasp for 'NIGERIA 1886-1897', unnamed.
$300-500   GORL

An early 19thC mahogany and brass campaign set, with gilt-brass inlaid cartouche to the lid engraved 'RSS', with accessories including a corkscrew, button hooks, razors, pen knife, scissors, scent bottle, brushes and strop, missing some items.

An officer's silver-plated cap badge, for the 1st VB Leicestershire Regiment, by J Gaunt & Son.
$250-350   W&W

Box 13in (34cm) long
$800-1,200   TEN

An early 19thC silver, steel and ivory campaign knife, fork and spoon, the three interlocking sections with cut-steel backs, the spoon with folding corkscrew, the fork with smaller knife, the spoon with Austro-Hungarian marks.
5in (13cm) long
$2,000-3,000   L&T

A rare NCO's bi-metal cap, for the Manchester Regiment, the title scroll reading 'EGYPT'.
$400-600   W&W

A Victorian silver and enamel vesta case, by Sampson Morden, London, the top decorated with four Gordon Highlanders pipers within a landscape, the reverse engraved 'James Luke Inverness'.
1890   *1.75in (4.5cm) wide*
$1,200-1,800   L&T

QUICK REFERENCE - MUSIC THROUGH THE AGES

- Cylinder music boxes were popular from the mid-19thC to the 1890s. Value is dependent on maker, with Nicole Frères being one of the most desirable, as well as case decoration, complexity and overall condition.
- Thomas Edison developed the phonograph, which could record and play sound, in the late 1870s. Larger examples are generally worth the most.
- A precursor to the record player, the gramophone was developed in 1887 by Emile Berliner. The most sought-after examples are made from brass, wood or decorated tin by companies such as HMV, Victor, Columbia or the Gramophone Company. Table-top gramophones with external horns are generally the most desirable.
- The golden age of radio design lasted from the 1930s to the 1950s. The most important indicator to value is the case. Look for Art Deco forms and bright colors, as these are likely to be most desirable. A good maker can also add value, with notable makers including FADA and EKCO.

A late 19thC Swiss cylinder music box, by Paillard, with lever-arm winding mechanism, playing eight airs, in a rosewood and ebonized case.

18in (46cm) wide

$700-1,000   CHT

A 19thC banded walnut musical box, serial no.21631, playing eight airs, with original tune card, the case inlaid to front and sides.

22in (56cm) wide

$1,000-1,500   FLD

A 19thC bells-in-sight music box, the 9.25in (23.5cm) cylinder playing eight airs, with Mandarin strikers, in a walnut case, with label reading 'Repaired Keith, Prowse & Co., Manufacturers, 48 Cheapside, London'.

Manufacturer, size and number of airs are some of the most important indicators to value for music boxes, but extra features, such as drums or bells, also add desirability and value. This example is unusual as it has detailed and decorative Mandarin-forms as strikers for the bells.

18.75in (47.5cm) wide

$4,000-6,000   LC

A 19thC bells-in-sight music box, playing eight airs, with Mandarin strikers, in a crossbanded walnut case, with replaced tune card.

19in (48cm) wide

$2,000-3,000   FLD

A late 19thC Swiss music box, the 7.5in (19cm) cylinder playing twelve airs, with four bells and bee strikers, in a walnut and mahogany banded case with stringing.

25in (64cm) wide

$1,200-1,800   AH

A late 19thC Swiss music box, 'The Victoria', with 73-tooth comb, double springs and three 13in (33cm) cylinders, in a walnut case with ebonized moldings and floral inlay.

33in (84cm) wide

$1,200-1,800   TRI

QUICK REFERENCE - POLYPHONS & SYMPHONIONS

- Polyphons and Symphonions were developed in Germany or Switzerland in the late 19thC. They reached the height of their popularity around the 1890s and were replaced by newer technologies during the first few decades of the 20thC.
- They have interchangeable revolving metal discs that are punctured to create small teeth that protrude from the bottom of the disc. As the disc revolves, these teeth strike a row of metal teeth mounted inside the box thus creating a different musical tone. The discs can be mounted horizontally or vertically and can exceed 24in (61cm) in size.
- Players of very large discs and those with highly decorative carved cases can fetch low to mid-thousands of dollars or more.
- Some Polyphons and Symphonions were made to stand in public areas, such as shops. A penny inserted into a slot on the side would make the device play a tune.

A German or Swiss Polyphon 11in (28cm) disc player, the quarter-veneered walnut lid with a marquetry rosewood panel and a monochrome printed picture of musical putti to the interior, with three teeth broken on comb, with a selection of metal discs.

16.25in (41cm) wide

$400-600   DN

A Ken-D automaton singing bird in cage, with wooden base, re-painted in gold.

c1900-10   13in (33cm) high

$250-350   DMC

A French automaton singing bird in cage, the base with molded bands of bead and foliate decoration, with some feather loss.

The value of these cages increases with the size, complexity and condition. The more birds there are, the more foliage and the greater the variety in movement and sound the better. French or Swiss examples from the late 19thC tend to be the best quality and are consequently worth more than many later examples.

c1900   10.25in (26cm) high

$400-600   LHA

A late 19thC German silver-cased 'singing bird' music box, by J D Schleissner & Söhne, Hanau, embossed with birds and foliate scrolls, the operating lever cast as a bird, with '930' standard mark.

Wind up these charming boxes, slide a lever and the central lid pops to reveal a bird that moves and sings. The quality of the movement, workmanship, and materials affects the value.

4in (10cm) wide

$3,000-4,000   GORL

A late 19thC German Polyphon 8in (20.5cm) disc player, in walnut case, the lid interior with original colorful label, with eleven metal discs.

10in (25.5cm) wide

$800-1,200   DA&H

A late 19thC Edison Bell 'Gem' phonograph, no.9421, in an oak case, with spun-aluminum horn and a box of 32 cylinders.

$400-600   GORL

A late 19thC Edison 'Gem' phonograph, in a curved oak case with transfer, with spun-aluminum horn and a box of 35 cylinders.

9.5in (24cm) wide

$400-600   DA&H

MUSIC THROUGH THE AGES

An unusual mahogany piano-shaped gramophone, with stylus and winding handle.

37in (94cm) high

$650-850   LC

A late 19thC Continental gramophone, contained in an ebonized Aesthetic-style stand with an embossed-metal frieze of cherubs playing musical instruments, with large tin horn.

$700-1,000   LC

An early 20thC Continental oak-cased table-top gramophone, the front with applied embossed brass decoration, with blue-painted tin horn.

14.5in (37cm) wide

$400-600   FLD

An early 20thC HMV mahogany-cased '103' table-top gramophone, with a no.4 reproducer and a re-finished case.

$80-120   DN

A CLOSER LOOK AT A REPRODUCTION

Nearly all brass gramophone horns are reproductions.

The wooden case of a reproduction will either show no signs of wear at all or the main case and horn will appear oily and dirty but areas such as the feet will be without authentic signs of wear and age.

The applied transfer on the front of a reproduction gramophone is usually too bright or has been varnished to give the effect of age. Look closely and you will be able to see the pixels.

The case, mechanism, soundbox and turntable are usually more poorly constructed than those of authentic period examples. They are also usually different colors and occasionally made from different materials.

A late 20thC/early 21stC replica HMV table-top gramophone, with wooden case and brass horn.

15in (38cm) wide

$40-60   FLD

A 1920s-30s HMV wind-up portable gramophone, the case with record storage inside, spare needles and a quantity of 78rpm records.

$70-100   BATE

A Thorens Excelda portable gramophone, with soundbox, crank and tone arm, the crackle-finish camera-form metal case with strap, with manufacturer's instructions.

1935-47   11in (28cm) long

$120-180   DMC

A 1940s E K Cole Ltd. 'EKCO' type Bakelite-cased electric radio receiver, designed by Wells Coates in 1940, serial no.AD6655, supplied by W H Rossiter & Co., Bradford-on-Avon, with two hairline cracks to case.

A rare General Electric 'Radiola-I' 'ER753a' crystal receiver, in mahogany case.

1922   *10in (25.5cm) high*

$120-180   DMC

This radio was first released in January 1940 with a price of £7 7s 0d. It was then re-released in October 1946 priced at £11 11s 0d plus £2 9s 8d purchase tax. It is part of a highly desirable range of round radios designed by Wells Coates and often known as Bournville radios, because they appeared in a period advertisement for the drink.

14.25in (36cm) diam

$1,200-1,800   DN

A mid-1930s E K Cole Ltd. 'EKCO' 'AC64' Bakelite-cased radio receiver, designed by Serge Chermayeff in 1933, with MW/LW Mtrs, interchangeable tuning scale.

15in (40cm) high

$400-600   FLD

An E K Cole Ltd. 'EKCO' 'RS2' Bakelite-cased radio receiver, designed by J K White in 1931, with original knobs.

Visually, the 'RS2' is the same radio as the 'M23', which was designed by J K White in 1932. The reason for this external similiary is that a fire destroyed the tooling for the 'RS2' in late 1931, so a new model was rapidly designed and built with a slightly different speaker configuration. Due to its very short production lifespan, the 'RS2' is rarer than the 'M23'.

1931 15.5in (39cm) high

$200-300   MHC

A 1960s Kuba 'Tango' stereo radio in an angular cabinet, the inlaid front opening to reveal a long wave, short wave and FM radio, five loudspeakers and record changer for ten discs.

German company Kuba also made the famous and outrageously styled 'Komet' radio, turntable and television from 1957 until 1961.

1959-62   *47.5in (120cm) wide*

$1,000-1,500   PC

A CLOSER LOOK AT A RADIO

This radio was designed by famous and influential designers Livio and Pier Giacomo Castiglioni, who are best known for their radical furniture designs.

The Castiglionis designed the 'Phonola 547' to fit in with office equipment on a desk. The radio was often compared to an intercom system.

The radio was also made in other colors. Green and red are considerably rarer and more valuable than this black variation. There is also an unproven rumour of the existence of a blue model.

The case is prone to cracking and the area around the push buttons is often damaged. Damage reduces value dramatically.

An Luigi Caccia Dominioni Bakelite-cased 'Phonola 547' radio receiver, designed by Livio and Pier Giacomo Castiglioni in 1939, marked 'PHONOLA Radio, MILANO, S.A. RIMI - SARONNO, MODELLO 547'.

10.5in (26.5cm) wide

$5,000-7,000   QU

A Matsushita Electrical Industries Panasonic green plastic-cased 'R-70' 'Panapet' transistor radio, made for the Western market.

Purple is the rarest and most desirable color for this radio and examples can fetch more than twice the value of any other color of 'Panapet'. Always examine the case carefully as scuffs, scratches and cracks seriously devalue the radio.

4in (10cm) high

$50-70   PC

MUSIC THROUGH THE AGES

A late 1960s Brionvega plastic-cased 'TS 502' radio, designed by Marco Zanuso and Richard Sapper in 1964.

Open 10.25in (26cm) wide

$500-700   **QU**

Four 1970s Marelli plastic-cased 'RD 339' radios, each marked 'RADIOMARELLI resp. WEST EXPORT', designed in 1971.

11in (28cm) wide

$1,000-1,500   **QU**

A Braun plastic- and metal-cased 'Audio 2 TC 45' compact radio and record player, designed by Dieter Rams in 1964.

25.5in (65cm) long

$400-600   **QU**

A 1980s Tomy plastic-cased 'Mr DJ' robot radio.

Look out for yellow and red examples, as these can fetch over 50% more than the blue version shown. The original box will increase the value by a similar amount.

7in (18cm) high

$25-35   **PC**

A Yamaha plastic-cased 'TC 800 D' cassette recorder, designed by Mario Bellini in 1976.

1976-78   *12.5in (32cm) wide*

$300-500   **QU**

A Seeburg chrome-plated 'Select-o-matic' High Fidelity 200 jukebox, serial no.13454, model no.201DH, the sound box grill applied with simulated tail-fin brake lights, one side panel replaced.

1958

$2,500-3,500   **GORL**

A late 1970s Wurlitzer 200 jukebox, with multicolored panels against a black ground, with chrome banding.

$800-1,200   **GORB**

An NSM 'City ES 160' jukebox, the front with inset panel showing a horse race.

This is an unusual panel for this jukebox - the design is usually either a New York skyline, scenes of Paris or London's Houses of Parliament.

1981   *40in (100cm) high*

$400-600   **SWO**

CHINESE REIGN PERIODS & MARKS

Imperial reign marks were adopted during the Ming dynasty, and some of the most common are illustrated here. Certain emperors forbade the use of their own reign mark, lest they should suffer the disrespect of a broken vessel bearing their name being thrown away. This is where the convention of using earlier reign marks comes from – a custom that was enthusiastically adopted by potters as a way of showing their respect for their predecessors.

It is worth remembering that a great deal of Imperial porcelain is marked misleadingly, and pieces bearing the reign mark for the period in which they were made are, therefore, especially sought after.

EARLY PERIODS & DATES

Xia Dynasty	c2000 - 1500BC	Three Kingdoms	221 - 280	The Five Dynasties	907 - 960
Shang Dynasty	1500 - 1028BC	Jin Dynasty	265 - 420	Song Dynasty	960 - 1279
Zhou Dynasty	1028 - 221BC	Northern & Southern Dynasties	420 - 581	Jin Dynasty	1115 - 1234
Qin Dynasty	221 - 206BC	Sui Dynasty	581 - 618	Yuan Dynasty	1260 - 1368
Han Dynasty	206BC - AD220	Tang Dynasty	618 - 906		

EARLY MING DYNASTY REIGNS

Hongwu	1368 - 1398	Zhengtong	1436 - 1449
Jianwen	1399 - 1402	Jingtai	1450 - 1457
Yongle	1403 - 1424	Tianshun	1457 - 1464
Hongxi	1425 - 1425	Chenghua	1465 - 1487
Xuande	1426 - 1435		

MING DYNASTY MARKS

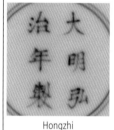
Hongzhi
1488–1505

Zhengde
1506–21

Jiajing
1522–66

Wanli
1573–1619

Chongzhen
1628–44

QING DYNASTY MARKS

Kangxi
1662–1722

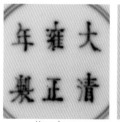
Yongzheng
1723–35

Qianlong
1736–95

Jiaqing
1796–1820

Xianfeng
1851–61

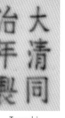
Tongzhi
1862–74

Guangxu
1875–1908

Xuantong
1909–11

Hongxian
1915–16

ORIENTAL

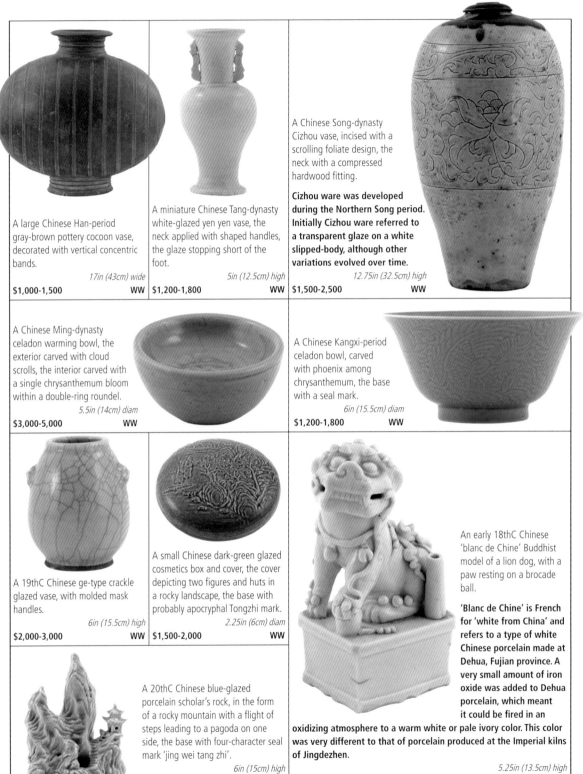

A large Chinese Han-period gray-brown pottery cocoon vase, decorated with vertical concentric bands.

17in (43cm) wide

$1,000-1,500   WW

A miniature Chinese Tang-dynasty white-glazed yen yen vase, the neck applied with shaped handles, the glaze stopping short of the foot.

5in (12.5cm) high

$1,200-1,800   WW

A Chinese Song-dynasty Cizhou vase, incised with a scrolling foliate design, the neck with a compressed hardwood fitting.

Cizhou ware was developed during the Northern Song period. Initially Cizhou ware referred to a transparent glaze on a white slipped-body, although other variations evolved over time.

12.75in (32.5cm) high

$1,500-2,500   WW

A Chinese Ming-dynasty celadon warming bowl, the exterior carved with cloud scrolls, the interior carved with a single chrysanthemum bloom within a double-ring roundel.

5.5in (14cm) diam

$3,000-5,000   WW

A Chinese Kangxi-period celadon bowl, carved with phoenix among chrysanthemum, the base with a seal mark.

6in (15.5cm) diam

$1,200-1,800   WW

A 19thC Chinese ge-type crackle glazed vase, with molded mask handles.

6in (15.5cm) high

$2,000-3,000   WW

A small Chinese dark-green glazed cosmetics box and cover, the cover depicting two figures and huts in a rocky landscape, the base with probably apocryphal Tongzhi mark.

2.25in (6cm) diam

$1,500-2,000   WW

An early 18thC Chinese 'blanc de Chine' Buddhist model of a lion dog, with a paw resting on a brocade ball.

'Blanc de Chine' is French for 'white from China' and refers to a type of white Chinese porcelain made at Dehua, Fujian province. A very small amount of iron oxide was added to Dehua porcelain, which meant it could be fired in an oxidizing atmosphere to a warm white or pale ivory color. This color was very different to that of porcelain produced at the Imperial kilns of Jingdezhen.

5.25in (13.5cm) high

$300-500   WW

A 20thC Chinese blue-glazed porcelain scholar's rock, in the form of a rocky mountain with a flight of steps leading to a pagoda on one side, the base with four-character seal mark 'jing wei tang zhi'.

6in (15cm) high

$1,500-2,500   WW

Judith Picks

During the reign of Kangxi Emperor (1662–1722), the existing porcelain factory at Jingdezhen was reorganized and new colors and glazes were developed. The decoration on pieces from this period, such as this bowl, is particularly charming and accomplished. As a result, the Kangxi period is one of the most desirable of Chinese porcelain.

A Chinese Kangxi-period blue-and-white bowl, the flared rim with diaper pattern border, the bowl centrally painted with boys playing with a ball, the exterior painted with figural reserves, the base with six-character Kangxi mark.

7.75in (20cm) diam

$6,500-7,500   **L&T**

A 19thC Chinese blue-and-white bottle vase, the neck painted with rising plaintain leaves over a band with coin reserves, the body with two scrolling dragons and clouds, the base with apocryphal Kangxi four-character mark.

13.75in (35cm) high

$550-750   **L&T**

A Chinese blue-and-white vase, mark, painted with a mountainous landscape, the base with apocryphal Qianlong six-character mark.

8.75in (22cm) high

$700-1,000   **L&T**

A 19thC Chinese blue-and-white 'Hundred Boys' brush pot, painted with boys engaged in various pursuits.

6in (15.5cm) high

$700-1,000   **L&T**

A Chinese blue-and-white vase, mark, painted with a mountainous landscape.

A 19thC Chinese blue-and-white model of a bull, decorated with diaper patterns and scrolls, the base with apocryphal Qianlong seal mark, with later bone cover.

7.5in (19cm) long

$500-700   **L&T**

A 19thC Chinese silver-mounted blue-and-white jar, decorated with ladies and a boy in a fenced garden, the base with six-character mark, mounted with a lobed silver collar and cover with a flower and foliate finial, the silver stamped 'DG'.

6.25in (16cm) high

$550-750   **L&T**

A 19thC Chinese blue-and-white bottle vase, painted with floral scrolls.

8.75in (22cm) high

$1,200-1,800   **L&T**

A 19thC Chinese blue-and-white tulip vase, painted with a mountainous landscape.

10.5in (27cm) high

$550-750   **L&T**

A large late 19thC Chinese blue-and-white covered jar, decorated with a sage seated on a qilin with two boy attendants.

11.5in (29cm) high

$500-700   **L&T**

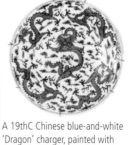

A 19thC Chinese blue-and-white 'Dragon' charger, painted with dragons among clouds chasing a flaming pearl, the reverse with apocryphal Kangxi mark.

15.75in (40cm) diam

$300-500   **L&T**

ORIENTAL

A Chinese Kangxi-period famille verte dish, painted with a gnarled willow, prunus and two swallows, the rim with panels of insects on a floral ground.

The famille verte palette consists of green and iron red with other overglaze colors. It originated from the Wucai style and is known to have first been used during the Kangxi period (1662-1722).

12.5in (32cm) diam

$1,000-1,500   WW

A Chinese Kangxi-period famille verte bowl, the ribbed body decorated with green and blue dragons and red phoenix above breaking waves, the interior decorated with a flaming pearl, the base with an artemesia mark.

7.75in (20cm) diam

$1,000-1,500   WW

An 18thC Chinese egg and spinach-glazed pottery figure of Budai He Shang.

5.75in (14.5cm) high

$1,500-2,500   WW

A 19thC Chinese famille verte figure of a boy, holding a vase of lotus, decorated with cranes and auspicious objects.

10.5in (26.5cm) high

$1,000-1,500   WW

A Chinese famille rose coffee pot and cover, decorated with figures in harbour landscapes.

The famille rose palette is comprised of predominantly rose-pink and purple shades. It was developed during the Yongzheng period (1723-35) and virtually replaced famille verte.

8.5in (21.5cm) high

$1,200-1,800   WHP

A Chinese famille rose figure of a reclining man, with a lacquered-wood stand.

c1800   *7.25in (18.5cm) long*

$300-500   WW

A 19thC Chinese Canton famille rose bottle vase, painted with an official and his attendants, cockerels, butterflies, fruit, flowers and figures on a floral ground.

13.5in (34.5cm) high

$1,000-1,500   WW

A 20thC Chinese famille rose figure of Budai He Shang.

10.25in (26cm) wide

$1,500-2,500   WW

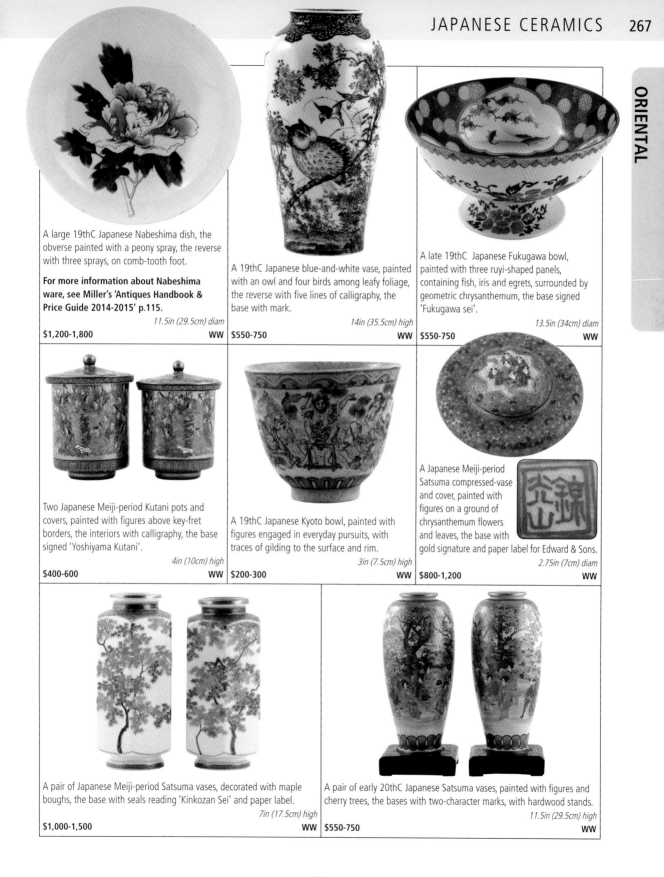

A large 19thC Japanese Nabeshima dish, the obverse painted with a peony spray, the reverse with three sprays, on comb-tooth foot.

For more information about Nabeshima ware, see Miller's 'Antiques Handbook & Price Guide 2014-2015' p.115.

11.5in (29.5cm) diam

$1,200-1,800   WW

A 19thC Japanese blue-and-white vase, painted with an owl and four birds among leafy foliage, the reverse with five lines of calligraphy, the base with mark.

14in (35.5cm) high

$550-750   WW

A late 19thC Japanese Fukugawa bowl, painted with three ruyi-shaped panels, containing fish, iris and egrets, surrounded by geometric chrysanthemum, the base signed 'Fukugawa sei'.

13.5in (34cm) diam

$550-750   WW

Two Japanese Meiji-period Kutani pots and covers, painted with figures above key-fret borders, the interiors with calligraphy, the base signed 'Yoshiyama Kutani'.

4in (10cm) high

$400-600   WW

A 19thC Japanese Kyoto bowl, painted with figures engaged in everyday pursuits, with traces of gilding to the surface and rim.

3in (7.5cm) high

$200-300   WW

A Japanese Meiji-period Satsuma compressed-vase and cover, painted with figures on a ground of chrysanthemum flowers and leaves, the base with gold signature and paper label for Edward & Sons.

2.75in (7cm) diam

$800-1,200   WW

A pair of Japanese Meiji-period Satsuma vases, decorated with maple boughs, the base with seals reading 'Kinkozan Sei' and paper label.

7in (17.5cm) high

$1,000-1,500   WW

A pair of early 20thC Japanese Satsuma vases, painted with figures and cherry trees, the bases with two-character marks, with hardwood stands.

11.5in (29.5cm) high

$550-750   WW

A 19thC Japanese ivory netsuke, in the form of Nitta no Shiro riding the boar, signed 'Minkoku'.

Nitta no Shiro was a warrior in the service of Minamoto no Yoritomo (Japan's military ruler from 1192). Reputedly, Nitta no Shiro saved Yoritomo from attack by a boar during a hunting expedition near Mount Fuji by jumping onto its back.

2in (5cm) long

$1,200-1,800   WW

A late 19thC Japanese ivory netsuke, in the form of Momotarō and his parents.

Momotarō (often translated as 'peach' 'boy') was found inside a giant peach. When he was older, he left to fight a band of marauding oni (demons), befriending a talking dog, a monkey and a pheasant on the way. Having defeated the oni, he returned home with their treasure. Momotarō was a popular proganda figure during World War II - he and the animals represented Japan's government and its citizens, while the oni represented the USA.

1.75in (4.5cm) long

$300-500   WW

A Japanese ivory netsuke, in the form of a karako beating a drum, the drum stand decorated with lotus leaves.

c1830   1.75in (4.5cm) high

$350-450   WW

A Japanese ivory netsuke, in the form of a monkey wearing a Noh mask, signed 'Mitsukide'.

c1830   1.5in (3.5cm) high

$450-550   WW

A Japanese ivory netsuke, in the form of Gama Sennin holding a toad and a gnarled staff, signed 'Kozan'.

c1860   2.25in (5.5cm) high

$1,200-1,800   WW

A Japanese wood and ivory shunga netsuke, in the form of an Onna-Daruma doll.

Daruma (male) and Onna-Daruma (female) dolls are lucky talismans. 'Shunga' is the Japanese term for erotic art - the erotic details are currently hidden, but can be revealed by removing the base of the netsuke!

c1900 2.5in (6cm) high

$400-600   WW

A Japanese wood netsuke, in the form of a shishi with forepaws resting on a mokugyo, with traces of lacquer.

c1820   1.5in (4cm) wide

$200-300   WW

A Japanese wood netsuke, in the form of a man dancing, signed 'Minko' but by a follower.

Tanaka Minko (1735-1816) was the founder of a small group of regional netsuke carvers in Tsu, Ise province.

c1820   2in (5cm) high

$350-450   WW

QUICK REFERENCE - NETSUKE

- Netsuke were originally carved as toggles for the sash (obi) on a kimono. They supported cords strung with containers (sagemono). Once the wearing of kimonos fell out of fashion, netsuke continued to be produced as artistic objects.
- Many are carved in the form of characters from mythology.
- Most are carved in ivory, although wood and bone were also used.
- Molded resin fakes began to appear on the market in the late 20thC. They typically have poorly defined details and, in comparison to real ivory, feel warm and light in weight.

An early 19thC Japanese wood netsuke, in the form of a woman carrying a child on her back and holding a kettle.

2in (5cm) high

$350-450   WW

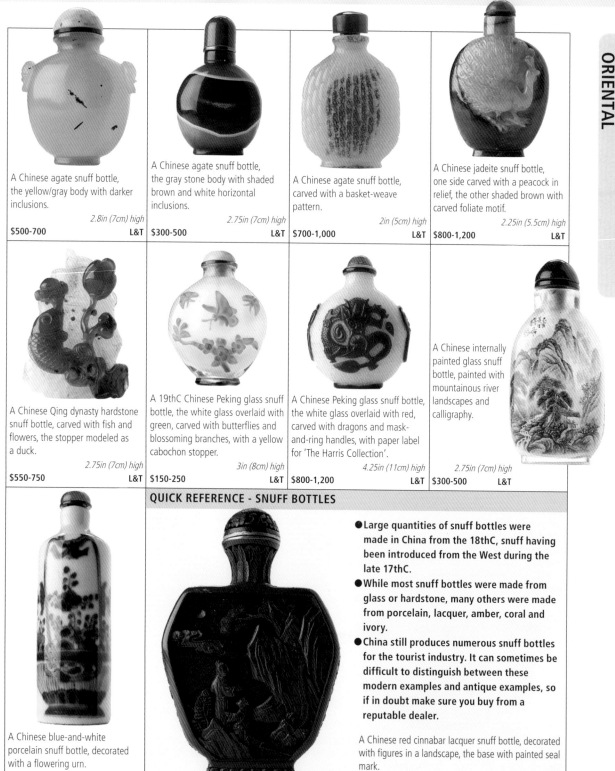

A Chinese agate snuff bottle, the yellow/gray body with darker inclusions.

2.8in (7cm) high

$500-700   L&T

A Chinese agate snuff bottle, the gray stone body with shaded brown and white horizontal inclusions.

2.75in (7cm) high

$300-500   L&T

A Chinese agate snuff bottle, carved with a basket-weave pattern.

2in (5cm) high

$700-1,000   L&T

A Chinese jadeite snuff bottle, one side carved with a peacock in relief, the other shaded brown with carved foliate motif.

2.25in (5.5cm) high

$800-1,200   L&T

A Chinese Qing dynasty hardstone snuff bottle, carved with fish and flowers, the stopper modeled as a duck.

2.75in (7cm) high

$550-750   L&T

A 19thC Chinese Peking glass snuff bottle, the white glass overlaid with green, carved with butterflies and blossoming branches, with a yellow cabochon stopper.

3in (8cm) high

$150-250   L&T

A Chinese Peking glass snuff bottle, the white glass overlaid with red, carved with dragons and mask-and-ring handles, with paper label for 'The Harris Collection'.

4.25in (11cm) high

$800-1,200   L&T

A Chinese internally painted glass snuff bottle, painted with mountainous river landscapes and calligraphy.

2.75in (7cm) high

$300-500   L&T

A Chinese blue-and-white porcelain snuff bottle, decorated with a flowering urn.

4in (10cm) high

$250-350   L&T

QUICK REFERENCE - SNUFF BOTTLES

- Large quantities of snuff bottles were made in China from the 18thC, snuff having been introduced from the West during the late 17thC.
- While most snuff bottles were made from glass or hardstone, many others were made from porcelain, lacquer, amber, coral and ivory.
- China still produces numerous snuff bottles for the tourist industry. It can sometimes be difficult to distinguish between these modern examples and antique examples, so if in doubt make sure you buy from a reputable dealer.

A Chinese red cinnabar lacquer snuff bottle, decorated with figures in a landscape, the base with painted seal mark.

3.25in (8cm) high

$200-300   L&T

A Chinese export silver pierced bowl, by Wang Hing, Hong Kong, with pierced decoration of dragons chasing a flaming pearl, the base marked 'WH' and '90' and with character mark.

Wang Hing & Co. was a late 19th/early 20thC maker and retailer of high-quality Chinese export silver. The company was patronized by Tiffany & Co. and Indian Maharajas.

c1890   3.5in (9cm) diam 3.3oz

$800-1,200   L&T

A Chinese export silver spill vase, by Wang Hing, Hong Kong, embossed with prunus tree blossom on a planished background, the base marked 'WH90'.

c1890   4.5in (11.5cm) high 1.5oz

$400-600   L&T

A Chinese export silver bowl, by Wang Hing, Hong Kong, engraved with prunus blossom, bamboo and birds, interior gilded, the base marked 'WH', '90' and with golfing presentation inscription.

c1896   4.5in (11.5cm) diam 5.4oz

$2,000-3,000   L&T

A Chinese export silver goblet, by Wang Hing, Hong Kong, on three twisted stems modeled as bamboo, the base marked 'WH', '90' and with character mark.

c1895   4.25in (11cm) high 2.8oz

$550-750   L&T

A Chinese export silver picture frame, by Wang Hing, Hong Kong, decorated with applied prunus-branch forms and engraving to frame, the tripod stand modeled as bamboo, with later sliding wooden back, the reverse marked 'WH', '90' and with character mark.

c1900

$1,000-1,500   L&T

A Chinese export silver card tray, by Wang Hing, Hong Kong, chased with dragons and suns and with pierced side, on four feet, the base marked 'WH', '90' and with character mark.

c1910   5.5in (14cm) wide 3.2oz

$700-1,000   L&T

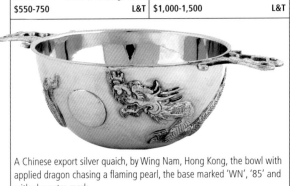

A Chinese export silver quaich, by Wing Nam, Hong Kong, the bowl with applied dragon chasing a flaming pearl, the base marked 'WN', '85' and with character mark.

c1895   With handles 6.25in (16cm) wide 4.7oz

$500-700   L&T

A Chinese export silver vase, engraved with birds in foliage above chased flowers and foliage and vacant shield cartouches, the base with mark.

c1900   7.5in (19cm) high 7.3oz

$700-1,000   L&T

A Chinese Canton export silver canister, decorated with fighting warriors within a landscape, the lid with fruiting vine and acanthus borders, with four pseudo London hallmarks.

c1850   4.25in (10.5cm) high 5.4oz

$2,000-3,000   L&T

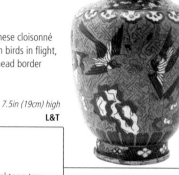

A miniature 17th/18thC Chinese cloisonné vase, with scrolling foliate design between bands of ruyi heads.

3.75in (9.5cm) high

$4,000-6,000　　**WW**

An 18th/19thC Chinese cloisonné vase, decorated with birds in flight, the neck with ruyi-head border and bats.

7.5in (19cm) high

$300-500　　**L&T**

A 19thC Japanese bronze model of an elephant, the underside with a four-character mark.

8.75in (22.5cm) high

$1,000-1,500　　**WW**

A Chinese paktong tray, decorated with figures in a pagoda and a rocky garden beneath pine trees, the reverse with a four-character mark 'bin sheng yuan ji'.

Paktong is an alloy of zinc, cooper and nickel, which resembles silver, but is slow to tarnish. It was developed in China and was imported to Europe during the 18thC. European smiths attempted to copy paktong with limited success until c1820 when 'German silver' was developed.

c1900　　*8.5in (21.5cm) wide*

$500-700　　**WW**

A 19thC Japanese silver-colored tea kettle and cover, the spout and handle formed as dragons, the base marked 'Arthur & Bond Yokohama Sterling'.

6.5in (16.5cm) high

$4,000-6,000　　**WW**

A 19th/20thC Japanese rootwood carving of a man.

22.5in (57cm) high

$550-750　　**WW**

A small 19thC Chinese hardwood traveling vanity box, the fitted drawer inlaid with mother-of-pearl, the double-hinged lid opening to reveal a mirror, with brass handles and mounts.

8in (20.6cm) wide

$400-600　　**WW**

Judith Picks

Prices for Chinese porcelain and works of art are still making headlines as wealthy Chinese businessmen continue to buy back their heritage. Imperial pieces, or those with a high level of detail, achieve the highest prices, but, with a large number of wealthy bidders all competing for the same pieces, even relatively plain 18thC objects can fetch high prices. Ten years ago, this small bowl was purchased for 30¢ at a hospital charity sale because nobody knew what it was. Today, it has been assessed as Qianlong and is worth thousands of dollars. Part of the rim had been slightly chipped and ground down - while this did not greatly deter bidders, if the bowl had been undamaged it would have been worth even more.

A Chinese Qianlong period pale celadon jade bowl, the base with four-character mark, the rim slightly ground.

4.75in (12.5cm) diam

$30,000-40,000　　**CAN**

A miniature glass paperweight, by Rick Ayotte, with a bird on branches with two trillium flowers, signed 'Ayotte M-25 '87', in excellent condition.

2in (5cm) diam

$500-700   JDJ

QUICK REFERENCE - PAPERWEIGHTS

- Paperweights were developed in Italy in around 1843, but it was the French who were responsible for the 'golden age' of the paperweight in the mid-19thC. Tens of thousands of very high quality weights were produced by the three major French factories Baccarat, Clichy and St Louis for around six years, until the early 1850s when paperweights fell out of fashion.
- Soon afterward many French paperweight artists immigrated to the USA, which, along with Scotland became a new hub for paperweight making when they began to return to fashion from the mid-20thC onward.
- Names such as Charles Kaziun Jnr., Emil Larson and Paul Stankard (see p.220 for an example of his work) are important USA makers. Paul Ysart, William Manson, and Peter Holmes are important Scottish makers.
- More recently artists including Steven Lundberg, Rick Ayotte and Victor Trabucco have developed a particular style of paperweight based on tiny, three-dimensional, lamp-worked natural vignettes.

A glass 'Floral Bouquet' paperweight, by Chris Buzzini, consisting of three pink blossoms with two blue foxglove flowers and five yellow buds, signed 'Buzzini '87 PFB1'.

Chris Buzzini (b.1949) is renowned for his delicate and lifelike floral glass constructions. He has studied and worked at many major studio glass companies in the USA including Correia Art Glass, the Lundberg Art Studios and Orient & Flume. His work is also in many important private and public collections.

3in (7.5cm) diam

$550-750   JDJ

A Baccarat carpet-ground glass paperweight, including silhouettes of an elephant, horse, monkey and goat and the signature canes 'B' and '1848', with some scratches to dome surface.

1848   *2.5in (7.5cm) diam*

$1,500-2,500   TOV

A Caithness limited edition glass 'Partridge in a Pear Tree' paperweight, designed by William Manson in 1983, from an edition of 500, with acid-etched mark.

1983   *3in (7.5cm) diam*

$100-150   JDJ

A mid-19thC Clichy concentric millefiori glass paperweight, with a central pink and green 'Clichy Rose' cane.

c1850   *1.5in (4cm) diam*

$300-500   PC

A glass 'Pansy' paperweight, by Charles Kaziun Jnr., the base signed with an internal gold 'K'.

2.25in (5.5cm) diam

$550-750   JDJ

A glass 'Rose' paperweight, by Charles Kaziun Jnr., the pink rope rose on an amethyst ground surrounded by a blue and white twist torsade, the base signed with an internal gold 'K'.

2in (5cm) diam

$250-350   JDJ

A glass 'Pond Lily' paperweight, by Steven Lundberg, signed 'Steven Lundberg Lundberg Studios 1985 050119' and with an 'LS85' signature/date cane.

1985   *3in (7.5cm) diam*

$250-350   JDJ

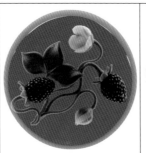

A glass 'Floral Bouquet' paperweight, by Steven Lundberg, the base signed 'Steven Lundberg Lundberg Studios 1985 022830'.

1985   *3in (7.5cm) diam*

$250-350   **JDJ**

A glass floral paperweight, by William Manson, the flower over a yellow sand ground, the base signed with a 'WM '81' signature/date cane and '43/150'.

1981   *2.75in (7cm) diam*

$200-300   **JDJ**

A glass 'Strawberry' paperweight, by Gordon Smith, the berries on a translucent blue ground, signed 'GES 1987'.

1987   *3in (7.5cm) diam*

$500-700   **JDJ**

A glass 'Rose Bouquet' paperweight, by Victor Trabucco, the base signed 'Trabucco 1994' and with 'VT' signature cane.

1994   *4in (10cm) diam*

$700-1,000   **JDJ**

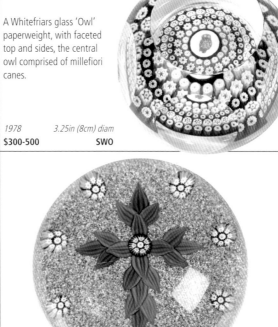

A Whitefriars glass 'Owl' paperweight, with faceted top and sides, the central owl comprised of millefiori canes.

1978   *3.25in (8cm) diam*

$300-500   **SWO**

A glass 'Floral Bouquet' paperweight, by Victor Trabucco, signed 'Trabucco 1987' and with 'VT' signature cane.

Victor Trabucco began working with glass in 1974. His finely detailed and hyper-realistic work has a sculptural element. It can be found in many collections, including the Corning Museum of Glass.

1987   *3.75in (9.5cm) diam*

$1,000-1,500   **JDJ**

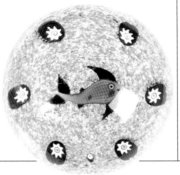

A Harland Studio glass paperweight, by Paul Ysart, with 'H' signature cane, with adhesive label, with original box.

2.75in (7cm) diam

$250-350   **DN**

A Harland Studio glass paperweight, by Paul Ysart, with 'H' signature cane, with adhesive label.

Master paperweight-maker Paul Ysart (1904-91) worked from a small studio at Harland in Wick, northern Scotland 1970-79, having moved to the area in 1962 to accept a role as training officer at the newly founded Caithness Glass. This paperweight is unusual, as well as being well designed and well made.

2.75in (7cm) diam

$650-850   **DN**

PENCILS & PENS

QUICK REFERENCE – PENCILS & PENS

- Although the origins of the first pen can be traced to Prehistoric times when sharpened implements were used to scratch lines into stone, it was the Ancient Egyptians who first used papyrus (a form of paper), ink and the reed brush. It is not known exactly when it was introduced, but the quill pen, made from a cut sharpened feather, was the predominant writing instrument from the Dark Ages until the 19thC when the steel nib took over.

- Writing instruments dating from the 17thC to the 19thC are widely collected today. Such instruments include portable writing sets and dip pens made to hold quill- or steel nibs, propelling pencils and early attempts at fountain pens. The first propelling pencil was developed in 1822 by Joseph Hawkins and Sampson Mordan. Mordan's silver- and gold-cased 'Everpoint' pencils have a strong collecting base today. Quality, date, materials used and the importance of the maker are the most important indicators of value with any antique writing tool.

- The first commercially successful fountain pens date from the 1880s, with the fountain pen enjoying a 'golden age' from the 1920s to the 1950s. The market is dominated by top names such as Parker, Waterman, Montblanc and Dunhill Namiki. Due to lively trading on the internet and the ease of mailing vintage pens, pens by smaller, previously lesser-known brands have risen in popularity and value. It is also likely that collectors are turning to these lesser-known pens due to the increasing scarcity of the best and most sought-after pens by the biggest names.

- Traditionally, collectors have been primarily interested in pens from the 1920s-50s, but, as good examples have become scarcer, attention has also turned to more modern pens from the 1960s onward. Such pens have consequently risen steeply in value over the past five years.

- A considerable premium is usually paid for pens that have never been used and are in mint condition with their boxes and paperwork. Condition is particularly important when considering modern limited edition pens. A used pen without its accompanying box and paperwork can fetch well under 50 percent of the value of a similar example that has never even been opened. Always look for top names, an appealing design and as small a limited edition as possible.

- Fountain pens were mass-produced in large quantities, so many common or unremarkable examples are worth less than $50, even with a gold nib. Pens should be complete and in working order to appeal to collectors. Avoid cracked or chipped examples and try to ensure replaceable parts, such as nibs or clips, are correct for the pen.

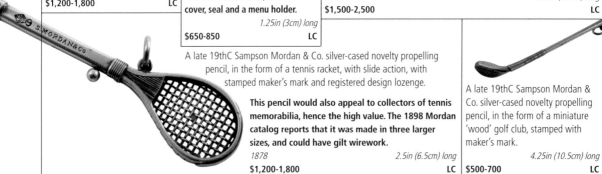

A late 19thC Sampson Mordan & Co. silver-cased novelty propelling pencil, in the form of a fish, stamped with maker's mark on the shaft.

2.25in (6cm) long

$1,200-1,800   LC

A late 19thC Sampson Mordan & Co. silver-cased novelty propelling pencil, in the form of an owl, with inset colored glass eyes, stamped with maker's mark.

The owl was one of Mordan's most popular and prolifically produced novelty forms. Other owl-shaped items produced by Mordan included a bookmark, inkwell cover, seal and a menu holder.

1.25in (3cm) long

$650-850   LC

A late 19thC Sampson Mordan & Co. silver-cased novelty telescopic pencil, in the form of a Muscovy drake's head, stamped with maker's mark and registered design no.'16538'.

This form is extremely rare and is not shown in the 1898 Mordan catalog. This is the only catalog from the company that survives following the 1941 air raid that destroyed the factory.

1898

2.25in (5.5cm) long

$1,500-2,500   LC

A late 19thC Sampson Mordan & Co. silver-cased novelty propelling pencil, in the form of a tennis racket, with slide action, with stamped maker's mark and registered design lozenge.

This pencil would also appeal to collectors of tennis memorabilia, hence the high value. The 1898 Mordan catalog reports that it was made in three larger sizes, and could have gilt wirework.

1878   *2.5in (6.5cm) long*

$1,200-1,800   LC

A late 19thC Sampson Mordan & Co. silver-cased novelty propelling pencil, in the form of a miniature 'wood' golf club, stamped with maker's mark.

4.25in (10.5cm) long

$500-700   LC

A late 19thC Sampson Mordan & Co. silver-cased novelty propelling pencil, in the form of a flintlock pistol, with a scroll-decorated butt, stamped with maker's mark and '353-6th July 1840'.

This form is one of the more commonly found examples of Mordan's novelty propelling pencils - it is also found with a toothpick replacing the pencil. The date '6th July 1840' refers to the date the design was registered.

2in (5cm) long

$250-350   LC

A Sampson Mordan & Co. silver-cased novelty seven-draw conical telescopic pencil, in a thimble by another maker, the pencil mechanism stamped 'S.MORDAN & CO.', the thimble with another (indistinct) maker's mark and hallmarked.

It is unusual that the thimble is by another maker, given Mordan's skills at producing novelty silver cases. This model appears in Mordan's 1898 catalog, numbered 789.

1907

$500-700

1in (2.5cm) long

LC

A late 19thC silver-cased novelty telescopic pencil, in the form of a champagne bottle, the label enameled 'LOUIS ROEDERER REIMS... for GT.BRITAIN', unmarked.

A number of makers produced pencils in the form of champagne bottles. This shape must have been popular as it is one of the more commonly found novelty forms. Champagne brands vary – as well as Louis Roederer, shown here, Perrier-Jouët, Heidsieck Monopole and Wachter's are also popular.

2in (5cm) high

$300-500   LC

A rare late 19thC silver-cased novelty telescopic pencil, in the form of a clinker-built rowing boat, unmarked.

On this rare form, the hull has been molded, but all the other parts, from the seats to the rowlocks and oars, have been made separately and soldered into place around the tube containing the mechanism.

1.75in (4.5cm) long

$700-1,000   WW

Mark Picks

This is an extremely rare novelty pencil and it's by Sampson Mordan & Co., the most important and sought after maker of novelty pencils. It doesn't appear in Mordan's catalog of 1898, but the first page of the catalog states that Mordan '...are always glad to consider proposals for the introduction of new inventions...' for pencils and other goods, so this may have been a special commission. The complex form and enameled and gilt face showcase the quality and skills of Mordan's workmen. As well as being sought-after by pencil collectors and Mordan collectors, this pencil would be of great interest to clock collectors. I can't help wondering if it was originally commissioned by a wealthy and well-to-do clockmaker, who showed it off to his peers and friends.

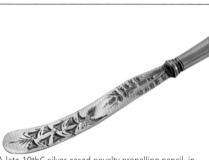

A late 19thC Sampson Mordan & Co. silver-cased novelty propelling pencil, in the form of a tallcase clock, with enameled dial and engraved gilt face, the shaft stamped with maker's mark.

1.75in (4.5cm) long

$2,500-3,500   LC

A late 19thC silver-cased novelty propelling pencil, in the form of a knife, probably American, maker's mark 'H.G.&S. Ltd.', with an acanthus-capped pistol handle and engraved scimitar blade, stamped '.925,SS'.

4.45in (11cm) long

$500-700   LC

A Sampson Mordan & Co. silver-cased propelling pencil, in the form of a Dickensian figure, stamped with maker's mark and registered design lozenge for 13th December 1882.

2.5in (4cm) high

$800-1,200   WW

PENCILS & PENS

A Sampson Mordan & Co. reeded silver-cased telescopic propelling pencil, London, with inset intaglio crest on the terminal, the body stamped 'S. MORDAN & CO. MAKERS & PATENTEES' and with 'SM GR' makers' mark.

Sampson Mordan (SM) was in partnership with wealthy stationer Gabriel Riddle (GR) 1823-36. During this period, pencils were stamped with a combined 'SM GR' makers' mark. The 'S. MORDAN & CO. MAKERS & PATENTEES' wording was used 1830-36. Without Riddle's financial input so early in his career, it's unlikely that Mordan would have grown into the success he was.

1831   *3.5in (9cm) long*
$250-350   **LC**

A Sampson Mordan & Co. silver-cased combined propelling pencil and dip pen, London, with engine-turning and chased floral borders, stamped 'S. MORDAN & CO's. PATENT' and with 'SM GR' makers' mark.

Combined pencil and pen holders are scarcer than propelling pencils and are usually more valuable, particularly if the body decoration is more decorative than simple reeding.

1828   *4in (10cm) long*
$300-500   **LC**

A Sampson Mordan & Co. silver-cased combined propelling pencil and dip pen, London, with reeded body, stamped 'S. MORDAN & CO's PATENT' and with 'SM GR' makers' mark.

1829   *3.75in (9.5cms) long*
$250-350   **LC**

A CLOSER LOOK AT A PENNER

A penner is a very rare writing tool, which was used from the late 17thC to the late 18thC. It enabled an educated gentleman, noble or scribe to write in ink wherever and whenever.

The long shaft contained quills, accessed by pulling the top off, and the wide tapered base unscrewed to hold ink. Later examples became more complex and contained more items, such as a quill knife.

Less fine quality examples were made from boiled leather or heated horn, hence the penner's other name 'inkhorn'. The owner of this silver penner must have been wealthy.

The maker's 'IC' mark has been found on other penners, but it is unknown whose mark it is. The style indicates that this penner was probably produced in London in around 1670-80.

A late 17thC silver penner, maker's mark 'IC' above a pellet in a heart, with a trefoil column to hold quills, a pull-off end cap and a flared trefoil ink vessel, with spiral reeded borders.

1670-80   *6in (15cm) long*
$6,500-7,500   **LC**

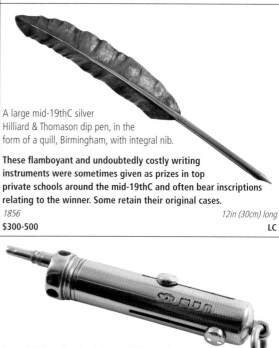

A large mid-19thC silver Hilliard & Thomason dip pen, in the form of a quill, Birmingham, with integral nib.

These flamboyant and undoubtedly costly writing instruments were sometimes given as prizes in top private schools around the mid-19thC and often bear inscriptions relating to the winner. Some retain their original cases.

1856   *12in (30cm) long*
$300-500   **LC**

A small William Hornby silver-cased three-color propelling pencil, London, with enameled black, red and blue spots on the slider buttons to represent the lead colors, with suspension ring, with maker's mark.

1903   *1.75in (4cm) long*
$120-180   **LC**

QUICK REFERENCE - DISCOLORATION

- The celluloid on this pen has discolored over time. When it was sold originally (over 80 years ago!), it was a light and bright marbled beige with vibrant red streaks. Unfortunately, the vulcanized hard rubber parts and the rubber ink sack inside the barrel have released chemicals over time that have caused the celluloid to take on dark amber tones. This is not reversible.
- Black hard rubber can sometimes take on biscuit-brown tones as a result of exposure to moisture, sweat and light. This process is known as oxidization or oxidation and is not reversible. The oxidized surface can be polished away to reveal the underlying black, but this will also result in any engine-turned detail or imprints being polished away in the process.
    - Discolored celluloid does not greatly affect value, as it is typical. Oxidisation reduces value by over 75% in most cases.

A 1930s Wade cellulose-decorated figurine of a 'Conchita', designed by Jessie van Halen, the base with printed marks.

8in (21.5cm) high

$120-180   LSK

A Conklin chased black hard-rubber crescent-filler, with sprung clip and Conklin 'Toledo' no.3 14ct gold nib, in excellent condition.

Conklin were the only company to use a metal crescent to squeeze the internal rubber ink sack in order to fill it with ink. The hard-rubber swiveling locking ring then ensured that the crescent was not depressed when in a pocket or in use. Conklin were founded in 1898 after founder Roy Conklin developed 'The Crescent Filling System' in 1897. The system was used until c1929 and counted Mark Twain among its fans. Although the company closed in 1938, pens continued to be made under the name until 1948. The brand was revived in 2009, along with the 'Crescent Filler'.

c1918

$120-180   PC

A late 1940s-50s Waterman's black no.503 lever-filler, with medium Waterman's W-2A nib, in unused, mint condition with original shop price band.

$50-70   BPH

A 1970s French Waterman's gold-plated CF 'Vague' convertor or cartridge-filler, with fine Waterman's 18ct integral gold nib, in mint condition.

c1976

$100-150   BPH

A 1930s De La Rue Onoto 'The Pen No. 1332' black hard-rubber lever-filler, with 14ct 'Warranted' no.22 gold nib, with shop display band, in mint condition.

$65-85   BPH

A late 1940s-50s Valentine pearl-marbled celluloid lever-filler, with a Valentine 14ct gold nib, in near mint condition.

$100-150   PC

PENCILS & PENS

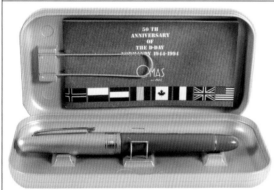

An OMAS limited edition 'Ferrari 348 Challenge' fountain pen, from a limited edition of 3000, in mint condition, with aluminum tube, card outer and instructions.

The aluminum tube box is in the form of the titanium torsion bar on Ferrari's Formula 1 cars. This pen was originally sold to Ferrari clients and owners of the Ferrari 348 Berlinetta.

1993
$400-600   DN

A set of three OMAS limited production 'Italia 90' commemorative pens, comprising a fountain pen, ballpoint pen and pencil, each with hexagonal vegetal resin body, the fountain pen with Omas 14ct gold nib, with presentation box and outer card packaging and paperwork.
1990
$300-500   DN

An OMAS limited edition 'D-Day' commemorative fountain pen, numbered 620 from an edition of 5300, with military-green barrel, rhodiated-bronze cap and 18ct gold nib, with aluminum presentation box, outer card packaging, paperwork and marketing ephemera.

This pen was limited to 5,300 pieces for the 5,300 ships that made the crossing from Britain to Normandy, France, as part of Operation Neptune (D-Day) in 1944.

1994
$300-500   DN

An OMAS limited edition 'Marconi - 100 Anni di Radio 1895-1995' commemorative fountain pen, numbered 1 from a Russian edition of 154, with dark gray cap and barrel, two color 18ct gold nib and intermittent gold-plated bands and clip, with boxes and paperwork.

This pen was designed to commemorate 100 years of radio and the inventions and experiments of Guglielmo Marconi. The clip was designed to resemble a stylized Morse code wireless telegraphy key.
1995
$500-700   DN

QUICK REFERENCE - LIMITED EDITION NUMBERS

- **Low numbers from a limited edition are usually more desirable and slightly more valuable than later numbers. Some numbers are also important to certain cultures or nationalities. For example, Chinese collectors will often pre-order or seek out any number with an 8 in it as 8 is seen as an auspicious and lucky number in China. Hence, the most sought after pen from any edition will be numbered 888, if the edition size allows it.**
- **Always aim to buy limited edition pens from as small an edition size as possible.**
- **The subject also counts: it should appeal generally or specifically to collectors of pens.**
- **This pen by Italian company OMAS was designed to commemorate the Trimillenium anniversary of the city of Jerusalem, and is the result of 108 hours of hand craftsmanship.**

An OMAS limited edition 'Jerusalem 3000' commemorative fountain pen, numbered 2 from an edition of 3000, the red resin barrel overlaid with a silver decorated with cast reliefs of sites in Jerusalem, stamped '.925', with an 18ct white gold nib.
1996
$550-750   DN

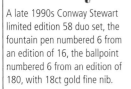

A late 1990s Conway Stewart limited edition 58 duo set, the fountain pen numbered 6 from an edition of 16, the ballpoint numbered 6 from an edition of 180, with 18ct gold fine nib.

Limited edition ballpens and pencils are often made in larger edition sizes than fountain pens, as they (ballpens and pencils) are more affordable, so more tend to be sold.

$250-350   DN

A Conway Stewart silver limited edition 'Dinkie' fountain pen and ballpoint set, each numbered 10 from an edition of 14, with chased barleycorn pattern, with a black leather travel wallet containing two stamps and a 1955 farthing.

Founded in 1905, Conway Stewart became one of the best-loved names in British pen making with many people growing up using them during the 1920s-60s. The company closed in 1975, but the brand was revived in the 1990s. The diminutive 'Dandy' was another of their most popular pens, particularly with ladies who could pop it in a purse or bag.
c1998

$650-850   DN

A 1990s Conway Stewart limited edition chased black hard-rubber 'Churchill' lever-filler, no.14 of a limited edition produced for the Writing Equipment Society's 20th anniversary, with broad Conway Stewart 18ct gold nib.
2000

$250-350   PC

Mark Picks

The Montblanc 149 is perhaps the most iconic fountain pen in the world. The largest and 'flashiest' Montblanc produced, it rose to prominence in the 1980s, the 'Age of Greed', where it was seen wielded by the likes of fictional Wall Street financier Gordon Gecko. Despite this association with the '80s, the 149 was actually introduced in 1952 and vintage examples made before the late 1960s are more sought-after and valuable than 1980s equivalents.

Earlier 149s were made from hand-turned celluloid, rather than a cast plastic. They also used a two-stage piston-filler mechanism that used primarily brass parts and needed a short pull before it engaged the piston to prevent leaks. The thin cap bands were silver, not gold, and the ink window is often a different color. The model number '149' is also often stamped onto the piston knob. More recent versions will often fetch less than half of the value shown below.

A Montblanc limited edition 'Semiramis' fountain pen, from the 'Patron of the Arts' series, numbered 1997 from an edition of 4810, the black resin body encased in a cage of gold plated fretwork, with an 18ct gold nib, with box, international service certificate and outer card packaging.
$4,000-6,000   DN

A Classic Pens CP5 limited edition 'Parker Duofold' fountain pen, numbered 397 from an edition of 1888, with moiré pattern sterling silver overlay, with a fine Duofold 'banner' nib.

Classic Pens was a company run by Andreas Lambrou, the noted vintage fountain pen author and expert. Although the edition size of this 'Parker Duofold' was intended to be 1,888 (the year Parker was founded), only 500 pens were made.
1997

$500-700   DN

A Montblanc black 'Meisterstück 149' piston-filler, with rolled gold trim, the cap band with outer silver bands, amber transparent ink window and 14ct gold nib, with a Montblanc box.
c1952

$800-1,200   DN

PLASTICS & BAKELITE

A mottled brown Bakelite lidded box, unmarked.

6in (15.5cm) diam

$100-150   P&I

A 1930s mottled Bakelite fruit bowl.

12in (30cm) diam

$50-70   WHP

A 1930s-50s E K Cole brown Bakelite table lamp, model no.1126, manufactured by ESC, with moving arm and hemispherical shade on a universal ball joint, with original switch.

This superb Modernist lamp was produced after 1930 by Czechoslovakian company ESC for E K Cole. The design is most likely to have been by Eric Kirkman Cole (1901-66), who founded his eponymous company in 1926.

14.25in (36cm) high

$500-700   QU

A 1930s yellow and green marbled Catalin-covered box.

3.25in (8cm) high

$350-450   PC

A 1930s brown Bakelite fruit bowl, with a pierced silver-plated rim.

9in (23cm) diam

$120-180   LSK

A 1930s-40s Polaroid Co. brown Bakelite desk lamp, model no.112, with yellow-tinted diffuser and mirrored reflector.

7.7in (19.5cm) high

$200-300   DN

A 1930s-50s Smiths brown Bakelite mechanical mantel clock.

Smiths was established in 1931. Clocks that are identical to this example and marked 'Enfield' date from after 1933. Clocks marks 'Smiths' Enfield' examples after 1949.

8in (20cm) high

$70-100   PC

A set of 1930s green and black Catalin salt and pepper shakers.

2.25in (6cm) high

$100-150   PC

A 1930s yellow Catalin Scottie dog napkin ring, with applied black eyes.

3in (7.5cm) wide

$25-35   PC

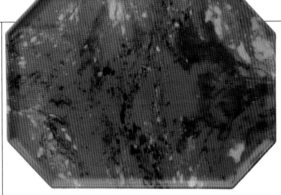

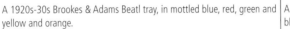

A 1920s-30s Linga Longa marbled white and yellow Beatl 'Diadem' tray.

This color combination is very rare.

12.5in (32cm) long

$70-100   P&I

A 1920s-30s Brookes & Adams Beatl tray, in mottled blue, red, green and yellow and orange.

12in (30.5cm) long

$80-120   P&I

A 1930s Brookes & Adams mottled blue and cream Bandalasta beaker.

3.75in (9.5cm) high

$30-50   BETH

A mid-1930s Dunlop Rubber Co. ashtray, manufactured by Roanoid Ltd., with folding black Bakelite cigarette-rests and base, with mottled green and cream urea formaldehyde top.

Produced in a number of mottled colors, this is a wonderful Art Deco design produced at a time when smoking was seen as healthy! The three black cigarette rests fold back inside to make a complete sphere. When they are open, a hole for ash is revealed. Always examine these ashtrays closely as they are often cracked.

5in (12cm) diam

$80-120   PC

A 1980s-90s Tacman plastic table lamp, in the form of a dog, designed by Fernando Cassetta, with molded marks.

8.25in (21cm) high

$300-500   WW

A 1960s Old Timer Ferrari plastic 'Tucano' lamp, designed by Design Verona, with molded marks.

8in (20cm) high

$120-180   WW

A 1930s-50s Lucite dice, mounted on a laminated colored Lucite base with a (bent) metal pin.

3.25in (9cm) high

$50-70   BETH

A set of five 1930s French Art Deco celluloid buttons.

1in (2.5cm) diam

$15-25   PC

POSTMODERN DESIGN

QUICK REFERENCE - POSTMODERN DESIGN

- Postmodernism is the name given to the group of styles that grew in the 1970s as a reaction to the Modernist and Modern styles of the first half of the 20thC. It actively rejected many of the ideas behind those earlier styles, such as function governing form.
- Key themes include surface decoration for the sake of it, historical or popular cultural references, handicrafts, a mixture of materials and often an irreverent sense of humor.
- Architecture was also an important inspiration and many Postmodern designers, such as Ettore Sottsass (1917-2007) and Michael Graves (b.1934), were also architects.

A Poltronova yellow 'Yantra - Y 33b' earthenware vase, designed by Ettore Sottsass in 1968, probably manufactured by Filigna di Prato, the base with factory marks and designer's facsimile signature.

12.5in (31.5cm) high

$1,500-2,500   QU

A Poltronova green 'Yantra - Y 15' earthenware vase, designed by Ettore Sottsass in 1968, probably manufactured by Filigna di Prato, the base with factory marks and designer's facsimile signature.

19.5in (50cm) high

$1,500-2,500   QU

A Memphis earthenware 'Carrot' vase, designed by Nathalie du Pasquier in 1985, manufactured by Flavia (Bitossi), the base printed 'MEMPHIS MILANO, made in Italy by FLAVIA Montelupo F.no, Designed by NATHALIE DU PASQUIER'.

11.5in (29.5cm) high

$650-850   QU

A Memphis earthenware vase, designed by Ettore Sottsass in 1986, manufactured by Flavia (Bitossi), the base marked 'SOTTSASS 1986, le ceramiche di BITOSSI Made in Italy by FLAVIA s.p.A. Montelupo FIRENZE'.

At the time of writing, this design is still being produced by the company.

18in (46cm) high

$1,200-1,800   QU

A Memphis porcelain 'Ladoga' vase, designed by Matteo Thun in 1982, the base with stamped mark.

In the same year he designed this piece, Thun also designed the porcelain 'Manitoba' tray. The four corners contained a salt shaker, a pepper shaker a toothpick holder and an appetizer holder. The dotted decoration and many of the forms seen on the 'Ladoga' vase also appeared on those four components.

10in (25.5cm) high

$550-750   WW

A mid-late 1980s Rosenthal Studio Line teapot, burner and milk jug, designed by Dorothy Hafner in 1982, from the 'Flash' range.

From 1973 until 1988, painter and sculptor Dorothy Hafner (b.1952) produced around twelve different designs of tableware for Tiffany & Co. and Rosenthal. Her striking 'Flash' range for Rosenthal was perhaps her most commercially successful. Teapots, coffee pots, vases and bowls are sought after. The burner is extremely rare.

Teapot 7.75in (19.5cm) high

$300-500   DRA

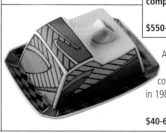

A mid-late 1980s Rosenthal Studio Line butter dish and cover, designed by Dorothy Hafner in 1982, from the 'Flash' range.

7.5in (19cm) wide

$40-60   PC

POSTMODERN DESIGN

A Rosenthal limited edition coffee set, designed by Marcello Morandini in 1987, from an edition of 250, the bases with factory marks and designer's facsimile signature, with original wooden box.

c1988   *Coffee pot 9.25in (23.5cm) high*
$3,000-4,000   **QU**

A Zani & Zani plastic and aluminum 'Vesuvio' coffee maker, designed by Gaetano Pesce in 1988-89, the base marked 'Caffetiera Espresso Vesuvio Progetto di Gaetano Pesce per zani & zani Made in Italy' and with facsimile designer's signature.

14.25in (36cm) high
$500-700   **QU**

A Next Interiors bowl, designed by Janice Tchalenko, the base with printed marks.

c1986   *4.75in (12cm) high*
$30-50   **PC**

A Next Interiors cone vase, designed by Janice Tchalenko, the base with printed marks.

The vase and bowl on this page are uncharacteristically brown - look out for Tchalenko's more commonly seen, and more desirable, vibrant pinks contrasted against grays, blues and other colors. For more information about Janice Tchalenko, see p.99 and p.131.

c1986   *8.75in (22cm) high*
$30-50   **PC**

A pair of Swid Powell silver-plated brass 'Silvershade' candlesticks, designed by Ettore Sottsass in 1986, the bases stamped 'c SWID POWELL, E. Sottsass, SILVER PLATED MADE IN ITALY'.

c1987
Taller 13in (33cm) high
$2,000-3,000   **QU**

An 1980s Acme cloisonné pin, designed by Ettore Sottsass, marked 'SOTTSASS FOR ACME STUDIOS'.

2in (5cm) wide
$250-350   **QU**

A Memphis long-sleeved cotton 'Zambia' shirt, designed by Nathalie du Pasquier, with woven Memphis label.

$50-70   **WW**

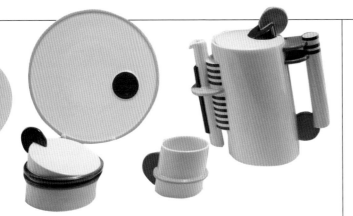

A mid-late 1980s Rosenthal Studio Line 'Flash One' pattern tri-form bowl, designed by Dorothy Hafner in c1982, from the 'Flash' range, the base with printed marks.

12.5in (30cm) wide
$120-180   **FLD**

POSTERS

QUICK REFERENCE - FILM POSTERS

- Posters for films that captured the public's imagination or that are considered to be cult classics tend to be the most desirable and valuable. Posters for little known or unpopular films, or those that have faded from the public's mind, are less valuable unless they have striking artwork, or artwork by a notable designer.
- An image or style with great eye-appeal will usually add to the value of a poster. Look out for designs that sum up the drama, emotion or story of a film, or that portray key characters or scenes.
- Although many collectors buy posters because they love the films depicted, other collectors focus on the work of one designer, such as Saul Bass or Robert Peal. Others focus on a series of films, such as the James Bond series, or films by key directors, such as Stanley Kubrick or Alfred Hitchcock, or those that feature particular actors.
- The most popular sizes are the American one-sheet - 27in (68.5cm) by 41in (104cm) - and the UK quad - 30in (76cm) by 40in (84cm). Posters from other countries can be in different sizes and can bear different artwork to the USA or UK versions. Posters from the film's country of origin tend to be the most desirable.
- Posters produced before a film is released are known as 'Teasers'. They usually have a different design to the main release poster, often a critical scene from the film, and can be rare. Posters are often issued if the film is re-released and, again, designs may differ from the original artwork.
- Always beware of photographic reproductions on shiny paper, as these are usually not valuable. Buy in the best condition possible. While folds and tears can be repaired, they should ideally not affect the image.

'2001 ODYSEJA KOSMICZNA' [2001 A Space Odyssey], a Polish one-sheet cinema poster, designed by Wiktor Gorka, in near mint condition, linen-backed.

Wiktor Górka (1922-2004) was one of Poland's most important and influential poster designers. Known for his use of collage, he designed dramatic posters that are highly desirable today. His most famous design is perhaps the poster for 'Kabaret' (1973), which depicts Sally Bowles' legs as a swastika.

1973   *33in (84cm) high*
$650-850   SAS

'BATTLE BEYOND THE STARS', a British quad poster, printed by W E Berry.

Inspired by the success of Star Wars, 'Battle Beyond the Stars' was a rehash of 'The Magnificent Seven' in outer space.

1980   *39.75in (101cm) wide*
$80-120   WW

'Battlestar GALACTICA', a British quad poster, printed by Leonard Ripley & Co., London, folded.

This poster promoted the first episode of the American TV series, which was released as a film in Canada, South America and some European countries, including the UK, in order to recoup the huge production costs.

1978   *40in (102cm) wide*
$120-180   WW

'DR NO', a British James Bond quad poster, designed by David Chasman and illustrated by Mitchell Hooks, printed by Stafford & Co., with folds and pin-holes to corners.

1962 40in (101cm) wide
$6,500-8,500   WW

'JAMES BOND 007 JAGT DR. NO' [Dr. No], a German James Bond one-sheet poster for the 1980 re-release, with folds, otherwise in excellent condition.

1980   *33in (84cm) high*
$50-70   SAS

'FROM RUSSIA WITH LOVE', a British James Bond quad film poster, with artwork by Renato Fratiniand and Eric Pulford, printed by Charles & Read.

1963   *40in (101cm) wide*

$5,500-6,500   **WW**

'GOLDFINGER', a British James Bond quad poster, printed by Stafford & Co, folded and with pin holes.

1964   *40in (101cm) wide*

$5,000-7,000   **WW**

'DER MANN MIT DEM GOLDENEN COLT' [The Man With The Golden Gun], a German James Bond poster, in very good condition.

Although there are exceptions to this rule, British Bond posters are the most desirable and valuable, followed by large American versions. Other country's posters are generally less sought after.

1974   *46in (117cm) high*

$100-150   **SAS**

'THE SPY WHO LOVED ME', a British James Bond quad poster, printed by Lonsdale & Bartholomew, in very good condition, folded.

1977   *40in (101cm) wide*

$400-600   **WW**

'BUCK ROGERS IN THE 25th CENTURY', a British quad poster, designed by Gadino, printed by W E Berry Ltd., Bradford, folded.

1979   *40in (101cm) wide*

$100-150   **WW**

Judith Picks

Like posters from other countries, posters produced for the re-release of a film can be much less expensive than the original UK or USA poster. Although the artwork is typically different than that used for the original, a re-release poster will still have a strong flavour of the film. This example invokes the romance and drama of the classic film 'Casablanca', featuring a large image of both stars. The inserted shot of the famous finale at the airport hints at the photomontage style of the original American one-sheet poster from 1942. If you wanted to buy one of those in similar condition, it could cost you over $40,000!

'CASABLANCA', an American half-sheet poster for the 1956 re-release, in excellent condition.

1956   *28in (71cm) wide*

$120-180   **SAS**

'EAST OF EDEN', an American one-sheet poster, in good condition, with pin holes to corners, wear from folds and minor paper loss.

1955   *41in (104cm) wide*

$650-850   **SAS**

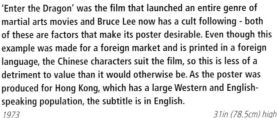

['Enter the Dragon'], a Chinese Hong Kong movie poster, in very good condition.

'Enter the Dragon' was the film that launched an entire genre of martial arts movies and Bruce Lee now has a cult following - both of these are factors that make its poster desirable. Even though this example was made for a foreign market and is printed in a foreign language, the Chinese characters suit the film, so this is less of a detriment to value than it would otherwise be. As the poster was produced for Hong Kong, which has a large Western and English-speaking population, the subtitle is in English.

1973
$200-300   SAS

'FLASH GORDON', a British quad film poster, printed by W E Berry Ltd., Bradford, with folds.
1980   40in (101cm) wide
$200-300   WW

'FRANCUSKI Ł CZNIK' ['The French Connection'], a Polish one-sheet poster, designed by Andrzej Krajewski, in excellent condition.

Posters by Krajewski (b.1933) are increasingly sought after and valuable. 2,500 copies of this poster were printed for distribution across Communist Poland.

1973   31.5in (80cm) high
$120-180   SAS

'easy rider', a French one-sheet poster, in excellent condition, with slight surface marking, linen-backed.
1969
$120-180   SAS

QUICK REFERENCE - REBOOTS

- Keep an eye on movie magazines and rumour sites to see if old movies are being rebooted. When this happens, prices for memorabilia connected to the older films in the franchise often rise dramatically. For example, the release of 'The Amazing Spider-Man' (2012), starring Andrew Garfield, caused prices to rise for memorabilia from Tobey Maguire's stint as Spidey.
- The 2014 release of the new Godzilla film directed by Gareth Edwards will undoubtedly affect Godzilla memorabilia since his first apperance in 1954.
- Whatever the film, always look out for pieces that sum up or are evocative of the franchise. The fantastic, eye-catching and bold artwork of this poster is a great example!

'ZABRANJENA PLANETA' ['Forbidden Planet'], a Yugoslav one-sheet poster.
1956   27in (69cm) high
$400-600   DS

'GODZILLA', a French one-sheet poster, in excellent condition, with folds and some staining.
1954
33in (84cm) high
$400-600   SAS

'LE BON LA BRUTE LE TRUAND', ['The Good, the Bad and the Ugly'], a French one-sheet poster, printed by Ets St. Martin, with folds.
1966
$400-600   DS

'HELL BELOW ZERO' a British quad poster, printed by Stafford & Co. Ltd., folded and with some losses.

1954   *40in (101cm) wide*

$120-180   **WW**

'THE HUSTLER', an American one-sheet pre-release promotional poster, framed and glazed.

This pre-release poster is more valuable and desirable than the actual release poster as a result of its eye-catching and bold artwork.

1964   *41.5in (104cm) high*

$500-700   **SWO**

'INDIANA JONES et le TEMPLE MAUDIT' ['Indiana Jones and The Temple of Doom'], a French one-sheet poster, with artwork by Jouin, in excellent condition, with folds.

1984   *63in (160cm) high*

$100-150   **SAS**

'An Inspector Calls', a British quad poster, with Quebec censor stamp, folds, with some holes to fold crosses.

1954   *40in (100cm) high*

$300-500   **SWO**

'DOBAR POSAO U ITALIJI' ['The Italian Job'], a Yugoslavian poster, in very good condition, with folds.

1969   *27.5in (70cm) high*

$100-150   **SAS**

'JAWS', a British quad film poster, printed by W E Berry Ltd, Bradford, folded.

1975   *40in (101.5cm) wide*

$100-150   **WW**

'The Jungle Book', a British quad poster, printed by S & D S Ltd., England, with folds.

1967   *40in (101cm) wide*

$120-180   **WW**

'Lawrence of Arabia', a British quad poster, in near mint condition, with folds.

1969   *40in (101cm) wide*

$150-250   **SAS**

'THE MAGNIFICENT SEVEN', a British quad poster, printed by Stafford & Co.

1960   *40in (101.5cm) wide*

$500-700   **WW**

'THE MAN WHO KNEW TOO MUCH', an American half-sheet poster, hole-punched to one edge, with 1.5in (4cm) edge tear and general surface marking.

1956   *28in (71cm) wide*

$120-180   **SAS**

'OCEAN'S 11', a Japanese poster, in excellent condition, with minor edge damage, linen-backed.

1960   *29in (73.5cm) high*

$300-500   **SAS**

'WALT DISNEY'S Pinoccchio', a British quad poster, printed by W E Berry, in very good condition, with folds.

1978

40in (101cm) wide

$120-180   **WW**

A CLOSER LOOK AT A FILM POSTER

Polish film posters have become highly sought after in the past decade. Those by the best artists can now fetch thousands of dollars.

Photomontage and collage are two typical techniques used in Polish posters. Here they are used to superb, jarring and disorientating effect that recalls the films' content.

This is from the 'golden age' of Polish film posters, which lasted from the mid-1950s to the 1960s.

Zdeněk Ziegler (b.1932) is an up-and-coming name among collectors.

In general double-bill posters are less valuable than posters for the primary release of a film. This example of a double-bill poster is more desirable than many as the two films are both well known and have a large crossover fan base.

'REAR WINDOW', an American one-sheet poster for the re-release double-bill of 'Psycho' and 'Rear Window', in very good condition, with folds, pin holes and edge nicks.

1962

$120-180   **SAS**

'PSYCHO', an American one-sheet re-release poster, in excellent condition.

The design of the re-release poster is the same as for the original 1960 poster, but with an additional 'IT'S BACK' box. The original can fetch over $3,000!

1965

$500-700   **SAS**

Hitchcock is a very popular director and memorabilia associated with him and his films is widely collected. He is shown clearly on the poster, which (given that he is an important figure in his own right) is a desirable feature.

'PTA'CI/PSYCHO' ['The Birds'/'Psycho'], a Czech poster for the re-release double-bill of 'The Birds' and 'Psycho', designed by Zdeněk Ziegler, in excellent condition, with folds.

1966   *16in (40.5cm) high*

$100-150   **SAS**

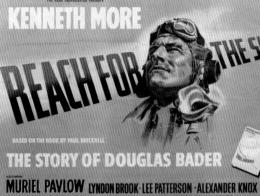

'REACH FOR THE SKY', a British quad poster, printed in colors by W E Berry Ltd., with folds and holes.
1956   *40in (100cm) wide*
$1,000-1,500   SWO

A CLOSER LOOK AT A FILM POSTER

The film was originally titled 'Return of the Jedi', but this was changed to 'Revenge of the Jedi' after screenwriter Lawrence Kasdan suggested 'Return' was a 'weak title'.

Luke and Vader are shown with the wrong color lightsabers. Vader's should be red, rather than blue, while Luke's should be green!

Before the film was released George Lucas changed the name back to 'Return of the Jedi' as he felt revenge was not appropriate for an honorable Jedi, but by then thousands of promotional pre-release posters had already been printed and many distributed. The remaining stocks were sold off to Star Wars fan club members.

This example does not bear the dated tagline for the American release, which means that it was intended for foreign cinemas. Undated examples are more rare and desirable than those with the dated tagline.

Almost all authentic examples of this poster were machine-folded - rolled examples are very rare and likely to be fakes. Fakes typically contain the image of fold lines (copied from the original), a 'cloudy' bottom right corner and a very pale 20th Century Fox logo.

'REVENGE OF THE JEDI', a one-sheet pre-release poster, designed by Drew Struzan, with folds and hole to bottom left, framed.
1983   *41.25in (103cm) high*
$700-1,000   SWO

'ROCKY and ROCKY II Together.', an American one-sheet poster for the double-bill of 'Rocky' and 'Rocky II', with folds.
1980   *41in (104cm) high*
$120-180   WW

'THIS SPORTING LIFE', a British quad poster, printed by Charles & Read Ltd., London.
1963   *40in (101cm) wide*
$70-100   WW

'DIE ROTE LOLA' ['Stagefright'], an Italian poster, printed by F P Druck Fotopress, with folds, linen-backed.
1950   *30in (76cm) high*
$120-180   WW

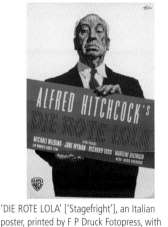

'ULYSSES', an American one-sheet poster, in very good condition, with folds.
1967   *40.5in (103cm) high*
$100-150   WW

'Young at Heart', an American quad poster, in excellent condition, with folds, framed.
1954   *40.25in (102cm) high*
$100-150   SWO

POSTERS

QUICK REFERENCE - TRAVEL POSTERS

- Travel posters can be found for most of the major forms of travel, including cruise liners, railways and airlines. Buses, ferries and other less glamorous forms of transport tend to attract considerably smaller audiences and lower values.
- Cruise line posters tend to date from the late 1910s into the 1930s. The 'golden age' of the railway poster dates from the 1920s and 1930s, while airline posters generally date from the 1930s to the 1970s. Following World War II, posters were superseded by other forms of advertising, such as magazine, radio and television adverts.
- A number of factors contribute toward value, including the visual appeal, theme, company, and designer.
- Look for posters that sum up the romance or excitement of that form of transport or the destination shown. Posters in the Art Deco style are usually highly prized. Bright colors, attractive and evocative scenes and popular company names will usually add value. Values can also vary between different railways and airlines, with posters produced for the Great Western Railway and Air France often being the most desirable in their categories.
- The work of notable and influential designers, such as Cassandre (Adolphe Mouron), Jean Carlu and Tom Purvis, is usually highly valued.
- Always consider condition, as tears, scuffs, folds and other damage will affect value.

'ABERYSTWYTH', a Railway Executive Western Region poster, designed by Claude Buckle, printed by Jordison & Co.

1960   *40.25in (102cm) high*

$400-600   **GWRA**

'BLACKPOOL', a London, Midlands & Scottish Railway poster, designed by Lewis Baumer, printed by Charles & Read Ltd., in very good condition.

Lewis Baumer (1870-1963) was a notable illustrator and caricaturist for 'Punch' magazine. Here he shows Blackpool as being full of elegant, fashionable and healthy people being sociable on the beach.

50in (127cm) wide

$3,000-4,000   **DN**

'CARDIGAN BAY RESORTS for Glorious Sea and Country Holidays TRAVEL BY TRAIN', a British Railways Western Region poster, designed by Harry Riley, printed by R B Macmillan Ltd.

40.25in (102cm) high

$350-450   **GWRA**

'NORTH EAST DALES', a London & North Eastern Railway poster, designed by Edwin Byatt, printed by Waterlow and Sons Ltd., with later 'TAKE HOLIDAYS EARLY' sticker, in very good condition.

50in (127cm) wide

$650-850   **GWRA**

'DUNFERMLINE', a British Railways Scottish Region poster, designed by Kenneth Steel, printed by Nathaniel Lloyd & Co., in excellent condition, with a central fold.

40.25in (102cm) high

$300-500   **GWRA**

'GLOUCESTER CATHEDRAL', a joint Gloucestershire Warwickshire Railway and London, Midland and Scottish Railway poster, designed by Claude Buckle, printed by Beck and Inchbold Ltd., with folds but otherwise in excellent condition.

40.25in (102cm) high

$650-850   **GWRA**

'ARRIVE EARLIER BY TRAIN ON THE HAMPSHIRE COAST', a British Railways Southern Region poster, designed by Bromfield, printed by Whitehead & Co., in very good condition.

40.25in (102cm) high

$50-70   **GWRA**

'PASS OF GLENCOE WESTERN HIGHLANDS ON THE ROUTE OF THE LOCH ETIVE, GLEN ETIVE AND GLENCOE CIRCULAR TOUR', a British Railways Scottish Region poster, designed by Frank Sherwin, printed by McCorquodale.

50in (127cm) wide

$1,200-1,800   **GWRA**

A CLOSER LOOK AT A RAILWAY POSTER

Store Street station was rebuilt in 1960 at the height of the post-war re-building boom and was renamed Piccadilly.

During the late 1950s/early 1960s images of modern buildings were being printed on postcards and posters to show that Britain was recovering from the war, growing and adopting new, modern ways of living and working.

Claude Henry Buckle (1905-73) was a painter who produced many railway poster designs during the 1930s-50s. His work is sought after by collectors.

A trained architect, he specialized in producing images of buildings.

'MANCHESTER'S NEW STATION', a British Railways London Midlands Region poster, designed by Claude Buckle, printed by Waterlow, in very good condition.

1960   *50in (127cm) wide*

$250-350   **GWRA**

'Lytham St Annes', a 1950s Railway Executive London Midland Region poster, designed by Johnston, printed by London Lithographic Co., in excellent condition, with a few minor edge tears.

40.25in (102cm) high

$500-700   **GWRA**

'MABLETHORPE AND SUTTON-ON-SEA', a British Railways East Region poster, designed by Blake, printed by Jordison & Co., in excellent condition, with one fold.

40.25in (102cm) high

$250-350   **GWRA**

'Ramsgate', a British Railways poster, designed by Alan Durman (1905-63), printed by the Baynard Press, in excellent condition.

c1955   *39.5in (100cm) high*

$300-500   **DN**

POSTERS

Judith Picks

This striking poster, featuring a Gresley V2 locomotive steaming across a bridge in a picturesque landscape, has more to recommend it than just its appearance! It was designed by one of the greatest and most celebrated British railway poster designers ever, Terence Cuneo. In fact, it was the first poster he produced for the newly formed British Railways.

The notable East Coast location, well-known designer, evocative scene, hallmark locomotive under steam and the rarity of this design combine to make this an excellent buy. I think the price will only appreciate.

'ROYAL BORDER BRIDGE BERWICK-ON-TWEED', a Railway Executive North Eastern Region poster, designed by Terence Cuneo, printed by Chromoworks, in good condition, mounted on acid-free paper, with some tape staining.

c1950   *50in (127cm) wide*
$1,000-1,500   **GWRA**

'ROYAL DEESIDE SEE SCOTLAND BY TRAIN', a British Railways Scottish Region poster, designed by Kenneth Steel, printed by Jarrold & Sons, in excellent condition, with very minor edge crinkling.

This is a well-known and desirable poster.

1951   *40.25in (102cm) high*
$400-600   **GWRA**

'PULLMAN DIESEL SERVICES', a British Railways Western Region poster, designed by an unknown designer, printed by Waterlow, with some tape damage and loss around the edges.

Although it's not as visually striking as other railway posters, this poster is interesting in that it typifies the post-war move away from glamour and into speed and efficiency. Three timetables are superimposed over the new Pullman diesel locomotive.

     40.25in (102cm) high
$80-120   **GWRA**

'ROYAL ROTHESAY THE HOLIDAY CAPITAL OF THE CLYDE COAST', a joint London, Midland and Scottish Railway and London and North Eastern Railway poster, designed by Cecil King, printed by Jordison, in good condition, with some edge crinkling.

50in (127cm) wide
$500-700   **GWRA**

'PROGRESS', a British Transport Commission poster, designed by Terence Cuneo, printed by Waterlow, with minor edge tears.

This poster shows the construction of a Warship Class locomotive and the restoration of a steam locomotive at Swindon Works.

50in (127cm) wide
$500-700   **GWRA**

'THORNTON CLEVELEYS ON THE LANCASHIRE COAST', a British Railways London Midland Region poster, designed by Kenneth Steel, printed by R B Macmillan, in excellent condition.

1950   *40in (102cm) high*
$550-750   **GWRA**

'I SHOULD HAVE SENT IT- LUGGAGE IN ADVANCE', a British Railways poster, designed by Kroll, printed by Stafford & Co.

40in (102cm) high
$300-500   **WW**

A London Underground poster for the University Boat Race, designed by Percy Drake Brookshaw (1907-93), printed by the Baynard Press, linen-backed.

The colors, flat planes of color and geometric style recall prints by contemporary artists at the Grosvenor School of Modern Art. Today, Grosvenor School prints can fetch tens of thousands of dollars.

1928	*18in (46.5cm) wide*
$1,500-2,500	**DN**

QUICK REFERENCE - LONDON UNDERGROUND

- From the 1910 to the 1930s, Frank Pick (1878-1941) oversaw a golden age of advertising and design management for the London Underground and London Transport.
- Pick helped develop the typeface and the recognisable circle and bar logo.
- He also employed numerous avant garde artists, including Frederick Herrick, to produce eye-catching, modern posters.
- Often less common than other railway posters, London Underground posters attract legions of fans today.
- Frederick Herrick's (1887-1970) posters are typified by an elegant Art Deco style. Indeed, he participated in the famed 1925 Exposition Internationales des Arts Decoratifs et Industriels Modernes in Paris that launched the Art Deco style.
- Herrick was also in charge of the Baynard Press in London.

'THE OPEN GATE THAT LEADS FROM WORK TO PLAY', a London Underground poster, designed by Frederick Herrick, printed by the Baynard Press, matted and framed, with minor losses and restoration.

1925	*41in (104cm) high*
$1,000-1,500	**SWA**

A London Underground poster for the University Boat Race, designed by Percy Drake Brookshaw, in good condition.

1937	*12.25in (31.5cm) wide*
$1,200-1,800	**DN**

'CUP FINAL WEMBLEY-APRIL 21st AT 3PM FROM ANY UNDERGROUND STATION', a London Underground poster, designed by Percy Drake Brookshaw, printed by the Baynard Press, with creases, mounted on black paper.

1928	*18in (46.5cm) wide*
$1,200-1,800	**DN**

'WHILE OTHERS WAIT - A SEASON TAKES YOU THROUGH', a London Underground poster, designed by Percy Drake Brookshaw, printed at the Baynard Press, with creased corners.

1928	*18in (46.5cm) wide*
$800-1,200	**DN**

'THE ZOO', a London Underground poster, designed by Gwynedd M Hudson, printed by John Waddington Ltd., with professional restoration and overpainting.

1925	*40.25in (102cm) high*
$800-1,200	**SWA**

'THE TOWER OF LONDON', a London Transport poster, designed by Edward McKnight Kauffer, printed by Vincent Brooks Day & Son Ltd., from an edition of 1,500, in good condition.

1934	*40in (102cm) high*
$1,200-1,800	**GWRA**

POSTERS

'LE PALAIS DE FONTAINEBLEAU', a Paris-Lyon-Méditerranée poster, designed by Julien Lacaze, in good condition, linen-backed.

40.25in (102cm) high

$500-700   GWRA

'VENICE SIMPLON ORIENT-EXPRESS', an Orient Express poster, designed by Pierre Fix-Masseau, framed and glazed.

This is one of a set of six posters designed by Fix-Masseau to commemorate the restoration of the Venice-Simplon Orient Express in 1981.

1979   *36.5in (92.7cm) high*

$120-180   CAPE

'BESANÇON', a Paris-Lyon-Méditerranée poster, designed by Roger Broders, printed by Lucien Serre & Cie, in excellent condition, linen-backed.

Roger Broders (1883-1953) was a notable French illustrator and poster designer. Highly sought after today, his work is typified by strong perspective, simple lines and bold colors. The PLM (c1858-1938) was the Paris to Lyon and Mediterranean railway.

c1930   *39in (100cm) high*

$1,200-1,800   BLO

'To See France go by train' and 'FRENCH RAILWAYS', two mid-late 20thC Société Nationale des Chemins de fer Francais posters, in excellent condition.

40in (102cm) high

$25-35 each   GWRA

A CLOSER LOOK AT A POSTER

The approved style of Soviet art in the 1930s was Social Realism, which largely depicted strong and far-sighted revolutionaries, sturdy factory workers or farmers on tractors. This unusual Art Deco poster was produced by Intourist, the Soviet state tourism agency. They correctly assumed that the Art Deco style would be more appealing to Western tourists than Social Realism.

The style is similar to contemporary Western travel posters.

The design, featuring a stylish sports car, speeding train and vast viaduct, is intended to highlight Soviet engineering skills.

Modern technology is shown in front of the beauty of the Armenian landscape, creating a combined image of glamorous tourism.

'RHEINGOLD-EXPRESS', designed by Eugene Max Cordier, printed by Carl Gerber, Munich, with minor restoration to edges.

Named after Richard Wagner's opera due to its route along the Rhine, this luxury service ran 1928-38 and from 1951 onward.

1953   *40in (102cm) high*

$650-850   SWA

'SCANDINAVIAN EXPRESS', a Netherlands railway poster, printed by J Van Boekhoven for Propaganda Sect Neth Railways 447, in good condition, with missing corner.

$200-300   GWRA

'SOVIET ARMENIA', an English-language Intourist railway poster, in very good condition, with slight discoloration and minor restoration.

c1935   *35.25in (89.5cm) high*

$6,500-7,500   SWA

'SOUTHERN PACIFIC'S NEW Daylight', a Southern Pacific poster, designed by Sam Hyde Harris, in very good condition, with minor creases and abrasions.

Streamlined trains were one of the most visible, striking and easily accessible examples of American Modernism. Harris captures their solidity, power and speed in this dramatic poster. English-born Harris (1889-1917) began his career as a commercial artist and was hired in 1920 by Atchison, Topeka & Santa Fe Railway Company. He also worked for Southern Pacific.

1937   *23in (58cm) high*
$10,000-15,000   **SWA**

'GO BY TRAIN at low fares to FLORIDA', a Pennsylvania Railroad poster, in very good condition, with abrasions, restored loss and other restoration.
c1941   *40.25in (102cm) high*
$1,200-1,800   **SWA**

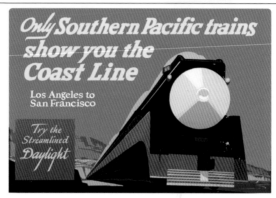

'Only Southern Pacific trains show you the Coast Line', an original tempera-on-board railway poster design, designed by Sam Hyde Harris, in very good condition, with chips and flaking to image, framed.
c1937   *39.5in (100cm) wide*
$8,000-12,000   **SWA**

'JAPAN', designed by Munetsugu Satomi, printed by Seihan Printing Co., Osaka, in excellent condition.

Note how even the telephone poles bend to the train's speed and power. Unusually for a railway poster, the train itself is not depicted. Instead the poster gives a passenger's perspective of the train's speed.

1937   *35in (89cm) high*
$5,000-7,000   **SWA**

['Osaka Railways'], a Japanese railway poster, designed by Toyonosuke Kurozumi, in very good condition, with some repaired tears and minor creases and abrasion.

This very rare and surprisingly (given the date) modern poster advertises the fast trains from Osaka and Yamada.

c1935   *42in (107cm) high*
$6,500-7,500   **SWA**

'THE NORTH CHINA RAILWAY CO.', a Japanese railway poster, designed by an unknown designer, in very good condition, with repaired tears, creases and overpainting.

This poster was published by the Japanese Government, which built the railway in occupied China.

c1940   *40.25in (102cm) high*
$5,000-7,000   **SWA**

['Long Live the Engineer of the Locomotive of Revolution - Comrade Stalin!'], a Soviet railway poster, designed by an unknown designer, in very good condition, with repaired tears in margins and creases.

As with the poster on the previous page, the style of this Soviet poster has an unusual Art Deco feel.

1938   *40.5in (103cm) high*
$8,000-12,000   **SWA**

'HOLLAND-AMERICA LINE', designed by Willem Ten Broek, printed by Joh. Enschede en Zonen, Haarlem, in very good condition, with some repaired tears and restoration.

Ten Broek was clearly influenced by Cassandre's famous poster for the 'Normandie'.

1936   *38in (96.5cm) high*
$5,000-7,000   SWA

'Cruise the GREAT LAKES', a Canadian Pacific poster, designed by Peter Ewart, in very good condition, with some repaired tears.

Ewart worked for the Canadian Pacific Railway for 20 years and created more than 24 different posters for the company, including two promoting the company's cruises on the Great Lakes. This is the rarer of the two.

c1940   *35.75in (91cm) high*
$2,500-3,500   SWA

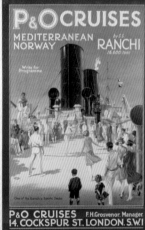

'P & O CRUISES', designed by Ellis Silas, printed by Philip Reid, in very good condition, with creases and abrasions in margins and image and some restoration, linen-backed.

60in (152cm) high
$6,500-7,500   SWA

'SOUTHERN RAILWAY'S SOUTHAMPTON DOCKS', designed by Leslie Carr, printed by J Weiner Ltd., depicting the RMS 'Queen Mary', numbered '3325', linen-backed, framed.

50in (127cm) wide
$1,200-1,800   GORL

'SAIL WHITE EMPRESS TO EUROPE', designed by Roger Couillard, published by Canadian Pacific, in very good condition, with repaired tears, paper-mounted.

1950   *36in (91.5cm) high*
$2,000-3,000   SWA

'Italian Line', an Italian Line poster, designed by Paolo Federico Garretto, printed in the USA, in very good condition, with repaired tears.

1937   *36.5in (92.5cm) high*
$2,500-3,500   SWA

'LONDON', a Royal Mail Steam Packet Company poster, designed by Kenneth Denton Shoesmith, in very good condition, with some folds and restoration.

c1921   *40in (102cm) high*
$1,200-1,800   SWA

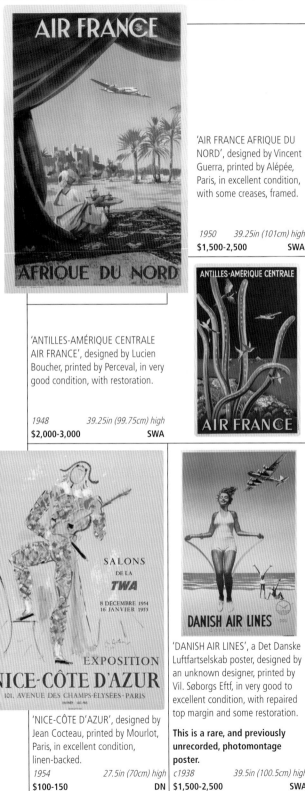

'AIR FRANCE AFRIQUE DU NORD', designed by Vincent Guerra, printed by Alépée, Paris, in excellent condition, with some creases, framed.

1950   39.25in (101cm) high
$1,500-2,500   **SWA**

'ANTILLES-AMÉRIQUE CENTRALE AIR FRANCE', designed by Lucien Boucher, printed by Perceval, in very good condition, with restoration.

1948   39.25in (99.75cm) high
$2,000-3,000   **SWA**

'AIR FRANCE FLY TO PARIS', designed by Raymond Gid, printed by Bedos & Cie, Paris, with creases and restoration.

Air France posters are among the most collectible of all airline posters. The brief for this rare poster asked for an image 'whose contagious cheerfulness attracts people to the capital'.

1953   39in (99cm) high
$2,500-3,500   **SWA**

'NICE-CÔTE D'AZUR', designed by Jean Cocteau, printed by Mourlot, Paris, in excellent condition, linen-backed.

1954   27.5in (70cm) high
$100-150   **DN**

'DANISH AIR LINES', a Det Danske Luftfartselskab poster, designed by an unknown designer, printed by Vil. Søborgs Eftf, in very good to excellent condition, with repaired top margin and some restoration.

This is a rare, and previously unrecorded, photomontage poster.

c1938   39.5in (100.5cm) high
$1,500-2,500   **SWA**

'RÉGIE AIR AFRIQUE', designed by F Haudepin, printed by Fehrenbach & Cie., Paris, in excellent condition, with minor restoration to margin, framed.

c1936   31in (78.75cm) high
$1,200-1,800   **SWA**

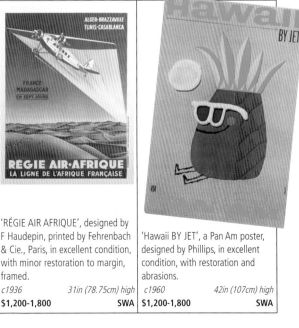

'Hawaii BY JET', a Pan Am poster, designed by Phillips, in excellent condition, with restoration and abrasions.

c1960   42in (107cm) high
$1,200-1,800   **SWA**

POSTERS

'NORWAY THE HOME OF SKI-ING', a Norwegian tourism and skiing poster, designed by Trygve Davidsen, printed by Hagen & Kornmann, Oslo, lithograph in colors, in excellent condition, linen-backed.

Painter and illustrator Trygve Davidsen (1895-1978) was inspired by religious subjects and Norwegian mythology, both of which can be seen in this design.

c1930   39in (99cm) high
$1,200-1,800   BLO

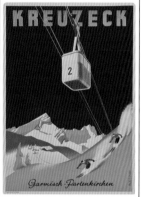

'KREUZECK Garmisch-Partenkirchen', a German skiing poster, designed by Plenert, printed by Carl Lipp, Münich, lithograph in colors, in excellent condition, linen-backed.

c1936   23.5in (60cm) high
$800-1,200   BLO

'Superbagnères', a French SNCF skiing poster, designed by Roland Hugon, printed by Paul Martial, lithograph in colors, in excellent condition, linen-backed.

1937   39in (99cm) high
$1,000-1,500   BLO

'Let's go skiing! USE THE NEW HAVEN R.R. Snow Trains', an American skiing poster, designed by Sascha Maurer, printed by McCandlish Lithograhpic Corporation, Philadelphia, lithograph in colors, with restoration and repairs.

The New Haven Railroad's Ski Trains, which began operating in 1933, were self-contained ski trips on wheels. The train itself was used as a ski lodge and people ate in the dining car. This is the larger of two formats this poster was available in.

1936   42in (106.5cm) high
$2,500-3,500   SWA

'PRAHA' (Prague), a Czech tourism poster, designed by Zden k Rykr, printed by Melantrich, Prague, lithograph in color, in excellent condition.

Largely a self-taught artist, Rykr was a set designer at the National Theatre in Prague, as well as an illustrator, painter, journalist and graphic designer. He is best remembered for his packaging designs for Orion, a Czech chocolate company, as well as for his corporate designs for Bata and Skoda.

c1935   37.25in (94.5cm) high
$3,000-5,000   SWA

'AROSA', a Swiss tourism poster, designed by Henel, in very good condition, with horizontal folds, some losses and restoration.

c1930   49.25in (125cm) high
$1,200-1,800   SWA

'SUMMER SPORTS IN USSR', a Soviet tourism poster, designed by Maria Nesterova-Berzina, in very good condition, with some repairs.

c1935   40in (102cm) high
$1,500-2,500   SWA

'Nice Travail & Joie', a French tourism poster, designed by Henri Matisse, printed by Mourlot, Paris, in excellent condition, linen-backed.

This design shows the bold collage style that Henri Matisse (1869-1954) used at this time, as well as his hallmark vibrant colors. Matisee moved to Cimiez, near Nice, in 1917 and died there in 1954.

1947   *39.5in (100cm) high*

$1,200-1,800   **DN**

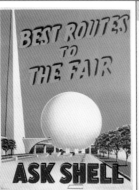

'BEST ROUTES TO THE FAIR ASK SHELL', a Shell promotional and travel poster, in very good condition, with restoration, creases and light foxing in margins.

1939   *54in (137cm) high*

$2,000-3,000   **SWA**

A CLOSER LOOK AT A POSTER

With its clean lines, simplified forms and use of shadow tones, this image crosses Art Deco and Modernist styles.

In 1938, it was awarded first prize in the poster competition for the fair.

Austrian graphic designer Joseph Binder (1898-1972) immigrated to the USA in the mid-1930s where he worked for United Airlines and the American Red Cross and was Art Director for the American Navy.

It shows the Trylon and the Perisphere, the key buildings at the heart of the fair, towering above a typical Manhattan-style skyline, a train and cruise liner.

'NEW YORK WORLD'S FAIR 1939', a promotional poster, designed by Joseph Binder, printed by Grinnell Litho. Co., Inc., New York City, in excellent condition, with creases and light stains.

1939   *20in (51cm) high*

$2,500-3,500   **SWA**

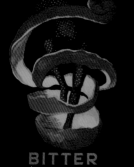

'BITTER CAMPARI', designed by Leonetto Cappiello, printed by by Devambez, Turin, marked 'L. Cappiello, Stampato in Italia, Riproduzione vietata, Devambez-edit-Paris-Torino unico concessionario dei nuovi AFFICHES CAPPIELLO', designed 1921.

43.5in (100cm) high

$4,000-6,000   **QU**

'CAMPARI', designed by Marcello Nizzoli, printed by Edizioni Star, Milan, marked 'Nizzoli, Edizioni Star, Autorizzato dalla R. Questura di Milano' and with a tax stamp, designed 1926.

55in (140cm) high

$1,500-2,500   **QU**

'Bitter CAMPARI', a two-part poster, designed by Nino Nanni, printed by Ripalta Industrie Grafiche, Milan, marked 'Nanni, RIPALTA Industrie Grafiche Milano Via Aulossi 17, 1958'.

1958   *55.5in (139.5cm) high*

$1,500-2,500   **QU**

'FERNET-BRANCA', designed by Leonetto Cappiello, printed by P Vercasson & Cie., Paris, marked 'Mod. Nr. 668, CREATION P. VERCASSON, PARIS. Imp. Publ. Etab. Vercasson, 6, Rue Martel, Paris'.

1909   *78.5in (200.5cm) high*

$1,200-1,800   **QU**

'ZOOLOGISCHER GARTEN BASEL', a Swiss zoo advertising poster, designed by Urs Eggenschwiler, published by Wassermann AG, Basel, line-backed, framed.

50in (127cm) high

$650-850   WW

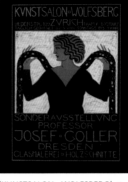

'KUNSTSALON - WOLFSBERG', a German exhibition poster, designed by Josef Goller, printed by J E Wolfensberger, Zürich, lithograph in colors, with vertical and horizontal folds, matted and framed.

Josef Goller (1868-1947) was a German designer, book designer and teacher. He is mainly known for his work in stained glass, which clearly influenced the design of this poster.

c1911   *39in (99cm) high*

$2,500-3,500   SWA

A poster card for Maison Prunier, designed by A M Cassandre (Adolphe Mouron, 1901-1968), lithograph in colors.

This famous image was used with the restaurant title at the side of the table and 'The Famous Paris Restaurant' arranged in a semi-circle over the fish. These cards were produced for display on tables, theatres or in glass fronted wall cases. The image was also produced as a larger poster.

1934   *7.5in (19cm) high*

$300-500   DN

'Visitez LE PALAIS ROYAL', a French Art Nouveau tourism poster, designed by Pal (Jean de Paléologue, 1860-1942), faded, yellowed, with losses to edges, corners and center of image, framed.

This poster could have fetched over three times as much had it not been so damaged. The areas of loss within the image are particularly detrimental.

c1900   *55in (139cm) high*

$250-350   SWO

'BRITON OR BOER', a British political and wartime poster, lithograph in colors.

c1900

$300-500   FLD

'THE MODEL RAILWAY EXHIBITION', a British event advertising poster, in excellent condition, linen-backed.

1936   *30in (76cm) high*

$500-700   GWRA

'Newmann THE GREAT', a card poster for a magician.

C A Newmann 'The Great' (1880-1952) was a noted hypnotist and mentalist who was also known for owning what was, at the time, the largest library of magic books in the USA. He began performing in front of the public in 1896 (aged 16) and continued until 1950, clocking up over five decades of amazing performances.

14in (35.5cm) high

$40-60   BLO

QUICK REFERENCE - POT LIDS

● Pot lids were one of the first examples of visually attractive packaging. Made from pottery that had been transfer-printed with a design, they were used to cover pots containing products such as food, toothpaste or bears' grease (a hair product). They were mainly produced in Staffordshire by companies such as F & R Pratt, who were granted a related patent in 1848, and J Ridgway.

● The first lids were produced during the 1820s and were mainly blue and white. Production grew in the 1830s and multi-colored lids were introduced during the early 1840s. It isn't possible to date most lids with any accuracy as they are undated and most were produced for long periods. Those that commemorate specific events, such as an exhibition, a war or the death of a personality can be dated more closely.

● Before 1860, lids tended to be flat in profile and lightweight and they often had a simple screw threaded flange. From the 1860s to mid-1870s, lids became heavier in weight and more domed and after 1875 they became even heavier but regained their flatter profiles. Early lids from the 1860s tend to be more desirable as the quality of the design and manufacture are typically higher.

● Pot lids first appeared at auction in 1924. Although they have fallen from fashion in recent years, pot lids still attract a group of dedicated collectors. Pieces from major 20thC collections, such as the Crowther or Cashmore collections, are particularly sought after.

● Condition is very important. Damaged or restored lids will fetch lower sums than lids in good condition. Always consider the quality of the design in terms of the colors and level of detail – the best and boldest designs will usually be the most sought after. Different sizes and unusual variations, such as the design of the border, will also often affect value.

● The numbers given in captions relate to those used in K V Mortimer's standard reference work on pot lids, 'Pot Lids Reference & Price Guide', published by the Antique Collectors Club in 2003.

A Staffordshire transfer-printed 'GENUINE RUSSIAN BEAR'S GREASE.' pot lid.

$120-180   H&C

A Staffordshire transfer-printed 'GENUINE BEARS GREASE' pot lid, by Patey & Co.

2.75in (7cm) diam

$450-650   H&C

A Staffordshire transfer-printed 'JAMES ATKINSON'S BEARS GREASE' pot lid, the transfer including price '2S 6D'.

2.5in (6cm) diam

$150-250   H&C

A Staffordshire blue and white transfer-printed 'RIMMEL'S GENUINE BEARS GREASE.' pot lid.

Eugene Rimmel (1820-87) founded his first perfume company with his father at the tender age of 14 in 1834. A great marketeer, known as the 'Prince of Perfumers', he was awarded ten Royal Warrants for his innovative products, which were landmarks in the development of cosmetics. He also contributed greatly to improving standards of 19thC hygiene. His company survives today and is owned by Coty Inc.

$500-700   H&C

A mid-late 19thC Staffordshire transfer-printed pot lid and base, 'VERITABLE GRAISSE D'OURS' (Authentic Bears' Grease), produced for the French market.

$400-600   H&C

A CLOSER LOOK AT A POT LID

This tiny lid, without any border, is classified as 'extra small' and is very rare.

Variations can occur in the color of certain characters' clothes. This does not usually affect the value.

The original watercolor was by Jesse Austin (1806-79), who worked primarily for the F & R Pratt factory and painted hundreds of watercolors to be used for pot lid designs.

The image of a glass dome can sometimes be found to the left of the bear, but the value of the lid remains roughly the same whether it is there or not.

An 'extra small' Staffordshire 'The Bear Pit' domed pot lid, no.6, without image of glass dome on left of image.

1.5in (4cm) diam

$800-1,200   H&C

A Staffordshire 'Bears Reading Papers' pot lid and base, no.7, possibly by J Ridgway & Co.

Surprisingly, the less colorful variation of this design is more valuable, primarily as it is considerably harder to find. It can fetch around 25% more than this colorful version.

2.75in (7cm) diam

$1,200-1,800   DN

A Staffordshire 'Performing Bear' pot lid and base, no.12, possibly by J Ridgway & Co.

The quality of the decoration is of great importance. Lids lacking the detail on this example, and with bluish colors, are usually worth around half the value of this example.

2.75in (7cm) diam

$1,500-2,500   DN

A Staffordshire 'Bear in a Ravine' pot lid, no.14, probably produced by J Ridgway for Whitaker & Co., with a small restored chip.

This very early, very rare lid is known in this 'small' size and a 'very small' size, which is around 2.25in (6cm) diam. They are both usually worth around the same. This example would have fetched more had it not been damaged and restored. The delicacy of the colors and details are much admired by collectors.

2.75in (7cm) diam

$3,000-5,000   H&C

A Staffordshire 'ALL BUT TRAPPED' pot lid, no.20, by T J & J Mayer.

The presence or lack of a fancy border does not usually affect the value of this rare lid. The angry and cornered crowned bear represents Russia during the Crimean War. This is a rare lid and political themes, such as this, are also very desirable.

2.75in (7cm) diam

$2,500-3,500   H&C

A Staffordshire 'A Very Great Bear' pot lid, no.23, probably by J Ridgway & Co., with damage and restoration.

This lid was known as 'The Gay Dog' and numbered 268 until the image was identified as having been taken from Alfred Elwes' book 'The Adventures of a Bear', published in 1853. So the dandy beast wearing his master's clothing is a bear, not a dog.

2.75in (7cm) diam

$1,200-1,800   H&C

A medium-sized Staffordshire 'ENGLAND'S PRIDE' pot lid, no.149, with a green ground.

A later version with a black border and Queen Victoria in purple robes is usually worth around a third the value of this version.

4in (10cm) diam

$500-700   H&C

A large Staffordshire 'Queen Victoria on Balcony' pot lid, no.165, with gold-lined rim, framed.

This design was copied from a Baxter print. The 5.5in (14cm) diam 'very large' version is usually worth over double the value of this 'large' size.

4.75in (12cm) diam

$250-350   H&C

A large Staffordshire 'ALMA' pot lid, no.203, with fancy border and portraits of (clockwise from top) Omar Pasha, the Duke of Cambridge, Lord Raglan and Marshal Saint-Arnaud.

The most valuable version has a fancy border highlighted in gold - it's usually worth around double the value of the version with a simple line border and about 20% more than this version.

4.75in (12cm) diam

$650-850   H&C

A Staffordshire 'Peabody' pot lid, no.160, probably by F & R Pratt.

Philantropist George Peabody (1795-1869) was born in Massachussetts, USA, and moved permanently to London in 1837. He is best remembered today for the Peabody Estate Housing and the Peabody Trust. It is estimated that during his lifetime he provided benefactions worth over $8 million - the equivalent of Bill Gates's or Warren Buffett's billions today.

$450-550   H&C

A CLOSER LOOK AT A POT LID

This early example has bold, vibrant colors - compare it to the less valuable example in 'Miller's Collectibles Handbook 2010-2011', p.316.

Examples with poorer, less vibrant colors are later in date and are usually worth under a third of the value of this example.

This lid is named after three key battles in the Crimean war (1853-56). Military subjects are very popular with pot lid collectors, who are also often men.

The portraits are of (clockwise from top) the Earl of Cardigan, the Duke of Cambridge, Lord Raglan and General Simpson, who were the four British commanders during the Crimean war.

A Staffordshire 'BALAKLAVA, INKERMAN, ALMA' pot lid, no.204, by T J & J Mayer.

4.75in (12cm) diam

$650-850   H&C

A Staffordshire 'Harriet Beecher Stowe' pot lid, no.159, by T J & J Mayer, framed.

Harriet Beecher Stowe (1811-96) was an American author best known for her anti-slavery novel and play 'Uncle Tom's Cabin', published in 1852. It caused a sensation at the time and this lid was probably made to commemorate her visit to England in 1853.

5.5in (14cm) diam

$800-1,200   H&C

POT LIDS

A Staffordshire 'Shakespeare's Birthplace, Exterior' pot lid, no.226, with leaf and scroll border.

The version with the line and dot border is generally worth around a third of this version, which has a more complex border.

4in (10cm) diam

$120-180   H&C

A Staffordshire 'Anne Hathaway's Cottage' pot lid, no.228, with leaf and scroll border.

Look out for the most desirable and valuable version, which has gold lines and a pearl dot border, as this can fetch four times more than this version.

4in (10cm) diam

$150-250   H&C

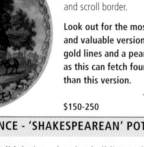

A Staffordshire 'Shakespeare's Birthplace, Interior' pot lid, no.227, with leaf and scroll border.

Note the bust of Shakespeare on the chest on the left.

4in (10cm) diam

$150-250   H&C

QUICK REFERENCE - 'SHAKESPEAREAN' POT LIDS

●**There are six pot lid designs showing buildings related to Shakespeare. This connection makes them very popular with collectors, both of pot lids, and of Shakespeare memorabilia. It is likely that they were all produced around 1864, the tri-centenary of Shakespeare's birth. Most were made by F & R Pratt. Later, in the 20thC, Cauldon reproduced the designs on ceramics. This design, showing Holy Trinity, is the rarest of the Shakespeare scenic lids, particularly if it has a super-rare leaf and scroll border shown here.**

A Staffordshire 'The Great Exhibition of 1851, Opening Ceremony' pot lid, no.147, by T J & J Mayer.

5.5in (14cm) diam

$400-600   H&C

A very rare Staffordshire 'CHURCH OF THE HOLY TRINITY' pot lid, no. 229, by F & R Pratt, with leaf and scroll border, with restoration.

5in (13cm) diam

$1,000-1,500   SAS

A Staffordshire 'Pegwell Bay, S. Banger, Shrimp Sauce Manufacturer' pot lid, no.40, with rim chips, framed.

This lid would have been worth nearly twice as much had it not been damaged. It is a rare lid, particularly in 2.75in (7cm) 'small' and 4in (10cm) 'medium sizes.

4.75in (12cm) diam

$300-500   H&C

A CLOSER LOOK AT A POT LID

Only a handful of examples of the first issue of this lid have been found, making it extremely rare.

This first issue can be identified by the wall of the well and the bucket, which were replaced by a rock and basket for the more common, later second issue of this lid. The second issue is generally worth under $120.

This example has an unusual fancy border with a gold band. Others have a plain white and gold band, but the border type does not affect the value as the image is so rare that it is always desirable.

The flange has been removed, and it has been restored. Had the lid been in undamaged, original condition, it could have fetched more than $3,000.

A Staffordshire 'Second Appeal' pot lid, no.135, first issue, with wide gold banded border, with flange removed and restoration.

4.75in (12cm) diam

$1,000-1,500   H&C

A Staffordshire 'The Mirror' pot lid, no.101, by F & R Pratt.

2.75in (7cm) diam

$200-300   H&C

A Staffordshire 'Old Jack' pot lid, no.218, probably by Bates, Brown-Westhead, Moore & Co., with fancy border.

2.75in (7cm) diam

$250-350   H&C

A late 19thC Staffordshire 'The Quarry' pot lid, no.313, by F & R Pratt.

The design was taken from a painting called 'The Landscape' by Dutch painter Philips Wouwerman (c1619-68).

4.75in (12cm) diam

$150-250   H&C

A Staffordshire 'Cattle and Ruins' pot lid, no.275, by F & R Pratt, with black mottled flange, and gold lined border.

4.75in (12cm) diam

$150-250   H&C

A Staffordshire 'The Ornamental Garden' pot lid, no.115, with gold-lined border.

This lid is from the noted Cashmore pot lid collection.

2.75in (7cm) diam

$800-1,200   H&C

A small-medium Staffordshire 'The Garden Terrace' pot lid, no.113, with molded floral border and beehive, with gold-lined rim.

The smaller 2.75in (7cm) diam 'small' size has no molded border and is considerably rarer. In undamaged, original condition, a small example could fetch more than twice the value of this example.

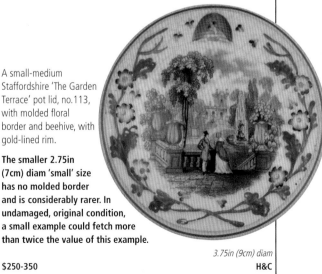

3.75in (9cm) diam

$250-350   H&C

QUICK REFERENCE - RAILWAYANA

- Harking back to the 'golden age' of steam and the excitement of rail travel from the 1910s-50s, railwayana has many fans. Many buyers choose to collect one type of object, such as locomotive signs, but most collect different items connected to one railway.
- The prime collecting period is from c1924, when the many railways in the UK were merged into four groups under the 1921 Railways Act, until 1948, when the railways were nationalized and merged into British Rail. The four groups were the Great Western Railway (GWR), the London, Midland & Scottish (LMS), the Southern Railway (SR) and the London & North-Eastern Railway (LNER).

- Memorabilia from some railways is more sought after than others. For example, the Great Western Railway tends to be the most popular railway. Memorabilia from smaller, short-lived railways, which can be rare, can also fetch high prices.
- Some objects are more desirable than others. Signs and posters tend to be the most valuable items, with tickets, carriage prints and timetables being more affordable.
- Pieces from the 1950s-60s are popular, but are currently not as valuable as much pre-war memorabilia. As such, they may be a good bet for the future as much of the market is driven by nostalgia.

'BARRY ISLAND', a British Railways Western Region totem sign, in very good condition.

Although already a popular holiday destination, the resort of Barry Island was given a major boost as a result of being used as the setting of the hugely popular British TV series 'Gavin & Stacey' 2007-10.

36in (91cm) wide

$2,000-3,000   **GWRA**

'BAT AND BALL', a British Railways Southern Region totem sign, in very good condition, with well-executed crease repairs.

In 1950 'Sevenoaks Bat and Ball' station was renamed 'Bat and Ball'.

36in (91cm) wide

$800-1,200   **GWRA**

'CARPENDERS PARK', a British Railways Midlands Region totem sign, in excellent condition, converted to a wall-fixed type.

36in (91cm) wide

$300-500   **GWRA**

'DINGWALL', a British Railways Scottish Region totem sign, with three crease repairs.

36in (91cm) wide

$250-350   **GWRA**

'HAWICK', a British Railways Scottish Region totem sign, in near-mint condition.

36in (91cm) wide

$3,000-5,000   **GWRA**

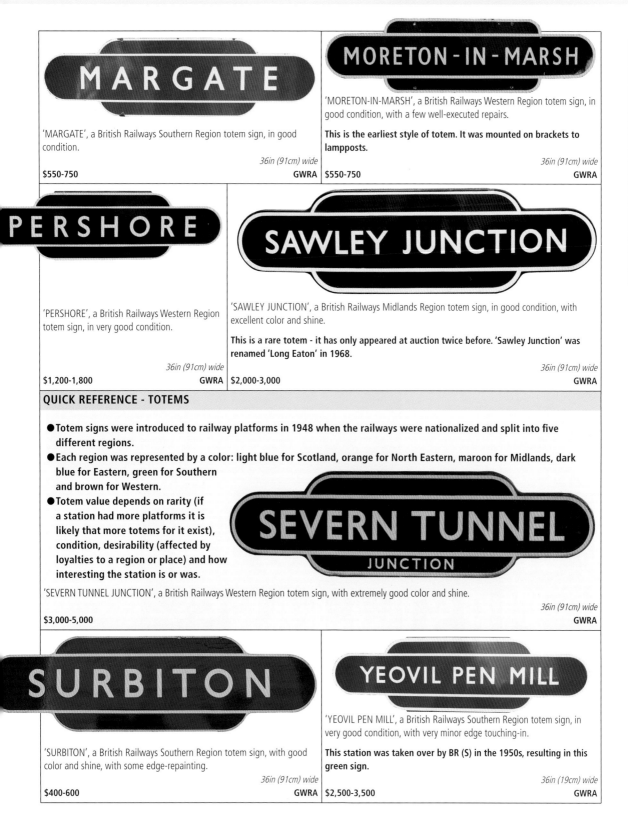

'BEWARE OF TRAINS.', a Midland Railway sign, with scalloped corners, without restoration.

$150-250   GWRA

'TO THE STATION', a late 19thC enameled-metal sign, in very good condition.

29in (74cm) wide

$400-600   GWRA

'BOOKING OFFICE', a rare Taff Vale Railway door sign, with original brown and cream paintwork.

19in (48cm) wide

$300-500   GWRA

'GENTLEMEN', a British Railways Midlands Region enameled-metal door sign, in excellent condition, with good color and shine.

'Gentlemen' door signs are extremely rare for some reason...

18in (46cm) wide

$300-500   GWRA

'STATION MASTER', a British Railways Southern Region enameled-metal door sign, in excellent condition, with good color and shine.

18in (46cm) wide

$300-500   GWRA

'LADIES' ROOM FIRST CLASS', a Midland Railway enameled-metal door sign, with some damage around the bolt holes.

$400-600   GWRA

'DRINKING WATER', a very rare British Railways Western Region enameled-metal sign, in excellent condition.

9in (23cm) wide

$400-600   GWRA

'TO CAR PARK', a cast-alloy double-sided street sign, with attached brackets.

21in (53cm) wide

$100-150   GWRA

A Caledonian Railways mahogany-cased wall clock, the deadbeat movement with Harrison's maintaining power movement, in full working order, used at the Coupar Angus station.

62in (157cm) high

$1,500-2,500 GWRA

A South Eastern Railway oak-cased fusee drop-dial clock, supplied by Gillett & Baxter of London, the front plate, pendulum and bob scratched '722', the dial painted with 'S.R JOHN WALKER 1, SOUTH MOLTON ST LONDON 722.S.E', the oak case stamped '722' and '722SE', used at Canterbury and Lancing stations.

c1890

$3,000-5,000 GWRA

A British Railways Southern Region mahogany-cased fusee clock, supplied by Grimshaw, Baxter & J J Elliott Ltd., the dial painted 'BR(S) 11158', in working condition, used at Ashford Kent Medical Office.

1951 *8in (20.5cm) diam*

$800-1,200 GWRA

One of a pair of Great Western Railway painted cast-iron platform-seat ends, in the 'Script' pattern, reputedly from Neath Station in South Wales.

$800-1,200 pair GWRA

One of a pair of Great Western Railway painted cast-iron 'Roundel'-style platform-seat ends, without restoration, with original paint layers and with some original bolts.

$800-1,200 pair GWRA

A South Eastern Railways station wall-lamp, with 'LYDD' lamp tablet, interior reservoir, globe and reflector, in original condition with original paint.

This lamp was mounted under a bridge, which is why it's in such good condition today. The station closed to passengers in 1967 and to freight in 1971.

$1,200-1,800 GWRA

A Great Western Railways cast-iron umbrella stand, with original top and frame, the bottom face embossed with company initials, missing drip tray.

$400-600 GWRA

A London Brighton & South Coast Railway hand bell, stamped 'LB&SCR', with wooden handle, with later mahogany display stand.

Station bells are rare and desirable. Each station would have only had one and they bring back nostalgic memories.

12in (30.5cm) high

$1,200-1,800 GWRA

A Tyer's oak-cased signal-box block instrument, the double dial with one wire.

This type was used by a number of smaller companies, notably the Barry, North Staffordshire and Furness railways. It is most likely that this is from the Furness Railway.
$500-700   GWRA

A rare Midland Railway brass and steel Annett's key, engraved 'SANDIACRE POINT KEY', from a Nottinghamshire location near the Toton Depot.

Patented by J E Annett in 1875, the Annett's key locks certain parts of signaling equipment. Without it, the signals cannot be operated.
$250-350   GWRA

A single-line bronze Tyer's no.9 key token, stamped 'MILLBURN ROSE STREET 2'.

This key was created as part of a 1986 scheme to revise signaling in Inverness. It was never used as logistical delays meant the project was overtaken by the installation of Radio Electronic Token Block.
$70-100   GWRA

A Glasgow & South Western Railway Stranraer-line aluminum single-line Tyer's no.6 tablet, stamped 'GIRVAN - PINWHERRY 2', in good condition.
$700-1,000   GWRA

'BROMSGROVE', a London, Midland & Scottish wooden box board, with cast letters, from the up platform signal box from Lickey Incline, with some original maroon paint.

58in (147cm) wide
$1,000-1,500   GWRA

Mark Picks

While I appreciate the importance of our railways, I've never been tempted to collect railwayana myself - until I saw a selection of these finials displayed in a collector's home while I was filming 'Collectaholics' with Mel Giedroyc for BBC2. Originally made to stand on top of signal posts, these finials look great when grouped together, due to variety of forms, colors and sizes. Now, I'm seriously considering investing!

Signals are obviously crucially important for safety, but during the 19thC and early 20thC, railway companies decided they should be embellished with these cast-iron ornaments. The spikes also protected the top of the signal post from rot as a result of rain and from birds, who might choose to perch or nest there, leaving 'deposits' behind. Most railway companies had their own designs and color combinations, meaning there's a good variety to collect today.

A rare Somerset & Dorset Joint Railway signal finial, painted white and yellow.
28in (71cm) high
$200-300   GWRA

A London & South Western Railway painted cast-iron signal finial, the base and one upright with company initials, one upright with 'BPRS Ltd.' maker's name, in excellent condition, reputedly from Barnstaple Junction.
$150-250   GWRA

A London Chatham & Dover Railway painted cast-iron signal finial, one fin with company initials 'LCD' and '349', with restoration.
$250-350   GWRA

A pair of signal-box level-crossing wicket-gate control levers, with brass 'Up Wicket' and 'Down Wicket' lever plates, from Oldbury & Langley Green West signal box, situated between Rowsley and Smethwick in the Midlands.
$1,200-1,800   GWRA

QUICK REFERENCE - LOCOMOTIVE NAMEPLATES

- Locomotive nameplates are among the most desirable and valuable pieces of railwayana, mainly as there are rarely more than two of them per locomotive.
- They tend to fetch more than cabplates as they are large, visually impressive and clearly display the name of the locomotive.
- Those from famous locomotives can fetch tens of thousands of dollars.

'FARNLEY HALL', a Great Western Railway locomotive left-hand nameplate, stamped 'L 6943'.

This 4-6-0 locomotive was built in Swindon in 1942 and allocated to Worcester. It was then moved to Hereford, then to Cardiff Canton and finally Gloucester Horton Road. It was then withdrawn from service in 1963 and scrapped in March 1964.

$10,000-15,000   GWRA

'9020', a Great Western Railways brass cabside numberplate, from a Dukedog Class locomotive in operation in Oswestry and then Machynlleth 1938-57, marked 'Machynlleth'.

$3,000-4,000   GWRA

'9657', a Great Western Railways cast-iron cabside numberplate, from a 0-6-PT locomotive operational in Shresbury 1946-66, broken in several places, with some losses and poor repairs.

$200-300   GWRA

'SHARP STEWART & CO. LIMITED ATLAS WORKS 4822 - 1902 GLASGOW', a North Western Railway worksplate, from a B class 0-4-2T locomotive, used on the narrow gauge Kalka Simla Railway as No 11.

1902

$1,200-1,800   GWRA

'B. R. (W) 5-308 5000 GALLONS SWINDON', a British Railways Western Region painted cast-iron locomotive tender plate, from an ex-Ministry of Supply 2-8-0 locomotive built in Glasgow, with restoration.

$650-850   GWRA

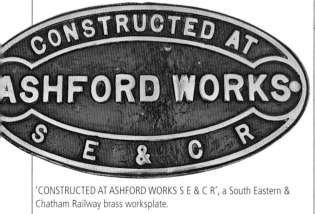

'CONSTRUCTED AT ASHFORD WORKS S E & C R', a South Eastern & Chatham Railway brass worksplate.

This type of plate was fitted to most SE&CR locomotives built at Ashford.

$2,000-3,000   GWRA

'SOUTH AFRICAN RAILWAYS' '2037 14CRM', a South African Railways single-language painted-brass cabside numberplate, from a 14 4-6-6 locomotive built by the Montreal Locomotive Company, works number 63076.

1922   20in (50cm) wide

$1,200-1,800   GWRA

'LMS BUILT 1940 DERBY', a London Midlands & Scottish Railway worksplate, from a 0-6-0 Diesel Shunter numbered LMS '7100', which went to the War Department Egypt.

1909

$200-300   GWRA

RAILWAYANA

'16J', a painted cast-iron shedplate, used at Rowsley until March 1967.

$250-350   GWRA

'51F', a painted cast-iron shedplate, used at West Auckland until February 1965, with restoration to face.

$200-300   GWRA

'56D', a painted cast-iron shedplate, used at Mirfield until April 1967, with restoration to face.

This shedplate is not particularly rare and generally sells for the value shown below, but in 2013 an example sold for $1,200!

$80-120   GWRA

'61B', a painted cast-iron shedplate, used at Aberdeen until May 1973.

$300-500   GWRA

'64B', a painted cast-iron shedplate, used at Haymarket until May 1973.

$200-300   GWRA

'66A', a painted cast-iron shedplate, used at Polmadie until May 1967 for steam, with restoration to face.

Polmadie was the major depot for main line workings from Glasgow. It boasted Coronation Pacifics, Princess Royal Pacifics, Royal Scots, Jubilees, Clans and Britannias to name but a few.

$150-250   GWRA

QUICK REFERENCE - SHEDPLATES

- Shedplates indicated a locomotive's home depot or garage. They were fitted to the front of locomotives below the smoke box.
- The number indicates a railway area, which is not always a geographic area.
- The letter indicates the size of the locomotive shed. 'A' is the main shed for the area, with letters lower down the alphabet indicating smaller regional sheds.
- The value depends on demand, which is based on the popularity of the shed and the area it is in, as well as the rarity of the shed. Condition is also important.
- Smaller sheds held fewer locomotives, so plates for them are rarer.

'67A', a painted cast-iron shedplate, used at Corkerhill until May 1967, with restoration to face.

Corkerhill was once a large Glasgow & South Western depot, which had a substantial allocation of locomotives in the days of steam.

$150-250   GWRA

'86E', a painted cast-iron shedplate, used at Severn Tunnel Junction.

This plate was obtained by a driver from the Severn Tunnel shed.

$550-750   GWRA

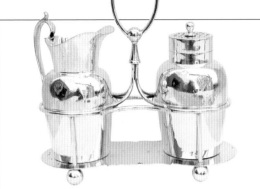

A Station Hotel Wick electroplated cruet set, comprising a cream jug and sugar shaker on a stand, each marked 'Station Hotel Wick' within a garter and 'RR Sheffield'.

8in (20.5cm) high

$300-500 GWRA

A pair of Great Northern Railway silver-plated cake tongs, manufactured by Walk & Hall, stamped 'G.N.R.R.'.

The letters in the stamp stand for Great Northern Reception Rooms. These tongs are believed to have come from Melton Constable Station.

7in (18cm) long

$60-80 GWRA

A pair of Great Western Railway silver-plated sugar tongs, stamped with full railway crest.

Small, easily pocketable items from the tea and dining table, such as teacups and cutlery, are commonly found today. Sugar tongs are slightly rarer and more valuable than other cutlery items, as there were fewer of them in a carriage.

$150-250 GWRA

A Pullman brass table lamp, stamped 'Hercules'.

This very rare lamp is valuable as it is an unusual design and is from the 'Hercules' Pullman parlor car. The 'Hercules' car was ordered as part of a set in 1938, but not delivered until 1951 due to the war. It formed part of the Pullman 'Golden Arrow' service exhibited at Victoria Station as part of the Festival of Britain.

$2,000-3,000 GWRA

A pair of London Chatham & Dover Railway silver-plated sugar tongs, manufactured by Mappin & Webb, stamped 'LCDR Mappin & Webb' and with the railway crest, in excellent condition.

$120-180 GWRA

A Great Eastern Railway Hotels copper 'Tolly Ale, Tolly Stout' advertising ashtray, with integral matchbox holder.

4in (10cm) high

$250-350 GWRA

A Great Central Railway tea plate, manufactured by Copeland, from a Directors' Saloon.

$250-350 GWRA

A Great Central Railway tinplate advertising vesta case, with fold-out wind-proof hood, printed with advertisements for 'RAPID TRAVEL IN LUXURY GREAT CENTRAL RAILWAY' and 'BARCLAY'S' ale, with an empty box of 'BRYANT & MAY' brand matches.

$250-350 GWRA

RAILWAYANA

A London & South Western Railway guard's pocket watch, manufactured by Waltham, USA, the reverse engraved 'L&S.W.R. 25', the movement numbered '2273520', in excellent, working condition.

Waltham were well known for their highly reliable railway watches.
$200-300   GWRA

A Great Western Railway pocket watch, manufactured by Rotherham & Sons, the reverse engraved 'GWR 1698', the front printed 'GWR', in working order, the back with dent.

This watch was made and used before the Grouping Act of 1923 that amalgamated the 120 railways around the country into four large groups known as the 'Big Four'. Alone amongst 120 railways, GWR retained its name. Collectors often refer to pieces from before 1923 with the words 'pre-grouping'.
$350-450   GWRA

A British Railways Western Region enamel and gilt-metal 'INSPECTOR' cap badge.
$60-80   GWRA

A CLOSER LOOK AT A TRUNCHEON

The South Devon Railway ran between Exeter and Plymouth and was broad gauge throughout.

These truncheons were owned and used by railway police in the 19thC. They are sought after today, if in good condition with their original painted details.

This rare truncheon dates from before 1876 when the South Devon Railway amalgamated with the Great Western Railway.

Some have a broad red band, as railway police sometimes also acted as signalmen.

The world record price for a railway police truncheon is $5,000 for a fine example from the Canterbury & Whitstable Railway.

A mid-late 19thC South Devon Railway police truncheon, with painted details, in good condition.
$1,200-1,800   GWRA

A rare Midland Railway button whistle, the sides with two Midland Railway nickel buttons, in excellent condition.
$200-300   GWRA

A Great Western Railway leather cash bag, with brass plate stamped 'GWR MALVERN ROAD', in very good condition.

This bag is from Cheltenham Spa Malvern Road station, which closed in January 1966.
$450-650   GWRA

A Great Western Railway long-spout locoman's oiler and a British Railways Western Region locoman's oiler, stamped respectively 'GWR' and 'BR(W)'.
24in (61cm) long
$150-250   GWRA

A Great North of Scotland Railway silver pass, one side with the railway name around a coat-of-arms, the other numbered '619' and with owner's name.

This railway pass is more valuable and desirable than typical examples as it is marked for two railways: the Great North of Scotland Railway and the Caledonian Railway (Cal Rly).

1in (2.5cm) diam

$1,500-2,500　　　　　　　　　**GWRA**

A brass locomotive whistle, from a locomotive numbered 9637 and later 78637, in use 1944-63, the boss stamped 'WD 1944 AUS 8F 90634'.

1944　　　*16in (40.5cm) high*

$350-450　　　　　　　　　**GWRA**

A London & North Western Railway wooden first-aid box and a London, Midland & Southern tin first-aid box.

$15-25 each　　　　　**GWRA**

A 1930s London, Midland & Scottish Railways bottle of 'Royal Scot Whisky', the original label with rampant lions and 'LMS' beneath within a scroll, unopened, with original cork.

$400-600　　　　**GWRA**

A London & North Eastern Railways leather horse bridle, with four horsebrasses, in excellent condition.

$150-250　　　　　　　　　**GWRA**

A 1920s Augier Frères & Co. bottle of cognac, for the Great Western Railway, unopened and with original sealed cork and label.

Bottles bearing the name 'Augier' are extremely rare and valuable today. Augier cognacs were all distilled in traditional Charentais Stills and aged naturally, making them of top quality.

$1,200-1,800　　　　**GWRA**

A transfer-printed commemorative pottery jug, depicting the entrance to the Liverpool & Manchester Railway, with minor chips to the spout.

5in (13cm) high

$150-250　　　　　　　　　**GWRA**

A late 19thC American cast-iron sad-iron, in the form of a locomotive, with brass finish, marked 'EB Cosby, Pat. Oct. 23, 88' and 'Dec. 17, 89'.

Early American railroadiana is highly sought after. This iron is both rare and desirable.

8.75in (22.5cm) high

$6,500-7,500　　　　**DRA**

ROCK & POP

QUICK REFERENCE - ROCK & POP

- The enduring popularity of major rock and pop artists across many generations means that there is a healthy market for related memorabilia. Items connected to globally famous artists, such as the Beatles, Elvis Presley, the Rolling Stones and Queen, tends to garner the most interest, but pieces produced for cult bands can also command good prices.
- The highest prices are reserved for those pieces directly connected with an artist, such as clothes or instruments. If the item was used at a famous or notable performance, so much the better. The provenance (or proof that links the piece with the artist and performance) is critical to value. It must be cast iron and unquestionable.
- Away from the hundreds of thousands or even millions of dollars paid for the best pieces, there is plenty to interest all collectors regardless of the size of the budget. Artists

had their names and faces applied to a truly dizzying range of memorabilia and some pieces can start from as little as a few dollars. Much of this level of memorabilia was poor quality and was not made to last, so look out for rarities. Always aim to buy in the best, unopened condition possible.

- A collection can be built up almost immediately by starting with ticket stubs, tour programs, posters, t-shirts and other memorabilia. Aim to buy pieces that represent the artist or their music.
- Although some artists may prove to be eternally popular, the market is also driven by nostalgia and the current popularity of the artist. Although they are not yet in the collecting mainstream, buying memorabilia related to some boy bands may prove to be a wise investment when today's teenagers grow into tomorrow's collectors.

A bronzed cast-resin figure of John Lennon, after the bronze statue designed by Tom Murphy that stands in the check-in hall of Liverpool's John Lennon Airport.

19.5in (50cm) high

$300-500   SAS

A set of four bronzed cast-resin busts of The Beatles, designed by Tom Murphy in 2003.

$200-300   SAS

QUICK REFERENCE - FAN-MADE MERCHANDIZE

- The low price of this cabinet shows the difference between official merchandize and pieces created by fans - had this cabinet been produced officially it would have been worth over ten times this amount.
- The clues here that this a fan-made piece are in the design of the paper (which is a well-known 1960s wallpaper) and the fact that the facsimile signatures are cut off by the side of the cabinet! No official merchandizer would have allowed the design to do this.

A 1960s Newfeld Ltd. rubber 'Paul McCartney' 'Bendy' doll, in very good condition.

It's hard to find these dolls in good condition, as the paint has usually flaked or been rubbed away and the foamy material often degrades, becoming powdery.

$300-500   SAS

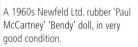

An early 1960s glass-topped coffee table, the top with individual printed images of the four Beatles with the wording 'The BEATLES', with screw-in legs.

24in (61cm) long

$400-600   SAS

A late 1950s-60s customized record cabinet, the drop-down front with applied printed wallpaper showing The Beatles, the interior with fitted record rack.

$80-120   SAS

A late 1990s Apple Corps. limited edition 'Pick Up' portable radio and compact disc player, modeled on a 1960s Dansette-type record player, in full working order, with instruction booklet.
c1998
$250-350   SAS

A rare set of three Beatles promotional stickers, produced for the concert at Rizal Memorial Stadium, the Philippines, on July 4th 1966, in excellent condition.

The concert venue was changed from the Araneta Coliseum to this stadium due to its larger capacity.
$500-700   SAS

Six Zippo and Apple Corps. Beatles commemorative brushed-steel lighters, comprising 'Beatles Playing', 'Beatles Band', 'Beatles Help', 'Beatles Revolver', 'Beatles Song' and 'The Beatles', all in excellent condition, all with tins, instructions and card slip-cover.
c2007
$120-180   SAS

Twelve packets of commemorative 'BEATLES INSECT REPELLENT MOTHBALLS', mounted on their original shop display card, manufactured by Charles Vincent Commercial, Manila, Philippines, in mint condition.
c1966
$150-250   SAS

A 1960s Show Souvenir program and an unused 1960s Beatles transfer-sheet.
$50-70   SAS

'HELP!', an American one-sheet film poster, in very good condition.
1965
$250-350   SAS

'Let It Be', a UK boxset, by The Beatles, published by Apple, PSX 1, in very good condition.
1970
$400-600   SAS

A handwritten letter, from and signed by George Harrison to Carol Bedford, offering advice on how to contact the rock journalist Al Aronowitz, written on the back of a blank recording sheet and signed 'Have B o L George'.

A personal friend of Harrison's, Carol Bedford was an Apple Scruffs member and author of the book 'Waiting For The Beatles' (An Apple Scruffs Story) in which this letter is illustrated. This letter is worth what it is because of the personal connection and the importance of the book. The subject matter is also relevant to The Beatles and interesting.
$3,500-4,500   SAS

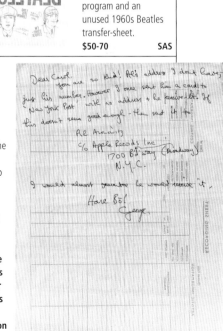

'ABBA THE MOVIE', a UK quad film poster, folded, with distributors label to top right corner and small ink censor stamp, in very good condition.
1977   *30in (76cm) wide*
$120-180   **SAS**

'Can't Help Thinking About Me'/'And I Say to Myself', a UK single, by David Bowie, published by Pye Records, 7N 17020, with original paper slip case, in very good condition.
1966
$400-600   **SAS**

'CLIFF GIGANTIC Color PORTRAIT PRESENTED WITH BOYFRIEND', a late 1950s magazine poster, from 'Boyfriend' magazine.
$50-70   **SAS**

A signed photograph, signed by Elvis Presley and dedicated to 'Mandy' (?), with a later 'ELVIS' annotation in red ballpoint pen to top.
7in (17.5cm) high
$2,000-3,000   **WHYT**

A CLOSER LOOK AT A WATCH

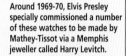

Around 1969-70, Elvis Presley specially commissioned a number of these watches to be made by Mathey-Tissot via a Memphis jeweller called Harry Levitch.

Like his 'Taking Care of Business' 'TCB' lightening bolt, these watches were given as gifts by Presley to members of his family, close friends and key staff.

The bezel has the words 'ELVIS PRESLEY' in raised letters above four stars and identified the wearer as close to Elvis, granting them special access at events.

Up to a few dozen were commissioned, but nobody knows the exact number. They rarely come on to the market as most people kept their very special gift.

A Mathey-Tissot gilt-metal watch, the bezel marked 'ELVIS PRESLEY' in raised letters above four stars, with date aperture, with its original box, Mathey-Tissot Certificate of Guarantee (no.17465) and certificate of authenticity from the Elvis Presley Museum.

For another watch owned and worn by Elvis, see p.303 of Miller's 'Antiques Handbook & Price Guide 2014-2015'.
c1969
$12,000-18,000   **WHYT**

A 1970s Elvis scarf, with a facsimile 'Elvis Presley' signature, with a letter of provenance from Nancy Rook, Elvis's maid at Graceland.

These would be thrown into the audience by Elvis at concerts during the 1970s.
33.5in (83.5cm) wide
$1,000-1,500   **WHYT**

'Elvis Presley as he appears in the M-G-M film "It Happened at the World's Fair"', a magazine poster, from 'Reveille Magazine', in very good condition, with folds, with some tape reside to corners.
1963   *60in (152.5cm) high*
$300-500   **SAS**

'Born This Way', a picture disc, signed by Lady Gaga, mounted with a photograph and framed.

2011   *27in (68.5cm) wide*

$300-500   **SAS**

'How Sweet It Is To Be Loved By You', a signed UK album, by Marvin Gaye, published by Tamla Motown, TML 11004, signed to front of sleeve 'Peace, Marvin Gaye'.

Provenance: From the collection of Roger St Pierre, DJ, presenter and author.

1965

$700-1,000   **SAS**

'Axis Bold As Love', a UK mono album, by The Jimi Hendrix Experience, published by Track, 612 003, with gatefold laminated sleeve, all in very good condition.

Produced to fulfil a contract that required two albums in 1967, this album has a gatefold sleeve that varies depending on the country. This desirable British version has a Donald Silverstein black-and-white photograph inside and the lyrics printed on an insert. The USA issue has only the lyrics on the inside, while the Polydor European version has a white border around the photograph and the French version simply a sleeve bearing a photograph of the group.

1967

$150-250   **SAS**

'THE Jimi Hendrix EXHIBITION', a New Zealand one-sheet poster for an exhibition in Auckland from October 30th to November 28th 1992, in excellent condition.

1992   *28in (71cm) high*

$30-50   **SAS**

'Moonwalker The Storybook', by Michael Jackson, published by William Heinemann, signed on the title page by Jackson.

1988

$1,000-1,500   **WHYT**

'MICHAEL JACKSON CORK', a rare poster advertising Jackson's concert at Páirc Uí Chaoimh, Cork in 1988.

60in (150cm) high

$3,000-4,000   **WHYT**

'Kinks', a UK mono album, by The Kinks, published by Pye, first press, NPL 18096, all in very good condition.

1984

$150-250   **SAS**

A set of four 1960s Monkees toy figures, each complete with original accessory, in excellent condition.

5in (12.5cm) high

$200-300   **SAS**

ROCK & POP

'I Want It All', a signed 7in (17.5cm) single sleeve, by Queen, signed to front by all four band members, in very good condition, in card mount, with certificate of authenticity.

$400-600   SAS

A Rolling Stones program, for the 1966 UK tour, supporting artists including Ike & Tina Turner, and The Yardbirds, in excellent condition.

1966

$300-500   SAS

'Let's Spend The Night Together', a UK quad film poster, in very good condition, with folds.

This was a live concert film, documenting The Rolling Stones's 1981 North American Tour.

30in (76cm) wide

$50-70   SAS

A very early T-Rex flyer, for their short 13-date tour of May 1971, in very good condition, with folds, with neat annotation about ticket availability to reverse.

$200-300   SAS

'Ritchie Valens', a UK album, by Ritchie Valens, published by London Records, first press, 1232, in very good condition.

This album was released one month after Valens's death in a plane crash, which also claimed the lives of fellow musicians Buddy Holly and J P 'The Big Bopper' Richardson. The day of the accident has become known as the 'Day the Music Died'.

1959

$120-180   SAS

Judith Picks

I must declare an 'interest': I'm a major Bruce fan and have seen him play over 40 times on both sides of the Atlantic in the last five years alone. That's because The Boss is THE Boss, and Bruce and the E Street Band is the greatest show on earth!. Of course, I'm not alone: a huge multi-generation fan base means Springsteen memorabilia is much in demand.

All Springsteen gigs are great, but some are positively historic, and good photographs from these command a premium. In addition to Slane Castle in '85, other particularly notable examples include: Hammersmith '75; Cleveland '78; Los Angeles '81; Leipzig '88; Madison Square Garden '00, and Helsinki '12, to name but a few!

One of four performance photographs of Bruce Springsteen, by Trevor Looney, taken at Slane Castle on 1 June 1985, one signed and titled on the mount by Looney and framed.

$400-600 set   **WHYT**

'My Generation', a UK mono album, by The Who, published by Brunswick, LAT 8616, with sleeve in excellent condition, the vinyl in very good condition.

1965

$200-300   SAS

A Bath Festival of Blues card ticket, for the festival on 28th June 1969.

This was the first Bath Festival. Acts included Led Zeppelin, Fleetwood Mac, The Nice, Taste, Chicken Shack, John Mayall. Tickets were torn in half on entry.

4in (10cm) wide

$100-150   SAS

An Edwardian silver novelty pin cushion, in the form of a chick, by H C Freeman, Chester.

1909   *1.5in (3.5cm) high*

$150-250   **LC**

A silver novelty pin cushion, in the form of a pig, Birmingham.

1918   *1.5in (3.5cm) high*

$250-350   **CHT**

A George III silver pin cushion, in the form of a wicker basket of flowers, by Samuel Pemberton, Birmingham.

c1800   *1.5in (3cm) high*

$350-450   **LC**

An Edwardian silver novelty pin cushion, in the form of a ballroom shoe, by Adie & Lovekin, Birmingham, the sole with a compartment for pins.

1903   *2.5in (6.5cm) long*

$300-500   **LC**

A 19thC French silver-mounted sewing set, in the form of a mussel, containing scissors, a needle case, a bodkin, a scent bottle, a thimble and another item, with crack to mussel shell.

3.5in (9cm) long

$400-600   **DN**

A late 19thC French gold sewing set, containing a thimble, needle case, (damaged) pair of scissors and another item, with a fitted ivory case with a monogram, missing bodkin.

The quality of this set is clear from the fine materials and quality of the carved case. Even though it may be hard to find a bodkin to match perfectly, it should be possible to find a relatively good replacement. Other missing items might be more difficult to replace.

4.25in (11cm) long

$800-1,200   **DN**

A silver novelty sewing nécessaire, in the form of a suitcase with straps, by Sampson Mordan & Co., London, the gilt interior containing two bobbins, a needle case and a tape measure, the exterior with monogram.

It's the esteemed and high-quality maker, level of detail and rare novelty form (which suggests the main use of a nécessaire i.e. to carry things) that makes this piece as valuable as it is.

1874   *2in (5cm) long 2oz*

$1,000-1,500   **LC**

A 19thC velvet-covered-card scissor case, containing four sets of sewing scissors, including a small fancy example inlaid with piqué work.

$150-250   **FLD**

A late Victorian gold thimble, with fitted case.

0.14oz

$250-350   **DN**

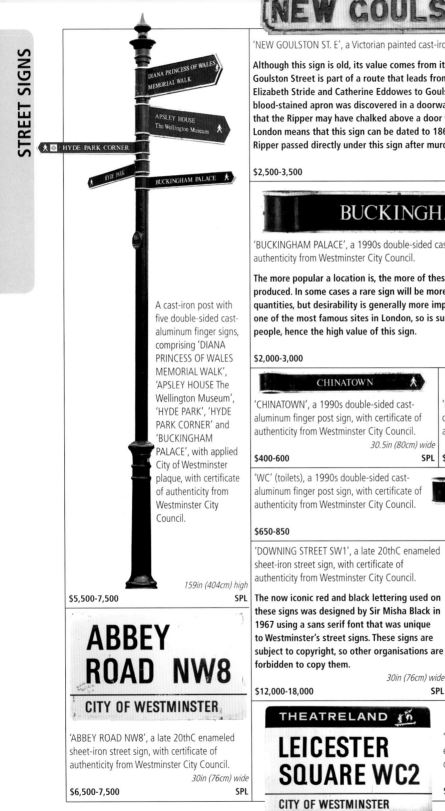

'NEW GOULSTON ST. E', a Victorian painted cast-iron street sign.

Although this sign is old, its value comes from its association with Jack the Ripper. New Goulston Street is part of a route that leads from the scenes of the 1888 murder of Elizabeth Stride and Catherine Eddowes to Goulston Street where a piece of Eddowes's blood-stained apron was discovered in a doorway, and the famous 'Goulston Street Grafitti' that the Ripper may have chalked above a door was found. The 'E.' suffix for this area of London means that this sign can be dated to 1866-1917. It is thus possible that Jack the Ripper passed directly under this sign after murdering Stride and Eddowes...

50.75in (129cm) wide

$2,500-3,500   D&H

'BUCKINGHAM PALACE', a 1990s double-sided cast-aluminum finger post sign, with certificate of authenticity from Westminster City Council.

The more popular a location is, the more of these finger post signs are likely to have been produced. In some cases a rare sign will be more valuable than one available in greater quantities, but desirability is generally more important than rarity. Buckingham Palace is one of the most famous sites in London, so is sure to have a huge appeal to a great many people, hence the high value of this sign.

30.5in (80cm) wide

$2,000-3,000   SPL

A cast-iron post with five double-sided cast-aluminum finger signs, comprising 'DIANA PRINCESS OF WALES MEMORIAL WALK', 'APSLEY HOUSE The Wellington Museum', 'HYDE PARK', 'HYDE PARK CORNER' and 'BUCKINGHAM PALACE', with applied City of Westminster plaque, with certificate of authenticity from Westminster City Council.

CHINATOWN

'CHINATOWN', a 1990s double-sided cast-aluminum finger post sign, with certificate of authenticity from Westminster City Council.

30.5in (80cm) wide

$400-600   SPL

HOUSES OF PARLIAMENT

'HOUSES OF PARLIAMENT', a 1990s double-sided cast-aluminum finger post sign, with certificate of authenticity from Westminster City Council.

30.5in (80cm) wide

$1,200-1,800   SPL

'WC' (toilets), a 1990s double-sided cast-aluminum finger post sign, with certificate of authenticity from Westminster City Council.

WC

30.5in (80cm) wide

$650-850   SPL

159in (404cm) high

$5,500-7,500   SPL

'DOWNING STREET SW1', a late 20thC enameled sheet-iron street sign, with certificate of authenticity from Westminster City Council.

The now iconic red and black lettering used on these signs was designed by Sir Misha Black in 1967 using a sans serif font that was unique to Westminster's street signs. These signs are subject to copyright, so other organisations are forbidden to copy them.

30in (76cm) wide

$12,000-18,000   SPL

DOWNING STREET SW1

CITY OF WESTMINSTER

ABBEY ROAD NW8

CITY OF WESTMINSTER

'ABBEY ROAD NW8', a late 20thC enameled sheet-iron street sign, with certificate of authenticity from Westminster City Council.

30in (76cm) wide

$6,500-7,500   SPL

THEATRELAND

LEICESTER SQUARE WC2

CITY OF WESTMINSTER

'LEICESTER SQUARE WC2', a late 20thC enameled sheet-iron street sign, with certificate of authenticity from Westminster City Council.

34in (86cm) wide

$1,200-1,800   SPL

QUICK REFERENCE - SILVER

- Although it fluctuates, the value of an ounce of silver has remained strong since 2009, rising to heights of over $50. This has caused many run-of-the-mill and common silver items, from tea sets to vesta cases, to be reappraised for their scrap value, rather than for their collectible or historical value. As a consequence, many such pieces have been melted down and lost forever. This has strengthened the values of smaller silver items produced from the early 19thC onward. As these pieces tend to be light in weight due to their size, their 'scrap value' is low, so the value of the type of object, maker, date, quality and condition are more important.
- Most collectors tend to focus on one type of item, such as pepperettes or card cases. In all instances, the quality of manufacture and decoration of a piece counts toward value. In general, the more finely detailed and highly worked a piece is, the higher its value. Additional features, such as enameling or inset stones, will usually raise value. If a piece has cross-market interest, for example, if it appeals to collectors of railway or sporting memorabilia as well as to collectors of silver, that increased interest can also push the price upward.

- Learn how to recognize makers' marks, particularly those for notable and sought after makers, such as Nathaniel Mills, Walker & Hall, Hester Bateman and Sampson Mordan. The maker's mark is usually a set of initials inside a small shape, which, along with the assay office stamp, the date letter and the duty mark, forms a hallmark. All items of British silver should bear a hallmark. It may be worth investing in a book of marks, such as Miller's 'Antiques Marks', to help you with identification.
- Many small silver objects were made to be used and were used heavily. Silver is a comparatively soft metal and some antique pieces are likely to have acquired dents, splits and general wear caused by rubbing after years of use. Be aware that cleaning 'dirty' silver removes a microscopically thin (oxidized) layer of metal. As such, repeated cleaning will reduce levels of detail over time.
- Although there are still numerous collectors of small silver novelties across the world, many objects remain undiscovered. As such, searching through small cabinets and drawers in antiques centers, shops and at fairs can yield some surprising treasures – particularly for the knowledgeable hunter.

A Victorian silver double sovereign case, by William Sharman, London, with gilt interior and button catch.

This case is curved to fit easily in a pocket.

1885   2.25in (5.5cm) wide 1.5oz
$500-700   LC

A late Victorian silver triple sovereign case, by Deakin & Francis, Chester, with plain finish, button catch and swivel ring.

1896
2.5in (6.5cm) wide 1.5 oz
$650-850   LC

A late Victorian silver engine-turned sovereign case, maker's mark 'JSW', Birmingham, with a slider to push out a coin, opening to refill.

1901   1.25in (3cm) diam 0.8oz
$650-850   LC

An Edwardian silver combined double sovereign, half sovereign and stamp case, by Martin Hall & Co., Birmingham.

1908   2.25in (5.7cm) wide
$600-800   GORL

An Edwardian silver double sovereign case, for full and half sovereigns, by Deakin & Francis, Birmingham, with hammered decoration.

1909   2.5in (6.5cm) wide
$200-300   GORB

A George V silver 'fob' sovereign case, by W Neale Ltd., Birmingham, with plain finish and gilt interior.

1912   1.25in (3.5cm) diam 1oz
$200-300   LC

An early 20thC silver 'fob' sovereign holder, by W H Haselar, Birmingham, with a button catch and a 'spring' coin clip.

1913   1.25in (3cm) diam 0.4oz
$350-450   LC

SILVER

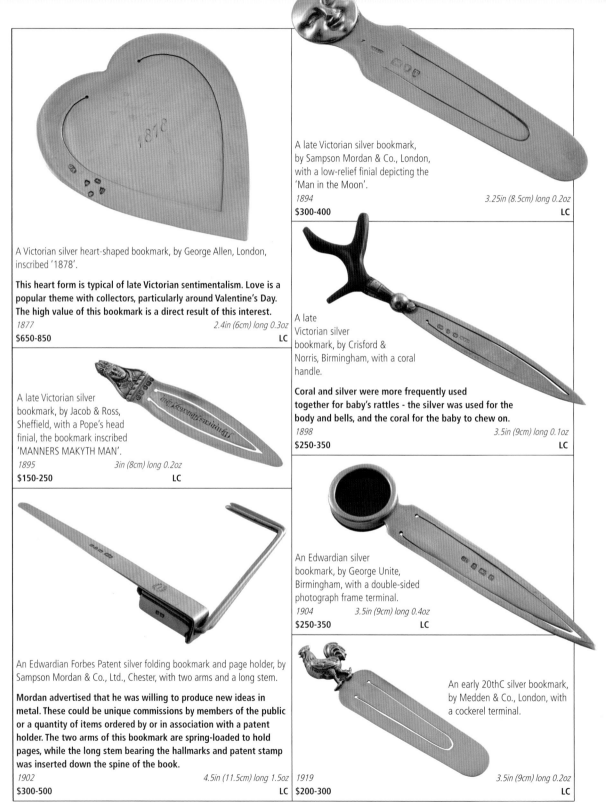

A Victorian silver heart-shaped bookmark, by George Allen, London, inscribed '1878'.

This heart form is typical of late Victorian sentimentalism. Love is a popular theme with collectors, particularly around Valentine's Day. The high value of this bookmark is a direct result of this interest.

1877   *2.4in (6cm) long 0.3oz*

$650-850   **LC**

A late Victorian silver bookmark, by Jacob & Ross, Sheffield, with a Pope's head finial, the bookmark inscribed 'MANNERS MAKYTH MAN'.

1895   *3in (8cm) long 0.2oz*

$150-250   **LC**

An Edwardian Forbes Patent silver folding bookmark and page holder, by Sampson Mordan & Co., Ltd., Chester, with two arms and a long stem.

Mordan advertised that he was willing to produce new ideas in metal. These could be unique commissions by members of the public or a quantity of items ordered by or in association with a patent holder. The two arms of this bookmark are spring-loaded to hold pages, while the long stem bearing the hallmarks and patent stamp was inserted down the spine of the book.

1902   *4.5in (11.5cm) long 1.5oz*

$300-500   **LC**

A late Victorian silver bookmark, by Sampson Mordan & Co., London, with a low-relief finial depicting the 'Man in the Moon'.

1894   *3.25in (8.5cm) long 0.2oz*

$300-400   **LC**

A late Victorian silver bookmark, by Crisford & Norris, Birmingham, with a coral handle.

Coral and silver were more frequently used together for baby's rattles - the silver was used for the body and bells, and the coral for the baby to chew on.

1898   *3.5in (9cm) long 0.1oz*

$250-350   **LC**

An Edwardian silver bookmark, by George Unite, Birmingham, with a double-sided photograph frame terminal.

1904   *3.5in (9cm) long 0.4oz*

$250-350   **LC**

An early 20thC silver bookmark, by Medden & Co., London, with a cockerel terminal.

1919   *3.5in (9cm) long 0.2oz*

$200-300   **LC**

A Victorian silver castle-top card case, by Yapp & Woodward, Birmingham, the front embossed and chased with a building framed by trees, the reverse decorated with flowers and scrolling foliage.

c1850   *2.5in (9cm) long*

$1,200-1,800   **TOV**

A Victorian silver card case, by George Unite, Birmingham, engraved with trailing vines and bunches of grapes, with a fitted case.

1885   *5in (10cm) long*

$400-600   **WW**

A late Victorian silver card case, by George Unite, Birmingham, engraved with vignettes of birds and a boy playing a horn by a stile, with a scrollwork ground, monogrammed, with a silk-lined interior.

George Unite (1798-1896) was apprenticed to notable Georgian silversmith Joseph Wilmore and registered his first maker's mark (G.U) in 1832. His business was highly successful and he is known for complex designs that reflected the detailed High Victorian taste for pattern and diverse inspirations.

1899   *4in (10cm) long*

$300-500   **LC**

A CLOSER LOOK AT A CARD CASE

Moving the slide with your thumb releases a card. This mechanical feature is unusual and adds value.

The floral decoration, particularly with its curving buds, is typical of the Art Nouveau movement, which was inspired by nature and blossomed at the time this case was made.

Along with the lily, the poppy was a popular flower during the Art Nouveau period. It was used by many makers, particularly the highly prolific German maker WMF.

Had it not been engraved with the original owner's initials, this case could be worth more.

An Edwardian silver patent card case, by Horton & Allday, Birmingham, with a sprung cover and a thumb-operated slide action for dispensing cards, engraved with poppies, with engraved initials.

1903   *4in (10cm) long 2.5oz*

$500-700   **LC**

An early 20thC silver card case, by H Matthews, Birmingham, embossed with floral and curving foliate designs, with a vacant cartouche on each side.

1913   *4in (10cm) long 1.8oz*

$150-250   **LC**

An early 20thC silver curved card case, maker's mark 'THH', Birmingham, hand-engraved with a scrolling foliate design, with a vacant cartouche.

1913   *3.25in (8cm) long 1oz*

$150-250   **LC**

An early 20thC silver engine-turned card case, in the form of an envelope, by Mappin & Webb, Birmingham, with a vacant cartouche and gilt interior.

1915   *3.75in (9.5cm) long 2.3oz*

$200-300   **LC**

An early 20thC silver patent 'sprung' card case, by Deakin & Francis, Birmingham, the cartouche engraved with the initial 'A'.

Cards are released by squeezing the sides.

1929   *3.5in (9cm) long 2oz*

$150-250   **LC**

SILVER

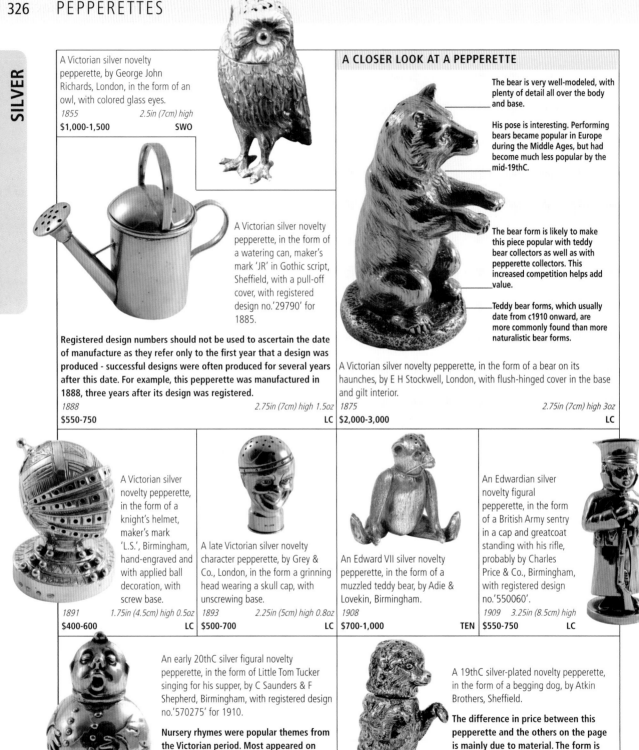

A Victorian silver novelty pepperette, by George John Richards, London, in the form of an owl, with colored glass eyes.

1855   *2.5in (7cm) high*

$1,000-1,500   **SWO**

A Victorian silver novelty pepperette, in the form of a watering can, maker's mark 'JR' in Gothic script, Sheffield, with a pull-off cover, with registered design no.'29790' for 1885.

Registered design numbers should not be used to ascertain the date of manufacture as they refer only to the first year that a design was produced - successful designs were often produced for several years after this date. For example, this pepperette was manufactured in 1888, three years after its design was registered.

1888   *2.75in (7cm) high 1.5oz*

$550-750   **LC**

A CLOSER LOOK AT A PEPPERETTE

The bear is very well-modeled, with plenty of detail all over the body and base.

His pose is interesting. Performing bears became popular in Europe during the Middle Ages, but had become much less popular by the mid-19thC.

The bear form is likely to make this piece popular with teddy bear collectors as well as with pepperette collectors. This increased competition helps add value.

Teddy bear forms, which usually date from c1910 onward, are more commonly found than more naturalistic bear forms.

A Victorian silver novelty pepperette, in the form of a bear on its haunches, by E H Stockwell, London, with flush-hinged cover in the base and gilt interior.

1875   *2.75in (7cm) high 3oz*

$2,000-3,000   **LC**

A Victorian silver novelty pepperette, in the form of a knight's helmet, maker's mark 'L.S.', Birmingham, hand-engraved and with applied ball decoration, with screw base.

1891   *1.75in (4.5cm) high 0.5oz*

$400-600   **LC**

A late Victorian silver novelty character pepperette, by Grey & Co., London, in the form a grinning head wearing a skull cap, with unscrewing base.

1893   *2.25in (5cm) high 0.8oz*

$500-700   **LC**

An Edward VII silver novelty pepperette, in the form of a muzzled teddy bear, by Adie & Lovekin, Birmingham.

1908

$700-1,000   **TEN**

An Edwardian silver novelty figural pepperette, in the form of a British Army sentry in a cap and greatcoat standing with his rifle, probably by Charles Price & Co., Birmingham, with registered design no.'550060'.

1909   *3.25in (8.5cm) high*

$550-750   **LC**

An early 20thC silver figural novelty pepperette, in the form of Little Tom Tucker singing for his supper, by C Saunders & F Shepherd, Birmingham, with registered design no.'570275' for 1910.

Nursery rhymes were popular themes from the Victorian period. Most appeared on transfer-printed ceramics made for use by children. Such pieces were known as 'nursery ware'.

1912   *2.25in (6cm) high 0.5oz*

$500-700   **LC**

A 19thC silver-plated novelty pepperette, in the form of a begging dog, by Atkin Brothers, Sheffield.

The difference in price between this pepperette and the others on the page is mainly due to material. The form is appealing, but the fact that it is only silver-plate, rather than silver, means that value drops by over 90 percent!

2.5in (8.5cm) high

$60-80   **FLD**

Mark Picks

Stamp cases, which were often hung from the chains of pocket watches or chatelaines, were fashionable from the late 19thC until the late 1910s.

Most are plain or have engraved or engine-turned decoration - enameled designs are much rarer. Such designs might depict wording or images of stamps, as in the example shown.

The penny lilac was in use 1881-1901 and is not commonly found on stamp cases. When it is, values tend to be high. As well as a rare image, this stamp case also benefits from a detailed, well-painted design, which covers nearly all of the side. It is also in superb condition.

A late Victorian silver stamp case, by George Heath, London, enameled in lilac and white with a one-penny stamp, the interior with a spring-loaded stamp compartment.
1890   *1.25in (3cm) long 0.7oz*
$3,000-4,000   LC

A late-Victorian silver triple-stamp box, by Grey & Co., Birmingham, the hinged cover set with three Victorian stamps, the base with gadrooned border.
1896   *3.25in (8.5cm) long*
$500-700   WW

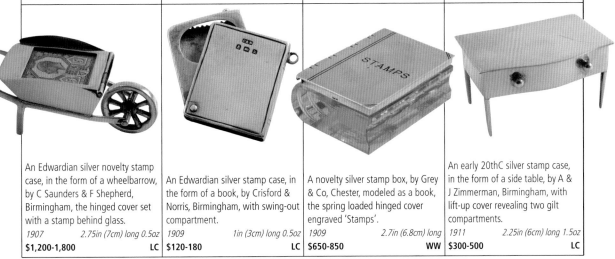

An Edwardian silver stamp box, importer's mark of George Edward and Son, Glasgow, the cover embossed with two cherubs kissing.
1903   *2.5in (7cm) long 1.7oz*
$700-1,000   WW

An Edwardian novelty silver stamp box, by Samuel Jacob, London, in the form of a shoe-shine box, with registration number.
1904   *4in (10cm) wide*
$800-1,200   WW

An Edwardian silver double-sided stamp case, in the form of an envelope, by G Vale & Co., Birmingham, one flap enameled '1/2D', the other '1D'.
1905   *1in (3cm) long 0.2oz*
$550-750   LC

An Edwardian silver double-section stamp box, by Matthew John Jessop, Birmingham.
1906   *2.5in (6.5cm) wide*
$220-280   GORL

An Edwardian silver novelty stamp case, in the form of a wheelbarrow, by C Saunders & F Shepherd, Birmingham, the hinged cover set with a stamp behind glass.
1907   *2.75in (7cm) long 0.5oz*
$1,200-1,800   LC

An Edwardian silver stamp case, in the form of a book, by Crisford & Norris, Birmingham, with swing-out compartment.
1909   *1in (3cm) long 0.5oz*
$120-180   LC

A novelty silver stamp box, by Grey & Co, Chester, modeled as a book, the spring loaded hinged cover engraved 'Stamps'.
1909   *2.7in (6.8cm) long*
$650-850   WW

An early 20thC silver stamp case, in the form of a side table, by A & J Zimmerman, Birmingham, with lift-up cover revealing two gilt compartments.
1911   *2.25in (6cm) long 1.5oz*
$300-500   LC

SILVER

QUICK REFERENCE - THE FORK

- Forks were first used in Ancient Egyptian times. The English word 'fork' comes from the latin word 'furca' meaning 'pitchfork'.
- By the 11thC, the fork had made its way into Europe via Italy through trade networks. It became widely used among the Italian upper and merchant classes by the late 16thC. Elsewhere in Europe, forks were seen as effeminate or as a 'fancy' Italian affectation and were sporadically used. Many in the Catholic Church even viewed forks as 'excessive delicacy', advocating the knife or 'natural fork' of fingers.
- Many forks dating from before the 18thC have two or three tines (prongs), with the standard four-tine form being adopted in the early 19thC.
- Often fork tines and blades were made of steel, as silver was too soft for prolonged, repeated use.
- This handy combination fork and knife was probably made for an invalid or one-armed person, perhaps even an officer wounded in the Napoleonic Wars (1803-15), judging by the date of the hallmark.

A George III silver combined fork and knife, by Messrs. Eley & Fearn, London, the outer tine fitted with a removable steel blade, with ivory handle.

1811   *8.5in (21.5cm) long*
$1,200-1,800   LC

A George III silver campaign knife and fork, the handles and fork by T Phipps & E Robinson, London, the blade with maker's mark 'GL', the handles with bright-cut borders, inscribed 'CCK-Campbell'.

This fork and knife slot together for traveling.
c1798   Fork 6.5in (16.5cm) long 1.8oz
$800-1,200   LC

A silver orange peeler, by Hukin & Heath, London, stamped 'Patent No. 10066', with ivory handle.

This orange peeler is typical of the array of 'knick-knackery' that bedeviled the early 20thC dining table. Probably passed around after dinner, it demonstrates the Edwardian love for innovation, and probably made an interesting change from the silver-bladed pocket fruit knives that were usually used.
1910   4.75in (12cm) long
$250-350   LC

An 18thC silver apple corer, the screw-off ball finial with pierced decoration, unmarked.

5in (13cm) long
$800-1,200   WW

A pair of George III Irish silver sugar nips, marked with a Hibernia and harp, Dublin.

c1775   5in (12.5cm) long 1.1oz
$250-350   WW

An Edwardian silver egg topper, maker's mark 'PW', London.

The spiked interior is closed over the top of an egg and made to bite in through the shell, thus allowing the 'lid' to be made and removed with one, simple scissor action. Egg toppers can also be found in silver- or nickel-plate. These are generally worth under $30.
1903   4in (10cm) long 2oz
$700-1,000   LC

A Victorian silver novelty menu holder, in the form of a fox jumping a rustic five-bar gate, by L Emmanuel, Birmingham.
1898   1.5in (4cm) high 1oz
$400-600   LC

A pair of silver novelty menu holders, in the form of ship's lanterns, maker's mark 'JWB', Birmingham, one stamped 'PORT' with red enamel lens, the other stamped 'STARBOARD' with green enamel lens.

These menu holders were made during the golden age of cruise liners, when luxurious liners, such as the 'Normandie', were hitting the headlines.
1927   1.75in (4.5cm) high 1.75oz
$1,200-1,800   LC

A Victorian silver novelty mustard pot and spoon, the pot in the form of an owl, by George Richards, London, with inset red and black glass eyes, with gilt interior and blue glass liner, the spoon with a mouse finial.

Owl forms are relatively common for small silver objects, such as bookmarks, inkwells and menu-card holders. They were particularly widely used by Sampson Mordan & Co. The plumage and claws on this example are very finely modeled and the extra detail of the glass eyes and mouse on the spoon makes it even more appealing.
1850   4.25in (10.5cm) high 5oz
$3,500-4,500   LC

A George V silver novelty mustard pot, in the form of 'Humpty Dumpty', by C Saunders & F Shepherd, London, with blue glass liner and spoon.

1924/25   1.75in (4.5 cm) high 0.5oz
$500-700   LC

A Victorian silver novelty vesta case and striker, in the form of a top hat, by Thomas Johnson, London, ribbed on the underside of the brim.

The ribbed brim would have been used to strike matches.

1885 *2in (5cm) wide 0.75oz*
$800-1,200 LC

QUICK REFERENCE - VESTA CASES

- Vesta cases (or match safes) were popular for nearly a century from the 1830s until the 1920s when pocket petrol lighters were developed and began to be more affordable. Nearly everyone carried a vesta case, with poorer people using brass, tin or, later, Bakelite.

- Many early matches were prone to igniting accidentally when they rubbed against each other, so the small metal box prevented damage to clothing or property if this occurred. The box also provided a durable, textured surface for matches to be struck on.

- Vesta cases took their name from Vesta, the Roman goddess of the hearth. There was also an early brand of match called Vesta.

- Vesta cases have become one of the most widely collected types of small silver article, due to the vast number that have survived and the amazing diversity of forms and decoration.

- Figural or amusing forms tend to fetch the highest sums, as do those that are finely made.

- Always consider condition, as splits, worn details and patterns and major dents reduce value.

- Plain, engine-turned late Victorian or Edwardian examples can easily be found for less than $80.

An Edwardian silver vesta case, by Sampson Mordan & Co., Chester, with reeded decoration, with hinged lid and striker to base.

1904 *1.75in (4.5cm) long 0.5oz*
$400-600 LC

A Victorian silver vesta case, by George Unite, Birmingham, with a hobnail surface.

1889 *2in (5cm) high 0.7oz*
$400-600 LC

An Edwardian silver and enamel vesta case, by Liberty and Co., Birmingham, the front with an inter-twined Celtic motif.

1903 *2.5in (5cm) long*
$1,000-1,500 WW

A Victorian silver vesta case, in the form of a flask, by Martin Brothers, Birmingham.

1888 *2in (5cm) high 0.5oz*
$200-300 LC

A late Victorian silver and enamel vesta case, by George Unite, Birmingham, enameled with a bust of William Shakespeare.

1894 *2.25in (6cm) long*
$1,500-2,500 WW

A silver vesta case, by Henry & Arthur Vander, London, the brass hinged cover applied with the Royal cypher of King William IV, with steel striker plate.

1915 *2.25in (5.5cm) long 2.75oz*
$450-550 LC

A late Victorian silver vesta case, by W D Wilmot, Birmingham, decorated in relief to resemble bamboo stems, with registered design no.'144480' for 1890.

1890 *2in (5cm) high 0.5oz*
$100-150 LC

A miniature Victorian silver vesta case, by the Co-Op Wholesale Manufacturers Ltd., Birmingham.

1857 *1in (2.5cm) wide*
$250-350 A&G

SILVER

A Victorian silver military whistle, by Jennens & Co., Birmingham, with an acorn finial and a faceted, tapering sheath.
1854   3.5in (9cm) long 1.2oz
$300-500   LC

A Victorian novelty silver horn vinaigrette/whistle, by Sampson Mordan & Co., with a registration lozenge.
1870   2in (5cm) long 0.4oz
$450-550   WW

A Victorian silver hunting whistle, by Joseph Alexander, Birmingham, with a fox head terminal.
1881   1.75in (4.5cm) long 0.2oz
$400-600   LC

A late Victorian silver novelty whistle, in the form of a port/ale bottle, by W Gibson & G Langman, London, enameled with a red and white flag, initialed 'EDH'.

The well-painted red and white striped flag is unusual. Although they are similar, it seems not to be the flag of Burgundy or the flag or the Kingdom of Raiatea (1847-80).
1893   2.75in (7cm) long 1.2oz
$500-700   LC

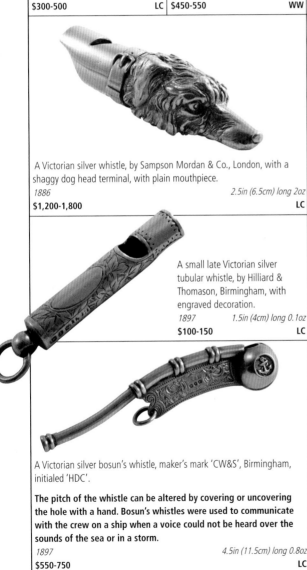

A Victorian silver whistle, by Sampson Mordan & Co., London, with a shaggy dog head terminal, with plain mouthpiece.
1886   2.5in (6.5cm) long 2oz
$1,200-1,800   LC

A small late Victorian silver tubular whistle, by Hilliard & Thomason, Birmingham, with engraved decoration.
1897   1.5in (4cm) long 0.1oz
$100-150   LC

A Victorian silver bosun's whistle, maker's mark 'CW&S', Birmingham, initialed 'HDC'.

The pitch of the whistle can be altered by covering or uncovering the hole with a hand. Bosun's whistles were used to communicate with the crew on a ship when a voice could not be heard over the sounds of the sea or in a storm.
1897   4.5in (11.5cm) long 0.8oz
$550-750   LC

Mark Picks

The Acme Whistle was developed in 1883 by Birmingham-based metalworker and toolmaker Joseph Hudson (1848-1930). Legend has it that he was inspired by the discordant sound his violin made when he dropped it on the floor. His pea-driven whistle soon gained a contract with the Metropolitan Police who were looking for a sounding alarm device to replace their rattle. Hudson's company, now known as Acme Whistles, still exists today and has sold millions of different types of whistle, many of which are still used by the armed forces and the police. Silver-plated whistles are relatively common and are usually worth well under $30. It's the highly collected Acme brand, combined with the precious material and the sought-after name of Sampson Mordan that makes this a whistle to listen out for!

A late Victorian silver patent 'ACME SIREN' whistle, by Sampson Mordan & Co., London.
1895   3in (8cm) long 1.3oz
$800-1,200   LC

A silver whistle, by J H & Co, Birmingham.
1963   2.5in (5.5cm) long 1.4oz
$250-350   WW

A George III silver vinaigrette, by T Phipps & E Robinson, London, the hinged grille pierced with drilled holes, with gilt interior.

1798   1.75in (4.5cm) long 1oz
$300-500   LC

A George III silver novelty vinaigrette, in the form of a flexible fish, by Lea & Co., Birmingham, the hinged head revealing a hinged grille and gilt interior.

1817   3.25in (8.5 cm) long 0.6oz
$1,500-2,500   LC

A Victorian silver novelty combined scent flask and vinaigrette, in the form of a horn, by Sampson Mordan & Co., London, with hinged cover and grille at one end and a screw cap at the other.

1872   3in (7.5 cm) long 1.2oz
$400-600   LC

A Victorian silver vinaigrette, by C Cheshire, Birmingham, with suspensory ring and gilt interior.

1886   1.5in (4cm) long 0.6oz
$400-600   LC

A George III silver novelty nutmeg grater, in the form of a vase and cover, by T Phipps & E Robinson, London, bright-engraved and initialed, with hinged cover and side.

1790   2.75in (7cm) high 1.5oz
$5,000-7,000   LC

A George III silver novelty nutmeg grater, in the form of a vase, by Cocks and Bettridge, Birmingham, engraved with festoons and foliate decoration, with pull-off cover and base.

1802   2.5in (3.5cm) high 0.3oz
$3,000-4,000   WW

A George IV silver engine-turned nutmeg grater, by Mary Ann & Charles Reily, London, with hinged cover and base.

1826   2.5in (5.5cm) long 1.4oz
$900-1,200   LC

A Victorian silver nutmeg grater, in the form of a melon, by Hilliard & Thomason, Birmingham, with hinged cover.

1869   1.5in (4cm) long 0.6oz
$1,500-2,500   LC

A late Victorian silver novelty stamp moistener, in the form of a flat-backed champagne bottle, by Sampson Mordan & Co., London, the label enameled 'Heidsieck & Co.', with screw cap and slot for a felt pad.

1897   4.25in (11cm) long 1.5 oz
$1,800-2,200   LC

SILVER

A small George III silver traveling inkwell, London, with a hinged, screw-down cover, no maker's mark.

1809   1.25in (3.5cm) wide 1.2oz
$350-450   LC

A Victorian silver traveling inkwell, in the form of an egg, by Henry William Dee, London, with a sprung cover with a button release, with gilt interior.

1874   2in (5cm) high 2oz
$550-750   LC

A Victorian silver novelty traveling inkwell, in the form of a milk can, by E H Stockwell, London, retailed by Thornhill & Co., with a button thumb press, gilt interior, and removable glass liner.

1875   2.25in (5.5cm) high 3oz
$550-750   LC

A late Victorian silver novelty traveling inkwell, in the form of a ship's lamp, by Samuel Jacob, London, inscribed 'PORT', with red glass lens, hinged cover and swing handle.

1899   4.25in (10.5cm) high 3oz
$650-850   LC

A George III silver pierced bougie box, by Richard Glanville, London, with reeded borders, with a swing-out handle, hinged cover and a pivoting crescent shaped closure.

The bougie box was designed to hold a coiled wax taper that could be pulled out of the center of the lid and cut with the small hook-shaped crescent device. The wax was then melted using a candle and dripped and stamped to seal a letter. Bougie boxes are usually solid metal, making this pierced example unusual.

1786   2in (5cm) diam 1.5oz
$1,200-1,800   LC

One of a pair of late Victorian Scottish silver beakers, in the form of thistle heads, by William Marshall, Edinburgh, with gilt interiors.

1895   2.5in (6.5cm) high 3.5oz
$550-750 pair   LC

A Victorian silver novelty beaker, in the form of an upturned thimble, by Hilliard & Thomason, Birmingham, with the applied letters 'JUST A THIMBLEFULL', with engraved monogram and gilt interior.

1876   2.25in (5.5cm) high 1.25oz
$400-600   LC

A miniature silver fireman's helmet, inscribed 'HONG KONG FIRE BRIGADE', with a chain chin strap, unmarked.

c1920   2.25in (6cm) high
$500-700   DN

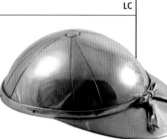

A Victorian silver novelty snuff box, in the form of a jockey cap, by E H Stockwell, London, with hinged cover and gilt interior.

1878   3in (7cm) long 2 oz
$1,200-1,800   LC

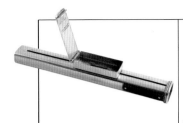

A late Victorian silver tubular sealing-wax holder, by H S Brown, London, with a slider, surmounted by a vesta case with a hinged cover and steel striker plate, with retailer's marks for 'Maurice, Piccadilly'.

Marks for good retailers in prestigious locations in city centers often indicate fine quality and can add value.

1900   5.5in (14cm) long 1.85oz
$500-700   LC

A small Edwardian novelty silver seal, topped with a model of a dog, by William Hornby, London, the base unscrewing to reveal a quill nib.

1907 is a very late date for a quill nib, a fact that suggests the nib may not have originally been part of this seal. By 1907, the quill had been superseded by the steel nib, which in turn was superseded by the fountain pen.

1907   1.75in (4.5cm) high 1oz
$250-350   LC

A small Victorian silver letter opener, by Henry Swann, Birmingham, with a tubular, wrythen handle.

1894   5.25in (13.5cm) long 0.25oz
$100-150   LC

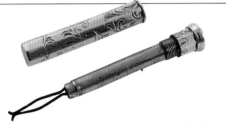

A Victorian silver traveling or pocket postal scale, by John Sheldon, Birmingham, made for the Indian market, with engraved details, the scale graduated for 'tola' (weight) and 'annar' (money).

John Sheldon was a noted inventor and maker of postal scales and similar items. Many of his pieces ingeniously combined other functions with their primary function of measuring weight. The more complex a pocket scale is, the more it is likely to be worth. Silver-plated versions were also produced, but are typically less valuable than solid examples.

1855   2in (5cm) long 2oz
$550-750   LC

A late Victorian silver portable reading lamp, by C & G Asprey, London, with telescopic stand, swing-out feet, hinged reflector, cover and hook for suspension, inscribed 'JLT from HJ. 12 March 1895', with original crocodile case.

This is a very rare item by one of London's greatest names in gold and silversmithing. It's so rare that it is possible that it was a unique commission. Quirky and indicative of the quality and eccentricity of a bygone age, pieces such as this are very popular today. This example is also very heavy, adding to its value.

Closed 6in (15cm) long 19.5oz

1894
$4,000-6,000   LC

A George III silver tongue scraper, maker's mark 'J.L' probably for Joseph Lock, London, with a stained-green ivory handle.

c1780   5in (11cm) long
$650-850   WW

A George IV silver 'Gibson's patent' caster oil/medicine spoon, by Charles Gibson, London, inscribed 'C. Gibson Inventor...', the enclosed bowl with a hinged cover in the center.

This form allows medicine to be fed to invalids lying in bed without spillage.

1828   5.25in (13cm) long 1oz
$800-1,200   LC

A 19thC silver posy holder, in the form of a flower bud, with a finger ring and pin, unmarked.

5in (12cm) long
$300-500   WW

A small Edwardian silver novelty scent bottle, in the form of a banana, by Levi & Salaman, Birmingham, with a hinged cover.

1904   2.25in (6cm) long 0.2oz
$400-600   LC

SMOKING

A 1950s Dunhill 'Aquarium' table lighter, the Lucite panels reverse-carved and painted with a fish among rocks and weeds, with silver-plated mount, in excellent condition.

4in (10cm) wide

$1,500-2,500   **HT**

A rare 1950s Dunhill 'Aquarium' table lighter, the Lucite panels with foil inclusions, reverse-carved and painted with the ships 'Royal William 1719' and 'HM Brig Watskerwitch', with silver-plated mount, with wear to plating and some flaking to paint.

4in (10.5cm) wide

$5,000-7,000   **HT**

QUICK REFERENCE - AQUARIUM LIGHTERS

- The most common motif in Dunhill's 1950s range of 'Aquarium' lighters is, as the name suggests, fish. Birds are rare and other motifs considerably rarer. This piece, which is possibly unique, would also appeal to collectors of automobilia as well as to collectors of smoking memorabilia.
- Always consider the condition of an 'Aquarium' lighter, as the paint can flake and bubble.

An extremely rare late 1950s Dunhill 'Aquarium' 'Donald Campbell Bluebird' table lighter, the Lucite panels reverse-carved and painted with the 'Bluebird CN7'.

4in (10cm) wide

$12,000-18,000   **SWO**

A Dunhill 'Unique A' silver combination cigarette lighter and watch, no.1198, with engine-turned decoration, with fold-out panel supporting a hinged watch case, with import hallmark for London 1927.

c1927   *1.75in (4.5cm) wide*

$1,500-2,500   **SWO**

A 1950s Dunhill silver-plated 'Unique Giant' table lighter, with engine-turned linear decoration and internal snuffer-arm spring, the base with stamped marks, with some wear.

4.25in (10.5cm) high

$250-350   **WW**

A 1980s Dunhill silver-plated 'Unique' gas-filled pocket lighter, decorated with vertical lines, the base with stamped marks, with instruction booklet guarantee and box.

During the 1960s, most lighters were filled with gas, rather than fluid.

2.5in (6.5cm) high

$150-250   **DN**

A late 1920s Dunhill silver 'Unique A' lighter and cigarette case, each decorated with fragments of eggshell in black lacquer, with marks for Dunhill Paris, with original Dunhill Paris fitted case (not shown).

The earliest Dunhill 'Unique' lighters have straight cylindrical arms with no Dunhill markings and a single striking wheel. This is an uncommon form of decoration.

Cigarette case 4in (10cm) wide

$5,500-6,500   **L&T**

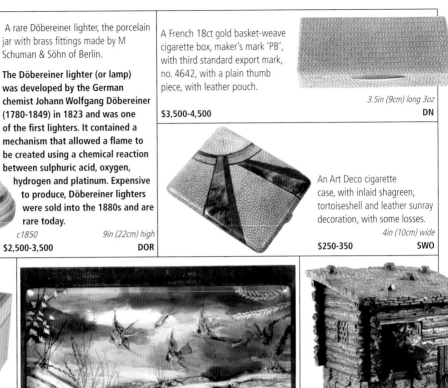

A rare Döbereiner lighter, the porcelain jar with brass fittings made by M Schuman & Söhn of Berlin.

The Döbereiner lighter (or lamp) was developed by the German chemist Johann Wolfgang Döbereiner (1780-1849) in 1823 and was one of the first lighters. It contained a mechanism that allowed a flame to be created using a chemical reaction between sulphuric acid, oxygen, hydrogen and platinum. Expensive to produce, Döbereiner lighters were sold into the 1880s and are rare today.

c1850   *9in (22cm) high*

$2,500-3,500   DOR

A French 18ct gold basket-weave cigarette box, maker's mark 'PB', with third standard export mark, no. 4642, with a plain thumb piece, with leather pouch.

3.5in (9cm) long 3oz

$3,500-4,500   DN

An Art Deco cigarette case, with inlaid shagreen, tortoiseshell and leather sunray decoration, with some losses.

4in (10cm) wide

$250-350   SWO

An Alfred Dunhill sycamore and marquetry cigar humidor, manufactured by David Linley, the lid with a central burr-elm panel and banded column border, the interior with three partitions, the back edge stamped 'LINLEY' and with a brass plaque.

13.5in (34cm) wide

$800-1,200   WW

A very rare 1950s Dunhill 'Aquarium' cigarette box, the lid inset with a reverse-carved and painted Lucite plaque depicting fish, the interior with Dunhill label.

'Aquarium' boxes are rarer than 'Aquarium' lighters, but often not as desirable since interest in the 'Aquarium' range comes mainly from lighter collectors.

8.5in (21cm) long

$5,500-6,500   SWO

A 19thC Black Forest cigar box, in the form of a log cabin, with door enclosing a vesta holder and wolf dressed in grandma's clothing from 'Little Red Riding Hood'.

8in (20cm) wide

$1,000-1,500   GORB

A Doulton Lambeth stoneware tobacco jar and cover, in the form of an ashes pot, inscribed 'BENJAMIN DUKE CREMATED A.D.', the interior decorated with scrolling foliage, the base with impressed marks.

c1874   *5.25in (13.5cm) high*

$150-250   WW

An early 20thC German molded-bisque comic ashtray, in the form of a head, probably by Shafer & Vater.

Shafer & Vater pieces are often (but not always) marked with an impressed mark of a crown above an 'R' in a star.

$80-120   CAPE

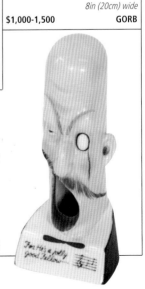

An FA Cup specimen gilt-metal winner's medal.

This piece was produced by the medal maker for the Soccer Association's approval before the main batch was produced.
c1900
$300-500   SAS

A rare pre-war 'ATWORTH F.C.' badge, the reverse with Miller's maker's mark.
$120-180   SAS

A signed Burnley claret and blue short-sleeved no.33 jersey, worn by Ian Wright in the match v Bury at Turf Moor 25th March 2000, the reverse signed, the collar torn.

Ian Wright ended his playing career at Burnley, which he joined in 2000 from Celtic. He made a total of 15 appearances for Burnley including 4 starts and scored 4 goals. On arrival at Turf Moor, Wright chose the squad number of 33, which was the number of England caps he had won in his illustrious playing career.

$800-1,200   GBA

QUICK REFERENCE - SOCCER

- Soccer is one of the most consistently popular sports in the UK and this creates a strong demand for memorabilia. Items connected to famous players and teams, such as Manchester United, are often the most valuable.
- Shirts, boots and other equipment can be extremely valuable, particularly if used during an important match or signed by the player. Items connected to legends, such as George Best, are likely to command a premium, but the shirts of today's top players can also fetch high sums as long as it can be proved that they were worn by the player.
- Programs are another popular area of collecting. Values vary greatly based on rarity and condition. Among the most desirable programs are those produced for pre-World War I games. Modern programs are printed in large numbers and are often kept in good condition. They can therefore be an affordable entry into soccer collecting.

A 1904 FA Cup 15ct winner's medal, awarded to Tommy Hynds of Manchester City FC, the reverse inscribed 'THE Soccer ASSOCIATION, MANCHESTER CITY, WINNERS, T. HINDS' (sic), the case by Whittle of Blackburn.

In 1903-04 Manchester City won the FA Cup, which was the first major honour in their history.
$10,000-15,000   GBA

A signed Everton black long-sleeved no.18 3rd choice jersey, signed by Wayne Rooney.

2000-03
$800-1,200   GBA

A West Bromwich Albion yellow and green short-sleeved no.20 away jersey, issued as spare jersey to Igor Bališ.
2003-04
$300-500   GBA

A pair of autographed Umbro Xai soccer boots, signed by Michael Owen.

These boots were donated by Michael Owen for a Sport Relief Charity Auction held at Sotheby's 18th July 2002.
$550-750   GBA

A very rare Nottingham Forest v Southampton FA Cup semi-final replay program, for the match played at the Crystal Palace Thursday 24th March 1898, the left-hand advertisement flap detached.

Following a 1-1 draw at Bramall Lane on Saturday 19th March 1898, the teams played this rematch at the Crystal Palace the following Thursday. As this was a work day, relatively few people attended, which would explain the rarity of this program.

$5,000-7,000   GBA

A Bradford City v Manchester City program, for the match played on 15th March 1913.

$700-1,000   GBA

A Portsmouth v Wolverhampton Wanderers FA Cup final program, for the match played on 29th April 1939.

$350-450   GBA

A set of 1947 Burnley FA Cup final and semi-final programs, for the Burnley v Charlton Athletic final played at Wembley and the Burnley v Liverpool semi-final played at Maine Road.

$200-300   GBA

A 1954 Hungary v Germany World Cup group match program, for the match played on 20th June 1954.

Hungary won this match 8-3. The teams later met in the final, where Germany famously won 3-2.

$200-300   SAS

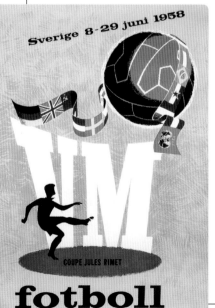

An official poster for the 1958 World Cup, designed by Beka, Swedish language, printed by Ervaco-Reklam, Dahlbergs, in good condition.

27.25in (69cm) high
$3,500-4,500   GBA

A signed soccer, signed by Pelé.

Pelé (born Edson Arantes do Nascimento) is a Brazilian soccerer, who is regarded by many experts and soccer fans as the best soccer player of all time. In 1999 he was named 'Athlete of the Century' by the International Olympic Committee and Reuters News Agency.

$400-600   NDS

A signed photograph of George Best and Rodney Marsh, signed by both in black marker, framed and glazed.

$70-100   SAS

Mark Picks

There are two tobacco cards that are considered the 'Holy Grails' of baseball card collecting – Honus Wagner and less famously this card depicting Edward 'Gettysburg Eddie' Plank. Both cards are astonishingly rare due to short print runs. In Wagner's case, legend has it that he demanded his image be removed because he would not encourage young people to smoke, while it seems likely that it was merely a broken plate that lead to small numbers of Plank's card being available.

The card depicts both Plank and the Philadelphia Athletics team he represented at the height of their powers. This example is also in very good condition, but it's the rarity that really justifies the value.

A T206 'Eddie Plank' baseball card, SGC graded 40 VG 3.
1910
$65,000-75,000   HER

A W511 '1. BABE RUTH' baseball card.

The 'W' class of cards are by far the most obscure section covered by the American Card Catalog: The Standard Guide on All Collected Cards and Their Values'. They have little obvious advertising or any confirmed sponsorship, so their origins remain unknown.
1926
$250-350   HER

An Exhibits '4 on 1' 'Lou Gehrig, Joe DiMaggio, Lefty Gomez and Tony Lazzeri' baseball card, SGC graded 70 EX+ 5.5.

Exhibit cards are generally common, except for these '4 on 1' cards. In 1937, Exhibit Supply Co. produced a card honouring each of the sixteen major league teams. This card features the New York Yankees.
1937
$2,000-3,000   HER

An Exhibits '4 on 1' 'Al Lopez, Bill Urbanski, Walter Berger and Danny MacFayden' baseball card, SGC graded 50 VG/EX 4.

1937
$120-180   HER

A Topps 'Roy Sievers' red-back baseball card, no.9, PSA graded Mint 9.

This is one of 23 examples of this card that exist. No higher grades are known.
1951
$70-100   HER

A Bowman 'Yogi Berra' baseball card, no.168, SGC graded 86 NM+ 7.5.
1955
$120-180   HER

A Topps 'Sandy Koufax' baseball card, no.79, PSA graded EX-MT 6.
1956
$150-250   HER

A Topps 'Yogi Berra' baseball card, no,21, PSA graded NM-MT 8.
1964
$80-120   HER

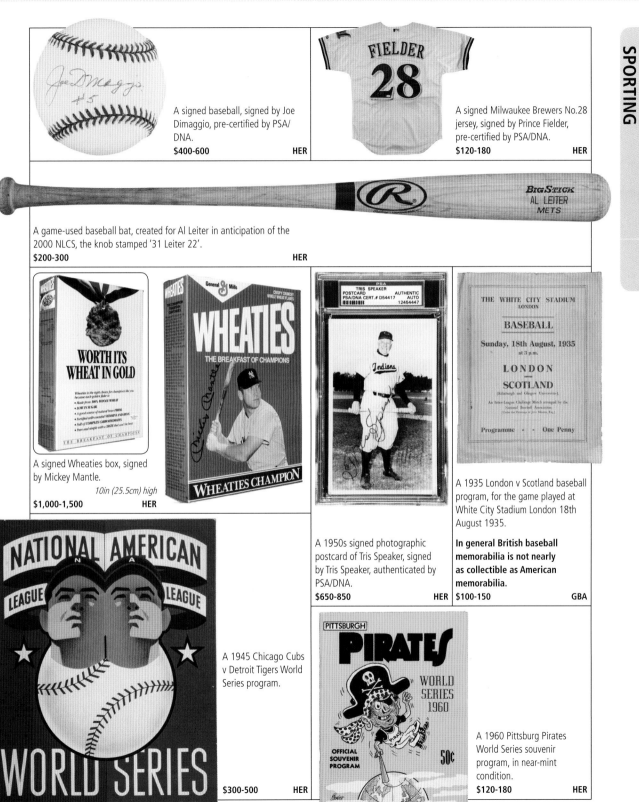

A signed baseball, signed by Joe Dimaggio, pre-certified by PSA/DNA.

$400-600 HER

A signed Milwaukee Brewers No.28 jersey, signed by Prince Fielder, pre-certified by PSA/DNA.

$120-180 HER

A game-used baseball bat, created for Al Leiter in anticipation of the 2000 NLCS, the knob stamped '31 Leiter 22'.

$200-300 HER

A signed Wheaties box, signed by Mickey Mantle.

10in (25.5cm) high

$1,000-1,500 HER

A 1950s signed photographic postcard of Tris Speaker, signed by Tris Speaker, authenticated by PSA/DNA.

$650-850 HER

A 1935 London v Scotland baseball program, for the game played at White City Stadium London 18th August 1935.

In general British baseball memorabilia is not nearly as collectible as American memorabilia.

$100-150 GBA

A 1945 Chicago Cubs v Detroit Tigers World Series program.

$300-500 HER

A 1960 Pittsburg Pirates World Series souvenir program, in near-mint condition.

$120-180 HER

A Fred Whiting 'Sandwich' oak mallet-head putter, with maker mark, with hide grip.
$250-350   MM

An unusual Korecta Reg. deep-faced putter, with raised top line and shaped aiming notch.
$150-250   MM

A Patrick Leven stained-beech long-nose curved-face short spoon, with original leather face-insert and ram's horn sole insert, with original hide grip.
c1880
$1,200-1,800   MM

A rare oversize pendulum dual-face mallet-head putter, in the style of the Hamilton patent, the beech head with two brace striking faces, with original leather grip.
Head 5.25in (13.5cm) wide
$300-500   MM

A mid-19thC hand-hammered gutty ball, with paint loss.
$500-700   GBA

A North British Rubber Co. pottery golf ball advertising model of a Scottie dog.

A pair of 1920s bronze and marble golfing bookends.
Taller 10in (25.5cm) high
$650-850   GBA

A Wileman & Co. Shelley match holder and striker, transfer-printed and hand-colored with a scene showing a golfer hitting a drive, the reverse with a crossed pair of drivers and four golf balls below 'Far and Sure', the base with registered number '360460'.
c1900   *2.5in (6.5cm) high*
$150-250   GBA

10.75in (27cm) high
$550-750   GBA

A 1908 London Olympic Games silvered-bronze steward's badge, by Vaughton & Son, Birmingham, inscribed 'OLYMPIC GAMES, LONDON 1908, STEWARD'.
$4,000-6,000   GBA

A 1912 Stockholm Olympic Games program, entitled (translated) 'Part 3 - Stadium and the Indoor Tennis 1912, in Images and Words'.
$400-600   GBA

A very rare Swedish printed-paper 'Olympiska Spelet 1912' parlor game, comprising a printed envelope and fold-out playing sheet printed with Olympic sports.

This is probably the first family parlor game inspired by the Olympic Games. On the throw of dice, players follow a numbered route around the 'board'.
$500-700   GBA

'VIIth OLYPIAD ANTWERP (BELGIUM)', an English-language poster for the 1920 Antwerp Olympic Games, designed by Martha van Kuyck and Walter van der Ven, with minor creases and tears.

1920   33.5in (85cm) high
$3,000-5,000   GBA

QUICK REFERENCE - OTL AICHER

- Otl Aicher (1922-91) established his own graphic design studio in 1948, having previously studied sculpture at the Munich Academy of Fine Arts.
- He was involved in the founding and development of the influential Ulm School of Design, which was open from 1953 until 1968.
- He is best known for his graphics for the 1972 Olympic Games in Munich. As well as his now-famous pictograms, Aicher and his team designed a series of posters for the Games, each depicting a different sport in the same color-saturated style. The first poster to be created showed the Olympic stadium and became the official poster for the 1972 Games.

'Munich 1972', an English-language poster for the 1972 Munich Olympic Games, designed by Otl Aicher, framed and glazed.
32.5in (82cm) high
$150-250   FLD

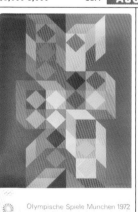

'Olympische Spiele München 1972', a German-language poster for the 1972 Munich Olympic Games, designed by Victor Vasarely.
39in (100cm) high
$200-300   WW

A signed 1996 Atlanta Olympic Games Team GB sprint suit, signed by John Regis and with dedication to the 'Sports Cafe'.
$200-300   GBA

SPORTING

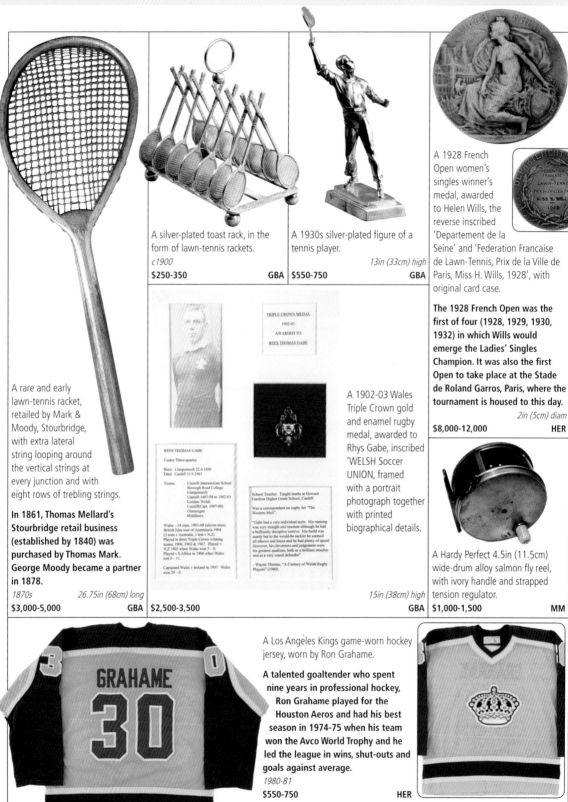

A silver-plated toast rack, in the form of lawn-tennis rackets.
c1900
$250-350   GBA

A 1930s silver-plated figure of a tennis player.
13in (33cm) high
$550-750   GBA

A 1928 French Open women's singles winner's medal, awarded to Helen Wills, the reverse inscribed 'Departement de la Seine' and 'Federation Francaise de Lawn-Tennis, Prix de la Ville de Paris, Miss H. Wills, 1928', with original card case.

The 1928 French Open was the first of four (1928, 1929, 1930, 1932) in which Wills would emerge the Ladies' Singles Champion. It was also the first Open to take place at the Stade de Roland Garros, Paris, where the tournament is housed to this day.
2in (5cm) diam
$8,000-12,000   HER

A rare and early lawn-tennis racket, retailed by Mark & Moody, Stourbridge, with extra lateral string looping around the vertical strings at every junction and with eight rows of trebling strings.

In 1861, Thomas Mellard's Stourbridge retail business (established by 1840) was purchased by Thomas Mark. George Moody became a partner in 1878.
1870s   26.75in (68cm) long
$3,000-5,000   GBA

TRIPLE CROWN MEDAL
1902-03
AWARDED TO
REES THOMAS GABE

REES THOMAS GABE
Centre Three-quarter
Born Llangennech 22.6.1880
Died   Cardiff 15.9.1967
Teams: Llanelli Intermediate School
               Borough Road College
               Llangennech
               Llanelli 1897-98 to 1902-03
               London Welsh
               Cardiff(Capt. 1907-08)
               Glamorgan
               Middlesex
Wales - 24 caps, 1901-08 (eleven tries).
British Isles tour of Australasia 1904
(3 tests v Australia, 1 test v N.Z)
Played in three Triple Crown winning
teams, 1900, 1902 & 1907. Played v
N.Z 1905 when Wales won 3 - 0.
Played v S.Africa in 1906 when Wales
lost 0 - 11.
Captained Wales v Ireland in 1907. Wales
won 29 - 0.

School Teacher. Taught maths at Howard
Gardens Higher Grade School, Cardiff.
Was a correspondent on rugby for "The
Western Mail".
"Gabe had a very individual style. His running
was very straight and resolute although he had
a brilliantly deceptive swerve. His build was
sturdy but to the would-be tackler he seemed
all elbows and knees and he had plenty of speed.
However, his cleverness and judgement were
his greatest qualities, both as a brilliant attacker
and as a very sound defender"
- Wayne Thomas, "A Century of Welsh Rugby
Players" (1980).

A 1902-03 Wales Triple Crown gold and enamel rugby medal, awarded to Rhys Gabe, inscribed 'WELSH Soccer UNION, framed with a portrait photograph together with printed biographical details.
15in (38cm) high
$2,500-3,500   GBA

A Hardy Perfect 4.5in (11.5cm) wide-drum alloy salmon fly reel, with ivory handle and strapped tension regulator.
$1,000-1,500   MM

A Los Angeles Kings game-worn hockey jersey, worn by Ron Grahame.

A talented goaltender who spent nine years in professional hockey, Ron Grahame played for the Houston Aeros and had his best season in 1974-75 when his team won the Avco World Trophy and he led the league in wins, shut-outs and goals against average.
1980-81
$550-750   HER

QUICK REFERENCE – TAXIDERMY

- Stuffed and mounted animals were popular decorative features during the mid-to-late Victorian and Edwardian eras. Taxidermy was then a display of wealth, travel and education, as it indicated that the owner was rich enough to travel and intelligent enough to hold an interest in the natural world.
- By the 1930s taxidermy had begun to go out of fashion and by the 1970s it was deemed both cruel and in bad taste. Most commercial outlets had also closed by this time.
- The past decade has seen a revival of interest in taxidermy, particularly among young people, who often use taxidermy as part of quirky, eclectic interiors.
- Fish and birds tend to be less controversial than other animals. Fish often also appeal to anglers, as well as to collectors of taxidermy. Exotic beasts tend to be rarer and are often more valuable than other stuffed animals.

- The quality of the preparation of the skin and the mounting is important – most towns had a taxidermist until the mid-20thC so quality varies widely. The work of notable taxidermists, such as Rowland Ward, John Cooper and Peter Spicer, is often the most valuable. In general, the more lifelike the animal looks, the better. A sense of drama or action can also add value.
- Condition is also important. Always consider the case, too, as this must also be in good condition, ideally with realistic backgrounds or settings. Some cases, such as glass domes, have a value in themselves.
- The sale and movement of many stuffed animals is strictly controlled, particularly with exotic species, so buyers and sellers should familiarize themselves with the relevant national and international laws.

A rare large stuffed and mounted salmon, by P D Malloch of Perth, in a barrel-fronted, glass-side case, the backboard inscribed 'CAUGHT IN THE 'PARRITCH HAUGH'. RIVER EARN. WITH FLY. 20th OCT. 1916. WEIGHT 40LBS. 4OZS.'.

P D Malloch was founded in 1871 and still exists today. It has been renowned for its expertise in, and fine quality equipment for, hunting and fishing for over a century.

1916   *54in (137cm) wide*
$4,000-6,000   L&T

A large stuffed and mounted salmon, in a glass-side oak case, the backboard painted '1903, BY P.M. COATS IN THE KILMOO HOLE UPPER STOBHALL WATER OF THE TAY. LENGTH 50 INCHES, GIRTH 32 INCHES, WEIGHT 51lbs. WINKINSON (NO.7) RECORD FOR SEASON.'.

1903   *51in (138cm) wide*
$1,500-2,500   L&T

A stuffed and mounted roach, by John Cooper & Sons, in a typical bowfront, glass-side case with gold line, with internal label reading 'Taken at Shepperton M.P. Heizman 17th Nov. 1878 wt 1lb 6 1/2 ozs'.

1878   *17.25in (44cm) wide*
$650-850   SWO

A stuffed and mounted trout, by John Cooper & Sons, in a typical bowfront, glass-side case with gold line, with internal trade and data label reading 'CAUGHT IN THE STAUNCH ST IVES, G A H MENCE, APRIL 5th 1899, WEIGHT 3 ½ lbs, PRESENTED TO ST IVES ANGLING SOCIETY'.

The Cooper family are renowned for their finely prepared fish, which, in many instances, still look as lifelike today as they did over a century ago.

1899   *25in (63cm) wide*
$800-1,200   SWO

A stuffed and mounted flying fish, attributed to Rowland Ward, mounted as if 'in flight' above simulated water, rock and weed, in an all-glass case.

Even though this is a very unusual fish and is possibly by the celebrated company of Rowland Ward, its value is relatively low. This is because the condition is poor and the remains are fragile. The wing tips are damaged and there are losses to the tail and back fins.

17in (43cm) wide
$300-500   SWO

Two stuffed and mounted rough-legged and common buzzards, by W A Macleay & Son, mounted on faux rocks with grass and fern groundwork, in a glass-front and -side case.

William Ashburton Macleay (1823-92) founded his company in Inverness, Scotland in 1854. He succeeded Lewis Dunbar, who was described as a 'bird stuffer'. His son, also William (1864-1932) continued the business. They are known to have stuffed many fish and birds, including a kiwi!

27in (68.5cm) high

$800-1,200   SWO

A pair of stuffed and mounted kingfishers, one mounted with open wings, mounted among reeds and grass, in a glass-front and -side case.

12in (30.5cm) high

$300-500   SWO

A stuffed and mounted green woodpecker, mounted on a branch with ferns and faux moss-covered rock, in a glass-front, -side and -top, wall-hanging case, with a trade label for Harrods Department Store, London.

Harrods employed top quality taxidermists to produce work for them. The case and mount are very fine quality.

17in (43cm) high

$500-700   SWO

A stuffed and mounted common buzzard, with a young rabbit prey, by E F Spicer, mounted on gorse and grass groundwork against a plate blue background, in a glass-front and -side hardwood case, with internal ivorine plaque, dated.

1927   24.5in (62cm) high

$250-350   SWO

A Victorian stuffed and mounted short-eared owl, mounted on a simulated wood stump and fern, under a glass dome, on an ebonized base with bun feet.

The style of the case and base indicates that this is a Victorian specimen.

22.5in (57cm) high

$400-600   SWO

A stuffed and mounted male copper pheasant and a male green pheasant, attributed to John Cooper & Sons, mounted among fern, moss and grass groundwork in a glass-side case with gold line, with crack to one side panel.

The gold line on the front of the case is a feature commonly associated with Cooper & Sons.

44.5in (113cm) wide

$300-500   SWO

Mark Picks

This lorikeet demonstrates much of the quality that one would expect to see from Ward, arguably the greatest name in taxidermy. It's mounted realistically, as if about to take flight, and the liveliness of the pose allows the full colors of the bird's wings to be displayed.

The bird was also well prepared and remains in great condition inside a fine quality all-glass case. The green taping on the case is a feature of Ward's taxidermy, as is the small ivorine identification label.

The appeal, color, condition and name all combine to make this a bird worth having in the hand!

A stuffed and mounted lorikeet, by Rowland Ward, mounted on a branch, in an all-glass case with green taping, with internal Ivorine trade label.

18.75in (48cm) high

$1,200-1,800   SWO

A stuffed and shoulder-mounted fox head, by F W Bartlett of Bunbury, mounted on an oak shield, the reverse with maker's label, also with inscription reading 'N.W.Hounds, Hunningham Coppice, Sept 1937'.

Fox heads are one of the most commonly found items of taxidermy. Unless of superb quality or by a major name known for fox heads, such as Spicer, the majority of fox heads currently sell for less than $150.
1937

$80-120 LC

Two stuffed and shoulder-mounted fox heads, one attributed to Hutchings of Aberystwyth, one with tail, both mounted on hardwood shields.

$150-250 SWO

A stuffed and shoulder-mounted melanistic roe deer head, by Rowland Ward, mounted on a hardwood shield, with ivorine plaque reading 'CAMBUSMORE OCTOBER 1929', the reverse with trade label.

Just as some cases have features that identify the taxidermist, the shape of the shield can also identify a taxidermist. This form of shield was only used by Rowland Ward.
1929 *Left antler 8in (20cm) long*

$300-500 SWO

QUICK REFERENCE - THE POLECAT

● The polecat used to be known as a 'foul mart' due to its strong smell. It has been hunted and persecuted for centuries and was commonly trapped for its fur, known as 'fitch'.

● This attitude and practice nearly drove the polecat to extinction during the late 19thC. It appeared to die out in Scotland and much of England, but was saved by World War I. Gamekeepers and hunters went off to fight and polecats gradually returned to England from the mountains in central Wales.

● This example is desirable and valuable because it is well mounted, in great condition, by a notable maker and because the redwing is an unusual prey.

A stuffed and mounted otter, by John Cooper & Sons, mounted on rockwork, with grass, reed and simulated water effect, in a bowfront, glass-side case with gold line, with internal trade label.

The pale blue background with a cloud is another feature commonly associated with Cooper's cases.
c1894 *43in (109.5cm) wide*

$300-500 SWO

A stuffed and mounted polecat, with redwing prey, by Hutchings of Aberystwyth, mounted on blue-tint rockwork, in a classic Hutchings-style case, missing trade label.
21.25in (54cm) high

$500-700 SWO

A Victorian stuffed and mounted wild rabbit, mounted sitting upright among grass and natural vegetation, in a glass dome with hardwood base and bun feet.
20.5in (52cm) high

$300-500 SWO

A late 19thC pair of stuffed and mounted red squirrels, mounted in a naturalistic setting, in a glass-front case.
21.75in (55cm) wide

$250-350 WW

TAXIDERMY

A stuffed and shoulder-mounted black buck head, mounted on a hardwood shield.

Left horn 17.75in (45cm) long

$250-350   SWO

A stuffed and shoulder-mounted red deer head, mounted on a hardwood polished shield, unlabeled.

Antler span 17.5in (44cm) long

$250-350   SWO

A stuffed and shoulder-mounted sassaby head, by Edward Gerrard & Sons, on mounted a hardwood shield with ivorine plaque reading 'SASSABY ZAMBESI 1904' and trade label.

1904   Left horn 13.5in (34cm) long

$300-500   SWO

A mounted set of warthog upper and lower horns, mounted on a hardwood shield, with inscribed brass shield.

This set of horns was acquired by Fritz Reinhard from the German infantry regiment 113 (Baden). Reinhard was appointed as captain of the protection unit for German East Africa and, before World War I, served in the German colonies where he also hunted.

c1913

$800-1,200   TEN

A stuffed and mounted snow leopard, mounted on faux rockwork, on later mahogany-effect plinth.

c1920   *19in (47cm) high*

$2,500-3,500   TEN

QUICK REFERENCE - CONDITION

- **A notable maker's name and the way an animal is prepared and mounted are vitally important to the desirability and value of a piece of taxidermy. However, the condition is also a major factor.**
- **As taxidermy went out of fashion in the second half of the 20thC, examples were often left to dry out or rot on display or were otherwise treated or stored badly.**
- **The open, snarling mouth and wrinkles on the nose suggest that this tiger's head may have been mounted by celebrated taxidermist Van Ingen & Van Ingen of Mysore, India (1900-90). However, the value is very low as the tiger lacks an ear and a couple of teeth and the fur is badly worn, particularly on the wrinkles and jaw. As this is almost impossible to restore properly, the value has been considerably reduced. If this piece had been in perfect condition, it could have been worth perhaps three times as much.**

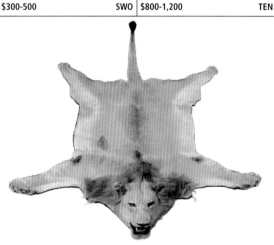

A lion skin rug, with head mount, the open jaw set with real teeth.

As this rug was prepared after 1945, it requires (and has) full CITES government licenses to be bought and sold. For more information about CITES, see 'Miller's Antiques Handbook & Price Guide 2014-2015', p.465.

1976   *117in (297cm) long*

$2,000-3,000   TEN

A stuffed and mounted tiger's head, with snarling expression and inset glass eyes, missing one ear and some teeth.

18.75in (48cm) high

$150-250   DN

QUICK REFERENCE - TEDDY BEARS

- Toy bears became known as teddy bears after American President Theodore (Teddy) Roosevelt refused to shoot a bear cub on a hunting trip in 1902. Entrepreneur Morris Michtom (who later founded the Ideal Novelty Company) made stuffed toys of 'Teddy's bear' and the craze began.
- The most prolific and famous makers were German and include Steiff, Schuco and Bing. Notable British makers include Chiltern, Merrythought and Chad Valley.

- Teddy bears made before World War II generally have long limbs, a pronounced snout and often a hump on their back. Post-war bears tend to be plumper, with shorter limbs and rounder heads. Be aware that many bears made from the 1980s onward are in the pre-war style.
- The shape of the head and its features will help to identify a maker, as will labels and their positioning. Always aim to buy in the best condition possible.

An unusual Steiff brown-mohair teddy bear, with black-stitched nose, mouth and claws, with jointed body, felt pads and larger than usual body, with 'FF' button, with two photographs of the original owner, one with this bear.

Photographs of the original owner with their bear will add desirability and value. This is also a rare, albeit faded, color.

c1908   16in (41cm) high

$1,500-2,500   SAS

A rare 1920s Bing white-mohair teddy bear, with glass eyes, pronounced clipped muzzle and brown-stitched nose, mouth and claws, with jointed body.

White mohair is rare.

21in (54cm) high

$3,000-4,000   SAS

A 1910s-20s German blond-mohair teddy bear, with replacement glass eyes, black re-stitched nose, mouth and claws and slotted-in ears, with swivel, jointed limbs, with replaced pads.

21in (54cm) high

$200-300   SAS

A 1920s German golden-mohair teddy bear, with glass eyes and black-stitched nose, mouth and claws, with jointed body, hump and inoperative growler, with wear and with replaced pads.

13.5in (34cm) high

$150-250   SAS

A 1920s American-type blond-mohair teddy bear, with glass eyes and black-stitched nose, mouth and claws, with jointed body and brown woven wool pads, with some wear.

20in (51cm) high

$120-180   SAS

A 1920s British golden-mohair teddy bear, with glass eyes and black-stitched nose, mouth and claws, with jointed body with cloth pads, with some wear and a few bald patches.

The form of the head and stitching suggests this bear may have been made by Chad Valley during the 1920s.

18in (46cm) high

$200-300   SAS

A 1920s red-mohair teddy bear, with boot-button eyes, black-stitched nose and mouth and 'slotted-in' ears with pink cloth linings, the jointed body and felt pads, with general wear and repairs to pads.

14.5in (37cm) high

$350-450   SAS

A 1930s pink-mohair teddy bear, possibly American, with glass eyes, black stitched nose and mouth and 'slotted-in' ears, with swivel head, with jointed body and felt pads, with inoperative growler and some slight wear.

24in (61cm) high

$500-700   SAS

A 1930s British golden-mohair teddy bear, with glass eyes and black-stitched nose, mouth and claws, with jointed body and cloth pads, with inoperative growler, slight wear and damaged pads.

27in (68cm) high

$120-180   SAS

A CLOSER LOOK AT A CHILTERN 'HUGMEE' BEAR

Chiltern produced their first teddy in 1916. The 'Hugmee' bear was introduced in 1923 and soon became the company's most popular and successful bear. _____

The shape of the head and the upturned paws are a characteristic of Chiltern's bears. _____

'Hugmee' bears from before World War II typically have shaven muzzles and two protruding stitches on top of the nose. _____

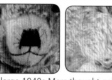

A large 1940s Merrythought golden-mohair teddy bear, with glass eyes, black-stitched nose, mouth, claws and webbed hand claws, with jointed body and brown felt pads, the foot with yellow printed label, with squeaker.

Even if the label was not present, it would still be possible to identify the maker of this bear. The characteristic stitching on the claws was only used by Farnell and Merrythought during this period. Merrythought's bears made at this time have less rounded heads than Farnell and have two stitches at the bottom of the nose, while Farnell's have two stitches on top of the nose.

28in (71cm) high

$300-500   SAS

Look out for pre-war 'Hugmee' bears in different colors. White and pastel blue, pink or green bears are rare and can be worth over three times the value of this bear.

A 1950s Chiltern blond-mohair 'Hugmee' musical teddy bear, with glass eyes and black-stitched nose, mouth and claws, with swivel head and jointed body, with velvet pads and pressure-operated musical mechanism.

17in (43cm) high

$300-500   SAS

A 1950s Chiltern beige-mohair 'Ting-a-Ling' teddy bear, with glass eyes and black-stitched nose, mouth and claws, with short-mohair pronounced inset muzzle and top of feet, with jointed body and Rexine pads, with inoperative growler, one replaced pad and general wear.

19in (48cm) high

$120-180   SAS

A rare 1920s British United Toy Manufacturing Company golden-mohair 'Omega Bear' on wheels, with glass eyes, black-stitched nose, mouth and claws and 'slotted-in' ears, on metal frame with wooden wheels.

14in (35cm) long

$300-500   SAS

A rare Steiff 'Molliette', with cream-mohair head, hands, feet and tail and orange-velvet body, with glass eyes and black-stitched nose, mouth and remains of claws, with swivel head and large 'FF' button, with wear, the ears re-attached.

A cross between a fabric doll and a teddy bear, the floppy, velvet-bodied 'Molliette' was produced by Steiff 1927-32. It can be found with a red, purpley-blue or green body.

c1929   *11in (28cm) high*
$250-350   SAS

A rare Steiff 'Rabbiette', with mohair head, hands and feet and velvet body, with glass eyes, pink-stitched nose and black-stitched mouth and claws, with swivel head, remains of suspension cord from head and large 'FF' button, with fading and wear.

c1929   *8in (21cm) high*
$250-350   SAS

A 1930s Norah Wellings beige-plush-wool rabbit, with glass eyes, with jointed neck, with integral light-blue velveteen trousers, the right foot with label, with fading, with hand-knitted green gym slip.

This rabbit and the mouse on this page were dressed in green knitted clothing by a collector. Most other collectors would prefer to remove this recent addition.

8.5in (22cm) high
$40-60   VEC

A Schuco character 'Mouse' tumbling figure, with black metal bead eyes, black horizontally-stitched nose, felt hands, feet and clothes, with hand-knitted gym slip with red sash.

3in (8cm) high
$60-80   VEC

A rare 1920s German gray-mohair squirrel, with boot-button eyes and brown-stitched nose and mouth, with jointed body and mohair wired tail.

This squirrel is virtually identical to the Steiff squirrel produced 1925-33, but this example does not have the tail joint. It is most probably by Strunz, as that company is well known for having copied Steiff products.

9.5in (23.5cm) high
$650-850   SAS

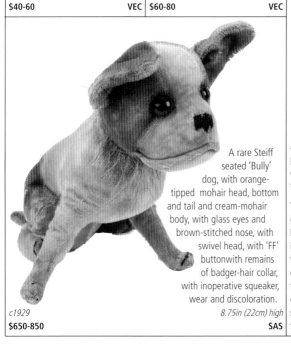

A rare Steiff seated 'Bully' dog, with orange-tipped mohair head, bottom and tail and cream-mohair body, with glass eyes and brown-stitched nose, with swivel head, with 'FF' button with remains of badger-hair collar, with inoperative squeaker, wear and discoloration.

c1929   *8.75in (22cm) high*
$650-850   SAS

A 1950s gold-plush 'Sooty' glove puppet, as used by Harry H Corbett on his BBC Television show during the late 1950s and early 1960s.

The size suggests that this is a genuine professional example to be used by an adult hand, as the length of the puppet is too large for a small child. A letter of authenticity was sold with the puppet explaining how it came to be in the vendor's son's possession.

$1,000-1,500   W&W

A rare 1930s Farnell Alpha 'Baby Bunting' rabbit-girl doll, with white-mohair body, hood and ears and pressed-felt face with painted features, with swivel head, with pink-velvet lining to ears and white-felt hands and feet pads, with inoperative squeaker, the foot with blue and white woven label.

22in (55.5cm) high
$550-750   SAS

TELEPHONES

A late Victorian 'Eiffel Tower'-style brass, ebony and lacquered telephone, with a hand crank, circular dial and two bells.

Developed in 1890, the 'skeleton' or 'Eiffel Tower' style of telephone was the world's first phone to be put into mainstream production. From 1892, L M Ericsson, who had invented the phone, sold parts for assembly to manufacturers around the world. In the USA, the 'Eiffel Tower' phone was made by Bell. In the UK, it was known as a GPO 'Type 16'.

c1890   *12in (30cm) high*
$500-700   **GHOU**

A Telefonbau & Normalzeit (Fuld & Co.) black Bakelite and brass telephone, designed at the Bauhaus, Dessau in 1928.

These phones were designed for the 'New Frankfurt' housing project. They were produced for sale in different variations into the 1930s.

5in (13cm) high
$1,200-1,800   **QU**

A Telefonbau & Normalzeit (Fuld & Co.) black Bakelite and brass telephone, designed at the Bauhaus, Dessau in 1928, marked '7801 FN 3/40B, 123028'.

5in (13cm) high
$1,200-1,800   **QU**

A Telefonbau & Normalzeit (Fuld & Co.) black Bakelite metal telephone exchange, designed at the Bauhaus, Dessau in 1928, with dark red and gray switches, marked 'Fuld, 7862, IN 12/2'.

5in (13cm) high
$1,200-1,800   **QU**

An early 1950s Siemens & Halske black Bakelite telephone, with a cylindrical vertically revolving dialing drum, designed in 1950.

The way this receiver is mounted means that it can be used equally well by left- and right-handed people. This phone is very rare in ivory and even rarer in green.

$300-500   **DOR**

A GPO black Bakelite 'Type 232' telephone, with dial and dialing-code drawer, dated.

1946
$80-120   **RW**

A 1950s GPO ivory Bakelite 'Type 312' telephone, with dial and dialing-code drawer.

6in (14.5cm) high
$150-250   **ROS**

A late 1950s-60s Ericsson red plastic 'Ericophone' telephone, with dialing mechanism inset into base.

The unusual shape of this phone has led to it being known as the 'Cobra' phone.

9in (22cm) high
$70-100   **WHP**

QUICK REFERENCE - TILES

- Glazed ceramic tiles have been produced as a resilient and decorative floor and wall covering from the earliest of times. They were often used in countries with a warm climate as they helped keep a room cool. Hubs of tile production grew in Persia and Turkey, but tiles were also produced in quantity across the Middle and Near East, and in northern Africa. The 15thC to the 18thC saw tin-glazed tiles also being produced in the Netherlands, England, Spain and, later, the USA.

- The golden age of tile production came during the 19thC. Industrialisation, new production methods and an improved distribution network were combined with a countrywide boom in house building, meaning that tiles were both desirable and easy to produce. This golden age continued until the mid-20thC, when many tile companies, or departments within larger companies, either went out of business or were merged into increasingly large companies, such as Richards Tiles or H & R Johnson. Designs tended to become less inventive after the 1930s.

- Interest in Victorian and Edwardian tiles was revived in the 1960s and '70s, when many Victorian buildings were pulled down, and their fixtures and fittings sold off.

- The work of leading designers, such as William De Morgan or A N W Pugin, tends to be the most desirable and valuable. Also look out for major makers, such as Minton, Maw and Wedgwood and American Arts & Crafts makers, such as Grueby and Rookwood. A tile that has a design that is typical of a particular style, particularly Aesthetic Movement, Arts & Crafts and Art Nouveau, is likely to be collectible.

- As tiles were usually affixed to a wall or floor at some point, consider damage carefully. Avoid those tiles that are chipped or, worse, cracked, unless rare.

A William De Morgan 'Persian' tile, Sand's End Pottery.

6in (15cm) wide

$800-1,200   WW

A William De Morgan 'Mongolian' tile, on a Poole Architectural blank, the reverse with impressed marks, with minor restoration to one corner.

William de Morgan (1839-1917) began designing tiles in the 1860s at his premises in Cheyne Row, Chelsea, London, and used blanks from companies including the Architectural Pottery Co. in Poole and later Carter & Co., until he began making blanks himself.

6in (15cm) wide

$300-500   WW

A William De Morgan tile, painted with boughs of foliage with blue berries, the reverse impressed 'No.5'.

De Morgan was influenced by ancient Turkish Iznik tiles and the work of Arts & Crafts champion William Morris, who was a close friend. This tile particularly shows Morris's influence.

6in (15cm) wide

$250-350   WW

A William De Morgan 'Flamingo' tile, on a Carter's Architectural blank, with chipped edge.

The flamingo is cleverly interwoven into the stylized floral and foliate design, but it can be seen on the bottom left.

6in (15cm) wide

$300-500   WW

A William De Morgan 'BBB' tile, Early Fulham period, decorated with ruby luster glaze, the reverse with impressed mark, with light surface wear.

6in (15cm) wide

$250-350   WW

A William De Morgan 'KL Rose' pattern tile, the reverse with impressed mark.

6in (15cm) wide

$300-500   WW

TILES

A large William De Morgan 'Marlborough' tile, Sand's End Pottery, the reverse with impressed mark.

8in (20.5cm) wide

$1,200-1,800   WW

A William De Morgan tile, painted with a carnation and segmented leaf design, on a Carter's Architectural blank, the reverse with impressed marks.

6in (15cm) wide

$300-500   WW

A William De Morgan tile, Late Fulham period, the reverse with impressed mark, with minor chips.

6in (15cm) wide

$120-180   WW

A William De Morgan 'Persian' tile, painted with a parrot perched in a tree bough, unsigned, with professional restoration.

This tile came from the collection of the notable De Morgan researcher and author Jon Catleugh.

6in (15cm) wide

$550-750   WW

A large William De Morgan 'Parrot' tile, Sands End Pottery, the reverse with impressed mark.

8in (20.5cm) wide

$1,200-1,800   WW

A William De Morgan 'Persian Eagle and Snake' tile, unmarked, with restoration.

6in (15cm) wide

$2,000-3,000   WW

A CLOSER LOOK AT A WILLIAM DE MORGAN TILE

Although De Morgan took inspiration from many places (see p.351), his designs featuring animals and mythical beasts are very much his own.

Some De Morgan tiles were inspired by Medieval illustrated manuscripts.

This dramatic scene has the flat planes of perspective and bold color typical of De Morgan's work.

Tiles with mythical beasts are much rarer than De Morgan's floral designs.

A William De Morgan 'Ornate Bird' tile, with blue spacer-tile border, framed.

Bird tile 6in (15cm) wide

$1,500-2,500   WW

A William De Morgan tile, Chelsea period, painted with a griffin attacking a cat-like creature, the reverse with impressed marks.

6in (15cm) wide

$5,000-7,000   WW

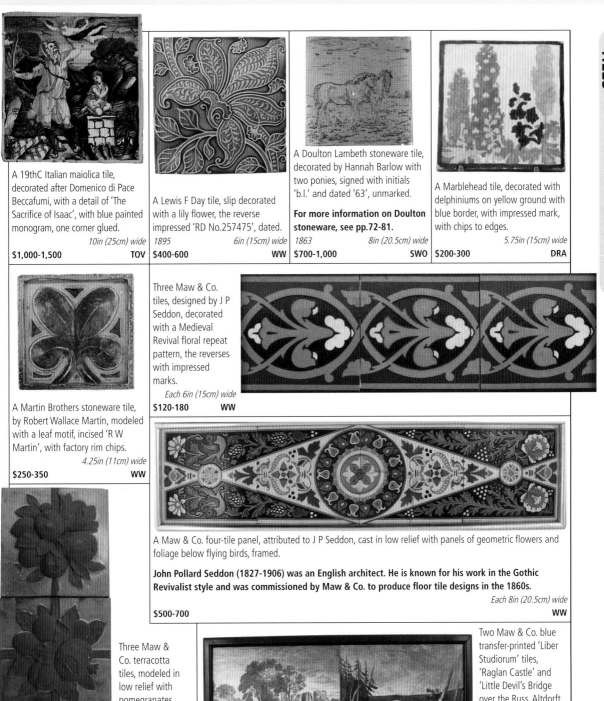

A 19thC Italian maiolica tile, decorated after Domenico di Pace Beccafumi, with a detail of 'The Sacrifice of Isaac', with blue painted monogram, one corner glued.

10in (25cm) wide

$1,000-1,500 TOV

A Lewis F Day tile, slip decorated with a lily flower, the reverse impressed 'RD No.257475', dated.

1895 *6in (15cm) wide*

$400-600 WW

A Doulton Lambeth stoneware tile, decorated by Hannah Barlow with two ponies, signed with initials 'b.l.' and dated '63', unmarked.

For more information on Doulton stoneware, see pp.72-81.

1863 *8in (20.5cm) wide*

$700-1,000 SWO

A Marblehead tile, decorated with delphiniums on yellow ground with blue border, with impressed mark, with chips to edges.

5.75in (15cm) wide

$200-300 DRA

A Martin Brothers stoneware tile, by Robert Wallace Martin, modeled with a leaf motif, incised 'R W Martin', with factory rim chips.

4.25in (11cm) wide

$250-350 WW

Three Maw & Co. tiles, designed by J P Seddon, decorated with a Medieval Revival floral repeat pattern, the reverses with impressed marks.

Each 6in (15cm) wide

$120-180 WW

A Maw & Co. four-tile panel, attributed to J P Seddon, cast in low relief with panels of geometric flowers and foliage below flying birds, framed.

John Pollard Seddon (1827-1906) was an English architect. He is known for his work in the Gothic Revivalist style and was commissioned by Maw & Co. to produce floor tile designs in the 1860s.

Each 8in (20.5cm) wide

$500-700 WW

Three Maw & Co. terracotta tiles, modeled in low relief with pomegranates, partially glazed in gray-green, the reverse with impressed marks, with minor chips.

Each 6in (15cm) wide

$80-120 WW

Two Maw & Co. blue transfer-printed 'Liber Studiorum' tiles, 'Raglan Castle' and 'Little Devil's Bridge over the Russ, Altdorft, Switzerland', after the original prints by J M W Turner, the reverses with impressed marks, framed.

Each 8in (20.5cm) wide

$300-500 WW

TILES

An Alfred Meakin ten-tile panel, slip decorated with a stylized callalily, in the manner of C F A Voysey, framed.

Each 6in (15cm) wide

$400-600   **WW**

A Mintons tile, designed by A W N Pugin, printed and painted with a geometric flower design, unmarked.

9in (23cm) wide

$300-500   **WW**

A Mintons Aesthetic Movement tile, painted with a frog among flowers.

6in (15cm) wide

$120-180   **WW**

A large Minton & Hollins tile, painted with a vase of pink and white peony flowers, the reverse with impressed marks, framed.

12in (30cm) wide

$150-250   **WW**

A Minton & Hollins tile, designed by Walter Crane, printed and painted with Little Bo Peep in a riverscape, signed 'CB', the reverse with impressed marks.

6in (15cm) wide

$150-250   **WW**

A Minton, Hollins & Co. tile, painted with a Medieval figure sowing seeds in an orchard landscape, indistinctly signed 'Fournier', the reverse with impressed marks.

11in (28cm) high

$1,000-1,500 WW

One of a set of sixteen Mintons terracotta tiles, attributed to Christopher Dresser, decorated with orange branches.

Each 4in (10cm) wide

$300-500 set   **DRA**

A Morris & Co. tile, painted with a paneled design of flowers and foliage sprays.

6in (15cm) wide

$50-70   **WW**

A Morris & Co. tin-glazed 'Scroll' pattern tile, unmarked, with damage.

6in (15cm) wide

$70-100   **WW**

A Herman Mueller tile, decorated with a ship at sea, the reverse with stamped marks, with chips to edges.

1910

6in (15cm) high

$600-800 **DRA**

Judith Picks

Edward Bawden (1903-89) is one of the 20thC's best illustrators and artists. Tiles by him are rare. These examples are visually appealing and are typical of his bold, linear style. They also have cross-market interest and would appeal to collectors of smoking memorabilia and Art Deco design, as well as collectors of Poole Pottery. As they were produced for the tea rooms at the pottery, rather than commercially, only a limited number were made and even fewer survive today. These factors mean these tiles should rise in value in the future - particularly the 'Pottery Making' tile!

Two Poole Pottery tiles, 'Ashtray' and 'Pottery Making (Handling)', designed by Edward Bawden for the Poole Pottery Tearooms.

c1932 *Each 5in (13cm) wide*

$550-750 **SWO**

A Pilkington's Royal Lancastrian tile, molded in low relief with a heraldic dragon, decorated in a copper luster on a blue ground, the reverse impressed 'P', with minor glaze nicks.

6in (15cm) wide

$250-350 **WW**

A Sherwin & Cotton 'The Monks' three-tile panel, designed by George Cartlidge, the reverse with impressed marks, framed.

12in (31.5cm) long

$200-300 **WW**

A set of four Ratton limited edition tiles, 'Frightened Fox', 'Woman and Lion', 'Hypnotising a Dog' and 'Woman and Marabou', designed by Paula Rego for the Tate Gallery, nos.49 and 45 from editions of 100, the reverses hand signed, framed, with original paper slipcases and certificates.

Each 5.5in (14cm) wide

$3,000-5,000 **WW**

A pair of large tile panels, each with two tiles decorated with allegorical figures in the manner of Walter Crane, framed.

Each 16.25in (41cm) high

$4,000-6,000 **WW**

An early Samuel Wright encaustic 'Marian' tile, probably designed by A W N Pugin for St Mary's College, Oscott, unsigned.

6in (15cm) wide

$500-700 **WW**

An Aesthetic Movement four-tile panel, printed with a wading crane in shades of green, framed.

11.5in (29.5cm) wide

$120-180 **WW**

QUICK REFERENCE - TOOLS

- Changing tastes in interior design and a growth in manufacturing during the late 17thC created the need for specialist tools to produce increasingly complex forms and patterns. Before this time, craftsmen generally made the tools they needed themselves.
- Tool making expanded in the 18thC and reached a peak in the 19thC. It declined in the 1930s-40s as ready-made furniture and parts began to be produced commercially.
- Planes are among the most collected tools and are often the most valuable. Makers such as Norris in the UK and Stanley in the USA have large followings.

- Although the value of tools is predominantly dependent on the quality and precision of their mechanical engineering, the age, design and decoration also count toward desirability. Tools that have a 'folk art' appearance may also be of interest to folk art collectors.
- The shape and purpose of a tool can help to date it, as can the material, methods of construction and any decorative features. Read specialist books to learn more.
- Always consider condition. Check for damaged or missing parts and woodworm in wooden parts, as this will reduce value. Original packaging is generally very rare.

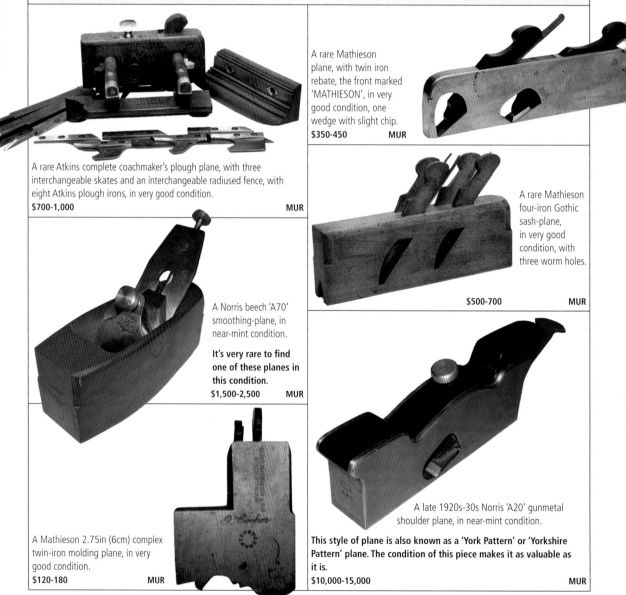

A rare Atkins complete coachmaker's plough plane, with three interchangeable skates and an interchangeable radiused fence, with eight Atkins plough irons, in very good condition.
$700-1,000   MUR

A rare Mathieson plane, with twin iron rebate, the front marked 'MATHIESON', in very good condition, one wedge with slight chip.
$350-450   MUR

A rare Mathieson four-iron Gothic sash-plane, in very good condition, with three worm holes.
$500-700   MUR

A Norris beech 'A70' smoothing-plane, in near-mint condition.

It's very rare to find one of these planes in this condition.
$1,500-2,500   MUR

A Mathieson 2.75in (6cm) complex twin-iron molding plane, in very good condition.
$120-180   MUR

A late 1920s-30s Norris 'A20' gunmetal shoulder plane, in near-mint condition.

This style of plane is also known as a 'York Pattern' or 'Yorkshire Pattern' plane. The condition of this piece makes it as valuable as it is.
$10,000-15,000   MUR

A CLOSER LOOK AT A PLANE

Its smaller toe allowed this plane to have greater access, making it sought-after by cabinet and instrument makers.

Norris was the only company to incorporate an adjuster on this style of plane.

This is a very rare plane. At this size (1 1/8) it cost 22/- in 1928.

It is extremely rare, and made more desirable and valuable, because it retains its original box and has never been used.

A late 1920s Norris gunmetal 'A27' bullnose plane, with rosewood handle, in mint condition, with original box.
$25,000-35,000   MUR

A Preston chamfer plane.
$120-180   MUR

A pair of Preston airtight casemaker's planes.
$150-250   MUR

A very rare Preston iron spill-plane, in good condition.
$200-300   MUR

A rare Spiers 1.25in (3cm) skew-mouthed shoulder plane, in dirty but very good condition.

Spiers made planes from c1840 until c1936.
$550-750   MUR

A Stanley 'No.97' plane, in good condition.

This number is also applied to a cabinetmaker's edge-plane by Stanley. That version is exceptionally rare and can fetch up to ten times this amount.
$400-600   MUR

A set of three brass violinmaker's planes, each blade stamped 'TN' for Thomas Norris, in very good condition.
$1,200-1,800   MUR

An unusual cast-iron chariot plane, with a brass lever-cap.
6.5in (16.5cm) long
$300-500   MUR

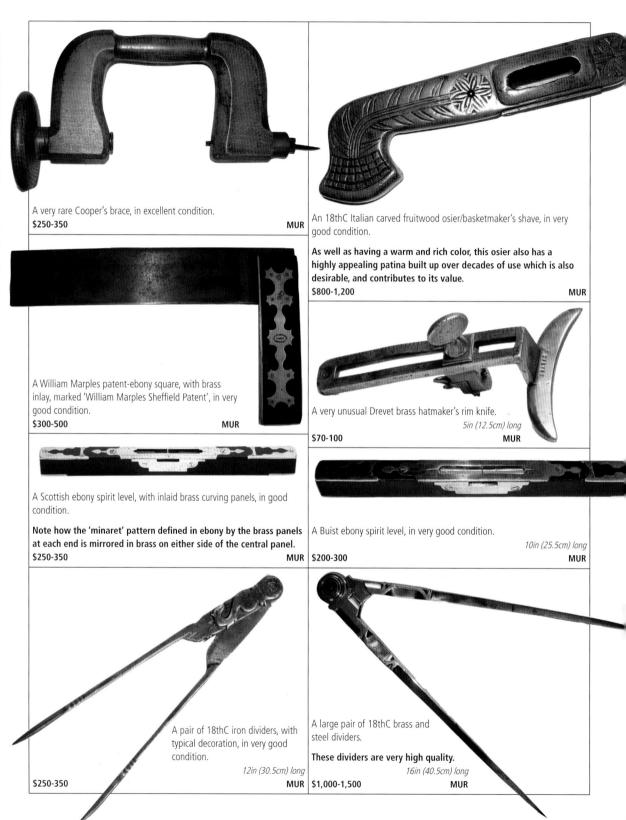

A very rare Cooper's brace, in excellent condition.

$250-350   MUR

An 18thC Italian carved fruitwood osier/basketmaker's shave, in very good condition.

As well as having a warm and rich color, this osier also has a highly appealing patina built up over decades of use which is also desirable, and contributes to its value.

$800-1,200   MUR

A William Marples patent-ebony square, with brass inlay, marked 'William Marples Sheffield Patent', in very good condition.

$300-500   MUR

A very unusual Drevet brass hatmaker's rim knife.

5in (12.5cm) long

$70-100   MUR

A Scottish ebony spirit level, with inlaid brass curving panels, in good condition.

Note how the 'minaret' pattern defined in ebony by the brass panels at each end is mirrored in brass on either side of the central panel.

$250-350   MUR

A Buist ebony spirit level, in very good condition.

10in (25.5cm) long

$200-300   MUR

A pair of 18thC iron dividers, with typical decoration, in very good condition.

12in (30.5cm) long

$250-350   MUR

A large pair of 18thC brass and steel dividers.

These dividers are very high quality.

16in (40.5cm) long

$1,000-1,500   MUR

TOOLS

TOOLS 359

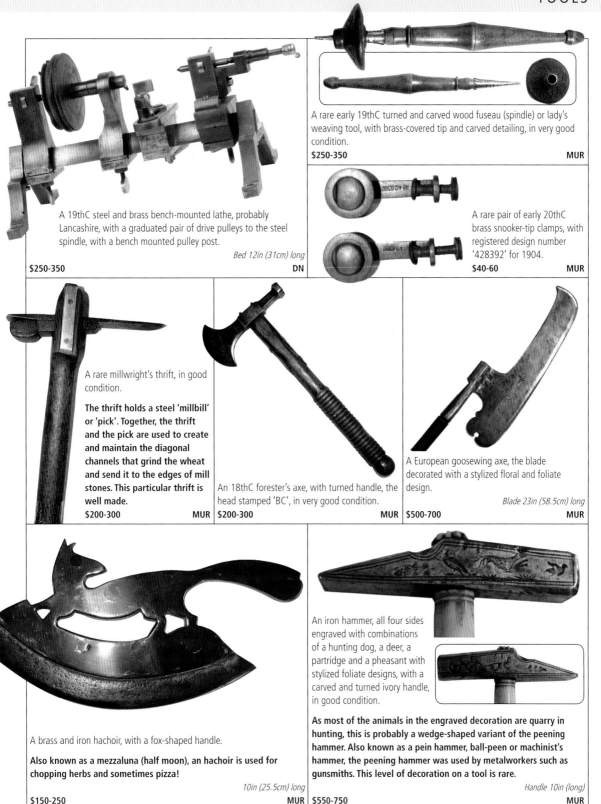

A 19thC steel and brass bench-mounted lathe, probably Lancashire, with a graduated pair of drive pulleys to the steel spindle, with a bench mounted pulley post.

Bed 12in (31cm) long

$250-350 · DN

A rare early 19thC turned and carved wood fuseau (spindle) or lady's weaving tool, with brass-covered tip and carved detailing, in very good condition.

$250-350 · MUR

A rare pair of early 20thC brass snooker-tip clamps, with registered design number '428392' for 1904.

$40-60 · MUR

A rare millwright's thrift, in good condition.

The thrift holds a steel 'millbill' or 'pick'. Together, the thrift and the pick are used to create and maintain the diagonal channels that grind the wheat and send it to the edges of mill stones. This particular thrift is well made.

$200-300 · MUR

An 18thC forester's axe, with turned handle, the head stamped 'BC', in very good condition.

$200-300 · MUR

A European goosewing axe, the blade decorated with a stylized floral and foliate design.

Blade 23in (58.5cm) long

$500-700 · MUR

A brass and iron hachoir, with a fox-shaped handle.

Also known as a mezzaluna (half moon), an hachoir is used for chopping herbs and sometimes pizza!

10in (25.5cm) long

$150-250 · MUR

An iron hammer, all four sides engraved with combinations of a hunting dog, a deer, a partridge and a pheasant with stylized foliate designs, with a carved and turned ivory handle, in good condition.

As most of the animals in the engraved decoration are quarry in hunting, this is probably a wedge-shaped variant of the peening hammer. Also known as a pein hammer, ball-peen or machinist's hammer, the peening hammer was used by metalworkers such as gunsmiths. This level of decoration on a tool is rare.

Handle 10in (long)

$550-750 · MUR

TOYS & GAMES

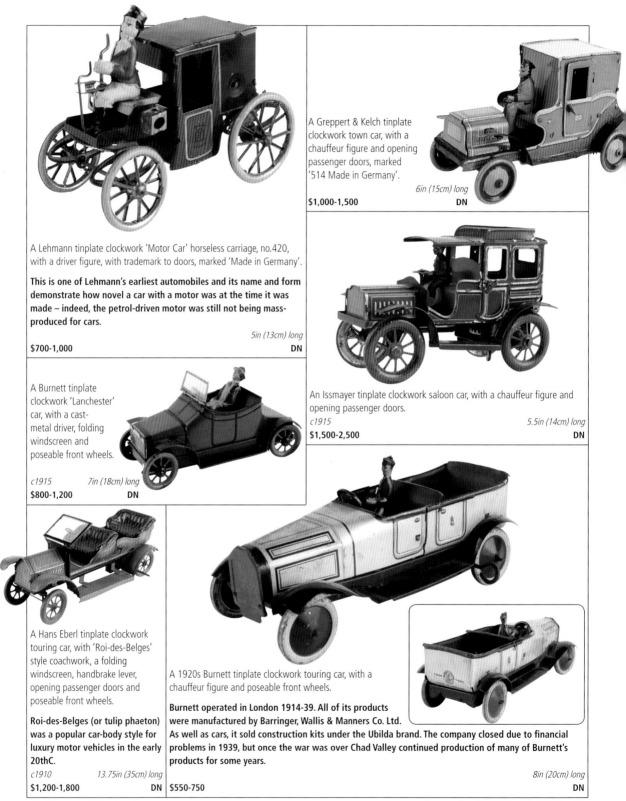

A Greppert & Kelch tinplate clockwork town car, with a chauffeur figure and opening passenger doors, marked '514 Made in Germany'.

6in (15cm) long

$1,000-1,500   **DN**

A Lehmann tinplate clockwork 'Motor Car' horseless carriage, no.420, with a driver figure, with trademark to doors, marked 'Made in Germany'.

This is one of Lehmann's earliest automobiles and its name and form demonstrate how novel a car with a motor was at the time it was made – indeed, the petrol-driven motor was still not being mass-produced for cars.

5in (13cm) long

$700-1,000   **DN**

A Burnett tinplate clockwork 'Lanchester' car, with a cast-metal driver, folding windscreen and poseable front wheels.

c1915   7in (18cm) long

$800-1,200   **DN**

An Issmayer tinplate clockwork saloon car, with a chauffeur figure and opening passenger doors.

c1915   5.5in (14cm) long

$1,500-2,500   **DN**

A Hans Eberl tinplate clockwork touring car, with 'Roi-des-Belges' style coachwork, a folding windscreen, handbrake lever, opening passenger doors and poseable front wheels.

Roi-des-Belges (or tulip phaeton) was a popular car-body style for luxury motor vehicles in the early 20thC.

c1910   13.75in (35cm) long

$1,200-1,800   **DN**

A 1920s Burnett tinplate clockwork touring car, with a chauffeur figure and poseable front wheels.

Burnett operated in London 1914-39. All of its products were manufactured by Barringer, Wallis & Manners Co. Ltd.
As well as cars, it sold construction kits under the Ubilda brand. The company closed due to financial problems in 1939, but once the war was over Chad Valley continued production of many of Burnett's products for some years.

8in (20cm) long

$550-750   **DN**

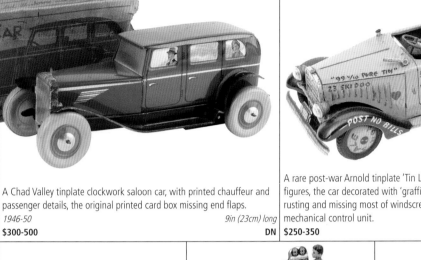

A Chad Valley tinplate clockwork saloon car, with printed chauffeur and passenger details, the original printed card box missing end flaps.

1946-50   *9in (23cm) long*

$300-500   DN

A rare post-war Arnold tinplate 'Tin Lizzy' car, with four composition figures, the car decorated with 'graffiti', in good condition, with some rusting and missing most of windscreen, with inoperative hand-held mechanical control unit.

$250-350   W&W

A rare Lineol clockwork tinplate World War II German army staff/field car, with battery-powered headlights, Ackermann steering and semaphore indicators, missing figures, windscreen and other small parts.

$200-300   W&W

A 1950s-60s TPS tinplate battery-operated 'Porsche 911' 'News Service Car', with 'WORLD NEWS' printed designs, with original box.

TPS (Tokyo Plaything Shokai) is a Japanese company, founded in 1956.

$200-300   W&W

A 1960s Taiyo tinplate 'VW Beetle', the rear seat printed 'Taiyo Made in Japan', with a battery-operated 'mystery' action.

9.5in (24.5cm) long

$80-120   DN

A Gunthermann 'Bluebird' tinplate clockwork racing car.

Bluebird was driven by Malcolm Campbell who held thirteen world speed records in the 1920s and 1930s. This model was produced by Gunthermann in two different sizes. This is the larger size and the most expensive, both at the time and now.

20in (51cm) long

$1,500-2,500   LC

A Kingsbury tinplate 'Golden Arrow' racing car, finished in gilt, with Dunlop Racking cord hard-rubber types, with some wear.

Designed by J S Irving and piloted by Major Henry Segrave, the 'Golden Arrow' won the land-speed record on 11th March 1929 by hitting 231.45mph on Daytona Sands. It never raced again. It can now be seen at the National Motor Museum in Beaulieu, UK.

1929   *19.25in (49cm) long*

$550-750   BATE

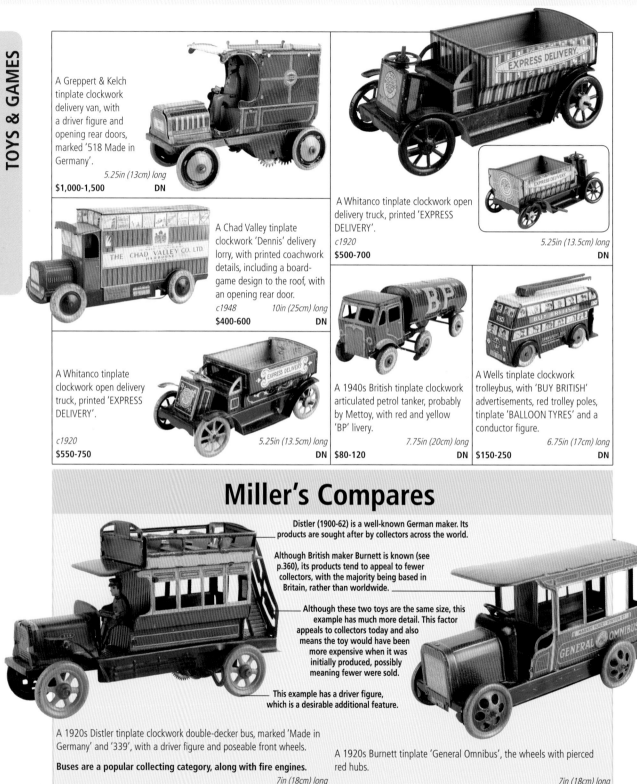

A Greppert & Kelch tinplate clockwork delivery van, with a driver figure and opening rear doors, marked '518 Made in Germany'.

5.25in (13cm) long

$1,000-1,500   DN

A Chad Valley tinplate clockwork 'Dennis' delivery lorry, with printed coachwork details, including a board-game design to the roof, with an opening rear door.

c1948   *10in (25cm) long*

$400-600   DN

A Whitanco tinplate clockwork open delivery truck, printed 'EXPRESS DELIVERY'.

c1920   *5.25in (13.5cm) long*

$550-750   DN

A Whitanco tinplate clockwork open delivery truck, printed 'EXPRESS DELIVERY'.

c1920

$500-700   DN

5.25in (13.5cm) long

A 1940s British tinplate clockwork articulated petrol tanker, probably by Mettoy, with red and yellow 'BP' livery.

7.75in (20cm) long

$80-120   DN

A Wells tinplate clockwork trolleybus, with 'BUY BRITISH' advertisements, red trolley poles, tinplate 'BALLOON TYRES' and a conductor figure.

6.75in (17cm) long

$150-250   DN

Miller's Compares

Distler (1900-62) is a well-known German maker. Its products are sought after by collectors across the world.

Although British maker Burnett is known (see p.360), its products tend to appeal to fewer collectors, with the majority being based in Britain, rather than worldwide.

Although these two toys are the same size, this example has much more detail. This factor appeals to collectors today and also means the toy would have been more expensive when it was initially produced, possibly meaning fewer were sold.

This example has a driver figure, which is a desirable additional feature.

A 1920s Distler tinplate clockwork double-decker bus, marked 'Made in Germany' and '339', with a driver figure and poseable front wheels.

Buses are a popular collecting category, along with fire engines.

7in (18cm) long

$2,000-3,000   DN

A 1920s Burnett tinplate 'General Omnibus', the wheels with pierced red hubs.

7in (18cm) long

$650-850   DN

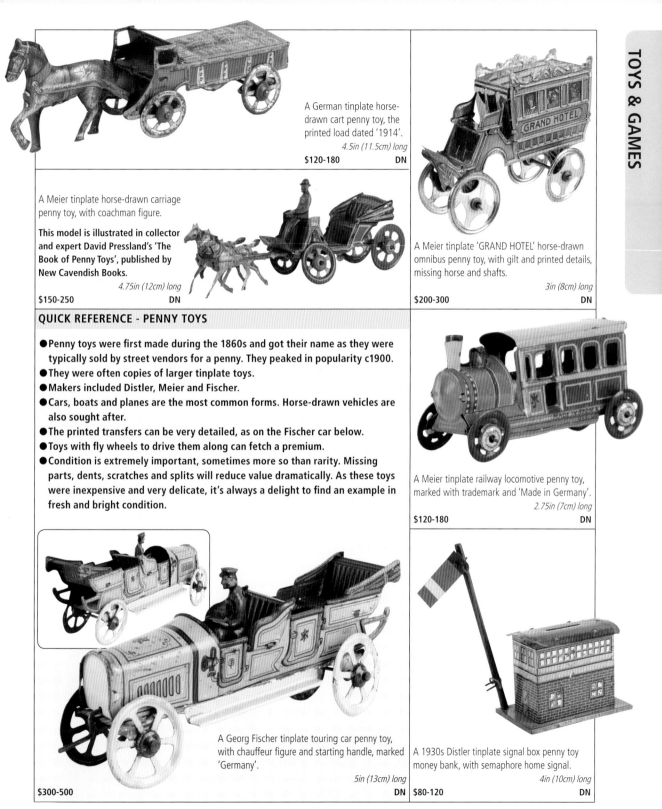

A German tinplate horse-drawn cart penny toy, the printed load dated '1914'.

4.5in (11.5cm) long

$120-180   DN

A Meier tinplate horse-drawn carriage penny toy, with coachman figure.

This model is illustrated in collector and expert David Pressland's 'The Book of Penny Toys', published by New Cavendish Books.

4.75in (12cm) long

$150-250   DN

A Meier tinplate 'GRAND HOTEL' horse-drawn omnibus penny toy, with gilt and printed details, missing horse and shafts.

3in (8cm) long

$200-300   DN

QUICK REFERENCE - PENNY TOYS

- Penny toys were first made during the 1860s and got their name as they were typically sold by street vendors for a penny. They peaked in popularity c1900.
- They were often copies of larger tinplate toys.
- Makers included Distler, Meier and Fischer.
- Cars, boats and planes are the most common forms. Horse-drawn vehicles are also sought after.
- The printed transfers can be very detailed, as on the Fischer car below.
- Toys with fly wheels to drive them along can fetch a premium.
- Condition is extremely important, sometimes more so than rarity. Missing parts, dents, scratches and splits will reduce value dramatically. As these toys were inexpensive and very delicate, it's always a delight to find an example in fresh and bright condition.

A Meier tinplate railway locomotive penny toy, marked with trademark and 'Made in Germany'.

2.75in (7cm) long

$120-180   DN

A Georg Fischer tinplate touring car penny toy, with chauffeur figure and starting handle, marked 'Germany'.

5in (13cm) long

$300-500   DN

A 1930s Distler tinplate signal box penny toy money bank, with semaphore home signal.

4in (10cm) long

$80-120   DN

TOYS & GAMES

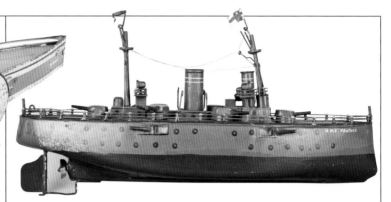

A German tinplate side-wheel gunboat, unmarked, with twin funnels and a revolving forward gun, the hull with further gun details, fitted with a clockwork motor.

c1920   *8.5in (21.5cm) long*

$300-500   **DN**

A Märklin tinplate battleship, with two masts, two funnels and six rotating twin-barreled guns, the superstructure removable, the bow later painted 'H.M.S. PANTHER', the lower hull and rudder repainted, the interior refitted with electrics.

Märklin is at the top of the tree of tinplate toys and its most desirable types include boats and airships. The larger and more detailed a Märklin boat is, the more it is likely to be worth, especially if it has its original finish.

c1910   *14.5in (37cm) long*

$8,000-12,000   **DN**

A Paton, Calvert & Co. tinplate 'MISS HAPPYNAK' speed boat, with an elastic-band-propelled mechanism, with a skipper figure and a hinged rudder, the original box with wear.

c1935   *11.25in (28.5cm) long*

$150-250   **DN**

A 1930s Hornby tinplate clockwork No. 3 'RACER III' speedboat, with both windshields, steering wheel and key, with box.

$200-300   **W&W**

A rare Sutcliffe tinplate clockwork 'VALIANT' battleship, complete with mast, flag and stand, in near-mint condition, with original box.

$200-300   **W&W**

A rare Sutcliffe tinplate clockwork 'DIANA' cruiser, in near-mint condition, with original box with applied label to lid.

$150-250   **W&W**

A rare late 1950s Sutcliffe tinplate clockwork 'BLUEBIRD II' boat, with plastic screen, key access, gold-painted exhaust covers, three Union flag decals, a period decal inscribed 'BLUEBIRD II SUTCLIFF MODEL MADE IN ENGLAND' to bow, in mint condition, with key and box.

This is a rare model, but it is only worth as much as it is because it is in mint condition.

$1,000-1,500   **W&W**

A very rare mid-late 1930s American lithographed-tinplate clockwork Popeye rowing boat, with original pipe, oars, and rudder, with decal inscribed 'POPEYE THE SAILOR NO.268 1935 KING FEATURES SYNDICATE', with some losses to the decal and paintwork.

$6,500-8,500   **MORP**

QUICK REFERENCE - THE 'GANG OF FIVE'

- The 'Gang of Five' is the name given to five early robot toys dating from the late 1950s to the early 1960s. They were all made by Masudaya under their Modern Toys brand, are battery powered and have boxy bodies that led to them becoming known as 'skirted' robots. All are very rare and demand outweighs supply many times.

- They were released at a time when science-fiction films and scientific advancements made it look like robots would soon be a reality.

- 'Machine Man' was only rediscovered in 1997, as it never appeared in catalogs. It is estimated that fewer than fifteen examples have survived. It is one of the rarest and sought-after robot toys in the world. An example once sold for over $70,000.

A Modern Toys painted and printed tinplate battery-operated 'Machine Man' robot, with several areas of oxidation and loss to the printed surface, with re-chroming to mouth, ears and eyes, in working condition.

15in (38cm) high

$55,000-75,000   **MORP**

A Modern Toys painted and printed tinplate battery-operated 'Radicon Robot', with some oxidation, flaking and discoloration, the battery box with re-sprayed interior.

Another of the 'Gang of Five', this was the world's first remote-controlled toy.

1957   *20in (51cm) high*

$13,000-18,000   **MORP**

A Modern Toys painted and printed tinplate battery-operated 'Giant Sonic/Train Robot', in near-mint condition, with one very small area of touch-up near switch and minor scratching where the arms move.

This robot (notably in near-mint condition!) is another of the 'Gang of Five'. It swings its arms as it moves forward and emits a train-like whistle. Terrifying!

15.25in (39cm) high

$10,000-15,000   **MORP**

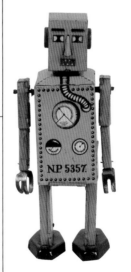

A KT painted and printed tinplate clockwork 'Lilliput Robot', with some minor crazing and scratching.

This was the first Japanese mass-produced robot and dates from the late 1940s. The name relates to how Gulliver appeared to the people of Lilliput.

6in (15.25cm) high

$6,000-8,000   **MORP**

A Modern Toys painted and printed tinplate battery-operated 'Target Robot', with a gun and two darts, in near mint condition.

Another of the 'Gang of Five', this robot shoots darts.

14.75in (37.5cm) high

$13,000-18,000   **MORP**

A Horikawa printed-tinplate and plastic battery-operated 'MR ZEROX' robot, in good condition, the original box in good condition.

9in (22.5cm) high

$200-300   **SAS**

A 1960s-70s Japanese tinplate and plastic battery-operated 'ENGINE ROBOT', in fair to good condition, with original box.

9in (23cm) high

$150-250   **AH**

A late 20thC Horikawa tinplate and plastic battery-operated 'STAR STRIDER' robot, with original box.

'Star Strider' robots were still being made by Horikawa until they closed in the late 1980s. The design was then taken over by Metal House, which continues to make them in tinplate today.

12in (31cm) high

$120-180   **BELL**

A 1960s-70s Markes & Co. metal and plastic battery-powered 'DUX-ASTROMAN' robot, with wire and controller, missing antenna on head, with original box.

12in (30.5cm) high

$700-1,000   **SWO**

A CLOSER LOOK AT A ROBOT

The small Japanese company of Asakusa only made one robot - the 'Thunder Robot'.

The artwork on the box is great and indicates what the robot's action is - it marches forward and raises its arms to fire before lowering them to carry on to find more to destroy.

Its unusual head/torso design makes the 'Thunder Robot' unique in terms of robot-toy design.

Reproductions are known. Most are produced by Ha Ha Toys in China. Differences between replicas and the originals include white instead of red guns in the hand and no Asakusa mark under the feet.

The mint condition of both the robot and the box implies that this could be old store stock. This great condition increases its value enormously.

An Asakusa Toy Company tinplate and plastic battery-operated 'THUNDER ROBOT', in near-mint condition, with original box and inserts.

1957   *10.75in (27cm) high*

$12,000-18,000   **MORP**

A Nomura printed and painted tinplate battery-operated 'Robby' 'MECHANIZED ROBOT', D-size battery version, with minor damage and repair, with original box and sales documents.

This is, of course, modeled on the famous Robby the Robot from the 1956 hit film 'Forbidden Planet'. The iconic 'Robby' was designed by Arnold 'Buddy' Gillespie, Mentor Huebner and Robert Kinoshita.

c1957   *111.75in (30cm) high*

$12,000-18,000   **MORP**

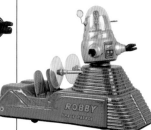

A Nomura printed-tinplate battery-operated 'ROBBY SPACE PATROL', in very good to excellent condition, with some crazing.

1957   *12.5in (32cm) high*

$3,000-5,000   **MORP**

A Horikawa printed-tinplate battery-operated 'FORKLIFT ROBOT', in near-mint and working condition, with original box, inserts and cardboard crate.

c1960   *12in (30.5cm) high*

$8,000-12,000   **MORP**

A 1920s-30s Bing tinplate clockwork 'Fordson' tractor, marked 'Bing Werke Germany', with driver figure.

8.5in (21.5cm) long

$550-750 DN

An American 1950s Louis Marx & Co. painted and printed tinplate 'G.Man' clockwork pursuit car, with signs of wear to extremities.

14in (35.5cm) long

$200-300 TRI

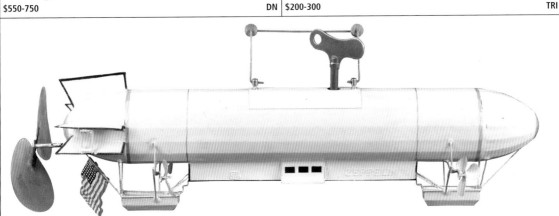

A rare Wells tinplate clockwork light aircraft, fitted with a twin-bladed propeller, in working condition.

8.75in (22cm) long

$150-250 W&W

A 1920s Märklin tinplate clockwork Zeppelin, model no.5404, embossed with logo, with celluloid rear propellers, with pulleys on for travel on stringing.

Zeppelins are among the rarest and most desirable of Märklin's tinplate toys. By the 1930s interest in Zeppelin models had already begin to decline in favor of planes, but the Hindenburg disaster of 6th May 1937 saw the sudden end of Zeppelins being produced as toys. This is a large example in excellent condition.

17in (43cm) long

$25,000-30,000 BER

A rare 1910s-30s Lehmann tinplate clockwork 'New Century Cycle', EPL345, with red white Japanese 'Sun' style decoration and Lehman's patent details, with working coil spring clockwork mechanism.

This toy was made in a number of color and pattern variations 1895-1938. It is known as the 'Am Pol' when the umbrella shows a map or part of a globe. This relates to Commander Peary's expedition to the North Pole.

5.25in (13.5cm) long

$400-600 W&W

A 1920s Gunthermann tinplate clockwork Arab on horseback figure.

4.75in (12cm) long

$550-750 DN

A Lehmann tinplate 'Autohutte Double Garage', no.772, with opeing roof.

c1934 *7in (18cm) long*

$120-180 TOV

QUICK REFERENCE - DIECAST TOYS

- Diecast toys are made from a metal alloy that can be cast in a mold, which is also known as a die, hence the name. Diecast toys have been made in many countries across the world since the early 20thC, but the most collectible and famous makers are Dinky, Corgi and Matchbox in the UK and Tootsie Toys and Hot Wheels in the USA.
- Dinky toys were first released as 'Modeled Miniatures' in 1931 and were intended as accessories to Hornby's model railways. The first car (No.23a) was produced in 1934, the same year the range was renamed 'Dinky'. Pre-war models are sought after.
- The range continued to expand after World War Two, and these models made from the 1950s-70s that are currently growing in value as the boys of then have become the grown up collectors of today.

- In 1956, Mettoy released the first Corgi toys to compete with Dinky. These models had realistic features such as windows, opening doors and 'Glidamatic' suspension.
- A number of factors contribute toward the value of a diecast toy, including the maker, the model, the period it was produced in, the color, any variations in design or decoration, and the condition. Variations in details, such as decals or interiors, can be rare and sought after.
- Ideally a model will be in 'mint and boxed' condition, which means that both the model and the original box will be in the same condition they left the factory in. Any wear or damage, such as scuffs, chips or customisation by the owner, will reduce the value. As a general rule, values given in specialist price guides are for a boxed model in the best condition.

A Dinky 'Rolls-Royce', no.30b, in dark blue with black plain closed-chassis and black ridged wheels, in mint condition.

Although this is not a particularly desirable model, the fact that it is in mint condition raises its value.

1946-50
$250-350   W&W

A Dinky 'Town Sedan', no.24c, in dark blue, the second-type criss-cross chassis with spare wheel slot, the plated wheels with white tyres, with unplated radiator as issued, in mint condition.

1934-38
$1,000-1,500   W&W

A Dinky 'British Salmson' four-seater, no.36f, in cream with sage-green criss-cross chassis, black smooth hubs, white tyres, tinplate windscreen and un-plated radiator/bumper as issued, in very good condition.

This is very unusual color combination for this model. Most examples are darker, often being combinations of blue or black.

1947-50
$1,000-1,500   W&W

A Dinky 'HILLMAN MINX SALOON', no.154, in tan with cream ridged hubs, in very near-mint condition, the good-condition box with two-tone variant illustration but correct factory color-dot stickers.

The most valuable variant of this model has a tan body and green hubs. It can fetch up to twice as much as the variant shown.

1954-56
$300-500   DN

A Dinky 'AUSTIN DEVON SALOON', no.152, in mid-blue over dark yellow, with mid-blue ridged hubs, in near-mint condition, with good-condition box.

Look out for examples with mid-blue bodies and hubs, or a tan bodies and green hubs, as these are the most valuable. They can fetch over twice as much as the variant shown.

1956-60
$300-500   DN

A rare 1960s French Dinky 'RENAULT 4L Dépannage "Autoroutes"', no.518A, in orange with gray interior, with 'AUTOROUTES' decals to doors, black plastic aerial and concave metal hubs, in mint condition, with near-mint condition box.

$500-700   VEC

A French Dinky 'MATRA SPORTS M 530', no.1403, in orange with light-brown interior and concave metal hubs, in near-mint condition, the excellent-condition card base and vacuform top with metal tyre but missing metal hook.

$100-150   VEC

A Dinky 'SCALE MODELS' '1:25 Ford Capri', no.2162, in metallic light-blue with matt black roof and light-blue interior, in mint condition, with mint-condition card base and vacuform top.
1973-76

$120-180   W&W

A Dinky 'SUNBEAM ALPINE SPORTS', no.107, in light blue with cream seats, with driver figure and windscreen, with racing number '26', with box.
1955-59

$100-150   W&W

A Dinky 'FORD CORTINA RALLY CAR', no.212, in white with black bonnet, with 'CASTROL' and 'DUNLOP' decals, roof light and spot lights, with '8' racing number, with box.
1965-70

$80-120   W&W

A Dinky 'JAGUAR TYPE D. RACING CAR', no.238, in turquoise with blue ridged hubs, in near-mint condition, with good-condition box.
1957-60

$250-350   DN

A late issue Dinky 'Alfa Romeo' single-seater racing car, no.232, in red, with red plastic wheel hubs and gray rubber tyres, with racing numbers, in mint condition.
1962-64

$120-180   W&W

A Dinky '"THUNDERBOLT" RACING CAR', no.23m, in silver with black detail, with smooth black hubs and white rubber tyres, with some fatigue, in good-condition box.
1938-41

$150-250   DN

TOYS & GAMES

A CLOSER LOOK AT A DINKY VAN

This rectangular style of front with its tinplate radiator is the first 'type' of front used by Dinky. It was used for the '28 series' of vans during 1933-35.

Dinky advertising vans are a popular collecting area, with rare pre-war examples being particularly sought after.

This model was only made for one year, making it rare. It is particularly desirable as it is mint condition, which is extremely unusual in such an early model.

Dinky models with more colorful wheels often command a premium from collectors.

A Dinky 'PICKFORD'S' delivery van, no.28b, in dark blue livery, the black die-cast wheels with white tyres, with first-type cab, in mint condition.
1935
$5,000-7,000   W&W

A Dinky 'TROJAN 15 CWT. VAN "DUNLOP"', no.451, in red with red ridged hubs, in very-near-mint condition, with good-condition box.
1954-57
$200-300   DN

A Dinky Supertoys 'GUY VAN' 'Slumberland', no.514, in red with decals to sides, with first-type cab, in very good condition, with box.
1950-52
$650-850   W&W

A rare Dinky Supertoys 'GUY VAN "GOLDEN SHRED"', no.919, in bright red with yellow wheels, in mint condition, with box.
1957-58
$1,200-1,800   W&W

A Dinky 'GUY VAN' 'LYONS SWISS ROLLS', no.514, in dark blue with mid-blue ridged hubs, with first-type cab, in very good condition, with good-condition box.
1952
$650-850   DN

A Dinky Supertoys 'GUY 4-TON LORRY', no.511, in red-brown with red-brown hubs, in very good condition, with box.

This example has an early 'Utility' box made of basic card with a printed label. This red-brown colorway was the first color used for this model.
1948-50
$150-250   W&W

A Dinky 'BEDFORD T.K. CRASH TRUCK', no.434, with metallic-red cab and light-gray back and interior, with cream plastic wheels and plastic tyres, with box.
1966-70
$120-180   W&W

A Dinky Supertoys 'LORRY-MOUNTED CONCRETE MIXER', no.960, in orange with gray mixer drum, with unusual blue flashes to cog wheel, black plastic wheel hubs and gray rubber tyres, with minor wear.

This model is based on the Albion Chieftain.

1960-68

$120-180   W&W

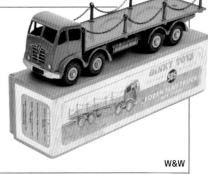

A Dinky Supertoys 'FODEN FLAT TRUCK', no.505, in dark green with mid-green wheels, with original chains, with box.

1954-56

$200-300   W&W

A Dinky Supertoys 'FODEN 14-TON TANKER', no.504, the first-type DG cab and chassis in dark blue, with mid-blue flash, tank and wheel hubs, with box.

1948-52

$500-700   W&W

A Dinky Supertoys 'FODEN 14-TON TANKER "REGENT"', no.942, in dark blue, red and white livery with red wheels, with box.

1955-57

$700-1,000   W&W

A Dinky Foden 'Mobilgas' 14-Ton Tanker, no.941, in red with matching grooved hubs, with second-type cab, in excellent condition, with card box base, missing lid.

1956

$200-300   DN

A Dinky AEC 'Lucas oil tanker', no.245, in green with black interior, gray opening tank covers, plated wheels with black rubber tyres, in mint condition, with card base and vacuform top.

This model is rare as it was issued for one year only as a promotion.

1977

$150-250   W&W

A Dinky 'BEDFORD ARTICULATED LORRY', no.409, in yellow with black cab mudguards and red hubs, in excellent condition, with good-condition box.

1956-63

$200-300   DN

A Dinky 'CAR CARRIER WITH TRAILER', no.983, in red with light gray load platforms, with 'DINKY AUTO SERVICE' decals to sides, in mint condition, with box and packing pieces.

1958-63

$400-600   W&W

A Dinky Supertoys 'MISSILE ERECTOR VEHICLE
with CORPORAL MISSILE and LAUNCHING PLATFORM', no.666, with
box, with packaging and instructions.

**Look out for the version with black missile fins and metal missile-
erector gears, as it is usually at least 50% more valuable than this
later version with all-white missile and plastic erector gears.**
1959-64
$300-500   W&W

A Dinky 'TANK TRANSPORTER', no.660, in olive green, in excellent
condition, with box.

**This model has open windows, which indicates a date of 1956-61.
If the windows are 'glazed' with plastic, the model was produced
between 1961 and 1964.**
1956-61
$120-180   TRI

A Dinky '25-POUNDER GUN UNIT' gift set, no.697, with box.
1957-71
$120-180   TRI

A Dinky Supertoys 'RECOVERY TRACTOR',
no.661, in olive green, with operable crane,
with box.

**The version with plastic wheels and yellow
'picture' box is usually worth up to twice the
value of the version shown.**
1957-65
$120-180   TRI

A Dinky Supertoys 'CENTURIAN TANK', no.651,
in olive green, with box.

**Look out for the American-export version,
which has a gold 'see-through' box, as it is
very rare and can fetch around twice the
price of this example.**
1954-70
$55-75   TRI

A French Dinky 'SINPAR 4 x 4 Gendarmerie
Militaire', no.815, in olive green, with plastic
tilt, concave hubs, black interior, with painted
driver figure, radio-operator figure, light-gray
radio, black aerial, in excellent condition, with
excellent-condition box.
$300-500   VEC

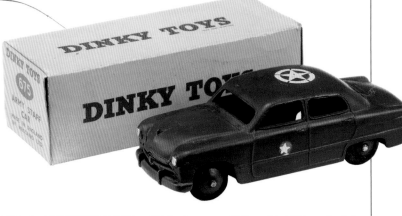

A Dinky Ford US 'ARMY STAFF CAR', no.675, in olive green, with five-pointed USA star decals, in
near-mint condition, with excellent-condition card box.
$650-850   VEC

A Corgi 'CHRYSLER "IMPERIAL"', no.246, in red with light-blue interior, with two figures, detailed cast hubs and golf trolley in the boot, in excellent condition, with excellent-condition box.

If this model was finished in rare metallic kingfisher-blue, rather than red, it could be worth twice as much as the price shown.
1965-68
$120-180   VEC

QUICK REFERENCE - WHIZZWHEELS

● Whizzwheels were released by Corgi in 1968 to keep up with competition from other diecast makers, who promoted the 'speed' of their models when pushed.
● The first 'Whizzwheels' had rubber tyres and brass hubs with low-friction red nylon centers. This configuration made Corgi models attractively distinctive and detailed. Unfortunately, 'red spot' wheels were expensive and time-consuming to produce, so they were phased out in 1970.
● Whizzwheels were eventually made entirely from plastic.
● Look out for 'red spot' Corgi models as they can be highly desirable and valuable.

A Corgi 'FORD CAPRI', no.311, in fluorescent orange with black interior, with Whizzwheels, in mint condition, with good-condition window box.
1970-72
$150-250   VEC

A Corgi 'CITROEN SM', no.C284, in metallic lime-green with light-blue interior, with spoked plastic wheels, in near-mint condition, with near-mint condition window box.
1970-76
$80-120   VEC

A Corgi 'ISO GRIFO 7 LITRE', no.301, in blue with black bonnet and cream interior, with Whizzwheels, in near-mint condition, with excellent-condition window box.
1956-69
$60-80   VEC

A Corgi 'LANCIA FULVIA SPORT ZAGATO', no.332, in metallic blue with blue interior, with detailed cast hubs, in near-mint condition, with excellent-condition box.
$80-120   VEC

A Corgi 'MARCOS MANTIS', no.312, in metallic red with white interior, with special spoked wheels, in excellent condition, with excellent-condition box.
1971-73
$40-60   VEC

A Corgi 'M.G.A. SPORTS CAR', no.302, in red, with smooth hubs, in near-mint condition, with good-condition box.
1957-64
$250-350   DN

A Corgi 'M.G.B. G.T.', no.327, in dark red with light blue interior, with spoked wire wheels, with black suitcase, in excellent condition, the near-mint condition box with pencil price to one end.

1967-69
$100-150   **VEC**

A Corgi 'MGC G.T. COMPETITION MODEL', no.345, in yellow and black, with racing number '4' accessory pack decals, with wire wheels, in excellent condition, with near-mint condition box and model club leaflet.

1969
$120-180   **VEC**

A Corgi 'MINI-COOPER WITH DE-LUXE WICKERWORK', no.249, in black and red with cream interior and 'wickerwork' decals to sides, with spun hubs, in excellent condition, with near-mint condition box.

1965-68
$250-350   **VEC**

A Corgi 'Mini Cooper Rally', no.227, in primrose yellow with white roof and bonnet and red interior, with flag decals to bonnet and '7' racing number, with spun hubs, in excellent condition.

The 'Mini Cooper' is a popular model with Corgi collectors, who typically aim to collect every variation. Monte Carlo rally examples are particularly sought after. This rally model can also be found in blue or primrose. Both variations are usually worth roughly the same.
1962-63
$120-180   **VEC**

A Corgi 'MINI COOPER', no.282, in white and black, with striped decal to roof and '177' decals to doors, with Whizzwheels, in excellent condition, with excellent-condition window box.

1971-74
$80-120   **VEC**

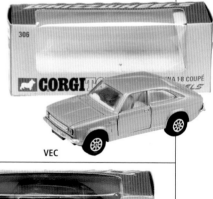

A Corgi 'MORRIS MARINA 1.8 COUPÉ', no.306, in metallic lime-green with cream interior, with Whizzwheels, in mint condition, with excellent-condition window box.

1971-73
$60-80   **VEC**

A Corgi James Bond 'FORD MUSTANG MACH 1', no.391, in red with a black plastic bonnet and white base, in excellent condition, with scratch to bonnet, with fair-condition window box, with fading, staining and torn acetate window.

The poor condition of the box and the scratch on the bonnet have reduced the value of this model dramatically. Taken from 'Diamonds Are Forever' (1971), the Ford Mustang is not the most iconic of Bond's cars, which also contributes to a relatively low price. The famous Aston Martin DB5 is generally much more sought after and valuable.
$120-180   **DN**

A Corgi 'RENAULT 16 T.S.', no.202, in metallic dark blue with deep yellow interior, with Whizzwheels, in near-mint condition, with excellent-condition window box.

1970-72
$60-80   **VEC**

A Corgi 'ROVER 2000 TC', no.281, in purple with orange interior, with Whizzwheels, in excellent condition, with very good-condition window box.

A gold-colored version of this model was also made, but it is very rare today. As such, it can fetch 50% more than this purple version.

1971-73

$80-120 VEC

A Corgi 'Simca '1000 COMPETITION MODEL', no.315, in dark blue with red interior, with '8' striped decal and spun hubs, in excellent condition, with excellent-condition card box.

This is the rarest and most valuable version of this model, which is usually found in silver with a red interior. The silver variation is usually worth around a third of the value of this version.

1964-66

$800-1,200 VEC

A Corgi 'Volkswagen 1300 Motor School Car', no.400, in metallic dark-blue body with lemon-yellow interior, with gold detailed cast hubs and roof wheel, with 'AUTO-ECOLE' decals to doors and 'L' decals bumpers, in excellent condition, with excellent-condition box.

This French-language version of the 'Motor School Car' is very hard to find, as is the German-language version. Either one is usually worth over twice the value of the version with English-language decals.

1974-77

$300-500 VEC

A Corgi Toys 'LOTUS RACING TEAM' gift set, no.37, comprising a 'Lotus Climax' racing car, a 'Lotus Elan Coupé', a 'Lotus Elan S.2', a 'Volkswagen Breakdown' van with winch and a 'Lotus Elan' chassis on trailer, with box and insert, with some wear.

1966-69

$250-350 W&W

Mark Picks

Even if it's not immediately obvious, toys often reflect the times they were made. This 'Land Rover' was produced between 1964 and 1966. Within this period, there were two British general elections. Both elections were won by the Labor party under Harold Wilson (1916-95), although the first was a very narrow victory indeed. Labor had a mere five-seat majority and, during 1965, this was reduced to a single seat as a result of by-election defeats! Fortunately for Labor, the political tide had changed by 1966 and Wilson quickly called another general election. This move paid off, as his majority was increased to 96. This toy is obviously a humorous take on the political campaigning that would have been seen by children on the street, on the TV and in newspapers at the time.

A Corgi Land Rover 'PUBLIC ADDRESS VEHICLE', no.472, in green and yellow, with two figures, with 'VOTE FOR CORGI' decals and spun hubs, in excellent condition, in excellent-condition box, missing internal packing.

1964-66

$150-250 VEC

A Corgi 'WALL'S ICE CREAM VAN', no.447, in light blue and cream, with ice-cream man figure, with box and display insert, missing boy-figure.

1965-66

$250-350 W&W

A Corgi 'KENNEL SERVICE WAGON', no.486, in white and red with light-blue interior, with four dog figures, in excellent condition, with some plating loss, with near-mint condition box.

1967-69

$120-180 VEC

QUICK REFERENCE - DIAPET

- Diapet toys were produced in Japan by Yonezawa after that company acquired Cherryca Phenix in 1965. Although diecast models had been made by Cherryca Phenix before this acquisition, the range was extended under Yonezawa.
- 'Pet' is the Japanese equivalent of 'small' or 'cute'.
- The quality of Diapet models varied widely. The top end included some excellent 1:40 scale reproductions of Japanese cars that were not produced by any other diecast toy company.
- Diapet toys sold well in Japan, despite competition from Tomy's Tomica range. Tomica toys generally sold better in markets outside Japan.
- Yonezawa's toy company was sold to Sega in 1994. The company discontinued the Diapet range around the same time.
- As with any diecast toy, the condition of the model and whether or not it has a box is of vital importance to value. Variations in color must also be considered.

A Diapet 'CROWN DELUXE' police car, no.D129, in black and white with light-blue interior, with red roof-light and white siren, in good condition, in excellent-condition box.
$1,000-1,500   VEC

A Diapet 'Lincoln Continental', in blue and cream with light-blue interior, in very good condition.
$250-350   VEC

A Diapet 'Chevrolet Impala', in blue and cream with turquoise interior, in excellent condition.
$550-750   VEC

A Diapet Datsun 'FAIRLADY', no.D113, in metallic light-blue with red interior, in excellent condition, with excellent-condition box.
$400-600   VEC

A Diapet 'DATSUN Sunny 1000', no.154, in turquoise with red interior, in good condition, with excellent-condition box.
$200-300   VEC

A Diapet 'Mercedes Benz 300SL', in metallic light-blue with red interior, in good condition.
$90-120   VEC

A Diapet 'NISSAN CEDRIC' police car, no.D134, in black and white with light-blue interior, with red roof-light and white siren, in good condition, with excellent-condition box.
$1,200-1,800   VEC

A Diapet 'NISSAN SILVIA', no.D137, in metallic green with light-blue interior, in excellent condition, with excellent-condition box.
$120-180   VEC

A Diapet 'NISSAN CEDRIC' custom, no.D120, in metallic light-blue with light-blue interior, in excellent condition, with very good-condition box.
$2,500-3,500   VEC

A Diapet 'PORSCHE 911', no.149, in red with light-blue interior, in good condition, with some signs of fatigue, with excellent-condition box.
$100-150   VEC

A Diapet Prince 'SKYLINE', no.D125, in metallic turquoise with light-blue interior in excellent condition, with excellent-condition box.
$300-500   VEC

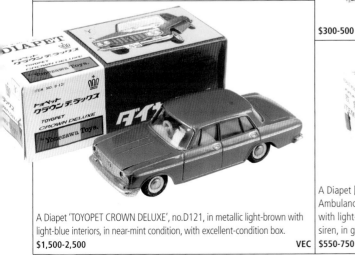

A Diapet 'TOYOPET CROWN DELUXE', no.D121, in metallic light-brown with light-blue interiors, in near-mint condition, with excellent-condition box.
$1,500-2,500   VEC

A Diapet ['Toyopet Crown Ambulance'], no.D151, in white with light-blue interior, with red cross to roof, red plastic light and white siren, in good condition, with excellent-condition box.
$550-750   VEC

A Budgie 'LONG DISTANCE REFRIGERATION TRUCK', no.202, in red and silver with silver plastic hubs, with 'COAST TO COAST REFRIGERATION', in excellent condition, with good-condition box.
$70-100   **DN**

A Gamda 'Ford Prefect', in cream, with bare metal hubs and black tyres, in excellent condition, with some splitting to tyres.
$250-350   **VEC**

A rare 1950s Budgie 'MINIATURE DIE-CAST MODELS By Budgie' gift set, no.12 comprising twelve vehicles including a Bedford refuse lorry, cement lorry, tipper, crane and a horse box, two petrol tankers, a Volkswagen first-type split screen and four other cars, the box with some wear.
$250-350   **W&W**

A Gamda 'Daimler Conquest', in light gray over gray, with plated metal hubs, in excellent condition, with plating-loss to hubs.
$500-700   **VEC**

A Gamda 'Israeli Army Willy's Jeep', in dark green and white with silver hubs, with logos to doors, in excellent condition, missing roof light.

Gamda toys were reputedly made in an Israeli kibbutz using molds from British and American diecast companies.
$800-1,200   **VEC**

A Matchbox Series 'G-1' gift set, comprising a 'PICKFORDS' removal van, Bedford 'Lomas' ambulance, 'Commer' milk van, 'Thames Trader' wreck truck, Foden 'TATE & LYLE' sugar container lorry, refreshment caravan, Routemaster bus and a 'Land Rover', with original box and insert.
$500-700   **W&W**

A Shackleton Toys 'Foden F.G.' flatbed lorry, in yellow with red wheel-arches, in good condition, with box, maintenance instructions, key and spanner.
$500-700   **DN**

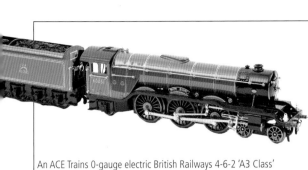

An ACE Trains 0-gauge electric British Railways 4-6-2 'A3 Class' locomotive and tender, 'BLINK BONNY', RN no.60051, with early British Railways crest to tender, in mint condition, with all packaging.

$700-1,000   **W&W**

A Bachmann 00-gauge London Midlands & Scottish Railway 'Jubilee Class' 4-6-0 locomotive and tender, 'GALATEA', no.31150A, RN no.5699, from a limited edition of 500, with box.

$150-250   **DN**

A Bassett-Lowke London Midlands & Scottish Railways 4-4-0 locomotive and tender, no.1106.

$300-500   **GORL**

A Hornby Dublo 2-rail 4-6-0 'Castle Class' locomotive and tender, 'CARDIFF CASTLE', no.2221, RN no.4075, with original box and internal packing piece.

$200-300   **W&W**

A Bing 0-gauge clockwork London & North West Railways 4-4-0 tank locomotive, RN no.44.

$500-700   **W&W**

A Hornby 0-gauge 3-rail Southern Railways 4-4-0 locomotive and tender, 'ETON'.

9in (23cm) long

$1,000-1,500   **SWO**

A Hornby 0-gauge 3-rail London Midlands & Scottish Railways 4-6-2 locomotive and tender, 'PRINCESS ELIZABETH'.

Produced for Hornby by Meccano around 1937, this was the company's flagship model and priced accordingly. As a result of this, few were sold and it is rare today.

Locomotive 14.25in (36cm) long

$2,500-3,500   **SWO**

Judith Picks

Issmayer was founded by Johann Issmayer in Nürnberg in 1861 and first made trains in 1879. Its lithographic printing is usually bright and shiny, as on this train, and its wares were typically produced using quick and economic 'tab and slot' construction methods - you can see this on the black roof. Much of their production was exported to the USA, hence the American shape of this locomotive. The company suffered under import bans around World War I and closed in 1932.

This is a bright, appealing toy that was produced during the golden age of German tinplate toys. The fact that it's in the shape of an American locomotive makes it even more collectible, particularly in this very good condition.

An Issmayer tinplate friction-driven floor model of a North American-style locomotive, marked '1000'.

c1910

6.75in (17.5cm) long

$250-350   **DN**

A Märklin 1-gauge clockwork 0-4-0 locomotive, with spring-activated brake, missing tender.

c1900

$500-700   **DN**

A Märklin 1-gauge clockwork 0-4-0 tender and locomotive, with spring-activated brake, with a Märklin four-wheel first-class passenger coach and box van.

c1900

$1,200-1,800   **DN**

A rare late 19thC H Wallwork & Co. cast-iron floor/carpet train, comprising a 4-4-0 locomotive and two six-wheeled coaches, one with brake, missing tender.

Established in 1856, H Wallwork & Co. of Redbank, Manchester, are an iron- and steel-foundry best known for making gears and related machinery, such as stationery gas engines. The company probably only produced toys for a small period of time.

$300-500   **W&W**

A Wrenn 00-gauge British Railways 'Lamport & Holt Line''Merchant Navy Class' 4-6-2 locomotive and tender, no.W2267, RN no.35026, the good-condition box stamped 'Packer No.3 / Ref. No.02305'.

$500-700   **DN**

A Wrenn 00-gauge British Railways 'Princess Coronation Class' 4-6-2 locomotive and tender, 'CITY OF MANCHESTER', no.W2229/A, RN no.46246, the good-condition box stamped 'Packer No.3'.

$400-600   **DN**

A 5in (12.5cm) gauge steam-powered London & North Eastern Railway locomotive and tender, no.984, missing boiler certificate.

This model was originally a Great Northern Railway Ivatt C2 'Klondyke' Atlantic 4-4-2.

Locomotive 38in (98.5cm) long

$9,000-12,000   **GWRA**

A 5in (12.5cm) gauge steam-powered model of a 0-6-0 tank engine, 'RIVER ROACH', missing boiler certificate.

30in (76cm) long

$3,000-5,000   **GWRA**

A 5in (12.5cm) gauge steam-powered Great Western Railway 'Prairie Tank', no.5109, missing boiler certificate, with detached grate, ashpan and brake cylinder.

41in (104cm) long

$12,000-18,000   **GWRA**

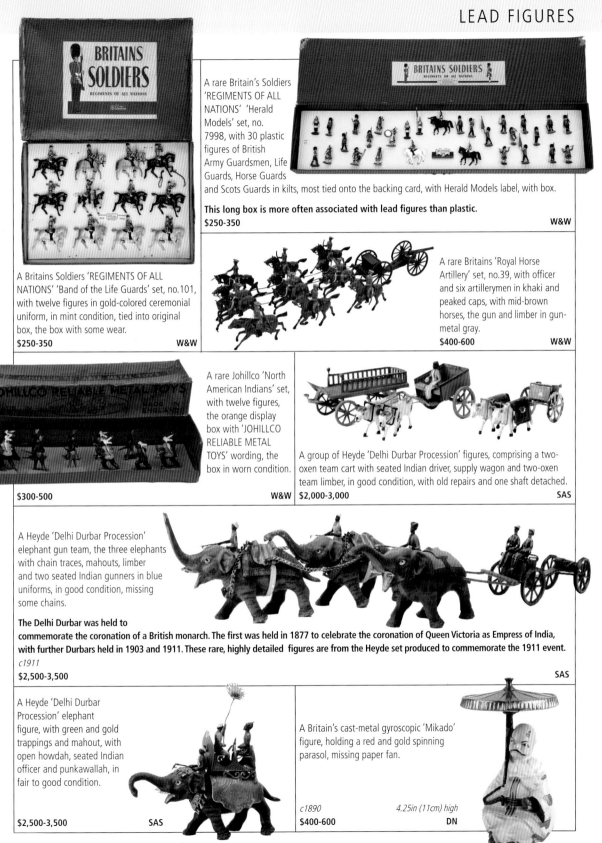

A rare Britain's Soldiers 'REGIMENTS OF ALL NATIONS' 'Herald Models' set, no. 7998, with 30 plastic figures of British Army Guardsmen, Life Guards, Horse Guards and Scots Guards in kilts, most tied onto the backing card, with Herald Models label, with box.

This long box is more often associated with lead figures than plastic.
$250-350   W&W

A Britains Soldiers 'REGIMENTS OF ALL NATIONS' 'Band of the Life Guards' set, no.101, with twelve figures in gold-colored ceremonial uniform, in mint condition, tied into original box, the box with some wear.
$250-350   W&W

A rare Britains 'Royal Horse Artillery' set, no.39, with officer and six artillerymen in khaki and peaked caps, with mid-brown horses, the gun and limber in gun-metal gray.
$400-600   W&W

A rare Johillco 'North American Indians' set, with twelve figures, the orange display box with 'JOHILLCO RELIABLE METAL TOYS' wording, the box in worn condition.
$300-500   W&W

A group of Heyde 'Delhi Durbar Procession' figures, comprising a two-oxen team cart with seated Indian driver, supply wagon and two-oxen team limber, in good condition, with old repairs and one shaft detached.
$2,000-3,000   SAS

A Heyde 'Delhi Durbar Procession' elephant gun team, the three elephants with chain traces, mahouts, limber and two seated Indian gunners in blue uniforms, in good condition, missing some chains.

The Delhi Durbar was held to commemorate the coronation of a British monarch. The first was held in 1877 to celebrate the coronation of Queen Victoria as Empress of India, with further Durbars held in 1903 and 1911. These rare, highly detailed figures are from the Heyde set produced to commemorate the 1911 event.
c1911
$2,500-3,500   SAS

A Heyde 'Delhi Durbar Procession' elephant figure, with green and gold trappings and mahout, with open howdah, seated Indian officer and punkawallah, in fair to good condition.

$2,500-3,500   SAS

A Britain's cast-metal gyroscopic 'Mikado' figure, holding a red and gold spinning parasol, missing paper fan.

c1890   4.25in (11cm) high
$400-600   DN

TOYS & GAMES

QUICK REFERENCE - DESIGNER TOYS

- A number of modern designers working during the 1920s-70s produced designs for children's toys, with some actually specializing in toys.
- Typically comprising well-proportioned, simple forms in bright colors, such toys were made to interest and encourage a child, as well as to withstand the rigours of play. Many have a therapeutic or medical element to their design, creation or intended use.
- Although some designer toys are still being produced, many are not and prices for those are rising against a limited supply. Many designer toys were expensive and difficult to get hold of in their day, making some rare.
- Most are hard to date precisely as designs and materials remained the same.
- Always look for those in the best condition, with their original paint.
- Today designer toys are becoming increasingly sought after by design-conscious parents or by those who want to add a fun, whimsical and colorful touch to their Mid-century Modern or Modernist interior.
- Ko Verzuu's (1901-71) range of toys was influenced by the De Stijl movement. They were handmade by patients in the local sanatorium, in an attempt to make their transition back into mainstream society easier, and were sold by Dutch company Ado during the 1930s-60s. They are highly collectible today.

An Ado painted-plywood locomotive and tender, designed by Ko Verzuu, the tender containing nine painted toy blocks, with 'ADO' badge.

c1934   *26.75in (68cm) long*
$650-850   QU

A 1970s Italian painted and turned wood 'Pinocchio' jointed puppet, reputedly designed by Marco Zanuso, in excellent condition.

During the mid-1950s, notable Italian furniture designer and architect Marco Zanuso (1916-2001) designed a number of buildings for the 'Pinocchio Park' in Collodi in Pescia, Italy. At the time, Zanuso reputedly also modernized the design of the character for the post-war era.

33.25in (86cm) high
QU
$1,500-2,500

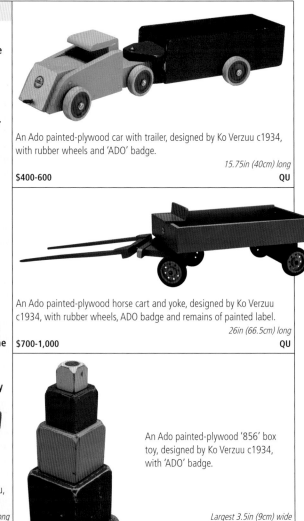

An Ado painted-plywood car with trailer, designed by Ko Verzuu c1934, with rubber wheels and 'ADO' badge.

15.75in (40cm) long
$400-600   QU

An Ado painted-plywood horse cart and yoke, designed by Ko Verzuu c1934, with rubber wheels, ADO badge and remains of painted label.

26in (66.5cm) long
$700-1,000   QU

An Ado painted-plywood '856' box toy, designed by Ko Verzuu c1934, with 'ADO' badge.

Largest 3.5in (9cm) wide
$650-850   QU

A painted and varnished wooden toy car, with four passengers, designed by Kay Bojesen c1942.

7.25in (18.5cm) long
$300-500   QU

Two 1950s teak articulated monkeys, designed by Kaj Bojesen in 1951, the larger stamped 'KAY BOJESEN DENMARK COPYRIGHT'.

For more information about these popular and sought-after 'toys', see p.386 of 'Miller's Collectibles Handbook 2012-2013'.

Larger 12.5in (31.5cm) high

$3,000-5,000   **DRA**

A small teak sitting monkey, designed by Kay Bojesen in 1951, branded 'KAY BOJESEN/DENMARK COPYRIGHT'.

5.5in (14cm) high

$300-500   **DRA**

A 1950s painted wooden zebra toy, designed by Kay Bojesen, with maker's marks.

6in (15.5cm) long

$250-350   **DRA**

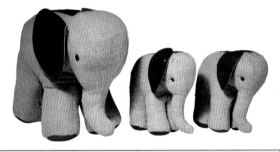

A set of three German jute and colored-leather elephants, designed by Renate Müller in 1968, with buttons eye.

Renate Müller's bright and colorful 1960s toy designs, launched at the Leipzig trade fair in 1967, were designed for mentally and physically handicapped children. They were used in activities to develop balance, sensory perception and coordination.

Largest 16.75in (42.5cm) high

$2,500-3,500   **QU**

A CLOSER LOOK AT A CAT TOY

This cat was part of a range of ten animals designed by Libuse Niklovà (1934-81) for Czech company Fatra. Such designs undoubtedly gave a light, bright relief to children in the dreary Communist block.

Although many were sold during the 1960s-80s, these cats were never mass-produced in their millions. This means there is a relatively small number on the market today.

Niklovà's designs were inexpensive and sold in packs for assembly and play. She also designed an inflatable elephant that a child could sit on.

Niklovà was inspired to use a plastic concertina body after seeing her colleagues develop the form for use in a lavatory flushing system.

A Fatra plastic 'Cat' toy, designed by Libuse Niklovà in 1963, with orange nose and white whiskers and squeezable squeaky body.

7.5in (19cm) high

$800-1,200   **QU**

An H Josef Leven jute and leather 'Hippopotamus' stuffed toy, designed by Renate Müller in 1969.

17.25in (44cm) long

$500-700   **QU**

An H Josef Leven jute and leather 'Hippopotamus' stuffed toy, designed by Renate Müller in c1973.

12.75in (32.5cm) long

$400-600   **QU**

A 1950s-60s Siegfried Lenz beech and laminated-plywood reversible 'Schaukelwagen' toy car and rocking chair, designed by Hans Brockhage and Erwin Andrä in 1950.

This design was influenced by Dutch Modernist architect and furniture designer Mart Stam, who made a comment about a rocking horse being useless when it fell over. This lead Brockhage to make the 'Schaukelwagen' reversible, thus also allowing a child to re-discover and 'change' their toy.

40in (100cm) long

$3,000-5,000   **QU**

A Star Wars 'Return of the Jedi' tri-logo 'AT-AT Commander' action figure, by Palitoy, retailed by General Mills, the 70-figure card back in excellent condition.
c1983
$150-250   **VEC**

A Star Wars 'Return of the Jedi' tri-logo 'Darth Vader' action figure, by Palitoy, retailed by General Mills, the 70-figure card back in excellent-plus to near-mint condition.
c1983
$250-350   **VEC**

QUICK REFERENCE - CARDED STAR WARS FIGURES

- The most valuable and desirable Star Wars figures are those that are 'carded' i.e. still sealed in their packaging.
- As well as the figure, the condition of the card counts toward value. This is especially true of more modern figures, where the presence of the small card tag that fills the shop display hole at the top of the card is also necessary if a carded figure is to be considered truly 'mint'.
- Always also pay attention to the card itself. The earliest have 12 figures on the back and are known as '12 backs'.

A Star Wars 'Return of the Jedi' tri-logo 'Chewbacca' action figure, by Palitoy, retailed by General Mills, the 70-figure card back in excellent-plus to near-mint condition.
c1983
$400-600   **VEC**

A Star Wars 'Return of the Jedi' tri-logo 'FX-7' action figure, by Palitoy, retailed by General Mills, the 70-figure card back in excellent condition.
c1983
$70-100   **VEC**

A Star Wars 'Return of the Jedi' tri-logo 'Han Solo' action figure, by Palitoy, retailed by General Mills, the 70-figure card back in near-mint condition.
c1983
$250-350   **VEC**

A Star Wars 'Return of the Jedi' tri-logo 'Luke Skywalker' action figure, by Palitoy, retailed by General Mills, the 70-figure card back in good condition.
c1983
$200-300   **VEC**

A Star Wars 'Return of the Jedi' tri-logo 'Ben (Obi-Wan) Kenobi' action figure, by Palitoy, retailed by General Mills, the 70-figure card back in good-plus to excellent condition.

The earliest, rarest and most sought-after Jawa figures had plastic capes, rather than the fabric capes worn by later, less valuable Jawas. Obi-Wan's cape (shown here) is the same as the Jawa plastic cape - so it is often cut down and used to re-clothe Jawas in an attempt to make them look more valuable!
c1983
$200-300   **VEC**

A Star Wars 'Return of the Jedi' 'Princess Leia Organa (Bespin gown)' action figure, by Kenner, the 77-figure card back in excellent to excellent-plus condition, the bubble yellowed.
c1983
$120-180   **VEC**

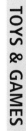

A Star Wars 'Return of the Jedi' tri-logo 'Artoo-Detoo (R2-D2) with pop-up Lightsabre' action figure, by Palitoy, retailed by General Mills, the 70-figure card back in good condition.

c1983

$250-350   VEC

A Star Wars 'The Empire Strikes Back' 'AT-AT', by Palitoy, in near-mint condition, with unapplied transfers, two instructions sheets and jaw gun, with excellent-condition box.

The 'AT-AT' was one of the most popular Star Wars vehicles. As a result, many 'AT-AT' toys were produced and sold, so it is only the boxed version in excellent condition with unapplied decals that fetches high prices. The same goes for the 'Millennium Falcon'. Unboxed, playworn versions of either toy are usually worth well under $50.

c1980

$150-250   VEC

A 'THE MAN FROM U.N.C.L.E.' 'Illya Kuryakin' action figure, by Gilbert, with black cotton jersey and trousers, black shoes, complete with firing pistol, in excellent-plus to near-mint condition, the illustrated box in good-plus to excellent condition, with instructions and Secret Agent card.

c1965

$150-250   VEC

A 'STARSKY & HUTCH' twin-pack of action figures, by Palitoy, with original clothing and guns, in near-mint to mint condition, the original box in good-plus to excellent condition, with inner card inserts.

$150-250   VEC

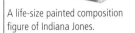

A life-size painted composition figure of Indiana Jones.

This figure was used at the ITV studios London South Bank première of the film 'Indiana Jones and the Kingdom of the Crystal Skull'.

c2008   *86.5in (220cm) high*

$700-1,000   FLD

A 'Muffin the Mule Junior' puppet, by Matchbox Moko, with string tail and metal hoop attachment to strings, in excellent-plus to near-mint condition, the box in good-plus to excellent condition.

$350-450   VEC

An art board with original ink and color images of Muffin the Mule, Louise the Lamb (x2), Peter the Pup, and Peter and Peregrine the Penguin (not shown), all probably by Molly Blake, with a handwritten and printed story by Annette Mills 'Mister Sea Serpent', a Muffin stage show poster, publicity photographs and other items.

$300-500   SAS

A silver National Television Award, awarded to Annette Mills for The Personality of the Year on Children's Television, by the Goldsmiths & Silversmiths Company Ltd., London, in the form of an early television with detail of Peter Pan, the sides with Comedy and Tragedy masks.

c1952   *9.75in (25cm) high*

$650-850   SAS

A miniature wooden cooking range, with hob, spirit burners, utensil rack, plate rack, bread oven and miniature metal cooking pots and accessories, with one door detached, with some wear, some of the utensils later.

c1900   *17.25in (44cm) high*
$400-600   **DW**

A 19thC Pollock's paper-covered wooden toy theatre, with printed-paper characters, props and scenery for plays such as 'Aladdin' and 'Blackbeard'.

                              13.5in (34cm) high
$200-300   **LC**

A large Tri-ang wooden Noah's Ark, painted in red and cream with stenciled windows, with Noah and his wife figures and 43 Lord Roberts wooden animals.

                              25in (63.5cm) long
$120-180   **SAS**

A 1920s Schoenhut & Co. painted wooden horse-drawn 'FINE BREAD' wagon, the wagon with decals of a woman baker, 'FINE BREAD' and 'No.44' to both sides, with a wooden driver figure in original clothing.

Schoenhut's (1872-1935) wooden toys are highly sought after in the USA, particularly if they are in as good condition as this example.
$5,500-6,500   **MORP**

A rare mid-19thC Perry & Co.'s Patent clockwork 'Automaton Dancers' jigging minstrel, the composition and wood articulated figure with wool hair and painted clothes, with printed label.

This toy is very similar to the automata made by Ives in the USA. Perry & Co. was a British wholesaler with an office in New York, so it is possible this toy was made by Ives.

                              10.5in (26.5cm) high
$500-700   **SAS**

A rare early 20thC Roullet & Decamps clockwork crocodile automaton, with painted papier-mâché body, glass eyes, cardboard teeth, kid covering at tail and neck joints, the mechanism causing him to move his head and tail from side to side and move forward.

                              18.5in (47cm) long
$650-850   **SAS**

A 1950s West German celluloid clockwork clown riding a scooter, missing one part.

$30-50   **QU**

A rare early 20thC Hudson Scott & Sons Ltd. zoetrope, the slotted metal drum patterned with passion flowers, the lid with pin to form the base, with four red and black printed motion strips.

Hudson Scott & Sons Ltd. was a lithographers and printers. It manufactured tins, including biscuit tins for Carr's.

                              5.75in (12.5cm) diam
$550-750   **DW**

A late 19thC French 'Loterie Parisienne' parlor toy, the fall-front box containing a selection of numbered prizes, with stencil-printed numbered paddles.

These popular games of chance were produced by Jeux et Jouets Francais (JJF) and offered in France's 'Etrennes' catalogs in the late 19thC and early 20thC. Spinning the wheel would win you a surprise gift from the selection. The value for this example is very high as it retains most of the original prizes and the box is in good condition.

c1900 *17.75in (45cm) wide*

$1,200-1,800 **DN**

An early 20thC Jaques & Son 'ASCOT' racing game, with six diecast racehorses attached to a string, the mahogany box with turning handle.

$650-850 **WHP**

A late 1920s Chad Valley '"BRUIN BOYS" PARADE' bagatelle game, with color-printed card pop-up Bruin Boys figures and green-finished wood box, in full working order, with replacement ball bearings and recent custom-made illustrated card box.

Box 21in (53cm) long

$350-450 **CBA**

A mahogany games compendium, the fitted interior with chess set, board and other games in two lift-out trays including draughts, backgammon, bezique, whist and dominoes.

c1910 *13in (33cm) wide*

$500-700 **HT**

A 1950s Allwin 'STRATO-PLAY' oak-cased and printed-glass wall slot machine, from an arcade.

19.5in (49cm) wide

$900-1,200 **SWO**

A Napoleonic prisoner-of-war bone games box, the sliding cover with painted pictures of an officer and a lady, the interior with an incomplete set of dominoes.

The value of this set is lifted by the painted portraits, presumably of the prisoner who carved the set and his much-missed beloved.

Box 6in (15cm) long

$300-500   LT

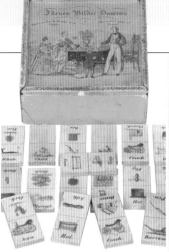

A mid-19thC German domino set, ['The Modern Game of Domino'], the wooden box with hand-colored and printed-paper covers featuring a family at play, the interior with an incomplete set of 61 wooden dominoes with printed-paper faces showing motifs such as a house, a fly and a coach.

Box 4.75in (12cm) wide

$200-300   DW

A set of early 19thC ivory alphabet counter discs, each painted with a letter of the alphabet, contained in a turned ivory cylinder with screw-off lid, the lid with the letter 'A' surrounded by painted floral and foliate designs, the cylinder with crack.

Cylinder 1.5in (4cm) high

$300-500   DW

A set of 82 late 18thC bone alphabet tiles, each stained red and with an incised letter on both sides (upper case on one side, lower on the other), comprising three sets of the alphabet and an extra set of vowels, the original wooden box with inset bone panel incised 'SPELLING ALPHABET'.

Box 4.25in (10.5cm) long

$600-800   DW

Mark Picks

Inexpensive toys aimed as quick treats for children, many of these dexterity games were produced many countries. Most examples are generally worth under a tenth of the value shown here, making them an affordable collectibles. Hunt through box lots at auctions or at flea markets for games with interesting themes that may raise the value, such as automobilia, fashion, advertising, sports or famous historical figures. This rare game, for example, is more valuable as it shows Paul Kruger (1825-1904). Kruger, better known as 'Uncle Paul', became the international face of the Boers in the Second Boer War (1899-1902). Once you've spotted and made your lucky purchase, I challenge you not to get addicted to the simple but terrifically difficult game itself!

A German dexterity game, the tin frame with a printed-card backing depicting Paul Kruger, with five white balls and holes for the balls to rest in to resemble his teeth.

c1900   *2.5in (6.5cm) diam*

$350-450   H&C

A group of thirteen late 19thC Scottish carpet bowls.

The age, condition, hand-applied colored patterns and colors of this set combine to make it valuable.

3in (8cm) diam

$2,000-3,000   L&T

QUICK REFERENCE - COQUILLA & TAGUA NUTS

- During the 19thC, many small items, such as snuff boxes, nutmeg graters and sewing utensils, were carved from coquilla nutshells or tagua nuts as well as wood.
- The coquilla nut is a tightly grained, dark-brown nut from the Brazilian Palm. As it is so dense it can be carved in great detail and polished up to a shine.
- When first carved, the tagua nut is a light creamy color. It takes on yellow and darker tones over time. As a consequence, it is often used as an inexpensive alternative to ivory.
- The humor, good level of detail and subject matter of this example make it as valuable as it is.

A German or Dutch coquilla nut snuffbox, in the form of an ape, with glass eyes, with hinged lid.
c1880   *3.5in (9cm) high*
$700-1,000   **HT**

An early 19thC German coquilla nut figural snuff box, in the form of a woman, hinge lacking pin.
4in (10cm) high
$300-500   **GORL**

An early 19thC Indian horn model of a Hindu merchant and his wife, possibly from Calcutta, with etched patterns to their clothing, hair and faces.
7.5in (19cm) high
$300-500   **WW**

A late 19thC lignum vitae inkwell, in the form of a Boxer dog's head, with inset glass eyes, the head opening to reveal a glass well.
4.75in (12cm) high
$300-500   **BATE**

A Robert 'Mouseman' Thompson oak ashtray, with carved mouse, inscribed and dated.
1941   *4in (10cm) long*
$120-180   **WHP**

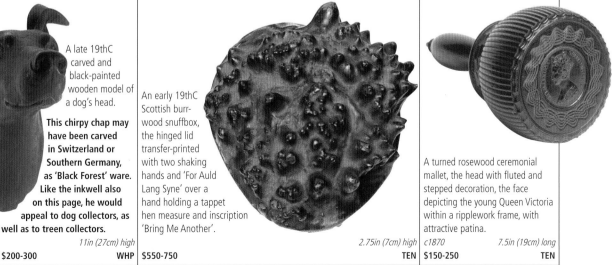

A late 19thC carved and black-painted wooden model of a dog's head.

This chirpy chap may have been carved in Switzerland or Southern Germany, as 'Black Forest' ware. Like the inkwell also on this page, he would appeal to dog collectors, as well as to treen collectors.
11in (27cm) high
$200-300   **WHP**

An early 19thC Scottish burr-wood snuffbox, the hinged lid transfer-printed with two shaking hands and 'For Auld Lang Syne' over a hand holding a tappet hen measure and inscription 'Bring Me Another'.
2.75in (7cm) high
$550-750   **TEN**

A turned rosewood ceremonial mallet, the head with fluted and stepped decoration, the face depicting the young Queen Victoria within a ripplework frame, with attractive patina.
c1870   *7.5in (19cm) long*
$150-250   **TEN**

QUICK REFERENCE - WALL MASKS

- Decorative ceramic masks made to be hung on a wall became fashionable in the 1920s, when new, typically suburban, houses sprang up around towns and cities across the world. Rather than being portraits of famous people, the majority were idealized faces that represented the Art Deco fashions of the day. As such, many wall masks were modeled with short, bobbed hair, stylish headwear and androgynous or stylized features and were decorated in bright, jazzy colors. Affordable and fun, they brightened up and added style to many city center apartments and suburban living rooms.
- Although wall masks were produced by many factories in Europe, the main centers of production were Germany, Czechoslovakia, Austria and the UK. One of the most notable and prolific factories was Goldscheider of Vienna (founded 1885), whose masks can fetch many hundreds of dollars. Highly stylized oval faces, applied tightly curled hair and vibrant green and orange glazes are typical features of Goldscheider masks, which were made from a red terracotta-like clay. Goldscheider masks marked 'Made in England' were produced by Myott & Sons from the 1930s onward and tend to be less desirable.
- Other notable factories include J H Cope in the UK (1887-1946), Goebel in Germany (founded 1871) and Lenci in Italy, which began producing ceramics in 1928. There were also many other factories whose names have been lost over time, primarily as they did not mark their ceramics.
- In all instances, the eye appeal of a wall mask will count toward its value. Pretty faces with character, decorated in bright colors and typifying the Art Deco style will always be sought after. If a mask is by a notable maker, its value will rise. Size also counts. Most wall masks measure around 7-12in (20-30cm) in height. Extra large and some miniature masks will often fetch more than standard pieces. The quality and level of detail of the modeling and glaze will also affect value. Any damage or restoration will reduce value by as much as 50%, particularly if the damage is serious.

A Goldscheider pottery wall mask, of a lady with a tulip flower, model no.6859, glazed in colors, the reverse with impressed and printed marks, with restoration to some locks of hair.

c1933   *8.25in (21cm) high*

$400-600   **WW**

A Goldscheider pottery wall mask, of a lady holding a bunch of grapes, model no.7527, the reverse with printed factory marks.

c1937   *12in (30.5cm) high*

$1,200-1,800   **DUK**

A Goldscheider pottery wall mask, of a lady with green bow and orange hair, model no.6911, the reverse with printed and impressed factory marks.

c1934   *11.5in (29cm) high*

$500-700   **PC**

A Goldscheider pottery wall mask, of a lady with a terrier dog, model no.7914, the reverse with impressed and printed marks.

The American import company Ebeling & Reuss imported a similar design from an unknown Czechoslovakian factory. These imported masks are marked 'ERPHILA', the 'E' and 'R' standing for the company name and the 'PHILA' indicating the city they were based in, Philadelphia. They are usually worth less than 50% of the value of this Goldscheider mask.

9.5in (24cm) high

$800-1,200   **WW**

A Goldscheider pottery wall mask, of a lady, model no.6660, with curly brown hair, green eyes and red lips, the reverse with printed mark.

11in (28.5cm) high

$400-600   **ROS**

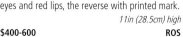

A Goldscheider pottery 'Tragedy' wall mask, of a lady with her face half concealed by a theatre mask, model no.6288, decorated in black and orange, the reverse with printed and incised marks.

14in (35cm) high
$550-750 **FLD**

A miniature Goldscheider pottery wall mask, of a lady gazing at a butterfly on her clasped hands, model no.7261, the reverse with printed and incised marks.

Miniature masks are often scarcer than full-size masks. This design was also produced in an 8.5in (22cm) high size.

c1936 *4.5in (11.5cm) high*
$400-600 **PC**

A Goldscheider pottery wall mask, of a girl wearing a bonnet and blue scarf, glazed in colors, the back with printed and impressed marks.

11in (28cm) high
$300-500 **WW**

A Goldscheider pottery wall mask, of a lady with flowing black hair and a blue scarf, model no.7784, the reverse with impressed and printed marks.

c1937 *11in (28cm) high*
$400-600 **WW**

A Goldscheider pottery wall mask, of a lady with blue hair and a gold-colored hair band, model no.3269, the reverse with impressed and printed marks, with rare original paper label to front.

c1940 *12in (30cm) high*
$300-500 **WW**

A Goldscheider pottery wall mask, of a lady wearing a shawl, model no.7813, designed by Kurt Goebel, the reverse with impressed and incised mark, designed 1937.

This mask was produced in a number of different color variations.

c1938 *13in (33cm) high*
$650-850 **L&T**

QUICK REFERENCE - GOLDSCHEIDER MARKS

- Most Goldscheider pieces are marked, with many bearing the mark shown here, which was used from 1918 onward. This mark could be printed onto or stamped into the back of a piece.
- The company's name curves over the top of a 'WM' monogram for Walter and Marcell Goldscheider, who ran the company from 1918. 'Wien' is German for Vienna.
- The 'Made In Austria' mark had to be included following the British Merchandize Act of 1887 and the various McKinley Tariff Act revisions of 1890-1921.
- The number that appears beneath the mark is the shape or model number. Many Continental ceramics had their shape or model numbers impressed, incised or molded into the bodies. Painted numbers tend to indicate something different, such as the decoration, decorator or even client or batch number.

A Czechoslovakian Art Deco-style wall mask, of a blonde lady with striped scarf.

7.75in (20cm) high

$120-180　　　　FLD

A rare 1920s-30s Czechoslovakian wall mask, of a singing girl, the reverse with printed mark.

8.75in (22cm) high

$1,200-1,800　　　　WW

An Erphila pottery wall mask, model no.11729, for the American market, the back with printed and impressed factory and importer marks.

This charming and almost naval-themed mask is scarce. The colors are vivid and she is not damaged in any way. For more information about the Czechoslovakian company Erphila, see p.390.

9in (24cm) high

$550-750　　　　WW

A miniature Czechoslovakian pottery wall mask, of a lady wearing a blue hat and with hollow eyes.

3in (7.5cm) high

$80-120　　　　CA

QUICK REFERENCE - HOLLYWOOD STARS & CZECHOSLOVAKIA

● **This mask was probably modeled on actress Joan Crawford (1904-77). A small but significant number of Czech wall masks were modeled on Hollywood film stars of the 1920s and '30s. Goebel made a mask that looked like Gracie Fields, while Royal Dux produced one of Bing Crosby, complete with his trademark pipe. Other stars immortalized in ceramic by (as yet unidentified) Czech factories include Ginger Rogers and Rita Hayworth. All production was primarily intended for export, mainly to the USA. Masks of celebrities can fetch slightly more than other masks, but eye appeal, quality, size and condition still count the most toward value.**

A Czechoslovakian Art Deco-style wall mask, of a red-haired lady with a blue spotted scarf, the reverse printed with 'Made in Czechoslovakia'.

7in (18cm) high

$120-180　　　　FLD

A 1930s Czechoslovakian wall mask, of a rather heavily-set lady with dark eye make-up, wearing a geometric patterned beret, the reverse with printed mark.

8.75in (22cm) high

$650-850　　　　WW

A 1930s Czechoslovakian wall mask, of a girl wearing a blue and green-edged bonnet, with 'googly' eyes, with some restoration.

Bulging, rounded 'googly' eyes were also commonly found on dolls made during the 1920s-30s.

8.5in (21.5cm) high

$100-150　　　　CA

A Royal Belvedere pottery wall mask, of a lady with brown hair, in the manner of Goldscheider.

Royal Belvedere was an Austrian company, which employed Stefan Dakon as a designer.

11in (28cm) high

$100-150　　　　CA

A 1930s Beswick 'Lady With Beret in Profile' wall mask, model no.277, glazed in yellow, white and navy blue, the reverse impressed '277'.

4.5in (11.5cm) high

$200-300 WW

A small 1930s Cope & Co. wall mask, of a lady with blonde hair and a green beret.

3in (7.5cm) high

$70-100 CA

A CLOSER LOOK AT A WALL MASK

Talented artist Sandro Vacchetti (1889-1974) worked at Lenci as a decorator and modeler from 1919, becoming its Art Director in 1922 and overseeing the company's 'golden age'. He left to found his own company, Essevi, in Turin in 1934 and produced similar, highly decorated, high quality figurines and masks.

This mask can be found in different colorways. This is one of the stronger and bolder combinations.

The unusual combination of elements, including a monkey, has no precedent and was not copied. It suggests a decadent Art Deco party.

A late 1930s Essevi pottery wall mask, of a lady wearing a large hat and black eye mask with a monkey on her hand, designed by Sandro Vacchetti, the reverse painted 'No.88 ESSEVI ITALIA-TORINO Lalla'.

10.5in (26.5cm) long

$1,500-2,500 PC

A 1950s Cortendorf wall mask, of a lady's profile, with black-glazed skin, blue hair and red lips, the reverse with marks.

10in (25.5cm) high

$70-100 CA

A 1930s Goebel wall mask, of a girl with black hair and flowers in her plaits, the reverse with marks.

The exotic look of the lady, and the bright colors of her adorned hair, make her popular with collectors.

7in (18cm) long

$150-250 CA

A Goebel wall mask, of a lady with blonde hair looking down, the reverse with mark.

The company that became known as Goebel was founded in Germany in 1871.

1928-34

8in (20cm) high

$250-350 PC

Miller's Compares

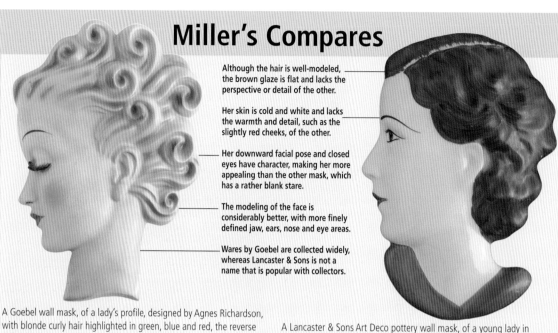

Although the hair is well-modeled, the brown glaze is flat and lacks the perspective or detail of the other.

Her skin is cold and white and lacks the warmth and detail, such as the slightly red cheeks, of the other.

Her downward facial pose and closed eyes have character, making her more appealing than the other mask, which has a rather blank stare.

The modeling of the face is considerably better, with more finely defined jaw, ears, nose and eye areas.

Wares by Goebel are collected widely, whereas Lancaster & Sons is not a name that is popular with collectors.

A Goebel wall mask, of a lady's profile, designed by Agnes Richardson, with blonde curly hair highlighted in green, blue and red, the reverse with mark.

8.5in (21.5cm) high

$200-300   **PC**

A Lancaster & Sons Art Deco pottery wall mask, of a young lady in profile, with brown hair and an orange collar.

7.25in (18.5cm) high

$50-70   **CA**

A Keramos wall mask, designed by Karl Grossl, the reverse with 'Keramia' stamp, impressed number '313' and 'Made in Czechoslovakia' mark.

The freelance modeler Karl Grossl also worked for Goldscheider, hence the similarity of this mask by Austrian company Keramos to designs more commonly associated with Goldscheider. As well as the hallmark Goldscheider curls, the mask has been glazed in similar colors to the Goldscheider equivalents. Although it's surprising to us today, no copyright laws could be used to prevent this happening, as this precise design is subtly different to those of Goldscheider. This mask is also clearly marked by Keramos, so it is not intended to be a forgery. This particular form is rare, as it was only made for a short period.

1934-35   *11in (27cm) high*

$500-700   **WW**

A 1930s Keramos double wall mask, of a young man and his female companion, the reverse with printed marks.

7.5in (19cm) high

$550-750   **WHP**

A 1930s Keramos terracotta 'Harlequinade' wall mask, of a young girl wearing a harlequin hat and yellow ruff, peering out from behind a mask, the reverse with printed factory mark.

Colorful harlequin characters are popular, particularly if they have pretty faces.

9.75in (25cm) high

$800-1,200   **WW**

A 1930s Lenci wall mask, of a lady in an Indian-patterned head scarf, modeled by Helen Konig Scavini, the reverse painted with 'Lenci Torino Made in Italy'.

The headscarf on this high quality mask can be found with different bright colors and different types of flower or motif.

12in (30cm) high

$800-1,200   **GORL**

A 1930s Italian terracotta face mask, in the manner of Goldscheider, as a lady's face with green coiled hair and stylized yellow and green shoulder, marked to reverse '1155 H.O Italy'.

11in (28cm) high

$120-180   FLD

A Continental Art Deco pottery wall mask, of an Oriental young girl with an exotic headdress painted in colors.

This appears to have been inspired by wall masks designed by Clarice Cliff, see p.70, but in plainer, less vibrant colors.

$150-250   SAS

A small Continental pottery wall mask, of a lady in a white hat and brown collar, the reverse marked 'Felt'.

5in (12.5cm) long

$50-70   CA

A 1930s Continental pottery wall mask, of Judy, unmarked.

This unusual subject matter would appeal to collectors of Punch and Judy memorabilia.

7.5in (19cm) high

$150-250   WHP

A 1950s hand-painted solid plaster wall mask, of a lady in profile with a ponytail and inset rhinestones.

9.5in (24cm) high

$70-100   MA

A 1950s hand-painted solid plaster Chinese girl wall mask, in mint condition.

Always examine these post-war plaster masks very closely. Any paint loss, even if 'touched up', reduces value dramatically. Only those in truly mint condition will fetch high sums. The more exotic the subject matter, the better.

11in (28cm) high

$80-120   MA

A 1950s Roskelly hand-painted solid plaster 'Carmen' wall mask, of a lady in a headscarf with flowers, with molded marks and name on the reverse.

8.5in (21.5cm) high

$50-70   PC

WATCHES

QUICK REFERENCE - WATCHES

- Although they were produced in small quantities earlier, wristwatches only really took hold shortly after World War I. They became immensely popular during the early 1920s and by the 1930s they had almost completely replaced the pocket watch.
- Watches can be dated from the style of features such as the case, hands and numbers. Be aware that some of today's makers produce watches in retro styles, so also pay attention to how a watch is made and signs of wear.
- The earliest wristwatches looked like small pocket watches with wire 'lugs' to attach the case to the strap. Rectangular or simple, circular cases with clean-lined faces usually date to the late 1920s-30s or from the 1950s. The late 1940s and 1950s saw shapes and designs become more extravagant and many watches took on the more ornamental styles of period jewelry.

- Factors that contribute toward value include the maker, the materials, the type and complexity of the movement and the style and date of the watch. Currently watches from the 1930s and 1950s-60s are in vogue. Complex watches by the best Swiss makers, such as Patek Philippe, tend to fetch the highest prices.
- Although brands such as Rolex, Cartier and Omega will always be valuable, it may also be worth looking at other brands that are lesser known. Attractive Longines watches often offer great value for money and American brands Hamilton and Elgin produced a wide range of styles during the 1920s-60s that make a great collection.
- Always check the movement is correct for the case and consider condition. Faces can be restored and metal parts re-plated, but it can be expensive and collectors always prefer watches in original condition.

A 1950s Banner stainless steel and gold-filled wristwatch, with 17-jewel Swiss Banner movement, with 'porthole' bezel, with subsidiary seconds dial.

This style of case was popular after World War II, with many other makers producing their own versions. For example, the page opposite has a similar watch by Elgin.

Case 1.25in (3cm) diam

$150-250   DN

A Benrus 14ct gold wristwatch, no.218246, the 17-jewel Benrus movement model BO 1, with subsidiary seconds dial, the case stamped '14k'.

c1950   Case 1.5in (3.5cm) wide

$300-500   DN

A Bulova stainless steel and gold-filled wristwatch, the 17-jewel Bulova movement cal.10AX, the dial with paste-set markers at 12, 3 and 9 and subsidiary seconds dial, with fancy knot lugs, with wear.

1942   Case 1.25in (3cm) wide

$200-300   DN

A Bulova gold-filled wristwatch, no.6794473, the 21-jewel Bulova movement cal.7AK, with Bulova 'Index' hands and subsidiary seconds dial, with some wear to plating.

c1946   Case 1.5in (3.5cm) wide

$120-180   DN

A late 1940s Bulova gold-filled wristwatch, no.9441067, the 17-jewel Bulova movement cal.8AE, with Bulova 'Modern' hands.

Case 1.5in (3.5cm) wide

$120-180   DN

A late 1940s-50s Bulova gold-filled wristwatch, no.8729996, the 21-jewel Bulova movement cal.10BH, with subsidiary seconds dial.

Bulova was founded in 1875 as a jewelry wholesaler in New York City, NY, USA. The company founded its first watch factory in Biel, Switzerland in 1912 and was mass-producing wristwatches by the early 1920s. Sales peaked in the 1930s and '40s when innovatively shaped cases were offered and again in the 1960s and '70s when sales were partly driven by the famous 'Accutron' watch.

Case 1.25in (3cm) wide

$200-300   DN

QUICK REFERENCE - ELGIN

- The Elgin National Watch Company was one of the largest and most successful watch companies in the USA. It operated 1864-1968, initially from a specially built factory in Elgin, Illinois.
- Elgin's first wristwatch was made in 1910. By the time the company closed it had produced over 60 million watches.
- Along with Waltham, Elgin firmly dominated the middle market, offering watches that adapted to the changing styles of the day.
- Elgin's more expensive range was branded 'Lord Elgin'. These watches contained better quality 21-jewel movements.
- Elgin produced two versions of this high-end watch, which were offered at a huge retail price of $95 in 1928. Both are much rarer than the strikingly similar Hamilton 'Piping Rock' of the same period, particularly in this great condition.

An Elgin 14ct white gold and enamel presentation wristwatch, model no.212, ref.577485, the 17-jewel Elgin movement cal.555 no.C649186, with subsidiary seconds dial.

1943   *Case 1.5in (4cm) wide*
$800-1,200   **DN**

An Elgin gold-filled and enamel wristwatch, ref.5532, no.U338828, the 19-jewel Elgin movement cal.672 no.K290339, with subsidiary seconds dial, with some wear to plates on edges.

Protruding 'fancy' lugs and cases were offered by a number of makers, including LeCoultre and Hamilton.

c1953   *Case 1.5in (3.5cm) wide*
$180-220   **DN**

A 1950s Elgin stainless steel and gold-filled wristwatch, the 15-jewel Elgin movement no.35555775, with port-hole bezel, with subsidiary seconds dial, with some wear to the plating.

Case 1.25in (3cm) diam
$120-180   **DN**

A late 1950s Elgin gold-filled mechanical 'Golf Ball' 'direct read' wristwatch, ref.9587, no.U271537, the 17-jewel Elgin movement cal.717, the dial with convex dimpled cover and aperture showing hours and minutes, with wear.

The time is read 'digitally', as the minute and hour dials move past the window. This dimpled 'golf ball' case is rare.

Case 1.25in (3cm) wide
$250-350   **DN**

A late 1950s Lord Elgin gold-filled mechanical 'direct read' wristwatch, ref.7775, no.X669348, the 17-jewel Elgin movement cal.719, the dial with aperture showing hours and minutes.

Case 1.25in (3cm) wide
$200-300   **DN**

A Lord Elgin white-gold-filled wristwatch, no.F849319, the 21-jewel Elgin movement cal.670 no.K762228, with subsidiary seconds dial, with minor wear.

1953   *Case 1.5in (3.5cm) wide*
$150-250   **DN**

A 1950s Lord Elgin 14ct gold wristwatch, ref.4508, no.F197171, the 21-jewel Elgin movement cal.626 no.H450623, with subsidiary seconds dial, the case stamped '14k', scuffed.

Case 1.5in (3.5cm) wide
$300-500   **DN**

WATCHES

A late 1950s-60s Gruen 14ct white gold wristwatch, no.M65 109, style no.335-855, the 21-jewel Gruen movement cal.335, the silvered dial with paste-set numerals and subsidiary seconds dial.

Case 1.5in (4cm) diam

$350-450   DN

A Hamilton 14ct white gold and enamel 'Spur' wristwatch, the 19-jewel Hamilton movement with screw-set jeweling, bi-metallic split balance and overcoil balance-spring, cal.979 no.2905684, with subsidiary seconds dial.

This watch was one of the earliest asymmetric Hamilton wristwatch designs and only 700 were produced. In 1992, a limited edition of 992 'Spur's were sold to commemorate Hamilton's 100th anniversary.

c1927   Case 1.5in (4cm) diam

$3,000-5,000   DN

A Hamilton gold-filled 'Medwick' driver's wristwatch, the 17-jewel Hamilton movement with monometallic balance and overcoil balance-spring, cal.980, no.G196094, with wear.

The small-sized 'Medwick' has a slightly curved case and hinged lugs so that it can be worn on the side of the wrist to make it visible when driving.

c1938   Case 1in (2.5cm) wide

$150-250   DN

QUICK REFERENCE - THE 'VENTURA'

- When it was released in 1957, the 'Ventura' was the world's first battery-powered electric wristwatch. It had taken over a decade of research to design a battery-powered electric movement that could be commercially produced.
- Early mechanisms were not reliable and the watch's reputation suffered, although it has subsequently become very popular.
- The asymmetric design by Richard Arbib was progressive and highly fashionable. Arbib had worked for General Motors, Century Boats and Harry Winston.
- The watch received a boost in popularity after it was worn by Elvis Presley in his 1961 film 'Blue Hawaii'.
- This gold version cost $200 in 1957.

A Hamilton 14ct gold 'Ventura' electric wristwatch, the Hamilton electric movement with flat-split magnetic balance and flat-balance spring, cal.500, the case stamped '14k gold', in good condition.

Case 2in (5cm) high

$1,500-2,500   DN

A Hamilton 14ct gold 'Polaris' electric wristwatch, the Hamilton Electric movement cal.500A, the bowtie case stamped '14k gold', in good condition.

c1965   Case 1.5in (4cm) diam

$300-500   DN

A Hamilton 14ct gold 'Savitar II' electric wristwatch, no.P708526, the Hamilton electric movement cal.505, the case stamped '14k'.

c1965   Case 1.5in (4cm) diam

$300-500   DN

A LeCoultre 10ct gold-filled 'Memovox' alarm wristwatch, the 17-jewel LeCoultre alarm automatic movement cal.K825 no.1778215, with central time-zone alarm disc and date aperture.

c1960   Case 1.75in (4.5cm) diam

$2,000-3,000   DN

A 1950s LeCoultre gold-filled wristwatch, no.372166, the 17-jewel Swiss LeCoultre movement cal.480/CW no.689128, with subsidiary seconds dial.
Case 1in (2.5cm) diam
$350-450   DN

A late 1940s-50s Longines gold-filled wristwatch, no.8675472, the 17-jewel Longines tonneau movement cal.9LT no.8723990, with convex glass, with subsidiary seconds dial.
Case 1.5in (4cm) wide
$200-300   DN

A 1950s Longines gold wristwatch, no.A71280, the 17-jewel Swiss Longines movement cal.32Z no.8051740, with subsidiary seconds dial, the American case stamped '14k'.
Case 1.25in (3cm) wide
$250-350   DN

An Omega 'Seamaster' stainless steel 'De Ville' wristwatch, the 24-jewel Omega automatic movement cal.565 no.2526747, with date aperture.
c1967   Case 1.5in (4cm) diam
$250-350   DN

An Omega stainless steel 'Chronostop' wristwatch, ref.145.009, the 17-jewel Omega movement with start and flyback work, cal.865 no.28092645, the tonneau case with two push-buttons, the sunken dial with luminous baton hands and red center seconds.

Introduced in 1966, the 'Chronostop' allows for times of up to sixty seconds to be measured. Push the button once to start the stopwatch hand, once again to stop it and once again to reset it. As there's no subsidiary dial, if you want to count minutes, you have to do that yourself! The heavy, curving style of this case is typical of the late 1960s and has become fashionable once again today.
c1967   Case 1.5in (4cm) diam
$1,200-1,800   DN

A 1970s Omega 'Seamaster' stainless steel wristwatch, ref.166036, the 24-jewel Omega automatic movement cal.752 no.27640556, the dial with date and day aperture.
Case 1.5in (4cm) diam
$650-850   DN

An Omega black stainless steel limited edition wristwatch, designed by Max Bill in 1987, from an edition of 999, with quartz movement, with date aperture, the case marked 'Omega, OMEGA ART COLLECTION MAX BILL 87, c OMEGA S.A., no. 50681 902'.

Max Bill (1908-94) was a Swiss architect and industrial and graphic designer. He studied at the Bauhaus in Dessau and helped found the Ulm School of Design. Most of his watches were designed for Junghans.
Case 1.5in (4cm) diam
$400-600   QU

A 1930s Rensie 14ct gold wristwatch, no.632268, with 17-jewel Rensie movement, the dial with luminous baton hands and center seconds, the case stamped '14k', in fair condition with replaced minute hand.
Case 1.5in (4cm) wide
$250-350   DN

A Rolex 9ct gold wristwatch, ref. 14163, with 15-jewel Rolex movement, the dial with luminous Arabic numerals, hands and subsidiary seconds dial, the 'Cushion' case engraved 'NM' to the reverse.

c1923   *Case 1.5in (3.5cm) wide*

$1,500-2,500   **DN**

A Rolex 'Oyster' stainless steel wristwatch, ref.2280, no.99818, the 15-jewel Rolex movement with signed patented 'Super' balance cal.620, the dial with luminous Arabic numerals, baton hands and subsidiary seconds dial.

c1940   *Case 1.5in (4cm) diam*

$800-1,200   **DN**

A 1950s Wittnauer stainless steel and gold-filled wristwatch, ref.2022, no.969054, the 17-jewel Wittnauer movement cal.9WNG, with subsidiary seconds dial, with some wear.

Case 1.25in (3cm) wide

$150-250   **DN**

A 1950s Tissot 14ct gold wristwatch, no.48392/78, the signed 17-jewel manual Tissot movement cal.414 no.172841, with subsidiary seconds dial, the case stamped ' MATHEW TISSOT', '14k' and with Swiss standard marks.

Case 1.5in (3.5cm) diam

$250-350   **DN**

A 1950s Wittnauer 14ct gold wristwatch, no.2207416, the 17-jewel Wittnauer movement cal.10ES, the case stamped '14k'.

Case 1in (2.5cm) wide

$300-500   **DN**

A CLOSER LOOK AT A TISSOT WATCH

Ettore Sottsass (1917-2007) was one of the late 20thC's greatest and most influential architects and designers. He was a founder and leader of the Postmodern movement during the 1970s and '80s.

Tissot was founded in the Swiss watchmaking town of Le Locle in 1853. It continues to produce innovative watches and mechanisms as part of the Swatch Group today.

The minimal color palette, the simple, modern forms and the use of matt and shiny surface effects all recall architectural features and are typical of Sottsass's design aesthetic.

Interest in and prices paid for Sottsass's designs have been rising, particularly since his death.

This watch is in mint condition and is complete with the packaging, which is desirable.

A Tissot stainless steel and 18ct gold wristwatch, designed by Ettore Sottsass in 1988, the case with facsimile signature and marked 'TISSOT, S 150 SWISS', '18 K GOLD BEZEL, S 150/250, SAPPHIRE CRYSTAL e.a.', with original box and paperwork.

c1988

$1,500-2,500   **QU**

A Zenith 18ct gold 'Stellina' wristwatch, no.115D796, the 17-jewel Zenith movement cal.2542, the dial with date aperture.

c1966   *Case 1.5in (4cm) diam*

$550-750   **DN**

A Vertex Art Deco diamond-set lady's wristwatch, ref.727/4601, with 16-jewel rectangular movement, monometallic balance and flat-bar screw.

Case 2.25in (6cm) high
$650-850 DN

An Art Deco platinum and diamond lady's wristwatch.

7in (17.5cm) long
$2,500-3,500 WW

A diamond- and seed-pearl-set lady's fob watch, the 16-jewel movement signed 'Ferrero S.A', the cover set with an old-cut diamond and bordered with seed pearls, on a bar pin set with a pearl and old eight-cut diamond cluster.

1.75in (4cm) high
$650-850 TEN

A silver and enamel fob watch, no.323988, with 15-jewel Swiss lever movement, the two-piece hinged case with engine-turned detail and flowers, with green and black enamel chain.

c1900 Case 1in (2.5cm) high
$800-1,200 DN

An Asprey Art Deco pendant watch, with 15-jewel Swiss 'Cord' lever movement, with skeleton-back case.

c1930 1in (2.5cm) high
$400-600 DN

A diamond-set lady's fob watch, the reverse set with graduated cushion-shaped diamonds, suspended from a diamond-set bow pin.

2in (5cm) high
$550-750 LC

An Art Deco enamel fob watch, the 15-jewel Swiss lever movement signed 'Speck Watch', the dial with Breguet hands, the spherical case with a band of brilliant-cut pastes, the double chain with blue enamel navette-shaped spacers.

Case 0.75in (2cm) diam
$650-850 DN

A Dent 18ct gold pocket watch, no.23974, the lever fusee movement with three-armed gold balance, flat-balance spring and Bosley-type regulator, with subsidiary seconds dial and marked 'Dent 35 Cockspur St, London', the case with London hallmarks.

1862 Case 1.75in (4.5cm) diam
$800-1,200 DN

An early 1950s Ingraham 'TOM CORBETT SPACE CADET' watch, on original card, with directions manual.

Tom Corbett appeared in the eponymous television series 1950-55, on the radio in 1952, in books 1952-56 and comics from 1952 onward. The character was revived in 2009 by Bluewater Productions.
$250-350 CBA

WATERLOO & WELLINGTON

QUICK REFERENCE - WATERLOO

- The year 2015 is the 200th anniversary of the Battle of Waterloo. Fought on 18th June 1815 in open countryside near Waterloo in Belgium, it was the decisive battle that saw the defeat of Emperor Napoleon (1769-1821) and led to the end of his rule and his subsequent exile to St Helena.
- The Anglo-allied army was led by Arthur Wellesley, the Duke of Wellington (1769-1852) and the Prussian army was led by Gebhard Leberecht von Blücher, Prince von Wahlstatt (1742-1819).
- According to Wellington, who became a national hero upon his return to Britain, the battle was 'the nearest run thing you ever saw in your life.'
- Pieces produced to commemorate the victory are often desirable. High sums are fetched by anything firmly connected directly to important people or moments in the battle or to the man himself.

An unusual pottery drainer, printed in blue with Wellington and his generals on horseback in the battlefield.

This drainer was probably manufactured by Jones & Sons of Hanley (1826-1828) who are recorded as producing a 'British History' series including a print entitled 'Battle of Waterloo'.

c1828   12in (30.5cm) wide
$650-850   H&C

A 19thC pearlware commemorative jug, molded with named equestrian portraits of Wellington and von Blücher beneath a molded canopy, with pink luster.

c1815   5.25in (13cm) high
$2,000-3,000   H&C

An early-mid 19thC Staffordshire 'Wellington With Cocked Hat' pot lid, by Mayer, no.182, without lettering, chipped and framed.

$800-1,200   H&C

A head and shoulders wax portrait of Wellington, mounted on (faded) red velvet, in its original hexagonal ebonized-wood frame.

6in (15cm) diam
$250-350   W&W

A hollow die-struck copper medallion, decorated with a bust of Wellington, the reverse with a commemorative inscription, the interior containing cartridge-paper discs of 'British Victories in Portugal, Spain & France, 1808-1815'.

c1815   1.75in (4.5cm) diam
$250-350   W&W

An 1815 Waterloo medal, awarded to William Pateman of the 1st Regiment Foot Guards, apparently not on the medal role list.

c1815
$3,000-5,000   GORL

A painted cast-iron door stop, in the form of Wellington, in good condition.

c1820   14in (35.5cm) high
$400-600   DN

'The London Gazette', July 1st 1815, original newspaper reporting the aftermath of the Battle of Waterloo, in very good condition.

8in (20.5cm) wide
$120-180   PC

A pair of late 1920s cast-iron nut crackers, the crackers in the form of a skull and the arms in the form of bones, with registered number 740410 for 1928.

The first metal nutcracker dates from the 3rdC or 4thC BC. By the Victorian 'age of invention', many elaborate and ingenious types were made, with those that used levers, screws and hammers being the most popular.

6in (15cm) long

$250-350   D&H

An unusual 19thC bronze ring, the tri-bulb club head on a tri-banded hoop with lozenge pattern.

The crude yet well-proportioned manufacture suggests this ring may have been made by a blacksmith or craftsman in his own workshop. It may have been cast for a loved one, with each of the three lobes perhaps representing a family member.

1.5in (4cm) long

$100-150   D&H

A mid-19thC sandstone gravestone in the form of a Latin cross, with recessed lozenge showing a monogram for 'SH' and further carved 'R.I.P.', with chips to two arms.

Although headstone forms became more diverse in the 19thC, Latin, Roman or Christian crosses remained popular. The shape is an obvious representation of Christ's cross and resurrection in the New Testament. Headstones are, unsurprisingly, rarely offered for sale.

c1850-70   *39in (99cm) high*

$550-750   D&H

A 1920s cast-iron 'Burdizzo' castration device.

The Burdizzo is a rather crude castration device used primarily on farm animals. It employs a large clamp designed to break the blood vessels leading into the testicles. Once the blood supply to the testicles is lost, testicular necrosis occurs and the testicles shrink, soften and eventually deteriorate completely.

16in (40.5cm) long

$40-60   D&H

QUICK REFERENCE - CRIMINAL MUGSHOTS

- The much-quoted statement that 'a picture speaks a thousand words' was the reason behind the development of criminal portraits, commonly known today as 'mugshots'. Written descriptions were simply too unreliable and vague. Robert Evan Roberts, Governor of Bedford Prison in the 1850s said 'Photography as an agent in discovering the antecedents of criminals, especially tramps and strangers, is unquestionably a very useful auxiliary and in my opinion should be brought into prison use generally.'
- The first mugshots were reputedly taken in Belgium in c1843 in an attempt to record known criminals.
- By 1857 the New York police had adopted the practice, opening a gallery so that the public could come in to see the daguerreotypes of 'hookers, stooges, grifters and goons.'
- Mugshots offer a rare insight into the lower and criminal classes of the late 19thC, who were otherwise rarely photographed. Photographic portraits were expensive so those that survive from this time are mainly of the gentry and middle classes.
- Like photographs of dead people or soon-to-be executed criminals, mugshots are hotly collected by a niche group of collectors.

Two pairs of 19thC American convict 'mugshot' photographs, showing a detained criminal arrested by the Boston Inspector's Office, each stamped 'The Inspectors Office, Boston, Massachusetts', framed.

Photographs 3.75in (9.5cm) high

$300-500 each pair   D&H

WEIRD & WONDERFUL

A pair of late 19thC Lancashire wooden and leather pitt clogs, later re-soled with iron.

The Lancashire clog was an adaptation of the all-wood sabot (clog) worn by the French and Dutch peasantry. It was introduced into Lancashire when the Flemish weavers settled in the Bolton area 'wearing wode shoon all of a peece', with the heydey of the clog between the 1840s and the 1920s. Leather 'uppers' replaced the all-wood shoe but the 'Lancashire clog' kept its wooden sole.

11in (28cm) long

$80-120   D&H

A mid-19thC French or German shadow-box framed reliquary, with paperolles work, paper filigree quilling, dried and tied flowers, beads and gilded scrolled papers in Latin text and silk cord with central paper cartouche depicting three figures and the crucifix and red rubber stamped seal, with ebonized reverse.

A reliquary (also referred to as a shrine or châsse) is a container for relics. These may be the physical remains of saints (such as bones), pieces of clothing or some other object associated with saints or other religious figures. This particular example is possibly a convent piece worked by cloistered nuns.

11in (28cm) wide

$500-700   D&H

A piece of toast from Prince Charles's wedding-day breakfast, baked sometime before and toasted on 29th July 1981.

'Acquired' by the vendor from Prince Charles's discarded breakfast tray in Buckingham Palace on the day of the wedding to Diana. The vendor was the mother of one of the maids at Buckingham Palace.

$500-700   HAN

A pair of jay's wings, from a bird shot by King George V at Elveden, November 1928, with a cartridge shot from the Kings gun and a note card reading 'Shot by King George at Elveden Nov.1928 and given by him to C.C (?)', in cardboard box.

$200-300   TRI

A late 20thC painted latex, rubber and fabric severed hand, from a fairground horror ride or show.

6.75in (17cm) long

$50-70   ANAA

A 17thC articulated iron dog collar, with spikes.

The spikes on this collar helped to protect the dog's vulnerable neck from attack from wolves, and even other dogs, when hunting. This form of collar is often mistakenly identified as a 'slave collar'.

20in (51cm) long

$300-500   ANAA

A rare set of four leather pony or donkey tennis-lawn boots, with straps and flower stampings.

These boots were worn by ponies pulling lawnmowers across lawns and lawn-tennis courts, with the idea being that they would stop the animal's hooves ruining the lawn.

4.75in (12cm) high

$300-500   PC

A 19thC-style hatter's tole trade sign.

Tole is thin tin or steel sheeting that is usually painted. Tradesmen's signs are highly collectible, particularly if they are authentic antique pieces that actually hung in the street.

The top hat was developed in the late 18thC and was accepted as a symbol of respectability after it was worn by Prince Albert in 1850.

40in (99cm) wide

$1,000-1,500   DN

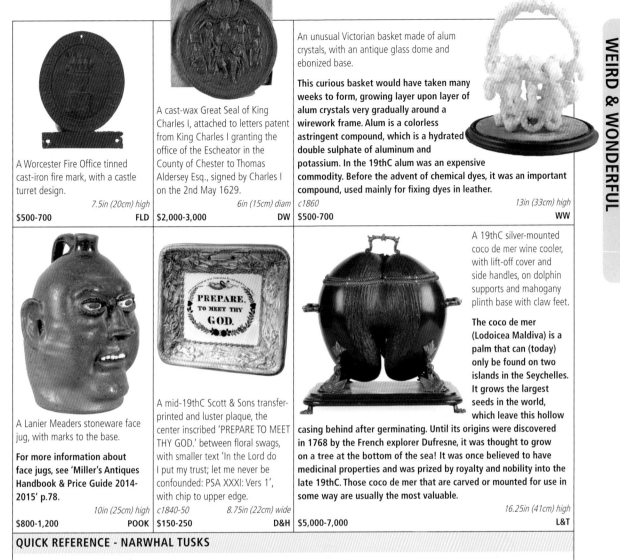

A Worcester Fire Office tinned cast-iron fire mark, with a castle turret design.

7.5in (20cm) high

$500-700   FLD

A cast-wax Great Seal of King Charles I, attached to letters patent from King Charles I granting the office of the Escheator in the County of Chester to Thomas Aldersey Esq., signed by Charles I on the 2nd May 1629.

6in (15cm) diam

$2,000-3,000   DW

An unusual Victorian basket made of alum crystals, with an antique glass dome and ebonized base.

This curious basket would have taken many weeks to form, growing layer upon layer of alum crystals very gradually around a wirework frame. Alum is a colorless astringent compound, which is a hydrated double sulphate of aluminum and potassium. In the 19thC alum was an expensive commodity. Before the advent of chemical dyes, it was an important compound, used mainly for fixing dyes in leather.

c1860   13in (33cm) high

$500-700   WW

A Lanier Meaders stoneware face jug, with marks to the base.

For more information about face jugs, see 'Miller's Antiques Handbook & Price Guide 2014-2015' p.78.

10in (25cm) high

$800-1,200   POOK

A mid-19thC Scott & Sons transfer-printed and luster plaque, the center inscribed 'PREPARE TO MEET THY GOD.' between floral swags, with smaller text 'In the Lord do I put my trust; let me never be confounded: PSA XXXI: Vers 1', with chip to upper edge.

PREPARE. TO MEET THY GOD.

c1840-50   8.75in (22cm) wide

$150-250   D&H

A 19thC silver-mounted coco de mer wine cooler, with lift-off cover and side handles, on dolphin supports and mahogany plinth base with claw feet.

The coco de mer (Lodoicea Maldiva) is a palm that can (today) only be found on two islands in the Seychelles. It grows the largest seeds in the world, which leave this hollow casing behind after germinating. Until its origins were discovered in 1768 by the French explorer Dufresne, it was thought to grow on a tree at the bottom of the sea! It was once believed to have medicinal properties and was prized by royalty and nobility into the late 19thC. Those coco de mer that are carved or mounted for use in some way are usually the most valuable.

16.25in (41cm) high

$5,000-7,000   L&T

QUICK REFERENCE - NARWHAL TUSKS

- This is the tusk of a narwhal or narwhale (Monodon monoceros), an Arctic-dwelling whale. The tusk has a characteristic helical, twisted appearance and can grow to over 10ft (3m) long.
- The Inuit believed that the narwhal was created when a female whale hunter struck a whale with her harpoon and was dragged into the ocean. She was transformed into a narwhal and her twisted hair became the tusk.
- As late as the mid-18thC, Europeans believed that they were unicorn horns. Unicorns could only be tamed by virgins and their horns were said to have magical and medicinal powers.
- This belief and the dramatic size and rarity of the horns meant that they were coveted by nobility and royalty.
- Narwhal tusks were used as symbols of royal power, as antidotes to poison, and were often set with gems and stored in treasuries.
- As the narwhal is an endangered species, trade in their tusks is governed by the international CITES laws.

A late 19thC narwhal tusk, with a modern metal fitting, mounted on a marble base.

78.5in (200cm) long

$15,000-20,000   L&T

WINE & DRINKING

A 1950s Czechoslovakian lemonade or water set, probably by Borské Sklo, all acid-etched and cut with stylized animals within abstract shapes, the jug with polished pontil mark.

Jug 10in (25.5cm) high

$120-180   **MA**

A set of six 1950s 'Girls Around The World' glasses, each transfer-printed with a glamorous lady wearing national costume surrounded by national icons.

New York and Paris tend to be the most popular and valuable individual glasses.

4.75in (12cm) high

$100-150   **MA**

A silver-plated presentation cocktail shaker, engraved with the 242 Squadron emblem of a flying boot marked '242' kicking a Nazi soldier, inscribed 'To Mack, from the Squadron, January 1941' and with 28 signatures, including that of Douglas Bader.

The connection with Bader and the Royal Canadian airforce raises the value of this cocktail shaker, which may have fetched less than half of this value had it not been autographed in this way.

10.5in (27cm) high

$500-700   **W&W**

An early 1960s 'Bamboo' lemonade or water set, all cut with a stylized bamboo pattern.

Glasses 6.5in (16.5cm) high

$100-150   **MA**

A set of six 1950s 'Hawaiian Melody' glasses, printed with Hawaiians swimming, dancing or welcoming visitors.

These are popular designs. Another set, called 'Bongo Rhythm', was also produced.

5in (12.5cm) high

$100-150   **MA**

A set of six 1950s glasses, printed with African-American jazz musicians playing instruments, with original box.

Box 14.75in (37.5cm) long

$120-180   **MA**

A 1950s pressed-glass 'Glamour Girl on Rug' mug or beer tankard, the reverse of the transfer showing her topless.

For a similar glass decorated with a different glamour girl, see 'Miller's Collectibles Handbook 2012-2013' p.196.

5in (12cm) high

$30-50   **MA**

A 1950s Old Jersey Glass of Milville New Jersey blue pressed-glass guitar-shaped tray, the two beakers molded with musical notes.

8.25in (21cm) long

$50-70   **MA**

A large James Dixon & Sons Ltd. silver, glass and crocodile-skin spirit flask, the silver with Sheffield hallmarks, the base pulling off to form a cup.

1934   6.75in (17cm) high

$400-600   DN

An oversized William Hutton & Sons Ltd. silver spirit flask, London, engraved 'HDW'.

1905   8.75in (22cm) high 20.25oz

$1,200-1,800   DN

A James Dixon & Sons electroplated brandy flask, in the form of a leather-bound book with silvered corners entitled 'A PLEASANT SURPRISE', one corner rotating to be released as a stopper.

Novelty-shaped flasks tend to be rare and highly sought after. The title of the 'book' is amusing and this probably contributed to the value.

5.75in (14.5cm) high

$650-850   CHEF

A late 1960s pear-shaped plastic ice bucket, with glass liner, the base marked 'REG DESIGN NO.918844' for 1964.

9in (23cm) high

$50-70   MA

A 1950s cast-metal 'Zulu' bar accessory, the heads fitted with a corkscrew and a bottle opener, the reverse impressed 'MADE IN ENGLAND'.

5.5in (14cm) high

$120-180   MA

A mid-19thC brass Thomason-type corkscrew, with turned bone handle and Coney patent tablet, missing brush.

Thomason's patent of 1802 used a double-helix mechanism, which meant that constant turning would both push the spiraling 'worm' into the cork and draw it out in one uninterrupted movement.

$250-350   DA&H

A late 19thC 'King's Screw' open-frame corkscrew, the ivory handle with brush and suspension ring.

7.25in (18.5cm) high

$250-350   DN

A Doulton Lambeth salt-glazed mask jug, the middle inscribed 'FILL WHAT YOU WILL AND DRINK WHAT YOU FILL', the base with impressed mark.

The form of this jug is based on the mid-16thC Bartmann or Bellarmine jug, which bears a bearded face on the neck. The name Bellarmine refers to the unpopular Cardinal Roberto Bellarmino (1542-1621), an opponent of Protestantism.

6.25in (16cm) high

$550-750   LOC

Every item illustrated in Miller's Collectibles by Judith Miller and Mark Hill has a letter code that identifies the dealer, auction house, or private collector that owns or sold it. In this way the source of the item can be identified. The list below is a key to these codes. In the list, auction houses are shown by the letter A, dealers by the letter D, and private collectors by the letters PC. Inclusion in this book in no way constitutes or implies a contract or a binding offer on the part of any of our contributors to supply or sell the goods illustrated, or similar items, at the prices stated.

A&G (A)
ANDERSON & GARLAND
Anderson House, Crispin Court,
Newbiggin Lane,
Westerhope,
Newcastle-upon-Tyne
Tyne and Wear, NE5 1BF, UK
Tel: 0044 191 430 3000
info@andersonandgarland.com
www.andersonandgarland.com

AH (A)
HARTLEY'S
Victoria Hall Salerooms,
Little Lane, Ilkley,
West Yorkshire, LS29 8EA, UK
Tel: 0044 1943 816 363
info@hartleysauctions.co.uk
www.andrewhartleyfinearts.co.uk

ANAA (D)
ANASTACIA'S ANTIQUES
617 Bainbridge Street,
Philadelphia, PA 19147
Tel: 215 928 9111
anastasciasantiques@gmail.com
www.anastasciasantiques.com

BATE (A)
BATEMANS
The Saleroom, Ryhall Road,
Stamford, Lincolnshire, PE9 1XF, UK
Tel: 0044 1780 766466
info@batemans-auctions.co.uk
www.batemans-auctions.co.uk

BELL (A)
BELLMANS
Newpound,
Wisborough Green,
Billingshurst,
West Sussex, RH14 0AZ, UK
Tel: 0044 1403 700 858
enquiries@bellmans.co.uk
www.bellmans.co.uk

BER (A)
BERTOIA
2141 De Marco Drive
Vineland, NJ 08360
Tel: 856 692 1881
toys@bertoiaauctions.com
www.bertoiaauctions.com

BETH (D)
BETH ADAMS
Stands G023-25/28-30
and SO59-60,
Alfies Antique Market,
13-25 Church Street,
Marylebone,
London, NW8 8DT, UK
Tel: 0044 7776 136 003
www.alfiesantiques.com

BEV (D)
BEVERLEY ADAMS
c/o Christique
11 West Street, Dorking,
Surrey, RH4 1BL, UK
Tel: 0044 1306 883 849
www.christique.com

BGL (P)(C)
BLOCK GLASS LTD.
blockglss@aol.com

BLO (A)
DREWEATTS & BLOOMSBURY
Bloomsbury House,24 Maddox
Street, London, W1S 1PP, UK
Tel: 0044 20 7495 9494
info@bloomsburyauctions.com
www.bloomsburyauctions.com

BPH (D)
BATTERSEA PEN HOME
PO Box 6128,
Epping, Essex, CM16 4GG, UK
Tel: 0044 1992 578 885
orders@penhome.co.uk
www.penhome.co.uk

CA (A)
CHISWICK AUCTIONS
1 Colville Road,
London, W3 8BL, UK
Tel: 0044 2089 924 442
info@chiswickauctions.co.uk
www.chiswickauctions.co.uk

CAN (A)
THE CANTERBURY AUCTION
GALLERIES
40 Station Road West,
Canterbury, Kent, CT2 8AN, UK
Tel: 0044 1227 763 337
www.thecanterburyauctiongalleries.com

CAPE (A)
CAPES DUNN
The Auction Galleries,
38 Charles Street,
Manchester, M1 7DB, UK
Tel: 0044 161 273 1911
capesdunn@googlemail.com
www.capesdunn.com

CBA (A)
COMIC BOOK AUCTIONS
PO Box 58386, London,
NW1W 9RE, UK
Tel: 0044 2074 240 007
www.compalcomics.com

CENC (D)
CENTRAL COLLECTABLES
sally@centralcollectables.com
www.centralcollectables.com

CHEF (A)
CHEFFINS
Clifton House,
1 & 2 Clifton Road,
Cambridge,
Cambridgeshire, CB1 7EA, UK
Tel: 0044 1223 213343
www.cheffins.co.uk

CHT (A)
CHARTERHOUSE
The Long Street Salerooms,
Sherborne,
Dorset, DT9 3BS, UK
Tel: 0044 1935 812 277
www.charterhouse-auction.com

CM (A)
CHARLES MILLER
11 Imperial Road,
London, SW6 2AG, UK
Tel: 0044 20 7806 5530
www.charlesmillerltd.com

COC (A)
COMIC CONNECT
873 Broadway, Suite 201,
New York, NY 10003
Tel: 212 895 3999
support@comicconnect.com
www.comicconnect.com

COTS (A)
COTSWOLD AUCTION COMPANY
Chapel Walk Saleroom,
Chapel Walk, Cheltenham,
Gloucestershire, GL50 3DS, UK
Tel: 0044 1242 256 363
info@cotswoldauction.co.uk
www.cotswoldauction.co.uk

CRIS (D)
CRISTOBAL
26 Church Street, Marylebone,
London, NW8 8EP, UK
Tel: 0044 2077 247 230
www.cristobal.co.uk

D&H (D)
DOE & HOPE
The Onion Barn, Shoe Cottage,
15 High Street, Blunham,
Bedfordshire, MK44 3NL, UK
Tel: 0044 7729 213 013
info@doeandhope.com
www.doeandhope.com

DA&H (A)
DEE, ATKINSON & HARRISON
The Exchange,
Exchange Street,
Driffield,
Yorkshire, YO25 6LD, UK
Tel: 0044 1377 253 151
www.dahauctions.com

DMC (A)
DUMOUCHELLES
409 East Jefferson Avenue,
Detroit, MI 48226
Tel: 313 963 6255
www.dumouchelles.com

DN (A)
DREWEATTS & BLOOMSBURY
Donnington Priory, Donnington,
Newbury, Berkshire, RG14 2JE, UK
Tel: 0044 1635 553 553
donnington@dnfa.com
www.dnfa.com

DOR (A)
DOROTHEUM
Palais Dorotheum,
Dorotheergasse 17,
1010 Vienna, Austria
Tel: 0043 1 51 56 00
www.dorotheum.com

DRA (A)
RAGO ARTS
333 North Main Street, Lambertville,
NJ 08530
Tel: 609 397 9374
info@ragoarts.com
www.ragoarts.com

DS (A)
DUNBAR SLOANE
7 Maginnity Street,
Wellington 6011, New Zealand
Tel: 0064 4 472 1367
info@dunbarsloane.co.nz
www.dunbarsloane.com

DUK (A)
DUKE'S
The Dorchester Fine Art Saleroom,
Weymouth Avenue, Dorchester,
Dorset, DT1 1QS, UK
Tel: 0044 1305 265 080
enquiries@dukes-auctions.com
www.dukes-auctions.com

DW (A)
DOMINIC WINTER
Mallard House, Broadway Lane,
South Cerney, Cirencester,
Gloucestershire, GL7 5UQ, UK
Tel: 0044 1285 860 006
info@dominicwinter.co.uk
www.dominicwinter.co.uk

ECGW (A)
EWBANK'S
Burnt Common Auction Rooms
London Road, Send, Woking
Surrey, GU23 7LN, UK
Tel: 0044 1483 223 101
antiques@ewbankauctions.co.uk
www.ewbankauctions.co.uk

FIS Ⓐ
DR FISCHER
Trappensee-Schlösschen
74074 Heilbronn,
Germany
Tel: 0049 71 31 15 55 70
info@auctions-fischer.de
www.auctions-fischer.de

FLD Ⓐ
FIELDING'S
Mill Race Lane,
Stourbridge,
West Midlands, DY8 1JN, UK
Tel: 0044 1384 444 140
info@fieldingsauctioneers.co.uk
www.fieldingsauctioneers.co.uk

FRE Ⓐ
FREEMAN'S
1808 Chestnut Street,
Philadelphia,
PA 19103
Tel: 215 563 9275
info@freemansauction.com
www.freemansauction.com

GAZE Ⓐ
T W GAZE
Diss Auction Rooms,
Roydon Road, Diss,
Norfolk, IP22 4LN, UK
Tel: 0044 1379 650 306
sales@dissauctionrooms.co.uk
www.twgaze.com

GBA Ⓐ
GRAHAM BUDD AUCTIONS
PO Box 47519,
London, N14 6XD, UK
Tel: 0044 2083 662 525
or 0044 7974 113 394
gb@grahambuddauctions.co.uk
www.grahambuddauctions.
co.uk

GC ⓅⒸ
GRAHAM COOLEY COLLECTION
Tel: 0044 7968 722 269
gc@itm-power.com

GHOU Ⓐ
GARDINER HOULGATE
9 Leafield Way, Corsham,
Bath, SN13 9SW, UK
Tel: 0044 1225 812 912
auctions@gardinerhoulgate
.co.uk
www.gardinerhoulgate.co.uk

GORB Ⓐ
GORRINGES
Terminus Road,
Bexhill-on-Sea,
East Sussex, TN39 3LR, UK
Tel: 0044 1424 212994
www.gorringes.co.uk

GORL Ⓐ
GORRINGES
Garden Street, Lewes,
East Sussex, BN7 1XE, UK
Tel: 0044 1424 478 221
gardenst@gorringes.co.uk
www.gorringes.co.uk

GROB Ⓓ
ROBINSON ANTIQUES
Stand G077-78 & G091-92
Alfies Antique Market,
13-25 Church Street,
Marylebone,
London, NW8 8DT, UK
Tel: 0044 7955 085 723
www.alfiesantiques.com

GWRA Ⓐ
GW RAILWAYANA AUCTIONS
The Willows,
Badsey Road,
Evesham,
Worcestershire, WR11 7PA, UK
Tel: 0044 1386 760 109
simon@gwra.co.uk
www.gwra.co.uk

H&C Ⓐ
HISTORICAL & COLLECTABLE
Kennetholme, Midgham
Reading, Berkshire, RG7 5UX, UK
Tel: 0044 1189 712 420
www.historicalandcollectable.com

HALL Ⓐ
HALLS
Battlefield, Shrewsbury,
Shropshire, SY4 3DR, UK
Tel: 0044 1743 450700
www.hallsestateagents.co.uk/
fine-art

HAN Ⓐ
HANSONS AUCTIONEERS
Heage Lane, Etwall,
Derbyshire, DE65 6LS, UK
Tel: 0044 1283 733 988
www.hansonsauctioneers.co.uk

HER Ⓐ
HERITAGE AUCTIONEERS
500 Maple Avenue, 17th Floor,
Dallas, Texas 75219-3941
Tel: 877 437 4824
www.ha.com

HT Ⓐ
HARTLEY'S
Victoria Hall Salerooms,
Little Lane, Ilkley,
West Yorkshire, LS29 8EA, UK
Tel: 0044 1943 816 363
info@hartleysauctions.co.uk
www.andrewhartleyfinearts.co.uk

HW Ⓐ
HOLLOWAYS
49 Parsons Street,
Banbury,
Oxfordshire, OX16 5NB, UK
Tel: 0044 1295 817 777
enquiries@hollowaysauctioneers.
co.uk
www.hollowaysauctioneers.co.uk

IMC Ⓐ
I M CHAIT
9330 Civic Center Drive
Beverly Hills,
CA 90210
Tel: 310 285-0182
chait@chait.com
www.chait.com

JDJ Ⓐ
JAMES D JULIA
203 Skowhegan Road,
Fairfield,
ME 04937
Tel: 207 453 7125
info@jamesdjulia.com
www.jamesdjulia.com

KAU Ⓐ
AUKTIONSHAUS KAUPP
Schloss Sulzburg,
Hauptstrasse 62,
79295 Sulzburg,
Germany
Tel: 0049 76 34 50 38 0
auktionen@kaupp.de
www.kaupp.de

KKO Ⓓ
KK OUTLET
42 Hoxton Square,
London, N1 6PB, UK
Tel: 0044 207 033 7680
www.kkoutlet.com

L&T Ⓐ
LYON & TURNBULL
33 Broughton Place,
Edinburgh, EH1 3RR, UK
Tel: 0044 131 557 8844
info@lyonandturnbull.com
www.lyonandturnbull.com

LC Ⓐ
LAWRENCES
The Linen Yard, South Street,
Crewkerne, Somerset,
TA18 8AB, UK
Tel: 0044 1460 73041
enquiries@lawrences.co.uk
www.lawrences.co.uk

LHA Ⓐ
LESLIE HINDMAN
1338 West Lake Street, Chicago,
IL 60607
Tel: 312 280 1212
www.lesliehindman.com

LOC Ⓐ
LOCKE & ENGLAND
18 Guy Street,
Leamington Spa,
Warwickshire, CV32 4RT, UK
Tel: 0044 1926 889 100
info@leauction.co.uk
www.leauction.co.uk

LOCK Ⓐ
LOCKDALES
52 Barrack Square, Martlesham
Heath, Ipswich, Suffolk, IP5 3RF, UK
Tel: 0044 1473 627 110
sales@lockdales.com
www.lockdales.com

LSK Ⓐ
LACY SCOTT & KNIGHT
10 Risbygate Street,
Bury St Edmunds,
Suffolk, IP33 3AA, UK
Tel: 0044 1284 748 623
fineart@lsk.co.uk
www.lskauctioncentre.co.uk

LT Ⓐ
LOUIS TAYLOR
Britannia House,
10 Town Road, Hanley,
Stoke-on-Trent,
Staffordshire, ST1 2QG, UK
Tel: 0044 1782 214 111
enquiries@louistaylorfineart.co.uk
www.louistaylorfineart.co.uk

MA Ⓓ
MANIC ATTIC
No Longer Trading

MAR Ⓐ
FRANK MARSHALL
Marshall House,
Church Hill, Knutsford,
Cheshire, WA16 6DH, UK
Tel: 0044 1565 653284
antiques@frankmarshall.co.uk
www.frankmarshall.co.uk

M20C Ⓓ
MID20C
63 West End, Redruth,
Cornwall, TR15 2SQ, UK
Tel: 0044 1209 315 949

MHC Ⓓ
MARK HILL COLLECTION
www.markhill.net

MDM Ⓓ
M&D MOIR
manddmoir@aol.com
www.manddmoir.co.uk

MLL Ⓐ
MALLAMS
Bocardo House,
St Michael's Street,
Oxford, Oxfordshire, OX1 2EB, UK
Tel: 0044 1865 241 358
oxford@mallams.co.uk
www.mallams.co.uk

MM Ⓐ
MULLOCK'S
Ludlow Racecourse,
Bromfield, Ludlow, Shropshire,
SY8 2BT, UK
Tel: 0044 1694 771 771
auctions@mullocksauctions.co.uk
www.mullocksauctions.co.uk

MODO Ⓓ
MODO ITALIA
Alfies Antique Market,
13-25 Church Street,
Marylebone, London,
NW8 8DT, UK
Tel: 0044 7796 061 901
info@modo-italia.co.uk
www.modo-italia.co.uk

MORP Ⓐ
MORPHY AUCTIONS
2000 North Reading Road,
Denver, PA 17517
Tel: 717 335 3435
morphy@morphyauctions.com
www.morphyauctions.com

MUR Ⓐ
TONY MURLAND ANTIQUE TOOLS
78 High Street, Needham Market,
Suffolk, IP6 8AW, UK
Tel: 0044 1449 722 992
Email: tony@antiquetools.co.uk
www.antiquetools.co.uk

NDS Ⓐ
NATE D SANDERS
11901 Santa Monica Boulevard,
Suite 555, Los Angeles,
CA 90025
Tel: 310 440 2982
info@natedsanders.com
www.natedsanders.com

NWST ⓅⒸ
NICK WEST
Private Collector
Tel: 0044 771 529 4481
nicquest_uk@hotmail.com

ON Ⓐ
ONSLOWS
The Coach House, Manor Road,
Stourpaine, Dorset, DT11 8TQ, UK
Tel: 0044 1258 488 838
or 0044 7831 473 400
www.onslows.co.uk

P&I Ⓓ
PAOLA & IAIA
Stand S057,
Alfies Antiques Market,
13-25 Church Street,
London, NW8 8DT, UK
Tel: 0044 7751 084 135
paola_iaia_london@yahoo.com
www.alfiesantiques.com

PC ⓅⒸ
PRIVATE COLLECTION

PCOM Ⓐ
PHIL-COMICS AUCTIONS
PO Box 2157, Seaford,
West Sussex, BN25 9DR, UK
Tel: 0044 1323 654 497
phil@phil-comics.com
www.phil-comics.com

POOK Ⓐ
POOK & POOK
463 East Lancaster Avenue
Downingtown, PA 19335
Tel: 610 269 4040
info@pookandpook.com
www.pookandpook.com

QU Ⓐ
QUITTENBAUM KUNSTAUKTIONEN
Theresienstrasse 60,
D-80333 Munich,
Germany
Tel: 0049 89 2737021-25
info@quittenbaum.de
www.quittenbaum.de

REEM Ⓐ
REEMAN DANSIE
No. 8 Wyncolls Road,
Severalls Business Park,
Colchester,
Essex, CO4 9HU, UK
Tel: 0044 1206 754 754
auctions@reemandansie.com
www.reemandansie.com

RET Ⓓ
RETROPOLITAN
Tel: 0044 7870 422 182
enquiries@retropolitan.co.uk
www.retropolitan.co.uk

ROS Ⓐ
ROSEBERY'S
74-76 Knights Hill,
West Norwood,
London,
SE27 0JD, UK
Tel: 0044 2087 612 522
auctions@roseberys.co.uk
www.roseberys.co.uk

RW Ⓐ
RICHARD WINTERTON
The Old School House,
Hawkins Lane,
Burton-on-Trent,
Staffordshire,
DE14 1PT, UK
Tel: 0044 1283 511 224
burton@richardwinterton.co.uk
www.richardwinterton.co.uk

SCA Ⓓ
SCARAB ANTIQUES
Tel: 0044 2081 335895
dungbeetleantique@btinternet.com
www.scarabantiques.com

SAS Ⓐ
SPECIAL AUCTION SERVICES
81 New Greenham Park,
Newbury,
Berkshire, RG19 6HW, UK
Tel: 0044 1635 580 595
www.specialauctionservices.com

SPL Ⓐ
SUMMERS PLACE AUCTIONS
The Walled Garden, Stane Street,
Billingshurst,
West Sussex, RH14 9AB, UK
Tel: 0044 1403 331 331
www.summersplaceauctions.com

SWA Ⓐ
SWANN GALLERIES
104 East 25th Street,
New York, NY 10010
Tel: 212 254 4710
swann@swanngalleries.com
www.swanngalleries.com

SWO Ⓐ
SWORDERS
Stansted Mountfitchet Auction
Rooms, Cambridge Road,
Stansted Mountfitchet,
Essex, CM24 8GE, UK
Tel: 0044 1279 817 778
auctions@sworder.co.uk
www.sworder.co.uk

TEN Ⓐ
TENNANTS
The Auction Centre,
Leyburn,
North Yorkshire, DL8 5SG, UK
Tel: 0044 1969 623 780
enquiry@tennants-ltd.co.uk
www.tennants.co.uk

TOV Ⓐ
TOOVEY'S
Spring Gardens, Washington,
West Sussex, RH20 3BS, UK
Tel: 0044 1903 891 955
auctions@tooveys.com
www.rupert-toovey.com

TRI Ⓐ
TRING MARKET AUCTIONS
Brook Street, Tring
Hertfordshire, HP23 5EF, UK
Tel: 0044 1442 826 446
sales@tringmarketauctions.co.uk
www.tringmarketauctions.co.uk

UCT Ⓓ
UNDERCURRENTS
28 Cowper Street,
Old Street,
London, EC2A 4AS, UK
Tel: 0044 207 251 1537
shop@undercurrents.biz
www.undercurrents.biz

VEC Ⓐ
VECTIS
Fleck Way, Thornaby,
Stockton-on-Tees,
North Yorkshire, TS17 9JZ, UK
Tel: 0044 1642 750 616
www.vectis.co.uk

W&W Ⓐ
WALLIS & WALLIS
West Street Auction Galleries,
Lewes, East Sussex, BN7 2NJ, UK
Tel: 0044 1273 480 208
auctions@wallisandwallis.org
www.wallisandwallis.co.uk

WHP Ⓐ
W & H PEACOCK
26 Newnham Street
Bedford,
Bedfordshire, MK40 3JR, UK
Tel: 0044 1234 266366
info@peacockauction.co.uk
www.peacockauction.co.uk

WHYT Ⓐ
WHYTE'S
38 Molesworth Street,
Dublin 2, Ireland
Tel: 00353 1 676 2888
info@whytes.ie
www.whytes.ie

WW Ⓐ
WOOLLEY & WALLIS
51-61 Castle Street,
Salisbury, Wiltshire, SP1 3SU, UK
Tel: 0044 1722 424 500
enquiries@woolleyandwallis
.co.uk
www.woolleyandwallis.co.uk

If you wish to have any item valued, it is advisable to contact the dealer or specialist in advance to check that they will carry out this service and whether there is a charge. While most dealers will be happy to help you with an enquiry, do remember that they are busy people with businesses to run. Telephone valuations are not possible. Please mention the Miller's Collectibles Handbook & Price Guide by Judith Miller and Mark Hill when making an enquiry.

ADVERTISING

Phil & Karol Atkinson
May-Oct:
713 Sarsi Trail, Mercer,
PA 16137
Tel: 724 475 2490
and Nov-Apr:
7188 Drewry's Bluff Road,
Bradenton, FL 34203
Tel: 941 755 1733

The Nostalgia Factory
Original Movie Posters &
Related Ephemera.
5 Guest Street,
Brighton, MA 02135
Tel: 617 779 5996
or 800 479 8754
posters@nostalgia.com
www.nostalgia.com

**Time Matters
Antique Mall & Awsum
Auctions**
2684 North Reading Road,
Reinholds, PA 17569
Tel: 717 484 1514
or 732.331.2951
awsumadvertising@aol.com
www.tias.com/stores/awsumadv

AMERICAN

Bucks County Antique Center
5791 Old York Road,
Lahaska, PA 18931
Tel: 215 794 9180

Lawrence Elman
PO Box 415, Woodland Hills,
CA 91365

Olde Hope Antiques
PO Box 718,
New Hope, PA 18938
Tel: 215 297 0200
info@oldehope.com
www.oldehope.com

**Stauble and Chambers
Antiques**
180 Main Street,
Wiscasset, ME 04578
Tel: 207 882 6341
pstauble@roadrunner.com or
ss.chambers@comcast.net
www.staublechambers
antiques.com

The Splendid Peasant
992 Foley Road,
Sheffield,
MA 01257
Tel: 413 229 8800
folkart@splendindpeasant.com
www.splendidpeasant.com

AUTOGRAPHS

**Professional Autograph
Dealers Association**
PO Box 1729W,
Murray Hill Station,
New York,
NY 10016
www.padaweb.org

AUTOMOBILIA

Dunbar's Gallery
54 Haven Street,
Milford,
MA 01757
Tel: 508.634.8697
dunbarsgallery@
comcast.net
www.dunbarsgallery.com

BOOKS

Abebooks
www.abebooks.com

Aleph-Bet Books
85 Old Mill River Road,
Pound Ridge,
NY 10576
Tel: 914 764 7410
helen@alephbet.com
www.alephbet.com

Bauman Rare Books
535 Madison Avenue,
between 54th & 55th Streets,
New York,
NY 10022
Tel: 212 751 0011
www.baumanrarebooks.com

Deer Park Books
609 Kent Road, (route 7),
Gaylordsville,
CT 06755
Tel: 860 350 4140
info@deerparkbooks.com
www.deerparkbooks.com

CANADIANA

Toronto Antiques on King
284 King Street West,
Toronto,
Ontario, M5V 1J2
Canada
Tel: 416 260 9057
askcynthia@cynthiafindlay.com
www.torontoantiques
onking.com

CERAMICS

Charles & Barbara Adams
(By appointment only)
289 Old Main Street,
South Yarmouth,
MA 02664
Tel: 508 760 3290
adams2430@gmail.com

**Mark & Marjorie Allen
Antiques**
300 Bedford Street,
Suite 421, Manchester,
NH 03101
Tel: 603 644 8989
mandmallen@antiquedelft.com
www.antiquedelft.com

British Collectibles
900 Chicago Avenue,
Suite104, Evanston,
Illinois 60202
Tel: 800 634 0431
www.britishcollectibles.net

Cynthia Findlay
Toronto Antiques on King
284 King Street West,
Toronto,
Ontario, M5V 1J2
Canada
Tel: 416 260 9057
askcynthia@cynthiafindlay.com
www.torontoantiquesonking.com

Greg Walsh
103 Ridgewood Avenue,
Keene, NH 03431
Tel: 603 903 3069
(New England) or
315 322 3520 (Northern NY)
gwalsh1889@hotmail.com
www.walshauction.com

Happy Pastime
1800 Parmenter Street,
Middleton,
WI 53562
Tel: 608 831 4200
shop@happypastime.biz
www.happypastime.net

Hi & Lo Modern
artsponge@gmail.com
www.hiandlomodern.com

Ken Forster
(Art Pottery)
5501 Seminary Road,
Suite 1311 South,
Falls Church,
VA 22041
Tel: 703 379 1142
kencforster@aol.com

Mary's Memories
PO Box 2342
Centreville,
VA 20122
www.tias.com/stores/mm

Mellin's Antiques
PO Box 1115,
Redding
CT 06875
Tel: 203 938 9538
info@mellinsantiques.com
www.mellinsantiques.com

**Mary Ann's Antiques &
Collectibles**
2930 North 5th Street
Highway,
Reading,
PA 19605
Tel: 610 939 1344

Pascoe & Company
Tel: 800 872 0195
www.pascoeandcompany.com

Rago Arts
333 North Main Street,
Lambertville,
NJ 08530
Tel: 609 397 9374
info@ragoarts.com
www.ragoarts.com

SPECIALISTS

TOJ Gallery
Susan L Tillipman
420 Annapolis Street,
MD 21403
Tel: 410 626 0770
susan@tojgallery.com
www.tojgallery.com

CHARACTER COLLECTIBLES
What A Character!
hugh@whatacharacter.com
www.whatacharacter.com

COMICS
Carl Bonasera
All-American Comic Shops,
3576 West 95th Street,
Evergreen Park,
IL 60805
Tel: 708 425 7555
alamcarl@ameritech.net
www.allamericancomic
shops.com

Comic Connect
873 Broadway, Suite 201,
New York,
NY 10003
Tel: 212 895 3999
support@comicconnect.com
www.comicconnect.com

Comic Gallery Collectibles
www.stores.ebay.com/
comic-gallery-collectibles

Metropolis Collectibles
873 Broadway, Suite 201,
New York,
NY 10003
Tel: 212 260 4147
orders@metropoliscomics.com
www.metropoliscomics.com

COSTUME & ACCESSORIES
Fayne Landes Antiques
3300 Darby Road. Apt. 7209,
Haverford,
PA 19041
Tel: 610 658 0566
fayne@comcast.net

Lofty Vintage
530 Nepperhan Avenue,
Yonkers, New York,
NY 10701
andrea@loftyvintage.com
www.loftyvintage.com

Vintage Eyewear of New York City Inc.
Tel: 917 721 6546
vintageeyes60@yahoo.com

Vintage Swank
212 East Main Street,
Front Royal,
VA 22630
Tel: 540 636 0069
www.vintageswank.com

COSTUME JEWELRY
Aurora Bijoux
www.aurorabijoux.com

Barbara Blau Collectables
29 North 2nd Street,
Philadelphia, PA 19106
Tel: 215 923 3625
bbjools@msn.com

The Junkyard Jeweler
sales@junkyardjeweler.com
www.junkyardjeweler.com

Melody Rodgers LLC
The Manhattan Art &
Antique Center,
1050 2nd Avenue,
Gallery 10A,
New York,
NY 10022
Tel: 212 758 3164
info@melodyrodgers.com
www.melodyrodgers.com

Roxanne Stuart
Langhorne PA
Tel: 215 750 8868
gemfairy@aol.com

Vintique Vintage Jewelry
Tel: 612 968 4600
www.rubylane.com/shop/
sparkles

Bonny Yankauer
Tel: 201 825 7697
bonnyy@aol.com

DISNEYANA
MuseumWorks
222 Merchandise Mart Plaza,
Suite 1850,
Chicago,
IL 60654
Tel: 970 544 6113
robertcasterline@aol.com
www.mwgalleries.com

Sign of the Tymes
Mill Antiques Center,
12 Morris Farm Road,
Lafayette,
NJ 07848
Tel: 973 383 6028
www.millantiques.com/
happle.htm

DOLLS
All Dolled Up
Kitchener, Ontario,
Canada
Tel: 519 745 2122
jenn@alldolledup.ca
www.alldolledup.ca

FIFTIES & SIXTIES
Deco Etc
The Show Place,
40 West 25th Street,
3rd Floor, New York,
NY 10010
Tel: 347 423 6446
vanstrou@aol.com
www.nyshowplace.com

Incogeeto
6 Division Street,
Somerville, NJ 08876
Tel: 908.722.4600

Jack's
1883 Amherst,
Montreal, Quebec,
H2L 3L6
Canada

Kathy's Korner
Tel: 516 624 9494
kathckoch@yahoo.com

Modcats
info@modcats.com
www.modcats.com

Vintage Swank
212 East Main Street,
Front Royal, VA 22630
Tel: 540 636 0069
www.vintageswank.com

FILM MEMORABILIA
Wonderful World of Animation
9517 Culver Boulevard,
Culver City,
CA 90232
Tel: 310 836 4992
www.wonderfulworldof
animation.com

GLASS
Blockglass Ltd.
blockglass@aol.com
www.blockglass.com

City Scavenger Vintage Glass & Goods
1667 South 55th Street,
Milwaukee, WI 53214
Tel: 414 763 5734
jmazzone@wi.rr.com

The End of History
548 1/2 Hudson Street,
New York, NY 10014
Tel: 212 647 7598
historyglass@gmail.com
www.theendofhistoryshop.
blogspot.com

Cynthia Findlay
Toronto Antiques on King
284 King Street West,
Toronto, Ontario, M5V 1J2,
Canada
Tel: 416 260 9057
askcynthia@cynthiafindlay.com
www.torontoantiquesonking.
com

Hi & Lo Modern
artsponge@gmail.com
www.hiandlomodern.com

Mary Ann's Antiques & Collectibles
2930 North 5th Street
Highway, Reading, PA 19605
Tel: 610 939 1344

Past-Tyme Antiques
12845 Potomac, Overlook
Lane, Leesburg, VA 20176
Tel: 703 777 8555
pasttymeantiques@aol.com

Jeffrey F Purtell
(Steuben Glass)
31 Pleasant Point Drive,
Portsmouth, NH 03801
Tel: 800 973 4331
jfpurtell@steubenpurtell.com
www.steubenpurtell.com

Paul Reichwein
2321 Hershey Avenue,
East Petersburg, PA 17520
Tel: 717 569 7637
paulrdg@aol.com

Retro Art Glass
Murrieta, California
Tel: 951 639 3032
retroartglass@verizon.net
www.retroartglass.com

Paul Stamati Gallery
1050 2nd Avenue,
New York, NY 10022
Tel: 212 754 4533
gallerymail@stamati.com
www.stamati.com

Antiques of Suzman
23 Winterberry Lane,
Rehoboth, MA 02769
Tel: 508 252 5729
suzmanf@comcast.net

HOLIDAY MEMORABILIA

Sign of the Tymes
Mill Antiques Center,
12 Morris Farm Road,
Lafayette, NJ 07848
Tel: 973 383 6028
jhap@nac.net
www.millantiques.com/happle.
htm

INUIT ART

Waddington's
111 Bathurst Street,
Toronto, Ontario, M5V 2R1.
Canada
Tel: 416 504 9100
www.waddingtons.ca

LIGHTING

Chameleon Fine Lighting
223 East 59th Street,
New York, NY 10022
Tel: 212 355 6300
mail@chameleon59.com
www.chameleon59.com

LUNCH BOXES

Seaside Toy Center
Joseph Soucy
179 Main Street,
Westerly, RI 02891
Tel: 401 596 0962

MARBLES

CollectibleMarbles.com
Steve Gorin, PO Box 773
Diablo, CA 94528
Tel: 925 785 9172
marblemania@aol.com
www.collectiblemarbles.com

MECHANICAL MUSIC

Mechantiques
Eureka Springs, Arizona
info@mechantiques.com
www.mechantiques.com

The Music Box Shop
6102 North 16th Street,
Phoenix, AZ 85016
Tel: 888 266 4464
inforders@themusic
boxshop.com
www.themusicboxshop.com

MILITARIA

International Military Antiques
1000 Valley Road,
Gillette, NJ 07933
Tel: 908 903 1200
www.ima-usa.com

PENS & WRITING EQUIPMENT

Fountain Pen Hospital
10 Warren Street,
New York, NY 10007
Tel: 800 253 7367
info@fountainpenhospital.com
www.fountainpenhospital.com

Go Pens - Fine Vintage Pens
16 Mulberry Road,
Woodbridge, CT 06525
Tel: 203 389 5295
garylehrer@aol.com
www.gopens.com

David Nishimura
PO Box 41452
Providence, RI 02940
Tel: 401 351 7607
pen.info@vintagepens.com
www.vintagepens.com

Pendemonium
619 Avenue G,
Fort Madison,
IA 52627
Tel: 319 372 0881
info@pendemonium.com
www.pendemonium.com

PLASTICS

Malabar Enterprises
172 Bush Lane,
Ithaca,
NY 14850
Tel: 607 266 0690
abbynash@gmail.com

POSTCARDS

Harry R. McKeon, Jr.
(Pre 1940)
18 Rose Lane,
Flourtown,
PA 19031
Tel: 215 233 4094
toyspost@aol.com

POSTERS

Chisholm Larsson Gallery
145 8th Avenue,
New York,
NY 10011
Tel: 212 741 1703
info@chisolm-poster.com
www.chisolm-poster.com

Posteritati
239 Center Street,
New York, NY 10013
Tel: 212 226 2207
mail@posteritati.com
www.posteritati.com

Vintage Poster Works
PO Box 784, Woodstock,
NY 12498
Tel: 845 704 7506
debra@vintageposterworks.com
www.vintageposterworks.com

RADIOS

Catalin Radios
5439 Schultz Drive,
Sylvania,
OH 43560
sales@catalinradio.com
www.catalinradio.com

ROCK & POP

Hein's Rare Collectibles
PO Box 179,
Little Silver,
NJ 07739
Tel: 732 219 1988
garymhein@comcast.net
www.beatles4me.com

Todd Hutchinson
PO Box 915,
Griffith,
IN 46319
Tel: 219 923 8334
toddtcb@aol.com
Ebay ID: toddtcb

SCENT BOTTLES

Oldies But Goldies
860 NW Sorrento Lane,
Port St Lucie, FL 34986
Tel. 772 873 0968
oldgood@comcast.net
www.oldgood.com

Monsen & Baer Inc
PO Box 529,
Vienna, VA 22183
Tel: 703 938 2129
monsenbaer@erols.com

SCIENTIFIC & TECHNICAL, INCLUDING OFFICE & OPTICAL

George Glazer Gallery
28 East 2nd Street,
New York, NY 10021
Tel: 212 535 5706
worldglobe@georgeglazer.com
www.georgeglazer.com

KARS Unlimited
PO Box 895340,
Leesburg, FL 34789
Tel: 352 365 0229
karsunltd@aol.com
www.kars-unlimited.com

Lee Richmond
(American reresentative for
Auction Team Breker)
Tel: 703 796 5544
breker@thebestthings.com
www.breker.com

The Olde Office
Branford House Antiques,
6691 US Route 7,
Brandon, VT 05733
Tel: 802 483 2971
www.branfordhouse
antiques.com

Harry Poster
New Jersey
tvs@harryposter.com
www.harryposter.com

Tesseract
mail@etesseract.com
www.etesseract.com

SMOKING

Ira Pilossof
Vintage Lighters NJ
vintageltr@aol.com
www.vintagelightersnj.com

Richard Weinstein
The International Vintage Lighter Exchange
3450 Asheville Highway,
Hendersonville,
NC 28791
Tel: 828 693 3212
info@vintagelighters.com
www.vintagelighters.com

SPORTING MEMORABILIA

Larry Fritsch Cards Inc.
(Baseball Cards)
735 Old Wasau Road,
PO Box 863,
Stevens Point,
WI 54481
Tel: 715 344 8687
www.fritschcards.com

Golf For All Ages
Tel: 214 377 8421
chuckfurjanic@hotmail.com
www.golfforallages.com

Hall's Nostalgia
PO Box 408,
Arlington,
MA 02476
Tel: 800 367 4255
hallsnost@aol.com
www.hallsnostalgia.com

SPECIALISTS

Vintage Sports Collector
3920 Via Solano,
Palos Verdes Estates,
CA 90274
Tel: 310 375 1723

TEDDY BEARS & SOFT TOYS

The Calico Teddy
Tel: 410 433 9202
calicteddy@aol.com
www.calicoteddy.com

TOYS & GAMES

Atomic Age
318 East Virginia Road,
Fullerton,
CA 92831
Tel: 714 446 0736

Barry Carter
Knightstown Antiques Mall,
136 West Carey Street,
Knightstown,
IN 46148
Tel: 765 345 5665
indytoysoldier@hotmail.com

Bertoia Auctions
2141 DeMarco Drive,
Vineland,
NJ 08360
Tel: 856 692 1881
www.bertoiaauctions.com

France Antique Toys
40 Maplewood Drive,
Northport,
NY 11768
Tel: 631 754 1399

Roger Johnson
9321 Massey Road
Pilot Point, TX 76258
Tel: 940 368 7874
czarmann@aol.com

Kitsch-n-Kaboodle
1513 Hancock Street,
Philadelphia,
PA 19104
Tel: 267 970 5221

Harry R. McKeon, Jr.
18 Rose Lane,
Flourtown,
PA 19031
Tel: 215 233 4094
toyspost@aol.com (Tin Toys)

The Old Toy Soldier Home
977 South Santa Fe,
Suite 11,
Vista,
CA 92083
Tel: 760 758 5481
oldtoysoldierhome@earthlink.net
www.oldtoysoldierhome.com

Trains & Things
210 East Front Street,
Traverse City,
MI 49684
Tel: 231 947 1353
info@tctrains.com
www.traversehobbies.com

WATCHES

Mark Laino
'Mark of Time'
132 South 8th Street,
Philadelphia, PA 19107
Tel: 215 922 1551
ebay ID: lecoultre

Texas Time
3076 Wauneta Street,
Newbury Park, CA 91320
Tel: 805 498 5644
paklonn@verizon.net

WEIRD & WONDERFUL

Anastacia's Antiques
617 Bainbridge Street,
Philadelphia, PA 19147
Tel: 215 928 9111
anastaciasantiques@gmail.com
www.anastaciasantiques.com

WINE & DRINKING

Donald A. Bull
dbull@bullworks.net
www.bullworks.net

Steve Visakay
Cocktail Shakers
visakay@optonline.net
www.visakay.com

The following list of general antiques and collectibles centers and markets has been organized by region. Any owner who would like to be listed in our next edition, space permitting, or who wishes to update their contact information, should email Miller's at info@millers.uk.com.

USA
ALABAMA
Antique Attic
5037 Fortner Street,
Dothan, AL 36305
Tel: 334 792 5040
warren@antiqueattic
dothan.com
www.antiqueatticdothan.com

ALASKA
The Pack Rat Antiques
1068 West Fireweed Lane,
Anchorage, AK 99503
Tel: 907 522 5272
packratantiques@hotmail.com
www.thepackratantiques.com

ARIZONA
American Antique Antiques
3130 East Grant Road,
Tucson,
AZ 85716
Tel: 520 326 3070
dwightandchristy@
americanantiquemall.com
www.americanantiquemall.com

The Antique Centre
2012 Scottsdale Road,
Scottsdale,
AZ 85257
Tel: 480 675 9500
www.arizonaantiquecentre.com

ARKANSAS
I-40 Antique Center
Interstate 40,
Exit 142,
13021 Long Fisher Road,
Maumelle (NLR),
AR 72113
Tel: 501 851 0039
i40antiquecenter@gmail.com
www.i40antique.com

CALIFORNIA
San Francisco Antique and Design Mall
701 Bayshore Boulevard,
San Francisco,
CA 94124
Tel: 415 656 3530
info@sfantique.com
www.sfantique.com

Ocean Beach Antique Mall
4926 Newport Avenue,
San Diego,
CA 92107
Tel: 619 223 6170
antiquesinsandiego@cox.net
www.antiquesinsandiego.com

COLORADO
Colorado Country Antique Mall
2109 West Broadway,
Colorado Springs,
CO 80904
Tel: 719 520 5680

CONNECTICUT
The Antique & Artisan Center
69 Jefferson Street,
Stamford,
CT 06902
Tel: 203 327 6022
antiqueartisan@gmail.com
www.stamfordantiques.com

DELAWARE
Lewes Mercantile Antiques
109 Second Street,
Lewes, DE 19958
Tel: 302 645 7900
www.antiqueslewes.com

FLORIDA
Inglenook Antiques & Collectibles
3607 North Scenic Highway,
Lake Wales,
FL 33898
Tel: 863 678 1641
inglenookantiques@ymail.com

Avonlea Antique Mall
8101 Philips Highway,
Jacksonville,
FL 32256
Tel: 904 636 8785
info@avonleamall.com
www.avonleamall.com

GEORGIA
Athens Antique Mall
4615 Atlanta Highway,
Bogart,
GA 30622
Tel: 706 354 0108

HAWAII
Antique Alley
1347 Kapiolani Boulevard,
Honolulu,
HI 96814
Tel: 808 941 8551
apake@hawaiiantel.net
www.portaloha.com/
antiquealley

IDAHO
Antique World Mall
Country Club Plaza,
4544 Overland Road,
Boise,
ID 83705
Tel: 208 342 5350
www.antiqueworldmall.com

ILLINOIS
Second Time Around Antique Market
151 South Will Road,
Braidwood, IL 60408
Tel: 815 458 2034
info@2xaroundantiques.com
www.2xaroundantiques.com

INDIANA
Manor House Antique Mall
5454 South East Street,
Indianapolis,
IN 46227
Tel: 317 782 1358
Manorhouse007z@aol.com
www.manorhouseantiques.com

IOWA
The Brass Armadillo Des Moines
701 NE 50th Avenue,
Des Moines,
IA 50313
Tel: 515 282 0082
www.brassarmadillo.com/
desmoines

KANSAS
Flying Moose Antique Mall
9223 West Kellogg Drive,
Wichita,
KS 67209
Tel: 316 721 6667
info@flying-moose.com
www.flying-moose.com

KENTUCKY
The Red Door Antiques
35 US Highway 641 North,
Eddyville,
KY 42038
Tel: 270 388 1957
red_door@bellsouth.net
www.thereddoorantiques.com

LOUISANA
Magazine Antique Mall
3017 Magazine Street,
New Orleans,
LA 70115
Tel: 504 896 9994
www.magazineantiquemall.com

MAINE
Cornish Trading Company
19 Main Street,
Cornish,
ME 04020
Tel: 207 625 8387
antiques@cornishtrading.com
www.cornishtrading.com

MARYLAND
Historic Savage Mill Antique Center
8600 Foundry Street,
Savage,
MD 20763
Tel: 410 880 0918
or 301.369.4650
www.antique-cntr-savage.com

MASSACHUSETTS
Showcase Antiques Center
Old Sturbridge Village,
Route 20,
Sturbridge,
MA 01566
Tel: 508 347 7190
sales@showcaseantiques.com
www.showcaseantiques.com

MICHIGAN
Michiana Antique Mall
2423 South 11th Street,
Niles, MI 49120
Tel: 269 684 7001
michianaantiquemall@
compuserve.com
www.michianaantiquemall.com

MINNESOTA
Lindström Antique Mall
12740 Lake Boulevard,
PO Box 668,
Lindström,
MN 55045
Tel: 651 257 3340

MISSISSIPPI
Boone's Camp Antique Mall
101 East Church Street,
Booneville,
MS 38829
Tel: 662 728 2227
www.boonescamp
antiquemall.com

MISSOURI
Antique Treasures
920 East Woodlawn Drive,
Farmington,
MO 63640
Tel: 573 431 4866
www.missouriantiquemalls.
com/AntiqueTreasures.aspx

MONTANA
The Montana Antique Mall
331 W Railroad Street,
Missoula,
MT 59802
Tel: 406 721 5366
www.montanaantiquemall.com

NEBRASKA
Platte Valley Antique Mall,
1 80 Exit 420,
Greenwood,
NE 68366
Tel: 402 944 2949
www.plattevalley
antiquemall.com

NEVADA
Cheshire Antiques
1423 Main Street,
Highway 395,
Gardnerville, NV 89410
Tel: 775 782 9117
www.cheshireantiques.com

NEW HAMPSHIRE
Antiques at Colony Mill Marketplace
The Colony Mill Marketplace,
222 West Street,
Keene, NH 03431
Tel: 603 358 6343
www.colonymillnh.com

Fern Eldridge & Friends
800 First NH Turnpike
(Route 4), Northwood,
NH 03261
Tel: 603 942 5602

NEW JERSEY
Lafayette Mill Antiques Center
12 Morris Farm Road
(Just off Route 15),
Lafayette, NJ 07848
Tel: 973 383 0065
themill@earthlink.net
www.millantiques.com

Somerville Center Antiques
34 West Main Street,
Somerville, NJ 08876
Tel: 908 595 1887
www.somervilleantiques.net

NEW MEXICO
Antique Connection Mall
12815 Central NE,
Albuquerque,
NM 87123
Tel: 505 296 2300
jane@antiqueconnectionmall.com
www.antiqueconnectionmall.com

NEW YORK
L W Emporium Co-op
6355 Knickerbocker Road,
Ontario, NY 14519
Tel: 315 524 8841
lwemporium@verizon.net
www.lwemporium.com

The Manhattan Art and Antiques Center
1050 Second Avenue
at 56th Street,
New York, NY 10022
Tel: 212 355 4400
info@the-maac.com
www.the-maac.com

The Showplace Antique and Design Center
40 West 25th Street,
New York, NY 10010
Tel: 212 633 6063
info@nyshowplace.com
www.nyshowplace.com

NORTH CAROLINA
Fifteen Ten Antiques
1510 Central Avenue,
Charlotte, NC 28205
Tel: 704 342 9005
info@1510-antiques.com
www.1510-antiques.com

NORTH DAKOTA
Blue Moon Antiques
1008 9th St NW,
Cooperstown, ND 58425
Tel: 701 797 3292

OHIO
Grand Antique Mall
9701 Reading Road,
Reading, OH 45215
Tel: 513 554 1919
grandantiquemall@aol.com
www.grandantiquemall.com

Hartville Market Place and Flea Market
1289 Edison Street NW,
Hartville, OH 44632
Tel: 330 877 9860
www.hartvillemarketplace.com

OKLAHOMA
Antique Co-op
1227 N May Avenue,
Oklahoma City,
OK 73107
Tel: 405 942 1214
www.antiqueco-op.com

OREGON
Old Town Antique Mall
324 SW Sixth Street,
Grants Pass,
OR 97526
Tel: 541 474 7525
www.grantspassantiques.com

PENNSYLVANIA
Antiquarian's Delight
615 South 6th Street,
Philadelphia, PA 19147
Tel: 215 592 0256

Antiques Showcase & German Trading Post at The Black Horse
2180 North Reading Road,
PO Box 343, Denver,
PA 17517
Tel: 717 336 8447
www.blackhorselodge.com/
Antiques.asp

RHODE ISLAND
Rhode Island Antiques Mall
345 Fountain Street,
Pawtucket,
RI 02860
Tel: 401 475 3400
scott@riantiquesmall.com
www.riantiquesmall.com

SOUTH CAROLINA
Charleston Antique Mall
4 Avondale at Savannah
Highway,
Charleston,
SC 29407
Tel: 843 769 6119
www.charlestonantiquemall.net

SOUTH DAKOTA
Bag Ladies Antiques Mall
524 6th Street,
Rapid City,
SD 57701
Tel: 605 341 5299
bhbagladies@yahoo.com

TENNESSEE
Goodlettsville Antique Mall
213 N Main Street,
Goodlettsville,
TN 37072
Tel: 615 859 7002
info@goodlettsville
antiquemall.com
www.goodlettsville
antiquemall.com

TEXAS
Antique Pavilion
2311 Westheimer Road,
Houston,
TX 77098
Tel: 713 520 9755
contact@antique-pavilion.com
www.antique-pavilion.com

Forestwood Antiques Mall
5333 Forest Lane,
Dallas,
TX 75244
Tel: 972 661 0001
info@forestwoodantiquemail.
com
www.forestwoodantiquemall.
com

Snider Plaza Antiques
6817 Hillcrest Avenue,
Dallas,
TX 75205
Tel: 214 373 0822
www.sniderplaza.net

UTAH
Capital City Antique Mall
959 S West Temple,
Salt Lake City,
UT 84101
Tel: 801 521 7207
www.capitalcityantiquemall.com

VERMONT

The Vermont Antique Mall
Quechee Gorge Village,
US Route 4, PO Box 730,
Quechee, VT 05059
Tel: 802 281 4147
www.quecheegorge.com/
vermont-antique-mall.php

VIRGINIA

Antique Village
10203 Chamberlayne Road,
Mechanicsville,
VA 23116
Tel: 804 746 8914
www.antiquevillageva.com

WASHINGTON

Antique Gallery Mall
117 Glen Avenue,
Snohomish, WA 98290
Tel: 360 568 7644

WEST VIRGINIA

South Charleston Antique Mall
617 D Street,
South Charleston,
WV 25303
Tel: 304 744 8975
www.southcharleston
antiquemall.com

WISCONSIN

Red Shed Antiques
1525W County Road B,
Hayward,
WI 54843
Tel: 715 634 6088
www.redshed.com

WYOMING

Cy Avenue Antique Mall
1905 CY Avenue,
Casper, WY 82604
Tel: 307 237 2293

CANADA

Toronto Antiques on King
284 King Street West, Toronto,
Ontario, M5V 1J2
Tel: 416 260 9057
askcynthia@cynthiafindlay.com
www.torontoantiques
onking .com

Antique Market
1324 Franklin Street
(at Clark Drive), Vancouver,
BC V5L 1N9
Tel: 604 875 1434
www.antiquesdirect.ca

Post Office Antique Mall
340 Esplanade
(Trans Canada Highway),
Ladysmith,
BC V9G 1A3
Tel: 250 245 7984
www.postoffice
antiquemall.com

Vanity Fair Antique & Collectables Mall
1044 Fort Street,
Victoria, BC V8V 3K4
Tel: 250 380 7274
lyon1848@gmail.com
www.vanityfairantiques.com

Green Spot Antiques
49 Cedar Street, Cambridge,
Ontario, N1S 7V4
Tel: 519 623 4050
info@greenspotantiques.com
www.greenspotantiques.com

Ganaraska Picker's Market
50 John Street, Port Hope,
Ontario L1A 2Z2
Tel: 905 885 7979

The following list of auctioneers who conduct regular sales by auction is organized by region. Any auctioneer who would like to be listed in the our next edition, space permitting, or to update their contact information, should email Miller's at info@millers.uk.com.

USA

ALABAMA

High as the Sky Auction Company
725 US Highway 231,
Wetumpka, AL 36093
Tel: 334 478 3843
highastheskyauctioncompany@
yahoo.com
www.highastheskyauction
company.com

ARIZONA

Brian Lebel's Old West Show & Auction
PO Box 2038,
Carefree, AZ 85377
Tel: 602 432 7602
brian@denveroldwest.com
www.codyoldwest.com

ARKANSAS

Ponders Auctions
1504 South Leslie,
Stuttgart, AR 72160
Tel: 870 673 6551
pondersauctions@centurytel.net
www.pondersauctions.com

CALIFORNIA

Aurora Galleries International
30 Hackamore Lane, Suite 2,
Bell Canyon, CA 91307
Tel: 818 884 6468
vcampbell@auroraauctions.com
www.auroragalleriesonline.com

Bonhams & Butterfield
7601 Sunset Boulevard,
Los Angeles, CA 90046
Tel: 323 850 7500
and
220 San Bruno Avenue,
San Francisco, CA 94103
Tel: 415 861 7500
info.us@bonhams.com
www.butterfields.com

Clark's Fine Art Gallery & Auctioneers
14931 Califa Street,
Sherman Oaks, CA 91411
Tel: 818 783 3052
info@clarkart.com
www.estateauctionservice.com

I M Chait Gallery/ Auctioneers
9330 Civic Center Drive,
Beverly Hills,
CA 90210
Tel: 310 285 0182
chait@chait.com
www.chait.com

eBay Inc.
Whitman Campus,
2065 Hamilton Avenue,
San Jose,
CA 95125
Tel: 408 376 7400
www.ebay.com

Ingrid O'Neil Sports & Olympic Memorabilia
PO Box 265,
Corona Del Mar,
CA 92625
Tel: 949 715 9808
ingrid@ioneil.com
www.ioneil.com

Malter Galleries
17003 Ventura Boulevard,
Encino,
CA 91316
Tel: 818 784 7772
mike@maltergalleries.com
www.maltergalleries.com

PBA Galleries
133 Kearny Street, 4th Floor,
San Francisco,
CA 94108
Tel: 415 989 2665
online@pbagalleries.com
www.pbagalleries.com

Poster Connection Inc.
43 Regency Drive,
Clayton, CA 94517
Tel: 925 673 3343
sales@posterconnection.com
www.posterconnection.com

Profiles in History
26901 Agoura Road, Suite 150,
Calabasis Hills, CA 91301
Tel: 310 859 7701
info@profilesinhistory.com
www.profilesinhistory.com

Nate D Sanders
11901 Santa Monica
Boulevard, Suite 555,
Los Angeles, CA 90025
Tel: 310 440 2982
info@natedsanders.com
www.natedsanders.com

San Rafael Auction Gallery
634 Fifth Avenue,
San Rafael, CA 94901
Tel: 415 457 4488
info@sanrafaelauction.com
www.sanrafael-auction.com

Signature House
818 North Mountain Avenue,
Upland, CA 91786
Tel: 909 920 9500
editor@signaturehouse.net
www.signaturehouse.net

Slawinski Auction Company
5015 Scotts Valley Drive,
Scotts Valley, CA 95066
Tel: 831 335 9000
antiques@slawinski.com
www.slawinski.com

COLORADO

Aristocrat
1229 South Broadway,
Denver, CO 80210
Tel: 303 997 9969
john@aristocratservices.com

CONNECTICUT

Alexander Historical Auctions
860 Canal Street, 2nd Floor,
Stamford, CT 06902
Tel: 203 276 1570
auctions@alexautographs.com
www.alexautographs.com

Heckler
79 Bradford Corner Road,
Woodstock Valley, CT 06282
Tel: 860 974 1634
info@hecklerauction.com
www.hecklerauction.com

Lloyd Ralston Gallery
549 Howe Avenue,
Shelton, CT 06484
Tel: 203 924 5804
lrgallery@sbcglobal.net
www.lloydralstontoys.com

DELAWARE

Reagan-Watson Auctions
1507 Middleford Road,
Seaford, DE 19973
Tel: 302 628 7653
and
115 N Washington Street,
Milford,
DE 19963
Tel: 302 422 2392
scott@reagan-watsonauctions.
com
www.reagan-watsonauctions.com

FLORIDA

Auctions Neapolitan
1100 1st Avenue South,
Naples, FL 34102
Tel: 239 262 7333
sales@auctionsn.com
www.auctionsneapolitan.com

Burchard Galleries
2528 30th Avenue North,
St Petersburg,
FL 33713
Tel: 727 821 1167
mail@burchardgalleries.com
www.burchardgalleries.com

Kincaid Auction Company
3809 East CR 542,
Lakeland,
FL 33801
Tel: 800 970 1977
kincaid@kincaid.com
www.kincaid.com

GEORGIA

Great Gatsby's
5180 Peachtree Industrial
Boulevard, Atlanta, GA 30341
Tel: 770 457 1903
internet@greatgatsbys.com
www.greatgatsbys.com

My Hart Auctions Inc.
Tel: 419 773 8244
myhart@prodigy.net
www.myhart.net

Red Baron's Antiques
6450 Roswell Road,
Atlanta, GA 30328
Tel: 404 252 3770
info@rbantiques.com
www.redbaronsantiques.com

AUCTIONEERS

IDAHO

The Coeur D'Alene
Art Auction,
8836 North Hess Street,
Suite B, Hayden, ID 83835
Tel: 208 772 9009
info@cdaartauction.com
www.cdaartauction.com

ILLINOIS

Bloomington Auction Gallery
300 East Grove Street,
Bloomington, IL 61701
Tel: 309 828 5533
bloomingtonauction@
frontier.com
www.bloomington
auctiongallery.com

Legendary Auctions
17542 Chicago Avenue,
Lansing, IL 60438
Tel: 708 889 9380
customerservice@
legendaryauctions.com
www.legendaryauctions.com

Leslie Hindman
1338 West Lake Street,
Chicago, IL 60607
Tel: 312 280 1212
www.lesliehindman.com

L H Selman Ltd.
410 South Michigan Avenue,
Suite 207, Chicago, IL 60605
Tel: 800 538 0766
info@paperweight.com
www.theglassgallery.com

Wright
1440 W Hubbard
Chicago, IL 60642
Tel: 312 563 0020
consign@wright20.com
www.wright20.com

INDIANA

Curran Miller
4424 Vogel Road,
Evansville, IN 47715
Tel: 800 264 0601
cmar@curranmiller.com
www.curranmiller.com

Lawson Auction Service
1731 Central Avenue,
Colombus, IN 47201
Tel: 812 372 2571
www.lawsonauction.com

Stout Auctions
529 State Road 28 East,
Williamsport, IN 47993
Tel: 765 764 6901
info@stoutauctions.com
www.stoutauctions.com

Strawser Auction Group
200 North Main Street,
PO Box 332, Wolcottville,
IN 46795
Tel: 260 854 2859
info@strawserauctions.com
www.strawserauctions.com

IOWA

Jackson's
2229 Lincoln Street,
Cedar Falls, IA 50613
Tel: 319 277 2256
jessib@jacksonsauctions.com
www.jacksonsauction.com

Tom Harris Auctions
203 South 18th Avenue,
Marshalltown, IA 50158
Tel: 641 754 4890
tom@tomharrisauctions.com
www.tomharrisauctions.com

Tubaugh Auctions
1702 8th Avenue,
Belle Plaine,
IA 52208
Tel: 319 444 2413
jerry@tubaughauctions.com
www.tubaughauctions.com

KANSAS

Manion's International Auction House
4411 North 67th Street,
Kansas City,
KS 66104
Tel: 866 626 4661
collecting@manions.com
www.manions.com

Woody Auction
PO Box 618,
317 South Forrest,
Douglass, KS 67039
Tel: 316 747 2694
info@woodyauction.com
www.woodyauction.com

KENTUCKY

Hays & Associates
120 South Spring Street,
Louisville, KY 40206
Tel: 502 584 4297
kenhays@haysauction.com
www.haysauction.com

LOUISIANA

Neal Auction Company
4038 Magazine Street,
New Orleans, LA 70115
Tel: 504 899 5329
clientservices@nealauction.com
www.nealauction.com

New Orleans Auction Galleries
801 Magazine Street,
New Orleans, LA 70130
Tel: 800 501 0277
info@neworleansauction.com
www.neworleansauction.com

MAINE

James D Julia Auctioneers Inc.
203 Skowhegan Road,
Fairfield, ME 04937
Tel: 207 453 7125
info@jamesdjulia.com
www.jamesdjulia.com

Thomaston Place
Auction Galleries
PO Box 300,
Thomaston, ME 04861
Tel: 207 354 8141
auction@kajav.com
www.thomastonauction.com

MARYLAND

Guyette & Schmidt
24718 Beverly Road,
PO Box 1170,
St. Michaels, MD 21663
Tel: 410 745 0485
decoys@guyetteandschmidt.com
www.guyetteandschmidt.com

Hantman's Auctioneers & Appraisers
PO Box 59366,
Potomac, MD 20859
Tel: 301 770 3720
hantman@hantmans.com
www.hantmans.com

Isennock Auctions Center
10912 York Road,
Cockeysville, MD 21030
Tel: 410 557 8052
cspotinc@aol.com
www.isennockauction.com

Sloans & Kenyon
7034 Wisconsin Avenue,
Chevy Chase, MD 20815
Tel: 301 634 2330
info@sloansandkenyon.com
www.sloansandkenyon.com

Theriault's
PO Box 151
Annapolis, MD 21404
Tel: 800 638 0422
info@theriaults.com
www.theriaults.com

MASSACHUSETTS

Eldred's
PO Box 796, 1483 Route 6A,
East Dennis, MA 02641
Tel: 508 385 3116
info@eldreds.com
www.eldreds.com

Grogan & Company
22 Harris Street,
Dedham, MA 02026
Tel: 781 461 9500
grogans@groganco.com
www.groganco.com

Simond & Oakes
1085 Commonwealth Avenue,
Suite 301,
Boston, Massachusetts 02215
Tel: 617 275 4393
info@simondoakes.com
www.simondoakes.com

Skinner Inc.
63 Park Plaza,
Boston, MA 02116
Tel: 617 350 5400
www.skinnerinc.com
and
274 Cedar Hill Street,
Marlborough, MA 01752
Tel: 508 970 3000
www.skinner.com

Willis Henry Auctions
22 Main Street,
Marshfield, MA 02050
Tel: 781 834 7774
wha@willishenry.com
www.willishenry.com

MICHIGAN

DuMouchelles
409 East Jefferson Avenue,
Detroit, MI 48226
Tel: 313 963 6255
www.dumouchelles.com

MINNESOTA

Luther Auctions
2556 7th Avenue E,
North Saint Paul, MN 55109
Tel: 651 770 6175
tluther@lutherauctions.com
www.lutherauctions.com

AUCTIONEERS

MISSISSIPPI

Edens
3720 Flowood Drive,
Flowood,
MS 39232
Tel: 601 896 0345
www.edensauctions.com

MISSOURI

Ivey-Selkirk
7447 Forsyth Boulevard,
Saint Louis,
MO 63105
Tel: 314 726 5515
iveyselkirk@iveyselkirk.com
www.iveyselkirk.com

MONTANA

Allard Auctions Inc.
PO Box 1030,
St Ignatius,
MT 59865
Tel: 406 745 0500
info@allardauctions.com
www.allardauctions.com

NEBRASKA

Helberg & Nuss
1145 M Street,
Gering,
NE 69341
Tel: 308 436 4056
www.helbergnussauction.com

NEVADA

Lightning Auctions, Inc.
870 South Rock Boulevard,
Sparks,
Nevada 89431
Tel: 775 331 4222
information@lightningauctions.
com
www.lightningauctions.com

NEW HAMPSHIRE

Northeast Auctions
93 Pleasant Street,
Portsmouth,
NH 03801
Tel: 603 433 8400
contact@northeastauctions.com
www.northeastauctions.com

NEW JERSEY

Bertoia Auctions
2141 DeMarco Drive,
Vineland,
NJ 08360
Tel: 856 692 1881
www.bertoiaauctions.com

Nye & Co.
225 Belleville Avenue,
Bloomfield, NJ 07003
Tel: 973 984 6900
info@dawsonandnye.com
www.dawsonandnye.com

**Rago Arts
and Auction Center**
333 North Main Street,
Lambertville, NJ 08530
Tel: 609 397 9374
info@ragoarts.com
www.ragoarts.com

NEW MEXICO

Manitou Galleries
123 West Palace Avenue,
Santa Fe, NM 87501
Tel: 800 283 0440
www.manitougalleries.com

NEW YORK

Christie's
20 Rockefeller Plaza,
New York, NY 10020
Tel: 212 636 2000
info@christies.com
www.christies.com

Bonhams
580 Madison Avenue,
Manhattan, NY 10022
Tel: 212 644 9001
info.us@bonhams.com
www.bonhams.com

Comic Connect
873 Broadway, Suite 201,
New York, NY 10003
Tel: 212 895 3999
support@comicconnect.com
www.comicconnect.com

Cottone Auctions
120 Court Street,
Geneseo, NY 14454
Tel: 585 243 3100
scottone@rochester.rr.com
www.cottoneauctions.com

Doyle New York
175 East 87th Street,
New York, NY 10128
Tel: 212 427 2730
info@doylenewyork.com
www.doylenewyork.com

Guernsey's Auctions
108 East 73rd Street,
New York, NY 10021
Tel: 212 794 2280
auctions@guernseys.com
www.guernseys.com

Phillips
450 Park Avenue,
New York,
NY 10022
Tel: 212 940 1300
www.phillips.com

Sotheby's
1334 York Avenue
at 72nd Street,
New York,
NY 10021
Tel: 212 606 7000
www.sothebys.com

Swann Galleries
104 East 25th Street,
New York,
NY 10010
Tel: 212 254 4710
swann@swanngalleries.com
www.swanngalleries.com

Philip Weiss Auctions
1 Neil Court,
Oceanside,
NY 11572
Tel: 516 594 0731
info@weissauctions.com
www.weissauctions.com

NORTH CAROLINA

Brunk Auctions
PO Box 2135,
Asheville,
NC 28802
Tel: 828 254 6846
auction@brunkauctions.com
www.brunkauctions.com

**Raynor's Historical
Collectible Auctions**
1687 West Buck Hill Road
Burlington,
NC 27215
Tel: 336 584 3330
bob@hcaauctions.com
www.hcaauctions.com

NORTH DAKOTA

Curt D Johnson
Auction Company
PO Box 13911,
Grand Forks,
ND 58208
Tel: 701 746 1378
curtdjohnson@gmail.com
www.curtdjohnson.com

OHIO

Belhorn Auction Services
9387 South Old State Road,
Lewis Center, OH 43025
Tel: 614 921 9441
auctions@belhorn.com
www.belhornauctions.com

Cincinnati Art Galleries
225 East 6th Street
Cincinnati, Ohio 45202
Tel: 513 381 2128
sandlers@cincyart.com
www.cincinnatiartgalleries.com

Cowan's Auctions
6270 Estate Avenue,
Cincinnati, OH 45232
Tel: 513 871 1670
info@cowans.com
www.cowanauctions.com

DeFina Auctions
1009 Bridge Street,
Ashtabula, OH 44004
Tel: 440 964 0054
info@definaauctions.com
www.definaauctions.com

Garth's Auctions
2690 Stratford Road,
PO Box 369,
Delaware, OH 43015
Tel: 740 362 4771
info@garths.com
www.garths.com

**Metropolitan Galleries
at Shaker Square**
13119 Shaker Square,
Cleveland, OH 44120
Tel: 216 491 1111
info@metropolitangalleries.com
www.metropolitangalleries.com

OKLAHOMA

Buffalo Bay Auction Co.
825 Fox Run Trail,
Edmond, OK 73034
Tel: 405 285 8990
admin@buffalobayauction.com
www.buffalobayauction.com

OREGON

**Antique & Auction Company
of Southern Oregon**
347 South Broadway,
(Hwy 101 So),PO Box 1159,
Coos Bay, OR 97420
Tel: 541 267 5361
info@oregonauctionhouse.com
www.oregonauctionhouse.com

PENNSYLVANIA

**Alderfer Auction
& Appraisal**
501 Fairgrounds Road,
Hatfield, PA 19440
Tel: 215.393.3023
info@alderferauction.com
www.alderferauction.com

Noel Barrett
Vintage Toys @ Auction
PO Box 300,
Carversville,
PA 18913
Tel: 215.297.5109
toys@noelbarrett.com
www.noelbarrett.com

Dargate Auction Galleries
326 Munson Avenue,
McKees Rocks, PA 15136
Tel: 412.771.8700
admin@dargate.com
www.dargate.com

Freeman's
1808 Chestnut Street,
Philadelphia, PA 19103
Tel: 215.563.9275
info@freemansauction.com
www.freemansauction.com

Hunt Auctions
256 Welsh Pool Road,
Exton, PA 19341
Tel: 610.524.0822
info@huntauctions.com
www.huntauctions.com

Morphy Auctions
2000 North Reading Road,
Denver, PA 17517
Tel: 717 335 3435
morphy@morphyauctions.com
www.morphyauctions.com

Pook & Pook Inc.
463 East Lancaster Avenue,
Downington,
PA 19335
Tel: 610 269 4040
info@pookandpook.com
www.pookandpook.com

Stephenson's
1005 Industrial Boulevard,
Southampton,
PA 18966
Tel: 215 322 6182
info@stephensonsauction.com
www.stephensonsauction.com

RHODE ISLAND

Web Wilson
Tel: 800 508 0022
hww@webwilson.com
www.webwilson.com

SOUTH CAROLINA

Charlton Hall
7 Lexington Drive,
West Columbia,
SC 29170
Tel: 803 799 5678
www.charltonhallauctions.com

SOUTH DAKOTA

**Girard Auction &
Land Brokers, Inc.**
PO Box 358
Wakonda, SD 57073
Tel: 605 267 2421
www.girardauction.com

TENNESSEE

**Berenice Denton Estate
Sales and Appraisals**
162 Belle Forest Circle,
Nashville, TN 37221
Tel: 615 292 5765
www.berenicedenton.com

Kimball M Sterling Inc.
125 West Market Street,
Johnson City, TN 37604
Tel: 423 928 1471
kimballsterling@earthlink.net
www.sterlingsold.com

TEXAS

Austin Auction Gallery
8414 Anderson Mill Road,
Austin, TX 78729
Tel: 512 258 5479
info@austinauction.com
www.austinauction.com

Dallas Auction Gallery
2235 Monitor Street,
Dallas, TX 75207
Tel: 214 653 3900
info@dallasauctiongallery.com
www.dallasauctiongallery.com

Heritage Auctions
3500 Maple Avenue,
17th Floor, Dallas, TX 75219
Tel: 214 528 3500
bid@ha.com
www.ha.com

Heritage-Slater Americana
3500 Maple Avenue,
17th Floor, Dallas,
TX 75219
Tel: 214 528 3500
www.heritagegalleries.com

UTAH

America West Archives
PO Box 100,
Cedar City,
UT 84721
Tel: 435 586 9497
awa@netutah.com
www.americawestarchives.com

VERMONT

Uriah Wallace
Auction Service
3428 Middlebrook Road,
Fairlee, VT 05045
Tel: 802 333 4386
uriah@uriahwallace.com
www.uriahwallace.com

VIRGINIA

Freeman's
126 Garrett Street,
Charlottesville,
VA 22902
Tel: 434 296 4096
info@freemansauction.com
www.freemansauction.com

**Green Valley Auctions
& Moving Inc.**
2259 Green Valley Lane,
Mt Crawford,
VA 22841
Tel: 540 434 4260
info@greenvalleyauctions.com
www.greenvalleyauctions.com

**Ken Farmer Auctions
& Appraisals**
105 Harrison Street,
Radford,
VA 24141
Tel: 540 639 0939
info@kfauctions.com
www.kfauctions.com

Phoebus Auction Gallery
14 East Mellen Street,
Hampton,
VA 23663
Tel: 757 722 9210
bill@phoebusauction.
hrcoxmail.com
www.phoebusauction.com

Quinn's Auction Galleries
431 North Maple Avenue,
Falls Church, VA 22046
Tel: 703 532 5632
info@quinnsauction.com
www.quinnsauction.com

WASHINGTON

**Pacific Galleries Auction
House**
241 S. Lander Street,
Seattle,
WA 98134
Tel: 206 441 9990
www.pacgal.com

WASHINGTON DC

Weschler's
909 East Street,
NW Washington, DC 20004
Tel: 202 628 1281
info@weschlers.com
www.weschlers.com

WEST VIRGINIA

**Cozart Auction
& Appraisal Services**
PO Box 11, New Martinsville,
WV 26155
Tel: 304 455 4720
tcozart@suddenlink.net
www.cozartauction.com

WISCONSIN

Krueger's Auctions
N2954 Highway 22 South,
Montello, WI 53949
Tel: 920 229 7229
mkrueger@centurylink.net
www.kruegersauctions.com

Schrager Auction Galleries
2915 North Sherman Boulevard,
Milwaukee, WI 53210
Tel: 414 873 3738
askus@schragerandassoc.com
www.schragerandassoc.com

WYOMING

Western Auction
3745 E. Lincolnway, Cheyenne,
WY 82001
Tel: 307 637 4150
zwonit@aol.com
www.westernauctioneer.com

AUCTIONEERS

CANADA
ALBERTA
Arthur Clausen & Sons, Auctioneers
11802 - 145 Street,
Edmonton, T5L 2H3
Tel: 780 451 4549
www.clausenauction.com

Hodgins Art Auctions Ltd
5240 1A Street S.E.,
Calgary, T2H 1J1
Tel: 403 640 12 44
art@hodginsauction.com
www.hodginshalls.com

Lando Art Auctions
11130-105 Avenue N.W.,
Edmonton, T5H 0L5
Tel: 780 990 1161
mail@landoartauctions.com
www.landoartauctions.com

BRITISH COLUMBIA
Maynards Fine Art Auction House
1837 Main Street
Vancouver, V5T 3B8
Tel: 604 876 6787
www.maynards.com

Heffel Fine Art
2247 Granville Street,
Vancouver, V6H 3G1
Tel: 604 732 6505
mail@heffel.com
www.heffel.com

ONTARIO
Empire Auctions
165 Tycos Drive,
Toronto,
M6B 1W6
Tel: 416 784 4261
toronto@empireauctions.com
www.empireauctions.com

Grand Valley Auctions
154 King Street East,
Cambridge,
N3H 3M4
Tel: 888 824 4243
www.grandvalleyauctions.ca

Ritchies
777 Richmond Street West,
Toronto, Ontario
M6J 2L8
Tel: 416 364 1864
www.ritchies.com

A Touch of Class
92 College Crescent,
Barrie,
L4M 5C8
Tel: 888 891 6591
www.atouchofclassauctions.com

Waddington's
275 King Street East,
Toronto,
M5A 1K2
Tel: 416 504 9100
www.waddingtons.ca

Walkers
Tudor Hall,
3750 North Bowesville Road,
Ottawa,
K1V 1B8
Tel: 613 224 5814
jeff@walkersauctions.com
www.walkersauctions.com

Robert Deveau Galleries, Robert Fine Art Auctioneers
299 Queen Street,
Toronto,
M5A 1S7
Tel: 416 364 6271
www.deveaugalleries.com

Heffel Fine Art Auction House
13 Hazelton Avenue,
Toronto,
M5R 2E1
Tel: 416 961 6505
mail@heffel.com
www.heffel.com

Sotheby's
9 Hazelton Avenue,
Toronto,
M5R 2E1
Tel: 416 926 1774
toronto@sothebys.com
www.sothebys.com

QUEBEC
Empire Auctions
5500, rue Paré,
Montréal,
H4P 2M1
Tel: 514 737 6586
montreal@empireauctions.com
www.montreal.empire
auctions.com

Iegor - Hôtel des Encans
872, rue Du Couvent,
Angle Saint-Antoine Ouest,
Montréal,
H4C 2R6
Tel: 514 344 4081
www.iegor.net

Montreal Auction House
5778 St Lawrent Boulevard,
Montréal,
H2T 1S8
Tel: 514 278 0827
pages.videotron.com/encans

CLUBS & SOCIETIES

The following list is organized by the type of collectible. If you would like your club, society or organization to appear in our next edition, or would like to update details, please contact us at email info@millers.uk.com.

ADVERTISING
Antique Advertising Association of America
PO Box 76, Petersburg, IL 62675
www.pastimes.org

Coca-Cola Collectors Club
www.cocacolaclub.org

AMERICANA
American Political Items Collectors
PO Box 55, Avon, NY 14414
www.apic.us

Folk Art Society of America
PO Box 17041, Richmond, VA 23226
Tel: 800 527 3655
fasa@folkart.org
www.folkart.org

AUTOGRAPHS
International Autograph Dealers' Alliance & Collectors' Club
11435 Lake Shore Drive, Hollywood, FL 33026
www.iada-cc.com

Universal Autograph Collectors Club
PO Box 1392, Mount Dora, FL 32756
www.uacc.org

AUTOMOBILIA
Automobile Objets d'Art Club
252 N. 7th Street, Allentown, PA 18102-4204
Tel: 610 432 3355
oldtoy@aol.com

BOOKS
Antiquarian Booksellers' Association of America
20 West 44th Street, #507, New York, NY 10036
Tel: 212 944 8291
www.abaa.org

CERAMICS
American Art Pottery Association
www.aapa.info

American Ceramic Circle
PO Box 224, Williamsburg, VA 23187
acc@acc.hrcoxmail.com
www.amercercir.org

Homer Laughlin China Collectors' Association
PO Box 721, North Platte, NE 69103
info@hlcca.org
www.hlcca.org

M.I. Hummel Club
www.mihummelclub.com

National Shelley China Club
591 West 67th Avenue, Anchorage, AK 99518
www.shelleychinaclub.com

COINS & BANKNOTES
International Bank Note Society
www.theibns.org

International Bond and Share Society
www.scripophily.org

COSTUME JEWELRY
Jewelcollect
www.jewelcollect.org

DISNEYANA
Disneyana Fan Club
PO Box 19212, Irvine, CA 92623
Tel: 714 731 4705
info@disneyanafanclub.org
www.disneyanafanclub.org

EPHEMERA
American Business Card Club US
5503 215th Street SW, Mountlake Terrace, WA 98043
Tel: 425 774 1458
smokeyhill44@yahoo.com
www.suzann.com/abcc

American Matchcover Collecting Club
PO Box 18481, Asheville, NC 28814
bill@matchcovers.com
www.matchcovers.net

FIFTIES & SIXTIES
Head Hunters Newsletter
www.headvasecollector.com

FILM & TV MEMORABILIA
The Lone Ranger Fan Club
Circle C Enterprises, c/o Tex Holland, PO Box 1253, Salisbury, MD 21802
www.lonerangerfanclub.com

GLASS
American Carnival Glass Association
www.myacga.com

Land of Sunshine Depression Glass Club
5512 Edgewater Drive, Orlando, FL 32810
Tel: 407 298 3355
milliesglass@webtv.net

HATPINS
American Hatpin Society
info@americanhatpinsociety.com
www.americanhatpinsociety.com

HOUSEHOLD
American Lock Collectors Association
admin@alcalocks.com
www.alcalocks.com

Antique Fan Collectors Association
president@fancollectors.org
www.fancollectors.org

KITCHENALIA
Ice Screamers
Info@icescreamers.com
www.icescreamers.com

MECHANICAL MUSIC
The Musical Box Society International
info2010@mbsi.org
www.mbsi.org

MILITARIA
Association of American Military Uniform Collectors
AAMUC FOOTLOCKER, PO Box 1876, Elyria, OH 44036
Tel: 440 365 5321
aamucfl@comcast.net
www.naples.net/clubs/aamuc/

OPTICAL, MEDICAL, SCIENTIFIC & TECHNICAL
Antique Wireless Association (AWA)
N2EVG@arrl.net
www.antiquewireless.org

PENS & WRITING
Pen Collectors of America
www.pencollectorsofamerica.com

The Society of Inkwell Collectors
2203 39th Street SE, Puyallup, WA 98372
Tel: 253 841 4197
soic@soic.com
www.soic.com

PEZ
Pez Collectors News
PO Box 14956, Surfside Beach, SC 29587
info@pezcollectorsnews.com
www.pezcollectorsnews.com

SCENT BOTTLES
International Perfume Bottle Association
www.perfumebottles.org

National Association of Avon Collectors
PO Box 7006, Kansas City, MO 64113

SMOKING
On The Lighter Side
PO Box 1733, Quitman, Texas 75783
Tel: 903 763 2795
www.otls.com

Pocket Lighter Preservation Guild
www.plpg.org

SNOWDOMES
Snowdome Collectors' Club
2205 California Street NW,
Washington DC 20008
Tel: 202 234 7484

SPORTING MEMORABILIA
Golf Collectors' Society
Attn. Karen Bednarski
PO Box 2386
Florence,
OR 97439
Tel: 541 991 7313
kbednarski@golfcollectors.com
www.golfcollectors.com

National Fishing Lure Collectors' Club
www.nflcc.org

Society for American Baseball Research
4455 East Camelback Road,
Suite D-140, Phoenix,
AZ 85018
Tel: 800 969 7227
info@sabr.org
www.sabr.org

TEDDY BEARS & SOFT TOYS
Steiff Club – North America
www.steiffusa.com

TEXTILES & COSTUME
The Costume Society of America
390 Amwell Road,
Suite 402,
Hillsborough,
NJ 08844
Tel: 908 359 1471
national.office@costumesocietyamerica.com
www.costumesocietyamerica.com

International Old Lacers
www.internationaloldlacers.org

TOYS & GAMES
Annalee Doll Society
Todd Watson,
71 NH Route 104,
Meredith,
NH 03253
Tel: 800 433 6557
customerservice@annalee.com
www.annalee.com

Chess Collectors' International
lichness@aol.com
www.chesscollectors.com

National Model Railroad Association
4121 Cromwell Road,
Chattanooga, TN 37421
Tel: 423 892 2846
www.nmra.org

Toy Soldier Collectors of America
c/o Charlie Duval,
PO Box 179,
New Ellenton,
South Carolina 29809
Tel: 803 652 7932
toysoldiercollectorsamerica@yahoo.com
www.toysoldiercollectors.homestead.com

United Federation of Doll Clubs
10900 North Pomona Avenue,
Kansas City,
MO 64153
Tel: 816 891 7040
ufdc@aol.com
www.ufdc.org

WATCHES
Early American Watch Club
www.nawcc-ch149.com

National Association of Watch & Clock Collectors
514 Poplar Street,
Columbia, PA 17512
Tel: 717 684 8261
www.nawcc.org

WINE & DRINKING
International Correspondence of Corkscrew Addicts
www.corkscrewnet.com/icca.htm

Collectibles are particularly suited to online trading. When compared with many antiques, most collectibles are easily defined, described and photographed, while shipping is relatively easy, due to average sizes and weights. Collectibles are also generally more affordable and accessible, and the internet has provided a cost-effective way of buying and selling without the overheads of shops and auction rooms. A huge number of collectibles are offered for sale and traded daily over the internet, with websites varying from global online marketplaces, such as eBay, to specialist dealers' sites.

• There are a number of things to be aware of when searching for collectibles online. Some items being sold may not be described accurately, meaning that general category searches, and even purposefully misspelling a name, can yield results. If something looks, or sounds, too good to be true, it probably is. Using this book should give you a head start in getting to know your market, and also enable you to tell the difference between a real bargain, and something that sounds like one. Good color photography is absolutely vital – try to find online listings that include as many images as possible, including detail shots, and check them carefully. Be aware that colors can appear differently between websites, and even between computer screens.

• Always ask the vendor questions about the object, particularly regarding condition. If no image is supplied, or you want to see another aspect of the object, ask for more information. A good seller should be happy to cooperate if approached politely and sensibly.

• As well as the 'e-hammer' price, you will very likely have to pay additional transactional fees such as packing, shipping and possibly state or national taxes. Ask the seller for an estimate of these additional costs before leaving a bid, as this will give you a better idea of the overall amount you will end-up paying.

• In addition to large online auction sites, such as eBay, there are a host of other online resources for buying and selling. The internet can also be an invaluable research tool for collectors, with many sites devoted to providing detailed information on a number of different collectibles – however, it is always best to use trusted names or compare information between sites.

INTERNET RESOURCES

Miller's Antiques & Collectibles
www.millersonline.com
Miller's website is the ultimate one-stop destination for collectors, dealers, or anyone interested in antiques and collectibles. Join the Miller's Club to search through a catalog containing many thousands of authenticated antiques and collectibles, each illustrated in full color and accompanied by a full descriptive caption and price range. Browse through practical articles written by Judith Miller, Mark Hill, and a team of experts to learn tips and tricks of the trade, as well as learning more about important companies, designs, and the designers behind them. Read Judith's blog, and order the full range of Millers books. You can also search the best fully illustrated A-Z of specialist terms on the internet; a dealer, appraiser and auctioneer database; a guide to silver hallmarks; and learn about care and repair of your antiques and collectibles. The site is continually updated, so check back regularly to see what's new.

Live Auctioneers
www.liveauctioneers.com
A free online service that allows users to search catalogs from selected auction houses in Europe, the USA and the United Kingdom. Visitors to the site can bid live via the internet into salerooms as auctions happen. Registered users can also search through an archive of past catalogs and receive a free e-mail newsletter.

The Saleroom.com
www.the-saleroom.com
A free online service that allows users to search catalogs from selected auction houses in Europe, the USA and the United Kingdom. Visitors to the site can bid live via the internet into salerooms as auctions happen. Registered users can also search through an archive of past catalogs and receive a free e-mail newsletter.

eBay
www.ebay.com
Undoubtedly the largest and most diverse of the online auction sites, allowing users to buy and sell in an online marketplace with over 78 million registered users from across the world.

ArtFact
www.artfact.com
Provides a comprehensive database of worldwide auction listings from over 2,000 art, antiques and collectibles auction houses. User can search details of both upcoming and past sales and also find information on a number of collectors' fields. Basic information is available free, access to more in depth information requires a subscription. Online bidding live into auctions as they happen is also offered.

The Antiques Trade Gazette
www.antiquestradegazette.com
The online edition of the UK antiques and collectibles trade newspaper, including British auction and fair listings, news and events.

Maine Antique Digest
www.maineantiquedigest.com
Online version of the US antiques and collectibles trade newspaper including news, articles, fair and auction listings and more.

La Gazette du Drouot
www.drouot.com
The online home of the magazine listing all auctions to be held in France at the Hotel de Drouot in Paris. An online subscription enables you to download the magazine online.

Auction.fr
www.auction.fr
An online database of auctions at French auction houses. A subscription allows users to search past catalogs and prices realized.

Go Antiques/Antiqnet
www.goantiques.com
www.antiqnet.com
An online global aggregator for art, antiques and collectibles dealers. Dealers' stock is showcased online, with users able to browse and buy.